An Introduction to Database Systems

VOLUME I

Fourth Edition

C. J. DATE

ADDISON-WESLEY PUBLISHING COMPANY

Reading, Massachusetts • Menlo Park, California
Don Mills, Ontario • Wokingham, England • Amsterdam • Bonn • Sydney
Singapore • Tokyo • Madrid • Bogota • Santiago • San Juan

WORLD STUDENT SERIES EDITION

This book is in the
Addison-Wesley Systems Programming Series

Consulting Editors: IBM Editorial Board
Sponsoring Editor: James T. DeWolf
Project Editor: Marion E. Howe
Packaging Service: Superscript Associates
Text Designer: Quadrata, Inc.
Cover: Marshall Henrichs
Manufacturing Supervisor: Hugh Crawford

ISBN 0-201-19215-2
CDEFGHIJ-HA-8987

For Lindy

THE SYSTEMS PROGRAMMING SERIES

* Published

Foreword

The field of systems programming primarily grew out of the efforts of many programmers and managers whose creative energy went into producing practical, utilitarian systems programs needed by the rapidly growing computer industry. Programming was practiced as an art where each programmer invented unique solutions to problems with little guidance beyond that provided by immediate associates. In 1968, the late Ascher Opler, then at IBM, recognized that it was necessary to bring programming knowledge together in a form that would be accessible to all systems programmers. Surveying the state of the art, he decided that enough useful material existed to justify a significant codification effort. On his recommendation, IBM decided to sponsor The Systems Programming Series as a long-term project to collect, organize, and publish those principles and techniques that would have lasting value throughout the industry.

The Series consists of an open-ended collection of text-reference books. The contents of each book represent the individual author's view of the subject area and do not necessarily reflect the views of the IBM Corporation. Each is organized for course use but is detailed enough for reference. Further, the Series is organized in three levels: broad introductory material in the foundation volumes, more specialized material in the software volumes, and very specialized theory in the computer science volumes. As such, the Series meets the needs of the novice, the experienced programmer, and the computer scientist.

Taken together, the Series is a record of the state of the art in systems programming that can form the technological base for the systems programming discipline.

The Editorial Board

v

About the Author

C. J. Date is an independent author, lecturer, and consultant, specializing in relational database systems. He is currently based in Saratoga, California.

Mr. Date joined IBM in 1967 in England, where he worked on the integration of database functions into PL/I. Later (1974) he moved to the IBM Development Center in California, where he was responsible for the design of a database language known as UDL (Unified Database Language). More recently, he was involved in technical planning and externals design for the IBM relational products SQL/DS (announced in 1981 for DOS and in 1983 for VM) and DB2 (announced in 1983 for MVS). He left IBM in May 1983.

Mr. Date has been active in the field of database for over fifteen years. He was one of the first people anywhere to recognize the significance of Codd's pioneering work on the relational model. He has lectured widely on technical subjects—principally on database topics, and especially on relational database—throughout the United States and also in Europe, Australia, Latin America, and the Far East. In addition to the present book, his publications include *An Introduction to Database Systems: Volume II* (1982), which covers a range of more advanced aspects of the subject; *Database: A Primer* (1983), which treats database systems (from micros to mainframes) specifically from the nonspecialist's point of view; and *A Guide to DB2* (1984), a description of the IBM relational product DB2 and its companion products QMF and DXT. He has also produced numerous technical papers and articles and has made a number of contributions to database theory. He is currently conducting a series of professional seminars on database technology, both in the United States and elsewhere.

Preface
to the
Fourth Edition

The fourth edition of this book is so different from all previous editions that it is to all intents and purposes a brand new book. Even the structure has changed, as will be explained below. But of course the overall objective is still the same as it always was—namely, to provide the basis for a solid education in the fundamentals of database technology. The general style and level of exposition are also still very much the same; the book is still intended primarily as a textbook rather than as a work of reference, and it still retains its introductory and tutorial flavor.

Readers are assumed to be professionally interested in some aspect of data processing. They may, for example, be systems analysts or designers, application programmers, systems programmers, students following a university or similar course in computer science, or teachers of such a course. Readers are expected to have a reasonable appreciation of the capabilities of a modern computer system, with particular reference to the file-handling features of such a system; they should also have some knowledge of at least one high-level programming language. Since these prerequisites are not particularly demanding, however, I am hopeful that the book will prove suitable as an introductory text for anyone concerned with using or implementing a database system, or for anyone who simply wishes to broaden a general knowledge of the computer science field.

The book is divided into six major parts:

1. Basic Concepts
2. A Sample Relational System
3. Relational Database Management
4. The Database Environment
5. Nonrelational Systems
6. Some Current Developments

Each part in turn is subdivided into a number of chapters:

- Part 1 (three chapters) provides a broad introduction to the concepts of database systems in general, and in particular distinguishes between relational and nonrelational systems. At the time of writing it is still the case that the majority of installed systems are nonrelational. However, this state of affairs is unlikely to persist for very much longer—relational products are being developed and installed at an ever-increasing rate; indeed, it is a fact that almost all modern products are relational. Furthermore, almost all current research and development is based on relational ideas. The emphasis of this book is therefore heavily on the relational approach.

- Part 2 (six chapters) consists of a tutorial treatment of the major concepts of relational systems, using the IBM system DB2 as a vehicle for illustrating those concepts.

- Part 3 (eight chapters), which is the longest part of the book (indeed, it is almost a book within a book) consists of a detailed examination of the ideas, both theoretical and pragmatic, underlying relational systems such as DB2. Part 3 also includes a detailed discussion of another relational system, namely INGRES, which is significantly different from DB2 in a number of ways.

- Part 4 (three chapters) then goes on to discuss certain other aspects of database systems (relational or otherwise)—recovery, concurrency, security, integrity, and so on.

- Next, Part 5 (three chapters) introduces the major nonrelational approaches (inverted list, hierarchic, and network), and describes a representative set of nonrelational systems: DATACOM/DB, IMS, and IDMS.

- Finally, Part 6 (two chapters) discusses some current research directions in the database field.

Note: The six parts have deliberately been written to be somewhat independent of one another; Part 3 (at least Chapters 11–14) can be studied before Part 2 if the reader wishes, and Part 5 can be studied before Parts 2 and 3 or after Part 6. However, my own recommendation is to read the material in sequence as written.

Most chapters are followed by a set of exercises and (usually) answers also; often the answers give additional information about the subject of the exercise. Most chapters are also followed by an extensive list of references, most of them annotated. References are identified in the text by numbers in square brackets. For example, [11.1] refers to the first item in the list of references at the end of Chapter 11, namely, a paper by E. F. Codd published in *Communications of the ACM* (CACM), Vol. 13, No. 6 (June 1970).

For readers who may be familiar with the third edition, the major differences from that edition are summarized below.

Part 1: The old introductory chapter (Chapter 1) has been expanded into two chapters (1 and 2) and made a little more gentle. The old Chapter 2 on storage structures (now Chapter 3) has been completely rewritten and greatly expanded. The old Chapter 3 on different data models has been dropped; however, all the material of that chapter still survives (indeed, in expanded form) at other points in the book.

Part 2: Chapters 4-9 replace Chapters 5-10 from the third edition. The material on the System R prototype has been replaced throughout by material on the DB2 product.

Part 3: This part is largely new, or at least considerably improved over the third edition. Chapter 10 (new) describes the INGRES system in some detail. Chapters 11-14 present a significantly expanded and improved treatment of the relational model (replacing the old Chapters 4 and 11-13); in particular, the integrity aspects of the model are covered in depth. Chapter 15 (new) discusses a number of practical aspects of relational systems. Chapter 16 (new) is an introduction to relational query optimization. Finally, Chapter 17 is a revised and extended version of the old Chapter 14 on further normalization.

Part 4: This part is also new. It consists of three new chapters. Chapter 18 discusses transaction processing (in particular, recovery and concurrency considerations); Chapter 19 describes the problems of security and integrity in a database system; and Chapter 20 discusses a number of auxiliary (frontend) systems—report writers, business graphics systems, natural language interfaces, application generators, and so on.

Part 5: This part replaces Parts 3-5 from the third edition. It consists of three long chapters, one for each of the major nonrelational approaches (inverted list, hierarchic, and network). Each chapter first discusses the relevant data model and then goes on to describe a typical system supporting that model. Chapter 21 (new) covers DATACOM/DB; Chapter 22 (revised and condensed version of the old Chapters 15-22) covers IMS; and Chapter 23 (revised and condensed version of the old Chapters 23-26) covers IDMS. Note that Chapter 23 in particular now describes an (important) concrete system instead of just the "official" CODASYL specifications, which were never fully implemented. Chapters 21 and 23 also include material on the new "relational" extensions to DATACOM/DB and IDMS.

Part 6: This part is also new. Chapter 24 describes distributed database systems and also briefly discusses database machines. Chapter 25 presents an introduction to semantic modeling; in particular, it describes the entity/relationship model and the extended relational model RM/T.

In addition, the old chapters 27 and 28 have been dropped, though much of the material from those chapters is preserved at various points throughout the book.

Why all these changes? There are several major reasons:

1. First, the promise of relational systems—foretold as far back as the first edition of this book (1975)—is at last beginning to come to fruition. As already mentioned, almost every modern database product is relational, and almost all database research is relational-based. Furthermore, most of the older (nonrelational) products are currently being extended to provide some kind of relational support. Given the intended audience for this book, therefore, it no longer seems necessary or appropriate to give "equal time" to the nonrelational approaches.

2. Following on from the previous point: Given the widespread acceptance of the relational approach, a solid understanding of the fundamentals of that approach is now more important than ever, for both researchers and practitioners—in fact, for anyone involved in any aspect of database management, in any capacity whatsoever. The relational portions of the book have therefore been completely rewritten, and at the same time consolidated and greatly expanded, with the aim of providing a basis for that solid understanding.

3. In addition, the "coming of age" of relational systems has made it possible to base most examples and discussions on commercially available products, instead of just on research prototypes as in earlier editions. (It goes without saying, of course, that commercial products are subject to continual change; details of specific systems are thus not guaranteed to be accurate as of the most recent release. Furthermore, inclusion or exclusion of a particular product in this book should not be construed as either endorsement or otherwise of the product in question—the purpose of including any specific system is merely to use it to make some specific point or illustrate some specific idea.)

4. The reduced coverage of nonrelational systems has made it possible to include material on a number of topics for which there was no room in the third edition. Specifically, the book now includes at least an introduction to all of the following: query optimization, recovery, concurrency, security, integrity, forms-based systems, natural language interfaces, report writing, graphics interfaces, application generators, semantic modeling (including entity/relationship modeling), distributed databases, and database machines. Note: Many of these topics are treated in more detail in Volume II (see below).

One result of all these changes, incidentally, is that the prefaces to the previous editions are no longer very relevant. They have therefore been dropped from this edition.

As indicated above, this book has a sequel, namely *An Introduction to Database Systems: Volume II* (first edition, Addison-Wesley, 1982)—referred to throughout the present text as simply *Volume II*. Volume II provides a more thorough treatment of some of the topics introduced in Parts 3, 4, and 6 of the present book (hereinafter referred to as *Volume I*). However, I hope the discussions above make it clear that this fourth edition of Volume I is far more than just a rehash of material from the previous (third) edition and Volume II; on the contrary, it contains a great deal of new material, and a significantly different emphasis on much of the existing material. Equally, of course, it is not intended to replace Volume II, which goes into considerably more detail (on its own topics) than is necessary or appropriate for the present volume.

Acknowledgments: As always, it is a great pleasure to acknowledge my debt to the many people involved, directly or indirectly, in the production of this book. First, the text has benefited enormously from the comments of numerous students on seminars I have taught based on this material. It has also benefited from the comments of several reviewers of the third edition: Randell Flint, Alan Hevner, Larry Rowe, Sharon Salveter, Stewart Shen, Paul Spirakis, Philip Stone, Richard Walters, and most especially Dave DeWitt. My thanks also to the following, each of whom reviewed at least some portion of the manuscript of this edition or made technical material available or otherwise helped me find answers to my many technical questions: Paul Butterworth, Roger Buchanan, Don Casey, Ted Codd, Dave DeWitt, Guy Egerton, Ron Fagin, Randell Flint, Robin Haines, Doug Hembry, Peter Kreps, Jack Nevison, Larry Rowe, Phil Shaw, Mike Stonebraker, and Sharon Weinberg. I would also like to thank Relational Technology Inc. for permission to base certain portions of Chapter 20 on an article that I wrote for them some time ago on the Visual Programming tools of INGRES. Finally, this book would never have been possible without the support and assistance of my long-suffering family, nor (obviously) without the professional expertise of my editor Elydia Siegel and everyone involved at Addison-Wesley. To them all, my heartfelt appreciation and thanks.

Saratoga, California   C. J. Date

Contents

16   Query Optimization   333

17   Further Normalization   361

PART 4
The Database Environment   411

18   Recovery and Concurrency   413

Part 1
Basic Concepts

Part 1 consists of three introductory chapters. Chapter 1 sets the scene by explaining what a database is and why database systems are generally desirable. It also briefly discusses the difference between relational and nonrelational systems. Next, Chapter 2 presents a general architecture for a database system (the so-called ANSI/SPARC architecture); that architecture serves as a framework on which all later chapters in the book will build. Then Chapter 3 provides an introduction to a number of techniques for physically arranging the data in the stored database. Note, however, that it is normal to shield users from all such physical-level details and to allow them to view the database in some logical form that is more suited to their specific application requirements; the primary purpose of Chapter 3 is to give some idea as to what has to go on "under the covers," not to describe material that users actually need in order to use the system.

1
An Overview
of
Database Management

1.1 AN INTRODUCTORY EXAMPLE

A database system is essentially nothing more than a *computerized record-keeping system*. The database itself can be regarded as a kind of electronic filing cabinet—that is, as a repository for a collection of computerized data files. The user of the system will be given facilities to perform a variety of operations on such files, including the following among others:

- Adding new (empty) files to the database;
- Inserting new data into existing files;
- Retrieving data from existing files;
- Updating data in existing files;
- Deleting data from existing files;
- Removing existing files (empty or otherwise) permanently from the database.

By way of illustration, we show in Fig. 1.1 a very small database containing a single file, the CELLAR file, which in turn contains information concerning the contents of a wine cellar. Figure 1.2 shows an example of a retrieval operation against that database, together with the data (more accurately, results) returned from that retrieval.

Figure 1.3 gives some further examples, all more or less self-explanatory, of operations on the CELLAR file. Examples of adding files to and removing files from the database are given later, in Chapter 4 and elsewhere.

To conclude this introductory section, a few final remarks:

- First, for obvious reasons, computerized files such as CELLAR in the example are frequently referred to as *tables* rather than as files, and we shall frequently

3

The CELLAR file:

BIN	WINE	PRODUCER	YEAR	BOTTLES	READY	COMMENTS
2	Chardonnay	Buena Vista	83	1	85	
3	Chardonnay	Louis Martini	81	5	84	
6	Chardonnay	Chappellet	82	4	85	Thanksgiving
11	Jo.Riesling	Jekel	84	10	86	
12	Jo.Riesling	Buena Vista	82	1	83	Late Harvest
16	Jo.Riesling	Sattui	82	1	83	very dry
21	Fume Blanc	Ch.St.Jean	79	4	83	Napa Valley
22	Fume Blanc	Robt.Mondavi	78	2	82	
25	Wh.Burgundy	Mirassou	80	6	82	
30	Gewurztraminer	Buena Vista	80	3	82	
43	Cab.Sauvignon	Robt.Mondavi	77	12	87	
50	Pinot Noir	Mirassou	77	3	85	Harvest
51	Pinot Noir	Ch.St.Jean	78	2	86	
64	Zinfandel	Mirassou	77	9	86	Anniversary
72	Gamay	Robt.Mondavi	78	2	83	

Fig. 1.1 The wine cellar database.

```
SELECT  WINE, BIN, PRODUCER
FROM    CELLAR
WHERE   READY = 85 ;
```

Result (printed or displayed on the screen):

WINE	BIN	PRODUCER
Chardonnay	2	Buena Vista
Chardonnay	6	Chappellet
Pinot Noir	50	Mirassou

Fig. 1.2 Sample retrieval against the wine cellar database.

Inserting new data:

```
INSERT INTO CELLAR
VALUES (53,'Pinot Noir','Franciscan',79,1,86,'for Joan') ;
```

Updating existing data:

```
UPDATE CELLAR
SET     BOTTLES = 4
WHERE   BIN = 3 ;
```

Deleting existing data:

```
DELETE FROM CELLAR
WHERE   BIN = 2 ;
```

Fig. 1.3 INSERT, UPDATE, and DELETE examples.

follow that practice in this book. (In fact, they are *relational* tables. See Section 1.6.)

- Second, the rows of such a table may be regarded as representing the *records* of the file (sometimes referred to explicitly as *logical* records, to distinguish them from other kinds of record to be discussed later). Likewise, the columns may be regarded as representing the *fields* of those logical records. In this book we will use the terms "row" and "record" interchangeably, likewise the terms "column" and "field."

- Third, the SELECT, INSERT, UPDATE, and DELETE operations shown in Figs. 1.2 and 1.3 above are all, in fact, examples of statements from a database language known as SQL ("Structured Query Language"). SQL (usually pronounced "sequel") is the language supported by the IBM database products DB2, SQL/DS, and QMF (see Part II of this book), as well as by numerous database products from other vendors. SQL is treated in depth in Part 2, Chapters 4–9.

1.2   WHAT IS A DATABASE SYSTEM?

To repeat from Section 1.1: A database system is basically a computerized record-keeping system—that is, a system whose overall purpose is to maintain information and to make that information available on demand.[1] The information concerned can be anything that is deemed to be of significance to the individual or organization the system is intended to serve—anything, in other words, required by that individual or organization to assist in the process of making decisions. Figure 1.4 shows a greatly simplified view of a database system.

Figure 1.4 is intended to show that a database system involves four major components: data, hardware, software, and users. We consider each of these briefly below. Later, we will go on to discuss each one in much more detail.

Data

Database systems are now available on machines that range all the way from quite small micros to the largest mainframes. Of course, the facilities provided by any given system are to some extent determined by the size and power of the underlying machine. In particular, systems on large machines ("large systems") tend to be *multi-user,* whereas those on smaller machines ("small systems") tend to be *single-user.* A single-user system is one in which only one user can be operating at any given

---

1.   The terms "data" and "information" are treated as synonymous in this book. Some writers distinguish between the two, using "data" to refer to the values physically recorded in the database and "information" to refer to the *meaning* of those values as understood by some user. The distinction is clearly important—so important that it seems preferable to make it explicit, where relevant, instead of relying on a somewhat arbitrary differentiation between two essentially similar terms.

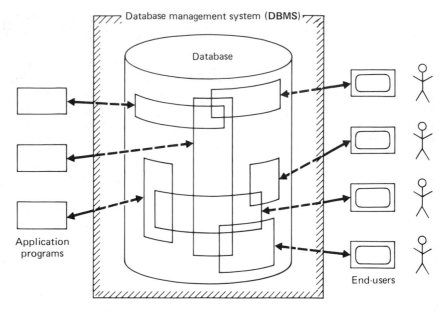

Fig. 1.4 Simplified picture of a database system.

time; a multi-user system is one in which multiple users can be operating concurrently. As Fig. 1.4 suggests, we will usually assume the latter case in this book, for reasons of generality, but in fact the distinction is largely irrelevant so far as most users are concerned: One of the objectives of most multi-user systems is precisely to allow each individual user to behave as if he or she were working with a *single*-user system. The special problems of multi-user systems are primarily problems that are internal to the system, not ones that are visible to the user (see Part 4 of this book).

Another preliminary remark: It is usually convenient to assume for the sake of simplicity that the totality of data stored in the system is all held in a single database, and we shall generally make this simplifying assumption, since it does not substantially invalidate any of the subsequent discussion. In practice, however, there may be good reasons, even in a small system, why the data should normally be split across several distinct databases. We will touch on some of those reasons later.

In general, then, the data in the database—at least in a large system—will be both *integrated* and *shared*. As will be seen in Section 1.4, these two aspects, integration and sharing, represent a major advantage of database systems in the "large" environment; and integration, at least, may be significant in the "small" environment too. Of course, there are many other advantages also (to be discussed later), even in the small environment. But first let us explain what we mean by the terms "integrated" and "shared."

■ By *integrated* we mean that the database may be thought of as a unification of several otherwise distinct data files, with any redundancy among those files either wholly or partly eliminated. For example, a given database might contain both an EMPLOYEE file, giving name, address, department, salary, etc., and an ENROLLMENT file, representing the enrollment of employees in training courses. Suppose that, in order to carry out the process of training course administration, it is necessary to know the department for each enrolled student. Then there is clearly no need to include that information, redundantly, in the ENROLLMENT file, because it can always be discovered by referring to the EMPLOYEE file instead.

■ By *shared* we mean that individual pieces of data in the database may be shared among several different users, in the sense that each of those users may have access to the same piece of data (and different users may use it for different purposes). As indicated earlier, different users may even be accessing the same piece of data *at the same time* ("concurrent access"). Such sharing (concurrent or otherwise) is partly a consequence of the fact that the database is integrated. In the EMPLOYEE/ENROLLMENT example cited above, the department information in the EMPLOYEE file would typically be shared by users in the Personnel Department and users in the Education Department—and, as suggested before, those two departments would typically be using the information for different purposes.

Another consequence of the same fact (that the database is integrated) is that any given user will normally be concerned only with some subset of the total database; moreover, different users' subsets will overlap in many different ways. In other words, a given database will be perceived by different users in a variety of different ways. In fact, even when two users share the same subset of the database, their views of that subset may differ considerably at a detailed level. This latter point is discussed more fully in Section 1.5 and also in the next chapter.

Hardware

The hardware consists of the secondary storage volumes—typically moving-head disks—on which the database physically resides, together with the associated I/O devices (disk drives, in the case of moving-head disks), device controllers, I/O channels, and so forth. This book does not concern itself very greatly with hardware aspects of the system, for the following reasons: First, those aspects form a major topic in their own right; second, the problems encountered in this area are not peculiar to database systems; and third, those problems have been very thoroughly investigated and documented in numerous other places. However, Chapter 3 does give a reasonably detailed overview of techniques for physically organizing the database on secondary storage, and Chapter 24 presents a very brief introduction to the topic of *database machines*—that is, hardware designed specifically to support a database system.

Software

Between the physical database itself (i.e., the data as actually stored) and the users of the system is a layer of software, the *database manager* (DB manager) or, more usually, *database management system* (DBMS). All requests from users for access to the database are handled by the DBMS; the facilities sketched in Section 1.1 for creating files (or tables), inserting data, retrieving data, etc., are all facilities provided by the DBMS. One general function provided by the DBMS is thus *the shielding of database users from hardware-level details* (much as programming-language systems shield application programmers from hardware-level details). In other words, the DBMS provides users with a view of the database that is elevated somewhat above the hardware level, and supports user operations (such as the SQL operations discussed briefly in Section 1.1) that are expressed in terms of that higher-level view. We shall discuss this function, and other functions of the DBMS, in considerably more detail throughout this book.

Users

We consider three broad classes of user. First, there is the *application programmer*, responsible for writing application programs that use the database, typically in a language such as COBOL or PL/I or some more modern language such as APL or Pascal. Those programs operate on the data in all the usual ways: retrieving information, creating new information, deleting or changing existing information. All of these functions are performed by issuing the appropriate request to the DBMS. The programs themselves may be conventional batch applications, or (increasingly) they may be *on-line* applications, whose function is to support an end-user (see below) who is accessing the database from an on-line terminal.

The second class of user, then, is the *end-user*, interacting with the system from an on-line terminal. A given end-user may access the database via one of the user-written on-line applications mentioned in the previous paragraph, or he or she may use an interface provided as an integral part of the system. Such interfaces are also provided by means of on-line applications, but those applications are *built-in*, not user-written. Most systems provide at least one such built-in application, namely an interactive *query language* processor, by which the user is able to issue high-level commands or statements (such as SELECT, INSERT, etc.) to the DBMS. The language SQL referred to several times already may be regarded as a typical example of a database query language.[2]

Note: Many systems also provide additional built-in interfaces, in which users are not required to issue explicit commands such as SELECT but instead operate by (for example) choosing items from a menu or filling in items on a form. Such *menu-* or *forms-driven* interfaces tend to be easier to use for people who do not

---

2. The term "query language," common though it is, is really a misnomer, inasmuch as the English verb "query" suggests *retrieval* (only), whereas query languages typically provide UPDATE, INSERT, and DELETE operations (and probably other operations) as well.

have a formal training in data processing. *Command-driven* interfaces (i.e., query languages), by contrast, do tend to require a certain amount of data processing expertise, though perhaps not a very great deal (obviously not as much as is needed to write an application program in COBOL or PL/I). Then again, a command-driven interface is likely to be more flexible than a forms- or menu-based one, in that query languages typically provide certain functions that are not supported by those other interfaces.

The third class of user (not shown in Fig. 1.4) is the *database administrator*, or DBA. Discussion of the DBA function is deferred to Sections 1.4 and 2.7.

This completes our preliminary description of the major aspects of a database system. We now go on to discuss these topics in somewhat more detail.

1.3 OPERATIONAL DATA

One of the earliest tutorials on the subject, a paper by Engles [1.10], refers to the data in a database as "operational data," distinguishing it from input data, output data, and other kinds of data. We give below a modified version of Engles' original definition of *database*:

■ A database is a collection of stored operational data used by the application systems of some particular enterprise.

This definition clearly requires some explanation. First, "enterprise" is simply a convenient generic term for any reasonably self-contained commercial, scientific, technical, or other organization. An enterprise can be a single individual (with a small private database), or a complete corporation or similar large body (with a large shared database), or anything in between. Some examples of enterprises are:

■ A manufacturing company;
■ A bank;
■ A hospital;
■ A university;
■ A government department.

Any enterprise must necessarily maintain a lot of data about its operation. This is its "operational data." The operational data for the enterprises above would typically include the following:

■ Product data;
■ Account data;
■ Patient data;
■ Student data;
■ Planning data.

As already mentioned, "operational data" does not include input or output data, work queues, temporary results, or indeed any purely transient information. "Input data" refers to information entering the system for the first time (typically from a terminal keyboard or card reader or similar device); such information may cause a change to be made to the operational data (it may *become* part of the operational data), but it is not initially part of the database itself. Similarly, "output data" refers to messages and results emanating from the system (typically printed or otherwise displayed on a terminal screen); again, such information may be *derived from* the operational data, but it is not itself considered to be part of the database. Analogous remarks apply to other kinds of transient information.

As an illustration of the concept of operational data, let us consider the case of a manufacturing company in a little more detail. Such an enterprise will typically wish to retain information about the *projects* it has on hand; the *parts* used in those projects; the *suppliers* who supply those parts; the *warehouses* in which the parts are stored; the *employees* who work on the projects; and so on. These are the basic *entities* about which information is to be recorded (the term "entity" is widely used in database circles to mean any distinguishable object that is to be represented in the database). See Fig. 1.5.

It is important to note that, in addition to the basic entities themselves, there will also be *relationships* linking those basic entities together. Such relationships are represented by connecting arrows in Fig. 1.5. For example, there is a relationship between suppliers and parts: Each supplier supplies certain parts, and conversely each part is supplied by certain suppliers (more accurately, each supplier supplies certain *kinds* of part, each *kind* of part is supplied by certain suppliers). Similarly, parts are used in projects, and conversely projects use parts; parts are stored in warehouses, and warehouses store parts; and so on. Note that these relationships are all *bidirectional*—that is, they can be traversed in either direction. For example, the relationship between employees and departments can be used to answer either or both of the following questions:

1. Given an employee, find the corresponding department;
2. Given a department, find the corresponding employees.

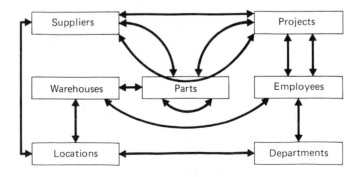

Fig. 1.5 An example of operational data.

The significant point about relationships such as those illustrated in Fig. 1.5 is that *they are just as much a part of the operational data as are the basic entities*. They must therefore be represented in the database. Later in this book we will consider various ways in which this can be done.

Figure 1.5 also illustrates a number of other points.

1. Although most of the relationships in the diagram involve *two* types of entity— i.e., they are *binary* relationships—it is by no means the case that all relationships must necessarily be binary in this sense. In the example there is one relationship involving three types of entity (suppliers, parts, and projects)—a *ternary* relationship. The intended interpretation is that certain suppliers supply certain parts to certain projects. Note carefully that this ternary relationship "suppliers supply parts to projects" is *not,* in general, equivalent to the combination of the three binary relationships "suppliers supply parts," "parts are used in projects," and "projects are supplied by suppliers." For example, the information that

a) Smith supplies monkey wrenches to the Manhattan project

tells us *more* than the combination

b) Smith supplies monkey wrenches,

c) monkey wrenches are used in the Manhattan project, and

d) the Manhattan project is supplied by Smith

— we cannot (validly!) deduce a) knowing only b), c), and d). More explicitly, if we know b), c), and d), then we can deduce that Smith supplies monkey wrenches to *some* project (say project Jz), that *some* supplier (say supplier Sx) supplies monkey wrenches to the Manhattan project, and that Smith supplies *some* part (say part Py) to the Manhattan project—but we cannot validly infer that Sx is Smith or that Py is monkey wrenches or that Jz is the Manhattan project. False inferences such as these are an illustration of what is sometimes called *the connection trap.*

2. The diagram also includes one arrow involving only *one* type of entity (parts). The relationship here is that certain parts include other parts as immediate components (the so-called *bill-of-materials* relationship)—for example, a screw is a component of a hinge assembly, which is also considered as a part and may in turn be a component of some higher-level part such as a lid. Note that this relationship is still binary; it is just that the two types of entity that are linked together (namely, parts and parts) happen to be one and the same.

3. In general, a given set of entity types may be linked together in any number of relationships. In the diagram, there are two arrows connecting projects and employees. One might represent the relationship "works on" (the employee works on the project), the other the relationship "is the manager of" (the employee is the manager of the project).

A relationship can be regarded as an entity in its own right. If we take as our definition of entity "any object about which we wish to record information," then a relationship certainly fits the definition. For instance, "part P4 is stored in warehouse W8" is an entity about which we may well wish to record information—for example, the corresponding quantity. In this book, therefore, we will tend to view relationships merely as a special kind of entity.

1.4 WHY DATABASE?

Why use a database system? What are the advantages? To some extent the answer to these questions depends on whether the system in question is single- or multi-user—or rather, to be more accurate, there are numerous *additional* advantages in the multi-user case. We consider the single-user case first. Refer back to the wine cellar example once again (Fig. 1.1), which we may regard as typical of a single-user database. Now, that particular database is so small and so simple that the advantages may not be very immediately obvious. But imagine a similar database for a large restaurant, with a stock of perhaps thousands of bottles and with very frequent changes to that stock; or think of a liquor store, with again a very large stock and with high turnover on that stock. (These would typically still be single-user systems, incidentally, even though the database is larger.) The advantages of a database system over traditional, paper-based methods of record-keeping will perhaps be more readily apparent in these examples. Here are some of them:

- *Compactness*: No need for possibly voluminous paper files.

- *Speed*: The machine can retrieve and change data far faster than a human can. In particular, ad hoc, spur-of-the-moment queries (e.g., "Do we have more Zinfandel than Pinot Noir?") can be answered quickly without any need for time-consuming manual or visual searches.

- *Less drudgery*: Much of the sheer tedium of maintaining files by hand is eliminated. Mechanical tasks are always better done by machines.

- *Currency*: Accurate, up-to-date information is available on demand at any time.

The foregoing benefits apply with even more force in a multi-user environment, where the database is likely to be much larger and much more complex than in the single-user case. However, there is one overriding additional advantage in such an environment, namely: *The database system provides the enterprise with centralized control of its operational data* (which, as the reader should realize from Section 1.3, is one of its most valuable assets). Such a situation contrasts sharply with that found in an enterprise without a database system, where typically each application has its own private files—quite often its own private tapes and disks, too—so that the operational data is widely dispersed and is therefore probably difficult to control in any systematic way.

Let us elaborate a little on the concept of centralized control. The concept implies that (in an enterprise with a database system) there will be some identifiable person who has this central responsibility for the operational data. That person is the *database administrator* (DBA) mentioned in Section 1.2. We shall be discussing the DBA function in more detail in Chapter 2; for the time being, it is sufficient to note that the job typically requires both a) a high degree of technical expertise and b) the ability to understand and interpret the requirements of the enterprise at a senior management level. In practice, the DBA function may well be performed by a team of several people, some managerial and some technical, instead of just by one person. For simplicity, however, it is convenient to assume that the DBA is indeed a single individual. It is important to realize that the position of the DBA within the enterprise is (or should be) a very senior one.

Following are some of the advantages that accrue from this notion of central-ized control:

- Redundancy can be reduced.

In nondatabase systems each application has its own private files. That fact can often lead to considerable redundancy in stored data, with resultant waste in storage space. For example, a personnel application and an education-records application may each own a file that includes department information for employees. As sug-gested in Section 1.2, those two files can be integrated, and the redundancy elimi-nated, *if* the DBA is aware of the data requirements for both applications—i.e., *if* the DBA has the necessary overall control.

Incidentally, we do not mean to suggest that *all* redundancy should necessarily be eliminated. Sometimes there are sound business or technical reasons for main-taining multiple copies of the same stored data. However, we do mean to suggest that any such redundancy should be carefully *controlled*—that is, the DBMS should be aware of it, if it exists, and should assume responsibility for "propagating up-dates" (see the next point below).

- Inconsistency can be avoided (to some extent).

This is really a corollary of the previous point. Suppose that a given fact about the real world—say the fact that employee E3 works in department D8—is repre-sented by two distinct entries in the stored database. Suppose also that the DBMS is not aware of this duplication (i.e., the redundancy is not controlled). Then there will be some occasions on which the two entries will not agree—namely, when one and only one of the two has been updated. At such times the database is said to be *inconsistent*. It is clear that a database that is in an inconsistent state is capable of supplying incorrect or conflicting information to its users.

It should also be clear that if the given fact is represented by a single entry (i.e., if the redundancy is removed), then such an inconsistency cannot occur. Alterna-tively, if the redundancy is not removed but is controlled (by making it known to the DBMS), then the DBMS could guarantee that the database is never inconsistent *as seen by the user*, by ensuring that any change made to either of the two entries is automatically applied to the other one also. This process is known as *propagating updates*—where (as is very frequently the case) the term "update" is taken to in-clude all of the operations of insertion, deletion, and modification. Note, however, that few commercially available systems today are capable of automatically propagating updates in this manner; that is, most current products do not support controlled redundancy at all, except in a few rather special cases.

- The data can be shared.

We discussed this point in Section 1.2, but for completeness we mention it again here. Sharing means not only that existing applications can share the data in the database, but also that new applications can be developed to operate against that same stored data. In other words, it may be possible to satisfy the data requirements of new applications without having to create any additional stored data.

- Standards can be enforced.

With central control of the database, the DBA can ensure that all applicable standards are observed in the representation of the data. Applicable standards may include any or all of the following: corporate, installation, departmental, industry, national, and international standards. Standardizing stored data formats is particularly desirable as an aid to *data interchange*, or migration between systems. Likewise, data naming and documentation standards are also very desirable as an aid to data sharing and understandability.

- Security restrictions can be applied.

Having complete jurisdiction over the operational data, the DBA a) can ensure that the only means of access to the database is through the proper channels, and hence b) can define security checks to be carried out whenever access is attempted to sensitive data. Different checks can be established for each type of access (retrieve, modify, delete, etc.) to each piece of information in the database. Note, however, that without such checks the security of the data might actually be *more* at risk than in a traditional (dispersed) filing system; that is, the centralized nature of a database system in a sense requires that a good security system be in place also.

- Integrity can be maintained.

The problem of integrity is the problem of ensuring that the data in the database is accurate. Inconsistency between two entries that purport to represent the same "fact" is an example of lack of integrity (see the discussion of this point above); of course, that particular problem can arise only if redundancy exists in the stored data. Even if there is no redundancy, however, the database may of course still contain incorrect information. For example, an employee might be shown as having worked 400 hours in the week instead of 40, or as belonging to a nonexistent department. Centralized control of the database can help in avoiding such problems— insofar as they can be avoided—by permitting the DBA to define integrity checks to be carried out whenever any update operation is attempted. (Again we are using the term "update" generically to cover all of the operations of modification, insertion, and deletion.)

It is worth pointing out that data integrity is even more important in a multi-user database system than it is in a "private files" environment, precisely because the database is shared. For without appropriate controls, it would be possible for one user to update the database incorrectly, thereby generating bad data and so "infecting" other innocent users of that data. It should also be mentioned that most current database products tend to be somewhat weak in their support for integrity controls.

■ Conflicting requirements can be balanced.

Knowing the overall requirements of the enterprise—as opposed to the requirements of any individual user—the DBA can structure the system to provide an overall service that is "best for the enterprise." For example, a representation can be chosen for the data in storage that gives fast access for the most important applications at the cost of comparatively poor performance for some other applications.

Most of the advantages listed above are probably fairly obvious. However, one further point, which may not be so obvious—although it is in fact implied by several of the others—needs to be added to the list, namely, *the provision of data independence*. (Strictly speaking, this is an *objective* for database systems, rather than an advantage necessarily.) The concept of data independence is so important that we devote a separate section to it.

1.5 DATA INDEPENDENCE

Data independence can most easily be understood by first considering its opposite. Many present-day applications are data-dependent. In other words, the way in which the data is organized in secondary storage and the way in which it is accessed are both dictated by the requirements of the application in question, and moreover *knowledge of that data organization and access technique is built into the application logic and code*. For example, it may be decided, for performance reasons, that a particular file is to be stored indexed on some particular field; e.g., the EMPLOYEE file might be stored indexed on the "employee number" field. (Indexing is explained in Chapter 3.) The application under consideration will then typically be aware of the fact that the index exists, and aware also of the file sequence as defined by that index, and the internal structure of the application will be built around that knowledge. In particular, the precise form of the various data access and exception-checking procedures within the application will depend very heavily on details of the interface presented by the file management software.

We say that an application such as this one is *data-dependent*, because it is impossible to change the storage structure (how the data is physically stored) or access strategy (how it is accessed) without affecting the application, probably drastically. For example, it would not be possible to replace the indexed file above by a hash-addressed file without making major modifications to the application. (Again, Chapter 3 explains the concept of hash-addressing.) What is more, the portions of the application requiring alteration in such a case are precisely those portions that communicate with the file management software; the difficulties involved

are quite irrelevant to the problem the application was originally written to solve—
i.e., they are difficulties *introduced* by the nature of the file management interface.

In a database system, however, it would be extremely undesirable to allow applications to be data-dependent, for at least the following two reasons:

1. Different applications will need different views of the same data. For example, suppose that before the enterprise introduces its integrated database, there are two applications, *A* and *B*, each owning a private file that includes the field "customer balance." Suppose, however, that application *A* records this value in decimal, whereas application *B* records it in binary. It will still be possible to integrate the two files (and to eliminate the redundancy), provided the DBMS is ready and able to perform all necessary conversions between the stored representation chosen (which may be decimal or binary or something else again) and the form in which each application wishes to see it. For example, if it is decided to store the value in decimal, then every access by *B* will require a conversion to or from binary.

This is a fairly trivial example of the kind of difference that might exist in a database system between the data as seen by a given application and the data as physically stored. Many other possible differences will be considered later.

2. The DBA must have the freedom to change the storage structure or access strategy (or both) in response to changing requirements, without having to modify existing applications. For example, new kinds of data may be added to the database; new standards may be adopted; application priorities (and therefore relative performance requirements) may change; new types of storage device may become available; and so on. If applications are data-dependent, such changes will typically require corresponding changes to be made to programs, thus tying up programmer effort that would otherwise be available for the creation of new applications. It is still not uncommon, even today, to find that 25 percent or even more of the programming effort available in the installation is devoted to this kind of maintenance activity—clearly a waste of a scarce and valuable resource.

It follows that the provision of data independence is a major objective of database systems. Data independence can be defined as *the immunity of applications to change in storage structure and access strategy*— which implies that the applications concerned do not depend on any one particular storage structure or access strategy. In Chapter 2, we present an architecture for a database system that provides a basis for achieving the data-independence objective. Before then, however, let us consider in more detail some examples of the types of change that the DBA may wish to make, and that we may therefore wish applications to be immune to.

We start by defining three terms: *stored field, stored record,* and *stored file.*

- A *stored field* is the smallest named unit of stored data. The database will, in general, contain many *occurrences* or *instances* of each of several *types* of stored field. For example, a database containing information about parts would probably include a stored field type called "part number," and there would be one occurrence of this stored field for each kind of part (screws, hinges, lids, etc.).

■   A *stored record* is a named collection of related stored fields. Again we distin-
    guish between type and occurrence. A stored record *occurrence* (or *instance*)
    consists of a group of related stored field occurrences. For example, a stored
    record occurrence in the "parts" database might consist of an occurrence of
    each of the following stored fields: part number, part name, part color, and
    part weight. We say that the database contains multiple occurrences of the
    "part" stored record *type* (again, one occurrence for each distinct kind of part).
        As an aside, we note that it is common to drop the qualifiers "type" and
    "occurrence" (both for stored fields and records and also for other kinds of
    field and record, to be discussed later), and to rely on context to indicate which
    of the two is meant. Although there is a slight risk of confusion, the practice
    is convenient, and we shall adopt it ourselves from time to time in this book.

■   Finally, a *stored file* is the named collection of all occurrences of one type of
    stored record. (We ignore the possibility of a stored file containing more than
    one type of stored record. This is yet another simplifying assumption that does
    not materially affect any of the following discussion.)

Now, in nondatabase systems it is usually the case that an application's logical
record is identical to some corresponding stored record. However, as we have already seen, this is not necessarily the case in a database system, because the DBA
may need to be able to make changes to the storage structure—that is, to the stored
fields, records, and files—while the corresponding logical structures do *not* change.
For example, the "part weight" field mentioned above might be stored in binary
to economize on storage space, whereas a given COBOL application might see it as
a PICTURE item (i.e., as a character string). And later the DBA may decide for
some reason to change the stored representation of that field from binary to decimal, and yet still allow the application to see it in character form.
    As stated earlier, a difference such as this one—involving data type conversion
on a particular field on each access—is comparatively minor, however; in general,
the difference between what the application sees and what is actually stored might
be quite considerable. To amplify this remark, we present below a list of aspects of
the database storage structure that might be subject to variation. (A more complete
list can be found in Engles [1.10].) The reader should consider in each case what
the DBMS would have to do to protect an application from such variation (and
indeed whether such protection can always be achieved).

■   Representation of numeric data

    A numeric field may be stored in internal arithmetic form (e.g., in packed dec-
imal) or as a character string. Either way, the DBA must choose an appropriate base
(e.g., binary or decimal), scale (fixed or floating point), mode (real or complex),
and precision (number of digits). Any of these aspects may be changed to improve
performance or to conform to a new standard or for many other reasons.

■   Representation of character data

A character string field may be stored in any of several distinct character codes (e.g., ASCII, EBCDIC).

■ Units for numeric data

The units in a numeric field may change—from inches to centimeters, for example, during a process of metrication.

■ Data coding

In some situations it may be desirable to represent data in storage by coded values. For example, the "part color" field, which an application sees as a character string ('Red' or 'Blue' or 'Green' ...), might be stored as a single decimal digit, interpreted according to the table 1 = 'Red', 2 = 'Blue', and so on.

■ Data materialization

Usually the logical field seen by an application will correspond to some unique stored field (although, as we have already seen, there may be differences in data type, units, and so on). In such a case, the process of materialization—that is, constructing an occurrence of the logical field from the corresponding stored field occurrence and presenting it to the application—may be said to be *direct*. Sometimes, however, a logical field will have no single stored counterpart; instead, its values will be materialized by means of some computation performed on a set of several stored field occurrences. For example, values of the logical field "total quantity" might be materialized by summing a number of individual stored quantity values. "Total quantity" here is an example of a *virtual* field, and the materialization process is said to be *indirect*. Note, however, that the user may see a difference between real and virtual fields, inasmuch as it will probably not be possible to create or modify an ocurrence of a virtual field, at least not directly.

■ Structure of stored records

Two existing stored records might be combined into one. For example, the stored records

```
(part number, color)     and     (part number, weight)
```
could be combined to form

```
(part number, color, weight) .
```

Such a change might occur as pre-database applications are brought into the database system. It implies that an application's logical record could consist of a subset of the corresponding stored record—that is, certain fields in that stored record would be invisible to the application in question.

Alternatively, a single stored record type might be split into two. Reversing the previous example, the stored record type

```
(part number, color, weight)
```
could be broken down into

```
(part number, color)     and     (part number, weight) .
```

Such a split would allow less frequently used portions of the original record to be stored on a slower device, for example. The implication is that an application's logical record might contain fields from several distinct stored records—that is, it would be a superset of any given one of those stored records.

■ Structure of stored files

A given stored file can be physically implemented in storage in a wide variety of ways. For example, it might be entirely contained within a single storage volume (e.g., a single disk), or it might be spread across several volumes on several different types of device; it might or might not be physically sequenced according to the values of some stored field; it might or might not be sequenced in one or more additional ways by some other means, e.g., by one or more indexes or one or more embedded pointer chains (or both); it might or might not be accessible via hash-addressing; the stored records might or might not be blocked; and so on. But none of these considerations should affect applications in any way (other than in performance, of course).

This concludes our list of aspects of the storage structure that are subject to possible change. The list implies (among other things) that the database should be able to *grow* without affecting existing applications; indeed, enabling the database to grow without logically impairing existing applications is probably the single most important reason for requiring data independence in the first place. For example, it should be possible to extend an existing stored record by the addition of new stored fields (representing, typically, further information concerning some existing type of entity or relationship; e.g., a "unit cost" field might be added to the "part" stored record). Such new fields should simply be invisible to existing applications. Likewise, it should be possible to add entirely new types of stored record (and hence new stored files), again without requiring any change to existing applications; such records would typically represent new types of entity or relationship (e.g., a "supplier" record type could be added to the "parts" database. Again, such additions should be invisible to existing applications.

We conclude this section by noting that data independence is not an absolute—different systems provide it in different degrees. To put this another way, few systems if any provide no data independence at all; it is just that some systems are more data-dependent than others. Modern systems tend to be more data-independent than older systems, but they are still not ideal, as we shall see in some of the chapters to come.

1.6 RELATIONAL SYSTEMS AND OTHERS

Almost all of the database systems developed over the past few years are *relational* (older systems, by contrast, are mostly not).[3] Furthermore, almost all current data-

---

3.   In most cases, however, the vendors of those older systems are currently trying to extend their product to incorporate some kind of relational support (with, we might add, varying degrees of success). This fact in itself may be seen as additional evidence in support of the claims of this paragraph.

base research is also based on relational ideas. In fact, there can be little doubt that the relational approach represents the dominant trend in the marketplace today, and that "the relational model" (see Part 3 of this book) is the single most important development in the entire history of the database field. For these reasons, plus the additional reason that relational ideas provide an extremely convenient vehicle for teaching purposes, the emphasis in this book is heavily on the relational approach. However, one part of the book, Part 5, does discuss other approaches, and in particular describes a number of commercially available nonrelational products.

What does it mean to say that a system is relational? It is not possible to answer this question fully at this early point in our discussion; however, it is possible (and desirable) to give a rough-and-ready answer, which we can make more precise later on (in Parts 2 and 3 of this book). Briefly, a relational system is a system in which:

1. the data is perceived by the user as tables (and nothing but tables); and

2. the operators at the user's disposal (e.g., for data retrieval) are operators that generate new tables from old. For example, there will be one operator to extract a subset of the rows of a given table, and another to extract a subset of the columns— and of course a row subset and a column subset of a table may both in turn be regarded as tables themselves.

As indicated, we will make this definition considerably more precise later, but it will serve for the time being. Figure 1.6 provides an illustration. The data—see

(a) Given table:	CELLAR	WINE	YEAR	BOTTLES
		Zinfandel	77	9
		Chardonnay	82	4
		Fume Blanc	78	2
		Pinot Noir	77	3

(b) Operators (examples):

1. Row subset: Result:

	WINE	YEAR	BOTTLES
SELECT WINE, YEAR, BOTTLES	Zinfandel	77	9
FROM CELLAR	Pinot Noir	77	3
WHERE YEAR = 77 ;			

2. Column subset: Result:

	WINE	BOTTLES
SELECT WINE, BOTTLES	Zinfandel	9
FROM CELLAR ;	Chardonnay	4
	Fume Blanc	2
	Pinot Noir	3

Fig. 1.6 Data structure and operators in a relational system (examples).

part (a) of the figure—consists of a single table, named CELLAR (in fact, it is a reduced version of the CELLAR table from Fig. 1.1, scaled down to make it a little more manageable). Two sample retrievals—one involving a row-subsetting operation and one a column-subsetting operation—are shown in part (b) of the figure. Note: Once again, the two retrievals are in fact examples of the SELECT statement of the language SQL first mentioned in Section 1.1.

We can distinguish a relational system from a nonrelational one as follows. As already stated, the user of a relational system sees the data as tables (and nothing but tables). The user of a nonrelational system, by contrast, sees other data structures, either instead of or in addition to the tables of a relational system. Those other structures, in turn, require other operators to manipulate them. For example, in IMS, which is a *hierarchic* system, the data is represented to the user in the form of a set of tree structures, and the operators provided for manipulating such structures include operators for traversing hierarchic paths up and down the trees.

In fact, we can conveniently categorize systems according to the data structures and operators they present to the user. The four major categories are *relational, inverted list, hierarchic,* and *network.* We conclude this section (and this whole introductory chapter) with a brief list of sample systems (all of them commercially available products) from each of the four categories. See Fig. 1.7.

	System	*Vendor*
Relational:	DB2	IBM
	SQL/DS	IBM
	INGRES	Relational Technology Inc.
	ORACLE	ORACLE Corp.
	Rdb/VMS	DEC
Inverted list:	MODEL 204	CCA
	ADABAS	Software AG
	DATACOM/DB	Applied Data Research
Hierarchic:	IMS	IBM
	System 2000	Intel
Network:	IDMS	Cullinet
	DMS 1100	Sperry
	TOTAL	Cincom Systems

Fig. 1.7 Some sample database products.

EXERCISES

1.1 Define the following terms:

concurrent access	DBMS
database	entity
database system	integration
data independence	integrity
DBA	operational data

query language	stored field
relationship	stored file
security	stored record
sharing	user

1.2 What are the advantages of using a database system?

1.3 What are the disadvantages of using a database system?

1.4 What do you understand by the term "relational system"? Distinguish between relational and nonrelational systems.

1.5 Show the effects of the following SQL retrieval operations on the wine cellar database of Fig. 1.1.

a) ```
SELECT WINE, PRODUCER
FROM   CELLAR
WHERE   BIN = 72 ;
```

b) ```
SELECT WINE, PRODUCER
FROM    CELLAR
WHERE   YEAR > 81 ;
```

c) ```
SELECT BIN, WINE, YEAR
FROM   CELLAR
WHERE   READY < 83 ;
```

d) ```
SELECT WINE, BIN, YEAR
FROM    CELLAR
WHERE   PRODUCER = 'Buena Vista'
AND     BOTTLES > 1 ;
```

1.6 Show the effects of the following SQL update operations on the wine cellar database of Fig. 1.1.

a) ```
INSERT INTO CELLAR
VALUES (80,'Merlot','Clos du Bois',78,12,85,'Christmas') ;
```

b) ```
DELETE
FROM    CELLAR
WHERE   READY > 84 ;
```

c) ```
UPDATE CELLAR
SET   BOTTLES = 10
WHERE   BIN = 43 ;
```

d) ```
UPDATE CELLAR
SET     BOTTLES = BOTTLES - 2
WHERE   BIN = 43 ;
```

1.7 Write SQL statements to perform the following operations on the wine cellar database.

a) Retrieve bin number, name of wine, and number of bottles for all Mirassou wines.

b) Retrieve bin number and name of wine for all wines for which there are more than five bottles in stock.

c) Retrieve bin number for all red wines.

d) Add three bottles to bin number 30.

e) Remove all Chardonnay from stock.

f) Add a record for a new case (12 bottles) of Mirassou Chardonnay: bin number 5, year 84, ready in 88, with a comment '1st prize'.

REFERENCES AND BIBLIOGRAPHY

1.1 CODASYL Systems Committee. "A Survey of Generalized Data Base Management Systems." Technical Report (May 1969). Available from ACM and IAG.

1.2 CODASYL Systems Committee. "Feature Analysis of Generalized Data Base Management Systems." Technical Report (May 1971). Available from ACM, BCS, and IAG.

These two lengthy documents (over 900 pages between them) complement each other in the following sense: Reference [1.1] consists of independent descriptions of a set of early systems (i.e., a separate chapter is devoted to each system); reference [1.2] consists of feature-by-feature comparisons of a (slightly different) set of systems. The following systems are covered: ADAM ([1.1] only), COBOL ([1.2] only), DBTG ([1.2] only), GIS, IDS, ISL-1 ([1.1] only), IMS ([1.2] only), MARK IV, NIPS/FFS, SC-1, TDMS, UL/1. The documents are now rather out-of-date (so are most of the systems described, for that matter), but they are interesting as a guide to database systems and thinking as they were in the late sixties.

1.3 CODASYL Systems Committee. "Introduction to 'Feature Analysis of Generalized Data Base Management Systems.'" *BCS Comp. Bull.* **15**, No. 4 (April 1971); also *CACM* **14**, No. 5 (May 1971).

Adapted from the initial section of reference [1.2] and published separately. A useful introduction to some of the basic concepts of a database system.

1.4 GUIDE/SHARE Data Base Task Force. "Data Base Management System Requirements." Available from SHARE Inc., 111 E. Wacker Drive, Chicago, Ill. 60601.

A detailed statement by representatives of the IBM user associations GUIDE and SHARE of the features they perceived (in 1971) as required in an ideal database system. Like references [1.1–1.3] above, now somewhat out-of-date, but still reasonably relevant.

1.5 Auerbach Publishers Inc. (eds.). *Practical Data Base Management*. Reston, Va.: Reston Publishing Company (1981).

As its title suggests, this book is aimed primarily at a management audience rather than at database technicians. Because of its very different perspective, it can be regarded as complementary to the present book.

1.6 Shaku Atre. *Data Base Management Systems for the Eighties* (looseleaf). QED Information Sciences, Inc., Wellesley, Mass. (1983).

A tutorial on database technology, database administration, and DBMS product evaluation, with the emphasis (as in reference [1.5]) on practical rather than theoretical aspects. Includes substantial detailed (and uniform) descriptions of a number of commercially available products: IMS, TOTAL, ADABAS, SYSTEM 2000, IDMS, DATACOM/DB, MODEL 204, and SQL/DS. The reader is cautioned that significant new releases of most, if not all, of these products have appeared since this book was published, also that many other commercially important systems now exist in the marketplace; however, the book does provide a convenient source for a lot of material that is otherwise available only in product manuals, which are often very bulky and can be difficult to obtain.

1.7 Digital Consulting Associates, Inc. "The 198*x* National Database and Fourth Generation Language Symposium: Proceedings" (new edition produced annually). Digital Consulting Associates, Inc., 6 Windsor St., Andover, Mass. 01810.

These proceedings include a foil presentation on database management and current product offerings, together with vendor-supplied material (typically one- or two-page marketing-oriented system descriptions) covering a wide range of commercially available products.

1.8 Joachim W. Schmidt and Michael L. Brodie (eds.). *Relational Database Systems: Analysis and Comparison*. New York: Springer-Verlag (1983).

A collection of working papers from the Relational Task Group (RTG) of the American National Standards Institute (ANSI). The RTG was chartered by the ANSI/X3/SPARC Study Group on Data Base Systems (see references [2.1–2.4] in Chapter 2) to investigate the suitability of establishing a project to develop standards in the area of relational database systems. Reference [1.9] below is the RTG Final Report. The recommendation of that report was that such a project should indeed be established, and at the time of writing the ANSI Database Committee (X3H2) is actively pursuing the definition of a proposed standard relational language based on SQL. The present reference [1.8] effectively does for certain relational systems what references [1.1–1.2] did for certain nonrelational ones—that is, it provides individual and feature-by-feature analyses of a set of relational systems (some commercially available, others only experimental). The systems in question are ASTRAL, IDAMS, the IDM, University INGRES, MRDS, MRS, NOMAD, ORACLE, PASCAL/R, PRTV, QBE, RAPID, RAPPORT, and System R.

1.9 Michael L. Brodie and Joachim W. Schmidt (eds.). Final Report of the ANSI/X3/SPARC DBS-SG Relational Database Task Group. *ACM SIGMOD Record* **12,** No. 4 (July 1982).

See the annotation to reference [1.8].

1.10 R. W. Engles. "A Tutorial on Data Base Organization." *Annual Review in Automatic Programming, Vol. 7* (eds., Halpern and McGee). Elmsford, N.Y.: Pergamon Press (1974).

A good early introduction to database concepts. The major topics included are a theory of operational data, a survey of storage structures and access techniques, and a discussion of data independence.

1.11 E. H. Sibley. "The Development of Data Base Technology." Guest Editor's Introduction to *ACM Comp. Surv.* **8,** No. 1: Special Issue on Data Base Management Systems (March 1976).

1.12 J. P. Fry and E. H. Sibley. "Evolution of Data Base Management Systems." *ACM Comp. Surv.* **8,** No. 1 (March 1976).

These two references [1.11–1.12] are included here because they provide a good illustration of how rapidly the database field moves. In 1976 it was still possible to write a survey paper that virtually ignored the existence of the relational approach entirely (these two papers do give relational systems a very brief mention, but the tone of that mention is almost dismissive). Today, as explained in Section 1.6, almost all research on database systems is founded on relational theory, and the vast majority of commercially available database products are relational. In fact, the relational approach is easily the single most important factor in the entire database field today, from both a marketing and an academic standpoint.

1.13 W. C. McGee. "Data Base Technology." *IBM Sys. J.* **25,** No. 5 (September 1981).

A survey of the evolution of database technology over the period 1955–1980, with special emphasis on the (often very significant) contributions made to the field by IBM researchers and developers during that period.

1.14 M. R. Stonebraker. "A Functional View of Data Independence." Proc. 1974 ACM SIGMOD Workshop on Data Description, Access and Control (May 1974).

This paper is an attempt to provide a precise framework for dealing with the subject of data independence. Seven classes of transformation of a stored database from one representation to another are identified and rigorously defined. The following examples give some idea of the types of transformation in each of the seven classes.

1. Physical relocation of stored files
2. Conversion of stored field values from one data type to another
3. Replacement of one hashing algorithm by another
4. Addition of indexes
5. Duplication of stored data
6. Splitting one stored record into two
7. Combining two stored records into one

It is suggested that a measure of the degree of data independence provided by a particular system may be obtained by considering the range of transformations supported (in a data-independent fashion) in each of the seven classes. The paper concludes with a brief examination of three (early) specific systems in the light of these ideas.

ANSWERS TO SELECTED EXERCISES

1.3 Security may be compromised
(without good controls)
Integrity may be compromised
(without good controls)
Additional hardware may be required
Performance overhead may be significant
Successful operation is crucial
(the enterprise may be highly vulnerable to failure)
System is likely to be complex
(though complexity should be concealed from the user)

1.5 a)

WINE	PRODUCER
Gamay	Robt.Mondavi

b)

WINE	PRODUCER
Chardonnay	Buena Vista
Chardonnay	Chappellet
Jo.Riesling	Jekel
Jo.Riesling	Buena Vista
Jo.Riesling	Sattui

c)

BIN	WINE	YEAR
22	Fume Blanc	78
25	Wh.Burgundy	80
30	Gewurztraminer	80

d)

WINE	BIN	YEAR
Gewurztraminer	30	80

1.6

a) Row for bin 80 added to the CELLAR table.

b) Rows for bins 2, 6, 11, 43, 50, 51, 64 (and 80) deleted from the CELLAR table.

c) Row for bin 43 has number of bottles set to 10.

d) Same as c).

1.7 a)
```
SELECT BIN, WINE, BOTTLES
FROM   CELLAR
WHERE  PRODUCER = 'Mirassou' ;
```
b)
```
SELECT BIN, WINE
FROM   CELLAR
WHERE  BOTTLES > 5 ;
```
c)
```
SELECT BIN
FROM   CELLAR
WHERE  WINE = 'Cab.Sauvignon'
OR     WINE = 'Pinot Noir'
OR     WINE = 'Zinfandel'
OR     WINE = 'Gamay'
OR     ...... ;
```

There is no short cut answer to this question, because "color of wine" is not explicitly recorded in the database.

d) UPDATE CELLAR
   SET   BOTTLES = BOTTLES + 3
   WHERE   BIN = 30 ;

e) DELETE FROM CELLAR
   WHERE   WINE = 'Chardonnay' ;

f) INSERT INTO CELLAR
   VALUES (5,'Chardonnay','Mirassou',84,12,88,'1st prize');

2
An Architecture
for a Database System

2.1 PURPOSE

We are now in a position to outline an architecture for a database system. Our aim in presenting this architecture is to provide a framework on which we can build in subsequent chapters. Such a framework is extremely useful for describing general database concepts and for explaining the structure of specific database systems—but of course we do not claim that every system can neatly be matched to this particular framework, nor do we mean to suggest that this particular architecture provides the only possible framework. "Small" (micro-based) systems, in particular, will certainly not support all aspects of the architecture. However, the architecture in question does seem to fit most systems (relational or otherwise) reasonably well; moreover, it is in broad agreement with that proposed by the ANSI/SPARC Study Group on Data Base Management Systems [2.1–2.4]. We choose not to follow the ANSI/SPARC terminology in every detail, however.

2.2 THE THREE LEVELS OF THE ARCHITECTURE

The architecture is divided into three general levels: internal, conceptual, and external (see Fig. 2.1). Broadly speaking:

1. the *internal* level is the one closest to physical storage—i.e., it is the one concerned with the way the data is actually stored;

2. the *external* level is the one closest to the users—i.e., it is the one concerned with the way the data is viewed by individual users; and

3. the *conceptual* level is a "level of indirection" between the other two.

   If the external level is concerned with *individual* user views, the conceptual level may be regarded as being concerned with a *community* user view. In other words,

29

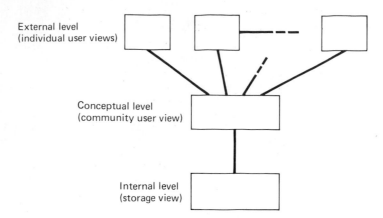

External level
(individual user views)

Conceptual level
(community user view)

Internal level
(storage view)

Fig. 2.1 The three levels of the architecture.

there will be many distinct "external views," each consisting of a more or less abstract representation of some portion of the total database, and there will be precisely one "conceptual view," consisting of a similarly abstract representation of the database in its entirety.[1] (Remember that most users will not be interested in the total database, only in some restricted portion of it.) Likewise, there will be precisely one "internal view," representing the total database as actually stored.

An example will help to make these ideas clearer. Figure 2.2 shows the conceptual view for a simple personnel database, the corresponding internal view, and two corresponding external views, one for a PL/I user and one for a COBOL user. Of course, the example is completely hypothetical—it is not intended to resemble any actual system—and many irrelevant details have deliberately been omitted.

We interpret Fig. 2.2 as follows.

- At the conceptual level, the database contains information concerning an entity type called EMPLOYEE. Each EMPLOYEE has an EMPLOYEE_NUMBER (six characters), a DEPARTMENT_NUMBER (four characters), and a SALARY (five decimal digits).

- At the internal level, employees are represented by a stored record type called STORED_EMP, eighteen bytes long. STORED_EMP contains four stored field types: a six-byte prefix (presumably containing control information such as flags or pointers—see Chapter 3), and three data fields corresponding to the three properties of employees. In addition, STORED_EMP records are indexed on the EMP# field by an index called EMPX.

---

1.   When we describe some representation as abstract, we mean merely that it involves user-oriented constructs such as logical records and fields instead of machine-oriented constructs such as bits and bytes.

```
External (PL/I)                    | External (COBOL)

DCL 1 EMPP,                        | 01 EMPC.
     2 EMP# CHAR(6),               |    02 EMPNO PIC X(6).
     2 SAL FIXED BIN(31);          |    02 DEPTNO PIC X(4).
-------------------------------------------------------------------

     Conceptual

     EMPLOYEE
          EMPLOYEE_NUMBER     CHARACTER (6)
          DEPARTMENT_NUMBER   CHARACTER (4)
          SALARY              NUMERIC   (5)
-------------------------------------------------------------------

     Internal

     STORED_EMP    LENGTH=18
          PREFIX   TYPE=BYTE(6),OFFSET=0
          EMP#     TYPE=BYTE(6),OFFSET=6,INDEX=EMPX
          DEPT#    TYPE=BYTE(4),OFFSET=12
          PAY      TYPE=FULLWORD,OFFSET=16
```

Fig. 2.2 An example of the three levels.

- The PL/I user has an external view of the database in which each employee is represented by a PL/I record containing two fields (department numbers are of no interest to this user and have therefore been omitted from the view). The record type is defined by an ordinary PL/I structure declaration in accordance with the normal PL/I rules.

- Similarly, the COBOL user has an external view in which each employee is represented by a COBOL record containing, again, two fields (this time, salaries have been omitted). The record type is defined by an ordinary COBOL record description in accordance with the normal COBOL rules.

- Notice that corresponding objects can have different names at each point. For example, the employee number is referred to as EMP# in the PL/I view, as EMPNO in the COBOL view, as EMPLOYEE_NUMBER in the conceptual view, and as EMP# (again) in the internal view. Of course, the system must be aware of the correspondences. For example, it must be told that the COBOL field EMPNO is derived from the conceptual object EMPLOYEE_NUMBER, which in turn is represented at the internal level by the stored field EMP#. Such correspondences, or *mappings*, are not shown in Fig. 2.2.

Note: It makes little difference for the purposes of the present chapter whether the system under consideration is relational or otherwise. However, it may be helpful to indicate briefly how the three levels of the architecture will typically be realized in a relational system. First, the conceptual level in such a system *will* definitely be relational, in the sense that the objects visible at that level will be relational tables (also, the operators will be the relational operators, i.e., operators that work on such tables). Second, a given external view will typically either be relational also, or else something very close to it; for example, the PL/I and COBOL records of Fig. 2.2 may be regarded as, respectively, the PL/I and COBOL representations of (a row within) a relational table. Third, the internal level will almost certainly *not* be "relational," because the objects at that level will normally not be just (stored) relational tables—instead, they will be the same kinds of object found at the internal level of other kinds of system (namely, stored records, pointers, indexes, hashes, etc.). In fact, relational theory as such has nothing to say about the internal level at all (it is, to repeat, concerned with how the database looks to the *user*).

We now proceed to examine the three levels of the architecture in considerably more detail, starting with the external level. Figure 2.3 shows the major components of the architecture and their interrelationships. That figure will be referenced repeatedly throughout the remainder of this chapter.

2.3 THE EXTERNAL LEVEL

The external level is the individual user level. As explained in Chapter 1, a given user can be either an application programmer or an on-line terminal user—i.e., an end-user—of any degree of sophistication. The DBA is an important special case. (Unlike ordinary users, however, the DBA will need to be interested in the conceptual and internal levels also. See the next two sections.)

Each user has a *language* at his or her disposal:

- For the application programmer, that language will be either one of the conventional programming languages, such as COBOL or PL/I, or else a proprietary programming language that is specific to the system in question (as found in, e.g., the systems NOMAD or Rdb/VMS or dBASE II).

- For the end-user, it will be either a query language or a special-purpose language, perhaps forms- or menu-based, tailored to that user's requirements and supported by some on-line application program.

For our purposes, the important thing about all such languages is that they will include a *data sublanguage*—i.e., a subset of the total language that is concerned specifically with database objects and operations. The data sublanguage (abbreviated DSL in Fig. 2.3) is said to be embedded within the corresponding *host language*. The host language is responsible for providing various nondatabase facilities, such as local (temporary) variables, computational operations, if-then-else logic, and so on. A given system may support multiple host languages and multiple data sublanguages.

Note: Although it is convenient for architectural purposes to distinguish between the data sublanguage and its containing host language, the two may in fact be indistinguishable so far as the user is concerned. Indeed, it is probably preferable from the user's point of view if they *are* indistinguishable. If they are, or if they can be separated only with difficulty, we say that the two are *tightly coupled*. If

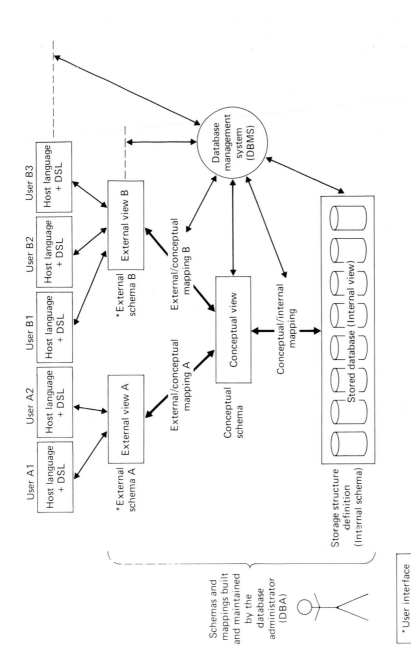

Fig. 2.3 Detailed system architecture.

they are clearly and easily separable, then we say they are *loosely* coupled. Most systems today support loose coupling only. A tightly coupled system will provide a more uniform set of facilities for the user, but obviously involves more effort on the part of the designers and developers of the system (which presumably accounts for the status quo). However, there is evidence to suggest that there will be a gradual movement toward more tightly coupled systems over the next few years.

In principle, any given data sublanguage is really a combination of at least two subordinate languages: a *data definition language* (DDL), which provides for the definition or description of database objects, and a *data manipulation language* (DML), which supports the manipulation or processing of those objects. Consider the PL/I user of Fig. 2.2 in Section 2.2. The data sublanguage for that user consists of those PL/I features that are used to communicate with the DBMS. The DDL portion consists of those declarative constructs of PL/I that are needed to declare database objects: the DECLARE (DCL) statement itself, certain PL/I data types, possibly special extensions to PL/I to support new objects that are not handled by existing PL/I. The DML portion consists of those executable statements of PL/I that transfer information to and from the database—again, possibly including special new statements. (Note: Current PL/I does not in fact include any specific database features. The "DML" statements are therefore typically just CALLs to the DBMS. This is because PL/I systems, like most other systems today, currently provide only very loose coupling between the data sublanguage and its host.)

To return to the architecture: We have already indicated that an individual user will generally be interested only in some portion of the total database; moreover, that user's view of that portion will generally be somewhat abstract when compared with the way the data is physically stored. The ANSI/SPARC term for an individual user's view is an *external view*.[2] An external view is thus the content of the database as it is seen by some particular user (that is, to that user the external view *is* the database). For example, a user from the Personnel Department may regard the database as a collection of department record occurrences plus a collection of employee record occurrences (and may be quite unaware of the supplier and part record occurrences seen by users in the Purchasing Department).

In general, then, an external view consists of multiple occurrences of multiple types of *external record*.[3] An external record is *not* necessarily the same as a stored

---

2. External views were called *data submodels* in the first edition of this book, and *external models* (following [2.1]) in the second. There is a great deal of confusion over terminology in this area. Following [2.2], we now prefer "view" for a set of occurrences and "schema" (or simply "view definition") for the definition of a view. As for the term "model" (or "data model"), we use it only in its original, theoretical sense; see Part 3 of this book.

3. For the time being, we assume that all information is represented in the form of records. In Part 5 of this book we will see that information may be represented in other ways as well, e.g., in the form of "links" or pointers. For a system using such alternative methods, the definitions and explanations given in this section will require suitable modification. Furthermore, these remarks apply to the conceptual and internal levels as well as to the external level (see Sections 2.4 and 2.5).

record. The user's data sublanguage is defined in terms of external records; for example, a DML "retrieve record" operation will retrieve an external record occurrence, not a stored record occurrence. We can now see, incidentally, that the term "logical record" used at several points in Chapter 1 actually referred to an external record. From this point on we will generally avoid the term "logical record."

Each external view is defined by means of an *external schema*, which consists basically of definitions of each of the various types of external record in that external view. The external schema is written using the DDL portion of the user's data sublanguage. (That DDL is therefore sometimes referred to as an *external DDL*.) For example, the employee external record type may be defined as a six-character employee number field plus a five-digit (decimal) salary field, and so on. In addition, there must be a definition of the *mapping* between the external schema and the underlying conceptual schema (described in the next section). We will discuss that mapping later, in Section 2.6.

Now we turn to the conceptual level.

2.4   THE CONCEPTUAL LEVEL

The *conceptual view* is a representation of the entire information content of the database, again (as with an external view) in a form that is somewhat abstract in comparison with the way in which the data is physically stored. It may also be quite different from the way in which the data is viewed by any particular user. Broadly speaking, the conceptual view is intended to be a view of the data "as it really is," rather than as users are forced to see it by the constraints of (for example) the particular language or particular hardware they are using.

The conceptual view consists of multiple occurrences of multiple types of *conceptual record*.[4] For example, it may consist of a collection of department record occurrences plus a collection of employee record occurrences plus a collection of supplier record occurrences plus a collection of part record occurrences. . . . A conceptual record is not necessarily the same as either an external record, on the one hand, or a stored record, on the other.

The conceptual view is defined by means of the *conceptual schema*, which includes definitions of each of the various types of conceptual record. The conceptual schema is written using another data definition language, the *conceptual DDL*. If data independence is to be achieved, then those conceptual DDL definitions must not involve any considerations of storage structure or access strategy—they must be definitions of information content *only*. Thus there must be no reference in the

---

4.   It should be pointed out that there may well be other ways of modeling the operational data of the enterprise at the conceptual level—ways, that is, that do not involve records as such at all, and that may be preferable in some respects for that very reason [2.11]. For example, instead of dealing in terms of "conceptual records," it may be more desirable to consider "entities," and perhaps "relationships" too, in some more direct fashion. However, such considerations are beyond the scope of this early part of the book. See Chapter 25.

conceptual schema to stored field representations, stored record sequence, indexing, hash-addressing, pointers, or any other storage/access details. If the conceptual schema is made truly data-independent in this way, then the external schemas, which are defined in terms of the conceptual schema (see Section 2.6), will necessarily be data-independent too.

The conceptual view, then, is a view of the total database content, and the conceptual schema is a definition of that view. However, it would be misleading to suggest that the conceptual schema is nothing more than a set of definitions much like the simple record definitions found in, for example, a COBOL program. The definitions in the conceptual schema are intended to include a great many additional features, such as the security checks and integrity checks mentioned in Chapter 1. Some authorities would go so far as to suggest that the ultimate objective of the conceptual schema is to describe the complete enterprise—not just its operational data, but also how that data is used: how it flows from point to point within the enterprise, what it is used for at each point, what audit or other controls are to be applied at each point, and so on [2.5]. It must be emphasized, however, that no system today actually supports a conceptual level of anything approaching this degree of comprehensiveness; in most existing systems the "conceptual schema" is really little more than a simple union of all individual external schemas, possibly with the addition of some simple security and integrity checks. But it seems clear that systems of the future will eventually be far more sophisticated in their support of the conceptual level. We will discuss this topic in more depth toward the end of this book (see Chapter 25).

2.5 THE INTERNAL LEVEL

The third level of the architecture is the internal level. The *internal view* is a low-level representation of the entire database; it consists of multiple occurrences of multiple types of *internal record*. "Internal record" is the ANSI/SPARC term for the construct that we have been calling a *stored* record (and we will generally continue to use this latter term). The internal view is thus still at one remove from the physical level, since it does not deal in terms of *physical* records (also called *pages* or *blocks*), nor with any device-specific considerations such as cylinder or track sizes. (Basically, the internal view assumes an infinite linear address space. Details of how that address space is mapped to physical storage are highly system-specific and are deliberately omitted from the architecture.)

The internal view is described by means of the *internal schema*, which not only defines the various types of stored record but also specifies what indexes exist, how stored fields are represented, what physical sequence the stored records are in, and so on. The internal schema is written using yet another data definition language—the *internal DDL*.

Note: In this book we will normally use the term "stored database" in place of "internal view," and the term "storage structure definition" in place of "internal schema."

As an aside, we remark that, in certain exceptional situations, application programs—in particular, applications of a "utility" nature (see Section 2.7)—might be permitted to operate directly at the internal level rather than at the external level. Needless to say, the practice is not recommended; it represents a security risk (since the security checks are bypassed) and an integrity risk (since the integrity checks are bypassed likewise), and the program will be data-dependent to boot; but sometimes it may be the only way to obtain the required function or performance—just as the user in a high-level programming language system might occasionally need to descend to assembler language in order to satisfy certain function or performance objectives.

2.6   MAPPINGS

Referring again to Fig. 2.3, the reader will observe two levels of *mapping* in the architecture, one between the external and conceptual levels of the system and one between the conceptual and internal levels. The *conceptual/internal* mapping defines the correspondence between the conceptual view and the stored database; it specifies how conceptual records and fields are represented at the internal level. If the structure of the stored database is changed—i.e., if a change is made to the storage structure definition—then the conceptual/internal mapping must also be changed accordingly, so that the conceptual schema may remain invariant. (It is the responsibility of the DBA to control such changes, of course.) In other words, the effects of such changes must be isolated below the conceptual level, in order that data independence may be preserved.

An *external/conceptual* mapping defines the correspondence between a particular external view and the conceptual view. The differences that may exist between these two levels are similar to those that may exist between the conceptual view and the stored database. For example, fields can have different data types, field and record names can be changed, multiple conceptual fields can be combined into a single (virtual) external field, and so on. Any number of external views can exist at the same time; any number of users can share a given external view; different external views can overlap. Incidentally, some systems permit the definition of one external view to be expressed in terms of others (in effect, via an *external/external* mapping), rather than always requiring an explicit definition of the mapping to the conceptual level—a useful feature if several external views are closely related to one another.

2.7   THE DATABASE ADMINISTRATOR

The *database administrator* (DBA), who has already been discussed to some extent both in this chapter and in Chapter 1, is the person (or group of persons) responsible for overall control of the total system. The responsibilities of the DBA include the following.

■   Deciding the information content of the database

It is the DBA's job to decide exactly what information is to be held in the database—in other words, to identify the entities of interest to the enterprise and to identify the information to be recorded about those entities.[5] Having done this, the DBA must then define the content of the database by writing the conceptual schema (using the conceptual DDL). The object (compiled) form of that schema is used by the DBMS in responding to access requests. The source (uncompiled) form acts as a reference document for the users of the system.

■   Deciding the storage structure and access strategy

The DBA must also decide how the data is to be represented in the database,[6] and must define that representation by writing the storage structure definition (using the internal DDL). In addition, the associated mapping between the internal and conceptual levels must also be defined. In practice, either the conceptual DDL or the internal DDL—most likely the former—will probably include the means for defining that mapping, but the two functions (defining the schema, defining the mapping) should be clearly separable. Like the conceptual schema, the internal schema and corresponding mapping will exist in both source and object form.

■   Liaising with users

It is the business of the DBA to liaise with users, to ensure that the data they require is available, and to write—or help the users write, as appropriate—the necessary external schemas, using the applicable external DDL (as already mentioned, a given system may support several distinct external DDLs). In addition, the mapping between any given external schema and the conceptual schema must also be defined. In practice, the external DDL will probably include the means for specifying that mapping, but the schema and the mapping should be clearly separable. Each external schema and corresponding mapping will exist in both source and object form.

■   Defining security and integrity checks

As already discussed, security and integrity checks can be regarded as part of the conceptual schema. The conceptual DDL will include facilities for specifying such checks.

■   Defining a strategy for backup and recovery

Once an enterprise is committed to a database system, it becomes critically dependent on the successful operation of that system. In the event of damage to any portion of the database—caused by human error, say, or a failure in the hardware or supporting operating system—it is essential to be able to repair the data concerned with the minimum of delay and with as little effect as possible on the rest of the system. For example, the availability of data that has *not* been damaged

---

5.   This process is usually referred to as *logical* (or sometimes *conceptual) database design.*
6.   This process is usually referred to as *physical* database design.

should ideally not be affected.[7] The DBA must define and implement an appropriate recovery strategy, involving, for example, periodic dumping of the database to backup storage and procedures for reloading the database when necessary from the most recent dump.

- Monitoring performance and responding to changing requirements

The DBA is responsible for so organizing the system as to get the performance that is "best for the enterprise," and for making the appropriate adjustments as requirements change. As already mentioned, any change to details of storage and access must be accompanied by a corresponding change to the definition of the mapping from the conceptual level, so that the conceptual schema can remain constant.

It is clear that the DBA will require a number of utility programs to help with the foregoing tasks. Such utilities are an essential part of a practical database system, though they were not shown in the architecture of Fig. 2.3. Here are some examples of the kind of utilities that are needed:

- Load routines (to create the initial version of the database from one or more nondatabase files).

- Dump/restore routines (to dump the database to backup storage for recovery purposes and to reload the database from such a backup copy). Note: The load routines mentioned above will in practice probably consist of the "restore" portion of these dump/restore routines.

- Reorganization routines (to rearrange the data in the database for various performance reasons—e.g., to cluster data together in some particular way, or to reclaim space occupied by data that has become obsolete).

- Statistics routines (to compute various performance statistics, such as file sizes and data value distributions).

- Analysis routines (to analyze the statistics just referred to).

One of the most important DBA tools—in many ways, in fact, the heart of the entire system, even though it is not shown in Fig. 2.3—is the *data dictionary* (also known as the system catalog; see Chapter 7). The data dictionary may be regarded as a database in its own right (but a system database, rather than a user database). The content of the dictionary can be regarded as "data about the data" (sometimes called "metadata")—that is, *descriptions* of other objects in the system, rather than simply "raw data." In particular, all the various schemas and mappings (external, conceptual, etc.) will physically be stored, in both source and object form, in the dictionary. A comprehensive dictionary will also include cross-reference informa-

---

7. This is one reason why it is a good idea to spread the operational data across multiple databases, incidentally, instead of keeping it all in one place. Nevertheless, we will continue to talk as if there were in fact only a single database, for reasons of simplicity.

tion, showing, for instance, which programs use which pieces of the database, which departments require which reports, what terminals are connected to the system, and so on. The dictionary may even (in fact, probably should) be integrated into the database it describes, and thus include its own description. It should certainly be possible to query the dictionary just like any other database, so that, for example, it is possible to tell which programs and/or users are likely to be affected by some proposed change to the system.

2.8   THE DATABASE MANAGEMENT SYSTEM

The *database management system* (DBMS) is the software that handles all access to the database. Conceptually, what happens is the following.

1. A user issues an access request, using some particular data sublanguage (e.g., SQL).
2. The DBMS intercepts that request and analyzes it.
3. The DBMS inspects, in turn, the external schema for that user, the corresponding external/conceptual mapping, the conceptual schema, the conceptual/internal mapping, and the storage structure definition.
4. The DBMS executes the necessary operations on the stored database.

For example, consider what is involved in the retrieval of a particular external record occurrence. In general, fields will be required from several conceptual record occurrences. Each conceptual record occurrence, in turn, may require fields from several stored record occurrences. Conceptually, at least, then, the DBMS must first retrieve all required stored record occurrences, then construct the required conceptual record occurrences, and then construct the required external record occurrence. At each stage, data type or other conversions may be necessary.

Note carefully, however, that the foregoing description is very much simplified. In particular, it suggests that the entire process is interpretive, which usually implies rather poor performance (severe execution-time overhead). In practice, it may be possible for access requests to be *compiled* in advance of execution time. See the discussion of this topic in Part 2 of this book (Chapter 4).

Another way of characterizing the function of the DBMS is to say that it provides the *user interface* to the database system. The user interface may be defined as a boundary in the system below which everything is invisible to the user. By definition, therefore, the user interface is at the external level. However, as we shall see later (Chapter 8), there are some situations in which the external view is unlikely to differ very significantly from (the relevant portion of) the underlying conceptual view.

2.9   DATA COMMUNICATIONS

We conclude this chapter with a brief mention of *data communications*. Database requests from an end-user are actually transmitted (from that user's terminal—which may be physically remote from the system itself—to some on-line application, built-in or otherwise, and thence to the DBMS) in the form of *communication messages.* Likewise, responses back to the user (from the DBMS and on-line application back to the user's terminal) are also transmitted in the form of such messages. All such message transmissions take place under the direction of another software system, the *data communications manager* (DC manager).

The DC manager is not a component of the DBMS but is an autonomous system in its own right. However, since the DC manager and the DBMS are clearly required to work harmoniously together, we sometimes regard them as equal partners in a higher-level cooperative venture called the *database/data-communications system* (DB/DC system), in which the DBMS looks after the database and the DC manager handles all messages to and from the DBMS, or more accurately to and from applications that use the DBMS. In this book, however, we shall have comparatively little to say about message-handling as such (it is a large subject in its own right). Chapter 24 does briefly discuss the question of communication *between distinct systems* (i.e., between distinct sites in a communications network), but that is really a separate topic.

EXERCISES

2.1 Draw a diagram of the database system architecture presented in this chapter.

2.2 Define the following terms:

conceptual DDL, schema, view
conceptual/internal mapping
data definition language
data dictionary
data manipulation language
data sublanguage
DC manager
external DDL, schema, view
external/conceptual mapping
host language
internal DDL, schema, view
storage structure definition
system catalog
user interface
utility

2.3 Explain the sequence of steps involved in retrieving a particular external record occurrence.

REFERENCES AND BIBLIOGRAPHY

2.1 ANSI/X3/SPARC Study Group on Data Base Management Systems. Interim Report. FDT (ACM SIGMOD bulletin) 7, No. 2 (1975).

2.2 D. C. Tsichritzis and A. Klug (eds.). "The ANSI/X3/SPARC DBMS Framework: Report of the Study Group on Data Base Management Systems." *Information Systems* 3 (1978).

These two documents [2.1, 2.2] are the Interim and Final Reports of the so-called ANSI/SPARC Study Group. The ANSI/X3/SPARC Study Group on Data Base Management Systems (to give it its full title) was established in late 1972 by the Standards Planning and Requirements Committee (SPARC) of ANSI/X3. ANSI/X3 is the American National Standards Committee on Computers and Information Processing. The objectives of the Study Group were to determine the areas, if any, of database technology for which standardization activity was appropriate, and to produce a set of recommendations for action in each such area. In working to meet these objectives, the Study Group took the position that *interfaces* were the only aspect of a database system that could possibly be suitable for standardization, and so defined a generalized architecture or framework for a database system and its various interfaces. The Final Report provides a detailed description of that architecture and of some of the 42 identified interfaces. The Interim Report is an earlier working document that is still of some interest; in some areas it provides additional detail.

2.3 D. A. Jardine (ed.). *The ANSI/SPARC DBMS Model*: Proceedings of the Second SHARE Working Conference on Data Base Management Systems, Montreal, Canada, April 26–30, 1976. North-Holland (1977).

The proceedings of a conference (papers and discussions) devoted to the ANSI/SPARC proposals as documented in the Interim Report [2.1].

2.4 B. Yormark. "The ANSI/X3/SPARC/SG DBMS Architecture." In [2.3].

An overview of the Interim Report [2.1].

2.5 J. J. van Griethuysen (ed.). *Concepts and Terminology for the Conceptual Schema and the Information Base*. International Standards Organization Document No. ISO/TC97/SC5-N695 (March 1982).

An interim report of an ISO Working Group (ISO/TC97/SC5/WG3) whose objectives include "the definition of concepts for conceptual schema languages." In particular, the report includes an introduction to three competing candidates (more accurately, three *sets* of candidates) for an appropriate conceptual schema formalism, and applies each of the three to a common example involving the activities of a hypothetical Car Registration Authority. The three sets of contenders are (1) "entity-attribute-relationship" approaches, (2) "binary relationship" approaches, and (3) "interpreted predicate logic" approaches. The report also includes a discussion of the fundamental concepts underlying the notion of the conceptual schema, and offers some principles for implementation of a system that properly supports that notion. Heavy going in places, but an important document for anyone seriously interested in the conceptual level of the system.

2.6 W. C. McGee. "Generalized File Processing." *Annual Review in Automatic Programming, Vol. 5* (eds., Halpern and Shaw). Elmsford, N.Y.: Pergamon Press (1969).

The paper that first introduced the term "schema" (though not with quite the ANSI/SPARC meaning). A most readable survey, with examples taken from a number of early database and "pre-database" systems.

2.7 Jay-Louise Weldon. *Data Base Administration*. New York, N.Y.: Plenum Press (1981).

This book provides a comprehensive description of the DBA function. The orientation is practical, not theoretical.

2.8 Data Dictionary Systems Working Party of the British Computer Society. Report. Joint Issue: *Data Base* (*ACM SIGBDP Newsletter*) **9,** No. 2; *SIGMOD Record* (*ACM SIGMOD Bulletin*) **9,** No. 4 (December 1977).

An excellent description of the role of the data dictionary; includes a brief but good discussion of the conceptual schema.

2.9 P. P. Uhrowczik. "Data Dictionary/Directories." *IBM Sys. J.* **12,** No. 4 (1973).

A good introduction to the basic concepts of a data dictionary system. An implementation is outlined using IMS physical and logical databases (see Part 5 of this book). The IBM Data Dictionary product in fact conforms to that broad outline.

2.10 H. C. Lefkovits, E. H. Sibley, and S. L. Lefkovits. *Information Resource / Data Dictionary Systems* (looseleaf). QED Information Sciences, Wellesley, Mass. (1983).

This publication is to the data dictionary what reference [1.6] is to the DBMS. It includes fairly detailed system descriptions for a number of dictionary products, namely, the IBM DB/DC Dictionary, DATAMANAGER, IDD, DATADICTIONARY, XDD, UCC10, and DCS.

2.11 W. Kent. *Data and Reality.* North-Holland (1978).

A stimulating and thought-provoking discussion of the nature of information, and in particular of the conceptual schema. The book may be regarded in large part as a compendium of real-world problems that (it is suggested) existing database formalisms—in particular, formalisms that are based on conventional record-like structures—have difficulty in dealing with. Recommended.

3
The Internal Level

3.1 INTRODUCTION

As explained in Chapter 2, the internal level of a database system is the level that is concerned with the way the data is actually stored. Physically, databases are almost invariably stored on direct access media—typically moving-head disks, though other media (e.g., drums, mass storage) may be used instead of, or in addition to, such disks in some systems. For simplicity we will use the term "disk" to stand generically for all such media. We will also assume, again for simplicity (though with some slight loss of generality), that the entire database can be stored on a single disk. Neither of these two simplifying assumptions materially affects any of the ideas to be presented in the remainder of the chapter.

The reader is assumed to have a basic familiarity with disk architecture and to understand what is meant by such terms as *seek time*, *rotational delay*, *cylinder*, *track*, *read/write head*, and so on. Good tutorials on such material can be found in many places; see, for example, references [3.5-3.6]. The basic point to be made here is that disk access times are *much* slower than main storage access times (typical disk access times range from about 400 milliseconds or more for a floppy disk on a micro to about 30 milliseconds or less for a large, "fast" disk on a large mainframe; main storage access is likely to be at least four or five orders of magnitude faster than disk access on any given system). An overriding performance objective in database systems is thus *to minimize the number of disk accesses* (disk I/O's). This chapter is concerned with techniques for achieving that objective—i.e., techniques for arranging stored data on the disk so that a required piece of data, say a required stored record, can be located in as few I/O's as possible.

Any given arrangement of data on the disk is referred to as a *storage structure*. Many different storage structures can be devised, and of course different structures have different performance characteristics; some are good for some applications,

45

others are good for others. There is no single structure that is optimal for all applications. It follows that a good system should support a variety of different structures, so that different portions of the database can be stored in different ways, and the storage structure for a given portion can be changed as performance requirements change or become better understood. The process of choosing an appropriate storage representation for a given database is referred to as *physical database design*. The point is worth emphasizing that, at least for a large and complex database, physical design can be a highly nontrivial task: It requires (among many other things) a good understanding of how the database will be used—in other words, a good understanding of the applications that will be run against the database, and also of the relative frequency of execution of those applications.

The examples in this chapter (and indeed in numerous subsequent chapters) are all based on a single database, the suppliers-and-parts database. A relational view of that database (with a sample set of data values) is shown in Fig. 3.1. Briefly, the database consists of three tables—table S, which represents suppliers, table P, which represents parts, and table SP, which represents shipments (the indicated suppliers are shipping, or supplying, the indicated parts). Each supplier has a unique *supplier number* (S#) and each part has a unique *part number* (P#). In addition, we assume that no two shipments can exist at the same time for the same supplier and the same part, so that each shipment has a unique supplier-number/part-number combination. In relational terminology (see Part 3), fields such as S# (for table S), P# (for table P), and the composite field (S#,P#) (for table SP) are called *primary keys*. Note: We will define this term rigorously in Chapter 12; for now, we will simply assume that it is well understood. The entire suppliers-and-parts example will be examined much more carefully in Chapter 4.

S	S#	SNAME	STATUS	CITY
	S1	Smith	20	London
	S2	Jones	10	Paris
	S3	Blake	30	Paris
	S4	Clark	20	London
	S5	Adams	30	Athens

P	P#	PNAME	COLOR	WEIGHT	CITY
	P1	Nut	Red	12	London
	P2	Bolt	Green	17	Paris
	P3	Screw	Blue	17	Rome
	P4	Screw	Red	14	London
	P5	Cam	Blue	12	Paris
	P6	Cog	Red	19	London

SP	S#	P#	QTY
	S1	P1	300
	S1	P2	200
	S1	P3	400
	S1	P4	200
	S1	P5	100
	S1	P6	100
	S2	P1	300
	S2	P2	400
	S3	P2	200
	S4	P2	200
	S4	P4	300
	S4	P5	400

Fig. 3.1 The suppliers-and-parts database.

The plan of the chapter is as follows. Following this introductory section, Section 3.2 explains in outline what is involved in the overall process of locating and accessing some particular record in the stored database, and identifies the major software components involved in that process. Section 3.3 then goes into a little more detail on two of those components, the file manager and the disk manager. Those two sections (3.2 and 3.3) need only be skimmed on a first reading, if the reader desires; a lot of the detail they contain is not really required for an understanding of the rest of the chapter. The next four sections (Sections 3.4–3.7) should not be just skimmed, however, since they represent the most important part of the entire chapter. They describe some of the most commonly occurring storage structures found in present-day systems, under the headings "indexing," "hashing," "pointer chains," and "compression techniques," respectively. Finally, Section 3.8 presents a brief conclusion.

Note: The emphasis throughout this chapter is on *concepts*, not detail. The intent is to explain the general idea behind such notions as indexing, hashing, etc., without getting too bogged down in the details of any specific system or technique. The reader who needs such detail is directed to the books and papers listed in the References and Bibliography section at the end of the chapter.

3.2 DATABASE ACCESS: AN OVERVIEW

Before we get into any discussion of storage structures per se, we first briefly consider what is involved in the overall process of database access in general. Locating a specific item of data in the database and presenting it to the user involves several layers of data access software. Of course, the details of those layers vary considerably from system to system, and so too does the terminology, but the principles are fairly standard and can be explained in outline as follows (refer to Fig. 3.2).

1. First, the DBMS decides what stored record is required, and asks the *file manager* to retrieve that record. (We assume for the purposes of this simple explanation that the DBMS is able to pinpoint the exact record desired ahead of time. In practice it may need to retrieve a set of multiple records and search through those records in main storage to find the specific one desired. In principle, however, this only means that the sequence of steps 1–3 must be repeated for each stored record in that set.)

2. The file manager in turn decides what *page* contains the desired record, and asks the *disk manager* to retrieve that page. The page is *the unit of I/O*—i.e., it is the amount of data transferred between the disk and main storage in a single disk access. Typical page sizes are 1024, 2048, or 4096 bytes.[1]

1. Sometimes, of course, the required page will already be in a buffer in main storage as the result of a previous retrieval, in which case it is obviously not necessary to retrieve it again.

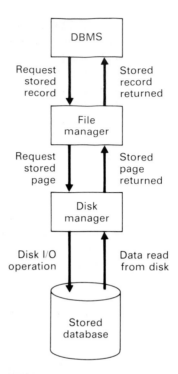

Fig. 3.2 The DBMS, file manager, and disk manager.

3. Finally, the disk manager determines the physical location of the desired page on the disk, and issues the necessary disk I/O operation.

Loosely speaking, therefore, the DBMS has a view of the database as a collection of stored records, and that view is supported by the file manager; the file manager, in turn, has a view of the database as a collection of pages, and that view is supported by the disk manager; and the disk manager has a view of the disk "as it really is." The three subsections below amplify these ideas somewhat. Section 3.3 then goes into more detail on the same topics.

Disk Manager

The disk manager is a component of the underlying operating system. It is the component responsible for all physical I/O operations (in some systems it is referred to as the "basic I/O services" component). As such, it clearly needs to be aware of *physical disk addresses*. For example, when the file manager asks to retrieve some specific page *p*, the disk manager needs to know exactly where page *p* is on the physical disk. However, the user of the disk manager—namely, the file manager—does not need to know that information. Instead, the file manager regards the disk simply as a logical collection of *page sets*, each one consisting of a collection of fixed-size pages. Each page set is identified by a unique *page set ID*. Each page, in turn, is identified by a *page number* that is unique within the disk; distinct page sets do not overlap (i.e., do not have any pages in common). The mapping between page numbers and physical disk addresses is understood and maintained by the disk manager. The major advantage of this arrangement (not the only one) is that all device-specific code can be isolated within a single system component, namely the disk manager, and all higher-level components—in particular, the file manager— can thus be device-independent.

As just explained, the complete set of pages on the disk is divided into a collection of disjoint subsets called *page sets*. One of those page sets, the *free space* page set, serves as a pool of available (i.e., currently unused) pages; the others are all considered to contain significant data. The allocation and deallocation of pages to and from page sets is performed by the disk manager on demand from the file manager. The operations supported by the disk manager on page sets—i.e., the operations the file manager is able to issue—include the following:

- Retrieve page p from page set s;
- Replace page p within page set s;
- Add a new page to page set s (i.e., acquire an empty page from the free space page set and return the new page number p);
- Remove page p from page set s (i.e., return page p to the free space page set).

The first two of these operations are of course the basic page-level I/O operations the file manager needs. The other two allow page sets to grow and shrink as necessary.

File Manager

The file manager uses the disk manager facilities just described in such a way as to permit its user (namely the DBMS) to regard the disk as a collection of *stored files* (remember from Chapter 1 that a stored file is the collection of all occurrences of one type of stored record). Each page set will contain one or more stored files. Note: The DBMS does need to be aware of the existence of page sets, even though it is not responsible for managing them in detail, for reasons sketched in the next subsection. In particular, the DBMS needs to know when two stored files share the same page set or when two stored records share the same page.

Each stored file is identified by a *file name* or *file ID*, unique at least within its containing page set, and each stored record, in turn, is identified by a *record number* or *record ID*, unique at least within its containing stored file. In practice, record IDs are usually unique, not just within their containing file, but actually within the entire disk, since they typically consist of the combination of a page number and some value that is unique within that page. See Section 3.3, later.

Aside: In some systems the file manager is a component of the underlying operating system, in others it is packaged with the DBMS. For our purposes the distinction is not important. However, we remark in passing that, although operating systems do invariably provide such a component, it is often the case that the general-purpose file manager provided by the operating system is not ideally suited to the requirements of the special-purpose "application" that is the DBMS. For more discussion of this topic, see reference [3.22].

The operations supported by the file manager on stored files (i.e., the operations the DBMS is able to issue) include the following:

- Retrieve stored record r from stored file f;
- Replace stored record r within stored file f;
- Add a new stored record to stored file f and return the new record ID r;
- Remove stored record r from stored file f;
- Create a new stored file f;
- Destroy stored file f.

Using these primitive file management operations, the DBMS is able to build and manipulate the storage structures that are the principal concern of this chapter (see Sections 3.4–3.7).

Clustering

We should not leave this overview discussion without a brief mention of the subject of data clustering. The basic idea behind clustering is to try and store records that are logically related (and are therefore frequently used together) physically close together on the disk. Physical data clustering is an extremely important factor in performance, as can easily be seen from the following. Suppose the stored record most recently accessed is record $r1$, and suppose the next stored record required is record $r2$. Suppose also that $r1$ is stored on page $p1$ and $r2$ is stored on page $p2$. Then:

1. If $p1$ and $p2$ are one and the same, then the access to $r2$ will not require any physical I/O at all, because the desired page $p2$ will already be in a buffer in main storage.

2. If $p1$ and $p2$ are distinct but physically close together— in particular, if they are physically adjacent—then the access to $r2$ will require a physical I/O, but the seek time involved in that I/O will be small (it will be *zero* if $p1$ and $p2$ are in the same cylinder), because the read/write heads will already be close to (or at) the desired position.

As an example of clustering, we consider the suppliers-and-parts database from Section 3.1:

- If sequential access to all suppliers in supplier number order is a frequent application requirement, then the supplier records should be clustered such that the supplier S1 record is physically next to the supplier S2 record, the supplier

S2 record is physically next to the supplier S3 record, and so on. This is an example of *intra-file* clustering: The clustering is applied within a single stored file.

■ If, on the other hand, access to some specific supplier together with all shipments for that supplier is a frequent application requirement, then supplier and shipment records should be stored interleaved, with the shipment records for supplier S1 physically next to the supplier S1 record, the shipment records for supplier S2 physically next to the supplier S2 record, and so on. This is an example of *inter-file* clustering: The clustering is applied across multiple stored files.

Of course, a given file (or set of files) can be physically clustered in one and only one way at any given time.

The DBMS can support clustering, both intra- and inter-file, by storing logically related records on the same page where possible and on adjacent pages where not. (This is why the DBMS must know about pages as well as stored files. When the DBMS creates a new stored record, the file manager must allow it to specify that the new record be stored "near"—i.e., on the same page as, or at least on a page logically near to—some existing record. The disk manager, in turn, will do its best to ensure that two pages that are logically adjacent are physically adjacent on the disk. See Section 3.3.) Of course, the DBMS can only know what clustering is required if the database administrator is able to tell it. A good DBMS should allow the DBA to specify different kinds of clustering for different files. It should also allow the clustering for a given file (or set of files) to be changed if the performance requirements change. If data independence is to be achieved, of course, any such change in physical clustering should not require any concomitant changes in application programs.

Observe, incidentally, how the foregoing discussion bears out the claim made in Section 3.1, to the effect that knowledge of how the data is going to be used is essential to the production of a good physical database design.

3.3 PAGE SETS AND FILES

As explained in the previous section, a major function of the disk manager is to allow the file manager to ignore all details of physical disk I/O and to think in terms of (logical) "page I/O" instead. This function of the disk manager is referred to as *page management*. We present a very simple example to show how page management is typically handled. Consider the suppliers-and-parts database once again. Suppose that the desired logical ordering of records within each table is as suggested by Fig. 3.1—that is, suppliers are required to be in supplier number order, parts in part number order, and shipments in part number order within supplier number order. To keep matters simple, suppose too that each stored file is stored in a page set of its own, and that each stored record, regardless of whether it is a supplier, a part, or a shipment, requires an entire page of its own. Suppose also that the disk contains a total of 64K = 65,536 pages (not at all unreasonable, by the way). Now consider the following sequence of events.

1. Initially the database contains no data at all. There is only one page set, the free space page set, which contains all the pages on the disk—except for page zero, which is special (see later). The remaining pages are numbered sequentially from one.

2. The file manager requests the creation of a page set for supplier records, and inserts the five supplier records shown in Fig. 3.1 (for suppliers S1–S5). The disk manager removes pages 1–5 from the free space page set and labels them "the suppliers page set."

3. Similarly for parts and shipments. Now there are four page sets: the suppliers page set (pages 1–5), the parts page set (pages 6–11), the shipments page set (pages 12–23), and the free space page set (pages 24, 25, 26, . . .). The situation at this point is as shown in Fig. 3.3.

To continue with the example:

4. Next, the file manager inserts a new supplier stored record (for a new supplier, supplier S6). The disk manager locates the first free page in the free space page set—namely, page 24—and adds it to the suppliers page set.

5. The file manager deletes the stored record for supplier S2. The disk manager returns the page for supplier S2 (page 2) to the free space page set.

6. The file manager inserts a new part stored record (for part P7). The disk manager locates the first free page in the free space page set—namely, page 2—and adds it to the parts page set.

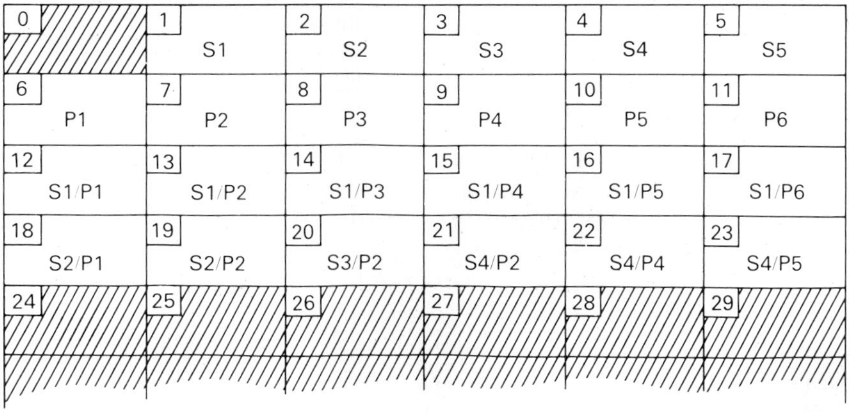

Fig. 3.3 Disk layout after creation and initial loading of the suppliers-and-parts database of Fig. 3.1.

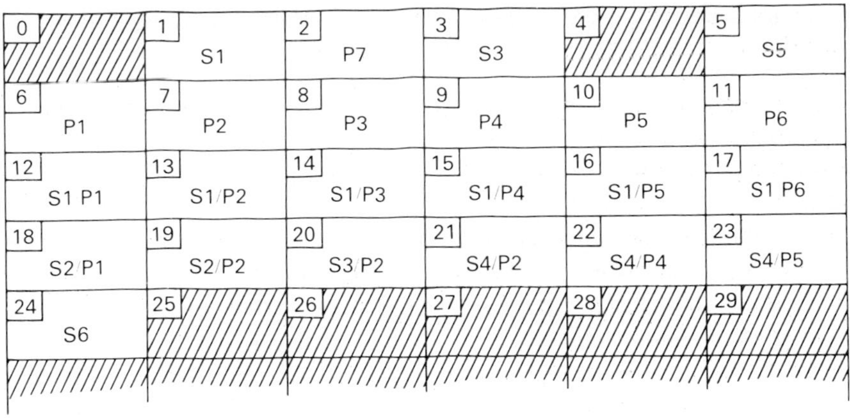

Fig. 3.4 Disk layout after inserting supplier S6, deleting supplier S2, inserting part P7, and deleting supplier S4.

7. The file manager deletes the stored record for supplier S4. The disk manager returns the page for supplier S4 (page 4) to the free space page set.

And so on. The situation now is as illustrated in Fig. 3.4. The point about that figure is the following: After the system has been running for awhile, it can no longer be guaranteed that pages that are logically adjacent are still physically adjacent (even if they started out that way). For this reason, the logical sequence of pages in a given page set must be represented, not by physical adjacency, but by *pointers*. Each page will contain a *page header*, i.e., a set of control information that includes (among other things) the physical disk address of the page that immediately follows that page in logical sequence. See Fig. 3.5.

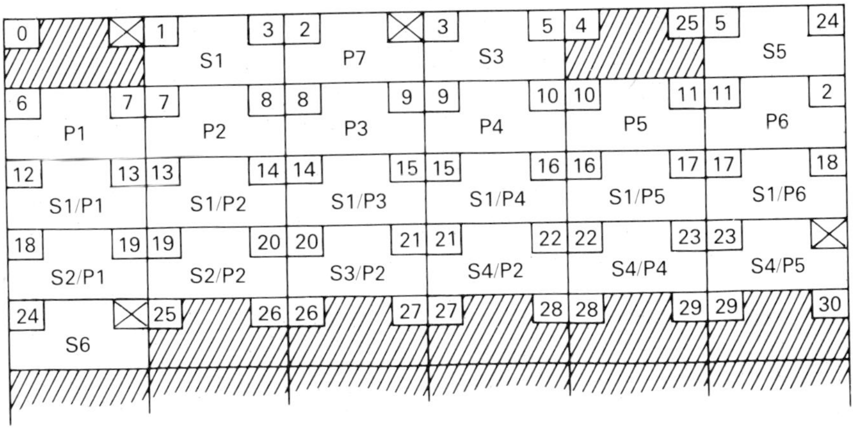

Fig. 3.5 Figure 3.4 revised to show ''next page'' pointers (top right corner of each page).

Some miscellaneous points arising from the foregoing example:

- The page headers—in particular, the "next page" pointers—are managed by the disk manager; they should be completely invisible to the file manager.

- Because (as explained in the subsection on clustering at the end of Section 3.2) it is desirable to have pages that are logically adjacent physically adjacent also so far as possible, the disk manager normally allocates and deallocates pages to and from page sets, not one at a time as suggested in the example, but rather in physically contiguous groups or "extents" of (say) 64 at a time.

- The question arises: How does the disk manager know where the various page sets are located?—or, more precisely, how does it know, for each page set, where the (logically) first page of that page set is located? (It is sufficient to locate the first page, of course, because the second and subsequent pages can then be located by following the pointers in the page headers.) The answer is that some fixed location on the disk—typically cylinder zero, track zero—is used to store a page that gives precisely that information. That page (variously referred to as "the disk table of contents," "the disk directory," "the page set directory," or simply "physical page zero") thus typically contains a list of the page sets currently in existence on the disk, together with a pointer to the first page of each such page set. See Fig. 3.6.

Now we turn to the file manager. Just as the disk manager allows the file manager to ignore details of physical disk I/O and to think for the most part in terms of logical pages, so the file manager allows the DBMS to ignore details of page I/O and to think for the most part in terms of stored files and stored records. This

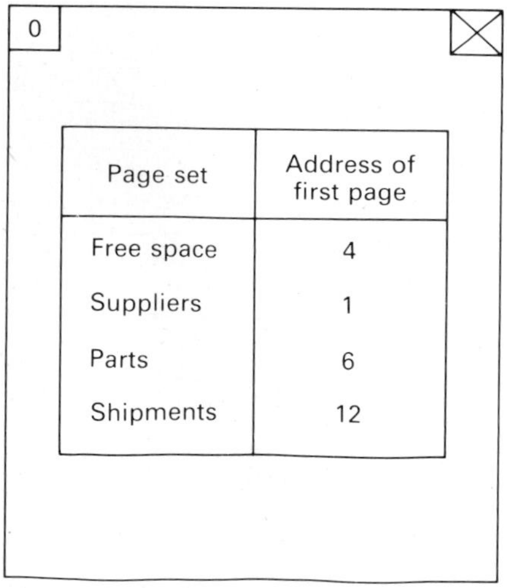

Page set	Address of first page
Free space	4
Suppliers	1
Parts	6
Shipments	12

Fig. 3.6 The disk directory (page zero).

function of the file manager is referred to as *stored record management*. We discuss that function very briefly here, once again taking the suppliers-and-parts database as the basis for our examples.

Suppose, then (rather more realistically), that a single page can accommodate multiple stored records, instead of just one as in the page management example. Suppose too that the desired logical order for supplier records is supplier number order, as before. Consider the following sequence of events.

1. First, the five stored records for suppliers S1–S5 are inserted and are stored together on some page p, as shown in Fig. 3.7. Note that page p still contains a considerable amount of free space.

2. Now suppose the DBMS inserts a new supplier stored record (for a new supplier, say supplier S9). The file manager stores this record on page p (because there is still space), immediately following the stored record for supplier S5.

3. Next, the DBMS deletes the stored record for supplier S2. The file manager erases the S2 record from page p, and shifts the records for suppliers S3, S4, S5, and S9 up to fill the gap.

4. Next, the DBMS inserts a new supplier stored record for another new supplier, supplier S7. Again the file manager stores this record on page p (because there is still space); it places the new record immediately following that for supplier S5, shifting the record for supplier S9 down to make room. The situation at this juncture is illustrated in Fig. 3.8.

And so on. The point of the example is that the logical sequence of stored records within any given page can be represented by *physical* sequence within that

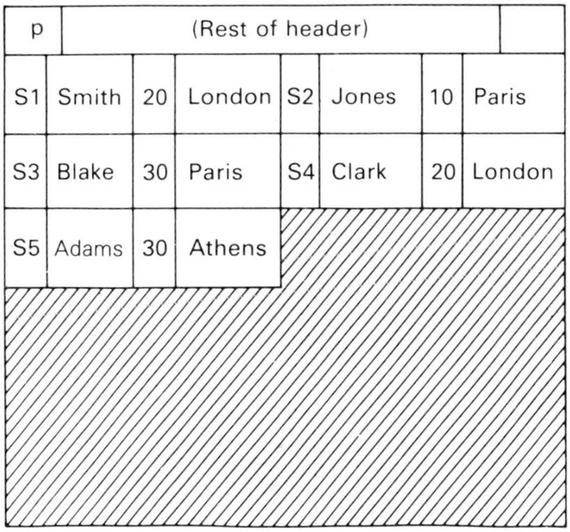

Fig. 3.7 Layout of page p after initial loading of the five supplier records of Fig. 3.1.

p	(Rest of header)							
S1	Smith	20	London	S3	Blake	30	Paris	
S4	Clark	20	London	S5	Adams	30	Athens	
S7	. . .	. .	. . . .	S9	. . .	. .	. . . .	

Fig. 3.8 Layout of page *p* after inserting supplier S9, deleting supplier S2, and inserting supplier S7.

page. The file manager will shift individual records up and down to achieve this effect, keeping all data records together at the top of the page and all free space together at the bottom. (The logical sequence of stored records *across* pages is of course represented by the sequence of those pages within their containing page set, as described in the page management example earlier.)

As explained in Section 3.2, stored records are identified internally by "record ID" or RID. Fig. 3.9 shows how RIDs are typically implemented. The RID for a stored record *r* consists of two parts: the page number of the page *p* containing *r*, and a byte offset from the foot of *p* identifying a slot that contains, in turn, the

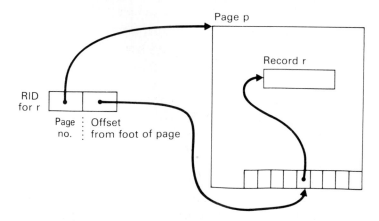

Fig. 3.9 Implementation of stored record IDs (RIDs).

byte offset of *r* from the top of *p*. This scheme represents a good compromise between the speed of direct addressing and the flexibility of indirect addressing: Records can be shifted up and down within their containing page, as illustrated in Figs.
3.7 and 3.8, without having to change RIDs (only the local offsets at the foot of
the page have to change); yet access to a given record given its RID is fast, involving
only a single page access. (It is desirable that RIDs not change, because they are
used elsewhere in the database as pointers to the records in question—for example,
in indexes. If the RID of some record did in fact change, then all such pointer
references elsewhere would have to be changed also.)

Note: Access to a specific stored record under the foregoing scheme might in
rare cases involve two page accesses (but never more than two). Two accesses will
be required if a varying length record is updated in such a way that it is now longer
than it was before, and there is not enough free space on the page to accommodate
the increase. In such a situation, the updated record will be placed on another "overflow" page, and the original record will then be replaced by a pointer (another
RID) to the new location. If the same thing happens again, so that the updated
record has to be moved to still a third page, then the pointer in the original page
will be changed to point to this newest location.

We are now almost ready to move on to our discussion of storage structures.
From this point on, we will assume for the most part (just as the DBMS normally
assumes) that a given stored file is simply a collection of stored records, each
uniquely identified by a record ID that never changes so long as that record remains
in existence. A few final points to conclude this section:

- Note that one consequence of the preceding discussion is that, for any given
  stored file, it is *always* possible to access all of the stored records in that stored
  file sequentially—where by "sequentially" we mean "stored record sequence
  within page sequence within page set" (i.e., typically ascending RID sequence).
  This sequence is often loosely referred to as *physical* sequence, though it should
  be clear that it does not necessarily correspond to any particular physical sequence on the disk. For convenience, however, we will adopt the same term.

- Notice that access to a stored file in "physical" sequence is possible even if
  multiple files share the same page set (i.e., if stored files are interleaved). Records that do not belong to the stored file in question can simply be skipped
  over during the sequential scan.

- It should be stressed that physical sequence is often at least adequate as an
  "access path" to a given stored file. Sometimes it may even be optimal. However, it is frequently the case that something better is needed. And, as indicated
  in Section 3.1, there is an enormous variety of techniques for achieving such a
  "something better."

- Henceforth, we will usually assume for simplicity that the (unique) "physical"
  sequence for any given stored file is *primary key sequence*. That is, files will be
  assumed to be physically sequenced on their unique identifier field (or field
  combination), barring any explicit statement to the contrary. Please note that

this assumption is made purely for the purpose of simplifying subsequent discussion; we recognize that there may be good reasons in practice for physically sequencing a given stored file in some other manner, e.g., by the value(s) of some other field(s), or simply according to time of arrival (*chronological sequence*).

■   Note that for various reasons a stored record will probably contain certain control information in addition to its user data fields. That information is typically collected together at the front of the record in the form of a *record prefix*. Examples of the kind of information found in such prefixes are the ID of the containing stored file (necessary if one page can contain records from multiple stored files), the record length (necessary for varying length records), a delete flag (necessary if records are not physically deleted at the time of a logical delete operation), pointers (necessary if records are chained together in any way), and so on. But of course all such control information should normally be concealed from the user (i.e., end-user or application programmer).

■   Finally, note that the user data fields in a given stored record will be of interest to the DBMS *but not to the file manager* (and not to the disk manager). The DBMS needs to be aware of those fields because it will use them as the basis for building indexes and the like. The file manager, however, has no need to be aware of them at all. Thus, another distinction between the DBMS and the file manager is that a given stored record has a known internal structure to the DBMS but is basically just a byte string to the file manager.

In the remainder of this chapter we describe some of the more important of the techniques for achieving the "something better" referred to above (i.e., an access path that is better than physical sequence). The techniques are discussed under the general headings of *indexing*, *hashing*, *pointer chains*, and *compression techniques*. One final general remark: The various techniques should not be seen as mutually exclusive. For example, it is perfectly feasible to have a stored file with (say) both hashed and indexed access to that file based on the same stored field, or with hashed access based on one field and pointer chain access based on another.

3.4   INDEXING

Consider the supplier table of Fig. 3.1 once again. Suppose the query "Find all suppliers in city C" (where C is a parameter) is an important one—i.e., one that is frequently executed and is therefore required to perform well. Given such a requirement, the DBA might choose the stored representation shown in Fig. 3.10. In that representation, there are two stored files, a supplier file and a city file (probably in different page sets); the city file, which is stored in city sequence (because CITY is the primary key—remember our assumption from the end of Section 3.3), includes pointers (RIDs) into the supplier file. To find all suppliers in London (say), the DBMS now has two possible strategies:

1. Search the entire supplier file, looking for all records with city value equal to London.

City file (index)   Supplier file (data)

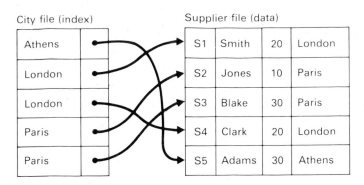

Fig. 3.10 Indexing the supplier file on CITY.

2. Search the city file for the London entries, and for each such entry follow the pointer to the corresponding record in the supplier file.

If the ratio of London suppliers to others is small, the second of these strategies is likely to be more efficient than the first, because 1) the DBMS is aware of the physical sequencing of the city file (it can stop its search of that file as soon as it finds a city that follows London in alphabetic ordering), and 2) even if it did have to search the entire city file, that search would still probably require fewer I/O's overall because the city file is physically smaller than the supplier file (because the records are smaller).

In this example, the city file is said to be an *index* to the supplier file; equivalently, the supplier file is said to be *indexed by* the city file. An index is a special kind of stored file. To be specific, it is a file in which each entry (i.e., record) consists of precisely two values, a data value and a pointer (RID);[2] the data value is a value for some field of the indexed file, and the pointer identifies a record of that file that has that value for that field.

From this point on, we shall refer to the city file of Fig. 3.10 more explicitly as "the CITY index." A note on terminology: An index on a primary key field—e.g., an index on field S# of the supplier file—is called a *primary* index. An index on any other field—e.g., the CITY index in the example—is called a *secondary* index.

How Indexes Are Used

The fundamental advantage of an index is that it speeds up retrieval. However, there is a converse disadvantage, too—namely, it slows down updates. (As in so many situations, there is an obvious tradeoff here.) For example, every time a new stored record is added to the indexed file, a new entry will also have to be added to the

---

2. It is called an index by analogy with a conventional book index, which also consists of entries containing "pointers" (page numbers) to facilitate the retrieval of information from an "indexed file" (i.e., the body of the book).

index. As a more specific example, consider what the DBMS must do to the CITY index of Fig. 3.10 if supplier S2 moves from Paris to London. In general, therefore, the question that must be answered when some field is being considered as a candidate for indexing is: Which is more important, efficient retrieval based on values of the field in question, or the update overhead involved in providing that efficient retrieval?

For the remainder of this section we concentrate on retrieval operations specifically.

Indexes can be used in essentially two different ways. First, they can be used for *sequential* access to the indexed file—where "sequential" means "in the sequence defined by values of the indexed field." For instance, the CITY index in the example above will allow records in the supplier file to be processed in city sequence. Second, indexes can also be used for *direct* access to individual records in the indexed file on the basis of a given value for the indexed field. The query "Find suppliers in London" discussed at the start of the section illustrates this second case.

In fact, the two basic ways of using an index just outlined can each be generalized slightly:

1. *Sequential*: The index can also help with *range* queries—for instance, "Find suppliers whose city is in some specified alphabetic range" (e.g., begins with a letter in the range L–R).
2. *Direct*: The index can also help with *list* queries—for instance, "Find suppliers whose city is in some specified list" (e.g., the list of cities London, Paris, and New York).

In addition, there are certain queries—basically *existence tests*—that can be answered from the index alone, without any access to the indexed file at all. As an example, consider the query "Are there any suppliers in Athens?" The response to this query is clearly "yes" if and only if an entry exists for Athens in the CITY index.

A given stored file can have any number of indexes. For example, the supplier stored file might have both a CITY index and a STATUS index (see Fig. 3.11). Those indexes could then be used to provide efficient access to supplier records on the basis of given values for either *or both* of CITY and STATUS. As an illustration of the "both" case, consider the query "Find suppliers in Paris with status 30." The CITY index gives the RIDs—*r2* and *r3*, say—for the suppliers in Paris; likewise, the STATUS index gives the RIDs—*r3* and *r5*, say—for suppliers with status 30. From these two sets of RIDs it is clear that the only supplier satisfying the original query is the supplier with RID equal to *r3* (namely, supplier S3). Only then does the DBMS have to access the supplier file per se, in order to retrieve the desired record.

More terminology: Indexes are sometimes referred to as *inverted lists*, for the following reason. First, a "normal" file—the supplier file of Figs. 3.10 and 3.11 may be taken as a typical "normal file"—lists, for each record, the values of the

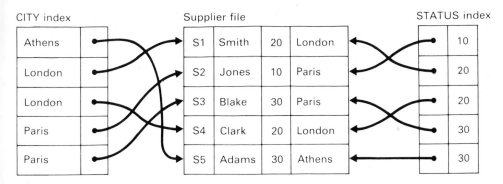

Fig. 3.11 Indexing the supplier file on both CITY and STATUS.

fields in that record. By contrast, an index lists, for each value of the indexed field, the records that contain that value. (The inverted-list database systems mentioned briefly at the end of Chapter 1 draw their name from this terminology, of course, as will be more fully explained later in this book.) And one more term: A file with an index on every field is sometimes said to be *fully inverted*.

Indexing on Field Combinations

It is also possible to construct an index on the basis of values of two or more fields in combination. For example, Fig. 3.12 shows an index to the supplier file on the combination of fields CITY and STATUS (in that order). With such an index, the DBMS could respond to the query discussed above—"Find suppliers in Paris with status 30"—in a single scan *of a single index*. If the combined index were replaced by two separate indexes, then (as described earlier) that query would involve two separate index scans. Furthermore, it might be difficult in that case to decide which of those two scans should be done first; since the two possible sequences could have very different performance characteristics, the choice could be significant.

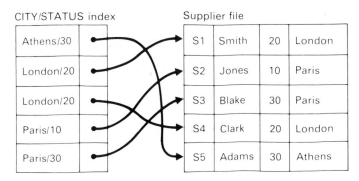

Fig. 3.12 Indexing the supplier file on the combined field CITY / STATUS.

Note that the combined CITY/STATUS index can also serve as an index on the CITY field alone, since all the entries for a given city are still consecutive within the combined index. (Another, separate index will have to be provided if indexing on STATUS is also required, however.) In general, an index on the combination of fields *F1*, *F2*, *F3*, . . . , *Fn* (in that order) will also serve as an index on *F1* alone, as an index on the combination *F1F2* (or *F2F1*), as an index on the combination *F1F2F3* (in any order), and so on. Thus the total number of indexes required to provide complete indexing in this way is not as large as might appear at first glance.

Dense vs. Nondense Indexing

As stated several times already, the fundamental purpose of an index is to speed up data retrieval—more specifically, to reduce the number of disk I/O's needed to retrieve some given stored record. Basically, this purpose is achieved by means of *pointers*; and up to this point we have assumed that all such pointers are *record* pointers (i.e., RIDs). In fact, however, it would be sufficient for the stated purpose if those pointers were simply *page* pointers (i.e., page numbers). It is true that, to find the desired record within a given page, the system would then have to do some additional work to search through the page in main storage, but the number of I/O's would remain unchanged.[3]

We can take this idea further. Remember that any given stored file has a single "physical" sequence, represented by the combination of 1) the sequence of stored records within each page and 2) the sequence of pages within the containing page set. Suppose the supplier file is stored such that its physical sequence corresponds to its logical sequence as defined by the values of some field, say the supplier number field; in other words, the supplier file is *clustered* on that field (recall the discussion of intra-file clustering at the end of Section 3.2). Suppose also that an index is required on that field. Then there is no need for that index to include an entry for every stored record in the indexed file (i.e., the supplier file, in the example). All that is needed is an entry for each *page*, giving the highest supplier number on the page and the corresponding page number. See Fig. 3.13 (where we assume for simplicity that a given page can hold a maximum of two supplier records).

As an example, consider what is involved in retrieving supplier S3 using this index. First the system must scan the index, looking for the first entry with supplier number greater than or equal to S3. It finds the index entry for supplier S4, which points to page *p* (say). It then retrieves page *p* and scans it in main storage, looking for the required stored record (which in this example will quickly be found, of course).

An index such as that of Fig. 3.13 is said to be *nondense*, because it does not contain an entry for every stored record in the indexed file. (By contrast, all indexes discussed in this section prior to this point have been *dense*.) One advantage of a

---

3. As a matter of fact, the book index analogy mentioned in an earlier footnote provides an example of an index in which the pointers are page pointers rather than "record" pointers.

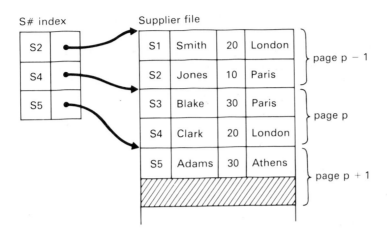

Fig. 3.13 Example of a nondense index.

nondense index is of course that it will occupy less storage than a corresponding dense index, for the obvious reason that it contains fewer entries. As a result, it will probably be quicker to scan also. A disadvantage is that it may no longer be possible to perform existence tests on the basis of the index alone (see the brief note on this topic under "How indexes are used" earlier in this section).

Note that a given stored file can have at most one nondense index, because such an index relies on the (unique) physical sequence of the file in question. All other indexes must necessarily be dense.

B-trees

A particularly common and important kind of index is the *B-tree*. Although it is true (as stated earlier) that there is no single storage structure that is optimal for all applications, there is little doubt that if a single structure must be chosen, then B-trees of one variety or another are probably the one to choose. B-trees do generally seem to be the best all-around performer (but see reference [3.26]). For this reason, incidentally, most relational systems support B-trees as their principal form of storage structure, and several support no other.

Before we can explain what a B-tree is, we must first discuss one additional preliminary notion, namely, the notion of a *multi-level* (or *tree-structured*) index.

The reason for providing an index in the first place is to remove the need for physical sequential scanning of the indexed file. However, physical sequential scanning is still needed in the *index*. If the indexed file is very large, then the index also can get to be quite sizable, and sequentially scanning the index can therefore itself get to be quite time-consuming. The solution to this problem is the same as before: Namely, we treat the index simply as a regular stored file, and build an index to it (an index to the index). This idea can be carried to as many levels as desired (three levels are common in practice; a file would have to be very large to require more than three levels of indexing). Each level of the index acts as a nondense index to the level below (it *must* be nondense, of course, for otherwise nothing would be achieved—level n would contain the same number of entries as level $n + 1$, and so would take just as long to scan).

Now we can discuss B-trees. A B-tree is a particular type of tree-structured index. B-trees as such were first described in a paper by Bayer and McCreight in 1972 [3.10]. Since that time, numerous variations on the basic idea have been proposed, by Bayer and by many other investigators; as already suggested, B-trees of one kind or another are now probably the commonest storage structure of all in modern database systems (relational or otherwise). Here we describe the variation given by Knuth [3.1]. We note in passing that the index structure of IBM's "Virtual Storage Access Method" VSAM [3.12] is very similar to Knuth's structure. However, the VSAM version was invented independently and includes additional features of its own, such as the use of compression techniques (see Section 3.7). In fact, a precursor of the VSAM structure was described by Chang as early as 1969 [3.13].

In Knuth's variation, the index consists of two parts, the *sequence set* and the *index set* (to use VSAM terminology).

1. The *sequence set* consists of a single-level index to the actual data; that index is normally dense, but could be nondense if the indexed file is clustered on the indexed field. The entries in the index are (of course) grouped into pages, and the pages are (of course) chained together, such that the logical ordering represented by the index is obtained by taking the entries in physical order in the first page on the chain, followed by the entries in physical order in the second page on the chain, and so on. Thus the sequence set provides fast *sequential* access to the indexed data.

2. The *index set*, in turn, provides fast *direct* access to the sequence set (and thus to the data too). The index set is actually a tree-structured index to the sequence set; in fact, it is the index set that is the real B-tree, strictly speaking. The combination of index set and sequence set is sometimes called "B-plus"-tree (B^+-tree). The top level of the index set consists of a single node (i.e., a single page, but of course containing multiple index entries, like all the other nodes). That top node is called the *root*.

A simple example is shown in Fig. 3.14.

We explain Fig. 3.14 as follows. The values 6, 8, 12, ..., 97, 99 are values of the indexed field, F say. Consider the top node, which consists of two F values (50 and 82) and three pointers (actually page numbers). Data records with F less than or equal to 50 can be found (eventually) by following the left pointer from this node; similarly, records with F greater than 50 and less than or equal to 82 can be found by following the middle pointer; and records with F greater than 82 can be found by following the right pointer. The other nodes of the index set are interpreted analogously; note that (for example) following the right pointer from the first node at the second level takes us to all records with F greater than 32 *and also less than*

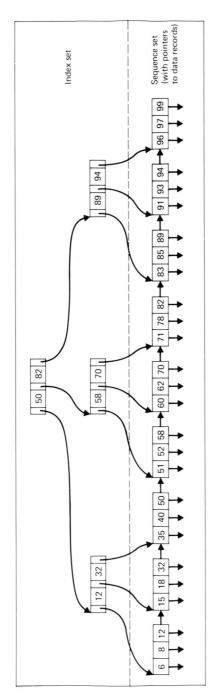

Fig. 3.14 Part of a simple B-tree (Knuth's variation).

or equal to 50 (by virtue of the fact that we have already followed the left pointer from the higher node).

The B-tree (i.e., index set) of Fig. 3.14 is somewhat unrealistic, however, for the following two reasons:

1. First, the nodes of a B-tree do not normally all contain the same number of data values;

2. Second, they normally do contain a certain amount of free space.

In general, *a B-tree of order n* has at least *n* but not more than 2*n* data values at any given node (and if it has *k* data values, then it also has *k* + 1 pointers). No data value appears in the tree more than once. We give the algorithm for searching for a particular value *V* in the structure of Fig. 3.14; the algorithm for the general B-tree of order *n* is a simple generalization.

```
set N to the root node ;
repeat until N is a sequence-set node ;
   let X, Y be the data values in node N /* X < Y */ ;
   if V <= X      then set N to the left   lower node of N ;
   if X < V <= Y then set N to the middle lower node of N ;
   if V > Y       then set N to the right  lower node of N ;
end repeat ;
if V occurs in node N then exit /* found */ ;
if V does not occur in node N then exit /* not found */ ;
```

A problem with tree structures in general is that insertions and deletions can cause the tree to become *unbalanced*. A tree is unbalanced if the leaf nodes are not all at the same level—i.e., if different leaf nodes are at different distances from the root node. Since searching the tree involves a disk access for every node visited.[4] search times can become very unpredictable in an unbalanced tree. The notable advantage of B-trees is that the B-tree insertion/deletion algorithm guarantees that the tree will always be balanced. (The "B" in "B-tree" is sometimes said to stand for "balanced" for this reason.) We briefly consider insertion of a new value, *V* say, into a B-tree of order *n*. The algorithm as described caters for the index set only, since, as explained earlier, it is the index set that is the B-tree proper; a trivial extension is needed to deal with the sequence set also.

■ First, the search algorithm is executed to locate, not the sequence set node, but that node (*N* say) at the lowest level of the index set in which *V* logically belongs. If *N* contains free space, *V* is inserted into *N* and the process terminates.

■ Otherwise, node *N* (which must therefore contain 2*n* values) is *split* into two nodes *N1* and *N2*. Let *S* be the ordered set consisting of the original 2*n* values plus the new value *V*, in their logical sequence. The lowest *n* values of set *S* are placed in the left node *N1*, the highest *n* values of that set are placed in the

---

4. Except that, in practice, the top one or two levels of the index will frequently be kept in main storage during most database processing.

right node *N2*, and the middle value, *W* say, is promoted to the parent node of *N*, *P* say, to serve as a separator value for nodes *N1* and *N2*. Future searches for a value *V'*, on reaching node *P*, will be directed to node *N1* if $V' <= W$ and to node *N2* if $W < V'$.

■ An attempt is now made to insert *W* into *P*, and the process is repeated.

In the worst case, splitting will occur all the way to the top of the tree; a new root node (parent to the old root, which will now have been split into two) will be created, and the tree will increase in height by one level (but even then will remain balanced).

The deletion algorithm is essentially the inverse of the insertion algorithm just described. Changing a value is handled by deleting the old value and inserting the new one.

3.5   HASHING

Hashing (also called *hash-addressing*) is a technique for providing fast *direct* access to a specific stored record on the basis of a given value for some field. The field in question is usually but not necessarily the primary key. In outline, the technique works as follows.

■ Each stored record is placed in the database at a location whose address (RID, or perhaps just page number) is computed as some function (the *hash function*) of some field of that record (the *hash field*). The computed address is called the *hash address*.

■ To store the record initially, the DBMS computes the hash address for the new record and instructs the file manager to place the record at that position.

■ To retrieve the record subsequently given the hash field value, the DBMS performs the same computation as before and instructs the file manager to fetch the record at the computed position.

As a simple illustration, suppose that 1) supplier number values are S100, S200, S300, S400, S500 (instead of S1, S2, S3, S4, S5) and 2) each stored supplier record requires an entire page to itself, and consider the hash function:

> hash address (i.e., page number) =
> remainder after dividing numeric part of S# value by 13

—a trivial example of a very common class of hash function called "division/remainder." (For reasons that are beyond the scope of this text, the divisor in a division/remainder hash is usually chosen to be prime, as in our example.) The page numbers for the five suppliers are then 9, 5, 1, 10, 6, respectively, giving us the representation shown in Fig. 3.15.

It should be clear from the foregoing description that hashing differs from indexing inasmuch as, while a given stored file can have any number of indexes, it

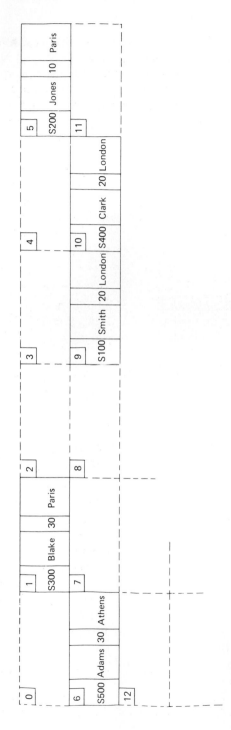

Fig. 3.15 Example of a hashed structure.

can have *at most one* hash structure.[5] To state this differently: A file can have any number of indexed fields, but only one hash field.

In addition to showing how hashing works, the example also shows why the hash function is necessary. It would theoretically be possible to use an "identity" hash function, i.e., to use the (numeric) primary key value for any given stored record directly as the hash address. Such a technique will generally be inadequate in practice, however, because the range of possible primary key values will usually be much wider than the range of available addresses. For instance, suppose that supplier numbers are in fact three digits wide, as in the example above. Then there would be 1000 possible distinct supplier numbers, whereas there may in fact be only ten or so actual suppliers. Thus, in order to avoid a considerable waste of storage space, we would ideally like to find a hash function that would reduce any value in the range 000–999 to one in the range 0–9 (say). To allow a little room for future growth, it is usual to extend the target range by 20 percent or so; that was why we chose a function that generated values in the range 0–12 rather than 0–9 in our example above.

The example also illustrates one of the disadvantages of hashing: The "physical sequence" of records within the stored file will almost certainly not be the primary key sequence, nor indeed any other sequence that has any sensible logical interpretation. (In addition, there may be gaps of arbitrary size between consecutive records.) In fact, the physical sequence of a stored file with a hashed structure is usually (not invariably) considered to represent no particular logical sequence,[6] thus, a hashed file usually does not have any intra-file clustering—which may be unfortunate, given that physical clustering is, as claimed earlier in this chapter, generally very desirable. (But see reference [3.26], which discusses an elegant hashing scheme that does preserve logical sequence in the file as stored.)

Another disadvantage of hashing in general is that there is always the possibility of running into *collisions*—that is, finding two distinct records that hash to the same address. For example, suppose the supplier file (with suppliers S100, S200, etc.) also includes a supplier with supplier number S1400. Given the "divide by 13" hash function discussed above, that supplier would collide (at hash address 9) with supplier S100. The hash function as it stands is thus clearly inadequate; it needs to be extended to deal with the collision problem somehow.

In terms of our original example, one possible extension is to treat the remainder after division by 13, not as the hash address per se, but rather as the start point for a sequential scan. Thus, to insert supplier S1400 (assuming that suppliers S100–S500 already exist), we go to page 9 and search forward from that position for the first free page. The new supplier will be stored on page 11. To retrieve that supplier

---

5.   Assuming the hash is direct. A file can have any number of *indirect* hashes (see reference [3.18]).

6.   Of course, it is always possible to *impose* any desired logical sequence on a hashed file by means of an index. Indeed, it is possible to impose multiple logical sequences, via multiple indexes.

subsequently, we go through a similar procedure. This *linear search* method may well be adequate if (as is more likely in practice) multiple records are stored on each page. Suppose each page can hold n stored records. Then the first n collisions at some hash address p will all be stored on page p, and a linear search through those collisions will be totally contained within that page. However, the next—i.e., $(n + 1)$th—collision will of course have to be stored on some distinct *overflow* page, and another I/O will be needed.

Another approach to the collision problem, perhaps more frequently encountered in practice, is to treat the result from the hash function, a say, as the storage address, not for a data record, but rather for an "anchor point." The anchor point at storage address a is then taken as the head of a chain of pointers (a *collision chain*) linking together all records—or all pages of records—that collide at a. Within any given collision chain, the collisions will typically be kept in hash field sequence, to simplify subsequent searching.

Extendable Hashing

Yet another disadvantage of hashing as described above is that as the size of the hashed file increases, so the number of collisions also tends to increase, and hence the average access time increases correspondingly (because more and more time is spent searching through sets of collisions). *Extendable* hashing [3.21] is a nice variation on the basic technique that alleviates this problem. In fact, extendable hashing guarantees that the number of disk accesses needed to locate a specific record (i.e., the record having a specific primary key value) is never more than two, and will usually be only one. Note: Values of the hash field must be unique in the extendable hashing scheme, which of course they will be if that field is in fact the primary key as suggested at the start of this section.

The scheme works as follows.

1. Let the basic hash function be h, and let the primary key value of some specific record r be k. Hashing k—i.e., evaluating $h(k)$—yields a value k' called the *pseudokey* of r. Pseudokeys are not interpreted directly as addresses but instead lead to storage locations in an indirect fashion as described below.

2. The stored file has a *directory* associated with it, also stored on the disk. The directory consists of a header, containing a value d called the *depth* of the directory, together with 2^d pointers. The pointers are pointers to data pages, which contain the actual stored records (multiple records per page). A directory of depth d can thus handle a maximum file size of 2^d distinct data pages.

3. If we consider the leading d bits of a pseudokey as an unsigned binary integer b, then the ith pointer in the directory ($1 <= i <= 2^d$) points to a page that contains all records for which b takes the value $i - 1$. In other words, the first pointer points to the page containing all records for which b is all zeros, the second pointer points to the page for which b is $0 \ldots 01$, and so on. (These 2^d pointers are typically not all distinct; that is, there will typically be fewer than 2^d distinct

data pages. See Fig. 3.16.) Thus, to find the record having primary key value k, we hash k to find the pseudokey k' and take the first d bits of that pseudokey; if those bits have the numeric value $i - 1$, we go to the ith pointer in the directory (first disk access) and follow it to the page containing the required record (second disk access).

   Note: In practice the directory will usually be sufficiently small that it can be kept in main storage most of the time. Thus the "two" disk accesses will usually reduce to one in practice.

4. Each data page also has a header giving the *local depth p* of that page ($p <\ =$ d). Suppose, for example, that d is three, and that the first pointer in the directory (the 000 pointer) points to a page for which the local depth p is two. Local depth

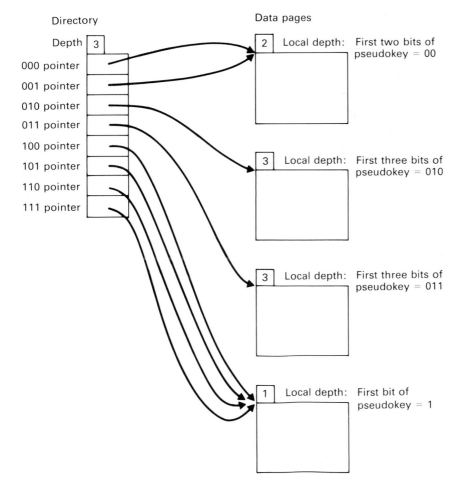

Fig. 3.16 Example of extendable hashing.

two here means that, not only does this page contain all records with pseudokeys starting 000, it contains *all* records with pseudokeys starting 00 (i.e., those starting 000 and also those starting 001). In other words, the 001 directory pointer also points to this page. Again, see Fig. 3.16.

5. Continuing the example from (3) above, suppose now that the 000 data page is full and we wish to insert a new record having a pseudokey that starts 000 (or 001). At this point the page is split in two; that is, a new, empty page is acquired, and all 001 records are moved out of the old page and into the new one. The 001 pointer in the directory is changed to point to the new page (the 000 pointer still points to the old one). The local depth p for each of the two pages will now be three, not two.

6. Again continuing the example, suppose that the data page for 000 becomes full again and has to split again. The existing directory cannot handle such a split, because the local depth of the page to be split is already equal to the directory depth. Therefore we "double the directory": that is, we increase d by one and replace each pointer by a pair of adjacent, identical pointers. The data page can now be split; 0000 records are left in the old page and 0001 records go in the new page; the first pointer in the directory is left unchanged (i.e., it still points to the old page), the second pointer is changed to point to the new page. Note that doubling the directory is a fairly inexpensive operation, since it does not involve access to any of the data pages.

Numerous further variations on the basic idea of hashing have been devised; see, for example, references [3.22–3.26].

3.6 POINTER CHAINS

Suppose again, as at the beginning of Section 3.4, that the query "Find all suppliers in city C" is an important one. Another stored representation that can handle that query reasonably well—possibly better than an index, though only marginally so— uses *pointer chains*. Such a representation is illustrated in Fig. 3.17. As can be seen, it involves two stored files, a supplier file and a city file, much as in the index representation of Fig. 3.10 (this time both files are probably in the same page set, for reasons to be explained in Section 3.7). In the pointer chain representation of Fig. 3.17, however, the city file is not an index but what is sometimes referred to as a "parent" file. The supplier file is accordingly referred to as the "child" file, and the overall structure is an example of "parent/child organization."

In the example, the parent/child structure is based on supplier city values. The parent (city) file contains one stored record for each distinct supplier city, giving the city value and acting as the head of a *chain* or *ring* of pointers linking together all child (supplier) records for suppliers in that city. Note that the city field as such has been removed from the supplier file. To find all suppliers in London (say), the DBMS can search the city file for the London entry and then follow the corresponding pointer chain.

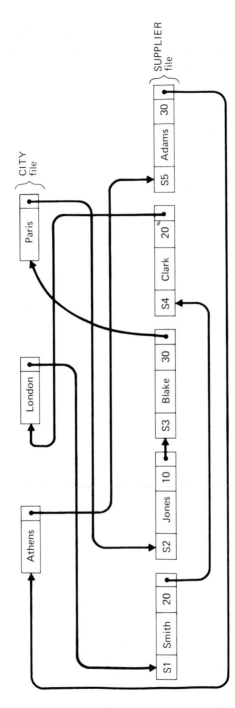

Fig. 3.17 Example of a parent/child structure.

The principal advantage of the parent/child (pointer chain) structure is that the insert/delete algorithms are somewhat simpler, and may conceivably be more efficient, than the corresponding algorithms for an index. Also, the structure will probably occupy less storage than the corresponding index structure, because each city value appears exactly once instead of multiple times. The principal disadvantages are as follows:

- For a given city, the only way to access the nth supplier is to follow the chain and access the 1st, 2nd, . . . , $(n - 1)$th supplier too. If the supplier records are not clustered appropriately, so that each access involves a seek operation, the time taken to access the nth supplier could be quite considerable.

- Although the structure may be suitable for the query "Find suppliers in a given city," it is of no help—in fact, it is a positive hindrance—with the converse query "Find the city for a given supplier" (where the given supplier is identified by a given supplier number). For this latter query, either a hash or an index on the supplier file is probably desirable; note that a parent/child structure based on supplier numbers would not make much sense (why not?). And even when the given supplier record has been located, it is still necessary to follow the chain to the parent record to discover the desired city (the need for this extra step is our justification for claiming that the parent/child structure is a hindrance for this class of query).

    Note, moreover, that the parent (city) file will probably require index or hash access too if it is of any significant size. Hence pointer chains alone are not really an adequate basis for a storage structure—other mechanisms such as indexes will almost certainly be needed too.

- Because the pointer chains actually run through the stored records (i.e., the record prefixes physically include the relevant pointers), and also because values of the relevant field are factored out of the child records and placed in the parent records instead, it is a nontrivial task to create a parent/child structure over an existing set of records. In fact, such an operation will typically require a database reorganization, at least for the relevant portion of the database (see Chapter 2, Section 2.7). By contrast, it is a comparatively straightforward matter to create a new index over an existing set of records. (Creating a new hash will also typically require a reorganization, incidentally.)

Several variations are possible on the basic parent/child structure. For example:

- The pointers could be made two-way. One advantage of this variation is that it simplifies the pointer adjustment necessitated by the operation of deleting a child record.

- Another extension would be to include a pointer (a "parent pointer" from each child record direct to the corresponding parent; this extension would reduce the amount of chain-traversing involved in answering the query "Find the city for a given supplier" (note, however, that it does not affect the requirement for a hash or index to help with that query).

▪ Yet another variation would be *not* to remove the city field from the supplier
   file but to repeat the field in the supplier records; certain retrievals (e.g., "Find
   the city for supplier S4") would then become more efficient. Note, however,
   that that increased efficiency is nothing to do with the pointer chain structure
   per se—also that a hash or index on supplier numbers is still probably required.

Finally, of course, just as it is possible to have any number of indexes over a
given stored file, so it is equally possible to have any number of pointer chains
running through a given stored file. (It is also possible, though unusual in practice,
to have both.) Figure 3.18 shows a representation for the supplier file that involves
two distinct pointer chains, and therefore two distinct parent/child structures, one
with a city file as parent (as in Fig. 3.17) and one with a status file as parent. The
supplier file is the child file for both of these structures.

3.7 COMPRESSION TECHNIQUES

Compression techniques are ways of reducing the amount of storage required for
a given collection of stored data. Quite frequently the result of such compression
will be, not only to save on storage space, but also (and probably more significantly)
to save on disk I/O; for if the data occupies less space, then fewer I/O operations
will be needed to access it. On the other hand, extra CPU operations will be needed
to decompress the data after it has been retrieved. On balance, however, the I/O
savings will probably outweigh the disadvantage of that additional CPU activity.

Compression techniques are designed to exploit the fact that data values are
almost never completely random but instead display a considerable amount of pre-
dictability. As a trivial example, if a given person's name in a name and address
file starts with the letter R, then it is extremely likely that the next person's name
will start with the letter R also—assuming, of course, that the file is in alphabetical
order by name.

A common compression technique is thus to replace each individual data value
by some representation of the difference between it and the value that immediately
precedes it—"differential compression." Note, however, that such a technique requires that the data in question be accessed sequentially, because to decompress any
given stored value requires knowledge of the immediately preceding stored value.
Differential compression thus has its main applicability in situations when the data
must be accessed sequentially anyway, as in the case of (for example) the entries in
a single-level index, or the stored records within a single page. Indexes in particular
almost always stand to gain from the use of compression. Note moreover that, in
the case of an index specifically, the pointers can be compressed as well as the data
values—for if the logical data ordering imposed by the index is the same as, or close
to, the physical ordering of the underlying file, then successive pointer values in the
index will be quite similar to one another, and pointer compression is likely to be
beneficial.

To illustrate differential compression, we depart for a moment from our usual
suppliers-and-parts example and consider a page of entries from an "employee

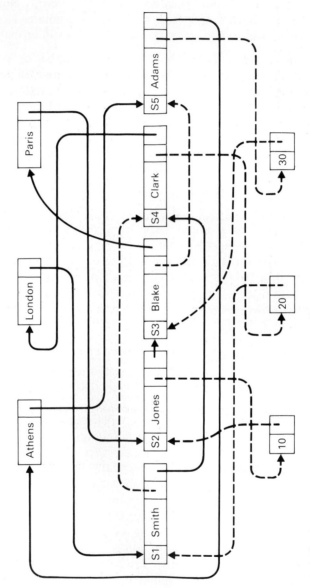

Fig. 3.18 Example of a multiple parent/child organization.

name'' index. Suppose the first four entries on that page are for the following employees:

```
ROBERTON
ROBERTSON
ROBERTSTONE
ROBINSON
```

Suppose also that employee names are 12 characters long, so that each of these names should be considered (in its uncompressed form) to be padded at the right with an appropriate number of blanks. One way to apply differential compression to this set of values is by replacing those characters at the front of each entry that are the same as those in the previous entry by a corresponding count: *front compression*. This approach yields:

```
0 - ROBERTONbbbb
6 - SONbbb
7 - TONEb
3 - INSONbbbb
```

(trailing blanks now shown explicitly as ''*b*'').

Another possible compression technique for this set of data is simply to eliminate all trailing blanks (again, replacing them by an appropriate count): an example of *rear compression*. Further rear compression can be achieved by dropping all characters to the right of the one required to distinguish the entry in question from its two immediate neighbors, as follows:

```
0 - 7 - ROBERTO
6 - 2 - SO
7 - 1 - T
3 - 1 - I
```

(where the first of the two counts in each entry is the same as in the example above, and the second is a count of the number of characters recorded). We have assumed that the next entry does not have ROBI as its first four characters when decompressed. Note, however, that we have actually lost some information from this index. That is, when decompressed, it looks like this:

```
ROBERTO?????
ROBERTSO????
ROBERTST????
ROBI????????
```

(where ''?'' represents an unknown character). Such a loss of information is obviously permissible only if the data is recorded in full *somewhere*—in the example, in the underlying employee file.

Hierarchic Compression

Suppose a given stored file is physically sequenced (i.e., clustered) by values of some stored field F, and suppose also that each distinct value of F occurs in several (consecutive) records of that file. For example, the supplier stored file might be clustered

by values of the city field, in which case all London suppliers would be stored together, all Paris suppliers would be stored together, and so on. In such a situation,
the set of all supplier records for a given city might profitably be compressed into
a single *hierarchic* stored record, in which the city value in question appears exactly
once, followed by supplier number, name, and status information for each supplier
that happens to be located in that city. See Fig. 3.19.

The stored record *type* illustrated in Fig. 3.19 consists of two parts: a fixed part
(the city field) and a varying part (the set of supplier entries). The latter part is
varying in the sense that the number of entries it contains (i.e., the number of suppliers in the city in question) varies from one occurrence of the record to another.
Such a varying set of entries within a record is usually referred to as a *repeating
group*. Thus we would say that the hierarchic record type of Fig. 3.19 consists of
a single city field and a repeating group of supplier information (and that, for any
given city, each instance of the group consists of a supplier number field, a supplier
name field, and a supplier status field).

Hierarchic compression of the type just described may be particularly appropriate in an index, where very often several successive entries will all have the same
data value (but of course different pointer values).

It follows from the foregoing that hierarchic compression of the kind illustrated
is feasible if and only if intra-file clustering is in effect. As the reader may already
have realized, however, a similar kind of compression can be applied with *inter*-file
clustering also. Suppose that suppliers and shipments are clustered as suggested at
the end of Section 3.2—that is, shipments for supplier S1 immediately follow the
supplier record for S1, shipments for supplier S2 immediately follow the supplier
record for S2, and so on. More specifically, suppose that supplier S1 and the shipments for supplier S1 are stored on page *p1*, supplier S2 and the shipments for
supplier S2 are stored on page *p2*, etc. Then an inter-file compression technique can
be applied as shown in Fig. 3.20. (Note, however, that although we describe this
example as "inter-file," it really amounts to combining the supplier and shipment
files into a single file and then applying *intra*-file compression to that single file.
Thus this case is not truly different in kind from the case already illustrated in Fig.
3.19.)

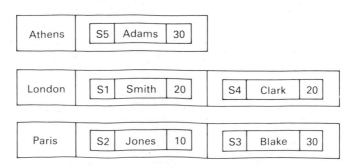

Fig. 3.19 Example of hierarchic compression (intra-file).

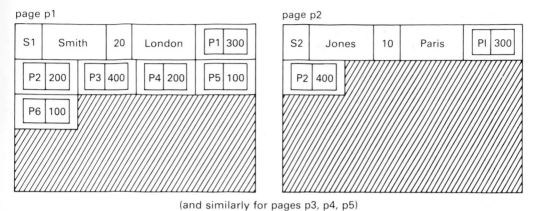

(and similarly for pages p3, p4, p5)

Fig. 3.20 Example of hierarchic compression (inter-file).

We conclude this subsection by remarking that the pointer chain structure of Fig. 3.17 can be regarded as a kind of inter-file compression that does not require a corresponding inter-file clustering (or, rather, the pointers provide the logical effect of such a clustering—so that compression is possible—but do not necessarily provide the corresponding physical performance advantage at the same time—so that compression, though possible, may not be a good idea).

Huffman Coding

"Huffman coding" [3.27] is a character encoding technique, little used in current systems, but one that can nevertheless result in significant data compression if different characters occur in the data with different frequencies (which is the normal situation, of course). The basic idea is as follows: Bit string encodings are assigned to represent characters in such a way that different characters are represented by strings of different lengths, and the most commonly occurring characters are represented by the shortest strings. Also, no character has an encoding (of n bits, say) such that those n bits are identical to the first n bits of some other character encoding.

As a simple example, suppose the data to be represented involves only the characters A, B, C, D, E, and suppose also that the relative frequency of occurrence of those five characters is as given in the following table (column two):

Character	Frequency	Code
E	35%	1
A	30%	01
D	20%	001
C	10%	0001
B	5%	0000

Character E has the highest frequency and is therefore assigned the shortest code, a single bit, say a 1-bit. All other codes must then start with a 0-bit and must be at least two bits long (a lone 0-bit would not be valid, since it would be indistinguishable from the leading portion of other codes). Character A is assigned the next shortest code, say 01; all other codes must therefore begin 00. Similarly, characters D, C, and B are assigned codes 001, 0001, and 0000, respectively (see column three above). Exercise: What English word does the following string represent?

    00110001010011

Given the encodings shown, the expected average length of a coded character, in bits, is

    0.35 * 1 + 0.30 * 2 + 0.20 * 3 + 0.10 * 4 + 0.05 * 4 = 2.15 bits,

whereas if every character were assigned the same number of bits, as in a conventional character coding scheme, we would need three bits per character (to allow for the five possibilities).

3.8   CONCLUDING REMARKS

In this chapter we have taken a lengthy, but by no means exhaustive, look at some of the most important storage structures used in current practice. We have also described in outline how the data access software typically functions, and have sketched the ways in which responsibility is divided up among the DBMS, the file manager, and the disk manager. Our purpose throughout has been to explain overall concepts, not to describe in fine detail how the various system components and storage structures actually work. Indeed, we have tried hard not to get bogged down in too much detail, though of course a certain amount of detail is unavoidable.

We conclude by stressing the point that most users are (or should be) unconcerned with most of this material most of the time. The only "user" who needs to understand these ideas in detail is the DBA, who is responsible for the physical design of the database and for performance monitoring and tuning. For other users, such considerations should preferably all be "under the covers," though it is true that those users will probably perform their job better if they have some idea of the way the system functions internally. For DBMS implementers, on the other hand, a working knowledge of this material (indeed, an understanding that goes much deeper than this introductory chapter does) is clearly desirable, if not mandatory.

EXERCISES

Exercises 3.1–3.9 may prove suitable as a basis for group discussion; they are intended to lead to a deeper understanding of various physical database design considerations. Exercises 3.10 and 3.11 have rather a mathematical flavor.

3.1 Investigate any database systems (the larger the better) that may be available to you. For each such system, identify the components that perform the functions ascribed in this chapter to, respectively, the disk manager, the file manager, and the DBMS proper. What kind of disks or other media does the system support? What is the page size? What are the disk capacities, both theoretical (in bytes) and actual (in pages)? What are the data rates? The access times? How do those access times compare with the speed of main storage? Are there any limits on file size or database size? If so, what are they? Which of the storage structures described in this chapter does the system support? Does it support any others? If so, what are they?

3.2 A company's personnel database is to contain information about the divisions, depart-ments, and employees of that company. Each employee works in one department; each de-partment is part of one division. Invent some sample data and sketch some possible corresponding storage structures. Where possible, state the relative advantages of each of those structures—i.e., consider how typical retrieval and update operations would be handled in each case. Hint: The constraints "each employee works in one department" and "each department is part of one division" are structurally similar to the constraint "each supplier is located in one city" (they are all examples of *many-to-one relationships*). A difference is that we would probably like to record more information in the database for departments and divisions than we did for cities.

3.3 Repeat Exercise 3.2 for a database that is to contain information about customers and items. Each customer can order any number of items; each item can be ordered by any num-ber of customers. Hint: There is a *many-to-many* relationship here between customers and items. One way to represent such a relationship is by means of a *double index*. A double index is an index that is used to index two data files simultaneously. A given entry corresponds to a pair of related data records, one from each of the two files, and contains two data values and two pointers. Can you think of other ways of representing many-to-many(-to-many-...) relationships?

3.4 Repeat Exercise 3.2 for a database that is to contain information about parts and com-ponents, where a component is itself a part and can have lower-level components. Hint: How does this problem differ from that of Exercise 3.3?

3.5 A stored file of data records with no additional access structure (i.e., no index, no hash, etc.) is sometimes called a *heap*. New records are inserted into a heap wherever there happens to be room. For small files—certainly for any file not requiring more than two or three pages of storage—a heap is probably the most efficient structure of all. Most files are bigger than that, however, and in practice all but the smallest files should have some additional access structure, say (at least) an index on the primary key. State the relative advantages and dis-advantages of an indexed structure when compared with a heap structure.

3.6 We have been tacitly assuming throughout this chapter that every file always has a unique identifier field (the primary key). Can you think of any situations where that assumption breaks down?

3.7 We referred several times in the body of this chapter to physical clustering. For example, it may be advantageous to store the supplier records such that their physical sequence is the same as (or close to) their logical sequence as defined by values of the supplier number field (the *clustering field*). How can the DBMS provide such clustering?

3.8 In Section 3.5 we suggested that one method of handling hash collisions would be to treat the output from the hash function as the start point for a sequential scan (the *linear search* technique). Can you see any difficulties with that scheme?

3.9 What are the relative advantages and disadvantages of the multiple parent/child organization? (It may help to review the advantages and disadvantages of the multiple index organization. What are the similarities? What are the differences?)

3.10 Define "complete indexing" to mean that an index exists for every distinct field combination in the indexed file. For example, complete indexing for a file with two fields A and B would require two indexes: one on the combination AB (in that order) and one on the combination BA (in that order). How many indexes are needed to provide complete indexing for a file defined on (a) 3 fields; (b) 4 fields; (c) N fields?

3.11 Consider a simplified B-tree (index set plus sequence set) in which the sequence set contains a pointer to each of N stored data records, and each level above the sequence set (i.e., each level of the index set) contains a pointer to every page in the level below. At the top (root) level, of course, there is a single page. Suppose also that each page of the index set contains n index entries. Derive expressions for the number of *levels* and the number of *pages* in the entire B-tree.

3.12 The first ten values of the indexed field in a particular indexed file are as follows:

```
ABRAHAMS,GK
ACKERMANN,LZ
ACKROYD,S
ADAMS,T
ADAMS,TR
ADAMSON,CR
ALLEN,S
AYRES,ST
BAILEY,TE
BAILEYMAN,D
```

(Each is padded with blanks at the right to a total length of 15 characters.) Show the values actually recorded in the *index* if the front and rear compression techniques described in Section 3.7 are applied. What is the percentage saving in space? Show the steps involved in retrieving (or attempting to retrieve) the stored records for "ACKROYD,S" and "ADAMS,V". Show also the steps involved in inserting a new stored record for "ALLINGHAM,M".

REFERENCES AND BIBLIOGRAPHY

The following references are organized into groups, as follows. References [3.1–3.6] are textbooks that either are devoted entirely to the topic of this chapter or at least include a detailed treatment of it. References [3.7–3.9] are attempts to provide a formal approach to the subject. References [3.10–3.17] are concerned specifically with indexing, especially B–trees; references [3.18–3.26] are concerned with hashing; references [3.27–3.28] discuss compression techniques; and, finally, references [3.29–3.34] address some miscellaneous techniques and related issues.

3.1 D. E. Knuth. *The Art of Computer Programming. Vol. III: Sorting and Searching.* Reading, Mass.: Addison-Wesley (1973).

Includes a comprehensive analysis of search algorithms (Chapter 6). For *database* searching, where the data resides in secondary storage, the most directly applicable sections are 6.2.4 (Multiway Trees), 6.4 (Hashing), and 6.5 (Retrieval on Secondary Keys).

3.2 J. Martin. *Computer Data-Base Organization* (2nd edition). Englewood Cliffs, N.J.: Prentice-Hall (1977).

> This book is divided into two major parts, "Logical Organization" and "Physical Organization." The latter part consists of an extensive description (well over 300 pages) of storage structures and corresponding access techniques.

3.3 J. D. Ullman. *Principles of Database Systems* (2nd edition). Rockville, MD.: Computer Science Press (1982).

> Includes a treatment of storage structures that is rather more theoretical than that of the present book.

3.4 T.J. Teorey and J. P. Fry. *Design of Database Structures.* Englewood Cliffs, N.J.: Prentice-Hall (1982).

> A tutorial and handbook on database design, both physical and logical. Over 200 pages are devoted to physical design.

3.5 G. Wiederhold. *Database Design* (2nd edition). New York, N.Y.: McGraw-Hill (1983).

> This book (15 chapters) includes a good survey of secondary storage devices and their performance parameters (one chapter, nearly 50 pages), and a comprehensive analysis of secondary storage structures (four chapters, over 250 pages).

3.6 T. H. Merrett. *Relational Information Systems.* Reston, VA.: Reston Publishing Company (1984).

> Includes an up-to-date introduction to, and analysis of, storage structures (about 100 pages), covering not only the methods described in the present chapter but also several others.

3.7 D. K. Hsiao and F. Harary. "A Formal System for Information Retrieval from Files." *CACM* **13**, No. 2 (February 1970).

> This paper is an attempt to unify the ideas of certain distinct storage structures—primarily indexes and pointer chains—into a general model, thereby providing a basis for a formal theory of such structures. A generalized retrieval algorithm is presented for retrieving records from the general structure that satisfy an arbitrary Boolean combination of "field = value" conditions.

3.8 D. G. Severance. "Identifier Search Mechanisms: A Survey and Generalized Model." *ACM Comp. Surv.* **6**, No. 3 (September 1974).

> This paper falls into two parts. The first part provides a tutorial on certain storage structures—basically hashing and indexing. The second part has points in common with reference [3.7]; like that paper, it defines a unified structure, here called a "trie-tree" structure, that combines and generalizes ideas from the structures discussed in the first part. The resulting structure provides a general model that can represent a wide variety of different structures in terms of a small number of parameters; it can therefore be used (and has in fact been used) to help in choosing a particular structure during the process of physical database design.
>
> A difference between this paper and reference [3.7] is that the "trie-tree" structure handles hashes but not pointer chains, whereas the proposal of reference [3.7] handles pointer chains but not hashes (loosely speaking). Note: The term "trie" derives from a paper by Fredkin [3.30].

3.9 M. E. Senko, E. B. Altman, M. M. Astrahan, and P. L. Fehder. "Data Structures and Accessing in Data-Base Systems." *IBM Sys. J.* **12,** No. 1 (1973).

This paper is in three parts:

I. Evolution of Information Systems;
II. Information Organization;
III. Data Representations and the Data Independent Accessing Model.

Part I consists of a short historical survey of the development of database systems prior to 1973. Part II describes "the entity set model," which provides a basis for describing a given enterprise in terms of entities and entity sets (it corresponds to the conceptual level in the ANSI/SPARC architecture). Part III is the most original and significant part of the paper. It forms an introduction to the Data Independent Accessing Model (DIAM), which is an attempt to describe a database in terms of four successive levels of abstraction: the entity set (highest), string, encoding, and physical device levels. These four levels can be thought of as a more detailed, but still abstract, definition of the lower portions of the ANSI/SPARC architecture. The three lower levels of the four can be briefly described as follows:

- *String level.* Access paths to data are defined as ordered sets or "strings" of data objects. Three types of string are identified: atomic strings (example: a string connecting stored field occurrences to form a part stored record occurrence), entity strings (example: a string connecting part stored record occurrences for red parts), and link strings (example: a string connecting a supplier stored record occurrence to part stored record occurrences for parts supplied by that supplier).
- *Encoding level.* Data objects and strings are mapped into linear address spaces, using a single simple representation primitive known as a basic encoding unit.
- *Physical device level.* Linear address spaces are allocated to formatted physical subdivisions of real recording media.

The aim of DIAM, like that of references [3.7–3.8], is (in part) to provide a basis for a systematic theory of storage structures and access methods. One criticism (which applies to the formalisms of references [3.7] and [3.8] also, incidentally) is that sometimes the best method of dealing with some given access request is simply to sort the data, and sorting is of course dynamic, whereas the structures described by DIAM (etc.) are by definition always static.

3.10 R. Bayer and C. McCreight. "Organization and Maintenance of Large Ordered Indexes." *Acta Informatica* **1,** No. 3 (1972).

3.11 D. Comer. "The Ubiquitous B-tree." *ACM Comp. Surv.* **11,** No. 2 (June 1979).

A good tutorial on B-trees.

3.12 R. E. Wagner. "Indexing Design Considerations." *IBM Sys. J.* **12,** No. 4 (1973).

Describes basic indexing concepts, with details of the techniques—including compression techniques—used in IBM's Virtual Storage Access Method, VSAM.

3.13 H. K. Chang. "Compressed Indexing Method." *IBM Technical Disclosure Bulletin* **II,** No. 11 (April 1969).

3.14 G. K. Gupta. "A Self-Assessment Procedure Dealing with Binary Search Trees and B-trees." *CACM* **27,** No. 5 (May 1984).

3.15 V. Y. Lum. "Multi-Attribute Retrieval with Combined Indexes." *CACM* **13,** No. 11 (November 1970).

The paper that introduced the technique of indexing on field combinations.

3.16 J. K. Mullin. "Retrieval-Update Speed Tradeoffs Using Combined Indices." *CACM* **14,** No. 12 (December 1971).

A sequel to reference [3.15] that gives performance statistics for the combined index scheme for various retrieval/update ratios.

3.17 B. Shneiderman. "Reduced Combined Indexes for Efficient Multiple Attribute Retrieval." *Information Systems* **2,** No. 4 (1976).

Proposes a refinement of Lum's combined indexing technique [3.15] that considerably reduces the storage space and search time overheads. For example, the index combination ABCD, BCDA, CDAB, DABC, ACBD, BDAC—see the answer to Exercise 3.10(b) —could be replaced by the combination ABCD, BCD, CDA, DAB, AC, BD. If each of A, B, C, D can assume 10 distinct values, then in the worst case the original combination would involve 60,000 index entries, the reduced combination only 13,200 entries.

3.18 R. Morris. "Scatter Storage Techniques." *CACM* **11,** No. 1 (January 1968).

This paper is concerned primarily with hashing as it applies to the symbol table of an assembler or compiler. Its main purpose is to describe an *indirect* hashing scheme based on *scatter tables.* A scatter table is a table of record addresses, somewhat akin to the directory used in extendable hashing [3.21]. As with extendable hashing, the hash function hashes into the scatter table, not directly to the records themselves; the records themselves can be stored anywhere that seems convenient. The scatter table can thus be thought of as a single-level *index* to the underlying data, but an index that can be accessed directly via a hash instead of having to be sequentially searched. Note that a given stored data file could conceivably have several distinct scatter tables, thus in effect providing hash access to the data on several distinct hash fields (at the cost of an extra I/O for any given hash access).

Despite its rather specialized orientation, the paper provides a useful survey of hashing techniques in general, and most of the material is applicable to database hashing also.

3.19 W. D. Maurer and T. G. Lewis. "Hash Table Methods." *ACM Comp. Surv.* **7,** No. 1 (March 1975).

A good tutorial, though now somewhat dated (it does not discuss any of the extendable methods). The topics covered include basic hashing techniques (not just division/remainder, but also random, midsquare, radix, algebraic coding, folding, and digit analysis techniques); collision and bucket overflow handling; some theoretical analysis of the various techniques; and alternatives to hashing (techniques to be used when hashing either cannot or should not be used). Note: A *bucket* in hashing terminology is the unit of storage—typically a page—whose address is computed by the hash function. A bucket normally contains multiple records.

3.20 V. Y. Lum, P. S. T. Yuen, and M. Dodd. "Key-to-Address Transform Techniques: A Fundamental Performance Study on Large Existing Formatted Files." *CACM* **14,** No. 4 (April 1971).

An investigation into the performance of several different basic (i.e., nonextendable) hashing algorithms. The conclusion is that the division/remainder method seems to be the best all-around performer.

3.21 R. Fagin, J. Nievergelt, N. Pippenger, and H. R. Strong. "Extendible Hashing—A Fast Access Method for Dynamic Files." *ACM TODS* **4,** No. 3 (September 1979).

3.22 G. D. Knott. "Expandable Open Addressing Hash Table Storage and Retrieval." *Proc. 1971 ACM SIGFIDET Workshop on Data Description, Access, and Control* (November 1971).

3.23 P. Larson. "Dynamic Hashing." *BIT* **18** (1978).

3.24 W. Litwin. "Virtual Hashing: A Dynamically Changing Hashing." *Proc. 4th International Conference on Very Large Data Bases* (September 1978).

3.25 W. Litwin. "Linear Hashing: A New Tool for File and Table Addressing." *Proc. 6th International Conference on Very Large Data Bases* (October 1980).

References [3.22–3.26] all present extendable hashing schemes of one kind or another. The proposals of [3.22] for "expandable" hashing pre-date (and are therefore of course quite independent of) all of the others. Nevertheless, expandable hashing is fairly similar to extendable hashing as defined in reference [3.21], and so too is "dynamic" hashing [3.23], except that both schemes use a tree-structured directory instead of the simple contiguous directory proposed in reference [3.21]. "Virtual" hashing [3.24] is somewhat different; see the paper for details. "Linear" hashing [3.25] is an improvement on virtual hashing.

3.26 W. Litwin. "Trie Hashing." *Proc. 1981 ACM SIGMOD International Conference on Management of Data.*

Presents an extendable hashing scheme with a number of desirable properties:

- It is *order-preserving* (that is, the "physical" sequence of stored records corresponds to the logical sequence of those records as defined by values of the hash field);
- It avoids the problems of complexity, etc., usually encountered with order-preserving hashes;
- An arbitrary record can be accessed (or shown not to exist) in a single disk access, even if the file contains many millions of records; and
- The file can be arbitrarily volatile (by contrast, many hash schemes, at least of the nonextendable variety, tend to work rather poorly in the face of high record insert volumes).

The hash function itself (which changes with time, as in all extendable hashing algorithms) is represented by a trie structure [3.30], which is kept in main storage whenever the file is in use and grows gracefully as the data file grows. The data file itself is, as already mentioned, kept in "physical" sequence on values of the hash field; and the logical sequence of leaf entries in the trie structure corresponds, precisely, to that "physical" sequence of the data records. Overflow in the data file is handled via a page-splitting technique, basically like the page-splitting technique used in a B-tree.

Trie hashing looks very promising. Like other hash schemes, it provides better performance than indexing for direct access (one I/O vs. typically two or three for a B-tree); and it is preferable to most other hash schemes in that it is order-preserving, which means that sequential access will also be fast. No B-tree or other additional structure is required to provide that fast sequential access. However, note the assumption that the trie will fit into main storage (probably realistic enough). If that assumption is invalid (i.e., if the data file is too large), or if the order-preserving property is not required, then linear hashing [3.25] or some other technique might provide a preferable alternative.

3.27 D. A. Huffman. "A Method for the Construction of Minimum Redundancy Codes." *Proc. IRE* **40** (September 1952).

3.28 B. A. Marron and P. A. D. de Maine. "Automatic Data Compression." *CACM* **10,** No. 11 (November 1967).

Gives two compression/decompression algorithms: NUPAK, which operates on numeric data, and ANPAK, which operates on alphanumeric or "any" data (i.e., any string of bits).

3.29 D. G. Severance and G. M. Lohman. "Differential Files: Their Application to the Maintenance of Large Databases." *ACM TODS* **1,** No. 3 (September 1976).

Discusses "differential files" and their advantages. The basic idea is that updates are not made directly to the database itself, but instead are recorded in a physically distinct file—the differential file—and are merged with the actual database at some suitable subsequent time. The following advantages are claimed for such an approach:

- Database dumping costs are reduced.
- Incremental dumping is facilitated.
- Dumping and reorganization can both be performed concurrently with updating operations.
- Recovery after a program error is fast.
- Recovery after a hardware failure is fast.
- The risk of a serious data loss is reduced.
- "Memo files" are supported efficiently. (A memo file is a kind of scratchpad copy of some portion of the database, used to provide quick access to data that is probably up to date and correct but is not guaranteed to be so.)
- Software development is simplified.
- The main file software is simplified.
- Future storage costs might be reduced.

One problem not discussed is that of supporting efficient sequential access to the data when some of the records are in the real database and some are in the differential file.

3.30 E. Fredkin. "TRIE Memory." *CACM* **3,** No. 9 (September 1960).

A "trie" is a tree-structured data file (rather than a tree-structured access path to such a file; that is, the data is represented *by* the tree, it is not pointed to *from* the tree—unless the "data file" is really an index to some other file, as it effectively is in trie hashing [3.26]). Each node in a trie logically consists of *n* entries, where *n* is the number of distinct symbols available for representing data values. For example, if each data item is a decimal integer, then each node will have exactly ten entries, corresponding to the ten symbols 0, 1, 2, . . . , 9. Consider the data item "4285." The (unique) node at the top of the tree will include a pointer in the "4" entry. That pointer will point to a node corresponding to all existing data items having "4" as their first digit. That node in turn (the "4 node") will include a pointer in its "2" entry to a node corresponding to all data items having "42" as their first two digits (the "42 node"). The "42" node will have a pointer in its "8" entry to the "428" node, and so on. And if (for example) there are no data items beginning "429," then the "9" entry in the "42" node will be empty (there will be no pointer); in other words, the tree is pruned to contain only nodes that are nonempty. (A trie is thus generally not a balanced tree.)

Note: The term "trie" derives from the word "retrieval," but is nevertheless usually pronounced "try." Tries are also known as *radix search trees* or *digital search trees*.

3.31 E. Wong and T. C. Chiang. "Canonical Structure in Attribute Based File Organization." *CACM* **14,** No. 9 (September 1971).

Proposes a novel storage structure based on Boolean algebra. It is assumed that all access requests are expressed as a Boolean combination of elementary "field = value" conditions, and that those elementary conditions are all known. Then the file can be partitioned into disjoint subsets for storage purposes. The subsets are the "atoms" of the Boolean algebra consisting of the set of all sets of records retrievable via the original Boolean access requests. The advantages of such an arrangement include the following:

- Set intersection (of atoms) is never necessary.
- An arbitrary Boolean request can easily be converted into a request for the union of one or more atoms.
- Such a union never requires the elimination of duplicates.

3.32 M. R. Stonebraker. "Operating System Support for Database Management." *CACM* **24,** No. 7 (July 1981).

Discusses reasons why various operating system facilities—in particular, the operating system file manager—frequently do not provide the kind of services required by the DBMS, and suggests some improvements to those facilities.

3.33 M. Schkolnick. "A Survey of Physical Database Design Methodology and Techniques." *Proc. 4th International Conference on Very Large Data Bases* (September 1978).

3.34 K. C. Sevcik. "Data Base System Performance Prediction Using an Analytical Model." *Proc. 7th International Conference on Very Large Data Base Systems* (September 1981).

ANSWERS TO SELECTED EXERCISES

3.5 The advantages of indexes are as follows:

a) They speed up direct access based on a given value for the indexed field or field combination. Without the index, a sequential scan would be required.

b) They speed up sequential access based on the indexed field or field combination. Without the index, a sort would be required.

The disadvantages are as follows:

a) They take up space on the disk. The space taken up by indexes can easily exceed that taken up by the data itself in a heavily indexed database.

b) While an index will probably speed up retrieval operations, it will at the same time slow down update operations. Any INSERT or DELETE on the indexed file or UPDATE on the indexed field or field combination will require an accompanying update on the index.

3.7 In order to maintain the desired clustering, the DBMS needs to be able to determine the appropriate physical insert point for a new supplier record. This requirement is basically the same as the requirement to be able to locate a particular record given a value for the clustering field. In other words, the DBMS needs an appropriate access structure—for example, an index—based on values of the clustering field. Note: An index that is used in this way to help maintain physical clustering is sometimes called a *clustering index*. By definition, a given stored file can have at most one clustering index.

3.8 Let the hash function be h, and suppose we wish to retrieve the record with hash field value k.

- One obvious problem is that it is not immediately clear whether the record stored at hash address $h(k)$ is the desired record or is instead a collision record that has overflowed from some earlier hash address. Of course, this question can easily be resolved by inspecting the value of the hash field in the stored record.
- Another problem is that, for any given value of $h(k)$, we need to be able to determine when to stop the process of sequentially searching for any given record. This problem can be solved by keeping an appropriate flag in the stored record prefix.
- Third, as pointed out in the introduction to the subsection on extendable hashing, when the stored file gets close to full, it is likely that most records will not be stored at their hash address location but will have overflowed to some other position. If record $r1$ overflows and is therefore stored at hash address $h2$, a record $r2$ that subsequently hashes to $h2$ may be forced to overflow to $h3$—even though there may as yet be no records that actually hash to $h2$ per se. In other words, the collision-handling technique itself can lead to further collisions. As a result, the average access time will go up, perhaps considerably.

3.10 (a) 3. (b) 6. For example, if the four field names are A, B, C, D, and if we denote an index by the appropriate ordered combination of field names, the following indexes will suffice: ABCD, BCDA, CDAB, DABC, ACBD, BDAC. (c) In general, the number of indexes required is i = the number of ways of selecting n elements from a set of N elements, where n is the smallest integer greater than or equal to $N/2$. For proof see Lum [3.15].

3.11 The number of *levels* in the B-tree is the unique positive integer k such that $n^{k-1} < N \le n^k$. Taking logs to base n, we have $k - 1 < \log_n N \le k$; hence

$$k = \text{ceil}(\log_n N),$$

where ceil(x) denotes the smallest integer greater than or equal to x.

Now let the number of pages in the ith level of the index be P_i (where $i = 1$ corresponds to the lowest level). We show that

$$P_i = \text{ceil}\left(\frac{N}{n^i}\right),$$

and hence that the total number of pages is

$$\sum_{i=1}^{i=k} \text{ceil}\left(\frac{N}{n^i}\right).$$

Consider the expression

$$\text{ceil}\ \frac{\text{ceil}\left(\dfrac{N}{n^i}\right)}{n} = x, \text{ say.}$$

Suppose $N = qn^i + r\ (0 \le r \le n^i - 1)$. Then

a) If $r = 0$,

$$x = \text{ceil}\left(\frac{q}{n}\right)$$

$$= \text{ceil}\left(\frac{qn^i}{n^{i+1}}\right)$$

$$= \text{ceil}\left(\frac{N}{n^{i+1}}\right).$$

b) If $r > 0$,

$$x = \text{ceil}\left(\frac{q+1}{n}\right).$$

Suppose $q = q'n + r'$ ($0 \leq r' \leq n - 1$). Then $N = (q'n + r')n^i + r = q'n^{i+1} + (r'n^i + r)$; since $0 < r \leq n^i - 1$ and $0 \leq r' \leq n - 1$,

$$0 < (r'n^i + r) \leq n^{i+1} - (n^i - n^i + 1) < n^{i+1};$$

hence ceil $\left(\dfrac{N}{n^{i+1}}\right) = q' + 1.$

But

$$x = \text{ceil}\left(\frac{q'n + r' + 1}{n}\right)$$

$$= q' + 1$$

since $1 \leq r' + 1 \leq n$. Thus in both cases (a) and (b) we have that

$$\text{ceil}\left(\frac{\text{ceil}\left(\dfrac{N}{n^i}\right)}{n}\right) = \text{ceil}\left(\frac{N}{n^{i+1}}\right).$$

Now, it is immediate that $P_1 = \text{ceil}\,(N/n)$. It is also immediate that $P_{i+1} = \text{ceil}(P_i/n)$, $1 \leq i < k$. Thus, if $P_i = \text{ceil}\,(N/n^i)$, then

$$P_{i+1} = \text{ceil}\left(\frac{\text{ceil}\left(\dfrac{N}{n^i}\right)}{n}\right) = \text{ceil}\left(\frac{N}{n^{i+1}}\right).$$

The rest follows by induction.

3.12   *Values recorded in index*   *Expanded form*

Values recorded in index	Expanded form
0 - 2 - AB	AB
1 - 3 - CKE	ACKE
3 - 1 - R	ACKR
1 - 7 - DAMS,T b	ADAMS,T c
7 - 1 - R	ADAMS,TR
5 - 1 - O	ADAMSO
1 - 1 - L	AL

Values recorded in index	*Expanded form*
1 – 1 – Y	A Y
0 – 7 – BAILEY,	BAILEY,
6 – 1 – M	BAILEYM

Notes

1. The two figures preceding each recorded value represent, respectively, the number of leading characters that are the same as those in the preceding value, and the number of characters actually stored.

2. The expanded form of each value shows what can be deduced from the index alone (via a sequential scan), without looking at the indexed records.

3. We assume that the next value of the indexed field does not have BAILEYM as its first seven characters.

The percentage saving in storage space is $100 * (150 - 35) / 150$ percent $= 76.67\%$.

The index search algorithm is as follows.

Let V be the specified value (padded with blanks if necessary to make it 15 characters long).

1. If no more entries exist in the index, no stored record for V exists. Go to exit.
2. Form the next expanded index entry; let N = corresponding length ($1 <= N <= 15$).
3. Compare the expanded index entry with the leftmost N characters of V.
4. If they are equal, go to Step 7.
5. If the index entry is high, no stored record for V exists. Go to exit.
6. Go to Step 1.
7. Retrieve the corresponding stored record and check V against the value stored therein. If they are equal, then this is the desired record; otherwise no stored record for V exists. Go to exit.

For "ACKROYD,S" we get a match on the third iteration; we retrieve the corresponding record and find that it is indeed the one we want.

For "ADAMS,V" we get "index entry high" on the sixth iteration, so no corresponding record exists.

For "ALLINGHAM,M" we get a match on the seventh iteration; however, the record retrieved is for "ALLEN,S", so it is permissible to insert a new one for "ALLINGHAM,M". (We are assuming here that the indexed field values are required to be unique.) Inserting "ALLINGHAM,M" involves the following steps.

1. Finding space and storing the new record
2. Adjusting the index entry for "ALLEN,S" to read

   1 – 3 – LLE

3. Inserting an index entry between those for "ALLEN,S" and "AYRES,ST" to read

   3 – 1 – I

Note that the preceding index entry has to be changed. In general, making a new entry in the index may affect the preceding entry or the following entry, or possibly neither—but never both.

Part 2
A Sample
Relational System

In this part of the book we examine some of the concepts and facilities of relational database systems specifically. To do this, we consider one particular system in some detail, namely the IBM system "IBM Database 2" (abbreviated DB2). DB2 is aimed at the large mainframe market, and for that reason is perhaps rather more sophisticated—or more complicated—internally than the majority of relational products currently available; however, most of that complication is concealed from the ordinary user (as of course it should be). From the user's point of view, therefore, DB2 can reasonably be regarded as a typical example of relational systems in general. In particular, its user language SQL is typical of relational languages in general (in fact, the same language SQL is actually used in numerous other relational products in addition to DB2). DB2 and SQL are therefore very suitable as a basis for illustrating relational concepts.

The structure of Part 2 is as follows. Chapter 4 provides an overview of the entire DB2 system, and in particular gives an outline description of the SQL language. Chapters 5 and 6 then describe in some detail how SQL is used to define and manipulate data in DB2. Chapter 7 discusses the system catalog, showing how SQL operations can be used to query and update that catalog. Chapter 8 then describes (the DB2 version of) a special relational facility called the *view* mechanism; and, finally, Chapter 9 explains how SQL can be used to write application programs. The entire set of chapters is intended to pave the way for a proper understanding and appreciation of the more theoretical material to be presented in Part 3. However, the reader may prefer to read that more theoretical material first and then come back to this part of the book—the order does not make all that much difference.

4

An Overview
of DB2

4.1 BACKGROUND

As explained in Chapter 1, the majority of present-day database systems are relational. In fact, a significant number of those systems (over 25 commercially available products at the time of writing) are not only relational, they are *SQL systems* specifically; that is, they support some dialect of the relational language SQL (which was the language used as the basis for the examples in Chapter 1; see, e.g., Figs. 1.2 and 1.3). A few general words on SQL are therefore appropriate here before we start getting into details.

SQL—originally spelled SEQUEL, and usually pronounced as if it still were— was first defined by Chamberlin and others at the IBM Research Laboratory in San Jose, California [4.5-4.8]. A prototype implementation of the language was built at the IBM San Jose Laboratory, under the name "System R" [4.11,4.12], and was subjected to a number of usability and performance tests, both inside IBM and elsewhere [4.6. 4.8,4.17]. The results of those tests were very encouraging, and the decision was made to go ahead with a family of IBM products based on the System R technology. Those products, now all generally available, are known as DB2, SQL/DS, and QMF [4.1-4.3]. All three products run on the IBM System/370 and similar machines. DB2 is a database management system for the MVS/370 and MVS/XA operating systems; SQL/DS is a database management system for the VM/CMS and DOS/VSE operating systems; and QMF is an ad hoc query and report-writing front-end product for both DB2 and SQL/DS (see Chapter 20).

No doubt encouraged by IBM's endorsement of the language, a number of other vendors have also produced systems that support SQL or something close to it; indeed, some of those other products were actually announced and made available before IBM's own products. In addition, SQL interfaces have been promised for a variety of other relational but "nonSQL" products. Furthermore, the American National Standards Database Committee (X3H2) is actively pursuing the definition of a proposed standard relational database language that is closely based on IBM SQL [4.9]. There can thus be no doubt that SQL is or soon will be an extremely important and widespread language.

Given all of the foregoing, it seems reasonable to use SQL as a vehicle for illustrating relational concepts, and so we do. One benefit of using SQL in this way is that it should be easy for the reader to obtain access to a working system, at least on a micro, on which to try out some of the examples and exercises. However, since different systems do support different SQL dialects, we fix our ideas by using the IBM dialect specifically (where it makes any difference; actually, the distinctions are mostly not important for our purposes). Even more specifically, we talk in terms of the MVS product DB2, simply in order to avoid repeated use of clumsy expressions like "QMF and/or SQL/DS and/or DB2." However, most statements made in this book regarding DB2 apply almost equally well to SQL/DS (and for the most part to System R too), and most of the ideas apply with only detail-level changes to many other relational systems as well. In fact, when we discuss a topic that truly is specific to the IBM products per se and is not of general applicability, we will make it very clear that such is the case.

A word of warning: DB2 and systems like it are "state-of-the-art" products, which is why we discuss them here. However, that statement should not be taken to mean that those systems are ideal in any absolute sense. In particular, they do *not* support all aspects of the underlying theory (i.e., the *relational model* — see Part 3 of this book). In certain respects, in fact, most present-day systems (including DB2 in particular) are regrettably ad hoc. Despite that fact, it still seems preferable to present the general ideas in terms of a concrete system first, before getting into the necessarily more abstract formulations of the underlying theory. But the reader is warned not to assume that, just because current products happen to behave in some particular manner, relational systems must necessarily behave in exactly that fashion. Primary keys (already touched on in Chapter 3) provide a good example—not the only one—of an aspect of the theory that current products typically do not support properly (see Chapters 12 and 15). For a more complete discussion of this topic in relation to SQL systems specifically, see reference [4.10].

4.2 RELATIONAL DATABASES

To repeat the definition from Section 1.6: *A relational database is a database that is perceived by its users as a collection of tables (and nothing but tables).* Figure 4.1 (a repeat of Fig. 3.1) shows an example of such a database, namely the suppliers-and-parts database. We will be using that database for most of our examples in this part of the book.

As the figure shows, the database consists of three tables, namely S, P, and SP.

■   Table S represents suppliers. Each supplier has a supplier number (S#), unique to that supplier; a supplier name (SNAME), not necessarily unique (though

S	S#	SNAME	STATUS	CITY
	S1	Smith	20	London
	S2	Jones	10	Paris
	S3	Blake	30	Paris
	S4	Clark	20	London
	S5	Adams	30	Athens

P	P#	PNAME	COLOR	WEIGHT	CITY
	P1	Nut	Red	12	London
	P2	Bolt	Green	17	Paris
	P3	Screw	Blue	17	Rome
	P4	Screw	Red	14	London
	P5	Cam	Blue	12	Paris
	P6	Cog	Red	19	London

SP	S#	P#	QTY
	S1	P1	300
	S1	P2	200
	S1	P3	400
	S1	P4	200
	S1	P5	100
	S1	P6	100
	S2	P1	300
	S2	P2	400
	S3	P2	200
	S4	P2	200
	S4	P4	300
	S4	P5	400

Fig. 4.1   The suppliers-and-parts database.

SNAME values do happen to be unique in Fig. 4.1); a rating or status value (STATUS); and a location (CITY). For the sake of the example, we assume that each supplier is located in exactly one city.

- Table P represents parts (more accurately, kinds of part). Each kind of part has a part number (P#), which is unique; a part name (PNAME); a color (COLOR); a weight (WEIGHT); and a location where parts of that type are stored (CITY). For the sake of the example, again, we assume that each kind of part comes in exactly one color and is stored in a warehouse in exactly one city.

- Table SP represents shipments. It serves in a sense to connect the other two tables together. For example, the first row of table SP in Fig. 4.1 connects a specific supplier from table S (namely, supplier S1) with a specific part from table P (namely, part P1); in other words, it represents a shipment of parts of kind P1 by the supplier called S1 (and the shipment quantity is 300). Thus, each shipment has a supplier number (S#), a part number (P#), and a quantity (QTY). For the sake of the example, once again, we assume that there can be at most one shipment at any given time for a given supplier and a given part; thus, for a given shipment, the combination of S# value and P# value is unique with respect to the set of shipments currently appearing in the SP table.

We remark that (to use the terminology of Section 1.3) suppliers and parts may be regarded as *entities*, and a shipment may be regarded as a *relationship* between a particular supplier and a particular part. Of course, the suppliers-and-parts database is extremely simple, much simpler than any real database is likely to be in practice; most real databases will involve many more types of entity and relationship than this one does. Nevertheless, the suppliers-and-parts database is at least adequate to illustrate most of the points that we need to make in this part of the book, and (as already stated) we will use it as the basis for most—not all—of our examples in the next few chapters.

We also remind the reader of the term "primary key," first introduced in Chapter 3, but not yet formally defined. We are still not ready to give such a formal definition (we will do so later, in Chapter 12); for now, we will continue to regard the primary key of a table simply as a unique identifier for the records of that table. The primary keys for the suppliers-and-parts database (to repeat from Chapter 3) are field S# for table S, field P# for table P, and the composite field (S#,P#) for table SP.

Note: There is nothing wrong with using more descriptive names (such as SUP-PLIERS, PARTS, and SHIPMENTS) in place of the rather terse names S, P, and SP used above; indeed, descriptive names are generally to be recommended in practice. But in the case of the suppliers-and-parts database specifically, the three tables are referenced so frequently in the chapters that follow that very short names seemed desirable. Long names tend to become irksome with much repetition.

A couple of points arising from the example are worth calling out explicitly:

■ First, note that all data values are *atomic*. That is, at every row-and-column position in every table there is always exactly one data value, never a set of values. Thus, for example, in table SP (looking at the first two columns only, for simplicity), we have

```
--    --
S#    P#
--    --
 .     .
S2    P1
S2    P2
 .     .
S4    P2
S4    P4
S4    P5
 .     .
 .     .
```

instead of

```
--    --------------
S#    P#
--    --------------
 .     .
S2    { P1, P2 }
 .     .
S4    { P2, P4, P5 }
 .     .
 .     .
```

A column such as P# in the second version of this table represents what is sometimes called a "repeating group" (we mentioned this term before, in Section 3.7). A repeating group can be regarded as a column (possibly composite) that contains *sets* of data values (different numbers of values in different rows), instead of just one value in each row. *Relational databases do not allow repeating groups.* The second version of the table above would not be permitted in a relational system. Reasons for this rule will be discussed in Chapter 11.

■   Second, note that the entire information content of the database is represented as *explicit data values*. This method of representation (as explicit values in column positions within rows of tables) is the *only* method available in a relational database. Specifically, there are no "links" or pointers connecting one table to another. For example, there is a relationship (as already pointed out) between the S1 row of table S and the P1 row of table P, because supplier S1 supplies part P1; but that relationship is represented not by pointers, but by the existence of a row in table SP in which the S# value is S1 and the P# value is P1. In nonrelational systems, by contrast, such information is typically represented by some kind of physical *link* or pointer that is explicitly visible to the user.

Of course, when we say that relational databases do not allow repeating groups or pointers, we mean specifically that *no such constructs are visible to the user.* We do not mean that such constructs may not exist at the physical level. Remember from Section 2.2 that when we say that a given system is relational, we mean that it supports relations *at the external and conceptual levels.* At the *internal* level, the system is free to use any structures it pleases, provided only that it is capable of representing those structures as relations at the higher levels. To repeat: A relational database is a database that is *perceived by its users* as a collection of tables. It is *not* just a database in which the data is physically stored as tables.

At this point the reader may be wondering why relational databases are called "relational" anyway. The answer is simple: "Relation" is just a mathematical term for a table (to be precise, a table of a certain specific kind—details to follow in Chapter 11). Thus, for example, we can say that the database of Fig. 4.1 consists of three *relations*. In this part of the book, in fact, we will generally use the terms "relation" and "table" interchangeably, as if they were synonymous. (In Part 3 we will be more precise.)

If it is true that a relation is basically just a table, then why not simply call it a table and have done with it? The answer is that (as already indicated) we very often do. However, it is worth taking a moment to understand why the term "relation" was introduced in the first place. Briefly, the explanation is as follows. As already mentioned, relational systems are based on an underlying set of theoretical ideas known as *the relational model.* The principles of the relational model were originally laid down by one man, Dr. E. F. Codd, at that time a member of the IBM San Jose Research Laboratory (where the System R work was subsequently done). It was late in 1968 that Codd, a mathematician by training, first realized that the discipline of mathematics could be used to inject some solid principles and rigor into a field—database management—that, prior to that time, was all too deficient in any such qualities. Codd's ideas were first widely published in a now classic paper, "A Relational Model of Data for Large Shared Data Banks" (Communications of the ACM, Volume 13, No. 6, June 1970). Since that time, those ideas (by now almost universally accepted) have had a wide-ranging influence on just about every aspect of database technology, and indeed on other fields as well, such as the field of artificial intelligence and natural language processing.

Now, the relational model as originally formulated by Codd very deliberately made use of certain terms—such as the term "relation" itself—that were not familiar in data processing circles at that time (even though the concepts in some cases were). The trouble was, many of the more familiar terms were very vague and fuzzy. They lacked the precision necessary to a formal theory of the kind that Codd was proposing. For example, consider the term "record." At different times that single term can mean either a record *instance* or a record *type*; a *COBOL-style* record (which allows repeating groups) or a *flat* record (which does not); a *logical* record or a *physical* record; a *stored* record or a *virtual* record; and so on. The formal relational model therefore does not use the term "record" at all; instead, it uses the term "tuple" (short for "*n*-tuple"), which was given a precise definition by Codd when he first introduced it. We do not give that definition here; for our purposes in the present part of the book, it is sufficient to say that the term "tuple" corresponds approximately to the notion of a *flat record instance* (just as the term "relation" corresponds approximately to the notion of a table). We will use the formal terms when we discuss the underlying theory in Part 3; for the present, however, we will stick for the most part to terms such as "record" that are reasonably familiar.

4.3   THE SQL LANGUAGE

Figure 4.1, the suppliers-and-parts database, is of course a representation of that database as it appears at some particular instant in time. It is a *snapshot* of the database. Fig. 4.2, by contrast, shows the database *structure*; in other words, it shows how the database is defined or described.[1]

Figure 4.2 includes one CREATE TABLE statement for each of the three tables. CREATE TABLE is an example of a SQL *data definition* statement (remember from Chapter 2 that any data sublanguage such as SQL will include both a data definition portion and a data manipulation portion). Each CREATE TABLE statement gives the name of the table to be created, the names of its columns, and the data types of those columns (possibly some additional information also, such as the "NOT NULL" specifications shown in Fig. 4.2).

It is not our purpose at this point to describe the CREATE TABLE statement in detail. That detailed description appears later, in Chapter 5. One point that does need to be stressed right at the outset, however, is that CREATE TABLE is an *executable statement*. (In fact, every statement in the SQL language is executable,

---

1.   Throughout this book we show data definition statements, data manipulation statements, etc., in upper case for clarity. In practice, it is usually more convenient to enter such statements in lower case. Most systems will accept both.

```
            CREATE TABLE S
                ( S#        CHAR(5)   NOT NULL,
                  SNAME     CHAR(20),
                  STATUS    SMALLINT,
                  CITY      CHAR(15) ) ;
            CREATE TABLE P
                ( P#        CHAR(6)   NOT NULL,
                  PNAME     CHAR(20),
                  COLOR     CHAR(6),
                  WEIGHT    SMALLINT,
                  CITY      CHAR(15) ) ;
            CREATE TABLE SP
                ( S#        CHAR(5)   NOT NULL,
                  P#        CHAR(6)   NOT NULL,
                  QTY       INTEGER ) ;
```

Fig. 4.2 The suppliers-and-parts database (data definition).

as we shall see.) If the three CREATE TABLEs in Fig. 4.2 are entered at a terminal, exactly as shown, the system will actually build the three tables, then and there. Initially, of course, the tables will be empty—that is, they will each contain just the row of column headings, no data rows as yet. However, we can immediately go on to insert such data rows (possibly via the SQL INSERT statement, to be discussed in Chapter 6), and, in just a few minutes' work, we can have a (probably small, but still useful and usable) database at our disposal, and can start doing some useful things with it. So this simple example illustrates right away one of the advantages of relational systems in general, and DB2 in particular: They are very easy to use (ease of "getting on the air" is of course just one aspect of ease of use in general).

To continue with the example: Having created the three tables, and loaded some records into them, we can now start doing useful work with them, using the SQL *data manipulation* statements. One of the things we can do is *data retrieval* (specified in SQL by means of the SELECT statement). An example of data retrieval is shown in Fig. 4.3.

a)   Interactive (DB2I):

```
        SELECT CITY                      Result:    CITY
        FROM   S                                    ------
        WHERE  S# = 'S4' ;                          London
```

b)   Embedded in PL/I (could be COBOL, FORTRAN, or Assembler):

```
 EXEC SQL SELECT CITY                     Result:    XCIT
          INTO   :XCIT                                ------
          FROM   S                                   London
          WHERE  S# = 'S4' ;
```

Fig. 4.3 A retrieval example.

A significant feature of SQL as implemented in DB2 (indeed, a significant feature of the data sublanguage in most relational systems) is that the same language is available at *two different interfaces*, namely an interactive interface ("DB2I," in the case of DB2) and an application programming interface. Figure 4.3 (a) shows an example of the interactive interface. Here, the user has entered the SELECT statement at a terminal, and the system has responded by displaying the result ("London") directly as that terminal. Figure 4.3 (b) shows essentially the same SELECT statement embedded in an application program (a PL/1 program, in the example). In this second case the statement will be executed when the program is executed, and the result "London" will be returned, not to a terminal, but to the program variable XCIT (by virtue of the INTO clause in the SELECT; XCIT is just an input area within the program—i.e., it is a PL/I variable).

As the example illustrates, therefore, SQL is both an *interactive query language* and a *database programming language.* Incidentally, this remark applies to the entire SQL language; that is, any SQL statement that can be entered at a terminal can alternatively be embedded in a program. Note in particular that the remark applies even to statements such as CREATE TABLE—it is perfectly possible to create tables from within an application program, if it makes sense to do so in the application in question (and if the user is authorized to perform such operations). In DB2, SQL statements can be embedded in programs written in any of the following languages: PL/I, COBOL, FORTRAN, and System/370 Assembler Language. IBM has also stated its intention of supporting other languages (BASIC, APL) at some future date.

Note: The prefix EXEC SQL is needed in Fig. 4.3 (b) to distinguish the SQL statement from the PL/I statements that surround it. Likewise, an INTO clause is needed to designate the input area, as we have seen, and the variable named in that clause must have a colon prefix in order to distinguish it from a SQL column-name. So, of course, it is not 100 percent true that the SELECT statement is the same at both interfaces. But it is broadly true, if we overlook the differences of detail.

We are now in a position to understand how the system looks to the user. By "user" here we mean (as usual) either an end-user at an on-line terminal or an application programmer; as already explained, both kinds of user will be using SQL to operate on tables. See Fig. 4.4.

The first point to be made concerning Fig. 4.4 is that there will normally be many users (of both kinds—both end-users and programmers), all operating on the same data at the same time. The system will automatically apply the necessary controls (basically locking; see Chapter 18) to ensure that those users are all protected from one another—that is, to guarantee that one user's updates cannot cause another user's operations to produce an incorrect result. As explained in Chapter 1, it is generally an objective of multi-user systems like DB2 to allow individual users to behave as if the system were single-user instead.

Next, note that the tables in the figure are also of two kinds, namely *base tables* and *views.* A base table is a "real" table—i.e., a table that physically exists, in the sense that there exist physically stored records, and possibly physical indexes also,

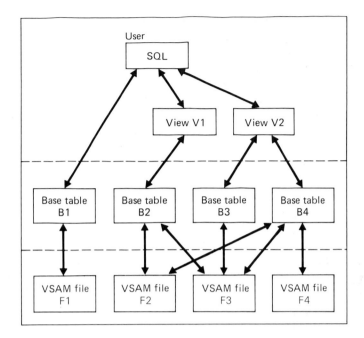

Fig. 4.4 User perception of the system.

in one or more VSAM files, that directly represent that table in storage.[2] By contrast, a view is a "virtual" table—i.e., a table that does not directly exist in physical storage, but looks to the user as if it did. Views can be thought of as different ways of looking at the "real" tables. As a trivial example, a given user might have a view of the suppliers base table S in which only those suppliers in London were visible. Views are defined, in a manner to be explained in Chapter 8, in terms of one or more of the underlying base tables.

Note: Of the various storage structures discussed in Chapter 3—indexes, hashes, pointer chains, and compressed structures—the only one currently supported by DB2 is indexes (actually B-trees). A given base table can have at most one *clustering* index (to control intrafile clustering: see Exercise 3.7) and any number (possibly zero) of additional, nonclustering indexes. As mentioned in Chapter 3, almost all

---

2. For the reader who may be familiar with VSAM, we note that the VSAM files in a DB2 database are all "entry-sequenced"; "key-sequenced" files are not used at all. Furthermore, those entry-sequenced files are not really conventional VSAM files anyway, because their internal structure is controlled by DB2, not VSAM. In the terminology of Chapter 3, DB2 uses VSAM not as the *file* manager but merely as the *disk* manager. The file manager function is performed by DB2 itself on top of the primitive VSAM entry-sequenced file construct. And DB2 indexes are not VSAM indexes but are (again) VSAM entry-sequenced files whose internal structure—controlled by DB2—happens to be an index structure.

relational systems support B-trees; a few—for example, INGRES (see Chapter 10)—support other structures, such as hashing, in addition.

Views, like base tables, can also be created at any time. The same is true of indexes. (The CREATE TABLE statement already discussed is for creating "real" or base tables. There is an analogous CREATE VIEW statement for creating views or "virtual" tables, and an analogous CREATE INDEX statement for creating indexes.) Similarly, base tables (and views and indexes) can be "dropped"—that is, destroyed—at any time, using DROP TABLE or DROP VIEW or DROP INDEX. With regard to indexes, however, note carefully that although the user—that is, *some* user, probably the database administrator—is responsible for creating and destroying them, the user is *not* responsible for saying when those indexes should be used. Indexes are never mentioned in SQL data manipulation statements such as SELECT. The decision as to whether or not to use a particular index in responding to, say, a particular SELECT operation is made by the system, not by the user. We shall have more to say on this topic in Section 4.4.

The user interface to the system is the SQL language. We have already indicated a) that SQL can be used in both interactive and programming environments, and b) that it provides both data definition and data manipulation functions (in fact, as we shall see later, it provides certain "data control" functions as well). The major data definition functions:

```
CREATE TABLE
CREATE VIEW
CREATE INDEX

DROP TABLE
DROP VIEW
DROP INDEX
```

have already been touched on. The major data manipulation functions (in fact, the only ones, if we temporarily disregard some embedded-SQL-only functions) are:

```
SELECT
UPDATE
DELETE
INSERT
```

We give examples (Fig. 4.5) of SELECT and UPDATE to illustrate an additional point, namely, the fact that SQL data manipulation statements typically operate on entire sets of records, instead of just on one record at a time. Given the sample data of Fig. 4.1, the SELECT statement (Fig. 4.5(a)) returns a set of four values, not just a single value; and the UPDATE statement (Fig. 4.5(b)) changes two records, not just one. In other words, SQL—like all relational data manipulation languages—is a *set-level language*.

Set-level languages such as SQL are sometimes described as "nonprocedural," on the grounds that users specify *what*, not *how* (i.e., they say what data they want, without specifying a procedure for getting it). In other words, the process of "navigating" around the physical database to locate the desired data is performed au-

```
a) SELECT  S#                    Result:  S#
   FROM    SP                             --
   WHERE   P# = 'P2' ;                    S1
                                          S2
                                          S3
                                          S4


b) UPDATE  S                     Result:  Status doubled
   SET     STATUS = 2 * STATUS            for S1 and S4
   WHERE   CITY = 'London' ;
```

Fig. 4.5 SQL data manipulation examples.

tomatically by the system, not manually by the user (relational systems are sometimes referred to as "automatic navigation" systems for this reason). In nonrelational systems, by contrast, such navigation is generally the responsibility of the user.

Actually, "nonprocedural" is not really a very satisfactory term—common though it is—because procedurality and nonprocedurality are not absolutes. The best that can be said is that some language *A* is either more or less procedural than some other language *B*. Perhaps a better way of putting matters is to say that relational languages such as SQL are at *a higher level of abstraction* than languages such as COBOL (or data sublanguages such as are typically found in nonrelational DBMS's). Fundamentally, it is this raising of the level of abstraction that is responsible for the increased productivity that relational systems provide.

We conclude this section by relating the functions provided by DB2 to the components of the ANSI/SPARC architecture discussed in Chapter 2. The correspondence is not entirely clear-cut, as will be seen, but it can nevertheless be useful as an aid to understanding.

1. The closest equivalent to the ANSI/SPARC "conceptual record type" is the *base table*. Base tables "really exist," in the sense that, for each row of a base table, there really is something physically stored—actually a stored record, possibly with a corresponding set of index entries, in one or more VSAM stored files. Of course, we do not mean to suggest that the stored version of a given base table is nothing but a straight copy of that table as seen by the user. There are numerous differences between a base table and its storage representation (for example, field values are stored in a variety of encoded forms). But the point is that users can always think of base tables as physically existing, without having to concern themselves with the details of how those tables are actually represented in storage.

2. A table as seen by the user can be a base table or it can be a *view*. The term "view" is used in SQL with a very specific meaning: A view is a (named) table that does not have any existence in its own right, but is instead derived from one or more underlying base tables. Note the distinction between a SQL view and an external view as defined in Chapter 2—in SQL a given user will typically be interacting with several views (and/or base tables) at the same time, whereas in Chapter 2 we defined

an external view to be the *totality* of data seen by the user in question. We will use "view" in the SQL sense, rather than in the ANSI/SPARC sense, whenever we are specifically concerned with SQL per se. Elsewhere we will generally rely on context to indicate our meaning.

3. At the internal level, as stated earlier, base tables are represented by VSAM stored files. The mapping is not just one base table to one VSAM stored file, however: Several base tables can share the same VSAM file, and one base table can be spread over several VSAM files. A given base table (as stored) can also have any number of indexes associated with it, also represented by VSAM stored files. Now, it is true that users above the internal level may conceivably be aware of the existence of such indexes; in that sense, indexes may not be completely "invisible" to users, as they ought to be if they were purely internal-level objects. However, there is no way users can directly reference those indexes in SQL access requests. As a result, indexes can be created and destroyed at any time without affecting users at all (other than in performance, of course). See the discussion of data independence in Chapter 1.

4. SQL is the system data sublanguage. As such, it includes both a data definition language (DDL) component and a data manipulation language (DML) component. As already indicated, the DML can operate at both the external and the conceptual level. The DDL, similarly, can be used to define objects at the external level (views), the conceptual level (base tables), and even the internal level (indexes). Moreover, SQL also provides certain "data control" facilities—that is, facilities that cannot really be classified as belonging to either the DDL or the DML. An example of such a facility is the GRANT statement, which allows one user to grant certain access privileges to another (see Chapter 19).

5. Application programs can access the database from a host language such as COBOL by means of embedded SQL statements. Embedded SQL represents a "loose coupling" between SQL and the host language (see Chapter 2). Basically, any statement that can be used in interactive SQL can be used in embedded SQL also. In addition, certain special statements (to be discussed in Chapter 9) are provided for use in the embedded environment only.

6. One particular on-line application, supplied with the DB2 system, is DB2I ("DB2 Interactive"). DB2I allows on-line users to access the database using SQL as an interactive query language. That is, DB2I accepts SQL statements from a terminal, passes them to DB2 for execution, and then passes the results from that execution back to the terminal. DB2I also provides access to various other DB2 facilities, beyond the scope of the present chapter; for example, it supports the interactive invocation of DB2 utilities, such as the database load utility.

(An aside for readers who are familiar with IBM systems: As explained in Chapter 2, communication between any on-line application and the user of that application (i.e., the end-user) is controlled by a system component referred to generically as a DC manager. In the particular case of DB2I (and also QMF, incidentally), the DC manager function is performed by the TSO component of MVS. In general, a given DB2 on-line application—user-written or built-in—can operate under any one (but only one) of the following DC managers: TSO, IMS/DC, or CICS. In the case of IMS/DC and CICS, the application is able to access IMS databases as well as DB2 databases. See Chapters 18 and 22.)

We will assume an interactive environment for most of our discussions of SQL, for reasons of simplicity. However, the embedded-SQL environment will be discussed in some detail in Chapter 9.

4.4 MAJOR SYSTEM COMPONENTS

The internal structure of DB2 is quite complex, as is only to be expected of a state-of-the-art system that provides all of the functions normally found in a modern DBMS (including, for example, recovery control, concurrency control, authorization control, and so on), and more besides. However, many of those functions, although of course crucial to the operation of the system as a whole, are of little or no direct interest to the ordinary user. From the user's point of view, in fact, the system can be regarded as consisting of just four major components, namely the *Precompiler*, *Bind*, the *Runtime Supervisor*, and the *Stored Data Manager*.[3] Briefly, the functions of those four components are as follows (refer to Fig. 4.6):

- The Precompiler is a preprocessor for application programs that contain embedded SQL statements. It collects those statements into a *Database Request Module* (DBRM), replacing them in the original program by host language CALLs to the Runtime Supervisor.

- The *Bind* component compiles one or more related DBRMs to produce an *application plan* (i.e., machine code instructions to implement the SQL statements in those DBRMs, including in particular machine code calls to the Stored Data Manager).

- The *Runtime Supervisor* oversees SQL programs during execution. When such a program requests some database operation, control goes first to the Runtime Supervisor, thanks to the CALL inserted by the Precompiler. The Runtime Supervisor then routes control to the application plan, and the application plan in turn invokes the Stored Data Manager to perform the required function.

- The *Stored Data Manager* manages the actual database, storing and retrieving records as requested by application plans. In other words, the Stored Data Manager is the component responsible for the kind of functions discussed in Chapter 3 of this book. It invokes other, lower-level components as necessary to perform

---

3. The other component of direct interest to the user is DB2I, of course. DB2I has already been discussed in Section 4.3.

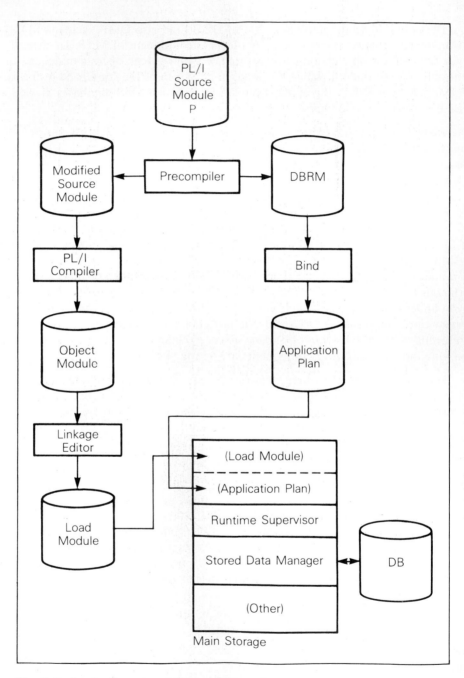

Fig. 4.6 Application preparation and execution.

detail-level functions such as buffering, locking, sorting, etc., during the performance of its basic task.

Let us examine the foregoing in a little more depth. Refer to Fig. 4.6 once again. That figure is intended to show the major steps involved in the preparation and execution of a DB2 application. To fix our ideas, we assume the original program *P* is written in PL/I (we take PL/I for definiteness; the overall process is of course essentially the same for other languages). The steps that program *P* must go through are as follows:

1. Before *P* can be compiled by the regular PL/I compiler, it must first be processed by the Precompiler. As explained above, the Precompiler is a preprocessor for the DB2 application programming languages (currently PL/I, COBOL, FORTRAN, and Assembler Language). Its function is to analyze a source program in any one of those languages, stripping out the SQL statements it finds and replacing them by host language CALL statements. At execution time those CALLs will pass control to the Runtime Supervisor. From the SQL statements it encounters, the Precompiler constructs a Database Request Module (DBRM), which subsequently becomes input to the Bind component. Note: The DBRM can be regarded as nothing more than a stylized representation of the original SQL statements (it consists basically of a parse-tree version of those statements). It does *not* consist of executable code.

2. Next, the modified PL/I program is compiled and link-edited in the normal way. Let us agree to refer to the output from this step as "PL/I load module *P*."

3. Now we come to the Bind step. As already suggested, Bind is really a *database compiler*: It converts high-level database requests—in effect, SQL statements—into System/370 machine code. (What is more, it is an *optimizing* compiler: The output from Bind is not just machine code, it is *optimized* machine code. We shall have more to say about optimization later in this section.) The input to Bind is a DBRM (or possibly multiple DBRMs, if the original program involved multiple separately compiled procedures). The output from Bind (i.e., the compiled code, which as already mentioned is called an application plan) is stored away in the system catalog, where it can be found when needed by the Runtime Supervisor. (The system catalog in DB2 is a special system database. See the brief discussion of the catalog—or "dictionary"—in Section 2.7. More details are given in Chapter 7.)

4. Finally, we come to execution time. Since the original program has effectively been broken into two pieces (load module and application plan), those two pieces must somehow be brought back together again at execution time. This is how it works (see Fig. 4.7). First, the PL/I load module *P* is loaded into main storage; it starts to execute in the usual way. Sooner or later it reaches the first of the CALLs inserted by the Precompiler. Control goes to the Runtime Supervisor. The Runtime Supervisor then retrieves the application plan from the catalog, loads it into main storage, and passes control to it. The application plan in turn invokes the Stored

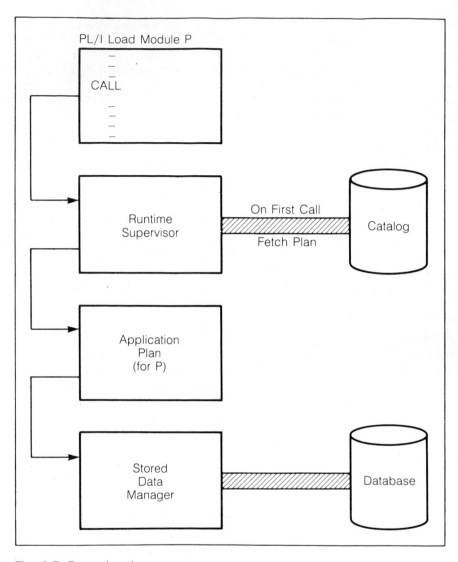

Fig. 4.7 Execution time.

Data Manager, which performs the necessary operations on the actual stored data and passes results back to the executing application as appropriate.

Optimization

Now we return to the important question of optimization. The optimizer is a major subcomponent of Bind. Its function is to choose, for each SQL manipulative statement processed by Bind, an efficient access strategy for implementing that statement. Remember that data manipulation statements such as SELECT specify only what data the user wants, not how to get to that data; the access path for getting to that data will be chosen by the optimizer ("automatic navigation"). Programs are thus independent of such access paths, which is of course desirable for reasons of data independence.

As an example of the foregoing, consider the following simple embedded SELECT statement (repeated from Fig. 4.3(b)):

```
EXEC SQL SELECT CITY
         INTO   :XCIT
         FROM   S
         WHERE  S# = 'S4';
```

Even in this very simple case, there are at least two ways of performing the desired retrieval:

1. By doing a physical sequential scan of (the stored version of) table S until the record for supplier S4 is found;

2. If there is an index on the S# column of that table—which in practice there probably will be—then by using that index and thus going directly to the S4 record.

The optimizer will choose which of these two strategies to adopt. More generally, given any particular SQL statement to be optimized, the optimizer will make its choice of strategy on the basis of considerations such as the following:

- which tables are referenced in the request (there may be more than one);
- how big those tables are;
- what indexes exist;
- how selective those indexes are;
- how the data is physically clustered on the disk;
- the form of the WHERE clause in the request;

and so on. Bind will then generate machine code that is *tightly bound to* (i.e., highly dependent on) the optimizer's choice of strategy. For example, if the optimizer decides to make use of some existing index, X say, then there will be machine code instructions in the application plan that refer explicitly to that index X. The generated code is thus tightly tailored to the original request and is therefore likely to be more efficient than more generalized, interpretive code would be.

Compilation and Recompilation

The foregoing discussion of the optimization process glosses over one extremely important point, which we now explain. First, as already indicated, DB2 is a *compiling system*. (So too is SQL/DS. By contrast, most other systems—certainly all nonrelational systems, to this writer's knowledge—are *interpretive* in nature, at least at the time of writing.) Now, compilation is certainly advantageous from the point of view of performance; it will nearly always yield better runtime performance than will interpretation (see reference [4.17]). However, compilation does suffer from one significant drawback: *It is possible that decisions made by the "compiler"* (actually Bind) *at compilation time may no longer be valid at execution time.* The following simple example illustrates the problem:

1. Suppose program *P* is compiled (bound) on Monday, and Bind decides to use an index, say index *X*, in its strategy for *P*. Then the application plan for *P* will include explicit references to *X*, as explained earlier.

2. On Tuesday, some user issues the statement

   `DROP INDEX X ;`

3. On Wednesday, some user tries to execute program *P*. What happens?

What does happen is the following. When an index is dropped, DB2 (actually the Runtime Supervisor) examines all application plans in the catalog to see which of them (if any) are dependent on that index. Any such plans that it finds it marks "invalid." When the Runtime Supervisor subsequently retrieves such a plan for execution, it sees the "invalid" marker, and therefore invokes Bind to produce a new plan—i.e., to choose some different access strategy and then to recompile the original SQL statements (which have also been kept in the catalog) in accordance with that new strategy. Provided the recompilation is successful, the new plan replaces the old one in the catalog, and the Runtime Supervisor continues with the new plan. Thus the entire rebind process (or "automatic bind" as it is called) is "transparent to the user"; the only effect that might be observed is a slight delay in the execution of the first SQL statement in the program.

Note carefully that the recompilation we are talking about here is a *SQL* recompilation, not a *PL/I* recompilation. It is not the PL/I program that is invalidated by the dropping of the index, only the application plan.

We can now see how it is possible for programs to be independent of physical access paths—more specifically, how it is possible to create and drop such paths without at the same time having to change programs. As stated earlier, SQL data manipulation statements such as SELECT and UPDATE never include any explicit mention of such access paths. Instead, they simply indicate what data the user is interested in; and it is the system's responsibility (actually Bind's responsibility) to choose a path for getting to that data, and to change to another path if the old path no longer exists. DB2 thus provides a high degree of data independence (specifically *physical* data independence, so called to distinguish it from *logical* data independence, which will be discussed in Chapter 8): Users and user programs are not dependent on the physical structure of the stored database—even though this is a compiling system.[4]

---

4. Data independence is easier to provide in an interpretive system, because the "Bind" process is effectively repeated every time the program is executed. But that repetition rep-

One further point concerning the foregoing: Our example was in terms of a dropped *index*, and perhaps that is the commonest case in practice. However, a similar sequence of events occurs when any object (not just an index) is dropped—likewise when an authorization is revoked (see Chapter 19). Thus, for example, dropping a table will cause all plans that refer to that table to be flagged as invalid. Of course, the automatic rebind will only work in this case if another table has been created with the same name as the old one by the time the rebind is done (and maybe not even then, if there are significant differences between the old table and the new one).

We conclude this section by noting that SQL is *always* compiled in DB2, never interpreted, even when the statements in question are submitted interactively. In other words, if the user enters (say) a SELECT statement at the terminal, then that statement will be compiled and an application plan generated for it; that plan will then be executed; and finally, after execution has completed, that plan will be discarded. Experiments have indicated that, even in the interactive case, compilation almost always results in better overall performance than interpretation (see reference [4.17]). The advantage of compilation is that the actual process of physically accessing the required data is made more efficient, since it is done by compiled code. The disadvantage is of course that there is a cost in doing the compilation, i.e., in producing that compiled code in the first place. But the advantage almost always outweighs the disadvantage, sometimes dramatically so.

REFERENCES AND BIBLIOGRAPHY

The following references have been arranged into groups. References [4.1–4.3] are introductory manuals on the IBM products DB2, SQL/DS, and QMF, respectively. Each of those manuals in turn includes references to further manuals on various specific aspects of the corresponding product. Reference [4.4] is another book by the present author; there is some overlap between that book and the present one, but that other book provides a much more extensive and thorough treatment of both the DB2 product per se and the IBM dialect of SQL than the present one does. References [4.5–4.10] are concerned with the definition of the SQL language. References [4.11–4.17] represent a careful selection from the rather extensive set of technical papers available on System R, the prototype forerunner of DB2 and SQL/DS. Much of the technical material contained in those System R papers applies with comparatively minor changes to DB2 and SQL/DS also. Finally, reference [4.18] consists of a set of overview papers on various aspects of DB2 and its implementation.

4.1 *IBM Database 2 General Information.* IBM Form No. GC26-4082.

4.2 *SQL/Data System for VSE: A Relational Data System for Application Development.* IBM Form No. G320-6590.

4.3 *Query Management Facility General Information.* IBM Form No. GC26-4071.

---

resents a significant overhead, of course, which is precisely why the IBM systems chose to go the compiling route.

4.4 C. J. Date. *A Guide to DB2*. Reading, Mass.: Addison-Wesley (1984).

4.5 D. D. Chamberlin and R. F. Boyce. "SEQUEL: A Structured English Query Language." *Proc. 1974 ACM SIGMOD Workshop on Data Description, Access and Control* (May 1974).

The original paper on the SEQUEL language. The name SEQUEL was subsequently changed to SQL for legal reasons.

4.6 P. Reisner, R. F. Boyce, and D. D. Chamberlin. "Human Factors Evaluation of Two Data Base Query Languages: SQUARE and SEQUEL." *Proc. NCC* **44** (May 1975).

The original SEQUEL language was based on an earlier language called SQUARE. The two languages are fundamentally the same, in fact, but SQUARE uses a rather mathematical syntax whereas SEQUEL is based on English keywords such as SELECT, FROM, WHERE, etc. The present paper [4.6] reports on a set of experiments that were carried out on the usability of the two languages, using college students as subjects. A number of revisions were made to SEQUEL as a result of that work (see the next reference).

4.7 D. D. Chamberlin et al. "SEQUEL 2: A Unified Approach to Data Definition, Manipulation and Control." *IBM J. R&D.* **20,** No. 6 (November 1976). See also errata: *IBM J. R&D.* **21,** No. 1 (January 1977).

Experience from an early prototype implementation of SEQUEL and results from the usability tests reported in reference [4.6] led to the design of a revised version of the language called SEQUEL 2. The language supported by System R is basically SEQUEL 2 (with the conspicuous absence of the so-called "assertion" and "trigger" facilities), plus certain extensions suggested by early user experience (see reference [4.8] below). The language referred to in this book as "IBM SQL"—i.e., the language supported by the IBM products DB2, SQL/DS, and QMF—is essentially the same as that supported by System R, with a few minor syntactic changes (for example, SELECT UNIQUE is replaced by SELECT DISTINCT).

4.8 D. D. Chamberlin. "A Summary of User Experience with the SQL Data Sublanguage." *Proc. International Conference on Databases, Aberdeen, Scotland* (1980). Also available as IBM Research Report RJ2767 (April 1980).

Discusses early user experience with System R SQL and proposes some extensions to the language in the light of that experience. A few of those extensions (EXISTS, LIKE, PREPARE, EXECUTE) were in fact implemented in the final version of System R.

4.9 X3H2 (American National Standards Database Committee). American National Standard Database Language SQL: Working Draft. Document X3H2-85-1 (December 1984). Available from American National Standards Institute Inc., 1430 Broadway, New York, NY 10018.

As explained in the annotation to references [1.8] and [1.9], the American National Standards Database Committee (X3H2) is currently at work on the definition of a proposed standard version of SQL. This document contains the current version of the X3H2 SQL definition. This version is under consideration (1/1/85) for distribution for public review.

4.10 C. J. Date. "A Critique of the SQL Database Language." *ACM SIGMOD Record* **14,** No. 3 (November 1984).

SQL is very far from perfect. This paper presents a critical analysis of the language's major shortcomings (primarily from the standpoint of formal computer languages in general, rather than database languages specifically).

4.11 M. M. Astrahan et al. "System R: Relational Approach to Database Management." *ACM TODS* **1,** No. 2 (June 1976).

The paper that first described the overall architecture of System R. The major components of System R were the *Relational Data System,* RDS (corresponding to the combination of Precompiler, Bind, and Runtime Supervisor in DB2); the *Relational* (or *Research*) *Storage System*, RSS (corresponding to the Stored Data Manager in DB2); and the *User Friendly Interface,* UFI (corresponding to the interactive SQL portions of DB2I in DB2). Note: The internal structure of SQL/DS is basically the same as that of System R. The internal structure of DB2 is rather different.

4.12 M. W. Blasgen et al. "System R: An Architectural Overview." *IBM Sys. J.* **20,** No. 1 (February 1981).

Describes the architecture of System R as it became by the time the system was fully implemented.

4.13 D. D. Chamberlin, A. M. Gilbert, and R. A. Yost. "A History of System R and SQL/ Data System." *Proc. 7th International Conference on Very Large Data Bases* (September 1981).

Discusses the lessons learned from the System R prototype and describes the evolution of that prototype into the first of IBM's relational product family, namely SQL/DS.

4.14 R. A. Lorie and B. W. Wade. "The Compilation of a High-Level Data Language." *IBM Research Report RJ2598* (August 1979).

Describes the compilation/recompilation scheme (which was pioneered by System R) in some detail, without however getting into any questions of optimization (see reference [4.16] for information on this latter topic).

4.15 R. A. Lorie and J. F. Nilsson. "An Access Specification Language for a Relational Data Base System." *IBM J. R&D.* **23,** No. 3 (May 1979).

Gives more details on one particular aspect of compilation in System R. For any given SQL statement, the System R optimizer generates a program in an internal language called ASL (Access Specification Language). That language serves as the interface between the optimizer and the *code generator*. (The code generator, as its name implies, converts an ASL program into System/370 machine code.) ASL consists of operators such as "scan" and "insert" on objects such as indexes and stored data files. The purpose of ASL was to make the overall translation process more manageable, by breaking it down into a set of well-defined subprocesses.

4.16 P. G. Selinger et al. "Access Path Selection in a Relational Database Management System." *Proc. 1979 ACM SIGMOD International Conference on Management of Data* (June 1979).

Describes the System R optimizer, showing in particular the criteria the optimizer uses in choosing access strategies. Optimization is another area in which System R was a pioneer. Note that the combined objectives of efficiency, data independence, and ease of use together imply that a relational system *must* include an optimizer component, at least in the large mainframe environment. For more information on this topic, see Chapter 16.

4.17 D. D. Chamberlin et al. "Support for Repetitive Transactions and Ad-Hoc Queries in System R." *ACM TODS* **6,** No. 1 (March 1981).

Gives some measurements of System R performance in both the ad hoc query and "canned transaction" environments. (A "canned transaction" is a simple application that accesses only a small part of the database and is compiled prior to execution time.) The measurements were taken on an IBM System 370 Model 158, running System R under the VM operating system. They are described as "preliminary"; with this caveat, however, the paper seems to show, among other things, that a) compilation is almost always superior to interpretation, even for ad hoc (interactive) queries, and b) a system like System R is capable of processing several canned transactions a second, provided appropriate indexes exist in the database.

4.18 *IBM Systems Journal* **23,** No. 2: Special Issue on DB2 (1984).

5

Data
Definition

5.1 INTRODUCTION

This chapter is concerned with the "data definition language" (DDL) statements of SQL. We deliberately restrict our attention to the "relational" portions of the DDL—i.e., we discuss only those aspects that are of direct interest to the user, not those aspects having to do purely with the internal level of the system, which are of course highly system-specific.[1] From the user's point of view, the principal DDL statements are as follows:

```
CREATE TABLE    CREATE VIEW    CREATE INDEX
ALTER TABLE
DROP TABLE      DROP VIEW      DROP INDEX
```

We defer discussion of CREATE and DROP VIEW to Chapter 8; the remaining statements are the subject of the present chapter.

5.2 BASE TABLES

A base table is an (important) special case of the more general concept "table." Let us therefore begin by making that more general concept a little more precise:

A *table* in a relational system consists of a row of *column headings*, together with zero or more rows of *data values* (different numbers of data rows at different times). For a given table:

---

1. The internal-level statements are the concern of the database administrator, of course. Briefly, they allow the DBA to specify such things as disk volume and storage space requirements, physical separation and affinity requirements, physical clustering details, and the like. The reader is referred to the appropriate IBM manuals for details.

a) The column heading row specifies one or more columns (giving, among other things, a data type for each of those columns);

b) Each data row contains exactly one data value for each of the columns specified in the column heading row. Furthermore, all the values in a given column are of the same data type, namely the data type specified in the column heading row for that column.

Two points arise in connection with the foregoing definition.

1.   Note that there is no mention of *row ordering*. Strictly speaking, the rows of a relational table are considered to be unordered. (A relation is a mathematical *set*— a set of rows — and sets in mathematics do not have any ordering.) It is possible, as we shall see in the next chapter, to *impose* an order on a set of rows when they are retrieved in response to a query, but such an ordering should be regarded as nothing more than a convenience for the user—it is not intrinsic to the notion of a table.

2.   In contrast to the first point, the columns of a table *are* considered to be ordered, left to right.[2] In table S of the suppliers-and-parts database, for example, column S# is the first column, column SNAME is the second column, and so on. In practice, however, there are very few situations in which that left-to-right ordering is significant, and even those can be avoided with a little discipline. Such avoidance is to be recommended, as we will explain later.

To turn now to base tables specifically: A base table is an *autonomous, named* table. By "autonomous" we mean that the table exists in its own right—unlike (e.g.) a view, which does not exist in its own right but is derived from one or more base tables (it is merely an alternative way of looking at those base tables). By "named" we mean that the table is explicitly given a name via an appropriate CREATE statement (CREATE TABLE or CREATE VIEW)—unlike a table that is merely constructed as the result of a query, which does not have any explicit name of its own and has only ephemeral existence (for examples of such unnamed tables, see the two result tables in Fig. 1.6 in Chapter 1).

CREATE TABLE

We are now in a position to discuss the CREATE TABLE statement in detail. The general format of that statement is as follows:

```
CREATE TABLE base-table-name
       ( column-definition [ , column-definition ] ... ) ;
```

where a "column-definition", in turn, takes the form:

```
column-name data-type [ NOT NULL ]
```

---

2.   At least, they are considered to be so ordered in most systems, including in particular DB2. Such an ordering is not part of the underlying theory, however; see Part 3 of this book.

Note: Barring explicit statements to the contrary, square brackets are used in syntactic definitions in this book to indicate that the material enclosed in those brackets is optional. An ellipsis (...) indicates that the immediately preceding syntactic unit may be repeated zero or more times. Material in capitals must be written exactly as shown; material in lower case must be replaced by specific values chosen by the user.

Here is an example (the CREATE TABLE statement for table S, repeated from Fig. 4.2):

```
CREATE TABLE S
      ( S#      CHAR(5)  NOT NULL,
        SNAME   CHAR(20),
        STATUS  SMALLINT,
        CITY    CHAR(15) ) ;
```

The effect of this statement is to create a new, empty base table called S. Entries describing that table are made in the system catalog. The table has four columns, called S#, SNAME, STATUS, and CITY, and having the indicated data types (data types are discussed below). Data can now be entered into the table via the INSERT statement of SQL (discussed in Chapter 6) or via the DB2 load utility.

Data Types

SQL supports the following data types:

INTEGER	signed fullword binary integer (31 bits precision)
SMALLINT	signed halfword binary integer (15 bits precision)
DECIMAL(p [,q])	signed packed decimal number of p digits precision, with assumed decimal point q digits from the right ($15 >= p >= q >= 0$; q is assumed to be 0 if omitted)
FLOAT	signed doubleword floating point number (characteristic c six bits and sign, fraction f fourteen hexadecimal digits and sign with an assumed radix point immediately to the left of the high-order digit; value $f * (16 ** c)$)
CHAR(n)	fixed length character string of length n characters
VARCHAR(n)	varying length character string of maximum length n characters

(These are the data types supported by DB2. Many other data types are possible, of course. Some common examples are: LOGICAL or BIT, MONEY, DATE and TIME, etc.)

Null Values

SQL supports the concept of a *null data value*. In fact, any column can contain null values *unless* the definition of that column in the CREATE TABLE statement explicitly specifies NOT NULL. Null is a special value that is used to represent "value unknown" or "value inapplicable." It is not the same as blank or zero. For example, a shipment record might contain a null QTY value (we know that the shipment exists but we do not know the quantity shipped); or a supplier record might contain a null STATUS value (perhaps STATUS does not apply to suppliers in San Jose for some reason).

Referring back to the CREATE TABLE for base table S, we have specified NOT NULL for S# (only). The effect of this specification is to guarantee that every supplier record in base table S will always contain a "genuine" (i.e., nonnull) supplier number value. By contrast, any or all of SNAME, STATUS, and CITY may be null in that same record. Our reasons for insisting that supplier numbers should not be null will be made clear in Part 3 of this book.

Aside: In DB2, a column that can accept null values is physically represented in the stored database by two columns, the data column itself and a hidden indicator column, one byte wide, that is stored as a prefix to the actual data column. An indicator column value of all ones indicates that the corresponding data column value is to be ignored (i.e., taken as null); an indicator column value of all zeros indicates that the corresponding data column value is to be taken as genuine (i.e., nonnull).

We do not discuss the properties of null in detail here, but content ourselves with noting that a) arithmetic expressions in which one of the operands is null evaluate to null, and b) comparison expressions in which one of the comparands is null evaluate to the "unknown" truth value (see Example 6.5.2 in Chapter 6 for an illustration of case b)). Volume II of this book describes (and incidentally criticizes) the concept of null values in considerable detail.

ALTER TABLE

Just as a new base table can be created at any time, via CREATE TABLE, so an existing base table can be *altered* at any time by the addition of a new column at the right, via ALTER TABLE:

```
ALTER TABLE base-table-name
     ADD column-name data-type ;
```

For example:

```
ALTER TABLE S
     ADD DISCOUNT SMALLINT ;
```

This statement adds a DISCOUNT column to the S table. All existing S records are expanded from four field values to five; the value of the new fifth field is null in every case (the specification NOT NULL is not permitted in ALTER TABLE). Note, incidentally, that this expansion of existing records does not mean that the records in the database are physically updated at this time—only their description in the catalog changes. An existing record is not physically changed until the next time it is the target of a SQL UPDATE statement (see Chapter 6).

Some systems support additional forms of ALTER TABLE. For example, some systems might allow the data type of a column to be changed from SMALLINT to INTEGER, say.

DROP TABLE

It is also possible to destroy an existing base table at any time:

```
DROP TABLE base-table-name ;
```

The specified base table is removed from the system (more precisely, the description of that table is removed from the catalog). All indexes and views defined on that base table are automatically dropped also.

5.3 INDEXES

Like base tables, indexes are created and dropped using SQL data definition statements. However, CREATE INDEX and DROP INDEX are basically the *only* statements in the SQL language that refer to indexes at all; other statements—in particular, data manipulation statements such as SELECT—deliberately do not include any such references. The decision as to whether or not to use an index in responding to a particular SQL request is made not by the user but by the system optimizer, as explained in Chapter 4.

CREATE INDEX takes the general form:

```
CREATE [ UNIQUE ] INDEX index-name
    ON base-table-name ( column-name [ order ]
                       [ , column-name [ order ] ] ... )
    [ CLUSTER ] ;
```

The optional CLUSTER specification means that this is a clustering index. A given base table can have at most one CLUSTER index (at any given time), as explained in Chapter 3.

Each "order" specification is either ASC (ascending) or DESC (descending); if neither ASC nor DESC is specified, then ASC is assumed by default. The left-to-right sequence of naming columns in the CREATE INDEX statement corresponds to major-to-minor ordering in the usual way. For example, the statement

```
CREATE INDEX X ON T ( P, Q DESC, R ) ;
```

creates an index (actually a B-tree) called X on the combination of columns (P,Q,R) of base table T. Entries in that index are ordered by ascending R-value within descending Q-value within ascending P-value. The columns P, Q, and R need not be contiguous within T, nor need they all be of the same data type, nor need they all be fixed length. Index X will be automatically updated to reflect updates on table T, until such time as X (or T) is dropped.

The UNIQUE option in CREATE INDEX specifies that no two records in the indexed base table will be allowed to take on the same value for the indexed field or field combination at the same time. In the case of the suppliers-and-parts database, for example, we would specify the following UNIQUE indexes:

```
CREATE UNIQUE INDEX XS  ON S  ( S# ) ;
CREATE UNIQUE INDEX XP  ON P  ( P# ) ;
CREATE UNIQUE INDEX XSP ON SP ( S#, P# ) ;
```

In general, indexes, like base tables, can be created and dropped at any time. In this example, however, we would probably want to create indexes XS, XP, and XSP at the time the underlying base tables S, P, and SP themselves are created; for if those base tables are nonempty at the time the CREATE INDEX statements are issued, the uniqueness constraints might already have been violated. An attempt to create a UNIQUE index on a table that does not currently satisfy the uniqueness constraint will fail.

Any number of indexes can be built on a single base table. Here is another index for table S:

```
CREATE INDEX XSC ON S ( CITY ) ;
```

UNIQUE has not been specified in this case because multiple suppliers can be located in the same city.

The statement to drop an index is

```
DROP INDEX index-name ;
```

The index is destroyed (its description is removed from the catalog). If an existing application plan depends on that dropped index, then (as explained in Chapter 4) that plan will be marked as invalid by the Runtime Supervisor. When that plan is next retrieved for execution, the Runtime Supervisor will automatically invoke Bind to generate a replacement plan that supports the original SQL statements without using the now vanished index. This process is completely hidden from the user.

Given that DB2 performs automatic rebinds if an existing index is dropped, the reader might wonder whether it will also do automatic rebinds if a new index is created. The answer is no, it will not. The reason for this state of affairs is that there can be no guarantee in that case that rebinding will actually be profitable; automatic rebind might simply mean a lot of unnecessary work (existing application plans might already be using an optimum strategy). The situation is different with DROP—a plan will simply not work if it relies on a nonexistent index, so rebind is mandatory in this case. Hence, if the DBA creates a new index, and suspects that some existing plan could profitably be replaced, then he or she must explicitly request that plan to be rebound by means of an explicit REBIND command. Of course, there is no guarantee even then that the rebound plan will in fact use the new index.[3]

---

3. Of course, it is quite possible that DB2 might be extended in some future release to perform automatic rebinds on index creation as well.

5.4   CONCLUDING REMARKS

The fact that data definition statements can be executed at any time makes DB2 a very flexible system. In older (i.e., nonrelational) systems, the addition of a new type of object, such as a new record type or a new index or a new field, is an operation not to be undertaken lightly. Typically it involves all of the following:

- Bringing the entire system to a halt;
- Unloading the database;
- Revising and recompiling the database definition; and finally
- Reloading the database in accordance with that revised definition.

In such a system it becomes highly desirable to perform the data definition process once and for all before starting to load and use the data—which means that a) the job of getting the system installed and operational can quite literally take months or even years of highly specialized people's time, and b) once the system is running, it can be difficult and costly, perhaps prohibitively so, to remedy early design errors.

In a system like DB2, by contrast, it is possible to create and load just a few base tables and then to start using that data immediately. Later, new base tables and new fields can be added in a piecemeal fashion, without having any effect on existing users of the database. It is also possible to experiment with the effects of having or not having particular indexes, again without affecting existing users at all (other than in performance, of course). Moreover, as we shall see in Chapter 8, it is even possible under certain circumstances to rearrange the structure of the database—e.g., to move a field from one table to another—and still not affect the logic of existing programs. In a nutshell, it is not necessary to go through the total database design process before any useful work can be done with the system, nor is it necessary to get everything right the first time.

EXERCISES

5.1 Fig. 5.1 shows some sample data values for an extended form of the suppliers-and-parts database, namely the *suppliers-parts-projects* database. Suppliers (S), parts (P), and projects (J) are uniquely identified by supplier number (S#), part number (P#), and project number (J#), respectively. The significance of an SPJ (shipment) record is that the specified supplier supplies the specified part to the specified project in the specified quantity (and the combination S#-P#-J# uniquely identifies such a record). Write a suitable set of CREATE TABLE statements for this database. Note: This database will be used in numerous exercises in subsequent chapters.

5.2 Write a set of CREATE INDEX statements for the database of Exercise 5.1 to enforce the required uniqueness constraints.

5.3 "Uniqueness" of a field or field combination is a logical property, but it is enforced in DB2 by means of an index, which is a physical construct. Discuss.

5.4 The table-name operand in CREATE INDEX must identify a base table, not a view. Why?

S	S#	SNAME	STATUS	CITY
	S1	Smith	20	London
	S2	Jones	10	Paris
	S3	Blake	30	Paris
	S4	Clark	20	London
	S5	Adams	30	Athens

P	P#	PNAME	COLOR	WEIGHT	CITY
	P1	Nut	Red	12	London
	P2	Bolt	Green	17	Paris
	P3	Screw	Blue	17	Rome
	P4	Screw	Red	14	London
	P5	Cam	Blue	12	Paris
	P6	Cog	Red	19	London

J	J#	JNAME	CITY
	J1	Sorter	Paris
	J2	Punch	Rome
	J3	Reader	Athens
	J4	Console	Athens
	J5	Collator	London
	J6	Terminal	Oslo
	J7	Tape	London

SPJ	S#	P#	J#	QTY
	S1	P1	J1	200
	S1	P1	J4	700
	S2	P3	J1	400
	S2	P3	J2	200
	S2	P3	J3	200
	S2	P3	J4	500
	S2	P3	J5	600
	S2	P3	J6	400
	S2	P3	J7	800
	S2	P5	J2	100
	S3	P3	J1	200
	S3	P4	J2	500
	S4	P6	J3	300
	S4	P6	J7	300
	S5	P2	J2	200
	S5	P2	J4	100
	S5	P5	J5	500
	S5	P5	J7	100
	S5	P6	J2	200
	S5	P1	J4	100
	S5	P3	J4	200
	S5	P4	J4	800
	S5	P5	J4	400
	S5	P6	J4	500

Fig. 5.1 The suppliers-parts-projects database.

ANSWERS TO SELECTED EXERCISES

```
5.1 CREATE TABLE S
      ( S#      CHAR(5)  NOT NULL,
        SNAME   CHAR(20),
        STATUS  SMALLINT,
        CITY    CHAR(15) ) ;
    CREATE TABLE P
      ( P#      CHAR(6)  NOT NULL,
        PNAME   CHAR(20),
        COLOR   CHAR(6),
        WEIGHT  SMALLINT,
        CITY    CHAR(15) ) ;
    CREATE TABLE J
      ( J#      CHAR(4)  NOT NULL,
        JNAME   CHAR(10),
        CITY    CHAR(15) ) ;
```

```
CREATE TABLE SPJ
     ( S#       CHAR(5)   NOT NULL,
       P#       CHAR(6)   NOT NULL,
       J#       CHAR(4)   NOT NULL,
       QTY      INTEGER ) ;
```

5.2
```
CREATE UNIQUE INDEX SX   ON S   ( S# )          CLUSTER ;
CREATE UNIQUE INDEX PX   ON P   ( P# )          CLUSTER ;
CREATE UNIQUE INDEX JX   ON J   ( J# )          CLUSTER ;
CREATE UNIQUE INDEX SPJX ON SPJ ( S#, P#, J# ) CLUSTER ;
```

In practice, it is strongly recommended that every table have at least a) a primary index, i.e., a UNIQUE index on its primary key, and b) a CLUSTER index, which may be either that primary index or some other (i.e., secondary) index.

5.3 An unfortunate state of affairs. DB2 is not quite as data independent as it ought to be.

5.4 CREATE INDEX defines an internal-level object, namely a physical access path. By definition, a physical access path must be an access path to a physically stored object. Now, in the case of a base table, a corresponding physically stored object does exist, namely the storage representation of that base table; in fact, it would be more accurate to say that the object indexed by an index in DB2 is not a base table per se but the *stored form* of that base table, perhaps better called a *stored table*. Views, by contrast, have no such corresponding physically stored object; views are *virtual*. See Chapter 8 for more details.

6
Data
Manipulation

6.1 INTRODUCTION

Now we turn to the data manipulation aspects of SQL. SQL provides four DML statements—SELECT, UPDATE, DELETE, and INSERT—and this chapter describes the major features of all four of them. As explained in Section 4.3, the tables manipulated by those DML statements can in general be either base tables or views; in this chapter, however, we concern ourselves with base tables only. Views are discussed in Chapter 8.

The plan of the chapter is as follows. Sections 6.2-6.5 are concerned with retrieval operations and Section 6.6 is concerned with update operations (where as usual we take the term "update operation" to include all of the operations UPDATE, DELETE, and INSERT). To be more specific:

- Section 6.2 introduces the major features of the basic SELECT statement.

- Section 6.3 shows how SELECT can be used to express various kinds of *join* (in particular, the so-called *natural* join).

- Section 6.4 discusses the *built-in functions* COUNT, SUM, AVG, etc.; in particular, it describes the use of the GROUP BY and HAVING clauses in connection with those functions.

- Section 6.5 describes a number of additional features: LIKE, the NULL predicate, subqueries, EXISTS, and UNION. These constructs, though in some cases quite important, tend to be used less often in practice than the constructs already described in Sections 6.2-6.4, and so are treated in a separate section of their own.

- Section 6.6 deals with the UPDATE, DELETE, and INSERT statements.

- Finally, in an attempt to tie together a number of the ideas introduced in the body of the chapter, Section 6.7 presents an example of a very complex query and shows in principle how that query might be executed.

We are not attempting to provide a comprehensive treatment of the SQL DML, merely to illustrate its major features. Nevertheless, the chapter is quite long, and the reader may like to take it one section at a time. Section 6.5 can be omitted on a first reading, if desired.

Note: Many of the examples that follow, especially those in Section 6.5, are quite complex. The reader should not infer that it is the SQL language itself that is complex. Rather, the point is that common operations are so simple in SQL (and indeed in most relational languages) that examples of such operations tend to be rather uninteresting, and do not illustrate the full power of the language. Of course, we do show a number of simple examples too. As usual, all examples are based on the suppliers-and-parts database.

6.2 SIMPLE QUERIES

We start with a simple example—the query "Get supplier numbers and status for suppliers in Paris," which can be expressed in SQL as follows:

```
SELECT S#, STATUS
FROM   S
WHERE  CITY = 'Paris' ;
```

Result:

```
--   ------
S#   STATUS
--   ------
S2      10
S3      30
```

This example illustrates the commonest form of the SQL SELECT statement—"*SE-LECT* specified fields *FROM* a specified table *WHERE* some specified condition is true." The first point to stress is that *the result of the query is another table*—a table that is derived in some way from the existing tables in the database. In other words, the user in a relational system is always operating in the simple tabular framework, a very attractive feature of such systems. (Because of this fact, we say that relational tables form a *closed system* under the retrieval operators of a language like SQL. We shall have more to say about closure in Part 3 of this book.)

Incidentally, we could equally well have formulated the query using *qualified field names* throughout:

```
SELECT S.S#, S.STATUS
FROM   S
WHERE  S.CITY = 'Paris' ;
```

A qualified field name consists of a table name and a field name (in that order), separated by a period. It is never wrong to use qualified names, and sometimes it is essential, as we shall see in Section 6.3.

The general form of the SELECT statement is as follows (ignoring numerous details, most of which will however be explained later in the chapter):

```
SELECT [ DISTINCT ] field(s)
FROM    table(s)
[ WHERE  predicate ]
[ GROUP  BY field(s) [ HAVING predicate ] ]
[ ORDER  BY field(s) ] ;
```

We now proceed to illustrate the major features of this statement by means of a rather lengthy series of examples.

6.2.1 Simple retrieval.   Get part numbers for all parts supplied.

```
SELECT P#
FROM    SP ;
```

Result:

```
--
P#
--
P1
P2
P3
P4
P5
P6
P1
P2
P2
P2
P4
P5
```

Notice the duplication of part numbers in this result. SQL does not eliminate duplicates from the result of a SELECT statement unless the user explicitly requests it to do so via the keyword DISTINCT, as in:

```
SELECT DISTINCT P#
FROM    SP ;
```

Result:

```
--
P#
--
P1
P2
P3
P4
P5
P6
```

6.2.2 Retrieval of expressions. For all parts, get the part number and the weight of that part in grams (part weights are given in table P in pounds).

```
SELECT P.P#, 'Weight in grams =', P.WEIGHT * 454
FROM    P ;
```

Result:

```
--  ------------------  ----
P#
--  ------------------  ----
P1  Weight in grams  =  5448
P2  Weight in grams  =  7718
P3  Weight in grams  =  7718
P4  Weight in grams  =  6356
P5  Weight in grams  =  5448
P6  Weight in grams  =  8626
```

In general, the items in the SELECT clause can be arbitrary expressions, involving field names and/or constants combined together by means of the usual arithmetic operators $(+,-,*,/)$, with optional parentheses to indicate a desired order of evaluation. Such expressions can also involve built-in functions (see Section 6.4).

6.2.3 Simple retrieval ("SELECT *"). Get full details of all suppliers.

```
SELECT *                                        /* or "SELECT S.*" */
FROM    S ;
```

Result: A copy of the entire S table. The star or asterisk is shorthand for a list of all field names in the table(s) named in the FROM clause, in the order in which those fields are defined in the relevant CREATE (and possibly ALTER) TABLE statement(s). The SELECT statement shown is thus equivalent to:

```
SELECT S.S#, S.SNAME, S.STATUS, S.CITY
FROM    S ;
```

The star notation is convenient for interactive queries, since it saves keystrokes. However, it is potentially dangerous in embedded SQL (i.e., SQL within an application program), because the meaning of "*" might change if the program is rebound and some change has been made to the definition of the table—in particular, if another column has been added—in the interim. In this book we will use "SELECT *" only in contexts where it is safe to do so (basically interactive contexts only), and we recommend that users do likewise in practice.

6.2.4 Qualified retrieval. Get supplier numbers for suppliers in Paris with status > 20.

```
SELECT S#
FROM    S
WHERE   CITY = 'Paris'
AND     STATUS > 20 ;
```

Result:

```
--
S#
--
S3
```

The condition or *predicate* following WHERE may include the comparison operators =, ~ =, >, ~ >, > =, <, ~ <, and < = (where the symbol ~ represents "not"); the Boolean operators AND, OR, and NOT; and parentheses to indicate a desired order of evaluation.

6.2.5 Retrieval with ordering. Get supplier numbers and status for suppliers in Paris, in descending order of status.

```
SELECT S#, STATUS
FROM    S
WHERE   CITY = 'Paris'
ORDER   BY STATUS DESC ;
```

Result:

```
--   ------
S#   STATUS
--   ------
S3       30
S2       10
```

In general, the result table is not guaranteed to be in any particular order. Here, however, the user has specified that the result is to be arranged in a particular sequence before being displayed. Ordering may be specified in the same manner as in CREATE INDEX (see Section 5.3)—that is, as

```
column-name [ order ] [ , column-name [ order ] ] ...
```

where, as in CREATE INDEX, "order" is either ASC or DESC, and ASC is the default.

It is also possible to identify columns in the ORDER BY clause by "column-number" instead of "column-name," where "column-number" refers to the ordinal (left-to-right) position of the column in question within the result table. This feature makes it possible to order a result on the basis of a column that does not have a name. For example, to order the result of Example 6.2.2 by ascending part number within ascending gram weight:

```
SELECT P.P#, 'Weight in grams =', P.WEIGHT * 454
FROM    P
ORDER   BY 3, P# ;                    /* or "ORDER BY 3, 1 ;" */
```

The "3" refers to the third column of the result table.

Result:

```
--   ------------------   ----
P#
--   ------------------   ----
P1   Weight in grams  =   5448
P5   Weight in grams  =   5448
P4   Weight in grams  =   6356
P2   Weight in grams  =   7718
P3   Weight in grams  =   7718
P6   Weight in grams  =   8626
```

6.3 JOIN QUERIES

The ability to "join" two or more tables is one of the most powerful features of relational systems. In fact, it is the availability of the join operation, almost more than anything else, that distinguishes relational from nonrelational systems (see Chapter 15). So what is a join? Loosely speaking, it is *a query in which data is retrieved from more than one table*. Here is a simple example.

6.3.1 Simple equijoin. Get all combinations of supplier and part information such that the supplier and part in question are located in the same city (i.e., are "colocated," to coin an ugly but convenient term).

```
SELECT S.*, P.*
FROM   S, P
WHERE  S.CITY = P.CITY ;
```

Notice that the field references in the WHERE clause here *must* be qualified by the names of the containing tables (because otherwise they would be ambiguous).

Result:

S#	SNAME	STATUS	S.CITY	P#	PNAME	COLOR	WEIGHT	P.CITY
S1	Smith	20	London	P1	Nut	Red	12	London
S1	Smith	20	London	P4	Screw	Red	14	London
S1	Smith	20	London	P6	Cog	Red	19	London
S2	Jones	10	Paris	P2	Bolt	Green	17	Paris
S2	Jones	10	Paris	P5	Cam	Blue	12	Paris
S3	Blake	30	Paris	P2	Bolt	Green	17	Paris
S3	Blake	30	Paris	P5	Cam	Blue	12	Paris
S4	Clark	20	London	P1	Nut	Red	12	London
S4	Clark	20	London	P4	Screw	Red	14	London
S4	Clark	20	London	P6	Cog	Red	19	London

(We have shown the two CITY columns in this result explicitly as S.CITY and P.CITY, for clarity.)

Explanation: It is clear from the English-language statement of the problem that the required data comes from two tables, namely S and P. In the SQL formulation of the query, therefore, we first name both those tables in the FROM clause, and we then express the connection between them (i.e., the fact that the CITY values must be equal) in the WHERE clause. To understand how this works, consider any two rows, one from each of the two tables—say the two rows shown here:

S#	SNAME	STATUS	CITY		P#	PNAME	COLOR	WEIGHT	CITY
S1	Smith	20	London		P1	Nut	Red	12	London

These two rows show that supplier S1 and part P1 are indeed "colocated" (since the CITY value is the same in both cases). They therefore generate the result row

S#	SNAME	STATUS	S.CITY	P#	PNAME	COLOR	WEIGHT	P.CITY
S1	Smith	20	London	P1	Nut	Red	12	London

(since they satisfy the predicate in the WHERE clause—namely, S.CITY = P.CITY). Similarly for all other pairs of rows having matching CITY values. Notice that supplier S5 (located in Athens) does not appear in the result, because there are no parts stored in Athens; likewise, part P3 (stored in Rome) also does not appear in the result, because there are no suppliers located in Rome.

The result of this query is said to be a *join* of tables S and P over matching CITY values. The term "join" is also used to refer to the operation of constructing such a result. The condition S.CITY = P.CITY is said to be a *join predicate*.

There is no requirement that the comparison operator in a join predicate be equality, incidentally, though it very often will be. Example 6.3.2 provides an illustration of a join involving "greater than." If the operator is equality, however, then the join is sometimes explicitly referred to as an *equijoin*. The equijoin by definition must produce a result containing two identical columns (see the example above). If one of those two columns is eliminated, then what is left is called the *natural* join. Here is a SQL example of natural join (the natural join of S and P over cities):

```
SELECT  S#, SNAME, STATUS, S.CITY   /* or P.CITY */,
        P#, PNAME, COLOR, WEIGHT
FROM    S, P
WHERE   S.CITY = P.CITY ;
```

Natural join is probably the single most useful form of join—so much so, that the unqualified term "join" is frequently used to mean the natural join specifically.

The following is an alternative (and helpful) way to think about how joins may conceptually be constructed. First, form the *Cartesian product* of the tables listed in the FROM clause. The Cartesian product of a set of *n* tables is the table consisting of all possible rows *r*, such that *r* is the concatenation of a row from the first table, a row from the second table, ..., and a row from the *n*th table. For example, the Cartesian product of table S and table P (in that order) is the following table:

S#	SNAME	STATUS	S.CITY	P#	PNAME	COLOR	WEIGHT	P.CITY
S1	Smith	20	London	P1	Nut	Red	12	London
S1	Smith	20	London	P2	Bolt	Green	17	Paris
S1	Smith	20	London	P3	Screw	Blue	17	Rome
S1	Smith	20	London	P4	Screw	Red	14	London
S1	Smith	20	London	P5	Cam	Blue	12	Paris
S1	Smith	20	London	P6	Cog	Red	19	London
S2	Jones	10	Paris	P1	Nut	Red	12	London
.	.	.	.	.	.	.	.	.
.	.	.	.	.	.	.	.	.
.	.	.	.	.	.	.	.	.
S5	Adams	30	Athens	P6	Cog	Red	19	London

(The complete table contains 5 * 6 = 30 rows.)

Now eliminate from this Cartesian product all those rows that do not satisfy the join predicate. What is left is the required join. In the case at hand, we eliminate all those rows in which S.CITY is not equal to P.CITY; and what is left is exactly the equijoin shown earlier.

6.3.2 Greater-than join. Get all combinations of supplier and part information such that the supplier city follows the part city in alphabetical order.

```
SELECT S.*, P.*
FROM   S, P
WHERE  S.CITY > P.CITY ;
```

Result:

S#	SNAME	STATUS	S.CITY	P#	PNAME	COLOR	WEIGHT	P.CITY
S2	Jones	10	Paris	P1	Nut	Red	12	London
S2	Jones	10	Paris	P4	Screw	Red	14	London
S2	Jones	10	Paris	P6	Cog	Red	19	London
S3	Blake	30	Paris	P1	Nut	Red	12	London
S3	Blake	30	Paris	P4	Screw	Red	14	London
S3	Blake	30	Paris	P6	Cog	Red	19	London

6.3.3 Join query with an additional condition. Get all combinations of supplier information and part information where the supplier and part concerned are co-located, but omitting suppliers with status 20.

```
SELECT S.*, P.*
FROM   S, P
WHERE  S.CITY = P.CITY
AND    S.STATUS ~= 20 ;
```

Result:

S#	SNAME	STATUS	S.CITY	P#	PNAME	COLOR	WEIGHT	P.CITY
S2	Jones	10	Paris	P2	Bolt	Green	17	Paris
S2	Jones	10	Paris	P5	Cam	Blue	12	Paris
S3	Blake	30	Paris	P2	Bolt	Green	17	Paris
S3	Blake	30	Paris	P5	Cam	Blue	12	Paris

The WHERE clause in a join-SELECT can include other conditions in addition to the join predicate itself.

6.3.4 Retrieving specified fields from a join. Get all supplier-number / part-number combinations such that the supplier and part in question are colocated.

```
SELECT S.S#, P.P#
FROM   S, P
WHERE  S.CITY = P.CITY ;
```

Result:

S#	P#
S1	P1
S1	P4
S1	P6
S2	P2
S2	P5
S3	P2
S3	P5
S4	P1
S4	P4
S4	P6

It is of course possible to SELECT just specified fields from a join, instead of necessarily having to SELECT all of them.

6.3.5 Join of three tables. Get all pairs of city names such that a supplier located in the first city supplies a part stored in the second city. For example, supplier S1 supplies part P1; supplier S1 is located in London, and part P1 is stored in London; so "London, London" is a pair of cities in the result.

```
SELECT DISTINCT S.CITY, P.CITY
FROM   S, SP, P
WHERE  S.S# = SP.S#
AND    SP.P# = P.P# ;
```

Result:

```
------  ------
S.CITY  P.CITY
------  ------
London  London
London  Paris
London  Rome
Paris   London
Paris   Paris
```

There is no intrinsic limit on the number of tables that can be joined together. Notice the use of DISTINCT in the example to eliminate duplicate city pairs.

6.3.6 Joining a table with itself.   Get all pairs of supplier numbers such that the two suppliers concerned are colocated.

```
SELECT FIRST.S#, SECOND.S#
FROM   S FIRST, S SECOND
WHERE  FIRST.CITY = SECOND.CITY
AND    FIRST.S#   < SECOND.S# ;
```

Result:

```
--  --
S#  S#
--  --
S1  S4
S2  S3
```

As can be seen, this query involves a join of table S with itself (over matching cities). Table S therefore appears twice in the FROM clause. To distinguish between the two appearances, we introduce arbitrary "aliases" FIRST and SECOND in that clause, and use those aliases as explicit qualifiers in the SELECT and WHERE clauses. Note: The purpose of the condition FIRST.S# < SECOND.S# is twofold: (a) It eliminates pairs of supplier numbers of the form (x,x); (b) it guarantees that the pairs (x,y) and (y,x) will not both appear.

This is the first example we have seen in which the use of aliases has been necessary. However, it is never wrong to introduce such aliases, even when their use is not essential, and sometimes they can help to make the statement clearer.

6.4   BUILT-IN FUNCTIONS

Although quite powerful in many ways, the SELECT statement as so far described is still inadequate for many practical problems. For example, even a query as simple as "How many suppliers are there?" cannot be expressed using only the constructs introduced up till now. SQL therefore provides a number of special *built-in functions* to enhance its basic retrieval power. The functions provided are COUNT, SUM, AVG, MAX, and MIN. Apart from the special case of "COUNT(*)" (see below), each of these functions operates on the collection of values in one column of some table—possibly a *derived* table, i.e., a table constructed as the result of some query—and produces a single value (defined as follows) as its result:

- COUNT— number of values in the column
- SUM   — sum of the values in the column
- AVG   — average of the values in the column
- MAX   — largest value in the column
- MIN   — smallest value in the column

For SUM and AVG the column must contain numeric values. In general, the argument of the function may optionally be preceded by the keyword DISTINCT, to indicate that redundant duplicate values are to be eliminated before the function is applied. For MAX and MIN, however, DISTINCT is irrelevant and has no effect. For COUNT, DISTINCT *must* be specified; the special function COUNT(*)—DISTINCT not allowed—is provided to count all rows in a table without any duplicate elimination.

Any null values in the argument column are always eliminated before the function is applied, regardless of whether DISTINCT is specified—except in the case of COUNT(*), where nulls are handled just like nonnull values. If the argument happens to be an empty set, COUNT returns a value of zero; the other functions all return null.

6.4.1 Function in the SELECT clause.   Get the total number of suppliers.

```
SELECT COUNT(*)
FROM    S ;
```

Result:

```
-

-
5
```

6.4.2 Function in the SELECT clause, with DISTINCT.   Get the total number of suppliers currently supplying parts.

```
SELECT COUNT (DISTINCT S#)
FROM    SP ;
```

Result:

```
-

-
4
```

6.4.3 Function in the SELECT clause, with a predicate.   Get the number of shipments for part P2.

```
SELECT COUNT (*)
FROM    SP
WHERE   P# = 'P2' ;
```

Result:

    -

    -
    4

6.4.4 Function in the SELECT clause, with a predicate. Get the total quantity of part P2 supplied.

```
SELECT SUM (QTY)
FROM    SP
WHERE   P# = 'P2' ;
```
Result:

    1000

6.4.5 Use of GROUP BY. Example 6.4.4 showed how it is possible to compute the total quantity supplied for some specific part. Suppose, by contrast, that it is desired to compute the total quantity supplied for *each* part: i.e., for each part supplied, get the part number and the total shipment quantity for that part.

```
SELECT P#, SUM (QTY)
FROM    SP
GROUP   BY P# ;
```
Result:

P#	
P1	600
P2	1000
P3	400
P4	500
P5	500
P6	100

Explanation: The GROUP BY operator logically rearranges the table represented by the FROM clause into partitions or *groups*, such that within any one group all rows have the same value for the GROUP BY field. (Of course, that grouping is purely conceptual; the table is not physically rearranged in the database.) In the example, table SP is grouped so that one group contains all the rows for part P1, another contains all the rows for part P2, and so on. The SELECT clause is then applied to each group of the partitioned table (instead of to each row of the original table). Each expression in the SELECT clause must be *single-valued per group*: i.e., it can be the GROUP BY field itself (or perhaps some arithmetic expression involving that field), or a constant, or a function such as SUM that operates on all values of a given field within a group and reduces those values to a single value.

A table can be grouped by any combination of its fields. Note that GROUP BY does not imply ORDER BY; to guarantee that the result in the foregoing example appears in P# order, the clause ORDER BY P# should be specified (after the GROUP BY clause).

6.4.6 Use of HAVING.   Get part numbers for all parts supplied by more than one supplier.

```
SELECT P#
FROM   SP
GROUP  BY P#
HAVING COUNT(*) > 1 ;
```

Result:

```
--
P#
--
P1
P2
P4
P5
```

HAVING is to groups what WHERE is to rows (if HAVING is specified, GROUP BY should also have been specified). In other words, HAVING is used to eliminate groups just as WHERE is used to eliminate rows. Expressions in a HAVING clause must be single-valued per group.

6.5   ADVANCED FEATURES

In this section we illustrate a variety of miscellaneous features of the SELECT statement. For want of a better term, we label those features "advanced," though they are not truly any more complicated than some of the concepts already discussed in the last three sections. In fact, some of them—especially EXISTS (see Examples 6.5.7–6.5.10)—are very fundamental; however, they are probably less frequently encountered in practice than the features discussed in Sections 6.2–6.4. For that reason the reader may choose to omit this section on a first reading.

6.5.1 Retrieval using LIKE.   Get all parts whose names begin with the letter C.

```
SELECT P.*
FROM   P
WHERE  P.PNAME LIKE 'C%' ;
```

Result:

P#	PNAME	COLOR	WEIGHT	CITY
P5	Cam	Blue	12	Paris
P6	Cog	Red	19	London

In general, a "LIKE predicate" takes the form

```
column-name LIKE character-string-constant
```

where "column-name" must designate a column of type CHAR or VARCHAR. For a given record, the predicate evaluates to *true* if the value within the designated column conforms to the pattern specified by the character string constant. Characters within that constant are interpreted as follows:

- The _ character (break or underscore) stands for *any single character*.
- The % character (percent) stands for *any sequence of n characters* (where *n* may be zero).
- All other characters simply stand for themselves.

In the example, therefore, the SELECT statement will retrieve records from table P for which the PNAME value begins with the letter C and has any sequence of zero or more characters following that C.

Here are some more examples of LIKE (and its converse, NOT LIKE):

```
ADDRESS LIKE '%Berkeley%'
```
— will evaluate to *true* if ADDRESS contains the string "Berkeley" anywhere inside it

```
S# LIKE 'S__'
```
— will evaluate to *true* if S# is exactly three characters long and the first is an "S"

```
PNAME LIKE '%c___'
```
— will evaluate to *true* if PNAME is four characters long or more and the last but three is a "c"

```
CITY NOT LIKE '%E%'
```
— will evaluate to *true* if CITY does not contain an "E"

6.5.2 Retrieval involving NULL. Suppose for the sake of the example that supplier S5 has a status value of null, rather than 30. Get supplier numbers for suppliers with status greater than 25.

```
SELECT S#
FROM    S
WHERE   STATUS > 25;
```

Result:

```
--
S#
--
S3
```

Supplier S5 does not qualify. When a null value is compared with some other value in evaluating a predicate, regardless of the comparison operator involved, the result of the comparison is *never* considered to be *true*—even if that other value is also null. In other words, if STATUS happens to be null, then none of the following comparisons evaluates to *true*:[1]

```
STATUS > 25
STATUS <= 25
STATUS = 25
STATUS ~ = 25
STATUS = NULL           /* This is illegal syntax. See below. */
STATUS ~ = NULL         /* So is this.                        */
```

A special predicate of the form

```
column-name IS [ NOT ] NULL
```

is provided for testing for the presence [or absence] of null values. For example:

```
SELECT S#
FROM   S
WHERE  STATUS IS NULL ;
```

Result:

```
--
S#
--
S5
```

The syntax "STATUS = NULL" is not permitted, because *nothing*—not even null itself—is considered to be equal to null.

6.5.3 Retrieval involving a subquery.   Get supplier names for suppliers who supply part P2.

```
SELECT SNAME
FROM   S
WHERE  S# IN
       ( SELECT S#
         FROM   SP
         WHERE  P# = 'P2' ) ;
```

Result:

```
-----
SNAME
-----
Smith
Jones
Blake
Clark
```

---

1.   Actually they all evaluate to the *unknown* truth value. In the presence of null values, it is necessary to adopt a three-valued logic, in which the truth values are *true, false,* and *unknown. (Unknown* is really the null truth value, as a matter of fact.) The SELECT statement retrieves records for which the WHERE predicate evaluates to *true,* i.e., not to *false* and not to *unknown.*

Explanation: A *subquery* is a SELECT – FROM – WHERE expression that is nested inside another such expression (loosely speaking). Subqueries are typically used to represent the set of values to be searched via an "IN predicate," as the example illustrates. The system evaluates the overall query by evaluating the nested subquery first. That subquery returns the set of supplier *numbers* for suppliers who supply part P2, namely the set ('S1','S2','S3','S4'). The original query is thus equivalent to the following simpler query:

```
SELECT SNAME
FROM   S
WHERE  S# IN ( 'S1', 'S2', 'S3', 'S4' ) ;
```

The WHERE clause in this simpler form evaluates to *true* if and only if S# has one of the values S1, S2, S3, S4; thus the overall result is as shown above.

Note, incidentally, that the original problem—"Get supplier names for suppliers who supply part P2"—can equally well be expressed as a *join* query, as follows:

```
SELECT S.SNAME
FROM   S, SP
WHERE  S.S# = SP.S#
AND    SP.P# = 'P2' ;
```

Explanation: The join of S and SP over supplier numbers consists of a table of 12 rows (one for each row in SP), in which each row consists of the corresponding row from SP extended with SNAME, STATUS, and CITY values for the supplier identified by the S# value in that row. Of these twelve rows, four are for part P2; the final result is thus obtained by extracting the SNAME values from those four rows.

The two formulations of the original query—one using a subquery, one using a join—are equally correct. It is purely a matter of taste as to which version a given user might prefer (except that—depending on the sophistication of the system optimizer—one might perform better than the other; in an ideal system, of course, the user should not have to worry about such considerations).

6.5.4 Subquery with multiple levels of nesting. Get supplier names for suppliers who supply at least one red part.

```
SELECT SNAME
FROM   S
WHERE  S# IN
         ( SELECT S#
           FROM   SP
           WHERE  P# IN
                    ( SELECT P#
                      FROM   P
                      WHERE  COLOR = 'Red' ) ) ;
```

Result:

```
-----
SNAME
-----
Smith
Jones
Clark
```

Subqueries can be nested to any depth. Exercise: Give an equivalent join formulation of this query.

6.5.5 Subquery with comparison operator other than IN.   Get supplier numbers for suppliers who are located in the same city as supplier S1.

```
SELECT  S#
FROM    S
WHERE   CITY =
        ( SELECT CITY
          FROM    S
          WHERE   S# = 'S1' ) ;
```

Result:

```
--
S#
--
S1
S4
```

If the user knows that a particular subquery will return exactly one value, a simple comparison operator (such as $=$, $>$, etc.) can be used in place of the more usual IN.

6.5.6 Function in a subquery.   Get supplier numbers for suppliers with status value less than the current maximum status value in the S table.

```
SELECT  S#
FROM    S
WHERE   STATUS <
        ( SELECT MAX (STATUS)
          FROM    S ) ;
```

Result:

```
--
S#
--
S1
S2
S4
```

6.5.7 Query using EXISTS.   Get supplier names for suppliers who supply part P2 (same as Example 6.5.3).

```
SELECT SNAME
FROM   S
WHERE  EXISTS
     ( SELECT *
       FROM   SP
       WHERE  S# = S.S#
       AND    P# = 'P2' ) ;
```

Explanation: EXISTS here represents the *existential quantifier*. The expression "EXISTS (SELECT * FROM ...)" evaluates to *true* if and only if the result of evaluating the "SELECT * FROM ..." is not empty—in other words, if and only if there exists a record in the FROM table of that "SELECT * FROM ..." satisfying the WHERE condition in that same "SELECT * FROM ...". Notice how the WHERE condition within the EXISTS expression refers to the FROM-table from the outer level of the query—namely, by means of an explicitly qualified column name (S.S#, in the example).

To see how the example works, consider each SNAME value in turn and see whether it causes the existence test to evaluate to *true*. Suppose the first SNAME value is "Smith" (so that the corresponding S# value is S1). Is the set of SP records having S# equal to S1 and P# equal to P2 empty? If the answer is no, then there exists an SP record with S# equal to S1 and P# equal to P2, and so "Smith" should be one of the values retrieved. Similarly for each of the other SNAME values. The entire query may thus be paraphrased: "Select supplier names for suppliers such that there exists a shipment relating them to part P2."

Although this particular example merely shows another way of formulating a query for a problem that we already know how to handle (using either join or a subquery), EXISTS is actually one of the most fundamental and most general constructs in the entire SQL language. (Note in particular that any query involving IN can always be reformulated to use EXISTS instead. The converse, however, is not true.) The negated form NOT EXISTS is especially important for a certain class of (rather complex) queries; we therefore give some examples of that negated form (Examples 6.5.8–6.5.10).

6.5.8 Query using NOT EXISTS. Get supplier names for suppliers who do not supply part P2 (inverse of Example 6.5.7).

```
SELECT SNAME
FROM   S
WHERE  NOT EXISTS
     ( SELECT *
       FROM   SP
       WHERE  S# = S.S#
       AND    P# = 'P2' ) ;
```

Result:

```
-----
SNAME
-----
Adams
```

The query may be paraphrased: "Select supplier names for suppliers such that there does not exist a shipment relating them to part P2." Note that this query could equivalently be expressed using the negated form of IN (see the formulation below); by contrast, the next example (Example 6.5.9) could not. (Exercise: Why not?)

```
SELECT  SNAME
FROM    S
WHERE   S# NOT IN
      ( SELECT  S#
        FROM    SP
        WHERE   P# = 'P2' ) ;
```

6.5.9 Query using NOT EXISTS.   Get supplier names for suppliers who supply all parts.

```
SELECT  SNAME
FROM    S
WHERE   NOT EXISTS
      ( SELECT  *
        FROM    P
        WHERE   NOT EXISTS
              ( SELECT  *
                FROM    SP
                WHERE   S# = S.S#
                AND     P# = P.P# ) ) ;
```

Result:

```
-----
SNAME
-----
Smith
```

The query may be paraphrased: "Select supplier names for suppliers such that there does not exist a part that they do not supply."

6.5.10 Query using NOT EXISTS.   Get supplier numbers for suppliers who supply at least all those parts supplied by supplier S2.

One way to tackle this rather complex problem is to break it down into a set of simpler queries and deal with them one at a time. Thus we can first discover the set of part numbers for parts supplied by supplier S2:

```
SELECT  P#
FROM    SP
WHERE   S# = 'S2' ;
```

Result:

```
--
P#
--
P1
P2
```

Using CREATE TABLE and INSERT (discussed in detail in the next section), it is possible to save this result in a table in the database, say table TEMP. Then we can go on to discover the set of supplier numbers for suppliers who supply all parts listed in TEMP (very much as in Example 6.5.9):

```
SELECT  DISTINCT S#
FROM    SP SPX
WHERE   NOT EXISTS
      ( SELECT *
        FROM    TEMP
        WHERE   NOT EXISTS
              ( SELECT *
                FROM    SP SPY
                WHERE   SPY.S# = SPX.S#
                AND     SPY.P# = TEMP.P# ) ) ;
```

Result:

```
--
S#
--
S1
S2
```

Note, however, that this query differs from that of Example 6.5.9 in that it is necessary to use at least one alias, since we are extracting S# values from table SP—instead of SNAME values from table S—and so need to be able to make two simultaneous but distinct references to table SP.

Table TEMP can now be dropped.

It is often a good idea to handle complex queries in this step-at-a-time manner, for ease of understanding. However, it is also possible to express the entire query as a single SELECT, eliminating the need for TEMP entirely:

```
SELECT  DISTINCT S#
FROM    SP SPX
WHERE   NOT EXISTS
      ( SELECT *
        FROM    SP SPY
        WHERE   S# = 'S2'
        AND     NOT EXISTS
              ( SELECT *
                FROM    SP SPZ
                WHERE   SPZ.S# = SPX.S#
                AND     SPZ.P# = SPY.P# ) ) ;
```

6.5.11 Query involving UNION. Get part numbers for parts that either weigh more than 16 pounds or are supplied by supplier S2 (or both).

```
SELECT  P#
FROM    P
WHERE   WEIGHT > 16
```

```
UNION
SELECT  P#
FROM    SP
WHERE   S# = 'S2' ;
```

Result:

```
--

--
P1
P2
P3
P6
```

UNION is the union operator of traditional set theory. In other words, *A* UNION *B* (where *A* and *B* are sets) is the set of all objects *x* such that *x* is a member of *A* or *x* is a member of *B* (or both). Redundant duplicates are always eliminated from the result of a UNION.

6.6 UPDATE OPERATIONS

The SQL DML includes three update operations: UPDATE (i.e., change or modify), DELETE, and INSERT. We first summarize the syntax and function of each of those statements, then present a number of examples.

- UPDATE

```
  UPDATE table
  SET       field = expression
        [, field = expression ] ...
[ WHERE   predicate ] ;
```

All records in "table" that satisfy "predicate" are modified in accordance with the assignments ("field = expression") in the SET clause.

- DELETE

```
  DELETE
  FROM    table
[ WHERE predicate ] ;
```

All records in "table" that satisfy "predicate" are deleted.

- INSERT

```
  INSERT
  INTO     table [ ( field [ , field ] ... ) ]
  VALUES ( constant [ , constant ] ... ) ;
```

or

```
  INSERT
  INTO     table [ ( field [ , field ] ... ) ]
  SELECT  ... FROM ... WHERE ... ;
```

In the first format, a row is inserted into "table" having the specified values for the specified fields (the ith constant in the list of constants corresponds to the ith field in the list of fields). In the second format, the SELECT . . . FROM . . . WHERE . . . is evaluated and a copy of the result (multiple rows, in general) is inserted into "table"; the ith column of that result corresponds to the ith field in the list of fields. In both cases, omitting the list of fields is equivalent to specifying a list of all fields in the table, in left-to-right order (as in "SELECT *").

6.6.1 Single-record UPDATE.   Change the color of part P2 to yellow, increase its weight by 5, and set its city to "unknown" (NULL).

```
UPDATE  P
SET     COLOR = Yellow',
        WEIGHT = WEIGHT + 5,
        CITY = NULL
WHERE   P# = 'P2' ;
```

For each record to be updated (i.e., each record that satisfies the WHERE predicate, or all records if the WHERE clause is omitted), references in the SET clause to fields within that record stand for the values of those fields before any of the assignments in that SET clause have been executed.

6.6.2 Multiple-record UPDATE.   Double the status of all suppliers in London.

```
UPDATE  S
SET     STATUS = 2 * STATUS
WHERE   CITY = 'London' ;
```

6.6.3 UPDATE with a subquery.   Set the shipment quantity to zero for all suppliers in London.

```
UPDATE  SP
SET     QTY = 0
WHERE   'London' =
      ( SELECT CITY
        FROM   S
        WHERE  S.S# = SP.S# ) ;
```

6.6.4 Multiple-table UPDATE.   Change the supplier number for supplier S2 to S9.

```
UPDATE  S
SET     S# = 'S9'
WHERE   S# = 'S2' ;

UPDATE  SP
SET     S# = 'S9'
WHERE   S# = 'S2' ;
```

It is not possible to update more than one table in a single statement. To put this another way, the UPDATE clause must specify *exactly one table*. In the example, therefore, we have a problem of *integrity* (more specifically, a problem of *referential* integrity), as follows: The database becomes inconsistent after the first update—it now includes some shipments for which there is no corresponding supplier record—and it remains in that state until after the second update. (Reversing the order of the updates does not solve the problem, of course.) It is therefore important to ensure that *both* updates are executed, not just one. This question (of maintaining integrity when multiple updates are involved) is discussed at some length in Chapter 18; in addition, the problem of referential integrity specifically is discussed in detail in Chapters 12 and 15.

6.6.5 Single-record DELETE.   Delete supplier S1.

```
DELETE
FROM    S
WHERE   S# = 'S1' ;
```

If table SP currently has any shipments for supplier S1, this DELETE will violate the consistency of the database (compare Example 6.6.4; as with UPDATE, there are no multiple-table DELETE operations). See Chapters 12, 15, and 18.

6.6.6 Multiple-record DELETE.   Delete all suppliers in Madrid.

```
DELETE
FROM    S
WHERE   CITY = 'Madrid' ;
```

6.6.7 Multiple-record DELETE.   Delete all shipments.

```
DELETE
FROM    SP ;
```

SP is still a known table ("DELETE all records" is not a DROP), but it is now empty.

6.6.8 DELETE with a subquery.   Delete all shipments for suppliers in London.

```
DELETE
FROM    SP
WHERE   'London' =
      ( SELECT CITY
        FROM    S
        WHERE   S.S# = SP.S# ) ;
```

6.6.9 Single-record INSERT.   Add part P7 (city Athens, weight 24, name and color at present unknown) to table P.

```
INSERT
INTO    P ( P#, CITY, WEIGHT )
VALUES ( 'P7', 'Athens', 24 ) ;
```

A new part record is created with the specified part number, city, and weight, and with null values for name and color. (Of course, these last two fields must not have been defined as NOT NULL in the CREATE TABLE statement for table P.) The left-to-right order in which fields are named in the INSERT statement does not have to be the same as the left-to-right order in which they were specified in the CREATE TABLE statement.

6.6.10 Single-record INSERT, with field names omitted. Add part P8 (name Sprocket, color Pink, weight 14, city Nice) to table P.

```
INSERT
INTO    P
VALUES ('P8', 'Sprocket', 'Pink', 14, 'Nice' ) ;
```

Omitting the list of fields is equivalent to specifying a list of all fields in the table, in the left-to-right order in which they were defined in the CREATE TABLE statement. As with "SELECT *", this shorthand may be convenient for interactive SQL; however, it is potentially dangerous in embedded SQL (i.e., SQL within an application program), because the assumed list of fields may change if the program is rebound and the definition of the table has changed in the interim.

6.6.11 Single-record INSERT. Insert a new shipment with supplier number S20, part number P20, and quantity 1000.

```
INSERT
INTO    SP ( S#, P#, QTY )
VALUES ('S20', 'P20', 1000 ) ;
```

Like UPDATE and DELETE, INSERT can cause referential integrity problems (in the absence of suitable controls—see Chapters 12, 15, and 18). In the case at hand, DB2 does not check that supplier S20 exists in table S or that part P20 exists in table P.

6.6.12 Multiple-record INSERT. For each part supplied, get the part number and the total quantity supplied of that part, and save the result in the database.

```
CREATE TABLE TEMP
       ( P#       CHAR(6),
         TOTQTY INTEGER ) ;

INSERT
INTO    TEMP ( P#, TOTQTY )
        SELECT P#, SUM(QTY)
        FROM    SP
        GROUP  BY P# ;
```

The SELECT is executed, just like an ordinary SELECT, but the result, instead of being returned to the user, is copied into table TEMP. Now the user can do anything he or she pleases with that copy—query it further, print it, even update it; none of those operations will have any effect whatsoever on the original data. Eventually, when it is no longer required, table TEMP can be dropped:

```
DROP TABLE TEMP ;
```

The foregoing example illustrates very nicely why the closure property of relational systems (discussed in the introduction to Section 6.2) is so important. The example works precisely because the result of a SELECT is another table. It would *not* work if the result was something other than a table.

It is not necessary for the target table to be initially empty for a multiple-record INSERT, incidentally, though for the foregoing example it is. If it is not, the new records are simply added to those already present.

6.7 CONCLUDING REMARKS

We have now covered all of the features of the SQL data manipulation statements to be illustrated in this book. To be specific, we have described:

- the basic SELECT clause itself, including the use of DISTINCT, constants and expressions, and "SELECT *"
- the FROM clause, including the use of aliases
- the use of ORDER BY to order the result table
- the WHERE clause, including:
  — comparison operators =, ~ =, >, > =, ~ >, <, < =, ~ <
  — join predicates
  — Boolean operators AND, OR, NOT
- the built-in functions COUNT, SUM, AVG, MAX, and MIN, and the use of the GROUP BY and HAVING clauses
- the special comparisons [NOT] LIKE ... and IS [NOT] NULL
- the use of subqueries and the [NOT] IN comparison operator
- the use of the existential quantifier EXISTS (especially the negated form NOT EXISTS)
- the UNION operator
- the update statements UPDATE, DELETE, and INSERT

It is worth pointing out that the fact that there are only four DML statements in SQL is one of the reasons for the comparative ease of use of that language. And the fact that there *are* only four such operations is a consequence of the simplicity of the relational data structure. As explained in Chapter 4, all data in a relational database is represented in exactly the same way, namely as values in column positions within rows of tables. Since there is only one way to represent anything, we need only one operator for each of the four basic functions (retrieve, change, insert, delete). By contrast, systems based on a more complex data structure fundamentally require $4n$ operations, where n is the number of ways that data can be represented in that system. In CODASYL-based systems, for example, where data can be represented either as records or as links between records (see Part 5 of this book), we typically find a STORE operation to create a record and a CONNECT operation to create a link; an ERASE operation to destroy a record and a DISCONNECT operation to destroy a link; a MODIFY operation to change a record and a RE-CONNECT operation to change a link; and so on.

By way of conclusion, we present a very contrived example that shows how many (by no means all) of the features of SQL discussed in this chapter can be used together in a single query (i.e., a single SELECT statement). We also give a conceptual algorithm for the evaluation of such a statement. Note that SELECT is in a sense the most fundamental of the four DML operations, since the other three must always be preceded—at least implicitly, if not explicitly—by an appropriate SELECT. For example, in the case of DELETE, the system must first execute an implicit SELECT in order to locate the data to be deleted.

Example: For all red and blue parts such that the total quantity supplied is greater than 350 (excluding from the total all shipments for which the quantity is less than or equal to 200), get the part number, the weight in grams, the color, and the maximum quantity supplied of that part; and order the result by descending part number within ascending values of that maximum quantity.

```
SELECT P.P#,  'Weight in grams =', P.WEIGHT * 454, P.COLOR,
              'Max shipped quantity =', MAX (SP.QTY)
       FROM    P, SP
       WHERE   P.P# = SP.P#
       AND   ( P.COLOR = 'Red' OR P.COLOR = 'Blue' )
       AND     SP.QTY > 200
       GROUP   BY P.P#, P.WEIGHT, P.COLOR
       HAVING  SUM (QTY) > 350
       ORDER   BY 6, P.P# DESC ;
```

Result:

```
--  -----------------  ----  -----  ----------------------  ---
P#                                  COLOR
--  -----------------  ----  -----  ----------------------  ---
P1  Weight in grams =  5448  Red    Max shipped quantity =  300
P5  Weight in grams =  5448  Blue   Max shipped quantity =  400
P3  Weight in grams =  7718  Blue   Max shipped quantity =  400
```

Explanation: The clauses of a SELECT statement are applied in the order suggested by that in which they are written—with the exception of the SELECT clause itself, which is applied after the HAVING clause (if any) and before the ORDER BY clause (if any). In the example, therefore, we can imagine the result being constructed as follows.

1. *FROM*. The FROM clause is evaluated to yield a new table that is the Cartesian product of tables P and SP.

2. *WHERE*. The result of Step 1 is reduced by the elimination of all rows that do not satisfy the WHERE clause. In the example, rows not satisfying the predicate

```
...     P.P# = SP.P#
AND ( P.COLOR = 'Red' OR P.COLOR = 'Blue' )
AND     SP.QTY > 200
```

are eliminated.

3. *GROUP BY*. The result of Step 2 is grouped by values of the field(s) named in the GROUP BY clause. In the example, those fields are P.P#, P.WEIGHT, and P.COLOR. (Note: In theory P.P# alone would be sufficient as the grouping field, since P.WEIGHT and P.COLOR are themselves single-valued per part number. However, DB2 is not aware of this latter fact, and will raise an error condition if P.WEIGHT and P.COLOR are omitted from the GROUP BY clause, because they are *included* in the SELECT clause. The basic problem here is that DB2 does not support primary keys. See Chapters 12 and 15, especially (the answer to) Exercise 15.1.)

4. *HAVING*. Groups not satisfying the condition

```
SUM (QTY) > 350
```

   are eliminated from the result of Step 3.

5. *SELECT*. Each group in the result of Step 4 generates a single result row, as follows. First, the part number, weight, color, and maximum quantity are extracted from the group. Second, the weight is converted to grams. Third, the two constants 'Weight in grams =' and 'Max shipped quantity =' are inserted at the appropriate points in the row.

6. *ORDER BY*. The result of Step 5 is ordered in accordance with the specifications of the ORDER BY clause to yield the final result.

Please understand that the algorithm just described is intended as a purely *conceptual* explanation of how the SELECT statement is evaluated. It is certainly correct, in the sense that it will definitely produce the correct result; indeed, it can be taken as a definition of what that result should be (in other words, it serves as a definition of the semantics of the original SELECT statement). However, it would probably be rather inefficient if actually executed. For example, it would be very unfortunate, for reasons of both storage space and execution time, if the system were actually to construct the Cartesian product as suggested in Step 1. Considerations such as these are exactly the reason why relational systems require an optimizer. Indeed, the task of the optimizer can be characterized as that of finding a procedure that will produce the same result as the definitional algorithm described above but is more efficient than that algorithm in terms of either space or time (and preferably both).

Finally, regarding the example query itself: It is of course true that the SELECT statement shown is quite complex—but think how much work it is doing. A conventional program to do the same job in a language such as COBOL could easily be nine pages long, instead of just nine lines as above, and the work involved in getting that program operational would be significantly greater than that needed to construct the SQL version shown. In practice, of course, most queries will be much simpler than this one anyway.

EXERCISES

All of the following exercises are based on the suppliers-parts-projects database (see the exercises in Chapter 5). In each one, you are asked to write a SQL statement (or set of SQL statements) for the indicated operation. For convenience, we repeat the structure of the database below:

```
S    ( S#, SNAME, STATUS, CITY )
P    ( P#, PNAME, COLOR, WEIGHT, CITY )
J    ( J#, JNAME, CITY )
SPJ ( S#, P#, J#, QTY )
```

Within each subsection, the exercises are arranged in approximate order of increasing difficulty. You should try at least some of the easy ones in each group. Numbers 34–40 are quite difficult.

Simple Queries

6.1 Get full details of all projects.

6.2 Get full details of all projects in London.

6.3 Get supplier numbers for suppliers who supply project J1, in supplier number order.

6.4 Get all shipments where the quantity is in the range 300 to 750 inclusive.

6.5 Get a list of all part-color / part-city combinations, with duplicate color / city pairs eliminated.

Joins

6.6 Get all supplier-number / part-number / project-number triples such that the indicated supplier, part, and project are all colocated.

6.7 Get all supplier-number / part-number / project-number triples such that the indicated supplier, part, and project are not all colocated.

6.8 Get all supplier-number / part-number / project-number triples such that no two of the indicated supplier, part, and project are colocated.

6.9 Get part numbers for parts supplied by a supplier in London.

6.10 Get part numbers for parts supplied by a supplier in London to a project in London.

6.11 Get all pairs of city names such that a supplier in the first city supplies a project in the second city.

6.12 Get part numbers for parts supplied to any project by a supplier in the same city as that project.

6.13 Get project numbers for projects supplied by at least one supplier not in the same city.

6.14 Get all pairs of part numbers such that some supplier supplies both the indicated parts.

Built-in Functions

6.15 Get the total number of projects supplied by supplier S1.

6.16 Get the total quantity of part P1 supplied by supplier S1.

6.17 For each part being supplied to a project, get the part number, the project number, and the corresponding total quantity.

6.18 Get part numbers of parts supplied to some project in an average quantity of more than 320.

Miscellaneous

6.19 Get all shipments where the quantity is nonnull.

6.20 Get project numbers and cities where the city has an "o" as the second letter of its name.

Subqueries

6.21 Get project names for projects supplied by supplier S1.

6.22 Get colors of parts supplied by supplier S1.

6.23 Get part numbers for parts supplied to any project in London.

6.24 Get project numbers for projects using at least one part available from supplier S1.

6.25 Get supplier numbers for suppliers supplying at least one part supplied by at least one supplier who supplies at least one red part.

6.26 Get supplier numbers for suppliers with a status lower than that of supplier S1.

6.27 Get project numbers for projects whose city is first in the alphabetic list of such cities.

6.28 Get project numbers for projects supplied with part P1 in an average quantity greater than the greatest quantity in which any part is supplied to project J1.

6.29 Get supplier numbers for suppliers supplying some project with part P1 in a quantity greater than the average shipment quantity of part P1 for that project.

EXISTS

6.30 Repeat Exercise 6.23 to use EXISTS in your solution.

6.31 Repeat Exercise 6.24 to use EXISTS in your solution.

6.32 Get project numbers for projects not supplied with any red part by any London supplier.

6.33 Get project numbers for projects supplied entirely by supplier S1.

6.34 Get part numbers for parts supplied to all projects in London.

6.35 Get supplier numbers for suppliers who supply the same part to all projects.

6.36 Get project numbers for projects supplied with at least all parts available from supplier S1.

For the next four exercises (6.37–6.40), convert the SQL SELECT statement shown back into an English equivalent.

```
6.37 SELECT  DISTINCT J#
     FROM    SPJ SPJX
     WHERE   NOT EXISTS
           ( SELECT  *
             FROM    SPJ SPJY
```

```
                WHERE   SPJY.J# = SPJX.J#
                AND     NOT EXISTS
                    ( SELECT *
                      FROM    SPJ SPJZ
                      WHERE   SPJZ.P# = SPJY.P#
                      AND     SPJZ.S# = 'S1' ) ) ;

6.38 SELECT DISTINCT J#
     FROM   SPJ SPJX
     WHERE  NOT EXISTS
          ( SELECT *
            FROM    SPJ SPJY
            WHERE   EXISTS
                  ( SELECT *
                    FROM    SPJ SPJA
                    WHERE   SPJA.S# = 'S1'
                    AND     SPJA.P# = SPJY.P# )
            AND     NOT EXISTS
                  ( SELECT *
                    FROM    SPJ SPJB
                    WHERE   SPJB.S# = 'S1'
                    AND     SPJB.P# = SPJY.P#
                    AND     SPJB.J# = SPJX.J# ) ) ;

6.39 SELECT DISTINCT J#
     FROM   SPJ SPJX
     WHERE  NOT EXISTS
          ( SELECT *
            FROM    SPJ SPJY
            WHERE   EXISTS
                  ( SELECT *
                    FROM    SPJ SPJA
                    WHERE   SPJA.P# = SPJY.P#
                    AND     SPJA.J# = SPJX.J# )
            AND     NOT EXISTS
                  ( SELECT *
                    FROM    SPJ SPJB
                    WHERE   SPJB.S# = 'S1'
                    AND     SPJB.P# = SPJY.P#
                    AND     SPJB.J# = SPJX.J# ) ) ;

6.40 SELECT DISTINCT J#
     FROM   SPJ SPJX
     WHERE  NOT EXISTS
          ( SELECT *
            FROM    SPJ SPJY
            WHERE   EXISTS
                  ( SELECT *
                    FROM    SPJ SPJA
                    WHERE   SPJA.S# = SPJY.S#
                    AND     SPJA.P# IN
                          ( SELECT P#
                            FROM    P
                            WHERE   COLOR = 'Red' )
```

```
AND        NOT EXISTS
             ( SELECT *
               FROM    SPJ SPJB
               WHERE   SPJB.S# = SPJY.S#
               AND     SPJB.J# = SPJX.J# ) ) ) ;
```

Union

6.41 Construct an ordered list of all cities in which at least one supplier, part, or project is located.

6.42 Show the result of the following SELECT:

```
SELECT P.COLOR
FROM    P
UNION
SELECT P.COLOR
FROM    P ;
```

Update operations

6.43 Change the color of all red parts to orange.

6.44 Delete all projects for which there are no shipments.

6.45 Delete all projects in Rome and all corresponding shipments.

6.46 Insert a new supplier (S10) into table S. The name and city are 'White' and 'New York', respectively; the status is not yet known.

6.47 Construct a table containing a list of part numbers for parts that are supplied either by a London supplier or to a London project.

6.48 Construct a table containing a list of project numbers for projects that are either located in London or are supplied by a London supplier.

ANSWERS TO SELECTED EXERCISES

The following solutions are not necessarily the only ones possible.

```
6.1 SELECT J#, JNAME, CITY                    /* or "SELECT *" */
    FROM   J ;

6.2 SELECT J#, JNAME, CITY                    /* or "SELECT *" */
    FROM   J
    WHERE  CITY = 'London' ;

6.3 SELECT DISTINCT S#
    FROM    SPJ
    WHERE   J# = 'J1'
    ORDER   BY S# ;

6.4 SELECT S#, P#, J#, QTY
    FROM    SPJ
    WHERE   QTY >= 300
    AND     QTY <= 750 ;
```

6.5 SELECT DISTINCT COLOR, CITY
    FROM   P ;

6.6 SELECT S#, P#, J#
    FROM   S, P, J
    WHERE S.CITY = P.CITY
    AND   P.CITY = J.CITY ;

6.7 SELECT S#, P#, J#
    FROM   S, P, J
    WHERE NOT
        (S.CITY = P.CITY AND P.CITY = J.CITY) ;

Or: SELECT S#, P#, J#
    FROM   S, P, J
    WHERE S.CITY ~= P.CITY
    OR   P.CITY ~= J.CITY ;

6.8 SELECT S#, P#, J#
    FROM   S, P, J
    WHERE S.CITY ~= P.CITY
    AND   P.CITY ~= J.CITY
    AND   J.CITY ~= S.CITY ;

6.9 SELECT DISTINCT P#
    FROM   SPJ, S
    WHERE SPJ.S# = S.S#
    AND   CITY = 'London' ;

6.10 SELECT DISTINCT P#
    FROM   SPJ, S, J
    WHERE SPJ.S# = S.S#
    AND   SPJ.J# = J.J#
    AND   S.CITY = 'London'
    AND   J.CITY = 'London' ;

6.11 SELECT DISTINCT S.CITY, J.CITY
    FROM   S, SPJ, J
    WHERE S.S# = SPJ.S#
    AND   SPJ.J# = J.J# ;

6.12 SELECT DISTINCT P#
    FROM   SPJ, S, J
    WHERE SPJ.S# = S.S#
    AND   SPJ.J# = J.J#
    AND   S.CITY = J.CITY ;

6.13 SELECT DISTINCT J.J#
    FROM   SPJ, S, J
    WHERE SPJ.S# = S.S#
    AND   SPJ.J# = J.J#
    AND   S.CITY ~= J.CITY ;

6.14 SELECT SPJX.P#, SPJY.P#
    FROM   SPJ SPJX, SPJ SPJY
    WHERE SPJX.S# = SPJY.S#
    AND   SPJX.P# > SPJY.P# ;

```
6.15 SELECT COUNT (DISTINCT J#)
     FROM    SPJ
     WHERE   S# = 'S1' ;

6.16 SELECT SUM (QTY)
     FROM    SPJ
     WHERE   P# = 'P1'
     AND     S# = 'S1' ;

6.17 SELECT P#, J#, SUM (QTY)
     FROM    SPJ
     GROUP   BY P#, J# ;

6.18 SELECT DISTINCT P#
     FROM    SPJ
     GROUP   BY P#, J#
     HAVING AVG (QTY) > 320 ;

6.19 SELECT S#, P#, J#, QTY
     FROM    SPJ
     WHERE   QTY IS NOT NULL ;
```

The foregoing is the "official" answer. However, the following will also work:

```
     SELECT S#, P#, J#, QTY
     FROM    SPJ
     WHERE   QTY = QTY ;

6.20 SELECT J#, CITY
     FROM    J
     WHERE   CITY LIKE '_o%' ;

6.21 SELECT JNAME
     FROM    J
     WHERE   J# IN
           ( SELECT J#
             FROM    SPJ
             WHERE   S# = 'S1' ) ;

6.22 SELECT DISTINCT COLOR
     FROM    P
     WHERE   P# IN
           ( SELECT P#
             FROM    SPJ
             WHERE   S# = 'S1' ) ;

6.23 SELECT DISTINCT P#
     FROM    SPJ
     WHERE   J# IN
           ( SELECT J#
             FROM    J
             WHERE   CITY = 'London' ) ;
```

```
6.24 SELECT  DISTINCT J#
     FROM    SPJ
     WHERE   P# IN
           ( SELECT  P#
             FROM    SPJ
             WHERE   S# = 'S1' ) ;

6.25 SELECT  DISTINCT S#
     FROM    SPJ
     WHERE   P# IN
           ( SELECT  P#
             FROM    SPJ
             WHERE   S# IN
                   ( SELECT  S#
                     FROM    SPJ
                     WHERE   P# IN
                           ( SELECT  P#
                             FROM    P
                             WHERE   COLOR = 'Red' ) ) ) ;

6.26 SELECT  S#
     FROM    S
     WHERE   STATUS <
           ( SELECT  STATUS
             FROM    S
             WHERE   S# = 'S1' ) ;

6.27 SELECT  J#
     FROM    J
     WHERE   CITY =
           ( SELECT  MIN (CITY)
             FROM    J ) ;

6.28 SELECT  J#
     FROM    SPJ
     WHERE   P# = 'P1'
     GROUP   BY J#
     HAVING  AVG (QTY) >
           ( SELECT  MAX (QTY)
             FROM    SPJ
             WHERE   J# = 'J1' ) ;

6.29 SELECT  DISTINCT S#
     FROM    SPJ SPJX
     WHERE   P# = 'P1'
     AND     QTY >
           ( SELECT  AVG (QTY)
             FROM    SPJ SPJY
             WHERE   P# = 'P1'
             AND     SPJY.J# = SPJX.J# ) ;
```

```
6.30  SELECT  DISTINCT P#
      FROM    SPJ
      WHERE   EXISTS
            ( SELECT  *
              FROM    J
              WHERE   J# = SPJ.J#
              AND     CITY = 'London' ) ;

6.31  SELECT  DISTINCT SPJX.J#
      FROM    SPJ SPJX
      WHERE   EXISTS
            ( SELECT  *
              FROM    SPJ SPJY
              WHERE   SPJY.P# = SPJX.P#
              AND     SPJY.S# = 'S1' ) ;

6.32  SELECT  J#
      FROM    J
      WHERE   NOT EXISTS
            ( SELECT  *
              FROM    SPJ
              WHERE   J# = J.J#
              AND     P# IN
                    ( SELECT  P#
                      FROM    P
                      WHERE   COLOR = 'Red' )
              AND     S# IN
                    ( SELECT  S#
                      FROM    S
                      WHERE   CITY = 'London' ) ) ;

6.33  SELECT  DISTINCT J#
      FROM    SPJ SPJX
      WHERE   NOT EXISTS
            ( SELECT  *
              FROM    SPJ SPJY
              WHERE   SPJY.J# = SPJX.J#
              AND     SPJY.S# ¬= 'S1' ) ;

6.34  SELECT  DISTINCT P#
      FROM    SPJ SPJX
      WHERE   NOT EXISTS
            ( SELECT  *
              FROM    J
              WHERE   CITY = 'London'
              AND     NOT EXISTS
                    ( SELECT  *
                      FROM    SPJ SPJY
                      WHERE   SPJY.P# = SPJX.P#
                      AND     SPJY.J# = J.J# ) ) ;
```

```
6.35 SELECT  DISTINCT S#
     FROM    SPJ SPJX
     WHERE   EXISTS
           ( SELECT  P#
             FROM    SPJ SPJY
             WHERE   NOT EXISTS
                   ( SELECT  J#
                     FROM    J
                     WHERE   NOT EXISTS
                           ( SELECT  *
                             FROM    SPJ SPJZ
                             WHERE   SPJZ.S# = SPJX.S#
                             AND     SPJZ.P# = SPJY.P#
                             AND     SPJZ.J# = J.J# ) ) ) ;
```

This rather complex SELECT statement may be paraphrased: "Get all suppliers
(SPJX.S#) such that there exists a part (SPJY.P#) such that there does not exist any project
(J.J#) such that the supplier does not supply the part to the project"—in other words, sup-
pliers such that there exists some part that they supply to all projects. Note the use of "SE-
LECT P# FROM . . ." and "SELECT J# FROM . . ." in two of the EXISTS references;
"SELECT *" would not be incorrect, but "SELECT P#" (for instance) seems a fraction
closer to the intuitive formulation—there must exist a *part* (identified by a part number), not
just a row in the shipments table.

```
6.36 SELECT  DISTINCT J#
     FROM    SPJ SPJX
     WHERE   NOT EXISTS
           ( SELECT  P#
             FROM    SPJ SPJY
             WHERE   SPJY.S# = 'S1'
             AND     NOT EXISTS
                   ( SELECT  *
                     FROM    SPJ SPJZ
                     WHERE   SPJZ.P# = SPJY.P#
                     AND     SPJZ.J# = SPJX.J# ) ) ;
```

6.37 Get project numbers for projects that use only parts that are available from supplier
S1.

6.38 Get project numbers for projects that are supplied by supplier S1 with some of every
part that supplier S1 supplies.

6.39 Get project numbers for projects such that at least some of every part they use is supplied to them by supplier S1.

6.40 Get project numbers for projects that are supplied by every supplier who supplies some
red part.

```
6.41 SELECT CITY FROM S
     UNION
     SELECT CITY FROM P
     UNION
     SELECT CITY FROM J
     ORDER  BY 1 ;
```

An ORDER BY clause in a SELECT statement involving UNION *must* identify the ordering column(s) by ordinal position, not by name, since the result columns in a SQL UNION are considered to be anonymous.

6.42 - - - - -

```
- - - - -
Red
Green
Blue
```

6.43
```
UPDATE P
SET     COLOR = 'Orange'
WHERE   COLOR = 'Red' ;
```

6.44
```
DELETE
FROM    J
WHERE   J# NOT IN
        ( SELECT   J#
          FROM     SPJ ) ;
```

6.45
```
DELETE
FROM    SPJ
WHERE   'Rome' =
        ( SELECT CITY
          FROM   J
          WHERE  J.J# = SPJ.J# ) ;
DELETE
FROM    J
WHERE   CITY = 'Rome' ;
```

6.46
```
INSERT
INTO    S ( S#, SNAME, CITY )
VALUES ('S10', 'White', 'New York' ) ;
```

Or:
```
INSERT
INTO    S ( S#, SNAME, STATUS, CITY )
VALUES ('S10', 'White', NULL, 'New York' ) ;
```

6.47
```
CREATE TABLE LP
     ( P# CHAR(6) ) ;

INSERT INTO LP ( P# )
        SELECT DISTINCT P#
        FROM   SPJ
        WHERE  S# IN
               ( SELECT S#
                 FROM   S
                 WHERE  CITY = 'London' )
        OR     J# IN
               ( SELECT J#
                 FROM   J
                 WHERE  CITY = 'London' ) ;
```

```
6.48 CREATE TABLE LJ
        ( J# CHAR(4) ) ;

   INSERT  INTO LJ ( J# )
           SELECT  J#
           FROM    J
           WHERE   CITY = 'London'
           OR      J# IN
                 ( SELECT  J#
                   FROM    SPJ
                   WHERE   S# IN
                         ( SELECT  S#
                           FROM    S
                           WHERE   CITY = 'London' ) ) ;
```

7
The System Catalog

7.1 INTRODUCTION

Recall from Chapter 2 that the system catalog can be thought of as a system database that contains information (sometimes called "descriptors") concerning various objects that are of interest to the system itself. Examples of such objects are base tables, views, indexes, users, application plans, access privileges, and so on. Descriptor information is essential if the system is to be able to do its job properly. For example, the optimizer uses catalog information about indexes (as well as other information) to choose a specific access strategy, as explained in Chapter 4. Likewise, the authorization subsystem (see Chapter 19) uses catalog information about users and access privileges to grant or deny specific user requests.

One of the nice features of a relational system like DB2 is that, in such a system, the catalog itself consists of relations or tables, just like the ordinary user data tables. In DB2 specifically, the catalog consists of some 20 or 25 such tables. Note that the catalog is not the same across different systems, because the catalog for a particular system necessarily contains a great deal of information that is specific to that system. For example, the DB2 and SQL/DS catalogs are different at the detail level, even though in many respects those systems do look very similar to one another (they are both SQL systems, of course).

It is not our purpose here to give an exhaustive description of the catalog as it actually appears in DB2, nor in any other specific system. Rather, we wish merely to give a basic introduction to the structure and content of a typical catalog, and to give some idea as to how the information in such a catalog can be helpful to the user as well as to the system. We use a simplified form of the DB2 catalog for these purposes. That simplified form contains the following catalog tables, among others:

- SYSTABLES

This catalog table contains a row for every table (base table or view) in the entire system. For each such table, it gives the table name (NAME), the name of the user that created the table (CREATOR), the number of columns in the table (COL-COUNT), and many other items of information.

■   SYSCOLUMNS

This catalog table contains a row for every column of every table in the entire system. For each such column, it gives the column name (NAME), the name of the table of which that column is a part (TBNAME), the data type of the column (COL-TYPE), and many other things besides.

■   SYSINDEXES

This catalog table contains a row for every index in the system. For each such index, it gives the index name (NAME), the name of the indexed table (TBNAME), the name of the user that created the index (CREATOR), and so on.

For example, the catalog structure for the suppliers-and-parts database might be as indicated in Fig. 7.1 (in outline; of course, almost all the details have been omitted). We assume for the sake of the example that the creator for all tables and indexes in that database is a user with user ID "Janice."

SYSTABLES	NAME	CREATOR	COLCOUNT	...
	S	Janice	4	...
	P	Janice	5	...
	SP	Janice	3	...

SYSCOLUMNS	NAME	TBNAME	COLTYPE	...
	S#	S	CHAR	...
	SNAME	S	CHAR	...
	STATUS	S	SMALLINT	...
	CITY	S	CHAR	...
	P#	P	CHAR	...
	PNAME	P	CHAR	...
	COLOR	P	CHAR	...
	WEIGHT	P	SMALLINT	...
	CITY	P	CHAR	...
	S#	SP	CHAR	...
	P#	SP	CHAR	...
	QTY	SP	INTEGER	...

SYSINDEXES	NAME	TBNAME	CREATOR	...
	XS	S	Janice	...
	XP	P	Janice	...
	XSP	SP	Janice	...
	XSC	S	Janice	...

Fig. 7.1 Catalog structure for the suppliers-and-parts database (outline).

7.2   QUERYING THE CATALOG

Since the catalog consists of tables just like ordinary user tables, it can be queried
by means of SQL SELECT statements just as ordinary tables can. For example, to
find out what tables contain an S# column:

```
SELECT TBNAME
FROM    SYSCOLUMNS
WHERE   NAME = 'S#' ;
```

Result:

```
------
TBNAME
------
S
SP
```

Another example: What columns does table S have?

```
SELECT NAME
FROM    SYSCOLUMNS
WHERE   TBNAME = 'S' ;
```

Result:

```
------
NAME
------
S#
SNAME
STATUS
CITY
```

And one more example: How many tables has user Janice created?

```
SELECT COUNT(*)
FROM    SYSTABLES
WHERE   CREATOR = 'Janice' ;
```

A user who is not familiar with the structure of the database can use queries
such as these to discover that structure. For example, a user who wishes to query
the suppliers-and-parts database (say), but does not have any detailed knowledge
as to exactly what tables exist in that database and exactly what columns they contain, can use catalog queries to obtain that knowledge first before going on to formulate the data queries per se.

Note that, in a traditional (nonrelational) system, those initial queries would
typically have to be directed to the system dictionary instead of to the database.
Indeed, the DB2 catalog can be regarded as a rudimentary dictionary (rudimentary,
in that it contains only information that is directly needed by DB2, whereas a full-
scale dictionary would typically contain much additional information, such as which
departments receive which reports). The important difference between the relational

approach and the traditional approach—and a significant ease-of-use benefit for relational systems such as DB2—is that in those systems the catalog and the database are queried through *the same interface*, namely the system's own query language (SQL, in the case of DB2). In traditional systems, by contrast, the dictionary and the database have always been distinct and have been accessed through different interfaces.

7.3   UPDATING THE CATALOG

We have seen how the catalog can be queried by means of the SQL SELECT statement. However, the catalog *cannot* be updated using the SQL UPDATE, DELETE, and INSERT statements (and the system will reject any attempt to do so). The reason is, of course, that allowing such operations would potentially be very dangerous: It would be far too easy to destroy information (inadvertently or otherwise) in the catalog so that the system would no longer be able to function correctly. Suppose, for example, that the statement

```
DELETE
FROM     SYSCOLUMNS
WHERE    TBNAME = 'S'
AND      NAME = 'S#' ;
```

were allowed. Its effect would be to remove the row

```
( 'S#', 'S', CHAR, ... )
```

from the SYSCOLUMNS table. *As far as the system is concerned, the S# column in the S table would now no longer exist*—i.e., the system would no longer have any knowledge of that column. Thus, attempts to access data on the basis of values of that column—e.g.,

```
SELECT CITY
FROM     S
WHERE    S# = 'S4' ;
```

—would fail (the system would produce some error message, such as "undefined column"). Perhaps worse, attempts to update supplier records could go disastrously wrong—for example, inserting a new record might cause the supplier number to be taken as the supplier name, the supplier name as the status, and so on.

For reasons such as these, UPDATE, DELETE, and INSERT operations are (as already stated) not permitted against tables in the catalog. Instead, it is the *data definition* statements (CREATE TABLE, CREATE INDEX, etc.) that perform such updates. For example, the CREATE TABLE statement for table S causes a) an entry to be made for S in the SYSTABLES table and b) a set of four entries, one for each of the four columns of S, to be made in the SYSCOLUMNS table. (It also causes a number of other things to happen too, which are however of no concern to us here.) Thus CREATE is in some ways the analog of INSERT for the catalog. Likewise, DROP is the analog of DELETE, and ALTER is the analog of UPDATE.

Note: The catalog will also include entries for the catalog tables themselves. However, those entries are not created by explicit CREATE TABLE operations. Instead, they are created automatically by the system itself as part of the system installation procedure (they are "hard-wired" into the system). In DB2 specifically, the user ID "SYSIBM" is used to designate the system itself; thus the "creator" for the catalog tables themselves is considered to be SYSIBM.

The COMMENT Statement

Although (as we have just seen) the regular SQL update statements cannot be used to update the catalog, there is one special statement, namely COMMENT, that does perform a kind of catalog updating function. The catalog tables SYSTABLES and SYSCOLUMNS each include a column—not shown in Fig. 7.1—called REMARKS, which can be used (in any particular row) to contain a text string that describes the object identified by the rest of that row. The COMMENT statement is used to enter such descriptions into the REMARKS column in those two tables. The following examples illustrate the two basic formats of the COMMENT statement.

```
COMMENT ON TABLE S IS
        'Each row represents one supplier' ;
```

The specified text string is stored in the REMARKS field in the row for the specified table (here table S) in the SYSTABLES table, replacing any value previously stored at that position. The specified table can be either a base table or a view.

```
COMMENT ON COLUMN P.CITY IS
        'Location of (unique) warehouse storing this part' ;
```

The specified text string is stored in the REMARKS field in the row for the specified column (here column P.CITY) in the SYSCOLUMNS table, replacing any value previously stored at that position. The specified column can be a column of either a base table or a view.

EXERCISES

7.1 Sketch the details of the catalog for the suppliers-parts-projects database. Include catalog entries for the catalog tables themselves, so far as you are able.

Now write SELECT statements for the following queries (numbers 7.2–7.8).

7.2 Which tables include a CITY column?

7.3 How many columns are there in the shipments table?

7.4 List the names of all catalog tables.

7.5 List the names of all users that have created a table with a CITY column, together with the names of the tables concerned.

7.6 List the names of all users that have created at least one table, together with the number of tables created in each case.

7.7 List the names of all tables that have at least one index.

7.8 List the names of all tables that have more than one index.

7.9 Write statements to do the following:

a) Create an appropriate comment on the SPJ table.

b) Change that comment to 'Ignore previous comment'.

c) Create an appropriate comment on the P# column of the SPJ table.

d) Create an appropriate comment on the XS index.

ANSWERS TO SELECTED EXERCISES

As usual the following solutions are not necessarily unique.

7.1 We show outline catalog entries for the catalog tables themselves only.

```
            ----------   --------   ---------   - - - -
SYSTABLES   NAME         CREATOR    COLCOUNT      ...
            ----------   --------   ---------   - - - -
            SYSTABLES    SYSIBM     ( >3 )        ...
            SYSCOLUMNS   SYSIBM     ( >3 )        ...
            SYSINDEXES   SYSIBM     ( >3 )        ...
            --------     ----------   --------   - - - -
SYSCOLUMNS  NAME         TBNAME       COLTYPE      ...
            --------     ----------   --------   - - - -
            NAME         SYSTABLES    CHAR         ...
            CREATOR      SYSTABLES    CHAR         ...
            COLCOUNT     SYSTABLES    SMALLINT     ...
            NAME         SYSCOLUMNS   CHAR         ...
            TBNAME       SYSCOLUMNS   CHAR         ...
            COLTYPE      SYSCOLUMNS   (?)          ...
            NAME         SYSINDEXES   CHAR         ...
            TBNAME       SYSINDEXES   CHAR         ...
            CREATOR      SYSINDEXES   CHAR         ...
```

```
7.2 SELECT TBNAME
    FROM   SYSCOLUMNS
    WHERE  NAME = 'CITY' ;

7.3 SELECT COLCOUNT
    FROM   SYSTABLES
    WHERE  NAME = 'SPJ' ;

7.4 SELECT NAME
    FROM   SYSTABLES
    WHERE  CREATOR = 'SYSIBM' ;

7.5 SELECT DISTINCT SYSTABLES.CREATOR, SYSTABLES.NAME
    FROM   SYSTABLES, SYSCOLUMNS
    WHERE  SYSTABLES.NAME = SYSCOLUMNS.TBNAME
    AND    SYSCOLUMNS.NAME = 'CITY' ;

7.6 SELECT CREATOR, COUNT (*)
    FROM   SYSTABLES
    GROUP  BY CREATOR ;
```

```
7.7 SELECT  TBNAME
    FROM    SYSINDEXES ;
7.8 SELECT  TBNAME
    FROM    SYSINDEXES
    GROUP   BY TBNAME
    HAVING  COUNT (NAME) > 1 ;
```
7.9

a) `COMMENT ON TABLE SPJ IS 'Appropriate comment' ;`

b) `COMMENT ON TABLE SPJ IS 'Ignore previous comment' ;`

c) `COMMENT ON COLUMN SPJ.P# IS 'Appropriate comment' ;`

d) Trick question! It is not possible to COMMENT ON an index.

8
Views

8.1 INTRODUCTION

At the external level of the ANSI/SPARC architecture, the database is perceived as an "external view," defined by an external schema. Different users can have different external views. As explained in Chapter 4, however, the term "view" is reserved in SQL to mean, specifically, a *named, derived table*; the SQL equivalent of an ANSI/SPARC external view is, in general, a collection of several tables, some of them views in the SQL sense and some of them base tables (and all of them named, by definition). The "external schema" consists of definitions of those views and base tables. In this chapter we examine views (in the SQL sense) in some detail.

The ANSI/SPARC framework is quite general and allows for arbitrary variability between the external and conceptual levels. In principle, even the *types* of data structure supported at the two levels could be different; for example, the conceptual level could be based on relations, while a given user could have an external view of the database as a hierarchy. In practice, however, most systems use the same type of structure as the basis for both levels, and SQL systems are no exception to this general rule—a view is still a table, like a base table. And since the same type of object is supported at both levels, the same manipulative language—i.e., the SQL DML—applies to both levels also.[1]

Recall from Chapter 4 that a view may be regarded as a *virtual table*—that is, a table that does not exist in its own right but looks to the user as if it did. (By contrast, a base table is a *real* table, in the sense that, for each row of such a table, there really is some stored counterpart of that row in physical storage. See Chapter

---

1. Indeed, the fact that a view is a table is one of the strengths of relational systems; it is important in just the same way that the fact that a subset is a set is important in mathematics.

4.) Views are not supported by their own, physically separate, distinguishable stored data. Instead, their *definition* in terms of other tables is stored in the catalog (in a table called SYSVIEWS, in the case of the DB2 catalog specifically). Here is an example:

```
CREATE VIEW GOOD_SUPPLIERS
     AS SELECT S#, STATUS, CITY
        FROM   S
        WHERE  STATUS > 15 ;
```

When this CREATE VIEW is executed, the SELECT–FROM–WHERE following the AS (which defines how the view is derived) is *not* executed; instead, it is simply saved in the catalog. But to the user it is now as if there really were a table in the database called GOOD_SUPPLIERS, with rows and columns as shown in the unshaded portions (only) of Fig. 8.1 below.

GOOD_SUPPLIERS is in effect a "window" into the real table S. Furthermore, that window is *dynamic*: Changes to S will be automatically and instantaneously visible through that window (provided, of course, that those changes lie within the unshaded portion of S); likewise, changes to GOOD_SUPPLIERS will automatically and instantaneously be applied to the real table S (see Section 8.3, later).

Now, depending on the sophistication of the user (and perhaps also on the application at hand), the user may or may not realize that GOOD_SUPPLIERS really is a view; some users may be aware of that fact and may understand that there is a real table S underneath, others may genuinely believe that GOOD_SUPPLIERS is a "real" table in its own right. Either way, it makes little difference: The point is, users may operate on GOOD_SUPPLIERS just as if it were a real table (with certain exceptions, to be discussed later). For instance, here is an example of a retrieval operation (i.e., SELECT statement) against GOOD_SUPPLIERS:

GOOD_SUPPLIERS	S#	SNAME	STATUS	CITY
	S1	Smith	20	London
	S2	Jones	10	Paris
	S3	Blake	30	Paris
	S4	Clark	20	London
	S5	Adams	30	Athens

Fig. 8.1 GOOD_SUPPLIERS as a view of base table S (unshaded portions).

```
SELECT *
FROM    GOOD_SUPPLIERS
WHERE   CITY ~= 'London' ;
```

Result:

```
--   ------   ------
S#   STATUS   CITY
--   ------   ------
S3       30   Paris
S5       30   Athens
```

This SELECT certainly looks and behaves just like a normal SELECT on a conventional base table. The system (actually Bind) handles such an operation by converting it into an equivalent operation on the underlying base table (or tables, plural—see Section 8.2). In the example, the equivalent operation is

```
SELECT  S#, STATUS, CITY
FROM    S
WHERE   CITY ~= 'London'
AND     STATUS > 15 ;
```

This new statement can now be compiled (i.e., bound) and executed in the usual way. The conversion is done, in effect, by *merging* the SELECT issued by the user with the SELECT that was saved in the catalog when the view was defined. From the catalog, the system knows that FROM GOOD_SUPPLIERS really means FROM S; it also knows that any selection from GOOD_SUPPLIERS must be further qualified by the WHERE condition STATUS > 15; and it also knows that "SELECT *" (from GOOD_SUPPLIERS) really means SELECT S#, STATUS, CITY (from S). Hence it is able to translate the original SELECT on the virtual table GOOD _SUPPLIERS into an equivalent SELECT on the real table S—equivalent, in the sense that the effect of executing that SELECT on the real table S is as if there really were a base table called GOOD_SUPPLIERS and the original SELECT were executed on that.

Update operations are treated in a similar manner. For example, the operation

```
UPDATE GOOD_SUPPLIERS
SET    STATUS = STATUS + 10
WHERE  CITY = 'Paris' ;
```

will be converted by Bind into

```
UPDATE S
SET    STATUS = STATUS + 10
WHERE  CITY = 'Paris'
AND    STATUS > 15 ;
```

Similarly for INSERT and DELETE operations.

8.2   VIEW DEFINITION

The general syntax of the SQL CREATE VIEW operation is

```
CREATE VIEW view-name
    [ ( column-name [, column-name ] ... ) ]
      AS subquery ;
```

Notice how, to use the ANSI/SPARC terminology, CREATE VIEW combines the "external schema" function (the view- and column-names describe the external object) and the "external/conceptual mapping" function (the subquery specifies the mapping of that object to the conceptual level).

In principle, any derivable table—i.e, any table that can be retrieved via a SELECT statement—can theoretically be defined as a view. In practice, this statement is not one hundred percent true so far as DB2 is concerned. Specifically, DB2 does not allow a view definition to include the UNION operator; however, there is no intrinsic reason for that restriction, it is merely a quirk of DB2 per se, which we can ignore for present purposes.

Note: The subquery in a view definition cannot include an ORDER BY specification. This apparent restriction is in fact not really a restriction at all, however. It is certainly not just an implementation quirk like the UNION restriction in DB2. The point is, ORDER BY in a view definition would make no sense, since the object being defined—i.e., the view—is a table, and tables by definition have no ordering (see Chapter 5). Of course, it is always possible to impose an ordering *dynamically* when data is retrieved from the view, by specifying ORDER BY in the SELECT that performs the retrieval in question.

Here are some examples of CREATE VIEW.

```
1. CREATE VIEW REDPARTS ( P#, PNAME, WT, CITY )
        AS SELECT P#, PNAME, WEIGHT, CITY
           FROM    P
           WHERE   COLOR = 'Red' ;
```

The effect of this statement is to create a view called REDPARTS, with four columns called P#, PNAME, WT, and CITY, corresponding respectively to the four columns P#, PNAME, WEIGHT, and CITY of the underlying base table P. If column names are not specified explicitly in the CREATE VIEW, then the view inherits column names from the source of the view in the obvious way (in the example, the inherited names would be P#, PNAME, WEIGHT, and CITY). Column names *must* be specified explicitly (for all columns of the view) if a) any column of the view is derived from a built-in function, an arithmetic expression, or a constant (and so has no name that can be inherited), or b) if two or more columns of the view would otherwise have the same name. See the next two examples for illustrations of each of these two cases.

```
2. CREATE VIEW PQ ( P#, TOTQTY )
       AS SELECT P#, SUM (QTY)
          FROM    SP
          GROUP   BY P# ;
```

In this example, there is no name that can be inherited for the second column, since that column is derived from a built-in function; hence column names must be specified explicitly, as shown. Notice that this view is not just a simple row-and-column subset of the underlying base table (unlike the views REDPARTS and GOOD_SUPPLIERS shown earlier). It might be regarded instead as a kind of statistical summary or compression of that underlying table.

```
3. CREATE VIEW CITY_PAIRS ( SCITY, PCITY )
       AS SELECT DISTINCT S.CITY, P.CITY
          FROM    S, SP, P
          WHERE   S.S# = SP.S#
          AND     SP.P# = P.P# ;
```

The meaning of this particular view is that a pair of city names (x,y) will appear in the view if a supplier located in city x supplies a part stored in city y. For example, supplier S1 supplies part P1; supplier S1 is located in London and part P1 is stored in London; and so the pair (London, London) appears in the view. Notice that the definition of this view involves a join, so that this is an example of a view that is derived from multiple underlying tables. Compare Example 6.3.5 in Chapter 6.

```
4. CREATE VIEW LONDON_REDPARTS
       AS SELECT P#, WT
          FROM    REDPARTS
          WHERE   CITY = 'London' ;
```

Since the definition of a view can be any valid subquery, and since a subquery can select data from views as well as from base tables, it is perfectly possible to define a view in terms of other views, as in this example.

The syntax of DROP VIEW is

```
DROP VIEW view-name ;
```

The specified view is dropped (i.e., its definition is removed from the catalog). Any views defined in terms of that view are automatically dropped too. Here is an example:

```
DROP VIEW REDPARTS ;
```

If a base table is dropped, all views defined on that base table (or on views of that base table, etc.) are automatically dropped too.

We conclude this section by noting that, in SQL, fields in a view inherit their data type from the underlying base table. Field STATUS of GOOD_SUPPLIERS, for instance, has data type SMALLINT, inherited from field STATUS of table S.

A more general view mechanism would permit fields in a view to have data types that differ from those in the base table.

8.3   DML OPERATIONS ON VIEWS

We have already explained in outline (Section 8.1) how operations on a view are converted into equivalent operations on the underlying base table(s). For *retrieval* operations (SELECT), that conversion process is quite straightforward, and works perfectly well in 100 percent of cases.[2] But the situation is different for update operations, as we now explain.

Note: The explanations that follow are extremely informal since, at this early point in the book, we lack the formal apparatus necessary for a more rigorous treatment of the problem. We shall have a little more to say on the question of updating views in Part 3 (Chapter 15), after we have discussed the relational model.

The basic point is the following: *Not all views are updatable.* (As usual, we are using "updatable" here to include INSERT and DELETE operations as well as UPDATE operations.) By way of illustration, consider the following two views, S#_CITY and STATUS_CITY, both of which are views of the same base table S:

```
CREATE VIEW S#_CITY                 CREATE VIEW STATUS_CITY
     AS SELECT S#, CITY                  AS SELECT STATUS, CITY
        FROM   S ;                          FROM   S ;
```

Of these two views, S#_CITY is theoretically updatable, while STATUS_CITY is not.[3] It is instructive to examine why this is so. In the case of S#_CITY:

a) We can insert a new record into the view, say the record ('S6','Rome'), by actually inserting the corresponding record ('S6',NULL,NULL,'Rome') into the underlying base table.

b) We can delete an existing record from the view, say the record ('S1','London'), by actually deleting the corresponding record ('S1','Smith',20,'London') from the underlying base table.

c) We can update an existing field in the view, say to change the city for supplier S1 from London to Rome, by actually making that same change to the corresponding field in the underlying base table.

In the case of STATUS_CITY, by contrast:

a) If we try to insert a new record into the view, say the record (40,'Rome'), the

---

2. At least in theory. In practice, unfortunately, certain retrievals do *not* work correctly in SQL systems such as DB2. However, this state of affairs is purely the result of certain quirks of the SQL language per se. Since such quirks are not particularly relevant to the present book, we will simply ignore them. See references [4.4,4.10] for further information.

3. Emphasis on "theoretically." Once again, we are getting into an area where most systems currently behave in a sadly ad hoc manner.

system will have to try to insert the corresponding record (NULL,NULL,40, 'Rome') into the underlying base table—and that operation will fail, because supplier numbers are defined to be NOT NULL. (And there is a good reason for that NOT NULL restriction, too. See Chapter 12.)

b) If we try to delete some existing record from the view, say the record (20,'London'), the system will have to try to delete some corresponding record from the underlying base table—but which one? The system has no way of knowing, because the supplier number has not been specified (and it cannot be, because the S# field is not part of the view).

c) If we try to update some existing record in the view, say to change the record (20,'London') to (20,'Rome'), the system will have to try to update some corresponding record in the underlying base table—but, again, which one?

Inspection of the two views S#_CITY and STATUS_CITY shows that the critical difference between them is that S#_CITY includes the primary key (namely S#) of the underlying table, while STATUS_CITY does not. In the case of S#_CITY, it is precisely the presence of the S# field that makes it possible to identify the "corresponding record" to be updated in the underlying table. Conversely, in the case of STATUS_CITY, it is precisely the absence of that field that makes it impossible to identify any such "corresponding record."

The two views S#_CITY and STATUS_CITY can both be characterized as "column subset" views—each of them consists of a subset of the columns of some one underlying table. As the examples demonstrate, a "column subset" view is theoretically updatable if and only if it preserves the primary key of the underlying table (assuming of course that the underlying table is updatable in the first place; it might in turn be a nonupdatable view itself). We briefly consider examples of three further cases: a "row subset" view, a join view, and a "statistical summary" view.

```
1. CREATE VIEW LONDON_SUPPLIERS
        AS SELECT S#, SNAME, STATUS, CITY
           FROM   S
           WHERE  CITY = 'London' ;
```

This view (a "row subset") does include the primary key of the underlying table (table S), and it is updatable. Consideration of the details is left as an exercise for the reader. See also the discussion of the CHECK option at the end of this section.

```
2. CREATE VIEW COLOCATED ( S#, SNAME, STATUS, SCITY,
                           P#, PNAME, COLOR, WEIGHT, PCITY )
        AS SELECT S#, SNAME, STATUS, S.CITY,
                  P#, PNAME, COLOR, WEIGHT, P.CITY
           FROM   S, P
           WHERE  S.CITY = P.CITY ;
```

This view is of course a join (actually an equijoin). For the set of joined records visible via this view given the usual set of data values for the underlying tables S,

P, and SP, see Example 6.3.1 in Chapter 6. From the standpoint of updatability, the COLOCATED view suffers from all kinds of problems. For example, suppose we try to update the record

```
('S1','Smith',20,'London','P1','Nut','Red',12,'London')
```

to

```
('S1','Allen',45,'London','P1','Nut','Red',12,'London')
```

It is very unclear as to whether this update should be allowed, and if it is, what its effect should be. And what if we try to delete the record instead? Or what if we try to insert the S1/Allen (etc.) version as a new record? Again, consideration of the details is left as an exercise for the reader.

```
3. CREATE VIEW PQ ( P#, TOTQTY )
       AS SELECT  P#, SUM (QTY)
          FROM    SP
          GROUP   BY P# ;
```

It is obvious that this view cannot support INSERT operations, nor UPDATE operations against field TOTQTY. DELETE operations, and UPDATE operations against field P#, theoretically *could* be defined to DELETE, or UPDATE, all corresponding records in table SP—but such operations could equally well be expressed directly in terms of table SP anyway. And it is at least arguable that a user issuing such operations should probably be interested in exactly which real records are affected by those operations.

From the foregoing examples, we see that some views are inherently updatable, whereas others are inherently not. Note the word "inherently" here. It is not just a question of some systems being able to support certain updates while others cannot. *No* system can consistently support updates on a view such as COLOCATED unaided (by "unaided" we mean "without help from some human user"). As a consequence of this fact, it is possible to classify views as indicated in the Venn diagram shown in Fig. 8.2.

Note carefully from the diagram that there do exist certain views that are theoretically updatable, but are not updatable in current systems such as DB2. The trouble is, although we know that such views exist, we do not know exactly which ones they are; it is a research problem to pin down exactly what it is that characterizes such views. For this reason, most current products either do not support view updating at all, or at best support updates against views that are either row subsets or column subsets (or a combination) of some single underlying base table. DB2 basically supports view updating of this "row-and-column-subset" kind, as do most current SQL systems.

The fact that not all views are updatable is frequently expressed as "You cannot update a join." That statement is *not* an accurate characterization of the situation, nor indeed of the problem: There are some views that are not joins that are not updatable, and there are some views that are joins that are (theoretically) updata-

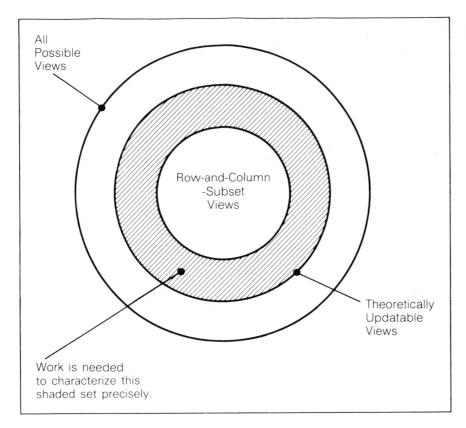

Fig. 8.2 Classification of views.

ble—although not updatable in today's products. But it is true that joins represent the "interesting case," in the sense that it would be very convenient to be able to update certain views whose definition involved a join. It should be clear from the foregoing discussion that such views may indeed be updatable in some future system or future release of one of today's systems.

We conclude this section by returning to the GOOD_SUPPLIERS view from Section 8.1 once again, in order to discuss a couple of remaining issues. The definition of that view (to repeat) is:

```
CREATE VIEW GOOD_SUPPLIERS
    AS SELECT S#, STATUS, CITY
       FROM    S
       WHERE   STATUS > 15 ;
```

This view is updatable (it is a row-and-column-subset of base table S). But note the following:

a) With the data values given in Fig. 4.1, supplier S2 will not be visible through the GOOD_SUPPLIERS view. But that does not mean that the user can IN-SERT a record into that view with supplier number value S2, or UPDATE one of the other records so that its supplier number value becomes S2. Such an operation must be rejected, just as if it had been applied directly to base table S.

b) Consider the following UPDATE:

```
UPDATE GOOD_SUPPLIERS
SET    STATUS = 5
WHERE  S# = 'S1' ;
```

Should this UPDATE be accepted? If it is, it will have the effect of removing supplier S1 from the view, since the S1 record will no longer satisfy the view-defining predicate (STATUS > 15). Likewise, the INSERT operation

```
INSERT
INTO   GOOD_SUPPLIERS ( S#, STATUS, CITY )
VALUES ( 'S8', 5, 'Stockholm' ) ;
```

(if accepted) will create a new supplier record, but that record will instantly vanish from the view. The SQL "CHECK option" is designed to deal with such situations. If the clause WITH CHECK OPTION is included in the definition of the view, as follows:

```
CREATE VIEW GOOD_SUPPLIERS
    AS SELECT S#, STATUS, CITY
       FROM   S
       WHERE  STATUS > 15
       WITH CHECK OPTION ;
```

then UPDATE and INSERT operations against the view will be checked to en-sure that the updated or inserted row satisfies the view-defining predicate STATUS > 15, in the example). If the CHECK option is not specified, then INSERTs and UPDATEs such as those illustrated above will be accepted, but the newly inserted or updated record will (as already indicated) immediately disappear from the view.

Note: DB2 does not in fact allow the CHECK option to be specified in all cases, even when the view in question is indeed updatable. The reason for this restriction is not inherent, but has to do with the implementation of DB2 spe-cifically. See reference [4.4] for details.

8.4   LOGICAL DATA INDEPENDENCE

We have not yet really explained what views are for. One of the things they are for is the provision of what is called *logical data independence*—so-called to distinguish it from physical data independence (see Sections 1.5 and 4.4). A system like DB2 is said to provide physical data independence because users and user programs are not dependent on the physical structure of the stored database. A system is said to provide *logical* data independence if users and user programs are also independent of the *logical* structure of the database. There are two aspects to this latter kind of independence, namely *growth* and *restructuring*.

Growth

As the database grows to incorporate new kinds of information, so the definition of the database must also grow accordingly. (Note: We discuss the question of growth in the database here only for completeness; it is important, but it has nothing to do with views as such.) There are two possible types of growth that can occur:

1. The expansion of an existing base table to include a new field (corresponding to the addition of new information concerning some existing type of object— for example, the addition of a DISCOUNT field to the supplier base table);

2. The inclusion of a new base table (corresponding to the addition of a new type of object—for example, the addition of project information to the suppliers-and-parts database).

Neither of these two kinds of change should have any effect on existing users at all.

Restructuring

Occasionally it may become necessary to restructure the database in such a way that, although the overall information content remains the same, the placement of information within that database changes—i.e., the allocation of fields to tables is altered in some way. Before proceeding further, we make the point that such restructuring is generally undesirable; however, it is sometimes unavoidable. For example, it may be necessary to split a table "vertically," so that commonly required fields can be stored on a faster device and less frequently required fields on a slower device. Let us consider this case in some detail. Suppose for the sake of the example that it becomes necessary (for some reason—the precise reason is not important here) to replace base table S by the following two base tables:

```
SX   ( S#, SNAME, CITY )
SY   ( S#, STATUS )
```

The crucial point to observe in this example is that *the old table S is the join of the two new tables SX and SY* (where by "join" we mean "natural join over supplier numbers". For example, in table S we had the record ('S1', 'Smith',20,'London'); in SX we now have the record ('S1','Smith','London') and in SY the record ('S1',20); join them together and we get the record ('S1','Smith',20,'London'), as before. So we create a *view* that is exactly that join, and we name it S:

```
CREATE VIEW S ( S#, SNAME, STATUS, CITY )
      AS SELECT SX.S#, SX.SNAME, SY.STATUS, SX.CITY
         FROM    SX, SY
         WHERE   SX.S# = SY.S# ;
```

Any program that previously referred to base table S will now refer to view S instead. SELECT operations will continue to work exactly as before (though they will require additional analysis during the bind process and may incur additional execution-time overhead). However, update operations will no longer work, because (as explained in Section 8.3) the system will not allow updates against a view that is defined as a join. In other words, a user performing update operations is not immune to this type of change, but instead must make some manual alterations to the update statements concerned (and then re-precompile and rebind them).

As a matter of fact, the view S (defined as the join of SX and SY) is a good example of a join view that *is* theoretically updatable. If we assume that there is a one-to-one correspondence between SX and SY at all times (so that any supplier appearing in SX also appears in SY, and vice versa), then the effect of all possible update operations on view S is clearly defined in terms of SX and SY. (Exercise: Do you agree with this statement?) Thus the example illustrates, not only why the ability to update join views would be a useful system feature, but also a case where such updating appears to be a feasible proposition.

8.5   ADVANTAGES OF VIEWS

We conclude this chapter with a brief summary of the advantages of views.

- They provide a certain amount of logical data independence in the face of re-structuring in the database, as explained in the previous section.

- They allow the same data to be seen by different users in different ways (at the same time).

This consideration is obviously important when there are many different categories of user all interacting with a single integrated database.

- The user's perception is simplified.

It is obvious that the view mechanism allows users to focus on just the data that is of concern to them and to ignore the rest. What is perhaps not so obvious is that, for retrieval at least, that mechanism can also considerably simplify the user's data manipulation operations. In particular, because the user can be provided with a view in which all underlying tables are joined together, the need for explicit operations to step from table to table can be greatly reduced. As an example, consider the view CITY_PAIRS (see Section 8.2), and contrast the SELECT needed to find cities storing parts that are available from London using that view with the SELECT needed to obtain the same result directly from the underlying base tables. In effect, the complex selection process has been moved out of the realm of data manipulation and into that of data definition (in fact, the distinction between "DDL" and "DML" is far from clearcut in relational languages like SQL).

- Automatic security is provided for hidden data.

"Hidden data" refers to data not visible through some given view. Such data is clearly secure from access through that particular view. Thus, forcing users to access the database via views is a simple but effective mechanism for authorization control. We will discuss this aspect of views in greater detail in Chapter 19.

EXERCISES

8.1 Create a view consisting of supplier numbers and part numbers for suppliers and parts that are not "colocated."

8.2 Create a view consisting of supplier records for suppliers that are located in London.

8.3 Define relation SP of the suppliers-and-parts database as a view of relation SPJ of the suppliers-parts-projects database.

8.4 Create a view from the suppliers-parts-projects database consisting of all projects (project number and city fields only) that are supplied by supplier S1 and use part P1.

8.5 Given the view definition:

```
CREATE VIEW HEAVYWEIGHTS ( P#, WT, COL )
     AS SELECT P#, WEIGHT, COLOR
        FROM P
        WHERE WEIGHT > 14 ;
```

show the operation actually executed (i.e., the converted form) for each of the following:

```
a) SELECT *
   FROM    HEAVYWEIGHTS
   WHERE   COL = 'Green' ;

b) SELECT P#, WT + 5
   FROM    HEAVYWEIGHTS
   ORDER   BY 2 ;

c) UPDATE HEAVYWEIGHTS
   SET     COL = 'White'
   WHERE   WT = 18 ;

d) DELETE
   FROM    HEAVYWEIGHTS
   WHERE   WT < 10 ;

e) INSERT
   INTO    HEAVYWEIGHTS ( P#, WT, COL )
   VALUES ('P99',12,'Purple') ;
```

8.6 Suppose we replace "WEIGHT" by "WEIGHT * 454" in the SELECT-clause portion (only) of the HEAVYWEIGHTS view definition. Now repeat Exercise 8.5.

ANSWERS TO SELECTED EXERCISES

```
8.1 CREATE VIEW NON_COLOCATED
        AS SELECT DISTINCT S#, P#
           FROM    S, P
           WHERE   S.CITY ~= P.CITY ;
```

8.2 CREATE VIEW LONDON_SUPPLIERS
      AS SELECT S#, SNAME, STATUS
         FROM   S
         WHERE CITY = 'London' ;

We have omitted the CITY field from the view, since we know its value must be 'London' for every record visible through the view. Note, however, that this omission means that any record inserted through the view will vanish instantly, since its CITY field will be set to null. The CHECK option would prohibit such insertions.

8.3 The problem here is: How should the field SP.QTY be defined? The sensible answer seems to be that, for a given (S#,P#) pair, SP.QTY should be the *sum* of all SPJ.QTY values, taken over all J#'s for that (S#,P#) pair.

```
    CREATE VIEW SP ( S#, P#, QTY )
        AS SELECT S#, P#, SUM (QTY)
           FROM    SPJ
           GROUP  BY S#, P# ;
```

8.4 CREATE VIEW JC (J#, CITY)
      AS SELECT J.J#, J.CITY
         FROM   J
         WHERE J# IN
                  (SELECT J#
                    FROM   SPJ
                    WHERE   S# = 'S1')
         AND   J# IN
                  (SELECT J#
                    FROM   SPJ
                    WHERE   P# = 'P1');

8.5

a) SELECT P#, WEIGHT, COLOR
   FROM   P
   WHERE   COLOR = 'Green'
   AND   WEIGHT > 14 ;

b) SELECT P#, WEIGHT + 5
   FROM   P
   WHERE   WEIGHT > 14
   ORDER   BY 2 ;

c) UPDATE P
   SET   COLOR = 'White'
   WHERE   WEIGHT = 18
   AND   WEIGHT > 14 ;

d) DELETE
   FROM   P
   WHERE   WEIGHT < 10
   AND   WEIGHT > 14 ;

e) INSERT
   INTO   P (P#, WEIGHT, COLOR)
   VALUES ('P99',12,'Purple') ;

8.6

a)
```
SELECT  P#, WEIGHT * 454, COLOR
FROM    P
WHERE   COLOR = 'Green'
AND     WEIGHT > 14 ;
```

b)
```
SELECT  P#, ( WEIGHT * 454 ) + 5
FROM    P
WHERE   WEIGHT > 14
ORDER   BY 2 ;
```

c)
```
UPDATE  P
SET     COLOR = 'White'
WHERE   ( WEIGHT * 454 ) = 18
AND     WEIGHT > 14 ;
```

d)
```
DELETE
FROM    P
WHERE   ( WEIGHT * 454 ) < 10
AND     WEIGHT > 14 ;
```

e) Fails. INSERT operations cannot be supported on such a view.

9
Embedded SQL

9.1 INTRODUCTION

As explained in Chapter 4, SQL is both an interactive query language and a database programming language. Up to this point, however, we have more or less ignored the programming aspects of SQL and have tacitly assumed (where it made any difference) that the language was being used interactively. Now we turn our attention to those programming aspects specifically and consider "embedded SQL" (as it is usually called).

The fundamental principle underlying embedded SQL, which we might call *the dual-mode principle*, is that *any SQL statement that can be used at the terminal can also be used in an application program*. Of course, as pointed out in Chapter 4, there are various differences of detail between a given interactive SQL statement and its corresponding embedded form, and SELECT statements in particular require significantly extended treatment in the programming environment (see Section 9.3); but the principle is nevertheless broadly true. (Its converse is not, however; that is, there are a number of SQL statements that are programming statements only and cannot be used interactively, as we shall see.)

Note clearly that the dual-mode principle applies to the entire SQL language, not just to the data manipulation operations. It is true that the data manipulation operations are far and away the most frequently used in a programming context, but there is nothing wrong in embedding (for example) a CREATE TABLE statement in a program, if it makes sense to do so for the application at hand.

Before we can discuss the statements of embedded SQL per se, it is necessary to cover a number of preliminary details. Most of those details are illustrated by the program fragment shown in Fig. 9.1. Note: To fix our ideas we assume that the host programming language is PL/I. Most of the ideas translate into other host languages with only minor changes.

```
DCL GIVENS# CHAR(5) ;
DCL RANK     FIXED BIN(15) ;
DCL CITY     CHAR(15) ;
DCL ALPHA    ... ;
DCL BETA     ... ;

EXEC SQL DECLARE S TABLE
                ( S#      CHAR(5) NOT NULL,
                  SNAME   CHAR(20),
                  STATUS  SMALLINT,
                  CITY    CHAR(15) ) ;

EXEC SQL INCLUDE SQLCA ;
.  .  .  .  .  .  .  .  .  .  .
IF ALPHA > BETA THEN
GETSTC:
EXEC SQL SELECT STATUS, CITY
         INTO   :RANK, :CITY
         FROM   S
         WHERE  S# = :GIVENS# ;
.  .  .  .  .  .  .  .  .  .  .
PUT SKIP LIST ( RANK, CITY ) ;
```

Fig. 9.1 Fragment of a PL/I program with embedded SQL.

Points arising:

1. Embedded SQL statements are prefixed by EXEC SQL, so that they can easily be distinguished from statements of the host language.

2. An *executable* SQL statement (from now on we will usually drop the "embedded") can appear wherever an executable host statement can appear. Note the "executable" qualifier: Unlike interactive SQL, embedded SQL includes some statements that are purely declarative, not executable. For example, DECLARE TABLE is not an executable statement, and neither is DECLARE CURSOR (see Section 9.3).

3. SQL statements can include references to host variables; such references are prefixed with a colon to distinguish them from SQL field names. Host variables can appear in embedded SQL (DML statements only) wherever a *constant* can appear in interactive SQL. They can also appear in an INTO clause to designate an input area for SELECT or FETCH (see later), and in certain embedded-only statements (details to follow).

4. Any tables (base tables or views) used in the program should be declared by means of an EXEC SQL DECLARE statement, in order to make the program more

self-documenting and to enable the Precompiler to perform certain syntax checks on the manipulative statements.

5. After any SQL statement has been executed, feedback information is returned to the program in an area called the SQL Communication Area (SQLCA). In particular, a numeric status indicator is returned in a field of the SQLCA called SQLCODE. A SQLCODE value of zero means that the statement executed successfully; a positive value means that the statement did execute, but constitutes a warning that some exceptional condition occurred (for example, a value of $+100$ indicates that no data was found to satisfy the request); and a negative value means that an error occurred and the statement did not complete successfully. In principle, therefore, every SQL statement in the program should be followed by a test on SQLCODE, and appropriate action taken if the value is not what was expected; however, we do not show this step in Fig. 9.1. (In practice such testing of SQLCODE values may be implicit, as we show in Section 9.4.)

The SQL Communication Area is included in the program by means of an EXEC SQL INCLUDE SQLCA statement.

6. Host variables must have a data type compatible with the SQL data type of fields they are to be compared with or assigned to or from. Data type compatibility is defined as follows: a) SQL character data is compatible with host character data, regardless of length and regardless of whether either length is varying; b) SQL numeric data is compatible with host numeric data, regardless of base (decimal or binary), scale (fixed or float), and precision (number of digits). DB2 will perform any necessary conversions. If significant digits or characters are lost on assignment (either to or from the program) because the receiving field is too small, an error indication is returned to the program.

7. Host variables and database fields can have the same name.

So much for the preliminaries. In the rest of this chapter we concentrate on the SQL data manipulation operations specifically. As already indicated, most of those operations can be handled in a fairly straightforward fashion (i.e., with only minor changes to their syntax). SELECT statements require special treatment, however. The problem is that executing a SELECT statement causes a *table* to be retrieved—a table that, in general, contains multiple records—and languages such as COBOL and PL/I are simply not equipped to handle more than one record at a time. It is therefore necessary to provide some kind of bridge between the set-at-a-time level of SQL and the record-at-a-time level of the host; and *cursors* provide such a bridge. A cursor is a new kind of SQL object, one that applies to embedded SQL only (because of course interactive SQL has no need of it). It consists essentially of a kind of *pointer* that can be used to run through a set of records, pointing to each of the records in the set in turn and thus providing addressability to those records one at a time. However, we defer detailed discussion of cursors to Section 9.3, and consider first (in Section 9.2) those statements that have no need of them.

9.2 OPERATIONS NOT INVOLVING CURSORS

The data manipulation statements that do not need cursors are as follows:

- "Singleton SELECT"
- UPDATE (except the CURRENT form—see Section 9.3)
- DELETE (again, except the CURRENT form—Section 9.3)
- INSERT

We give examples of each of these statements in turn.

9.2.1 Singleton SELECT. Get status and city for the supplier whose supplier number is given by the host variable GIVENS#.

```
EXEC SQL SELECT  STATUS, CITY
         INTO    :RANK, :CITY
         FROM    S
         WHERE   S# = :GIVENS# ;
```

We use the term "singleton SELECT" to mean a SELECT statement for which the retrieved table contains at most one row. In the example, if there exists exactly one record in table S satisfying the WHERE condition, then the STATUS and CITY values from that record will be delivered to the host variables RANK and CITY as requested, and SQLCODE will be set to zero. If no S record satisfies the WHERE condition, SQLCODE will be set to $+100$; and if more than one does, the program is in error, and SQLCODE will be set to a negative value. In these last two cases, the host variables RANK and CITY will remain unchanged.

The foregoing example raises another point. What if the SELECT statement does indeed select exactly one record, but the STATUS value or CITY value in that record happens to be null? With the SELECT statement as shown above, an error will occur (SQLCODE will be set to a negative value). If there is a chance that a field to be retrieved might be null, the user should supply an *indicator variable* for that field in the INTO clause as well as the normal target variable, as illustrated in the following example.

```
EXEC SQL SELECT  STATUS, CITY
         INTO    :RANK:RANKIND, :CITY:CITYIND
         FROM    S
         WHERE   S# = :GIVENS# ;
IF RANKIND < 0 THEN    /* STATUS was null */ ... ;
IF CITYIND < 0 THEN    /* CITY was null   */ ... ;
```

If the field to be retrieved is null and an indicator variable has been specified, then that indicator variable will be set to a negative value and the ordinary target variable will remain unchanged. Indicator variables are specified as shown—i.e., following the corresponding ordinary target variable and separated from that target variable by a colon. They should be declared as 15-bit signed binary integers.

For simplicity, we will ignore indicator variables and the possibility of null values throughout the remainder of this chapter.

9.2.2 UPDATE.   Increase the status of all London suppliers by the amount given
by the host variable RAISE.

```
EXEC SQL UPDATE S
         SET    STATUS = STATUS + :RAISE
         WHERE  CITY = 'London' ;
```

If no S records satisfy the WHERE condition, SQLCODE will be set to +100.

9.2.3 DELETE.   Delete all shipments for suppliers whose city is given by the host
variable CITY.

```
EXEC SQL DELETE
         FROM   SP
         WHERE  :CITY =
              ( SELECT CITY
                FROM   S
                WHERE  S.S# = SP.S# ) ;
```

Again SQLCODE will be set to +100 if no records satisfy the WHERE condition.

9.2.4 INSERT.   Insert a new part (part number, name, and weight given by host
variables PNO, PNAME, PWT, respectively; color and city unknown) into table P.

```
EXEC SQL INSERT
         INTO   P ( P#, PNAME, WEIGHT )
         VALUES ( :PNO, :PNAME, :PWT ) ;
```

9.3   OPERATIONS INVOLVING CURSORS

Now we turn to the case of a SELECT that selects a whole set of records, not just
one. As explained in Section 9.1, what is needed here is a mechanism for accessing
the records in the set one by one, and *cursors* provide such a mechanism. The process is illustrated in outline in the example of Fig. 9.2, which is intended to retrieve
supplier details (S#, SNAME, and STATUS) for all suppliers in the city given by
the host variable Y.

```
EXEC SQL DECLARE X CURSOR FOR          /* define cursor X       */
         SELECT S#, SNAME, STATUS
         FROM   S
         WHERE  CITY = :Y ;

EXEC SQL OPEN X ;                       /* execute the query     */
         DO WHILE ( more-records-to-come ) ;
             EXEC SQL FETCH X INTO :S#, :SNAME, :STATUS ;
                                        /* fetch next supplier   */

             .........
         END ;
EXEC SQL CLOSE X ;                      /* deactivate cursor X   */
```

Fig. 9.2 Retrieving multiple records.

Explanation: The DECLARE X CURSOR ... statement defines a cursor called X, with an associated query as specified by the SELECT that forms part of that DECLARE. The SELECT is not executed at this point; DECLARE CURSOR is a purely declarative statement. The SELECT *is* executed when the cursor is opened, in the procedural part of the program. The FETCH ... INTO ... statement is used to retrieve records one at a time from the result set, placing retrieved values into host variables in accordance with the specifications of the INTO clause in that statement. (For simplicity we have given the host variables the same names as the corresponding database fields. Note that the SELECT in the cursor declaration does not have an INTO clause of its own.) Since there will be multiple records in the result set, the FETCH will normally appear within a loop (DO ... END in PL/I); the loop will be repeated so long as there are more records still to come in that result set. On exit from the loop, cursor X is closed (deactivated) via an appropriate CLOSE statement.

Now let us consider cursors and cursor operations in more detail. First, a cursor is declared by means of a DECLARE CURSOR statement, which takes the general form

```
EXEC SQL DECLARE cursor-name CURSOR
         FOR embedded-SELECT-statement
      [ FOR UPDATE OF column-name [ , column-name ] . . . ] ;
```

For an example, see Fig. 9.2. As previously stated, the DECLARE CURSOR statement is declarative, not executable; it declares a cursor with the specified name and having the specified query (SELECT statement) permanently associated with it. Notice that the embedded query can include host variable references. If the cursor will be used in UPDATE CURRENT statements (see later in this section), then the declaration must include a FOR UPDATE clause, specifying all fields that will be updated via this cursor; if not (and only if not), then it may optionally include an ORDER BY clause, as in a conventional SELECT statement. That ORDER BY clause will control the order in which result rows are retrieved via FETCH. Note, therefore, that it is not possible to retrieve a set of records via a cursor in some specified order *and* update some of those records via that same cursor at the same time.

A program can include any number of DECLARE CURSOR statements, each of which must (of course) be for a different cursor.

Three executable statements are provided to operate on cursors: OPEN, FETCH, and CLOSE.

1. The statement

```
EXEC SQL OPEN x ;
```

(where x is a cursor name) opens or "activates" cursor x (which must not already be open). In effect, the query associated with cursor x is executed (using the current values for any host variables referenced within that query); a set of records is thus identified and becomes the current *active set* for cursor x. Cursor x also identifies a *position* within that active set, namely the position just before the first record in the set. (Active sets are always considered to have an ordering, so that the concept of position has meaning. The ordering is either that defined by the ORDER BY clause, or a system-determined ordering in the absence of such a clause.)

2. The statement

```
EXEC SQL FETCH x INTO host-variable [, host-variable ] ... ;
```

advances cursor *x* (which must be open) to the next record in the active set for *x* and then assigns field values from that record to host variables as specified in the INTO clause. As indicated earlier, FETCH is normally executed within a program loop, as shown in Fig. 9.2. If there is no next record when FETCH is executed, then SQLCODE is set to +100 and no data is retrieved.

Note, incidentally, that FETCH (i.e., "fetch *next*") is the *only* cursor movement operation. It is not possible to move a cursor (e.g.) "forward three positions" or "backward two positions," etc.

3. The statement

```
EXEC SQL CLOSE x ;
```

closes or "deactivates" cursor *x* (which must currently be open). Cursor *x* now has no current active set. However, cursor *x* can subsequently be opened again, in which case it will acquire another active set—probably not exactly the same set as before, especially if the values of any host variables referenced in the query associated with cursor *x* have changed in the meantime. Note that changing the values of those host variables while cursor *x* is open has no effect on the current active set.

Two further statements can include references to cursors. These are the CURRENT forms of UPDATE and DELETE. If a cursor, X say, is currently positioned on a particular record in the database, then it is possible to UPDATE or DELETE the "current of X," i.e., the record on which X is positioned. Syntax:

```
EXEC SQL UPDATE table-name
         SET    field-name = expression
            [, field-name = expression ] ...
         WHERE  CURRENT OF cursor-name ;

EXEC SQL DELETE
         FROM   table-name
         WHERE  CURRENT OF cursor-name ;
```

For example:

```
EXEC SQL UPDATE S
         SET    STATUS = STATUS + :RAISE
         WHERE  CURRENT OF X ;
```

UPDATE CURRENT and DELETE CURRENT are not permitted if the SELECT statement in the cursor declaration involves UNION or ORDER BY, or if

that SELECT statement would define a nonupdatable view if it were part of a CRE-
ATE VIEW statement (see Section 8.3 in Chapter 8). In the case of UPDATE CUR-
RENT, as explained earlier, the cursor declaration must include a FOR UPDATE
clause identifying all the fields that appear as targets of a SET clause in any UP-
DATE CURRENT statement for that cursor.

9.4   A COMPREHENSIVE EXAMPLE

We present a somewhat contrived, but comprehensive, example (Fig. 9.3) to illustrate the use of embedded SQL in detail. The program accepts four input values: a
part number (GIVENP#), a city name (GIVENCIT), a status increment (GIVEN-
INC), and a status level (GIVENLVL). The program scans all suppliers of the part
identified by GIVENP#. For each such supplier, if the supplier city is GIVENCIT,
then the status is increased by GIVENINC; otherwise, if the status is less than GIV-
ENLVL, the supplier is deleted, together with all shipments for that supplier. In all
cases supplier information is listed on the printer, with an indication of how that
particular supplier was handled by the program.

Points arising:

1. Note that the two DECLAREs for tables S and SP are basically nothing but
slight textual variations on the corresponding CREATE TABLE statements of SQL.
A special utility program, the declarations generator (DCLGEN), is provided to
construct such declarations on the user's behalf. Basically, DCLGEN uses the information in the system catalog to build either or both of the following:

- a DECLARE statement for the table;
- a corresponding PL/I or COBOL declaration for a structure the same shape as
  the table (to be used as a target for retrieval and/or a source for update).

For further details, see reference [4.4].

2. As explained in Section 9.2, every SQL statement should in principle be followed by a test of the returned SQLCODE value. The WHENEVER statement is
provided to simplify this process. The WHENEVER statement has the syntax:

```
EXEC SQL WHENEVER condition action ;
```

where "condition" is NOT FOUND, SQLWARNING, or SQLERROR, and "action" is either CONTINUE or a GO TO statement. WHENEVER is not an executable statement; rather, it is a directive to the Precompiler. "WHENEVER
condition GO TO label" causes the Precompiler to insert an "IF condition
GO TO label" statement after each executable SQL statement it encounters.
"WHENEVER condition CONTINUE" causes the Precompiler not to insert any
such statements (the implication being that the programmer will insert such state-

```
SQLEX: PROC OPTIONS (MAIN) ;

       DCL GIVENP#          CHAR(6) ;
       DCL GIVENCIT         CHAR(15) ;
       DCL GIVENINC         FIXED BINARY(15) ;
       DCL GIVENLVL         FIXED BINARY(15) ;
       DCL S#               CHAR(5) ;
       DCL SNAME            CHAR(20) ;
       DCL STATUS           FIXED BINARY(15) ;
       DCL CITY             CHAR(15) ;
       DCL DISP             CHAR(7) ;
       DCL MORE_SUPPLIERS BIT(1) ;

       EXEC SQL INCLUDE SQLCA ;

       EXEC SQL DECLARE S TABLE
                     ( S#      CHAR(5) NOT NULL,
                       SNAME   CHAR(20),
                       STATUS  SMALLINT,
                       CITY    CHAR(20) ) ;

       EXEC SQL DECLARE SP TABLE
                     ( S#      CHAR(5) NOT NULL,
                       P#      CHAR(6) NOT NULL,
                       QTY     INTEGER ) ;

       EXEC SQL DECLARE Z CURSOR FOR
               SELECT S#, SNAME, STATUS, CITY
               FROM    S
               WHERE   EXISTS
                   ( SELECT *
                     FROM    SP
                     WHERE   SP.S# = S.S#
                     AND     SP.P# = :GIVENP# )
               FOR UPDATE OF STATUS ;

       EXEC SQL WHENEVER NOT FOUND CONTINUE ;
       EXEC SQL WHENEVER SQLERROR CONTINUE ;
       EXEC SQL WHENEVER SQLWARNING CONTINUE ;

       ON CONDITION ( DBEXCEPTION )
       BEGIN ;
          PUT SKIP LIST ( SQLCA ) ;
          EXEC SQL ROLLBACK ;
          GO TO QUIT ;
       END ;
```

Fig. 9.3 A comprehensive example (part 1 of 2).

```
      GET LIST ( GIVENP#, GIVENCIT, GIVENINC, GIVENLVL ) ;
      EXEC SQL OPEN Z ;
      IF SQLCODE  ~= 0
      THEN SIGNAL CONDITION ( DBEXCEPTION ) ;
      MORE_SUPPLIERS = '1'B ;
      DO WHILE ( MORE_SUPPLIERS ) ;
         EXEC SQL FETCH Z INTO :S#, :SNAME, :STATUS, :CITY ;
         SELECT ;            /* a PL/I SELECT, not a SQL SELECT */
         WHEN ( SQLCODE = 100 )
            MORE_SUPPLIERS = '0'B ;
         WHEN ( SQLCODE  ~= 100 & SQLCODE  ~= 0 )
            SIGNAL CONDITION ( DBEXCEPTION ) ;
         WHEN ( SQLCODE = 0 )
            DO ;
               DISP = 'bbbbbb' ;
               IF CITY = GIVENCIT
               THEN
                  DO ;
                     EXEC SQL UPDATE S
                             SET    STATUS = STATUS + :GIVENINC
                             WHERE  CURRENT OF Z ;
                     IF SQLCODE  ~= 0
                     THEN SIGNAL CONDITION ( DBEXCEPTION ) ;
                     DISP = 'UPDATED' ;
                  END ;
               ELSE
                  IF STATUS < GIVENLVL
                  THEN
                     DO ;
                        EXEC SQL DELETE
                                FROM   SP
                                WHERE  S# = :S# ;
                        IF SQLCODE  ~= 0 & SQLCODE  ~=100
                        THEN SIGNAL CONDITION ( DBEXCEPTION ) ;
                        EXEC SQL DELETE
                                FROM   S
                                WHERE  CURRENT OF Z ;
                        IF SQLCODE  ~= 0
                        THEN SIGNAL CONDITION ( DBEXCEPTION ) ;
                        DISP = 'DELETED' ;
                     END ;
                  PUT SKIP LIST ( S#, SNAME, STATUS,
                                     CITY, DISP ) ;
            END ; /* WHEN ( SQLCODE = 0 ) ... */
         END ; /* PL/I SELECT */
      END ; /* DO WHILE */
      EXEC SQL CLOSE Z ;
      EXEC SQL COMMIT ;
QUIT: RETURN ;
   END ; /* SQLEX */
```

Fig. 9.3 A comprehensive example (part 2 of 2).

ments by hand). The three "conditions" are defined as follows (ignoring some minor DB2-specific details):

```
NOT FOUND      means     SQLCODE = 100
SQLWARNING     means     SQLCODE > 0 and SQLCODE ~= 100
SQLERROR       means     SQLCODE < 0
```

Each WHENEVER statement the Precompiler encounters on its sequential scan through the program text (for a particular condition) overrides the previous one it found (for that condition). At the start of the program text there is an implicit WHENEVER statement for each of the three possible conditions, specifying CONTINUE in each case.

In the sample program, all exception-testing is done explicitly, for tutorial reasons. If any exception occurs, control is passed to a procedure that prints diagnostic information (the SQL Communication Area, in the example), issues a ROLLBACK (see below), and then branches to the final RETURN.

3. When a program updates the database in some way, that update should initially be regarded as *tentative only*—tentative in the sense that, if something subsequently goes wrong, *the update may be undone* (either by the program itself or by the system). For example, if the program hits an unexpected error, say an overflow condition, and terminates abnormally, then the system will automatically undo all such tentative updates on the program's behalf. Updates remain tentative until one of two things happens: Either a) a COMMIT statement is executed, which makes all tentative updates firm ("committed"); or b) a ROLLBACK statement is executed, which undoes all tentative updates. Once committed, an update is guaranteed never to be undone (this is the definition of "committed").

In the example, the program issues COMMIT when it reaches its normal termination, but issues ROLLBACK if any SQL exception is encountered. Actually, that explicit COMMIT is not necessary; the system will automatically issue a COMMIT on the program's behalf for any program that reaches normal termination. It will also automatically issue a ROLLBACK on the program's behalf for any program that does not reach normal termination; in the example, however, an explicit ROLLBACK *is* necessary, because the program is designed to reach its normal termination even if a SQL exception occurs.

Note: This question of "committed updates" and the related notion of *transaction processing* is considered in more depth in Chapter 18.

9.5 DYNAMIC SQL

"Dynamic SQL" consists of a set of embedded SQL facilities that are provided specifically to allow the construction of on-line applications. (Recall from Chapter 1 that an on-line application is an application that supports access to the database from an on-line terminal.) The topic of this section is therefore somewhat specialized—the only people who really need to be familiar with it are people directly concerned with the writing of on-line applications. For that reason we content ourselves here with a brief introduction only.

Consider what a typical on-line application has to do. In outline, the steps it must go through are as follows.

1. Accept a command from the terminal.

2. Analyze that command.

3. Issue appropriate SQL statements to the database.

4. Return a message and/or results to the terminal.

If the set of commands the program can accept is fairly small, as in the case of (perhaps) a program handling airline reservations, then the set of possible SQL statements to be issued may also be small and can be "hardwired" into the program. In this case, Steps 2 and 3 above will consist simply of logic to examine the input command and then branch to the part of the program that issues the predefined SQL statement(s). If, on the other hand, there can be great variability in the input, then it may not be practicable to predefine and "hardwire" SQL statements for every possible command. Instead, it is probably much more convenient to *construct* the necessary SQL statements dynamically, and then to bind and execute those constructed statements dynamically. The facilities of dynamic SQL are provided to assist in this process.

The two principal dynamic statements are PREPARE and EXECUTE. Their use is illustrated in the following example.

```
         DCL      SQLSOURCE CHAR(256) VARYING ;
    EXEC SQL DECLARE SQLOBJ STATEMENT ;

         SQLSOURCE = 'DELETE FROM SP WHERE QTY < 100' ;
    EXEC SQL PREPARE SQLOBJ FROM :SQLSOURCE ;
    EXEC SQL EXECUTE SQLOBJ ;
```

Explanation: SQLSOURCE is a PL/I character string variable in which the program will construct the source form (i.e., character string representation) of some SQL statement (a DELETE statement, in our particular example). SQLOBJ, by contrast, is a *SQL* variable, not a PL/I variable, that will be used to hold the object form (i.e., machine code representation) of the SQL statement whose source form is given in SQLSOURCE. (The names SQLSOURCE and SQLOBJ are arbitrary.) The assignment statement "SQLSOURCE = ... ;" assigns to SQLSOURCE the source form of a SQL DELETE statement. (As suggested previously, the process of constructing such a source statement is likely to be much more complicated in practice, involving the input and analysis of some end-user command from the terminal.) The PREPARE statement then takes that source statement and precompiles and binds it to produce a machine code version, which it stores in SQLOBJ. Finally, the EXECUTE statement executes that machine code version and thus (in the example) causes the actual DELETE to occur. Feedback information from the DELETE will be returned in the SQLCA as usual.

Incidentally, the process just described is exactly what happens when SQL statements themselves are entered interactively, either through DB2I or through QMF (see Chapter 4). In each case, an on-line application is executing and is ready to accept an extremely wide variety of input, namely any valid (or invalid!) SQL statement. It uses the facilities of dynamic SQL to construct suitable *embedded* SQL statements corresponding to its input, to bind and execute those constructed statements, and to return messages and results back to the terminal.

For more information regarding dynamic SQL, see reference [4.4].

9.6 CONCLUDING REMARKS

We conclude our discussion of embedded SQL by offering a number of observations on the SQL approach to database application programming.

1. The use of essentially the same language for both interactive and programmed access to the database has one very significant consequence: It means that the database portions of an application program can be tested and debugged interactively. Using the interactive interface, it is very easy for a programmer to create some test tables, load data into them, execute (interactive versions of) the programmed SQL statements against them, query the tables and/or the catalog to see the effect of those statements, and so on. In other words, the interactive interface provides a very convenient *programmer debugging facility*. Of course, it is attractive for other reasons too; for example, the data definition process is normally carried out through that interface, and so too is the process of granting and revoking authorization (see Chapter 19).

2. Second, of course, that same fact (namely, that essentially the same language is used at both interfaces) greatly eases communication between end-users and application programmers (and with the DBA too, come to that). Moreover, embedded SQL is essentially the same regardless of what host language (COBOL, PL/I, etc.) it happens to be embedded in.

3. The fact that SQL manipulative operations are compiled (i.e., bound prior to run time), at least in the IBM systems, means that those systems enjoy a significant performance advantage over systems that adopt a more conventional interpretive approach. All of the following operations—

- parsing the original request
- detecting and reporting on syntax errors
- choosing an access strategy
- checking authorization
- generating machine code

— are removed from the run-time path. (Of these operations, the most significant from a performance point of view is choosing an access strategy—in a word, optimization.) The run-time path is thus considerably shorter than it would otherwise be; and since the instructions in the run-time path must be executed on every request, and since such requests frequently occur within program loops, the savings can be considerable.

4. Even in the case of dynamically prepared and executed statements, where all the operations mentioned above are necessarily in the run-time path, the compilation approach can still pay off. In System R it was found that, as soon as the system had to access more than quite a small number of records in order to respond to the request, then compilation outperformed interpretation, sometimes very significantly [4.17].

5. A disadvantage of SQL as an application programming language is that it is only "loosely coupled" to the host. In fact, of course, the two are totally different languages. SQL objects (e.g., tables, fields, cursors) are not known and cannot be referenced in the host environment; and host objects can be referenced in the SQL environment only in an ad hoc manner and in certain restricted contexts. The rules for such things as name formation, name resolution, name qualification, expression evaluation, and so forth all change every time the programmer crosses the host/SQL boundary. Perhaps more significant, SQL does not take advantage of constructs that already exist in the host language for such things as loop control, data structuring, exception handling, and argument passing. As a consequence, SQL programs tend to be rather unstructured and not very concise. See reference [4.10] for an elaboration of these points.

EXERCISES

9.1 Using the suppliers-parts-projects database, write a program with embedded SQL statements to list all supplier records, in supplier number order. Each supplier record should be immediately followed in the listing by all project records for projects supplied by that supplier, in project number order.

9.2 Why do you think the FOR UPDATE clause is required?

9.3 Revise your solution to Exercise 9.1 to do the following in addition: a) Increase the status by 50 percent for any supplier who supplies more than two projects; b) delete any supplier who does not supply any projects at all.

9.4 (Harder.) Given the tables

```
CREATE TABLE PARTS
     ( P# ... NOT NULL,
       DESCRIPTION ... ) ;

CREATE TABLE PART_STRUCTURE
     ( MAJOR_P# ... NOT NULL,
       MINOR_P# ... NOT NULL,
       QTY        ... ) ;
```

where PART_STRUCTURE shows which parts (MAJOR_P#) contain which other parts (MI-NOR_P#) as first-level components, write a SQL program to list all component parts of a given part, to all levels (the "parts explosion" problem). Note: The following sample values may help you visualize this problem:

MAJOR_P#	MINOR_P#	QTY
P1	P2	2
P1	P4	4
P5	P3	1
P3	P6	3
P6	P1	9
P5	P6	8
P2	P4	3

ANSWERS TO SELECTED EXERCISES

9.1 We define two cursors, CS and CJ, as follows:

```
EXEC SQL DECLARE CS CURSOR FOR
            SELECT S#, SNAME, STATUS, CITY
            FROM   S
            ORDER  BY S# ;

EXEC SQL DECLARE CJ CURSOR FOR
            SELECT J#, JNAME, CITY
            FROM   J
            WHERE  J# IN
                  ( SELECT J#
                    FROM   SPJ
                    WHERE  S# = :CS_S# )
            ORDER BY J# ;
```

where the host variable CS_S# contains a supplier number value, fetched via cursor CS. Procedural logic (in outline):

```
EXEC SQL OPEN CS ;
DO for all S records accessible via CS ;
    EXEC SQL FETCH CS INTO :CS_S#, :CS_SN, :CS_ST, :CS_SC ;
    print CS_S#, CS_SN, CS_ST, CS_SC ;
    EXEC SQL OPEN CJ ;
    DO for all J records accessible via CJ ;
        EXEC SQL FETCH CJ INTO :CJ_J#, :CJ_JN, :CJ_JC ;
        print CJ_J#, CJ_JN, CJ_JC ;
    END ;
    EXEC SQL CLOSE CJ ;
END ;
EXEC SQL CLOSE CS ;
```

Note: The problem with this exercise is that it effectively requires the computation of an *outer join* (see reference [13.9]). Since SQL does not provide direct support for such an operation, it is necessary to "hand-code" it by means of nested loops as shown above. As a result, the solution involves a certain amount of manual (as opposed to automatic) navigation through the database. See reference [4.4] for further discussion of this problem.

9.2 Suppose the program includes a DECLARE CURSOR statement of the form

```
EXEC SQL DECLARE C CURSOR FOR
          SELECT ...
          FROM    T
          ...... ;
```

The optimizer is responsible for choosing an access path corresponding to the cursor C. Suppose it chooses an index based on field F of table T. The set of records accessible via C when C is activated will then be ordered according to values of F. If the program were allowed to UPDATE a value of F via the cursor C—i.e., via an UPDATE statement of the form

```
EXEC SQL UPDATE T
          SET    F = ...
          WHERE CURRENT OF C ;
```

— then the updated record would probably have to be "moved" (logically speaking), because it would now belong in a different position with respect to the ordering of the active set. In other words, cursor C would effectively jump to a new position, with unpredictable results. To avoid such a situation, the user must warn the optimizer of any fields to be updated, so that access paths based on those fields will *not* be chosen.

9.3 "Note that cursor CS does not permit updates. Apart from this consideration, the solution is basically straightforward."

```
EXEC SQL UPDATE S
          SET     STATUS = STATUS * 1.5
          WHERE   S# = :CS_S# ;

EXEC SQL DELETE
          FROM    S
          WHERE   S# = :CS_S# ;
```

9.4 This is a good example of a problem that SQL in its current form does not handle well. The basic difficulty is as follows: We need to "explode" the given part to n levels, where the value of n is unknown at the time of writing the program. A comparatively straightforward way of performing such an n-level "explosion"—if it were possible—would be by means of a recursive program, in which each recursive invocation creates a new cursor, as follows:

```
          GET LIST ( GIVENP# ) ;
          CALL RECURSION ( GIVENP# ) ;
          RETURN ;

RECURSION: PROC ( UPPER_P# ) RECURSIVE ;
          DCL UPPER_P# ... ;
          DCL LOWER_P# ... ;
          EXEC SQL DECLARE C "reopenable" CURSOR FOR
                    SELECT MINOR_P#
                    FROM    PART_STRUCTURE
                    WHERE   MAJOR_P# = :UPPER_P# ;
          print UPPER_P# ;
```

```
EXEC SQL OPEN C ;
DO for all PART_STRUCTURE records accessible via C ;
    EXEC SQL FETCH C INTO :LOWER_P# ;
    CALL RECURSION ( LOWER_P# ) ;
END ;
EXEC SQL CLOSE C ;
END ; /* of RECURSION */
```

We have assumed here that the (fictitious) specification "reopenable" means that it is
legal to issue "OPEN C" for a cursor C that is already open, and that the effect of such an
OPEN is to create a new *instance* of the cursor for the specified query (using the current
values of any host variables referenced in that query). We have assumed further that references to C in FETCH (etc.) are references to the "current" instance of C, and that CLOSE
destroys that instance and reinstates the previous instance as "current." In other words, we
have assumed that a reopenable cursor forms a *stack*, with OPEN and CLOSE serving as
the "push" and "pop" operators for that stack.

Unfortunately, those assumptions are purely hypothetical today. There is no such thing
as a reopenable cursor in SQL today (indeed, an attempt to issue "OPEN C" for a cursor
C that is already open will fail). The foregoing code is illegal. But the example makes it clear
that "reopenable cursors" would be a very desirable extension to current SQL.

Since the foregoing procedure does not work, we give a sketch of one possible (but very
inefficient) procedure that does.

```
GET LIST ( GIVENP# ) ;
CALL RECURSION (GIVENP# ) ;
RETURN ;

RECURSION: PROC ( UPPER_P# ) RECURSIVE ;
    DCL UPPER_P# ... ;
    DCL LOWER_P# ... INITIAL ('bbbbbb' ) ;
    EXEC SQL DECLARE C CURSOR FOR
            SELECT MINOR_P#
            FROM    PART_STRUCTURE
            WHERE   MAJOR_P# = :UPPER_P#
            AND     MINOR_P# > :LOWER_P#
            ORDER   BY MINOR_P# ;

DO forever ;
    print UPPER_P# ;
    EXEC SQL OPEN C ;
    EXEC SQL FETCH C INTO :LOWER_P# ;
    IF not found THEN RETURN ;
    IF found THEN
    DO ;
        EXEC SQL CLOSE C ;
        CALL RECURSION (LOWER_P# ) ;
    END ;
END ;
END ; /* of RECURSION */
```

Note in this solution that the same cursor is used on every invocation of RECURSION.
(By contrast, new instances of UPPER_P# and LOWER_P# are created dynamically each

time RECURSION is invoked; those instances are destroyed at completion of that invocation.) Because of this fact, we have to use a trick—

```
... AND MINOR_P# > :LOWER_P# ORDER BY MINOR_P#
```

— so that, on each invocation of RECURSION, we ignore all immediate components (LOWER_P#s) of the current UPPER_P# that have already been processed.

See reference [4.8] for a discussion of some alternative approaches to this problem.

Part 3
Relational Database Management

In this part of the book we consider several aspects of relational database management in some depth. Chapter 10 is devoted to a description of another important relational system, namely INGRES (however, that description is much less detailed than the description of DB2 in Part 2 of this book). We choose to include INGRES here because it is a good example of a system in which the primary language, QUEL, is *not* SQL or "SQL-like"; indeed, there are some respects in which QUEL is clearly superior to SQL. (But in general there are many similarities between the two languages, as is only to be expected.) Both QUEL and SQL will be used as a basis for examples later in the book.

Next, we go on to examine the formal theory underlying systems such as INGRES and DB2. That theory is referred to as *the relational model of data*. When we describe some system as relational, what we mean, broadly speaking, is that the system in question is constructed in accordance with the principles—at least the major principles—of that underlying theoretical model. The relational model can be characterized as *a way of looking at data* — that is, a prescription for a way of representing data and for a way of manipulating that representation. More precisely, the relational model is concerned with three aspects of data: data *structure*, data *integrity*, and data *manipulation*. We consider each of those aspects in turn in the next few chapters: Chapter 11 discusses relational data structure; Chapter 12, relational data integrity; and Chapters 13 and 14, relational data manipulation. We devote two chapters to the last of these three topics because the manipulative part of the model can be realized in either of two distinct (but equivalent) fashions, referred to respectively as the *relational algebra* and the *relational calculus*.

After the somewhat theoretical material of Chapters 11–14, Chapter 15 then considers the more immediately practical question of what exactly it is that constitutes a relational *system*. Then Chapter 16 goes on to describe some approaches to the problem of query optimization in such systems. Finally, Chapter 17 discusses *further normalization*, and thereby provides an introduction to what is now called *dependency theory*. Note that this last topic, although (like the relational model itself) rather theoretical in nature, is not really part of the relational model per se; however, it does build very directly on that model, and for that reason it makes sense to treat it in this part of the book.

Note: It is quite possible to provide an overview of relational database management in just one or two pages. Indeed, it is a strength of the relational model that its basic ideas can be very easily explained and readily understood. However, a one- or two-page treatment cannot really do justice to the subject, nor truly illustrate its wide range of applicability. The considerable length of this part of the book should thus be seen not as a comment on the model's complexity, but rather as a tribute to its importance and to its success as a foundation for numerous far-reaching developments.

10
An Overview
of INGRES

10.1 BACKGROUND

While the System R prototype was being developed within IBM (in the mid to late 1970s), another major relational project was under way at the University of California at Berkeley. The result of that effort was the INGRES prototype ("INGRES" —pronounced "ingress"—was originally an acronym, standing for "Interactive Graphics and Retrieval System"). The INGRES prototype (now usually called "University INGRES" to distinguish it from the commercial version—see below) became widely available in university environments in the late 1970s and early 1980s, both in the United States and elsewhere. In addition, of course, an active program of INGRES-based research and development continues at Berkeley, just as similar activities based on System R continue within IBM.

In the early 1980s, a company called Relational Technology Inc. (RTI) was formed to develop and market a commercial version of INGRES [10.1]. University INGRES runs on DEC PDP machines under the UNIX operating system; Commercial INGRES runs on DEC VAX machines under either UNIX or VMS and also on a wide variety of MC68000-based and other machines under UNIX. In this book we will generally not bother to distinguish between the university and commercial versions, except where the distinctions are important; the generic name INGRES should thus be taken to refer to both, unless we explicitly state otherwise.

INGRES is *not* a SQL system.[1] The primary user language in INGRES is called QUEL ("Query Language"). QUEL may be regarded as a fairly "pure" implementation of the relational calculus (see Chapter 14); as such, it is a considerably less idiosyncratic language than SQL, and indeed is clearly superior to SQL in some ways. (For this reason, in fact, several currently available relational products sup-

---

1. However, RTI has stated its intention of providing a SQL interface to Commercial INGRES.

port a language that can best be characterized as "QUEL-like" rather than "SQL-like." Examples of such products include the ENCOMPASS system from TANDEM, the CA-UNIVERSE system from Computer Associates, and the "Intelligent Database Machine" (IDM) from Britton-Lee.) We examine QUEL in some detail in the sections that follow.

Like SQL, QUEL can be used both as an interactive query language (via the INGRES *Terminal Monitor*) and also as a database programming language embedded within a variety of host languages (via *Embedded QUEL* or EQUEL). In addition, Commercial INGRES specifically provides a number of built-in forms-based interfaces for such tasks as report-writing, business graphics, and so on. We shall have more to say about the forms-based interfaces in Chapter 20.

The reader of this chapter is expected to have at least a general appreciation of the facilities of DB2 (i.e., to have read Part 2 of this book), or else to have a good understanding of relational concepts in general. There are numerous parallels between INGRES and DB2; for example, INGRES also supports multiple users, includes a query optimizer component, allows dynamic data definition, supports the notion of "virtual relations" or views, and so on. We will not repeat the explanations of such basic ideas in this chapter. Rather, we will concentrate on those aspects of INGRES that are significantly different from the corresponding features of DB2.

One area of difference we mention right away. There is no notion in INGRES of a separate Bind component, as there is in DB2. The two operations of

1. producing an optimized "application plan" (called a "query plan" in INGRES) for a given request, and

2. executing that plan,

are not as sharply separated as they are in DB2. The advantage of not separating them is that the elaborate compiling/recompiling mechanism of DB2 is unnecessary in INGRES; the optimizer always produces code that is in accordance with the current state of the database, and operations such as dropping an index or other object do not require any additional system activity to track usage of the dropped object. Furthermore, the INGRES optimizer may in fact produce better code than the DB2 optimizer, precisely because it operates in terms of more current information. The disadvantage, of course, is that repetitively executed programs must be optimized every time they are run. (In Commercial INGRES, however, if a given *request* is to be executed multiple times during a single program run, that request need be optimized only on its first execution within that program run, not every time it is executed. See the discussion of the REPEAT option in Section 10.6.)

10.2   DATA DEFINITION

The QUEL "data definition language" (DDL) statements are as follows:

CREATE   — creates a base table
INDEX   — creates an index

```
DEFINE VIEW   — creates a view
DESTROY       — destroys a base table, index, or view
MODIFY        — changes the storage structure of a base table or index
```

There is no QUEL analog of the SQL "ALTER TABLE" function. We defer discussion of views to Section 10.5; the remaining statements are the subject of the present section.

CREATE

The general format of CREATE is as follows:

```
CREATE base-table-name
     ( column-definition [, column-definition ] ... )
```

where a "column-definition", in turn, takes the form:

```
column-name = data-type
```

For example (ignoring the fact that "#" is not a legal character in a QUEL name):

```
CREATE S ( S#     = TEXT(5),
           SNAME  = TEXT(20),
           STATUS = I2,
           CITY   = TEXT(15) )
```

QUEL supports the following data types:

I1, I2, I4	binary integers of 1, 2, 4 bytes respectively
F4, F8	floating point numbers of 4, 8 bytes respectively
MONEY	dollars and cents, 16 digits, with assumed decimal point two digits from the right
TEXT(n)	varying length text string of maximum length *n* bytes
DATE	date and time (year/month/day/hour/minute/second), representing either an absolute value such as "14-Mar-85 10:30 am" or an interval such as "3 months 14 days 10 hours 30 minutes"
Cn	character string of *n* bytes[2]

QUEL does not support SQL-style null values. If the user does not supply a value for some field when storing a new record, INGRES automatically sets the field to zero for numeric data types (i.e., the first three types listed above) and blank for the other types.

---

2. "*Cn*" was the original character string data type in University INGRES. Commercial INGRES added the TEXT data type in order to avoid certain problems with *Cn*—primarily the problem that *Cn* obeys somewhat strange comparison rules (details beyond the scope of this chapter). TEXT is usually a better choice in practice.

In INGRES (unlike DB2), different base tables can have significantly different storage structures. Tables are automatically created as "heaps" (that is, records are stored wherever there happens to be room). However, the storage structure for any given table can be changed to some more efficient form, say to an indexed (BTREE) structure, at any time after that table is created. Furthermore, the storage structure can subsequently be changed as often as desired. See the discussion of MODIFY below.

INDEX

The INDEX statement is used to create additional indexes on a base table, over and above the index (if any) that already exists as part of that base table's principal storage structure. The format is:

```
INDEX ON base-table-name IS index-name
                    ( column-name [ , column-name ] ... )
```

For example:

```
INDEX ON S IS XSC ( CITY )
```

An index created via an INDEX operation is initially stored as an ISAM structure (see the discussion of MODIFY below), but can later be modified to some other structure just as a base table can.

DESTROY

Format:

```
DESTROY name [ , name ] ...
```

where each "name" is the name of a base table or index (or view). Examples:

```
DESTROY XSC
DESTROY S, P, SP
```

If a base table is destroyed, any indexes defined on that table via an INDEX operation are automatically destroyed also. Any views defined on the table are flagged as no longer valid.

MODIFY

The MODIFY operation is used to change the storage structure for a base table or index (in other words, to reorganize that table or index in storage). The general format is:

```
MODIFY name TO structure [ UNIQUE ] [ ON column-name
                                [ , column-name ] ... ]
```

where "name" identifies a base table or an index, and "structure" is one of the following:

BTREE	CBTREE
HASH	CHASH
ISAM	CISAM
HEAP	CHEAP
HEAPSORT	CHEAPSORT

Explanation: The optional "C" prefix—as in, e.g., CBTREE—specifies that the data is to be compressed on the disk. BTREE, HASH, and HEAP are self-explanatory. (Note: HASH uses a standard system-supplied division/remainder algorithm.) ISAM ("indexed sequential access method") is somewhat similar to BTREE, but is a less dynamic structure (in practice BTREE is usually—but not invariably—preferable to ISAM). Finally, HEAPSORT causes the records to be sorted into a specified order at the time of the MODIFY; however, the sort order is not maintained in the face of subsequent updates (e.g., new records are still added wherever there happens to be room, as in HEAP).

Examples:

1. `MODIFY P TO CHEAP`

2. `MODIFY SP TO HEAPSORT ON S#:A, P#:D`

The records of table SP are physically sorted into descending P# order within ascending S# order. If neither ":A" nor ":D" is specified, ":A" is assumed by default; these specifications can be used only with HEAPSORT (and CHEAPSORT). UNIQUE cannot be specified for HEAPSORT (or CHEAPSORT), nor for HEAP (or CHEAP).

3. `MODIFY S TO BTREE UNIQUE ON S#`

Table S is sorted into S# order and a B-tree is built on that field. No two records of S are allowed to have the same S# value (the MODIFY will fail—i.e., the storage structure will remain unchanged—if that constraint is already violated by existing records).

4. `MODIFY SP TO CHASH UNIQUE ON S#, P#`

Table SP is reorganized into a hash-addressed structure, compressed, with hash access via values of the composite field (S#,P#). No two records of SP are allowed to have the same value for that composite field (the MODIFY will fail if that constraint is already violated by existing records).

Note: The MODIFY operation removes duplicate records from the table *in all cases* (i.e., regardless of whether UNIQUE is specified), except for HEAP and CHEAP. Furthermore, duplicate records can be introduced only into tables stored as HEAP or HEAPSORT (or CHEAP or CHEAPSORT). Tables in INGRES thus always satisfy a "no duplicate records" constraint, except for the various flavors of "heap" (which are best regarded as anomalous anyway, since most tables will usually have one of the other structures in practice). The optional UNIQUE specification represents a *stronger* constraint; in effect, it says that records are to be unique, not just on the combination of all of their fields, but rather on the combination of some subset of their fields.

Two further points:

1. MODIFY also includes certain additional parameters, not discussed here, that have to do with such things as the amount of free space to be left in each page on the disk. Of course, INGRES automatically applies appropriate default values if such parameters are left unspecified.

2. MODIFY automatically destroys any indexes on the table being modified. Thus it may be necessary to follow the MODIFY by an appropriate set of INDEX operations.

10.3 DATA MANIPULATION: RETRIEVAL OPERATIONS

The QUEL "data manipulation language" (DML) statements are listed below, with SQL analogs shown for reference:

```
RETRIEVE    -    SELECT
REPLACE     -    UPDATE
DELETE      -    DELETE
APPEND      -    INSERT
```

We illustrate these statements (in this section and the next) by means of a series of examples. In doing so, we pay particular attention to those aspects of QUEL that are significantly different from their SQL counterpart (or that do not have such a counterpart). Also, we give the number of the equivalent SQL example from Chapter 6, where applicable.

First, RETRIEVE. The general form of RETRIEVE is as follows:

```
    RETRIEVE [ UNIQUE ] ( target-list )
[ WHERE     predicate ]
[ SORT BY   field(s) ]
```

where "target-list" is basically a list of *assignments* of the form

```
[ unqualified-name = ] expression
```

separated by commas.[3] The "unqualified-name =" portion of such an assignment can be omitted only if the result of evaluating "expression" has an obvious inherited name (see Example 10.3.3 below). UNIQUE is the QUEL analog of DISTINCT in SQL; likewise, SORT BY is the QUEL analog of ORDER BY in SQL, except that SORT BY implies UNIQUE.

---

3.   The form *R*.ALL is also permitted as a shorthand for the list *R.F1, R.F2, ..., R.Fn*, where *F1, F2, ..., Fn* are all the fields of relation *R* (analogous to "SELECT *" in SQL).

Simple Retrievals and Joins

10.3.1 Qualified retrieval. Get supplier number and status for suppliers in Paris with status > 20. (Extended version of Example 6.2.4)

```
RETRIEVE ( S.S#, S.STATUS )
WHERE      S.CITY = "Paris"
AND        S.STATUS > 20
```

Notice that all references to fields in the database (in the target list and in the WHERE clause) must be appropriately qualified; in contrast to SQL, there is no FROM clause from which to derive any implicit qualification. The predicate in the WHERE clause may include the comparison operators =, !=(not equal), >, >=, <, and <=; the Boolean operators AND, OR, and NOT; and parentheses to indicate a desired order of evaluation.

10.3.2 Saving the result of a query. Get supplier number and status for suppliers in Paris with status > 20 (as in Example 10.3.1), and save the result in table TEMP.

```
RETRIEVE INTO TEMP ( S.S#, S.STATUS )
WHERE      S.CITY = "Paris"
AND        S.STATUS > 20
```

INGRES automatically creates a new table TEMP, with columns S# and STATUS, and saves the result of the query in that table. Table TEMP must not exist prior to execution of the RETRIEVE.

10.3.3 Retrieval of expressions. For all parts, get the part number and the weight of that part in grams (part weights are given in table P in pounds). (Example 6.2.2)

```
RETRIEVE ( P.P#, EXPLANATION = "Weight in grams =",
                 GMWT = P.WEIGHT * 454 )
SORT BY GMWT, P#:D
```

Result:

```
--  ------------------   ----
P#  EXPLANATION          GMWT
--  ------------------   ----
P5  Weight in grams =    5448
P1  Weight in grams =    5448
P4  Weight in grams =    6356
P3  Weight in grams =    7718
P2  Weight in grams =    7718
P6  Weight in grams =    8626
```

It is necessary to introduce names for the second and third columns of the result here, because there are no obvious names they can inherit. Notice that such introduced names can then be referenced in the SORT BY clause (but not in the WHERE clause, unfortunately).

The expressions in the target list can involve, not only field names and constants and the usual operators ($+$, $-$, $*$, $/$, parentheses), but also exponentiation, string concatenation, and a wide array of scalar built-in functions—e.g., SIN, COS, SQRT, INTERVAL (for date arithmetic), and so on. They can also involve aggregate operators such as SUM and AVG (see later).

10.3.4 Partial-match retrieval.   Get all parts whose names begin with the letter C. (Example 6.5.1)

```
RETRIEVE ( P.ALL )
WHERE     P.PNAME = "C*"
```

The following special characters can be used to specify partial match retrieval in a string comparison:[4]

- The character "?" matches any single character.
- The character "*" matches any sequence of zero or more characters.
- The string "[xyz]" (where xyz is any set of characters) matches any character in xyz.

10.3.5 Simple equijoin.   Get all combinations of supplier and part information such that the supplier and part in question are located in the same city. (Example 6.3.1)

```
RETRIEVE ( S.ALL, P.ALL )
WHERE     S.CITY = P.CITY
```

10.3.6 Join of three tables.   Get all pairs of city names such that a supplier located in the first city supplies a part stored in the second city. (Example 6.3.5)

```
RETRIEVE UNIQUE ( S.CITY, P.CITY )
WHERE     S.S# = SP.S#
AND       SP.P# = P.P#
```

Notice that this query references a table (SP) in the WHERE clause that is not mentioned in the target list.

10.3.7 Joining a table with itself.   Get all pairs of supplier numbers such that the two suppliers concerned are colocated. (Example 6.3.6)

```
RANGE OF FIRST IS S
RANGE OF SECOND IS S

RETRIEVE ( FIRST.S#, SECOND.S# )
WHERE     FIRST.CITY = SECOND.CITY
AND       FIRST.S#   < SECOND.S#
```

The two RANGE statements define FIRST and SECOND as *range variables*, each "ranging over" table S. QUEL's range variables are precisely analogous to

---

4.   A special character can be made to behave like an ordinary character—i.e., the special interpretation can be disabled—by preceding it by a backslash character.

what we called "aliases" in Chapter 6. As a matter of fact, QUEL *always* requires queries to be formulated in terms of range variables. If no such variables are specified explicitly, then QUEL assumes the existence of *implicit* variables with the same name(s) as the corresponding table(s). For example, the query

```
RETRIEVE ( S.ALL )
```

is treated by QUEL as if it had been expressed as follows:

```
RANGE OF S IS S
RETRIEVE ( S.ALL )
```

In the second of these two formulations, the symbol "S" in the expression "S.ALL" really means *range variable* S, not *table* S.

Aggregates and Aggregate Functions

Like SQL, QUEL provides the operators COUNT, SUM, etc., to operate on the collection of values in some column of some table. QUEL refers to such operators as *aggregates*. The available aggregates include COUNT, SUM, AVG, MAX, and MIN (as in SQL); COUNTU, SUMU, and AVGU, where the "U" stands for "unique" (e.g., QUEL "SUMU" is analogous to SQL "SUM (DISTINCT ...)"); and ANY (analogous to SQL "EXISTS"; we defer discussion of ANY until Example 10.3.16). The general syntax for an aggregate reference is as follows:

```
aggregate ( expression [ WHERE predicate ] )
```

Since an aggregate returns a single scalar value, it can appear in the target list or in the WHERE clause wherever a constant is allowed.

10.3.8 Aggregate in the target list.   Get the total number of suppliers. (Example 6.4.1)

```
RETRIEVE ( X = COUNT ( S.S# ) )
```

Note that a name (here X) must be supplied for the result.

10.3.9 Aggregate in the target list.   Get the total number of suppliers currently supplying parts. (Example 6.4.2)

```
RETRIEVE ( Y = COUNTU ( SP.S# ) )
```

10.3.10 Aggregate in the target list.   Get the total quantity of part P2 supplied. (Example 6.4.4)

```
RETRIEVE ( Z = SUM ( SP.QTY WHERE SP.P# = "P2" ) )
```

10.3.11 Aggregate in the WHERE clause.   Get supplier numbers for suppliers with status value less than the current maximum status value in the S table. (Example 6.5.6)

```
RETRIEVE ( S.S# )
WHERE     S.STATUS < MAX ( S.STATUS )
```

Note that there are two different "S"'s here (rather as in the corresponding SQL formulation). The following version makes the point explicit:

```
RANGE OF SX IS S, SY IS S

RETRIEVE ( SX.S# )
WHERE     SX.STATUS < MAX ( SY.STATUS )
```

In general, any range variables (implicit or explicit) appearing inside the argument to an aggregate are *purely local to that aggregate;* they are distinct from any range variable that may happen to have the same name but appears outside the aggregate—*unless* they are mentioned in a BY clause within the aggregate argument (see the next example).

10.3.12 Use of the BY clause.   For each part supplied, get the part number and the total shipment quantity for that part. (Example 6.4.5)

```
RETRIEVE ( SP.P#, X = SUM ( SP.QTY BY SP.P# ) )
```

The action of the BY clause is somewhat analogous to that of the GROUP BY clause in SQL—but only somewhat. We explain the example as follows. For simplicity we assume that the BY clause names only a single field; the generalization to multiple fields is straightforward.[5]

First, an aggregate operator whose argument includes a BY clause is known in QUEL as an aggregate *function.* The value of an aggregate function is not just a single scalar, but rather an entire set of values, one for each distinct value of the field identified in the BY clause. A query involving an aggregate function is (conceptually) evaluated in two stages.

1. First, the aggregate function itself is evaluated, to yield an intermediate result table (AF, say). In the example, table AF looks like this:

```
         --   ----
AF   by    agg
         --   ----
         P1    600
         P2   1000
         P3    400
         P4    500
         P5    500
         P6    100
```

Table AF contains two columns, one ("agg") giving the aggregated values (the sums, in the case at hand) and the other ("by") giving the corresponding values of the BY field.

---

5.   Like GROUP BY, BY permits the specification of multiple fields. Unlike GROUP BY, it also permits specifications of the form "BY R.ALL."

2. Now the original query is altered (again conceptually) to read as follows:

```
RETRIEVE UNIQUE ( SP.P#, X = AF.agg )
WHERE       SP.P# = AF.by
```

That is, a) a UNIQUE specification is inserted, unless one is already present; b) the aggregate function in the target list is replaced by a reference to the "aggregate values" column in table AF; and c) a WHERE clause is appended to the query, specifying an equality join condition between the BY field specified in the original query and the "by-values" column in table AF. The altered query is then evaluated to yield the desired overall result.

Note that the effect of appending the join condition to the query is to make range variables that are mentioned in a BY clause known outside the aggregate function. In other words, such variables are *not* purely local to the aggregate function. Any other range variables referenced inside the aggregate function are, however, still purely local.

10.3.13 Aggregate function in the WHERE clause.   Get part numbers for all parts supplied by more than one supplier. (Example 6.4.6)

```
RETRIEVE ( SP.P# )
WHERE       COUNT ( SP.S# BY SP.P# ) > 1
```

Note that this query required a HAVING clause in SQL. In QUEL, by contrast, all "HAVING-type" conditions are expressed by means of a conventional WHERE clause that includes an aggregate function (as in the example).

10.3.14 Nested aggregate functions.   Get the average of the total quantities in which each part is supplied.

```
RETRIEVE ( X = AVG ( SUM ( SP.QTY BY SP.P# ) ) )
```

This query cannot be expressed in a single SQL statement (SQL built-in functions cannot be nested).

10.3.15 Aggregate functions in an arithmetic expression.   For each supplier, get the supplier number and a count of the parts not supplied by that supplier.

```
RETRIEVE ( S.S#, X = COUNT ( P.P# ) -
                     COUNT ( SP.P# BY S.S#
                             WHERE SP.S# = S.S# ) )
```

The first COUNT returns the total number of parts, the second returns the number supplied by this supplier. As an aside, we remark that the field we choose to do the counting on in a COUNT reference is arbitrary; any field of the relevant table would suffice. QUEL does not currently permit a COUNT reference of the form "COUNT (R.ALL ...)."

Note: This is another example of a query that cannot be expressed in a single statement in SQL. (Why not?)

Quantification

10.3.16 Query involving existential quantification. Get supplier names for suppliers who supply part P2. (Example 6.5.7, also Example 6.5.3)

```
RETRIEVE ( S.SNAME )
WHERE      S.S# = SP.S#
AND        SP.P# = "P2"
```

Any range variable mentioned in the WHERE clause and not in the target list is considered to be *implicitly* quantified by the existential quantifier (EXISTS in SQL). Thus the query above can be paraphrased:

"Get supplier names such that there exists a shipment record with the same supplier number and with part number P2."

The aggregate function ANY can be used if desired to make the quantification more explicit:

```
RETRIEVE ( S.SNAME )
WHERE      ANY ( SP.S# BY S.S#
                 WHERE S.S# = SP.S#
                 AND   SP.P# = "P2" ) = 1
```

ANY returns the value 0 if its argument set is empty, the value 1 otherwise.[6,7] In practice there is little point in using the "ANY (...) = 1" form, since such a query can always be expressed more simply without using ANY at all, as the example above illustrates. However, the "ANY (...) = 0" form *is* sometimes necessary, since it is QUEL's analog of the *negated* form NOT EXISTS in SQL. See Examples 10.3.17–10.3.18 below.

10.3.17 Query using ANY (...) = 0. Get supplier names for suppliers who do not supply part P2. (Example 6.5.8)

```
RETRIEVE ( S.SNAME )
WHERE      ANY ( SP.S# BY S.S#
                 WHERE S.S# = SP.S#
                 AND   SP.P# = "P2" ) = 0
```

Note that the following formulation does *not* produce the desired result. (Why not? What does it produce?)

```
RETRIEVE ( S.SNAME )
WHERE      S.S# = SP.S#
AND        SP.P# != "P2"
```

---

6. The field over which we choose to compute the ANY function (field SP.S#, in the example) is arbitrary; any field of the relevant table would suffice. QUEL does not currently permit an ANY reference of the form "ANY (R.ALL ...)."

7. Note that the predicates ANY(...) = 0 and COUNT(...) = 0 are functionally identical. However, the ANY form is preferable, in that it is a more "natural" formulation (it is closer to the natural language expression "there does not exist any"). As a result, it also has the potential for more efficient evaluation.

10.3.18 Query using ANY (...) = 0.   Get supplier names for suppliers who supply all parts. (Example 6.5.9)

```
RETRIEVE ( S.SNAME )
WHERE   ANY ( P.P# BY S.S#
                  WHERE ANY ( SP.P# BY S.S#, P.P#
                              WHERE S.S# = SP.S#
                              AND   SP.P# = P.P# ) = 0 ) = 0
```

Querying the Catalog

INGRES, like DB2, has a system catalog that contains information concerning tables, columns, indexes, and so on. Users (again as in DB2) can query that catalog using the retrieval operator of their regular query language, in this case the RETRIEVE statement of QUEL. However, QUEL also provides a special HELP statement, which may be regarded as a convenient shorthand for certain predefined catalog RETRIEVE operations (except that HELP also displays its output in a slightly more readable format than the conventional RETRIEVE operation does). For example, the operation

```
HELP SP
```

displays information regarding table SP (its columns and their data types, its storage structure, etc.). Likewise, the operation

```
HELP
```

(with no operand) displays a list of all user tables (as opposed to system tables) in the database.

10.4   DATA MANIPULATION: UPDATE OPERATIONS

QUEL includes three update operations—REPLACE, DELETE, and APPEND—with syntax as follows:

```
REPLACE range-variable ( target-list ) [ WHERE predicate ]

DELETE range-variable [ WHERE predicate ]

APPEND TO table ( target-list ) [ WHERE predicate ]
```

10.4.1 Single-record REPLACE.   Change the color of part P2 to yellow and increase its weight by 5. (Modified version of Example 6.6.1)

```
REPLACE P ( COLOR = "Yellow", WEIGHT = P.WEIGHT + 5 )
WHERE   P.P# = "P2"
```

Note carefully that field names on the left of the equals signs must *not* be explicitly qualified. (They may be regarded as being implicitly qualified by the range variable name that appears following the keyword REPLACE.)

10.4.2 Multiple-record REPLACE.   Double the status of all suppliers in London. (Example 6.6.2)

```
REPLACE S ( STATUS = 2 * S.STATUS )
WHERE    S.CITY = "London"
```

10.4.3 REPLACE referring to another table. Set the shipment quantity to zero for all suppliers in London. (Example 6.6.3)

```
REPLACE SP ( QTY = 0 )
WHERE    SP.S# = S.S#
AND      S.CITY = "London"
```

10.4.4 Multiple-table REPLACE.   Change the supplier number for supplier S2 to S9. (Example 6.6.4)

```
REPLACE S ( S# = "S9" ) WHERE S.S# = "S2"

REPLACE SP ( S# = "S9" ) WHERE SP.S# = "S2"
```

10.4.5 Updating one table from another.   Suppose table SP has an additional field, TOTWT, representing total shipment weight. Compute the values for this field by multiplying the quantity for each shipment by the corresponding part weight.

```
REPLACE SP ( TOTWT = SP.QTY * P.WEIGHT )
WHERE    SP.P# = P.P#
```

This update cannot be done in SQL in a single statement (why not?).

10.4.6 Single-record DELETE.   Delete supplier S1. (Example 6.6.5)

```
DELETE S WHERE S.S# = "S1"
```

10.4.7 Multiple-record DELETE.   Delete all suppliers in Madrid. (Example 6.6.6)

```
DELETE S WHERE S.CITY = "Madrid"
```

10.4.8 Single-record APPEND.   Add part P7 (city Athens, weight 24, name and color at present unknown) to table P. (Example 6.6.9)

```
APPEND TO P ( P# = "P7", CITY = "Athens", WEIGHT = 24 )
```

The name and color in the new record will be set to blank, since no other value has been explicitly specified. As with REPLACE, field names on the left of the equals signs in an APPEND target list must *not* be explicitly qualified. (They may be regarded as being implicitly qualified by the table name that appears following the keyword APPEND.)

10.4.9 Multiple-record APPEND.   Suppose table NEWSP has the same fields (S#, P#, and QTY) as table SP. Copy all records of NEWSP for which the quantity is greater than 1000 into table SP.

```
APPEND TO SP ( S#  = NEWSP.S#,
               P#  = NEWSP.P#,
               QTY = NEWSP.QTY )
WHERE   NEWSP.QTY > 1000
```

10.5 VIEWS

Views in INGRES are fairly similar to the corresponding notion in DB2. Here is an example of a QUEL view definition:

```
DEFINE VIEW LONSUPPS
     ( S#     = S.S#,
       SNAME  = S.SNAME,
       STATUS = S.STATUS
       CITY   = S.CITY )
       WHERE   S.CITY = "London"
```

The general syntax is:

```
DEFINE VIEW view-name ( target-list ) [ WHERE predicate ]
```

Here is an example of a RETRIEVE operation against LONSUPPS:

```
RANGE OF LS IS LONSUPPS

RETRIEVE ( LS.ALL )
WHERE      LS.STATUS < 25
```

The process of converting such a retrieval into an equivalent retrieval on the underlying base table(s) is known in INGRES as *query modification* [10.4]. The converted form looks like this:

```
RANGE OF LS IS S

RETRIEVE ( S# = LS.S#, SNAME = LS.SNAME,
           STATUS = LS.STATUS, CITY = LS.CITY )
WHERE      LS.STATUS < 25
AND        LS.CITY = "London"
```

The converted form is then executed in the usual way, of course. In a similar manner, the update operation

```
RANGE OF LS IS LONSUPPS

REPLACE LS ( STATUS = LS.STATUS + 10 )
WHERE      LS.STATUS < 15
```

is converted by the query modification process into

```
RANGE OF LS IS S

REPLACE LS ( STATUS = LS.STATUS + 10 )
WHERE      LS.STATUS < 15
AND        LS.CITY = "London"
```

Similarly for APPEND and DELETE operations.

Views are dropped by the same DESTROY operation that is used to drop base tables and indexes. For example:

```
DESTROY LONSUPPS
```

The status of INGRES with respect to DML operations on views is similar but not identical to that of DB2. As far as retrieval operations are concerned, INGRES is definitely superior, because the syntax of QUEL is more systematic than that of SQL; thus, for example, many view retrievals that would fail in SQL [4.4] work perfectly well in QUEL. However, when it comes to update operations, INGRES is just as ad hoc—though in different ways—as DB2 is.

10.6 EMBEDDED QUEL

An "embedded QUEL" (EQUEL) preprocessor is available for the languages COBOL, FORTRAN, BASIC, Pascal, and C. Here is an example of an EQUEL statement:

```
##    REPLACE S ( STATUS = X )
##    WHERE    S.S# = Y
```

The ## characters are required in columns 1 and 2 for all source lines that are to be processed by the EQUEL preprocessor, including declarations of host language variables (such as X and Y in the example). For instance, if the REPLACE above were part of a FORTRAN program, then the corresponding declarative statements might look as follows:

```
##    DECLARE

##    INTEGER * 2     X
##    CHARACTER * 5   Y
```

The DECLARE statement is needed to warn the preprocessor that a block of declarations is to follow.

Host language variables can be used in EQUEL statements for any or all of the following:

- Target variables for RETRIEVE
- Range variable names
- Table and field names
- Field values and constants within expressions and predicates
- Complete expressions and predicates

For the first category, of course, host variables *must* be used, and they can be of any appropriate data type. For the remaining categories, the host variables must be of type character string.

The foregoing list of possibilities is considerably more extensive than the corresponding list for embedded SQL. Observe in particular that host language variables can be used to supply entire expressions and predicates. For example:

```
##    CHARACTER * 25    PRED

      PRED = ' S.CITY = "London" '

##    REPLACE S ( STATUS = 2 * S.STATUS )
##    WHERE    PRED
```

Of course, the fact that EQUEL is more flexible than embedded SQL in this regard is a consequence of the fact that embedded SQL is compiled prior to execution, whereas EQUEL is not "compiled" until run time.

Feedback information after execution of any EQUEL statement can be obtained via the special EQUEL operation INQUIRE_EQUEL. For example:

```
##   INQUIRE_EQUEL ( Z = ERRORNO )
```

The "error number" for the most recently executed EQUEL statement is returned in host variable Z. An error number of zero indicates successful execution. Another example:

```
##   INQUIRE_EQUEL ( N = ROWCOUNT )
```

The number of rows retrieved (or replaced or ...) in the most recently executed EQUEL statement is returned in host variable N.

In contrast to embedded SQL, EQUEL has no notion of cursors. Instead, the problem of multiple-record retrieval is handled by means of a construct called a *RETRIEVE loop*. For example (FORTRAN again):

```
##   DECLARE

##   CHARACTER * 5   X
##   INTEGER * 4     Y
##   CHARACTER * 6   Z

     Z = 'P5'

##   RETRIEVE ( X = SP.S#, Y = SP.QTY )
##   WHERE     SP.P# = Z
##   {
         process X and Y
##   }
```

It is assumed that all RETRIEVE operations are potentially multiple-record; there is no analog of the embedded SQL "singleton SELECT." In the example, the RETRIEVE is executed using the current value of the host variable Z ('P5', in the example). The code between the braces ("process X and Y") is then executed once for each record in the retrieved set. That code may not include any other database operations. When all records have been processed, control goes to the statement following the closing brace. The statement

```
##   ENDRETRIEVE
```

can be used to exit from the RETRIEVE loop "early," i.e., to force control to go the statement following the closing brace before all retrieved records have been processed.

It may be helpful to compare the foregoing ideas with the SQL cursor mechanism. The EQUEL RETRIEVE acts like a combination of the SQL cursor declaration and OPEN; exit from the loop (either explicitly, via ENDRETRIEVE, or implicitly, after all records have been processed) is analogous to CLOSE. FETCH is completely implicit; the target variables are specified in the "OPEN" (i.e., RE-TRIEVE), not in a separate FETCH statement. There is no analog of the SQL UPDATE/DELETE CURRENT operations; nor can any other database operation be executed from within the RETRIEVE loop. Note too that EQUEL imposes some *syntactic* constraints on the structure of the program. Specifically, the loop source code *must* immediately follow the RETRIEVE statement, and the statement to be executed first on exit from the loop *must* be the one immediately following the loop source code.

We should not conclude this brief look at EQUEL without some discussion of the REPEAT option. Normally, each EQUEL statement is processed by the INGRES optimizer at the time it is encountered during flow of control through the executing program. Thus, if the same statement is executed repeatedly (e.g., if it is inside a program loop), it will be optimized repeatedly also—clearly an undesirable state of affairs. The REPEAT option is intended to alleviate this problem. Consider the following example:

```
##   REPEAT REPLACE S ( STATUS = @X )
##              WHERE S.S# = @Y
```

The first time this statement is executed, it is optimized in the usual way. In addition, the REPEAT option causes the optimizer to *save the resulting query plan*. If the statement is subsequently encountered again, INGRES will then reuse the saved plan instead of generating a new one. In the example, host variables X and Y are considered to be *parameters* (indicated by the prefix "@" symbols); each time the statement is encountered, it will be executed using the current values of those variables. Parameters are allowed wherever QUEL permits constants to appear.

We may characterize the foregoing scheme, loosely, as "compile on first use." The optimization is still being done at run time, not prior to run time as in DB2, but it is done only once per program execution instead of once per *statement* execution.

In conclusion, a few miscellaneous points:

■ An EQUEL program can process only one INGRES database at a time. The EQUEL statement

```
##   INGRES database-name
```

must be executed to "open" the required database before it can be used. Likewise, the EQUEL statement

```
##   EXIT
```

must be used to "close" the database after it is finished with. (The program can then go on to open another database, if it chooses.)

■ Analogs of the SQL COMMIT and ROLLBACK operations are provided—details beyond the scope of this chapter.

- Embedded SQL includes a special set of facilities ("dynamic SQL") to assist in the writing of on-line applications (see Section 9.5). EQUEL has comparatively little need of such facilities, since EQUEL is *always* "dynamic" (in the sense that the various components of an EQUEL statement can all be represented by host variables whose values can change with time). The only difficulty occurs with target lists. For example, given only the facilities sketched in this section so far, there is no way to construct a RETRIEVE statement for which the number of fields retrieved per record is not known until run time. EQUEL therefore provides a special function, the PARAM function, for dealing with exactly this problem (i.e., PARAM supports the dynamic construction of target lists). For details, the reader is referred to the INGRES documentation [10.1].

- Finally, EQUEL also provides an extensive set of facilities known as EQUEL/ FORMS to assist in the construction of the screen and dialog management portions of an on-line application. Again, for details the reader is referred to the INGRES documentation.

EXERCISES

10.1 Write an appropriate set of QUEL definitional statements for the suppliers-parts-projects database.

10.2 Give QUEL solutions to Exercises 6.1–6.48 (where possible or appropriate).

10.3 Give EQUEL solutions to Exercises 9.1 and 9.3.

REFERENCES AND BIBLIOGRAPHY

10.1 Information regarding Commercial INGRES is available from Relational Technology Inc., 1080 Marina Village Parkway, Alameda, CA 94501.

10.2 G. D. Held, M. R. Stonebraker, and E. Wong. "INGRES—A Relational Data Base System." *Proc. NCC* **44** (May 1975).

  The first paper to describe University INGRES. Includes a preliminary definition of QUEL.

10.3 G. D. Held and M. R. Stonebraker. "Storage Structures and Access Methods in the Relational Data Base Management System INGRES." *Proc. ACM Pacific* (April 1975).

10.4 M. R. Stonebraker. "Implementation of Integrity Constraints and Views by Query Modification." *Proc. ACM SIGMOD International Conference on Management of Data* (May 1975).

10.5 Eric Allman, Michael Stonebraker, and Gerald Held. "Embedding a Relational Data Sublanguage in a General Purpose Programming Language." *Proc. ACM SIGPLAN/SIGMOD Conference on Data: Abstraction, Definition, and Structure* (March 1976). Joint Issue: *ACM SIGPLAN Notices* **11**, Special Issue / *ACM SIGMOD Bulletin FDT* **8**, No. 2 (1976).

10.6 M. R. Stonebraker, E. Wong, P. Kreps, and G. D. Held. "The Design and Implementation of INGRES." *ACM TODS* **1**, No. 3 (September 1976).

A detailed overview of University INGRES.

10.7 P. Hawthorn and M. R. Stonebraker. "Performance Analysis of a Relational Data Base Management System." *Proc. 1979 ACM SIGMOD International Conference on Management of Data* (May 1979).

> This paper reports on the conclusions drawn from running a set of benchmark queries against University INGRES. Queries are divided into two categories, "data-intensive" and "overhead-intensive." The benchmarks show that the two categories have such widely differing characteristics that it may be difficult to build a single system that can handle both well. However, the paper also shows that significant performance improvements are achievable in both cases by means of "some combination of" extended memory, read-ahead techniques (sometimes called *sequential prefetch*), and multiple processors.

10.8 M. R. Stonebraker. "Retrospection on a Data Base System." *ACM TODS* **5**, No. 2 (June 1980).

> An account of the history of the University INGRES project (to January 1979). The emphasis is on mistakes and lessons learned, rather than on successes.

10.9 Eric Allman and Michael Stonebraker. "Observations on the Evolution of a Software System." In [10.11].

10.10 Michael Stonebraker et al. "Performance Enhancements to a Relational Database System." *ACM TODS* **8**, No. 2 (June 1983).

> Analyzes the effects of four possible performance-motivated changes to University INGRES (or to its environment): dynamically compiling QUEL requests, implementing frequently executed INGRES routines in microcode, replacing the UNIX file system by a specially tailored (INGRES-specific) system, and replacing UNIX entirely by a special-purpose operating system. (The term "dynamic compilation" means compilation at run time. The idea is that, even though optimization is still done at run time instead of at some prior time, the optimizer should nevertheless produce compiled code instead of acting as a pure interpreter.) Benchmark experiments indicate that dynamic compilation and using a specially tailored file system would both be very beneficial, but that the other two changes would be of only limited usefulness. Note that Commercial INGRES does in fact use a form of dynamic compilation.

10.11 Michael Stonebraker (ed.). *The INGRES Papers: The Anatomy of a Relational Database Management System*. Addison-Wesley (1985).

ANSWERS TO SELECTED EXERCISES

```
10.1 CREATE S ( S#      = TEXT(5),
                SNAME   = TEXT(20),
                STATUS  = I2,
                CITY    = TEXT(15) )

     CREATE P ( P#      = TEXT(6),
                PNAME   = TEXT(20),
```

```
                COLOR   = TEXT(6),
                WEIGHT  = I2,
                CITY    = TEXT(15)  )

 CREATE J ( J#       = TEXT(4),
            JNAME    = TEXT(10),
            CITY     = TEXT(15)  )

 CREATE SPJ ( S#     = TEXT(5),
              P#     = TEXT(6),
              J#     = TEXT(4),
              QTY    = I4 )

MODIFY S TO BTREE UNIQUE ON S#

MODIFY P TO BTREE UNIQUE ON P#

MODIFY J TO BTREE UNIQUE ON J#

MODIFY SPJ TO BTREE UNIQUE ON S#, P#, J#
```

10.2 We have numbered the following solutions as 10.2.*n*, where *n* is the number of the original exercise in Chapter 6.

10.2.1 RETRIEVE (J.ALL)

10.2.2 RETRIEVE (J.ALL) WHERE J.CITY = "London"

10.2.3 RETRIEVE (SPJ.S#)
```
     WHERE    SPJ.J# = "J1"
     SORT BY  S#
```

10.2.4 RETRIEVE (SPJ.ALL)
```
     WHERE    SPJ.QTY >= 300
     AND      SPJ.QTY <= 750
```

10.2.5 RETRIEVE UNIQUE (P.COLOR, P.CITY)

10.2.6 RETRIEVE (S.S#, P.P#, J.J#)
```
     WHERE    S.CITY = P.CITY
     AND      P.CITY = J.CITY
     AND      J.CITY = S.CITY
```

10.2.7 RETRIEVE (S.S#, P.P#, J.J#)
```
     WHERE    S.CITY != P.CITY
     OR       P.CITY != J.CITY
     OR       J.CITY != S.CITY
```

10.2.8 RETRIEVE (S.S#, P.P#, J.J#)
```
     WHERE    S.CITY != P.CITY
     AND      P.CITY != J.CITY
     AND      J.CITY != S.CITY
```

```
10.2.9   RETRIEVE ( SPJ.P# )
         WHERE     SPJ.S# = S.S#
         AND       S.CITY = "London"

10.2.10  RETRIEVE ( SPJ.P# )
         WHERE     SPJ.S# = S.S# AND S.CITY = "London"
         AND       SPJ.J# = J.J# AND J.CITY = "London"

10.2.11  RETRIEVE ( S.CITY, J.CITY )
         WHERE     S.S# = SPJ.S# AND SPJ.J# = J.J#

10.2.12  RETRIEVE ( SPJ.P# )
         WHERE     SPJ.S# = S.S#
         AND       SPJ.J# = J.J#
         AND       S.CITY = J.CITY

10.2.13  RETRIEVE ( SPJ.J# )
         WHERE     SPJ.S# = S.S#
         AND       SPJ.J# = J.J#
         AND       S.CITY != J.CITY

10.2.14  RANGE OF SPJX IS SPJ

         RETRIEVE ( SPJ.P#, SPJX.P# )
         WHERE     SPJ.S# = SPJX.S#
         AND       SPJ.P# < SPJX.P#

10.2.15  RETRIEVE ( X = COUNTU ( SPJ.J# WHERE SPJ.S# = "S1" ) )

10.2.16  RETRIEVE ( Y = SUM ( SPJ.QTY WHERE SPJ.S# = "S1"
                                  AND    SPJ.P# = "P1" ) )

10.2.17  RETRIEVE ( SPJ.P#, SPJ.J#, Z = SUM ( SPJ.QTY BY
                                     SPJ.P#, SPJ.J# ) )

10.2.18  RETRIEVE ( SPJ.P# )
         WHERE     AVG ( SPJ.QTY BY SPJ.P#, SPJ.J# ) > 320
```

10.2.19 Not applicable.

```
10.2.20  RETRIEVE ( J.J#, J.CITY )
         WHERE     J.CITY = "?o*"

10.2.21  RETRIEVE ( J.JNAME )
         WHERE     J.J# = SPJ.J#
         AND       SPJ.S# = "S1"

10.2.22  RETRIEVE ( P.COLOR )
         WHERE     P.P# = SPJ.P#
         AND       SPJ.S# = "S1"

10.2.23  RETRIEVE ( SPJ.P# )
         WHERE     SPJ.J# = J.J#
         AND       J.CITY = "London"
```

10.2.24 RANGE OF SPJX IS SPJ

```
RETRIEVE ( SPJ.J# )
WHERE     SPJ.P# = SPJX.P#
AND       SPJX.S# = "S1"
```

10.2.25 RANGE OF SPJX IS SPJ, SPJY IS SPJ

```
RETRIEVE ( SPJ.S# )
WHERE     SPJ.P# = SPJX.P#
AND       SPJX.S# = SPJY.S#
AND       SPJY.P# = P.P#
AND       P.COLOR = "Red"
```

10.2.26 RANGE OF SX IS S

```
RETRIEVE ( S.S# )
WHERE     S.STATUS < SX.STATUS
AND       SX.S# = "S1"
```

10.2.27 RETRIEVE (J.J#)

```
WHERE     J.CITY = MIN ( J.CITY )
```

10.2.28 RETRIEVE (SPJ.J#)

```
WHERE     SPJ.P# = "P1"
AND       AVG ( SPJ.QTY BY SPJ.P#, SPJ.J# ) >
          MAX ( SPJ.QTY WHERE SPJ.J# = "J1" )
```

10.2.29 RETRIEVE (SPJ.S#)

```
WHERE     SPJ.P# = "P1"
AND       SPJ.QTY > AVG ( SPJ.QTY BY SPJ.P#, SPJ.J# )
```

10.2.30–31 Not applicable.

10.2.32 RETRIEVE (J.J#)

```
WHERE     ANY ( SPJ.S# BY J.J#
                WHERE SPJ.S# = S.S# AND S.CITY = "London"
                AND   SPJ.P# = P.P# AND P.COLOR = "Red"
                AND   SPJ.J# = J.J# ) = 0
```

10.2.33–36 Left as exercises for the reader.

10.2.37–40 Not applicable.

10.2.41 RETRIEVE INTO TEMP (S.CITY)

```
APPEND TO TEMP ( P.CITY )
APPEND TO TEMP ( J.CITY )
RETRIEVE ( TEMP.CITY ) SORT BY CITY
```

10.2.42 Not applicable.

10.2.43 REPLACE P (COLOR = "Orange") WHERE P.COLOR = "Red"

10.2.44 DELETE J WHERE COUNT (SPJ.S# BY J.J#

```
                        WHERE SPJ.J# = J.J# ) = 0
```

10.2.45 DELETE SPJ WHERE SPJ.J# = J.J# AND J.CITY = "Rome"

        DELETE J WHERE J.CITY = "Rome"

10.2.46 APPEND TO S (S# = "S10",
                      SNAME = "White",
                      CITY = "New York")

10.2.47 RETRIEVE INTO TEMP (SPJ.P#)
        WHERE   (SPJ.S# = S.S# AND S.CITY = "London")
        OR   (SPJ.J# = J.J# AND J.CITY = "London")

10.2.48 RETRIEVE INTO TEMP (J.J#)
        WHERE   J.CITY = "London"
        OR   (J.J# = SPJ.J# AND
                 SPJ.S# = S.S# AND
                 S.CITY = "London")

11
Relational
Data Structure

11.1 AN INTRODUCTORY EXAMPLE

In the next few chapters we will mostly be using formal relational terminology. Figure 11.1 shows some of the most important of those formal terms, using relation S from the suppliers-and-parts database by way of illustration. The terms in question are *domain*, *attribute*, *tuple*, *primary key*, and (of course) *relation* itself. We explain each one very informally here, then go on to give more formal definitions in subsequent sections.

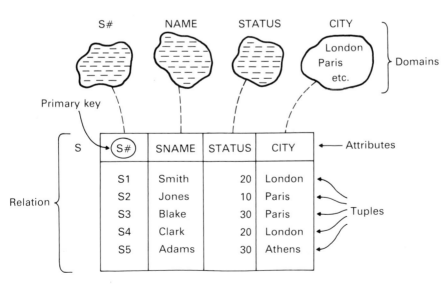

Fig. 11.1 The supplier relation S.

Briefly:

- A *relation* corresponds to what so far in this book we have generally been calling a table;

- A *tuple*[1] corresponds to a row of such a table and an *attribute* to a column;

- The *primary key* is a unique identifier for the table—that is, a column (or combination of columns) with the property that, at any given time, no two rows of the table contain the same value in that column (or combination of columns);

- Finally, a *domain* is a pool of values, from which one or more attributes (columns) draw their actual values. For example, the CITY domain is the set of all legal city names, and the set of values appearing in attribute CITY of relation S at any given time is a subset of that set. Likewise, the set of values appearing in attribute CITY of relation P at any given time is also a subset of that set.

To summarize:

Formal relational term	Informal equivalents
relation	table
tuple	row or record
attribute	column or field
primary key	unique identifier
domain	pool of legal values

Note 1: Please understand that these equivalences are all only approximate. We will explain the precise difference between (for example) a relation and a table in the sections that follow.

Note 2: The term "key" is one of the most overworked in the entire database field. In the relational model alone we find primary, candidate, alternate, and foreign keys. In other areas of database technology we meet index keys, hash keys, search keys, secondary keys, ordering keys, parent keys, child keys, and many other kinds of key. It therefore seems advisable to avoid use of the unqualified term "key" and always to state explicitly in any discussion of the subject just what kind of key is meant. However, if any one of that multiplicity of keys does deserve to be called just *the* key, it is clearly the primary key. The primary key is easily the most important one of all. In this book, therefore, if we ever use the term "key" without any further qualification, we will mean the primary key specifically.

Note 3: The notions of "domain" and "primary key" serve right away to illustrate the important point that *not all relational systems support all aspects of the relational model*. DB2, for example, does not support either of those concepts (indeed, nor do most other current systems). We will address this point in some detail in Chapter 15. Please understand, therefore, that prior to that chapter we are describ-

---

1. Usually pronounced to rhyme with "couple."

ing a theoretical model only; that model does not necessarily correspond in every last detail to the way in which any particular system actually works.

Now we proceed with our formal definitions.

11.2 DOMAINS

The smallest unit of data in the relational model is an individual data value, such as a supplier number or a shipment quantity. Such values are considered to be *atomic*—that is, they are nondecomposable so far as the model is concerned. A *domain* is a set of such values, all of the same type; for example, the domain of supplier numbers is the set of all possible supplier numbers, the domain of shipment quantities is the set of all integers greater than zero and less than 10,000 (say). Thus domains are *pools of values*, from which the actual values appearing in attributes are drawn. Note that, at any given time, there will typically be values included in a given domain that do not currently appear in any of the attributes that correspond to that domain. For example, the value S8 may well appear in the domain of supplier numbers—i.e., if it is a legal supplier number—but no supplier S8 actually appears in the relation S of Fig. 11.1.

Aside: Domains of atomic values are more accurately referred to as *simple* domains, to distinguish them from *composite* domains (to be discussed later). However, domains are invariably assumed to be simple unless explicitly stated to be otherwise, and we will follow that convention throughout this book. By the same token, attributes are also categorized as simple or composite (depending on whether the domain on which they are defined is simple or composite); attributes are likewise assumed to be simple unless explicitly stated to be otherwise.

Domains have a certain operational significance, as follows: If two attributes draw their values from the same domain, then comparisons—and hence joins, unions, etc.—involving those two attributes probably make sense, because they are comparing like with like. Conversely, if two attributes draw their values from different domains, then comparisons (etc.) involving those two attributes probably do not make sense. In SQL terms, for example, the query

```
SELECT P.*, SP.*
FROM   P, SP
WHERE  P.P# = SP.P# ;
```

probably does make sense. By contrast, the query

```
SELECT P.*, SP.*
FROM   P, SP
WHERE  P.WEIGHT = SP.QTY ;
```

probably does not, because, although it is true that WEIGHT and QTY values are both numbers, they are different *kinds* of numbers. (However, both of these SELECT statements are legal queries in SQL, because SQL has no notion of domains.)

Note that domains are primarily conceptual in nature. They may or may not be explicitly stored in the database as actual sets of values; in most cases, in fact, they probably will not be so stored. But they should be specified as part of the database definition (in a system that supports the concept at all—but most systems currently do not); and then each attribute definition should include a reference to the corresponding domain, so that the system is aware of which attributes are comparable with each other and which not. For example, Fig. 11.2 shows how the suppliers-and-parts database might be defined in a system that did support domains, using a hypothetical extended form of the SQL DDL ("pseudoDDL").

A given attribute may have the same name as the corresponding domain or a different name. Obviously it must have a different name if any ambiguity would otherwise result (in particular, if two attributes in the same relation are both based on the same domain; see the definition of "relation" in the next section, and note the phrase "not necessarily all distinct"). Generally speaking, however, it is a good idea if attributes do have the same name as the underlying domain wherever possible, or at least include the name of that domain as the trailing portion of their own name. We have followed this convention in the example of Fig. 11.2. We might additionally have followed another common convention and omitted the specifi-

```
CREATE DOMAIN S#      CHAR(5) ;
CREATE DOMAIN NAME    CHAR(20) ;
CREATE DOMAIN STATUS  SMALLINT ;
CREATE DOMAIN CITY    CHAR(15) ;
CREATE DOMAIN P#      CHAR(6) ;
CREATE DOMAIN COLOR   CHAR(6) ;
CREATE DOMAIN WEIGHT  SMALLINT ;
CREATE DOMAIN QTY     INTEGER ;

CREATE TABLE S
     ( S#      DOMAIN ( S# )      NOT NULL,
       SNAME   DOMAIN ( NAME ),
       STATUS  DOMAIN ( STATUS ),
       CITY    DOMAIN ( CITY ) ) ;

CREATE TABLE P
     ( P#      DOMAIN ( P# )      NOT NULL,
       PNAME   DOMAIN ( NAME ),
       COLOR   DOMAIN ( COLOR ),
       WEIGHT  DOMAIN ( WEIGHT ),
       CITY    DOMAIN ( CITY ) ) ;

CREATE TABLE SP
     ( S#      DOMAIN ( S# )      NOT NULL,
       P#      DOMAIN ( P# )      NOT NULL,
       QTY     DOMAIN ( QTY ) ) ;
```

Fig. 11.2 The suppliers-and-parts database definition (pseudoDDL, with domain support).

cation of the underlying domain altogether from the definition of any attribute that bears the same name as that domain. For example, the CREATE TABLE for table S might have been simplified to:

```
CREATE TABLE S
     ( S#      NOT NULL,
       SNAME DOMAIN ( NAME ),
       STATUS
       CITY  ) ;
```

Here is another example of the practical significance of domains. Consider the query:

"Which relations in the database contain any information pertaining to suppliers?"

This query can be phrased more precisely:

"Which relations in the database include an attribute that is defined on the supplier numbers domain?"

In a system that supports the domain concept, the query thus translates into a simple interrogation against the system catalog. In a system that does not support domains, it is obviously not possible to interrogate the catalog regarding domains per se—it is only possible to interrogate it regarding *attributes*. Only if the database designer has followed the naming convention recommended above—in other words, if he or she has in effect imposed the domain discipline on the database, without any support for that discipline from the system—will that latter interrogation serve the intended purpose. In fact, we tacitly assumed the existence of exactly such a self-imposed discipline in our first example of "querying the catalog" in Chapter 7 (Section 7.2). We remark that such a discipline has *not* been followed in DB2 in naming the attributes within the catalog itself; again, see Chapter 7.

Now we consider *composite* domains. A composite domain is defined as the Cartesian product of some collection of simple domains. For example, the composite domain DATE could be defined as the Cartesian product of the simple domains MONTH, DAY, and YEAR (in that order). If MONTH is the set (1,2, . . . ,12), DAY the set (1,2, . . . ,31), and YEAR the set (00,01, . . . ,99), then DATE would be the set

```
 1    1  00
 1    2  00
 1    3  00
 .    .  ..
 1   31  00
 2    1  00
 .    .  ..
 .    .  ..
12   31  99
```

(a total of 12 * 31 * 100 = 37,200 elements).[2] Any attribute defined on the DATE domain would in turn be a composite attribute, with component simple attributes defined on the MONTH, DAY, and YEAR domains, respectively. For example (pseudoDDL again):

```
CREATE DOMAIN MONTH CHAR(2) ;
CREATE DOMAIN DAY   CHAR(2) ;
CREATE DOMAIN YEAR  CHAR(2) ;
CREATE DOMAIN DATE ( MONTH, DAY, YEAR ) ;
CREATE TABLE EMPLOYEE
      ( EMP#   ....... NOT NULL,
        ENAME ....... ,
        HIREDATE DOMAIN ( DATE )
                 ( HIREMONTH, HIREDAY, HIREYEAR ),
        DEPT#  ....... ,
        SALARY ....... ) ;
```

DML statements should then be able to refer both to the composite attribute HIREDATE and to the simple attributes HIREMONTH, HIREDAY, and HIRE-YEAR. For example:

```
SELECT *
FROM   EMPLOYEE
WHERE  HIREYEAR < '84' ;

SELECT *
FROM   EMPLOYEE
WHERE  HIREDATE = '010184' ;
```

Note: It would of course be possible to support composite attributes without explicitly supporting domains at all. Unfortunately, however, few systems today, even those that do support domains, do in fact permit such composite attributes.

One further remark: The relational notion of domain is closely related to the programming language notion of *data type*, at least as that term is normally understood in modern programming languages. For example, the following is legal in the language Pascal:

```
type month = ( 1..12 ) ;
var  hiremonth: month ;
```

This example shows a "domain" (i.e., data type) called MONTH and an "attribute" (i.e., variable) defined on that domain called HIREMONTH. Note, however, that domains should generally be thought of as *semantic* data types. The point is, even SQL (for example) does support a very primitive notion of domain, since of course it does provide certain primitive data types (SMALLINT, FLOAT, etc.), but those primitive domains are basically syntactic in nature—they do not carry

---

2. Not all of those 37,200 elements are valid dates, of course. See Chapter 19 or Volume II for further discussion of this point.

much in the way of intended semantic interpretation with them, unlike (for example) the domain MONTH.

Finally, a caveat: It would be misleading to leave this subject without making the point that the domain concept is in fact considerably more complex than it might appear at first sight (which is perhaps why most systems currently do not support it). The point is, comparison operations (and purely intra-domain comparison operations at that) are by no means the end of the story:

- First, there may well be situations in which certain inter-domain comparison operations do make sense. In fact, the DATE examples shown earlier illustrate this point: Both of the two SELECT statements involve the comparison of a domain value (i.e., a typed value—a year value in the first case, a month/day/year value in the second) with a constant, whose domain is presumably just the primitive domain "character string."
- Second, it must obviously be possible (when appropriate) to combine values from different domains by means of a variety of arithmetic or other operators. For example, multiplying a VELOCITY value by a TIME value yields a DISTANCE value.

Full support for the domain concept would thus require all of the following (see McLeod [11.4] for further discussion):

1. The ability to specify the complete set of domains, D say, that apply to a given database. Note that D would have to be a closed set, in the sense that any element-level operation supported by the system (such as $-Z$ or $A + B$ or $X > Y$) would have to yield a value that belonged to some domain of the set D.

2. The ability to specify, for every domain Di belonging to the set D, exactly which unary operators apply to elements di from that domain Di.

3. The ability to specify, for every pair of domains Di and Dj (not necessarily distinct) belonging to the set D, exactly which binary operators apply to pairs of elements di and dj, where di belongs to Di and dj belongs to Dj.

4. The ability to specify, for every legal element-level expression, the domain of the result of evaluating that expression.

For simplicity, however, we will generally ignore these complications in what follows. In particular, we will normally assume that if two values are to be compared with each other, then they should be drawn from the same domain.

11.3 RELATIONS

We are now in a position to define the term "relation." A *relation* on domains $D1$, $D2$, ..., Dn (not necessarily all distinct) consists of a *heading* and a *body*.

- The *heading* consists of a fixed set of *attributes* $A1$, $A2$, . . . , An, such that each attribute Ai corresponds to exactly one of the underlying domains Di ($i = 1, 2, . . . , n$).

■ The *body* consists of a time-varying set of *tuples*,[3] where each tuple in turn consists of a set of attribute-value pairs $(Ai:vi)$ $(i = 1,2, \ldots ,n)$, one such pair for each attribute Ai in the heading. For any given attribute-value pair $(Ai:vi)$, vi is a value from the unique domain Di that is associated with the attribute Ai.

As an example, let us see how the supplier relation S of Fig. 11.1 measures up to this definition. The underlying domains are the domain of supplier numbers (S#), the domain of names (NAME), the domain of supplier status values (STATUS), and the domain of city names (CITY). The heading of S consists of the attributes S# (underlying domain S#), SNAME (domain NAME), STATUS (domain STATUS), and CITY (domain CITY). The body of S consists of a set of tuples (five tuples in Fig. 11.1, but this set varies with time as updates are made to the relation); and each tuple consists of a set of four attribute-value pairs, one such pair for each of the four attributes in the heading. For example, the tuple for supplier S1 consists of the pairs

```
( S#     : 'S1'      )
( SNAME  : 'Smith'   )
( STATUS : 20        )
( CITY   : 'London'  )
```

(though it is normal to elide the attribute names in informal contexts). And of course each attribute value does indeed come from the appropriate underlying domain; the value S1, for example, does come from the supplier number domain S#. So S is indeed a relation according to the definition.

Referring back to that definition, the value n (the number of attributes in the relation, or equivalently the number of underlying domains) is called the *degree* of the relation. A relation of degree one is called *unary*, a relation of degree two *binary*, a relation of degree three *ternary*, . . . , and a relation of degree n *n-ary*. In the suppliers-and-parts database, relations S, P, and SP have degrees 4, 5, and 3, respectively. Similarly, the number of tuples in the relation is called the *cardinality* of the relation; with the sample values shown in Fig. 4.1 (Chapter 4), the cardinalities of relations S, P, and SP are 5, 6, and 12, respectively. The cardinality of a relation changes with time, whereas the degree does not.[4]

Notice that the underlying domains of a relation are "not necessarily all distinct." Many examples have already been given (in Part 2 of this book) in which they are not all distinct; see, e.g., the result relation in Example 6.3.1 (Chapter 6), which includes two attributes both defined on the CITY domain. Another example (a repeat of the PART_STRUCTURE relation from the exercises in Chapter 9) is shown in Fig. 11.3.

---

3.   Or *n-tuples*. It is usual to drop the "*n-*" prefix.
4.   The SQL ALTER TABLE operation, which adds another column to a table, can be regarded, not as changing the degree of a relation from n to $n+1$, but rather as creating a new relation of degree $n+1$ from one of degree n.

```
                              --------  --------  ---
   PART_STRUCTURE    MAJOR_P#  MINOR_P#  QTY
                              --------  --------  ---
                        P1        P2        2
                        P1        P4        4
                        P5        P3        1
                        P3        P6        3
                        P6        P1        9
                        P5        P6        8
                        P2        P4        3
```

Fig. 11.3 The PART_STRUCTURE relation.

If the same domain is used more than once within some given relation, then (as already pointed out in Section 11.2) it is not possible to give all attributes of that relation the same name as the underlying domain. Figure 11.3 illustrates the recommended approach in such a situation: Generate distinct attribute names by prefixing a common domain name with distinct *role names* to indicate the distinct roles being played by that domain in each of its appearances. In fact, if we agreed always to follow this convention, and furthermore always to use some reserved distinguishing character (such as the underscore character) to separate the role name if present from the trailing domain name, then the specification "DOMAIN (domain name)" would never be explicitly needed in the definition of an attribute.

Properties of Relations

Relations possess certain important properties, all of them consequences of the definition of "relation" given at the start of this section. We first briefly state those properties, then discuss them in detail. The properties, four in number, are as follows. Within any given relation:

- There are no duplicate tuples;
- Tuples are unordered (top to bottom);
- Attributes are unordered (left to right);
- All attribute values are atomic.

1. *There are no duplicate tuples.*

This property follows from the fact that the body of the relation is a mathematical set (a set of tuples), and sets in mathematics by definition do not include duplicate elements.

An important corollary of this point is that *the primary key always exists.* Since tuples are unique, it follows that at least the combination of *all* attributes of the relation has the uniqueness property, so that at least the combination of all attributes can (if necessary) serve as the primary key. In practice, of course, it is usually not necessary to involve all of the attributes—some lesser combination is usually sufficient. Indeed, the primary key will be defined (in Chapter 12) not to include any attributes that are superfluous for the purpose of unique identification; thus, for example, the combination (S#,CITY), though "unique," is not the primary key for relation S, because CITY can be discarded without destroying that uniqueness. Note, however, that the primary key may still be composite, i.e., involve multiple simple attributes. Relation SP provides an example.

The importance of the primary key concept will be made clear in Chapter 12.

2. *Tuples are unordered (top to bottom).*

This property also follows from the fact that the body of the relation is a mathematical set. Sets in mathematics are not ordered. In Fig. 11.1, for example, the tuples of relation S could just as well have been shown in the reverse sequence—it would still have been the same relation. We defer to Chapter 15 our discussion of why such lack of ordering is desirable.

Aside: It is a slightly unfortunate consequence of the fact that relations are typically represented on paper in tabular form that that representation suggests something that is not actually true—namely, that the tuples do have a top-to-bottom ordering. It should be clearly understood that tables are a *concrete* representation of an *abstract* construct (namely, a relation); and certain aspects of that concrete representation are spurious, and do not correspond to anything in the underlying abstract construct. (See also the discussion of property number 3 below.) Despite this slight weakness, it is in fact a significant strongpoint of the relational model that its data structures do have a concrete representation that is so familiar and easy to understand. Such a representation greatly facilitates the process of reasoning about the effects of various operations on those structures. Indeed, it is a major contributor to the ease of use of relational systems.

3. *Attributes are unordered (left to right).*

This property follows from the fact that the heading of a relation is also defined as a set (a set of attributes). Strictly speaking, there is no such thing as (say) the *third* attribute of relation S; instead, there is a STATUS attribute, which is always referenced by name, never by position. As a result, the scope for errors and obscure programming is reduced. For example, there is—or should be —no way to subvert the system by somehow "flopping over" from one attribute into another. This situation contrasts with that found in many programming systems, where it often is possible to exploit the physical adjacency of logically discrete items (deliberately or otherwise) in a variety of subversive ways.

As indicated under the discussion of property number 2, this question of attribute ordering is another area where the concrete representation of a relation as a table suggests something that is not really true: The columns of a table obviously do have a left-to-right ordering, but the attributes of a relation do not.

Aside: This property (number 3) is not nearly so important in practice as numbers 1, 2, and 4. Indeed, relations are frequently defined in such a way that property number 3 does not hold. But we will continue to assume in this book that attributes are unordered, barring explicit statements to the contrary.

4. *All attribute values are atomic.*

This last property is more accurately stated: "All *simple* attribute values are atomic." It is, of course, a consequence of the fact that all underlying domains are simple in turn—i.e., contain atomic values only. (Even if composite attributes are involved, those composite attributes are of course nothing but simple concatenations of simple attributes.) We can state the property differently (and very informally) as follows: At every row-and-column position within the table, there always exists precisely one value, never a set of values. Or equivalently again: *Relations do not contain repeating groups*. A relation satisfying this condition is said to be *normalized*.[5]

The foregoing implies that *all* relations are normalized so far as the relational model is concerned, and indeed so they are. In fact, the unqualified term "relation" is always taken to mean "*normalized* relation" in the context of the relational model. The point is, however, that a *mathematical* relation need not be normalized. Consider relation BEFORE of Fig. 11.4. Mathematically speaking, BEFORE *is* a re-

BEFORE

S#	PQ	
	P#	QTY
S1	P1	300
	P2	200
	P3	400
	P4	200
	P5	100
	P6	100
S2	P1	300
	P2	400
S3	P2	200
S4	P2	200
	P4	300
	P5	400

AFTER

S#	P#	QTY
S1	P1	300
S1	P2	200
S1	P3	400
S1	P4	200
S1	P5	100
S1	P6	100
S2	P1	300
S2	P2	400
S3	P2	200
S4	P2	200
S4	P4	300
S4	P5	400

Fig. 11.4 An example of normalization.

5. Equivalently, such a relation is said to be in *first normal form*. Additional normal forms (second, third, . . .) are discussed in Chapter 17.

lation, of degree two, but it is a relation for which one of the underlying domains is *relation-valued*. Loosely speaking, a relation-valued domain is a domain whose elements are themselves relations.[6] In the example, attribute PQ is defined on a relation-valued domain, whose elements are binary relations; those binary relations in turn are defined on two simple domains, namely P# and QTY. The relational model does not permit relation-valued domains.

A relation like BEFORE must be replaced by some semantically equivalent but normalized relation. Relation AFTER in the figure is such a relation (in fact, of course, it is the familiar relation SP from the suppliers-and-parts database). The degree of relation AFTER is three, and the three underlying domains are all simple, as required.

A relation such as BEFORE is said to be *unnormalized*, and the process of converting BEFORE into AFTER is called *normalization*. As the example shows, it is a trivial matter to cast an unnormalized relation into an equivalent normalized form; however, we will have a lot more to say about the overall normalization process in Chapter 17.

The reason for insisting that all relations be normalized is as follows. Basically, a normalized relation is a *simpler structure*, mathematically speaking, than an unnormalized one. As a result, the corresponding operators are simpler too, and there are fewer of them. For example, consider the following two transactions:

T1. Create a new shipment for supplier S5, part P5, quantity 500.

T2. Create a new shipment for supplier S4, part P5, quantity 500.

With relation AFTER, there is no qualitative difference between these two transactions—each of them involves the insertion of a single tuple into the relation. With relation BEFORE, by contrast, transaction T1 involves the same kind of single-tuple insertion, but transaction T2 involves a totally different operation—namely, an operation to append a new entry to a set of entries within an existing tuple. Thus two qualitatively different "INSERT" operations are needed to support unnormalized relations. For exactly analogous reasons, two different SELECT operations, two different DELETE operations, etc., etc., are also needed. And note clearly that these remarks apply, not only to the data manipulation operations, but to *all* operations in the system; for example, additional data security operations are needed, additional data integrity operations are needed, etc., etc.

---

6. Do not confuse relation-valued and composite domains. The elements of a composite domain are merely concatenations of a set of atomic elements, one from each of the constituent simple domains; loosely speaking, in other words, the elements of a composite domain are *tuples*. The elements of a relation-valued domain, by contrast, are *sets* of tuples. Furthermore, those sets of tuples—i.e., the relations that are the values in the relation-valued domain—may themselves include relation-valued attributes; i.e., those relations may themselves be unnormalized in turn (see the definition of "unnormalized," later).

11.4 RELATIONAL DATABASES

We can now define a *relational database* as a database that is perceived by the user as a collection of time-varying, normalized relations of assorted degrees.[7] As pointed out earlier in this book, the phrase "perceived by the user" is important: The ideas of the relational model apply at the external and conceptual levels of the system, not the internal level. To put this another way, the relational model represents a database system at a level of abstraction that is somewhat removed from the details of the underlying machine—just as, for example, a language such as PL/I represents a programming system at a level of abstraction that is somewhat removed from the details of the underlying machine. (Indeed, the relational model can be regarded as a rather abstract programming language that is oriented specifically toward database applications. This interpretation of the model is explored in depth in Volume II.)

To sum up, we can say that, in traditional terms, a relation resembles a *file*, a tuple a *record* (occurrence, not type), and an attribute a *field* (type, not occurrence). Those correspondences are at best approximate, however. A relation should not be regarded as "just a file," but rather as a *disciplined* file—the discipline in question being one that results in a considerable simplification in the data structures with which the user must interact, and hence in a corresponding simplification in the operators needed to deal with those structures.

We conclude this chapter by summarizing the major features of relational "files" that distinguish them from traditional (undisciplined) files.

1. Each "file" contains only one record type.

2. The fields have no particular order, left to right.

3. The records have no particular order, top to bottom.

4. Every field is single-valued.

5. The records have a unique identifier field or field combination called the primary key.

REFERENCES AND BIBLIOGRAPHY

Most of the following references are applicable to all three aspects of the relational model, not just to its structural aspect.

---

7. By "time-varying," we mean of course that the set of tuples in any given relation changes with time. Note that, by contrast, the underlying domains are not time-varying in the same sense. The set of all *possible* supplier numbers (for example) obviously does not change with time—or rather, if it does, then the change is a *definitional* change, i.e., a change at the type level rather than the instance level.

11.1 E. F. Codd. "A Relational Model of Data for Large Shared Data Banks." *CACM* **13,** No. 6 (June 1970). Republished in *Milestones of Research—Selected Papers 1958-1982: CACM 25th Anniversary Issue, CACM* **26,** No. 1 (January 1983).

> The paper that started it all. Although now some 15 years old, it stands up remarkably well to repeated rereading. Of course, some of the ideas have been refined somewhat since the paper was first published, but by and large the changes have been evolutionary, not revolutionary, in nature. Indeed, there are numerous ideas in the paper whose implications have still not been fully explored.
>
> The paper is divided into two principal sections: "Relational Model and Normal Form" and "Redundancy and Consistency." The first section includes a discussion of data independence (especially the lack of such independence in systems available at the time the paper was written), relational data structure, normalization, linguistic aspects, and base relations vs. views vs. derivable relations. The second section introduces a number of relational operations—projection, join, etc.—and uses those operations as a basis for discussing various kinds of redundancy and consistency in a database.
>
> The definition of relation given in the paper is worth a brief discussion here. That definition runs as follows (paraphrasing slightly): Given sets $D1$, $D2$, ..., Dn (not necessarily distinct), R is a relation on those n sets if it is a set of n-tuples each of which has its first element from $D1$, its second element from $D2$, and so on. (The set Dj is said to be the jth *domain* of R.) More concisely, R is a subset of the Cartesian product $D1$ X $D2$ X ... X Dn.
>
> Although mathematically respectable, this definition can be criticized from a database standpoint (with, of course, 20:20 hindsight) on a number of counts:
>
> 1. First, it does not clearly distinguish between domains and attributes. (Later in the paper Codd does use the term "active domain" for the set of values from a given domain actually appearing in the database at the current time, but "active domain" is still not quite equivalent to "attribute" as that term is now used.) As a result, there has been widespread confusion over domains and attributes, and such confusion still persists, even today.
>
> 2. (Comparatively minor.) Next, a relation according to the definition in fact does have a left-to-right ordering among its domains. Again, Codd states later in the paper that users should not have to deal with relations per se but rather with "their domain-unordered counterparts," but that emendation seems to have escaped the attention of many database system designers.
>
> 3. Finally, the definition does not adequately distinguish between the static and dynamic (or time-independent and time-dependent) aspects of a relation (what we have called the "heading" and the "body" portions), although the distinction is clearly implied by later sections of the paper. This omission has also been a rich source of subsequent confusion.

11.2 E. F. Codd. "Derivability, Redundancy, and Consistency of Relations Stored in Large Data Banks." *IBM Research Report RJ599* (August 1969).

> A preliminary version of [11.1].

11.3 E. F. Codd. "Understanding Relations." Series of articles in FDT (previous title of SIGMOD Record: *Bulletin of ACM Special Interest Group on Management of Data [SIG-MOD,* previously *SIGFIDET]*), beginning with Vol. 5, No. 1 (June 1973).

11.4 D. J. McLeod. "High Level Definition of Abstract Domains in a Relational Data Base System." In *Computer Languages 2*: Pergamon Press (1977). An earlier version of this paper can be found in *Proc. ACM SIGPLAN/SIGMOD Conference on Data: Abstraction, Definition, and Structure* (March 1976): Joint Issue—*ACM SIGPLAN Notices* **11** (Special Issue) / *FDT (ACM SIGMOD Bulletin)* **8,** No. 2 (1976).

11.5 Raymond Reiter. "Towards a Logical Reconstruction of Relational Database Theory." In *On Conceptual Modelling: Perspectives from Artificial Intelligence, Databases, and Programming Languages* (eds., Michael L. Brodie, John Mylopoulos, and Joachim W. Schmidt). Springer-Verlag (1984).

An attempt to put the relational model on a somewhat different theoretical foundation, namely a "proof theoretic" foundation. A relational database can be regarded as a special theory of first order logic. Reiter shows how this interpretation can be extended to deal with (among other things) additional real-world semantics.

11.6 Jeffrey D. Ullman. *Principles of Database Systems,* Second Edition. Rockville, Md.: Computer Science Press (1982).

11.7 David Maier. *The Theory of Relational Databases*. Rockville, Md.: Computer Science Press (1983).

11.8 T. H. Merrett. *Relational Information Systems*. Reston, Va.: Reston Publishing Company (1984).

12
Relational
Integrity Rules

12.1 INTRODUCTION

The integrity part of the relational model consists of two general integrity rules, namely the *entity integrity* rule and the *referential integrity* rule. The rules are *general*, in the sense that they apply to every database that claims to conform to the prescriptions of the relational model. Of course, any given database will have additional, specific rules of its own, over and above the two general rules. For example, the suppliers-and-parts database might have a rule that shipment quantities must be greater than zero and less than 10,000 (say). But such specific rules are outside the scope of the relational model per se.

The two general rules have to do respectively with *primary keys* and *foreign keys*. We therefore examine these two concepts first.

12.2 PRIMARY KEYS

Primary keys are actually a special case of a more general construct, namely *candidate* keys. A candidate key is basically just a unique identifier. By definition every relation has at least one candidate key; in practice, most relations have *exactly* one, but it is possible that some may have two or more. For any given relation, we choose one of the candidate keys to be the primary key, and then the remainder (if any) are called alternate keys.

We now make these ideas more precise. Let R be a relation with attributes $A1$, $A2, \ldots, An$. The set of attributes $K = (Ai, Aj, \ldots, Ak)$ of R is said to be a *candidate key* of R if and only if it satisfies the following two time-independent properties:

1. *Uniqueness:*
   At any given time, no two distinct tuples of R have the same value for Ai, the same value for $Aj, \ldots$, and the same value for Ak.

2. *Minimality:*

None of $Ai, Aj, \ldots, Ak$ can be discarded from K without destroying the uniqueness property.

As explained above, every relation has at least one candidate key, because at least the combination of all of its attributes has the uniqueness property (see Chapter 11). For a given relation, one candidate key is (arbitrarily) designated as the *primary* key. Then the remaining candidate keys (if any) are called *alternate* keys.

Example: Suppose for the sake of the example that supplier names and supplier numbers are both "unique" (i.e., at any given time, no two suppliers have the same number or the same name). Then relation S has two candidate keys, S# and SNAME. We choose S# as the primary key; SNAME then becomes an alternate key.

Why are primary keys important? The answer is that they provide *the sole tuple-level addressing mechanism within the relational model.* That is, the *only* system-guaranteed way of pinpointing some individual tuple is via the combination (R,k), where R is the name of the containing relation and k is the primary key value for the tuple concerned.[1] Primary key values are used elsewhere in the database to serve as *references* to the tuples identified by those values (see Section 12.3 below). It follows, therefore, that primary keys are *absolutely fundamental* to the operation of the overall relational model, for exactly the same reason that main memory addresses are fundamental to the operation of the underlying machine [12.3]. It also follows that a system like DB2 or INGRES that has no knowledge of primary keys is bound to display behavior on occasion that is not "truly relational." For further discussion of this point, see reference [4.10] and the exercises in Chapter 15.

We conclude this section by noting that it has often been claimed that the relational model "requires associative addressing." Now, since all relational addressing—in particular, primary-key addressing—clearly *is* associative (i.e., value-based, not position-based), the claim is clearly true—*at the logical level.* But of course it does not follow (as has, unfortunately, also often been claimed) that the relational model requires associative *hardware.* As has been stated many times in this book already, the relational model is concerned with the logical level of the system, not the physical level. At the physical level, perfectly conventional I/O devices and perfectly conventional storage structures are quite adequate to support a relational system, as numerous relational implementations have clearly demonstrated.

12.3 FOREIGN KEYS

Refer once again to the suppliers-and-parts database, and consider attribute S# of relation SP. It is clear that a given value for that attribute, say the supplier number S1, should be permitted to appear in the database only if that same value also ap-

---

1.   Of course, this statement does not mean that access to a relation from a relational DML should be restricted to "access by primary key." The point is, however, that only "access by primary key" is guaranteed to return (at most) a single tuple.

pears as a value of the primary key S# of relation S (for otherwise the database cannot be considered to be in a state of integrity). For example, it would make no sense for relation SP to include a shipment for supplier S9 (say) if there were no supplier S9 in relation S. Likewise, a given value for attribute P# of relation SP should be permitted to appear only if the same value also appears as a value of the primary key P# of relation P; for again, it would make no sense for relation SP to include a shipment for part P9 (say) if there were no part P9 in relation P.

Attributes S# and P# of relation SP are examples of what are called *foreign keys*. In general, a foreign key is an attribute (or attribute combination) in one relation *R2* whose values are required to match those of the primary key of some relation *R1* (*R1* and *R2* not necessarily distinct). Note that a foreign key and the corresponding primary key should be defined on the same underlying domain (possibly composite, as usual).

Incidentally, there is no requirement for a foreign key to be a component of the primary key of its containing relation, although it does happen that attributes SP.S# and SP.P# in fact are (the primary key of relation SP is of course the composite attribute (S#,P#)). For a counterexample, consider the following departments-and-employees database:

```
DEPT  ( DEPT#, DNAME, MGR_EMP#, BUDGET )
EMP   ( EMP#, ENAME, DEPT#, SALARY )
```

Attribute EMP.DEPT# is a foreign key in relation EMP (matching the primary key DEPT.DEPT# of relation DEPT); however, it is not a component of the primary key EMP.EMP# of that relation EMP. Likewise, attribute DEPT.MGR_EMP# is a foreign key in relation DEPT (matching the primary key of relation EMP), and it is not a component of the primary key DEPT.DEPT# of that relation DEPT.

Note also in the definition of foreign key that the two relations *R1* and *R2* are "not necessarily distinct." Here is an example of where they are not (a revised version of the EMP relation above):

```
EMP ( EMP#, ENAME, MGR_EMP#, SALARY )
```

Here EMP# is the primary key, and MGR_EMP# (employee number of the employee's manager) is a foreign key matching the primary key of the same EMP relation. For instance, if the tuple

```
( '111','Smith','222', 20000 )
```

appears in the EMP relation, then another tuple with EMP# 222 should also appear in that relation to represent the manager of employee 111.

Foreign-to-primary-key matches represent *references* from one relation to another; they are the "glue" that holds the database together. Another way of saying this is that foreign-to-primary-key matches represent certain *relationships* between tuples. Note carefully, however, that not all such relationships are represented by foreign-to-primary-key matches. For example, there is a relationship ("colocation") between parts and suppliers, represented by the CITY attributes of relations S and

P, but those CITY attributes are not foreign keys. (Of course, they could *become* foreign keys if a relation with a CITY primary key were added to the database.)

12.4   THE TWO INTEGRITY RULES

We are now in a position to state the two integrity rules of the relational model (a modified version of the rules as originally formulated in reference [12.1]).

1. *Entity integrity*:
   No attribute participating in the primary key of a base relation is allowed to accept null values.

2. *Referential integrity:*
   If base relation *R2* includes a foreign key *FK* matching the primary key *PK* of some base relation *R1*, then every value of *FK* in *R2* must either (a) be equal to the value of *PK* in some tuple of *R1* or (b) be wholly null (i.e., each attribute value participating in that *FK* value must be null). *R1* and *R2* are not necessarily distinct.

A *base relation* corresponds to what SQL calls a base table—i.e., it is an autonomous, named relation (see Chapter 5 for further discussion). The null value, as usual, represents "property inapplicable" or "information unknown." Note, however, that it need not be the rather peculiar kind of null supported by SQL specifically. From the point of view of the two integrity rules, "null" simply means a value that is understood by convention not to stand for any real value in the applicable domain. A blank supplier number value could be considered as "null" in this sense, for example.

The justification for the entity integrity rule is as follows:

- Base relations correspond to entities in the real world. For example, base relation S corresponds to a set of suppliers in the real world.

- By definition, entities in the real world are distinguishable—that is, they have a unique identification of some kind.

- Primary keys perform the unique identification function in the relational model.

- Thus, a primary key value that was wholly null would be a contradiction in terms; in effect, it would be saying that there was some entity that had no *identity*—i.e., did not exist. (Hence the name "entity integrity.")

Analogous arguments can be used to show that *partially* null primary key values should also be prohibited.

As for the second rule ("referential integrity"): The basic intent of this rule is simply that, if some tuple *t2* references some tuple *t1*, then tuple *t1* must exist. It is clear, therefore, that a given foreign key value must have a matching primary key value somewhere in the referenced relation if that foreign key value is nonnull. Sometimes, however, it is necessary to permit the foreign key to accept null values. Suppose, for example, that in a given company it is legal for some employee to be currently assigned to no department at all. For such an employee, the department number attribute (which is a foreign key) would clearly have to be null in the tuple representing that employee in the database.

12.5 IMPLICATIONS OF THE TWO INTEGRITY RULES

Note carefully that the two integrity rules as presented in the previous section are framed purely in terms of database *states*. Any state of the database that does not satisfy the two rules is by definition incorrect; but how exactly are such incorrect states to be avoided? The rules themselves do not say.

One possibility is, of course, that the system can simply reject any operation that, if executed, would result in an illegal state. In many cases, however, a preferable alternative is for the system to accept the operation but to perform certain additional compensating operations (if necessary) in order to guarantee that the overall result is still a legal state. For example, if the user asks to delete supplier S1 from relation S, it should be possible to get the system to delete the shipments for supplier S1 from relation SP as well, without any further action on the part of the user (assuming that such a "cascading delete" effect is what is wanted).

It follows that, in a good system, it should be possible for the user (in this context, probably the *database designer*) to specify which operations should be rejected and which accepted, and, for those that are accepted, what compensating operations (if any) should be performed by the system. We therefore conclude this chapter with a brief discussion of that possibility. Note, however, that we are stepping outside the bounds of the relational model per se in this discussion. Note too that—regrettably—few systems today actually support anything resembling the following proposals.

To make the discussion reasonably concrete, we present the ideas in terms of further "pseudoDDL" extensions (PRIMARY KEY and FOREIGN KEY clauses) to the SQL CREATE TABLE statement. First the PRIMARY KEY clause—syntax:

```
PRIMARY KEY ( primary-key )
```

where "primary-key" is either a single attribute name, such as "S#", or a list of attribute names separated by commas, such as "S#,P#". For example:

```
CREATE TABLE S
       ( S#      ... ,
         SNAME   ... ,
         STATUS  ... ,
         CITY    ... )
         PRIMARY KEY ( S# ) ;
```

The effect of this PRIMARY KEY clause is to tell the system that S# is the primary key for relation S—in particular, the system is to enforce the "uniqueness" and NOT NULL constraints for S#, *without* the user explicitly having to create a UNIQUE index or explicitly having to specify NOT NULL. Any user operation that would violate either of those constraints is to be rejected.

Now for foreign keys. For each foreign key in the database, the database designer needs to answer three questions, as follows:

1. Can that foreign key accept null values? For example, does it make sense for a shipment to exist for which the supplier or the part is unknown? The answer in that case is, "Probably not." But in some other case the answer may well be different. For example (as suggested earlier), it might well be possible in the case of the departments-and-employees database for some employee to be currently assigned to no department at all. Note clearly that the answer to this question (as to whether nulls are allowed for a given foreign key) depends, not on the whim of the database designer, but on the policies in effect in the portion of the real world that is to be represented in the database. Similar remarks apply to questions 2 and 3 below, of course.

2. What should happen on an attempt to delete the target of a foreign key reference?—for example, an attempt to delete a supplier for which there exists at least one matching shipment? For definiteness let us consider this case explicitly. In general there are three possibilities:

- CASCADES   —The delete operation "cascades" to delete those matching shipments also
- RESTRICTED —The delete operation is "restricted" to the case where there are no such matching shipments (it is rejected otherwise)
- NULLIFIES —The foreign key is set to null in all such matching shipments and the supplier is then deleted (of course, this case could not apply if the foreign key cannot accept null values)

3. What should happen on an attempt to update the primary key of the target of a foreign key reference?—for example, an attempt to update the supplier number for a supplier for which there exists at least one matching shipment? For definiteness, again, we consider this case explicitly. In general there are the same three possibilities as for DELETE:

- CASCADES   —The update operation "cascades" to update the foreign key in those matching shipments also
- RESTRICTED —The update operation is "restricted" to the case where there are no such matching shipments (it is rejected otherwise)
- NULLIFIES —The foreign key is set to null in all such matching shipments and the supplier is then updated (of course, this case could not apply if the foreign key cannot accept null values)

For each foreign key in the design, therefore, the database designer should specify, not only the attribute or attribute combination constituting that foreign key and the target relation referenced by that foreign key, but also the answers to the foregoing three questions (i.e., the three constraints that apply to that foreign key). Hence our proposed syntax for the pseudoDDL FOREIGN KEY clause:

```
FOREIGN KEY ( foreign-key IDENTIFIES target
             NULLS [ NOT ] ALLOWED
             DELETE OF target effect
             UPDATE OF target-primary-key effect )
```

where:

1. "foreign-key" is the same as "primary-key" in the PRIMARY KEY clause—i.e., it is either a single attribute name or a list of attribute names separated by commas;

2. "target" is a relation name;

3. "target-primary-key" specifies the "primary-key" for "target"; and

4. "effect" is CASCADES or RESTRICTED or NULLIFIES.

Here is a sample pseudoDDL CREATE TABLE statement for the SP relation, showing a possible set of foreign key specifications:

```
CREATE TABLE SP
      ( S# ... , P# ... , QTY ... )
      PRIMARY KEY ( S#, P# )
      FOREIGN KEY ( S# IDENTIFIES S
                    NULLS NOT ALLOWED
                    DELETE OF S RESTRICTED
                    UPDATE OF S.S# CASCADES )
      FOREIGN KEY ( P# IDENTIFIES P
                    NULLS NOT ALLOWED
                    DELETE OF P RESTRICTED
                    UPDATE OF P.P# RESTRICTED )
```

The meaning of these specifications is intended to be self-explanatory.

REFERENCES AND BIBLIOGRAPHY

12.1 E. F. Codd. "Extending the Relational Database Model to Capture More Meaning." *ACM TODS* **4**, No. 4 (December 1979).

The overall purpose of this paper is (as the title indicates) to present some preliminary "semantic" extensions to the basic relational model (see Chapter 25). Before getting into details of the proposed extensions, however, the paper first establishes its starting point by summarizing the features of the basic model, and in so doing provides the first published statement of the two integrity rules (not however in quite the form given in the present chapter). The rules were implicit in the model as originally formulated in reference [11.1] but had not previously been spelled out explicitly.

12.2 C. J. Date. "Referential Integrity." *Proc. 7th International Conference on Very Large Data Bases* (September 1981).

Discusses some of the implications of the two integrity rules, much along the lines of Section 12.5 of the present chapter.

12.3 C. J. Date. "Why Relations Should Have Exactly One Primary Key." *ANS Database Committee (X3H2) Working Paper X3H2-84-118* (October 1984).

13
Relational Algebra

13.1 INTRODUCTION

The third and last part of the relational model, the manipulative part, itself divides into two subsidiary parts, namely:

1. a set of operators (such as *join*) that together make up what is called the *relational algebra*; and
2. an assignment operation (for instance, "C := A *join* B"), which assigns the value of some arbitrary expression of the algebra to some other relation.

In this introductory section we give a very brief overview of part 1, the algebraic operations, specifically. Subsequent sections then go over those operators again in considerably more detail. We defer discussion of the assignment operator to the very end of the chapter.

Each operator of the relational algebra takes either one or two relations as its input and produces a new relation as its output. Codd [13.1] originally defined eight such operators, two groups of four each:

1. the traditional set operations union, intersection, difference, and Cartesian product (all modified slightly to take account of the fact that their operands are relations, as opposed to arbitrary sets); and
2. the special relational operations select, project, join, and divide.

Numerous variations on the original algebra have been proposed since the publication of [13.1]; see, for example, references [13.6–13.8]. In this chapter we present a variation of our own—one that does not, however, depart very far from the original—and use it as the basis for discussing a number of related ideas.

The eight operations are shown symbolically in Fig. 13.1. We explain that figure as follows.

SELECT: Extracts specified tuples from a specified relation[1]
PROJECT: Extracts specified attributes from a specified relation
PRODUCT: Builds a relation from two specified relations consisting of all possible concatenated pairs of tuples, one from each of the two specified relations
UNION: Builds a relation consisting of all tuples appearing in either or both of two specified relations
INTERSECT: Builds a relation consisting of all tuples appearing in both of two specified relations
DIFFERENCE: Builds a relation consisting of all tuples appearing in the first and not the second of two specified relations
JOIN: Builds a relation from two specified relations consisting of all possible concatenated pairs of tuples, one from each of the two specified relations, such that in each pair the two tuples satisfy some specified condition
DIVIDE: Takes two relations, one binary and one unary, and builds a relation consisting of all values of one attribute of the binary relation that match (in the other attribute) all values in the unary relation

Observe that the output from each of the algebraic operations is (of course) another relation. This is the property of *closure*, first mentioned in Chapter 6. As a result of this property, it is possible (for example) to take a projection of a union, or a join of two selections, or the difference of a join and an intersection, etc., etc. In other words, it is possible to write *nested relational expressions* —that is, expressions in which the operands are themselves represented by expressions, instead of just by names. There is an obvious analogy here with nested arithmetic expressions in ordinary arithmetic; indeed, the fact that relations are closed under the algebra is important for exactly the same kind of reasons that the fact that numbers are closed under ordinary arithmetic is important.

Note: We assume throughout this chapter that the left-to-right order of attributes within a relation *is* significant—not because it is necessary to do so, but because it simplifies the discussion. A more formal treatment of the algebra that does not make that simplifying assumption can be found in Volume II.

---

1. Do not confuse the algebraic SELECT with the SQL SELECT. The SQL SELECT statement is considerably more powerful than the algebraic SELECT operation—in fact, the SQL SELECT includes the functionality of all eight of the algebraic operations, and more besides. The algebraic SELECT is sometimes referred to as RESTRICT, partly in order to avoid exactly this confusion. In this book we will use both terms, SELECT and RESTRICT, interchangeably.

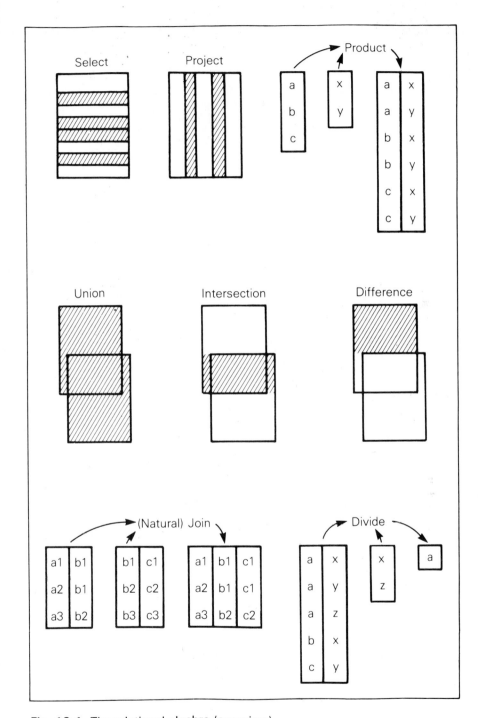

Fig. 13.1 The relational algebra (overview).

13.2   A SYNTAX FOR THE RELATIONAL ALGEBRA

In this section we introduce a concrete syntax for the operations of the relational algebra, in order to provide a basis for the discussions that follow in the rest of the chapter. The syntax is deliberately rather terse. It is defined by the BNF grammar of Fig. 13.2. Note that square brackets are used in that grammar, not as elsewhere in this book to indicate optional material, but rather as symbols in the language being defined.

```
rel-defn
    ::= DEFINE RELATION rel-name [ attr-name-commalist ]

alias-defn
    ::= DEFINE ALIAS rel-name FOR rel-name

expr
    ::= selection | projection | infix-expr

selection
    ::= primitive WHERE selection-pred

primitive
    ::= rel-name | ( expr )

projection
    ::= primitive | primitive [ attr-spec-commalist ]

attr-spec
    ::= attr-name | rel-name . attr-name

infix-expr
    ::= projection infix-op projection

infix-op
    ::= UNION | INTERSECT | MINUS | TIMES | JOIN | DIVIDEBY
```

Fig. 13.2 A BNF grammar for the relational algebra.

Some Notes on the Grammar

1. The grammar makes use of the following convenient shorthand: If "xyz" is a syntactic category, then "xyz-commalist" is a syntactic category consisting of a list of one or more "xyz"'s in which adjacent "xyz"'s are separated by a comma.

2. The categories *rel-name* and *attr-name* are both defined to be *identifiers* (a terminal category with respect to this grammar).

3. The category *selection-pred* represents a Boolean combination of *comparisons*, formed in accordance with the normal rules for Boolean expressions. The category *comparison*, in turn, represents a simple comparison between two *scalar-values*; and a *scalar-value* consists of either a constant or an attribute value (represented by an *attr-spec*, i.e., a qualified or unqualified attribute name).

4. We deliberately do not allow an "attr-spec" in a projection to be an operational expression such as *ATTR1 + ATTR2*, for reasons of simplicity. Likewise, we do not allow such expressions to appear as a comparand in a comparison. In practice, of course, such restrictions would be very undesirable.

5. Our grammar includes operations for the definition of relations and aliases. We include aliases in order to avoid a naming problem with the Cartesian product operator (see the discussion of that operator in Section 13.3 below).

Attribute Names for Derived Relations

Our version of the algebra includes rules for naming the attributes of result relations, an aspect that is frequently overlooked. Note: Despite the fact that we are considering attributes to be ordered left to right within a relation, we still rely on attribute names for purposes of reference, and we still require that no relation have two attributes with the same name. We assume that this constraint is automatically enforced for named—i.e., defined—relations. The rules for generating attribute names for *derived* relations (i.e., relations that are represented by expressions rather than by name) in accordance with the unique naming constraint are spelled out in Sections 13.3 and 13.4. Here we content ourselves with a few words regarding *named* relations.

First, let R be a named relation, and let A be the (unqualified) name of an attribute within R—i.e., an attribute listed within the "attr-name-commalist" appearing in the definition of R. Attribute A is considered to have the *qualified* name $R.A$.

Next, if R is a named relation and S is an alias for R, then: a) when the given relation is referenced by the name R, attribute A of that relation can be referenced as $R.A$; b) when the given relation is referenced by the name S, attribute A of that relation can be referenced as $S.A$.

An attribute of a named relation thus always has a qualified name. (However, such an attribute may also be referenced by its simple unqualified name if no ambiguity results from so doing.) Attributes of derived relations also always have qualified names, generated as described in the next two sections. Again, however, they may be referenced by their unqualified names if no ambiguity results.

Note: As stated earlier, a derived relation is a relation that is represented by an expression, rather than simply by name. In considering such derivations, we can obviously restrict our attention to expressions involving exactly one of the algebraic operators (since the operand(s) of that operator can in turn be derived relations).

13.3 TRADITIONAL SET OPERATIONS

The traditional set operations are union, intersection, difference, and product (more precisely, extended Cartesian product). Each operation takes two operands. For all except Cartesian product, the two operand relations must be *union-compatible*—that is, they must be of the same degree, *n* say, and the *i*th attribute of each (*i* = 1,2, . . . ,*n*) should be based on the same domain (they do not have to have the same name). The union-compatibility rule is imposed to ensure that the result is still a relation (i.e., to guarantee the closure property); for otherwise it would be possible (for example) to form the union of relation S and relation P, the result of which, while it would still be a set, would certainly not be a relation (it would be a heterogeneous mixture of S tuples and P tuples).

■ *Union*

The union of two (union-compatible) relations *A* and *B*, *A* UNION *B*, is the set of all tuples *t* belonging to either *A* or *B* (or both).

Example: Let *A* be the set of supplier tuples for suppliers in London, and let *B* be the set of supplier tuples for suppliers who supply part P1. Then *A* UNION *B* is the set of supplier tuples for suppliers who *either* are located in London *or* supply part P1 (or both).

We define the result of a UNION operation to have the same qualified attribute names as the first operand.

■ *Intersection*

The intersection of two (union-compatible) relations *A* and *B*, *A* INTERSECT *B*, is the set of all tuples *t* belonging to both *A* and *B*.

Example: Let *A* and *B* be as in the example under "Union" above. Then *A* INTERSECT *B* is the set of supplier tuples for suppliers who are located in London *and* supply part P1.

We define the result of an INTERSECT operation to have the same qualified attribute names as the first operand.

■ *Difference*

The difference between two (union-compatible) relations *A* and *B*, *A* MINUS *B*, is the set of all tuples *t* belonging to *A* and not to *B*.

Example: Let *A* and *B* again be as in the example under "Union" above. Then *A* MINUS *B* is the set of supplier tuples for suppliers who are located in London and do *not* supply part P1. (What is *B* MINUS *A*?)

We define the result of a DIFFERENCE operation to have the same qualified attribute names as the first operand.

■ *Extended Cartesian product*

The extended Cartesian product of two relations *A* and *B*, *A* TIMES *B*, is the set of all tuples *t* such that *t* is the concatenation of a tuple *a* belonging to *A* and a tuple b belonging to B. The *concatenation* of a tuple $a = (a1, \ldots, am)$ and a tuple $b = (b(m+1), \ldots, b(m+n))$—in that order—is the tuple $t = (a1, \ldots, am, b(m+1), \ldots, b(m+n))$.

Example: Let A be the set of all supplier numbers and B the set of all part numbers. Then A TIMES B is the set of all supplier-number/part-number pairs.

We define the result of a TIMES operation to have qualified attribute names as follows. Consider the product A TIMES B. Let the qualified attribute names for A and B, in their left-to-right order, be

$$A.A1, \ldots, A.Am \text{ and } B.B(m+1), \ldots, B.B(m+n),$$

respectively. Then the attributes of A TIMES B have exactly those qualified names (in left-to-right order).

Example: Let $A(X\#)$, $B(Y\#)$, and $D(X\#, Y\#)$ be three relations. Then A TIMES B has attributes $(A.X\#, B.Y\#)$. If we call this product C, then C TIMES D has attributes $(A.X\#, B.Y\#, D.X\#, D.Y\#)$.

As the example shows, attributes of a derived relation can have nonunique unqualified names, but their qualified names must be unique. Suppose we need to form the extended Cartesian product of a relation R with itself (where R has attributes $A1, \ldots, Am$, say). The expression R TIMES R is illegal, because it would violate the unique naming rule. Therefore we must introduce another name for R, S say, as follows:

    DEFINE ALIAS S FOR R

Now we can write R TIMES S, or S TIMES R, thus generating the required product without violating the unique naming rule.

Associativity

It is easy to verify that UNION is *associative*—that is, if X, Y, and Z are arbitrary "projections" (in the sense of Fig. 13.2), then the expressions

$$(X \text{ UNION } Y) \text{ UNION } Z$$

and

$$X \text{ UNION } (Y \text{ UNION } Z)$$

are equivalent. (Exercise: Verify this assertion.) For convenience, therefore, we allow a sequence of UNIONs to be written without any embedded parentheses; for example, each of the foregoing expressions can unambiguously be simplified to just

$$X \text{ UNION } Y \text{ UNION } Z .$$

Analogous remarks apply to INTERSECT and TIMES, but not to MINUS.

13.4   SPECIAL RELATIONAL OPERATIONS

■ *Selection*

Let *theta* represent any valid scalar comparison operator (for example, $=$, $\sim =$, $>$, $> =$, etc.). The theta-selection of relation R on attributes X and Y—

$$R \text{ WHERE } R.X \text{ } theta \text{ } R.Y$$

—is the set of all tuples t of R such that the comparison "$t.X$ *theta* $t.Y$" evaluates to *true*. (Attributes X and Y should be defined on the same domain, and the operation *theta* must make sense for that domain.) A constant value may be specified in place of either attribute X or attribute Y—for example:

$$R \text{ WHERE } R.X \text{ } theta \text{ } constant$$

Thus, the theta-selection operator yields a "horizontal" subset of a given relation— that is, that subset of the tuples of the given relation for which a specified comparison is satisfied.

Note: "Theta-selection" is often abbreviated to just "selection" (or "restriction"—see below). But remember that, as pointed out in Section 13.1, the algebraic "selection" operation is not the same as the SELECT operation of SQL.

The selection operation as just defined permits only a simple comparison in the WHERE clause. However, it is possible—by virtue of the closure property—to extend the definition unambiguously to the form described in Section 13.2 (in which the predicate consists of an arbitrary Boolean combination of such simple comparisons), as indicated by the following equivalences:

1. R WHERE *c1* AND *c2*

    is defined to be equivalent to

    (R WHERE *c1*) INTERSECT (R WHERE *c2*)

2. R WHERE *c1* OR *c2*

    is defined to be equivalent to

    (R WHERE *c1*) UNION (R WHERE *c2*)

3. R WHERE NOT *c*

    is defined to be equivalent to

    R MINUS (R WHERE *c*)

Henceforth we will assume that the predicate in the WHERE clause of a selection consists of such an arbitrary Boolean combination of simple comparisons. Such a predicate (i.e., a predicate that can be established as *true* or *false* for a given tuple by examining that tuple in isolation) is said to be a *restriction predicate*; and the selection operation is often referred to (correspondingly) as a *restriction* operation.

Some examples of selection are given in Fig. 13.3.

```
 -----------------------------------------------------------------
|                                                                 |
|                              --   -----   ------   ------       |
|  S WHERE CITY = 'London'     S#   SNAME   STATUS   CITY         |
|                              --   -----   ------   ------       |
|                              S1   Smith       20   London       |
|                              S4   Clark       20   London       |
|                                                                 |
|                              --   -----   -----   ------   ------ |
|  P WHERE WEIGHT < 14         P#   PNAME   COLOR   WEIGHT   CITY  |
|                              --   -----   -----   ------   ------ |
|                              P1   Nut     Red         12   London|
|                              P5   Cam     Blue        12   Paris |
|                                                                 |
|                              --   --   ---                      |
|  SP WHERE S# = 'S1'          S#   P#   QTY                      |
|        AND P# = 'P1'         --   --   ---                      |
|                              S1   P1   300                      |
|                                                                 |
 -----------------------------------------------------------------
```

Fig. 13.3 Three sample selections.

If R denotes the relation on which the selection is performed, then the result has exactly the same qualified attribute names as R. Note that R may be an arbitrary expression (enclosed in parentheses)—though if it is not just a simple name, then it cannot be used to qualify attribute names in the WHERE clause.

■ *Projection*

The projection of relation R on attributes, $X, Y, \ldots, Z$—

$$R [X, Y, \ldots, Z]$$

—is the set of all tuples $(x, y, \ldots, z)$ such that a tuple t appears in R with X-value x, Y-value y, . . . , and Z-value z. Thus, the projection operator yields a "vertical" subset of a given relation—that is, that subset obtained by selecting specified attributes, in a specified left-to-right order, and then eliminating redundant duplicate tuples within the attributes selected, if necessary. Since we are assigning significance to the order of attributes within a relation, projection provides us with a way of permuting (i.e., reordering) the attributes of a given relation, if desired.

Some examples of projection are given in Fig. 13.4.

If R denotes the relation on which the projection is performed, then the attributes of the result have exactly the same qualified names as they have within R. Note that R may be an arbitrary expression (enclosed in parentheses). No attribute may be specified more than once in the list of attributes in a projection operation. Omitting the list is equivalent to specifying a list containing all attributes of the given relation, in their correct left-to-right order. In other words, such a projection is identical to the given relation.

```
  --------------------------------------------------------------
|                                      ------                    |
|  S [ CITY ]                          CITY                      |
|                                      ------                    |
|                                      London                    |
|                                      Paris                     |
|                                      Athens                    |
|                                                                |
|                                      -----   ------  --  ------ |
|  S [ SNAME, CITY, S#, STATUS ]       SNAME   CITY    S#  STATUS |
|                                      -----   ------  --  ------ |
|                                      Smith   London  S1      20 |
|                                      Jones   Paris   S2      10 |
|                                      Blake   Paris   S3      30 |
|                                      Clark   London  S4      20 |
|                                      Adams   Athens  S5      30 |
|                                                                |
|                                      ------  -----             |
|  ( S TIMES P ) [ STATUS, COLOR ]     STATUS  COLOR             |
|                                      ------  -----             |
|                                          20  Red               |
|                                          10  Red               |
|                                          30  Red               |
|                                          20  Green             |
|                                          10  Green             |
|                                          30  Green             |
|                                          20  Blue              |
|                                          10  Blue              |
|                                          30  Blue              |
|                                                                |
  --------------------------------------------------------------
```

Fig. 13.4 Three sample projections.

■ *Join*

Let *theta* be as defined under "Selection" above. The theta-join of relation A on attribute X with relation B on attribute Y is the set of all tuples t such that t is the concatenation of a tuple a belonging to A and a tuple b belonging to B and the predicate "*a.X theta b.Y*" evaluates to *true*. (Attributes $A.X$ and $B.Y$ should be defined on the same domain, and the operation *theta* must make sense for that domain.) For example, the *greater-than join* of relation S on CITY with relation P on CITY is as shown in Fig. 13.5 (compare Example 6.3.2 in Chapter 6).

Theta-join is not a primitive operation; instead, it is always equivalent to taking the extended Cartesian product of the two relations and then performing an appropriate restriction (i.e., selection) on the result. The greater-than join illustrated in Fig. 13.5, for example, is equivalent to the following:

```
( S TIMES P ) WHERE S.CITY > P.CITY
```

```
 ---------------------------------------------------------------------
|                                                                     |
| --    -----    ------    ------    --    -----    -----    ------    ------  |
| S#    SNAME    STATUS    S.CITY    P#    PNAME    COLOR    WEIGHT    P.CITY  |
| --    -----    ------    ------    --    -----    -----    ------    ------  |
| S2    Jones        10    Paris     P1    Nut      Red          12    London  |
| S2    Jones        10    Paris     P4    Screw    Red          14    London  |
| S2    Jones        10    Paris     P6    Cog      Red          19    London  |
| S3    Blake        30    Paris     P1    Nut      Red          12    London  |
| S3    Blake        30    Paris     P4    Screw    Red          14    London  |
| S3    Blake        30    Paris     P6    Cog      Red          19    London  |
|                                                                     |
 ---------------------------------------------------------------------
```

Fig. 13.5 Greater-than join of S on CITY with P on CITY.

If *theta* is equality, the theta-join is called an *equijoin*. It follows from the definition that the result of an equijoin must include two identical attributes (see Example 6.3.1 in Chapter 6 for an illustration). If one of those two attributes is eliminated (which it can be via projection), the result is called the *natural* join. Thus the natural join is a projection of a restriction of a product; for example, the following expression—.

```
( ( S TIMES SP ) WHERE S.S# = SP.S# )
                [ S.S#, SNAME, STATUS, CITY, P#, QTY ]
```

—represents the natural join of relation S on S# with relation SP on S#. Natural join is easily the most important form of join in practice. For that reason, the grammar of Fig. 13.2 provides a special shorthand syntax for it—more precisely, for the special case of natural join in which common attributes of the two relations to be joined have the same unqualified names. For example, the natural join above can be written as simply

```
S JOIN SP
```

in that shorthand form. In general, the expression A JOIN B is defined if and only if, for every unqualified attribute name that is common to A and B, the underlying domain is the same for both relations. Let the qualified attribute names for A and B, in their left-to-right order, be

$$A.A1, \ldots, A.Am \text{ and } B.B(m+1), \ldots, B.B(m+n),$$

respectively; let $Ci, \ldots, Cj$ be the unqualified attribute names that are common to A and B; and let $Br, \ldots, Bs$ be the unqualified attribute names remaining for B (with their relative order undisturbed) after removal of $Ci, \ldots, Cj$. Then A JOIN B is defined to be equivalent to

```
( A TIMES B ) [ A.A1,...,A.Am,B.Br,...,B.Bs ]
              WHERE A.Ci = B.Ci
              AND    ......
              AND A.Cj = B.Cj
```

Please note: Henceforth in this chapter we take the unqualified term "join" to mean this form of natural join, unless we explicitly state otherwise.

Figure 13.6 shows the result of evaluating the expression

S JOIN SP

(including the qualified attribute names generated for the result).

S.S#	S.SNAME	S.STATUS	S.CITY	SP.P#	SP.QTY
S1	Smith	20	London	P1	300
S1	Smith	20	London	P2	200
S1	Smith	20	London	P3	400
S1	Smith	20	London	P4	200
S1	Smith	20	London	P5	100
S1	Smith	20	London	P6	100
S2	Jones	10	Paris	P1	300
S2	Jones	10	Paris	P2	400
S3	Blake	30	Paris	P2	200
S4	Clark	20	London	P2	200
S4	Clark	20	London	P4	300
S4	Clark	20	London	P5	400

Fig. 13.6 Result of evaluating S JOIN SP.

For convenience, we allow a sequence of JOINs to be written without any embedded parentheses; for example, the expressions

$$(X \text{ JOIN } Y) \text{ JOIN } Z$$

and

$$X \text{ JOIN } (Y \text{ JOIN } Z)$$

can both be unambiguously simplified to

$$X \text{ JOIN } Y \text{ JOIN } Z ,$$

since JOIN is associative. (Exercise: Prove this last statement.) We remark that, if A and B have no attribute names in common, then A JOIN B is equivalent to A TIMES B.

■ *Division*

The division operator divides a dividend relation A of degree $m + n$ by a divisor relation B of degree n, and produces a quotient relation of degree m. The $(m + i)$th attribute of A and the ith attribute of B ($i = 1,2, \ldots ,n$) should be defined on the same domain. Consider the first m attributes of A as a single composite attribute X, and the last n as another, Y; relation A can then be thought of as a set of pairs of values (x,y). Similarly, relation B can be thought of as a set of single values (*y*). Then the result of dividing *A* by *B*—that is, the result of evaulating the expression

A DIVIDEBY *B*

—is the relation *C*, with sole (composite) attribute *X*, such that every value *x* of *C.X* appears as a value of *A.X*, and the pair of values (*x,y*) appears in *A* for *all* values *y* appearing in *B*. The *m* attributes of the quotient have the same qualified names as the first *m* attributes of relation *A*.

Figure 13.7 shows some examples of division. The dividend (DEND) in each case is the projection of SP over S# and P#; the divisors (DOR) are as indicated in the figure.

```
+-----------------------------------------------------------------------+
|                   --    --                .    .                       |
|         DEND     S#    P#                 .    .                       |
|                   --    --                .    .                       |
|                  S1    P1               S2    P1                       |
|                  S1    P2               S2    P2                       |
|                  S1    P3               S3    P2                       |
|                  S1    P4               S4    P2                       |
|                  S1    P5               S4    P4                       |
|                  S1    P6               S4    P5                       |
|                   .    .                                               |
|                                                                        |
+-------------------------+------------------------+---------------------+
|                         |                        |                     |
|         --              |         --             |         --          |
|    DOR  P#              |    DOR  P#             |    DOR  P#          |
|         --              |         --             |         --          |
|         P1              |         P2             |         P1          |
|                         |         P4             |         P2          |
|                         |                        |         P3          |
|                         |                        |         P4          |
|                         |                        |         P5          |
|                         |                        |         P6          |
+-------------------------+------------------------+---------------------+
|                      DEND DIVIDEBY DOR                                  |
+-------------------------+------------------------+---------------------+
|                         |                        |                     |
|         --              |         --             |         --          |
|    S#                   |    S#                  |    S#               |
|         --              |         --             |         --          |
|    S1                   |    S1                  |    S1               |
|    S2                   |    S4                  |                     |
|                         |                        |                     |
+-------------------------+------------------------+---------------------+
```

Fig. 13.7 Three sample divisions.

13.5 EXAMPLES

13.5.1 Get supplier names for suppliers who supply part P2. (Example 6.5.3)

```
( ( S JOIN SP ) WHERE P# = 'P2' ) [ SNAME ]
```

Explanation: First the natural join of relation S on S# with relation SP on S# is constructed. That join is then restricted to just those tuples in which the P# value is P2. Finally, that restriction is projected over the SNAME attribute. The final result has a single attribute, with qualified name S.SNAME.

13.5.2 Get supplier names for suppliers who supply at least one red part. (Example 6.5.4)

```
( ( ( P WHERE COLOR = 'Red' ) [ P# ]
                        JOIN SP ) [ S# ]
                                JOIN S ) [ SNAME ]
```

Result attribute name: S.SNAME.

13.5.3 Get supplier names for suppliers who supply all parts. (Example 6.5.9)

```
( ( SP [ S#, P# ] DIVIDEBY P [ P# ] )JOIN S ) [ SNAME ]
```

Result attribute name: S.SNAME.

13.5.4 Get supplier numbers for suppliers who supply at least all those parts supplied by supplier S2. (Example 6.5.10)

```
SP [ S#, P# ] DIVIDEBY ( SP WHERE S# = 'S2' ) [ P# ]
```

Result attribute name: SP.S#.

13.5.5 Get supplier names for suppliers who do not supply part P2. (Example 6.5.8)

```
( ( S [ S# ] MINUS ( SP WHERE P# = 'P2' ) [ S# ] )
                                JOIN S ) [ SNAME
```

Result attribute name: S.SNAME.

13.5.6 Get all pairs of supplier numbers such that the two suppliers are located in the same city. (Example 6.3.6)

```
DEFINE ALIAS FIRST FOR S
DEFINE ALIAS SECOND FOR S

( ( FIRST TIMES SECOND ) WHERE FIRST.CITY = SECOND.CITY
                          AND   FIRST.S#   < SECOND.S# )
                              [ FIRST.S#, SECOND.S# ]
```

Result attribute names: FIRST.S#, SECOND.S#.

13.6 CONCLUDING REMARKS

To summarize this chapter so far: We have defined a *relational algebra*, i.e., a collection of high-level operations on relations. The operations in question are restriction (selection), projection, product, union, intersection, difference, join, and divide (basically the set that Codd originally defined in reference [13.1]). We have also presented a possible syntax for those operations. Note, however, that it would be highly desirable for any real implementation of the algebra to use a syntax that is much more "user-friendly" than ours; our syntax was introduced purely for expository reasons.

The reader should understand that the eight operations do not constitute a minimal set in any sense, nor were they ever intended to. In fact, of the eight, only five are primitive, namely restriction, projection, product, union, and difference. The other three can be defined in terms of those five. For example, the natural join is a projection of a restriction of a product, as explained in Section 13.4. In practice, however, those other three operations (especially join) are so useful that a good case can be made for supporting them directly, even though they are not primitive.

We should now clarify one extremely important point. Although we have never said as much explicitly, the body of the chapter prior to this point has certainly suggested that the primary purpose of the algebra is merely *data retrieval*. Such is not the case, however. The fundamental intent of the algebra is to allow *the writing of expressions*. Those expressions in turn are intended to serve a variety of purposes, including retrieval of course, but certainly not limited to that function alone. The following list indicates some possible applications for such expressions. (Basically, of course, the expressions represent *relations*, and those relations in turn define the scope for the retrieval, update, etc., operations shown in the list.)

- Defining a scope for retrieval—i.e., defining the data to be fetched as the result of a retrieval operation
- Defining a scope for update—i.e., defining the data to be modified or deleted as the result of an update operation (see below)
- Defining virtual data—i.e., defining the data to be visible in the form of a virtual relation or view
- Defining access rights—i.e., defining the data over which authorization of some kind is to be granted (see Chapter 19)
- Defining stability requirements—i.e., defining the data that is to be the scope of some concurrency control operation (see Chapter 18)
- Defining integrity constraints—i.e., defining some specific rule that the database must satisfy, over and above the two general rules that are part of the relational model and apply to *every* database (see Chapter 19)

In general, in fact, the expressions serve as *a high-level and symbolic representation of the user's intent* (with regard to a retrieval request, for example). And precisely because they are high-level and symbolic, they can be manipulated in accordance with a variety of symbolic *transformation rules*; for example, the expression

```
( S JOIN SP ) WHERE P# = 'P1'
```

can be transformed into the logically equivalent, but more efficient, expression

```
( S JOIN ( SP WHERE P# = 'P1' ) )
```

The algebra thus serves as a convenient basis for *optimization*. See Chapter 16. (Exercise: In what sense is the second of the two expressions above more efficient?)

We conclude this chapter with a brief note on the relational assignment operation. Basically, the assignment operation is provided to make it possible to "remember" the value of some algebraic expression, and thereby to change the database state. But relation assignment is somewhat of a sledgehammer operation, inasmuch as it supports only the wholesale replacement of an entire relation value. In practice, of course, some finer-precision update operations are clearly desirable. The assignment operation theoretically *could* be used as the basis for such finer-precision operations; for example, it would theoretically be possible to perform insertions and deletions as suggested by the following examples:

```
S    := S    UNION    { ('S6','Baker', 50,'Madrid') } ;
SP   := SP   MINUS    { ('S1','P1',300) } ;
```

(The first of these inserts the tuple for supplier S6 into relation S, the second deletes the shipment for supplier S1 and part P1 from relation SP.)

However, using UNION and MINUS in this manner as a substitute for explicit INSERT and DELETE operations is not really satisfactory, because UNION and MINUS do not handle error situations appropriately. To be specific, UNION and MINUS fail to balk at situations that are customarily treated as errors by INSERT and DELETE. UNION, for example, will not reject an attempt to insert a tuple that is a duplicate of one that already exists; and MINUS will not reject an attempt to delete a nonexistent tuple. In practice, therefore, a relational system should provide explicit INSERT and DELETE (and UPDATE) operations as well. For example (SQL):

```
DELETE FROM SP WHERE S# = 'S1' ;
```

Observe, incidentally, how this example illustrates our earlier remarks concerning algebraic expressions. The DELETE can be regarded as a) first applying an algebraic operation—actually a restriction, in this particular example—to identify the data to be deleted, followed by b) the actual deletion itself.

EXERCISES

13.1 The five primitive algebraic operations are union, difference, product, selection, and projection. Give definitions of join, intersection, and difference in terms of those five primitives.

13.2 Consider the expression A JOIN B. If A and B have no attribute names in common, this expression is equivalent to the expression A TIMES B. What is it equivalent to if instead A and B have *all* attribute names in common?—i.e., if all unqualified attribute names appearing in A also appear in B, and vice versa?

13.3 Given the standard suppliers-and-parts database, what is the value of the expression S JOIN SP JOIN P? (Warning: There is a trap here.)

13.4 Show that SQL is "relationally complete" (see Chapter 14), in the sense that, for any arbitrary expression of the relational algebra, there exists a semantically equivalent SQL expression. Is there a SQL equivalent of the relational assignment operation?

13.5 Let A and B be two relations. Assume that A and B are union-compatible, joinable, etc., as necessary. State the primary key for each of the following:

a) an arbitrary restriction of A;

b) an arbitrary projection of A;

c) the product A TIMES B;

d) the union A UNION B;

e) the intersection A INTERSECT B;

f) the difference A MINUS B;

g) the natural join A JOIN B;

h) the quotient A DIVIDEBY B.

13.6 Give algebraic solutions to Exercises 6.1–6.48 (where possible or appropriate).

13.7 Show that the five primitive operators of the algebra truly are primitive, in the sense that none of them can be expressed in terms of the other four.

13.8 Give a definition of the *outer join* operator in terms of the operators defined in the body of this chapter. (See the annotation to reference [13.9] for an informal explanation of outer join.)

REFERENCES AND BIBLIOGRAPHY

13.1 E. F. Codd. "Relational Completeness of Data Base Sublanguages." In *Data Base Systems*, Courant Computer Science Symposia Series, Vol. 6. Englewood Cliffs, N.J.: Prentice-Hall (1972).

Includes a formal definition of the relational algebra. See Chapter 14 (especially Section 14.4) for further discussion of this paper.

13.2 R. C. Goldstein and A. J. Strnad. "The MacAIMS Data Management System." *Proc. 1970 ACM SICFIDET Workshop on Data Description and Access.*

13.3 A. J. Strnad. "The Relational Approach to the Management of Data Bases." *Proc. IFIP Congress* 1971.

MacAIMS [13.2, 13.3] appears to have been the earliest example of a system supporting both *n*-ary relations and a set-level language. The language was algebraic. Two particularly interesting features of the system were the following.

■ The storage structure could vary from relation to relation. Each structure was managed by a "relational strategy module," specific to that particular structure, which hid the storage details of that structure from the rest of the system (and hence from the user).

■ Attributes were stored as "data element sets." Each data element (i.e., attribute value) was assigned a unique fixed-length *reference number*, and all references to the data element within any relation were via that reference number. The algorithm for assigning reference numbers was such that, if *A* and *B* belonged to the same data element set, then the reference number for *A* would be greater than that for *B* if and only if *A* was greater than *B*. As a result, any comparison operation between two data elements (from the same data element set) could be made directly on the corresponding reference numbers; moreover, the actual comparison itself was likely to be more efficient, because reference numbers were fixed-length whereas data elements could be variable-length. This point is particularly significant in view of the fact that such comparisons were easily the operations most frequently performed in the internals of the system (as indeed they probably are in any database system).

13.4 M. G. Notley. "The Peterlee IS/1 System." *IBM (UK) Scientific Centre Report UKSC-0018* (March 1972).

See the annotation to reference [13.5].

13.5 S. J. P. Todd. "The Peterlee Relational Test Vehicle—A System Overview." *IBM Sys. J.* **15**, No. 4 (1976).

The Peterlee Relational Test Vehicle, PRTV [13.5], was an experimental system developed at the IBM UK Scientific Centre in Peterlee, England. It was based on an earlier prototype called IS/1 [13.4]. It supported *n*-ary relations and a version of the algebra based on proposals documented in [13.6]. Three significant aspects of PRTV were the following:

- It incorporated some sophisticated optimization techniques (see Chapter 16).

- It included a delayed evaluation feature, which was important both for optimization and for the support of virtual relations (views).

- It provided "function extensibility"—i.e., the ability to extend the system to include an arbitrary set of user-defined computational functions.

13.6 P. A. V. Hall, P. Hitchcock, and S. J. P. Todd. "An Algebra of Relations for Machine Computation." *Conference Record of the Second ACM Symposium on Principles of Programming Languages* (1975).

13.7 A. L. Furtado and L. Kerschberg. "An Algebra of Quotient Relations." *Proc. 1977 ACM SIGMOD International Conference on Management of Data* (August 1977).

Presents a revised relational algebra for operating directly on "quotient relations." Given an *n*-ary relation *R*, a corresponding quotient relation can be derived from *R* by grouping tuples on the basis of the values of some attribute of *R* (along the lines of the GROUP BY operation in SQL or the BY operation in QUEL). For example, the quotient relation derived from the supplier relation S on the basis of CITY values is a set of three groups of tuples—one containing two London tuples, one containing two Paris tuples, and one containing a single Athens tuple. The authors claim that operating directly on such quotient relations leads both to more natural queries and to a potential for more efficient implementation.

13.8 T. H. Merrett. "The Extended Relational Algebra, A Basis for Query Languages." In *Databases: Improving Usability and Responsiveness* (ed., B. Shneiderman). New York: Academic Press (1978).

Proposes the introduction of quantifiers into the algebra — not just the existential and universal quantifiers of the calculus (see Chapter 14), but the more general quantifiers "the number of" and "the proportion of." These quantifiers allow the expression of such conditions as "at least three of," "not more than half of," "an odd number of," etc. See also Merrett's book [11.8].

13.9 C. J. Date. "The Outer Join." *Proc. 2nd International Conference on Databases (ICOD-2),* Cambridge, England (September 1983). Also available as *IBM Technical Report TR 03.181* (January 1982).

Outer join is an extended form of the ordinary (or *inner*) join operation in which tuples in one relation having no counterpart in the other appear in the result concatenated with an all-null tuple (instead of simply being ignored, as they are in the ordinary join). It is not a primitive operation; for example, the following "pseudoSQL" operation could be used to construct the outer join of suppliers and shipments on supplier numbers (it is only "pseudoSQL" because real SQL does not permit NULL to appear in a SELECT clause).

```
SELECT  S.*, SP.*
FROM    S, SP
WHERE   S.S# = SP.S#
UNION
SELECT  S.*, NULL, NULL, NULL
FROM    S
WHERE   NOT EXISTS
          ( SELECT *
            FROM    SP
            WHERE   SP.S# = S.S# ) ;
```

The result includes rows for suppliers who supply no parts, concatenated with null values in the SP.S#, SP.P#, and SP.QTY positions.

Although not primitive, outer join is needed very frequently in practice, and it would be desirable for the system to support it directly, instead of requiring the user to indulge in lengthy circumlocutions (see the example—which in any case is not legal SQL, as already explained). The paper [13.9] discusses the outer join problem in depth (it is not as trivial as the example above might suggest), and presents some proposals for supporting the operation in relational languages such as SQL. Note: Some systems today— for example, ORACLE—do provide some support for outer join, but no system (to this writer's knowledge) yet supports it in full generality.

13.10 P. A. V. Hall. "Relational Algebras, Logic, and Functional Programming." *Proc. 1984 ACM SIGMOD International Conference on Management of Data* (June 1984).

Presents a functional interpretation of the relational algebra, with the aims (paraphrasing from the paper) of a) providing a theoretical basis for the so-called "fourth generation languages" (see Chapter 20 of this book), and b) integrating functional, logic, and relational languages so that they can share implementation technology. The author claims that, whereas logic programming and databases have been moving toward each other for some time, to date the functional or applicative languages have paid little heed to database requirements or technology. The paper is therefore presented principally as a contribution toward a rapprochement between the latter two. One potential outcome is an approach to extending the relational algebra—i.e., to incorporate higher-level functions, such as the ability to perform arithmetic—that is systematic instead of ad hoc (as most such approaches regrettably seem to be at present).

ANSWERS TO SELECTED EXERCISES

13.1

a) *A* INTERSECT *B*
   = *A* MINUS (*A* MINUS *B*)
   = *B* MINUS (*B* MINUS *A*)

b) *A* DIVIDEBY *B* (where *A* has attributes *X* and *Y* and *B* has
                    attribute *Z* -- *X*, *Y*, and *Z* possibly composite)
   = *A* [*X*] MINUS ((*A* [*X*] TIMES *B*) MINUS *A*) [*X*]

13.2 *A* INTERSECT *B*

13.3 The trap is that the join involves the CITY attributes as well as the S# and P# attributes (because of our definition of the JOIN operator). Result:

S.S#	S.SNAME	S.STATUS	S.CITY	SP.P#	SP.QTY	P.PNAME	P.COLOR	P.WEIGHT
S1	Smith	20	London	P1	300	Nut	Red	12
S1	Smith	20	London	P4	200	Screw	Red	14
S1	Smith	20	London	P6	100	Cog	Red	19
S2	Jones	10	Paris	P2	400	Bolt	Green	17
S3	Blake	30	Paris	P2	200	Bolt	Green	17
S4	Clark	20	London	P4	200	Screw	Red	14

13.4 Let A and B be any two members of the given set of named relations. Further (unnamed) relations can be derived from A and B by means of unnested algebraic expressions involving exactly one of the algebraic operators and one or both, as appropriate, of A and B. For each such unnested expression it is fairly straightforward to find a semantically equivalent SQL SELECT expression, as indicated below. (Notation is intended to be self-explanatory.)

```
Algebra              SQL

A UNION B            SELECT  *
                     FROM    A
                     UNION
                     SELECT  *
                     FROM    B
A MINUS B            SELECT  *
                     FROM    A
                     WHERE   NOT EXISTS
                           ( SELECT  *
                             FROM    B
                             WHERE   all-fields-of-A =
                                     all-fields-of-B )
A TIMES B            SELECT  *
                     FROM    A, B
A WHERE p            SELECT  *
                     FROM    A
                     WHERE   p
A [x,y,...,z]        SELECT  DISTINCT x,y,...,z
                     FROM    A
```

We indicate in outline how we might prove that *any* relation that is derivable via a single (arbitrarily complex) algebraic expression can be derived via a single SQL expression (without however getting into the details, which are left as an exercise for the reader; but we remark that UNION is a little troublesome).

Step 1. (Already done.) Show that, if A and B are any two members of the given set of named relations, then any relation derivable via a single unnested algebraic expression involving exactly one of the algebraic operations and either one or both of A and B can be derived via a single SQL expression.

Step 2. Now let A and B be any two relations, either members of the given set of named relations or relations derivable from that set via possibly nested algebraic expressions. Further (unnamed) relations can be derived from A and B by means of expressions involving exactly one of the algebraic operators applied to one or both, as appropriate, of A and B. Show that *if* there exist SQL expressions representing A and B, *then* there exists a SQL expression representing each such derived relation.

Step 3. From Steps 1 and 2 together, the desired result follows.

Finally, consider the algebraic assignment

```
R := X ;
```

(where R is a named relation and X is an arbitrary expression). The sequence of SQL operations

```
DELETE FROM R ;
INSERT INTO R QX ;
```

(where QX is the SQL equivalent of X) has the same effect as the algebraic assignment, *provided* X is not a UNION. The SQL statement "INSERT ... SELECT" does not permit a UNION in the SELECT portion (for no very good reason).

13.5 Remember that the statement that (say) attribute K is the primary key for relation A is *time-independent*. It is not just a question of the values that happen to appear in the body of A at some particular time. With that caveat in mind:

a) The primary key of an arbitrary restriction of A is the same as the primary key of A.

b) If the projection includes the primary key of A, then its primary key is the same as that of A. Otherwise it is the combination of all attributes of the projection (in general— though it may be possible to be more specific if relation A satisfies certain additional time-independent constraints; see the discussion of functional dependence and further normalization in Chapter 17).

c) The primary key of the product A TIMES B is the combination of the primary keys of A and B.

d) The primary key of the union A UNION B is the combination of all attributes (in general).

e) Left as an exercise for the reader (intersection is not a primitive).

f) The primary key of the difference A MINUS B is the same as that of A.

g) We leave the general case as an exercise for the reader (natural join is not a primitive). However, in the particular case where the joining attribute in A is the primary key of A, the primary key of the join is the same as that of B.

h) Left as an exercise for the reader (division is not a primitive).

13.6 We have numbered the following solutions as 13.6.*n*, where *n* is the number of the original exercise in Chapter 6.

13.6.1   J

13.6.2   J WHERE CITY = 'London'

13.6.3   Ignoring ordering:

```
( SPJ WHERE J# = 'J1' ) [ S# ]
```

13.6.4   SPJ WHERE QTY >= 300 AND QTY <= 750

13.6.5   P [COLOR, CITY]

13.6.6
```
( ( S TIMES P TIMES J ) WHERE S.CITY = P.CITY
                        AND   P.CITY = J.CITY )
                                     [ S#, P#, J# ]
```

13.6.7
```
( ( S TIMES P TIMES J ) WHERE S.CITY ~= P.CITY
                        OR    P.CITY ~= J.CITY
                        OR    J.CITY ~= S.CITY )
                                     [ S#, P#, J# ]
```

13.6.8
```
( ( S TIMES P TIMES J ) WHERE S.CITY ~= P.CITY
                        AND   P.CITY ~= J.CITY
                        AND   J.CITY ~= S.CITY )
                                     [ S#, P#, J# ]
```

13.6.9   (SPJ JOIN (S WHERE CITY = 'London')) [P#]

13.6.10
```
( ( SPJ JOIN ( S WHERE CITY = 'London' ) ) [ P#, J# ]
          JOIN ( J WHERE CITY = 'London' ) ) [ P# ]
```

13.6.11
```
( ( S [ S#, CITY ] TIMES SPJ TIMES J [ J#, CITY ] )
          WHERE S.S# = SPJ.S#
          AND   SPJ.J# = J.J# ) [ S.CITY, J.CITY ]
```

13.6.12   (J [J#, CITY] JOIN SPJ JOIN S [S#, CITY]) [P#]

13.6.13
```
( ( J [ J#, CITY ] TIMES SPJ TIMES S [ S#, CITY ] )
          WHERE S.S# = SPJ.S#
          AND   SPJ.J# = J.J#
          AND   S.CITY ~= J.CITY ) [ J# ]
```

13.6.14
```
DEFINE ALIAS SPJX FOR SPJ
DEFINE ALIAS SPJY FOR SPJ
( ( SPJX TIMES SPJY ) WHERE SPJX.S# = SPJY.S#
                      AND   SPJX.P# < SPJY.P# )
                                  [ SPJX.P#, SPJY.P# ]
```

13.6.15–18 Cannot be done (they require the computational built-in functions SUM, AVG, etc.).

13.6.19 Cannot be done (it requires an operator called "maybe select"; see reference [12.1]).

13.6.20 (J WHERE CITY LIKE '_o%') [J#, CITY]
We have assumed that the SQL "LIKE" operator is a legal *theta*.

13.6.21 (J JOIN (SPJ WHERE S# = 'S1')) [JNAME]

13.6.22 (P JOIN (SPJ WHERE S# = 'S1')) [COLOR]

13.6.23 (SPJ JOIN (J WHERE CITY = 'London')) [P#]

13.6.24 (SPJ JOIN (SPJ WHERE S# = 'S1') [P#]) [J#]

13.6.25 (((SPJ JOIN (P WHERE COLOR = 'Red') [P#])
                    [S#] JOIN SPJ) [P#] JOIN SPJ) [S#]

13.6.26 DEFINE ALIAS SX FOR S
     DEFINE ALIAS SY FOR S
     ((SX TIMES SY) WHERE SX.S# = 'S1'
                   AND   SX.STATUS > SY.STATUS) [SY.S#]

13.6.27 DEFINE ALIAS JX FOR J
     DEFINE ALIAS JY FOR J
     JX [J#] MINUS
          ((JX TIMES JY) WHERE JX.CITY > JY.CITY) [JX.J#]

13.6.28–29 Cannot be done (they require the computational built-in functions).

13.6.30–31 Not applicable.

13.6.32 J [J#] MINUS
     (((S WHERE CITY = 'London') [S#]
          JOIN SPJ
          JOIN (P WHERE COLOR = 'Red') [P#]) [J#])

13.6.33 (SPJ WHERE S# = 'S1') [J#] MINUS
     (SPJ WHERE S# ~= 'S1') [J#]

13.6.34 SPJ [P#, J#] DIVIDEBY
                    (J WHERE CITY = 'London') [J#]

13.6.35 (SPJ [S#, P#, J#] DIVIDEBY J [J#]) [S#]

13.6.36 SPJ [J#, P#] DIVIDEBY (SPJ WHERE S# = 'S1') [P#]

13.6.37–40 Not applicable.

13.6.41 Ignoring ordering:

     S [CITY] UNION P [CITY] UNION J [CITY]

13.6.42–46 Not applicable.

13.6.47 (SPJ JOIN (S WHERE CITY = 'London')) [P#]
     UNION
     (SPJ JOIN (J WHERE CITY = 'London')) [P#]

13.6.48 (J WHERE CITY = 'London') [J#]
     UNION
     (SPJ JOIN (S WHERE CITY = 'London')) [J#]

13.7 We give an intuitive "proof" only.

- Product is the only operator that increases the number of attributes, so it cannot be simulated by any combination of the other operators. Therefore product is primitive.
- Projection is the only operator that reduces the number of attributes, so it cannot be simulated by any combination of the other operators. Therefore projection is primitive.

- Union is the only operator that increases the number of tuples, apart from product, and product increases the number of attributes as well. Let the two relations to be "unioned" be A and B. Note that A and B must be union-compatible, and their union has exactly the same attributes as each of them. If we form the *product* of A and B, and then use projection to reduce the set of attributes in the product to just the set of attributes in A (or in B), we simply get back to the original relation A (or B) again. Therefore union is primitive.

- Difference cannot be simulated via product (because product increases the number of tuples) or union (likewise) or projection (because projection reduces the number of attributes). Nor can it be simulated by restriction, because difference is sensitive to the values appearing in the second relation, whereas restriction cannot be (by virtue of the nature of a restriction predicate). Therefore difference is primitive.

- Restriction is the only operator that allows attribute values to be compared with externally specified constants (i.e., values that are not already part of some relation). Therefore restriction is primitive.

13.8 Let R $(A,B1)$ and S $(B2,C)$ be two relations with (possibly composite) attributes $R.A$, $R.B1$, $S.B2$, $S.C$ and with $R.B1$ and $S.B2$ defined on the same domain. Define T to be the theta-join of R on $B1$ with S on $B2$:

```
T = ( R TIMES S ) WHERE R.B1 theta S.B2
```

Define $R1$ and $S1$ as follows:

```
R1 = R MINUS ( T [ A,B1 ] )
S1 = S MINUS ( T [ B2,C ] )
```

Then the *left outer theta-join*, X say, of R on $B1$ with S on $B2$ is defined as follows:

```
X = T UNION ( R1 TIMES { ( ?,? ) } )
```

where the expression " { (?,?) }" represents a relation that is union-compatible with S and contains just one tuple, which consists entirely of null values. Likewise, the *right* outer theta-join, Y say, of R on $B1$ with S on $B2$ is defined as follows:

```
Y = T UNION ( { ( ?,? ) } TIMES S1 )
```

where the expression "{ (?,?) }" represents a relation that is union-compatible with R and contains just one tuple, which consists entirely of null values. The *full* or *symmetric* outer theta-join, Z say, of R on $B1$ with S on $B2$ is defined as follows:

```
Z = X UNION Y
```

Similarly, the full or symmetric outer *natural* join, Z' say, of R on $B1$ with S on $B2$ is defined as follows:

```
Z' = ( T [ A,B1,C ] ) UNION ( R1 TIMES { ( ? ) } )
                       UNION ( { ( ? ) } TIMES S1 )
```

where the first "{ (?) }" is union-compatible with S [C] and the second is union-compatible with R [A]. Left and right outer natural joins can be defined analogously.

A comprehensive discussion of outer join can be found in [13.9].

14

Relational
Calculus

14.1 INTRODUCTION

The relational calculus represents an alternative to the relational algebra as a candidate for the manipulative part of the model. The difference between the two is as follows: Where the algebra provides a collection of explicit operations—join, union, projection, etc.—that can actually be used to *build* some desired relation from the given relations in the database, the calculus merely provides a notation for formulating the *definition* of that desired relation in terms of those given relations. For example, consider the query "Get supplier numbers and cities for suppliers who supply part P2." An algebraic version of this query might look somewhat as follows:

Join relation S on S# with relation SP on S#;
Restrict the result of that join to tuples with P# = 'P2';
Project the result of that restriction on S# and CITY.

(We deliberately do not use the formal syntax of Chapter 13.) A calculus formulation, by contrast, might look something like this:

Get S# and CITY for suppliers such that there exists a shipment SP with the same S# value and with P# value 'P2'.

Here the user has merely stated the defining characteristics of the desired set, and it is left to the system to decide exactly what joins, projections, etc. must be executed in order to construct that set.[1]

---

1. Like the algebra, the calculus needs an associated assignment operator to permit the result of evaluating some arbitrary expression to be recorded in some more or less permanent manner (and in particular to serve as the basis for database update operations). We do not discuss that assignment operator in this chapter.

Superficially, at least, therefore, we might say that the calculus formulation is *descriptive* where the algebraic one is *prescriptive*: The calculus simply states what the problem *is*, the algebra gives a procedure for *solving* that problem. Or, *very* loosely: The algebra is procedural (admittedly high-level, but still procedural); the calculus is nonprocedural.

However, we stress the point that the foregoing distinctions *are* superficial. The fact is, *the algebra and the calculus are precisely equivalent to one another*. For every expression of the algebra, there is an equivalent expression in the calculus; likewise, for every expression of the calculus, there is an equivalent expression in the algebra. There is a one-to-one correspondence between the two. The different formalisms simply represent different styles of expression (the calculus is arguably closer to natural language, the algebra is perhaps more like a programming language). But—to repeat—all such distinctions are more apparent than real; in particular, neither approach is genuinely more nonprocedural than the other. We will examine this question of the equivalence between the two approaches in more depth in Section 14.4.

Relational calculus is founded on a branch of mathematical logic called the *predicate* calculus. The idea of using predicate calculus as the basis for a database language appears to have originated in a paper by Kuhns [14.1]. The concept of a *relational* calculus—i.e., an applied predicate calculus specifically tailored to relational databases—was first proposed by Codd in reference [14.2]; a language explicitly based on that calculus called "data sublanguage ALPHA" was also presented by Codd in another paper [14.3]. ALPHA itself was never implemented, but the language QUEL discussed in Chapter 10 is actually very similar to it (indeed, the design of QUEL was influenced by ALPHA).

A fundamental feature of the calculus as defined in reference [14.2] is the notion of the *tuple variable* (also known as a *range variable*, and introduced by that name in Chapter 10). Briefly, a tuple variable is a variable that "ranges over" some relation—i.e., a variable whose only permitted values are tuples of that relation. In other words, if tuple variable T ranges over relation R, then, at any given time, T represents some tuple t of R. For example, the query "Get supplier numbers for suppliers in London" can be expressed in QUEL as follows:

```
RANGE OF SX IS S
RETRIEVE ( SX.S# ) WHERE SX.CITY = "London"
```

The tuple variable here is SX, and it ranges over relation S. The RETRIEVE statement can be paraphrased: "For each possible value of the variable SX, retrieve the S# component of that value, if and only if the CITY component has the value London".[2]

---

2. The SQL formulation of this query—

```
SELECT  S.S#
FROM    S
WHERE   S.CITY = 'London' ;
```

Because of its reliance on tuple variables (and to distinguish it from the domain calculus—see below), the original relational calculus [14.2] has come to be known as the *tuple* calculus. The tuple calculus is described in detail in Section 14.2.

In reference [14.4], Lacroix and Pirotte proposed an alternative relational calculus called the *domain* calculus, in which tuple variables are replaced by domain variables—i.e., variables that range over a domain instead of a relation. A language called ILL based on that calculus is presented by the same authors in reference [14.5]. Other examples of domain calculus languages are FQL [14.6], DEDUCE [14.7], and Query-By-Example, QBE [14.8]. We sketch the domain calculus in Section 14.5 and discuss QBE briefly in Section 14.6.

14.2 TUPLE-ORIENTED RELATIONAL CALCULUS

As with the algebra in Chapter 13, we introduce a concrete syntax for the relational calculus, in order to provide a basis for the discussions that follow in the rest of the chapter. The syntax is defined by the BNF grammar of Fig. 14.1. Note that square brackets in that grammar (as in the algebraic grammar of Chapter 13) represent symbols in the language being defined, instead of indicating that the material they enclose is optional.

Some Notes on the Grammar

1. The term "commalist" is as defined in Section 13.2: If "xyz" is a syntactic category, then "xyz-commalist" is a syntactic category consisting of a list of one or more "xyz"s in which adjacent "xyz"s are separated by a comma. The term "semicolonlist" is defined analogously.

2. The categories *rel-name*, *vble-name*, and *attr-name* are each defined to be *identifiers* (a terminal category with respect to this grammar).

3. The category *comparison* represents (as in the algebra) a simple comparison between two *scalar-values*, and a *scalar-value* consists of either a constant or an attribute value (represented by an expression of the form *vble-name.attr-name*).

—does not require the explicit introduction of a tuple variable, but allows the relation name S to serve as an *implicit* tuple variable instead. But the underlying concept is the same. To understand how the SQL query is evaluated, it is necessary to imagine the *tuple variable* S ranging over the *relation* S. In effect, SQL simply has a default rule for the automatic definition of tuple variables that is adequate in simple cases. In more complex cases the user still has to introduce tuple variables explicitly; see, for instance, Example 6.3.6 in Chapter 6 (where we referred to such tuple variables, perhaps a trifle misleadingly, as "aliases"). In fact, QUEL also has such a default rule, as we already know. For example, the original QUEL query could have been expressed simply as

```
RETRIEVE ( S.S# ) WHERE S.CITY = "London"
```

```
rel-defn
    ::= DEFINE RELATION rel-name [ attr-name-commalist ]

vble-defn
    ::= RANGE OF vble-name IS expr-semicolonlist

expr
    ::= target-item-commalist
      | target-item-commalist WHERE wff

target-item
    ::= vble-name . attr-name

wff
    ::= comparison
      | ( wff )
      | NOT wff
      | wff AND wff
      | wff OR wff
      | EXISTS vble-name ( wff )
      | FORALL vble-name ( wff )
      | IF wff THEN wff
```

Fig. 14.1 A BNF grammar for the tuple calculus.

4. We deliberately do not allow a "target-item" to be an operational expression such as $T1.A1 + T2.A2$, for reasons of simplicity. Likewise, we do not allow such expressions to appear as a comparand in a comparison. In practice, of course, such restrictions would be very undesirable.

5. The category *wff* represents a "well-formed formula" (WFF, usually pronounced "weff"). WFFs are discussed in detail in the following subsections.

Tuple Variables

A tuple variable is defined by means of a statement of the form

```
RANGE OF T IS X1; X2; ...; Xn
```

where T is a tuple variable and $X1, X2, \ldots, Xn$ are tuple calculus expressions, representing relations $R1, R2, \ldots, Rn$ (say). Relations $R1, R2, \ldots, Rn$ must all be union-compatible, and corresponding attributes must be identically named in every relation listed.[3] Tuple variable T ranges over the union of those relations. Of course, if the "list of expressions" identifies just one named relation R (the normal case), then the tuple variable T ranges over just the tuples of that single relation R.

---

3.   Thus (as in the algebra) we need rules defining attribute names for an arbitrary derived relation. We also need an extended form of the DEFINE ALIAS operator of Chapter 13 to permit the renaming not only of relations, but also of attributes within those relations. The details are left as an exercise for the reader.

Throughout this chapter, we assume that the following variable definitions are in effect:

```
RANGE OF SX IS S
RANGE OF SY IS S
RANGE OF SZ IS S

RANGE OF PX IS P
RANGE OF PY IS P
RANGE OF PZ IS P

RANGE OF SPX IS SP
RANGE OF SPY IS SP
RANGE OF SPZ IS SP
```

Free and Bound Variables

Each occurrence of a tuple variable within a WFF is either *free* or *bound*. We explain this notion in purely syntactic terms first (with examples), then go on to discuss its significance later.

By "occurrence of a tuple variable" we mean an appearance of the variable name within the WFF under consideration. A tuple variable T occurs within a given WFF either in the context of an attribute reference (of the form $T.A$, where A is an attribute of the relation over which T ranges) or as the variable immediately following one of the "quantifiers" EXISTS and FORALL. Quantifiers are explained below.

1. Within a simple comparison, all tuple variable occurrences are free.

2. Tuple variable occurrences in the WFFs (f), NOT f are free/bound according as they are free/bound in f. Tuple variable occurrences in the WFFs f AND g, f OR g are free/bound according as they are free/bound in f or g (whichever of f or g they appear in).

3. Occurrences of T that are free in f are bound in the WFFs EXISTS T (f), FORALL T (f). Other tuple variable occurrences in f are free/bound in these WFFs according as they are free/bound in f.

4. The WFF

   ```
   IF f THEN g
   ```

   is defined to be precisely equivalent to the WFF

   ```
   ( NOT f ) OR g
   ```

   See Example 14.3.8 in Section 14.3.

Examples:

a) Simple comparisons:

```
SX.S# = 'S1'
SX.S# = SPX.S#
SPX.P# ~= PX.P#
```

All occurrences of SX, PX, SPX are free in these examples.

b) Boolean WFFs:

```
NOT SX.CITY = 'London'
SX.S# = SPX.S# AND SPX.P# ~= PX.P#
```

Again, all occurrences of SX, PX, SPX here are free.

c) Quantified WFFs:

```
EXISTS SPX ( SPX.S# = SX.S# AND SPX.P# = 'P2' )
```

The *existential quantifier* EXISTS is read as "there exists." The example can be read: "There exists an SP tuple with S# value equal to the value of SX.S#"—whatever that is—"and P# value equal to P2." Each occurrence of SPX in this example is bound. The (single) occurrence of SX is free.

```
FORALL PX ( PX.COLOR = 'Red' )
```

The *universal quantifier* FORALL is read as "for all." The example can be read: "For all P tuples, the COLOR is Red." The two occurrences of PX here are bound.

Note: The universal quantifier is included in the calculus purely for convenience; it is not essential—the identity

```
FORALL x ( f ) ≡ NOT EXISTS x ( NOT f )
```

shows that any WFF involving FORALL can always be replaced by an equivalent WFF involving EXISTS instead. For example, the (true) statement "For all integers x, there exists an integer y such that $y > x$" is equivalent to the statement "There does not exist an integer x such that there does not exist an integer y such that $y > x$." But it is frequently easier to think in terms of FORALL than in terms of EXISTS and a double negative.

Let us now examine the concept of free and bound variables a little more closely. Consider the following simple example:

```
EXISTS x ( x > 3 )
```

(where x ranges over the set of integers). The bound variable x in this WFF is a kind of *dummy*—it serves only to link the expression within the parentheses to the quantifier outside. The WFF states that there exists some integer, say x, that is greater than three. The meaning of the WFF would remain unchanged if all occurrences of x were replaced by some other variable y. In other words, the WFF

```
EXISTS y ( y > 3 )
```

is semantically identical to the one above.

Now consider the WFF

```
EXISTS x ( x > 3 ) AND x < 0
```

Here there are three occurrences of *x*, *referring to two different variables*. The first two occurrences are bound, and could be replaced by some other variable *y* without changing the overall meaning of the WFF. The third occurrence is free, and *cannot* be replaced with impunity. Thus, of the two WFFs below, the first is equivalent to the one above and the second is not:

```
EXISTS y ( y > 3 ) AND x < 0

EXISTS y ( y > 3 ) AND y < 0
```

Expressions

A tuple calculus expression is an expression of the form

$$T.A, U.B, \ldots , V.C \text{ WHERE } f$$

where *T*, *U*, . . . , *V* are tuple variables, *A*, *B*, . . . , *C* are attributes of the associated relations,[4] and *f* is a WFF containing exactly *T*, *U*, . . . , *V* as free variables. The value of this expression is defined to be a projection of that subset of the extended Cartesian product $T \times U \times \ldots \times V$ (where *T*, *U*, . . . , *V* range over all of their possible values) for which *f* evaluates to *true*—or, if "WHERE *f*" is omitted, a projection of that entire Cartesian product. The projection in question is of course taken over the components (attributes) indicated by the entries in the list *T.A*, *U.B*, . . . , *V.C*. No target item may appear more than once in that list.
Examples:

```
SX.S#
SX.S# WHERE SX.CITY = 'London'
SX.S#, SX.CITY WHERE EXISTS SPX ( SPX.S# = SX.S# AND
                                   SPX.P# = 'P2' )
```

The first of these denotes the set of all supplier numbers in relation S; the second denotes that subset of those supplier numbers for which the city is London. The third is a tuple calculus representation of the query "Get supplier numbers and cities for suppliers who supply part P2" (which is of course the sample query we started with, at the beginning of Section 14.1).

14.3 EXAMPLES

14.3.1. Get supplier numbers for suppliers in Paris with status > 20. (Example 6.2.4)

```
SX.S# WHERE SX.CITY = 'Paris' AND SX.STATUS > 20
```

---

4. Remember that, in general, the "associated relation" for a given tuple variable is the union of a set of relations that are in turn represented by tuple calculus expressions.

14.3.2. Get all pairs of supplier numbers such that the two suppliers are located in the same city. (Examples 6.3.6, 13.5.6)

```
SX.S#, SY.S# WHERE SX.CITY = SY.CITY AND SX.S# < SY.S#
```

14.3.3. Get supplier names for suppliers who supply part P2. (Examples 6.5.3, 13.5.1)

```
SX.SNAME WHERE EXISTS SPX ( SPX.S# = SX.S# AND
                            SPX.P# = 'P2' )
```

14.3.4. Get supplier names for suppliers who supply at least one red part. (Examples 6.5.4, 13.5.2)

```
SX.SNAME WHERE EXISTS SPX ( SX.S# = SPX.S# AND
                            EXISTS PX ( SPX.P# = PX.P# AND
                                        PX.COLOR = 'Red' ) )
```

Or equivalently (but in *prenex normal form*, in which all quantifiers appear at the front of the WFF):

```
SX.SNAME WHERE EXISTS SPX ( EXISTS PX ( SX.S# = SPX.S# AND
                                        SPX.P# = PX.P# AND
                                        PX.COLOR = 'Red' ) )
```

Prenex normal form is not inherently more or less correct than any other form, but with a little practice it does tend to become the most natural formulation in many cases. Furthermore, it introduces the possibility of reducing the number of parentheses, as follows. The WFF

```
quant-1 vble-1 ( quant-2 vble-2 ( wff ) )
```

(where "quant-1" and "quant-2" are quantifiers) can optionally, and unambiguously, be abbreviated to the form

```
quant-1 vble-1 quant-2 vble-2 ( wff )
```

Thus we can rewrite the calculus expression above (if desired) as

```
SX.SNAME WHERE EXISTS SPX EXISTS PX ( SX.S# = SPX.S# AND
                                      SPX.P# = PX.P# AND
                                      PX.COLOR = 'Red' )
```

For clarity, however, we will continue to show all parentheses in all remaining examples in this section.

14.3.5. Get supplier names for suppliers who supply at least one part supplied by supplier S2.

```
SX.SNAME WHERE EXISTS SPX ( EXISTS SPY ( SX.S# = SPX.S# AND
                                         SPX.P# = SPY.P# AND
                                         SPY.S# = 'S2' ) )
```

14.3.6. Get supplier names for suppliers who supply all parts. (Examples 6.5.9, 13.5.3)

```
SX.SNAME WHERE FORALL PX ( EXISTS SPX ( SPX.S# = SX.S# AND
                                        SPX.P# = PX.P# ) )
```

Or equivalently, but without using FORALL:

```
SX.SNAME WHERE NOT EXISTS PX ( NOT EXISTS SPX
                                 ( SPX.S# = SX.S# AND
                                   SPX.P# = PX.P# ) )
```

14.3.7. Get supplier names for suppliers who do not supply part P2. (Examples 6.5.8, 13.5.5; also contrast Example 14.3.3 above)

```
SX.SNAME WHERE NOT EXISTS SPX
                 ( SPX.S# = SX.S# AND SPX.P# = 'P2' )
```

14.3.8. Get supplier numbers for suppliers who supply at least all those parts supplied by supplier S2. (Examples 6.5.10, 13.5.4)

```
SPX.S# WHERE FORALL SPY ( SPY.S# ~= 'S2' OR
                    EXISTS SPZ ( SPZ.S# = SPX.S# AND
                                 SPZ.P# = SPY.S# ) )
```

Paraphrasing: "Get supplier numbers for shipments, say SPX, such that, for all shipments SPY, either that shipment is not from supplier S2, or if it is, then there exists a shipment SPZ of the SPY part from the SPX supplier."

We introduce another syntactic convention to help with complex queries such as this one, namely an explicit syntactic form for the *logical implication* operator. If *A* and *B* are WFFs, then the logical implication expression

```
IF A THEN B
```

is also defined to be a WFF, with semantics identical to those of the WFF

```
( NOT A ) OR B
```

The expression above can thus be rewritten (if desired):

```
SPX.S# WHERE FORALL SPY ( IF SPY.S# = 'S2' THEN
                    EXISTS SPZ ( SPZ.S# = SPX.S# AND
                                 SPZ.P# = SPY.S# ) )
```

Paraphrasing: "Get supplier numbers for shipments, say SPX, such that, for all shipments SPY, if that shipment SPY is from supplier S2, then there exists a shipment SPZ of the SPY part from the SPX supplier."

14.3.9. Get part numbers for parts that either weigh more than 16 pounds or are supplied by supplier S2, or both. (Example 6.5.11)

```
RANGE OF PU IS PX.P# WHERE PX.WEIGHT > 16 ;
               SPX.P# WHERE SPX.S# = 'S2'
PU.P#
```

14.4 RELATIONAL CALCULUS vs. RELATIONAL ALGEBRA

We claimed several times in the introduction to this chapter that the relational algebra and the relational calculus are fundamentally equivalent to one another. We now examine that claim in more detail. First, Codd proved in reference [14.2] that the algebra is at least as powerful as the calculus. (Note: For brevity, we will use the unqualified term "calculus" to refer to the tuple calculus specifically throughout this section.) He did this by giving an algorithm—"Codd's reduction algorithm"—by which an arbitrary expression of the calculus can be reduced to a semantically equivalent expression of the algebra. We do not present Codd's algorithm in detail here, but content ourselves with a reasonably complex example that illustrates in general terms how that algorithm works.

As a basis for our example we use, not the familiar suppliers-and-parts database, but the extended suppliers-parts-projects version from the exercises in Chapters 5 and 6 (and elsewhere). For convenience, we show in Fig. 14.2 a set of sample values for that database (repeated from Fig. 5.1.).

S	S#	SNAME	STATUS	CITY
	S1	Smith	20	London
	S2	Jones	10	Paris
	S3	Blake	30	Paris
	S4	Clark	20	London
	S5	Adams	30	Athens

P	P#	PNAME	COLOR	WEIGHT	CITY
	P1	Nut	Red	12	London
	P2	Bolt	Green	17	Paris
	P3	Screw	Blue	17	Rome
	P4	Screw	Red	14	London
	P5	Cam	Blue	12	Paris
	P6	Cog	Red	19	London

J	J#	JNAME	CITY
	J1	Sorter	Paris
	J2	Punch	Rome
	J3	Reader	Athens
	J4	Console	Athens
	J5	Collator	London
	J6	Terminal	Oslo
	J7	Tape	London

SPJ	S#	P#	J#	QTY
	S1	P1	J1	200
	S1	P1	J4	700
	S2	P3	J1	400
	S2	P3	J2	200
	S2	P3	J3	200
	S2	P3	J4	500
	S2	P3	J5	600
	S2	P3	J6	400
	S2	P3	J7	800
	S2	P5	J2	100
	S3	P3	J1	200
	S3	P4	J2	500
	S4	P6	J3	300
	S4	P6	J7	300
	S5	P2	J2	200
	S5	P2	J4	100
	S5	P5	J5	500
	S5	P5	J7	100
	S5	P6	J2	200
	S5	P1	J4	100
	S5	P3	J4	200
	S5	P4	J4	800
	S5	P5	J4	400
	S5	P6	J4	500

Fig. 14.2 The suppliers-parts-projects database.

Now consider the query: "Get names and cities for suppliers who supply at least one Athens project with at least 51 of every part." A calculus expression for this query is:

```
SX.SNAME, SX.CITY WHERE EXISTS JX FORALL PX EXISTS SPJX
                            ( JX.CITY = 'Athens' AND
                              JX.J# = SPJX.J# AND
                              PX.P# = SPJX.P# AND
                              SX.S# = SPJX.S# AND
                              SPJX.QTY > 50 )
```

where SX, PX, JX, SPJX are tuple variables ranging over S, P, J, SPJ, respectively. We now show how this expression can be evaluated to yield the desired result.

Step 1. For each tuple variable, retrieve the range (i.e., the set of possible values for that variable), restricted if possible. By "restricted if possible," we mean that there may be a restriction predicate embedded within the WHERE clause that can be used right away to eliminate certain tuples from all further consideration. In the case at hand, the sets of tuples retrieved are as follows:

SX : All tuples of S		5 tuples
PX : All tuples of P		6 tuples
JX : Tuples of J where CITY = 'Athens'		2 tuples
SPJX : Tuples of SPJ where QTY > 50		24 tuples

Step 2. Construct the Cartesian product of the ranges retrieved in Step 1, to yield:

S#	SN	STATUS	CITY	P#	PN	COLOR	WEIGHT	CITY	J#	JN	CITY	S#	P#	J#	QTY
S1	Sm	20	Lon	P1	Nt	Red	12	Lon	J3	Rd	Ath	S1	P1	J1	200
S1	Sm	20	Lon	P1	Nt	Red	12	Lon	J3	Rd	Ath	S1	P1	J4	700
.	.	.	.	.	.	.	.	.	.	.	.	.	.	.	.
.	.	.	.	.	.	.	.	.	.	.	.	.	.	.	.
.	.	.	.	.	.	.	.	.	.	.	.	.	.	.	.

(etc., etc.). The complete product contains 5 * 6 * 2 * 24 = 1440 tuples. Note: We have made a number of obvious abbreviations in the table above in the interests of space.

Step 3. Restrict the Cartesian product just built in accordance with the "join condition" portion of the WHERE clause. In the example, that portion is

```
JX.J# = SPJX.J# AND PX.P# = SPJX.P# AND SX.S# = SPJX.S#
```

We therefore eliminate tuples from the product for which the supplier S# value is not equal to the shipment S# value or the part P# value is not equal to the shipment P# value or the project J# value is not equal to the shipment J# value, to yield a subset of the Cartesian product consisting (as it happens) of just 10 tuples:

S#	SN	STATUS	CITY	P#	PN	COLOR	WEIGHT	CITY	J#	JN	CITY	S#	P#	J#	QTY
S1	Sm	20	Lon	P1	Nt	Red	12	Lon	J4	Cn	Ath	S1	P1	J4	700
S2	Jo	10	Par	P3	Sc	Blue	17	Rom	J3	Rd	Ath	S2	P3	J3	200
S2	Jo	10	Par	P3	Sc	Blue	17	Rom	J4	Cn	Ath	S2	P3	J4	500
S4	Cl	20	Lon	P6	Cg	Red	19	Lon	J3	Rd	Ath	S4	P6	J3	300
S5	Ad	30	Ath	P2	Bt	Green	17	Par	J4	Cn	Ath	S5	P2	J4	100
S5	Ad	30	Ath	P1	Nt	Red	12	Lon	J4	Cn	Ath	S5	P1	J4	100
S5	Ad	30	Ath	P3	Sc	Blue	17	Rom	J4	Cn	Ath	S5	P3	J4	200
S5	Ad	30	Ath	P4	Sc	Red	14	Lon	J4	Cn	Ath	S5	P4	J4	800
S5	Ad	30	Ath	P5	Cm	Blue	12	Par	J4	Cn	Ath	S5	P5	J4	400
S5	Ad	30	Ath	P6	Cg	Red	19	Lon	J4	Cn	Ath	S5	P6	J4	500

Step 4. Apply the quantifiers from right to left, as follows.

■ For the quantifier "EXISTS RX" (where RX is a tuple variable that ranges over some associated relation R), *project* the current intermediate result to eliminate all attributes of relation R.

■ For the quantifier "FORALL RX," *divide* the current intermediate result by the "restricted range" relation associated with RX (as retrieved in Step 1).

In the example, the quantifiers are:

EXISTS JX FORALL PX EXISTS SPJX

Hence:

1. Project out the attributes SPJ.S#, SPJ.P#, SPJ.J#, SPJ.QTY.

Result:

S#	SN	STATUS	CITY	P#	PN	COLOR	WEIGHT	CITY	J#	JN	CITY
S1	Sm	20	Lon	P1	Nt	Red	12	Lon	J4	Cn	Ath
S2	Jo	10	Par	P3	Sc	Blue	17	Rom	J3	Rd	Ath
S2	Jo	10	Par	P3	Sc	Blue	17	Rom	J4	Cn	Ath
S4	Cl	20	Lon	P6	Cg	Red	19	Lon	J3	Rd	Ath
S5	Ad	30	Ath	P2	Bt	Green	17	Par	J4	Cn	Ath
S5	Ad	30	Ath	P1	Nt	Red	12	Lon	J4	Cn	Ath
S5	Ad	30	Ath	P3	Sc	Blue	17	Rom	J4	Cn	Ath
S5	Ad	30	Ath	P4	Sc	Red	14	Lon	J4	Cn	Ath
S5	Ad	30	Ath	P5	Cm	Blue	12	Par	J4	Cn	Ath
S5	Ad	30	Ath	P6	Cg	Red	19	Lon	J4	Cn	Ath

2. Divide by relation P.

Result:

```
--  --  ------  ----  --  --  ----
S#  SN  STATUS  CITY  J#  JN  CITY
--  --  ------  ----  --  --  ----
S5  Ad      30  Ath   J4  Cn  Ath
```

We now have room to show this relation without any abbreviations:

```
--  -----  ------  ------  --  -------  ------
S#  SNAME  STATUS  CITY    J#  JNAME    CITY
--  -----  ------  ------  --  -------  ------
S5  Adams      30  Athens  J4  Console  Athens
```

3. Project out the attributes J#, JNAME, CITY.

Result:

```
--  -----  ------  ------
S#  SNAME  STATUS  CITY
--  -----  ------  ------
S5  Adams      30  Athens
```

Step 5. Project the result of Step 4 in accordance with the specifications in the target list. In our example, the target list is:

```
SX.SNAME, SX.CITY
```

Hence the final result is:

```
-----  ------
SNAME  CITY
-----  ------
Adams  Athens
```

This concludes the example. We note that numerous improvements are possible (see Chapter 16 for some ideas for such improvements), also that many details have been glossed over. However, the example should be adequate to give the general idea of how the reduction works. Incidentally, we are now able to explain one of the reasons (not the only one) why Codd defined precisely the eight algebraic operators he did: Those eight operators provide a convenient basis for a possible implementation of the calculus. But perhaps more important, they also provide a *yardstick* for measuring the expressive power of any given database language (existing or proposed). Let us examine this latter point in more depth.

First, a language is said to be *relationally complete* if it is at least as powerful as the relational calculus—that is, if its expressions permit the definition of any relation definable by the expressions of the relational calculus [14.2]. It follows from the existence of Codd's reduction algorithm that the relational algebra is complete in this sense. Relational completeness may be regarded as a basic measure of selective or expressive power for database languages in general.

Next, since the algebra is relationally complete, it follows that, to show that any given language L is also complete, it is sufficient to show that L includes analogs of each of the eight algebraic operations (indeed, it is sufficient to show that L includes analogs of the five *primitive* algebraic operations). SQL is an example of a language that is relationally complete (see Exercise 13.4 in Chapter 13), and QUEL is another. In practice, it will often be easier to show that a given language has equivalents of the algebraic operations than to show that it has equivalents of expressions of the calculus; thus the "yardstick" aspect of the algebra may be considered one of its most important characteristics.

Two further points concerning completeness:

1. The term "relationally complete" is frequently interpreted in a somewhat more demanding sense, to wit: A language is considered to be relationally complete if any relation definable via a *single expression* of the calculus is definable via a *single expression* of the language. The algebra is complete in this more demanding sense (as indeed are many relational languages). The calculus and the algebra thus both provide a basis for designing languages that provide this power of expressiveness *without having to resort to the use of loops*—a particularly important consideration in the case of a language that is intended for end-users, though it is not irrelevant for programming languages as well.

2. Of course, relational completeness does not necessarily imply any other kind of completeness. For example, it is desirable that a language provide "computational completeness" also (i.e., it should support all of the computational operators found in ordinary arithmetic; note that the calculus and the algebra as we have defined them are *not* complete in this sense, though in practice real database languages ought preferably to be so).

To return to the question of the equivalence of the algebra and the calculus: We have shown by example that any calculus expression can be reduced to an algebraic equivalent, and hence that the algebra is at least as powerful as the calculus. Conversely, it is possible to show that any algebraic expression can be reduced to a calculus equivalent, and hence that the calculus is at least as powerful as the algebra; for proof, see Ullman [11.6] or Maier [11.7]. It follows that the two formalisms are logically equivalent.

14.5 DOMAIN-ORIENTED RELATIONAL CALCULUS

As indicated in Section 14.1, the domain-oriented relational calculus (domain calculus for short) differs from the tuple calculus in that it has *domain* variables instead of tuple variables—i.e., variables that range over domains instead of over relations.[5] We discuss the domain calculus only rather briefly in this book.

---

5. "Element variable" would be a better name than "domain variable," since the values are domain *elements*, not domains themselves.

From a practical standpoint, the most immediately obvious distinction between the domain and tuple versions of the calculus is that the domain version supports an additional form of "comparison" (the term is not terribly apt in this context), which we will refer to as the *membership condition*. A membership condition takes the form

$$R \text{ (term, term, } \ldots \text{)}$$

where R is a relation name, and each term is a pair of the form $A{:}v$, where A in turn is an attribute of R and v is either a domain variable or a constant. The condition evaluates to true if and only if there exists a tuple in relation R having the specified values for the specified attributes. For example, the expression

```
SP ( S#:'S1', P#:'P1' )
```

is a membership condition, which evaluates to *true* if and only if there exists a tuple in relation SP with S# value S1 and P# value P1. Likewise, the membership condition

```
SP ( S#:SX, P#:PX )
```

evaluates to *true* if and only if there exists an SP tuple with S# value equal to the current value of domain variable SX (whatever that may be) and P# value equal to the current value of domain variable PX (again, whatever that may be).

For the remainder of this section we assume the existence of domain variables with names formed by appending X, Y, Z, . . . to the corresponding domain name— except that, for domains whose names end in "#", we drop that "#". We remind the reader that in the suppliers-and-parts database each attribute has the same name as its underlying domain, except for attributes SNAME and PNAME, for which the underlying domain is called simply NAME.

Examples of domain calculus expressions:

```
SX
SX WHERE S ( S#:SX )
SX WHERE S ( S#:SX, CITY:'London' )
SX, CITYX WHERE S ( S#:SX, CITY:CITYX )
          AND    SP ( S#:SX, P#:'P2' )
```

The first of these denotes the set of all supplier numbers;[6] the second denotes the set of all supplier numbers in relation S; the third denotes that subset of those supplier numbers for which the city is London. The last is a domain calculus representation of the query "Get supplier numbers and cities for suppliers who supply part P2" (note that the tuple calculus version of this query required an existential quantifier).

---

6. And may not be a supported query in an implemented system, given that domains per se are typically not stored in the database.

We give domain calculus versions of some of the examples from Section 14.3.

14.5.1. Get supplier numbers for suppliers in Paris with status > 20. (Example 14.3.1)

```
SX WHERE EXISTS STATUSX ( STATUSX > 20 AND
                  S ( S#:SX, STATUS:STATUSX, CITY:'Paris' )
```

Note that quantifiers are still needed. This particular example is somewhat clumsier than its tuple calculus counterpart. On the other hand, there are also cases where the reverse is true (see especially some of the more complex examples later).

14.5.2. Get all pairs of supplier numbers such that the two suppliers are located in the same city. (Example 14.3.2)

```
SX, SY WHERE EXISTS CITYZ
           ( S ( S#:SX, CITY:CITYZ ) AND
             S ( S#:SY, CITY:CITYZ ) AND
             SX < SY )
```

14.5.3. Get supplier names for suppliers who supply at least one red part. (Example 14.3.4)

```
NAMEX WHERE EXISTS SX EXISTS PX
           ( S ( S#:SX, SNAME:NAMEX )
           AND SP ( S#:SX, P#:PX )
           AND P ( P#:PX, COLOR:'Red' ) )
```

14.5.4. Get supplier names for suppliers who supply at least one part supplied by supplier S2. (Example 14.3.5)

```
NAMEX WHERE EXISTS SX EXISTS PX
           ( S ( S#:SX, SNAME:NAMEX )
           AND SP ( S#:SX, P#:PX )
           AND SP ( S#:'S2', P#:PX ) )
```

14.5.5. Get supplier names for suppliers who supply all parts. (Example 14.3.6)

```
NAMEX WHERE EXISTS SX ( S ( S#:SX, SNAME:NAMEX )
                  AND FORALL PX ( IF P ( P#:PX )
                      THEN SP ( S#:SX, P#:PX ) ) )
```

14.5.6. Get supplier names for suppliers who do not supply part P2. (Example 14.3.7)

```
NAMEX WHERE NOT EXISTS SX ( S ( S#:SX, SNAME:NAMEX )
                      AND SP ( S#:SX, P#:'P2' ) )
```

14.5.7. Get supplier numbers for suppliers who supply at least all those parts supplied by supplier S2. (Example 14.3.8)

```
SX WHERE FORALL PX ( IF SP ( S#:'S2', P#:PX ) THEN
                     SP ( S#:SX, P#:PX ) )
```

14.5.8. Get part numbers for parts that either weigh more than 16 pounds or are supplied by supplier S2, or both. (Example 14.3.9)

```
PX WHERE EXISTS WEIGHTX
           ( P ( P#:PX, WEIGHT:WEIGHTX )
               AND WEIGHTX > 16 )
     OR ∃P ( S#:'S2', P#:PX )
```

The domain calculus, like the tuple calculus, is formally equivalent to the relational algebra (i.e., it is relationally complete). For proof see Ullman [11.6] or Maier [11.7].

14.6 QUERY-BY-EXAMPLE

We conclude this chapter with a brief description of the relational language Query-By-Example, QBE [14.8]. QBE is supported by IBM as one of the two user interfaces to its query product QMF[7] (see reference [4.3]; the other, and primary, interface to QMF is SQL, of course). QBE can be regarded as a particularly attractive realization of the domain calculus—attractive in that its syntax is intuitively very simple, because it is based on the idea of making entries in tables instead of writing linear statements. For example, the QBE formulation of Example 14.5.4—"Get supplier names for suppliers who supply at least one part supplied by supplier S2" (a fairly complex query)—might look like this:

```
S   | S#  | SNAME       |   SP  | S#  | P#  |    SP  | S#  | P#  |
--- |-----|-------------|   ----|-----|-----|    ----|-----|-----|
    | _SX | P._NAMEX    |       | _SX | _PX |        | S2  | _PX |
```

Explanation: The user asks the system to display three "skeleton tables" on the screen, one for relation S and two for relation SP, and makes entries in them as shown.[8] Entries beginning with a leading underscore represent "examples" (i.e., domain variables); other entries represent constants. The user is asking the system to print or "present" ("P.") supplier name values (_NAMEX) such that, if the supplier is _SX, then _SX supplies some part _PX, and part _PX in turn is also supplied by supplier S2. Note that the existential quantifiers are all implicit (another reason why the syntax is intuitively easy to understand).

In the rest of this section we illustrate some of the highlights of QBE by showing a number of further examples. For convenience we give references (where applicable) to the SQL versions of the examples in Chapter 6.

---

7. The dialect of QBE supported in QMF is slightly different from that proposed by Zloof, the original designer of QBE [14.8], because QMF implements QBE by first translating it to SQL. In this book we restrict our attention (for the most part) to the QMF dialect specifically.
8. The system automatically displays the relation name and required attribute names. Attributes (columns) that are not relevant to the query at hand can simply be erased from the screen. Similarly, extra columns can be added if desired (see, e.g., Examples 14.6.4 and 14.6.5, later), and existing columns can be widened or narrowed as necessary.

14.6.1 Qualified retrieval, with ordering. Get supplier numbers and status for suppliers in Paris, in ascending supplier number order within descending status order. (Extended version of Example 6.2.5)

```
S    | S#          | SNAME  | STATUS     | CITY    |
-----|-------------|--------|------------|---------|
     | P.AO(2).    |        | P.DO(1).   | Paris   |
```

"AO." stands for ascending order, "DO." for descending order. The integers in parentheses indicate the major-to-minor sequence for ordering columns; in the example, STATUS is the major column and S# the minor column.

It is also possible to specify "P." against the whole row, as here:

```
S    | S#          | SNAME  | STATUS     | CITY     |
-----|-------------|--------|------------|----------|
P.   | AO(2).      |        | DO(1).     | Paris    |
```

which is shorthand for specifying "P." in every column, as here:

```
S    | S#          | SNAME  | STATUS     | CITY     |
-----|-------------|--------|------------|----------|
     | P.AO(2).    | P.     | P.DO(1).   | P.Paris  |
```

14.6.2 Retrieval involving AND. Get supplier numbers for suppliers in Paris with status > 20. (Example 6.2.4)

```
S    | S# | SNAME  | STATUS   | CITY     |
-----|----|--------|----------|----------|
     | P. |        | > 20     | Paris    |
```

14.6.3 Retrieval involving OR. Get supplier numbers and status for suppliers who either are located in Paris or have status > 20 or both.

Conditions specified within a single row are considered to be "ANDed" together, as Example 14.6.2 illustrates. To "OR" together two conditions, they must be specified in different rows, as here:

```
S    | S# | SNAME  | STATUS   | CITY     |
-----|----|--------|----------|----------|
     | P. |        |          | Paris    |
     | P. |        | > 20     |          |
```

Another approach to this query makes use of what is known as a *condition box*. A condition box allows the specification of conditions of any degree of complexity. For example:

```
S    | S# | SNAME  | STATUS   | CITY     |
-----|----|--------|----------|----------|
     | P. |        | _ST      | _SC      |

     |            CONDITIONS              |
     |-----------------------------------|
     | _SC = Paris OR _ST > 20           |
```

14.6.4 Retrieval involving multiple conditions on the same column ANDed together.   Get parts whose weight is in the range 16 to 19 inclusive.

```
P    | P# | PNAME | COLOR | WEIGHT  | WEIGHT  | CITY    |
-----|----|-------|-------|---------|---------|---------|
     | P. |       |       | >= 16   | <= 19   |         |
```

Notice the two WEIGHT columns.

14.6.5 Retrieval of expressions.   For all parts, get the part number and the weight of that part in grams (part weights are given in table P in pounds). (Example 6.2.2)

```
P    | P# | WEIGHT |                           |               |
-----|----|--------|---------------------------|---------------|
     | P. | _PW    | P. 'Weight in grams ='    | P. _PW * 454  |
```

14.6.6 Retrieving specified fields from a join.   Get all supplier-number / part-number combinations such that the supplier and part in question are colocated. (Example 6.3.4)

```
S    | S#  | CITY |      P    | P#  | CITY |           |     |     |
-----|-----|------|      -----|-----|------|      -----|-----|-----|
     | _SX | _CX  |           | _PX | _CX  |      P.   | _SX | _PX |
```

14.6.7 Joining a table with itself.   Get all pairs of supplier numbers such that the two suppliers concerned are colocated. (Example 6.3.6)

```
S    | S#  | CITY |      ----|-----|-----|
-----|-----|------|      P. | _SX | _SY |
     | _SX | _CZ  |
     | _SY | _CZ  |
```

A condition box can be used to specify the additional condition _SX < _SY, if desired (see Chapter 6 for a discussion of this point).

14.6.8 Retrieval involving existential quantification.   Get supplier names for suppliers who supply part P2. (Examples 6.5.3, 6.5.7)

```
S    | S#  | SNAME |      SP   | S#  | P# |
-----|-----|-------|      -----|-----|----|
     | _SX | P.    |           | _SX | P2 |
```

14.6.9 Retrieval involving union.   Get part numbers for parts that either weigh more than 16 pounds or are supplied by supplier S2 or both. (Example 6.5.11)

```
P    | P#  | WEIGHT |      SP   | S#  | P#  |      ----|-----|
-----|-----|--------|      -----|-----|-----|      P.  | _PX |
     | _PX | > 16   |           | S2  | _PY |      P.  | _PY |
```

14.6.10 Use of grouping. For each part supplied in an average quantity greater than 200, get the part number and the total quantity.

```
SP   | S# | P#   |     QTY   |       |  CONDITIONS   |
-----|----|------|-----------|       |---------------|
     |    | P.G. | P.SUM._QP |       | AVG._QP > 200 |
```

The "G." is the analog of the GROUP BY operator in SQL. Observe how the "HAVING" condition is specified.

14.6.11 Single-record update. Change the color of part P2 to yellow, increase its weight by 5, and set its city to null. (Example 6.6.1)

```
P    | P# | PNAME | COLOR    | WEIGHT |  WEIGHT   | CITY   |
-----|----|-------|----------|--------|-----------|--------|
     | P2 |       | U.Yellow | _WT    | U._WT + 5 | U.NULL |
```

The update operator is "U." In general, the records to be updated are all those that have the specified constant values in the specified columns. In the example, there is only one such record—namely, the one having part number equal to P2. Each "U." indicates that the value of the indicated field is to be replaced by the value of the specified expression.

14.6.12 Multiple-record update. Set the shipment quantity to zero for all suppliers in London. (Example 6.6.3)

```
SP  | S#  | QTY |     S    | S#  | CITY   |
----|-----|-----|          |-----|--------|
    | _SX | U.0 |          | _SX | London |
```

14.6.13 Multiple-record delete. Delete all suppliers in Madrid. (Example 6.6.6)

```
S    | S# | SNAME | STATUS | CITY   |
-----|----|-------|--------|--------|
D.   |    |       |        | Madrid |
```

Note that "D." (delete) applies to the entire row and so appears beneath the table name, whereas "U." applies to individual fields and so appears in the body of the table (i.e., within individual columns).

14.6.14 Single-record insert. Add part P7 (city 'Athens', weight 24, name and color at present unknown) to table P. (Example 6.6.9)

```
P    | P# | PNAME | COLOR | WEIGHT | CITY   |
-----|----|-------|-------|--------|--------|
I.   | P7 |       |       | 24     | Athens |
```

"I." (insert), like "D.", appears beneath the table name.

To conclude this section, we note that QBE as implemented in QMF is in fact not relationally complete. To be specific, QMF does not include a QBE analog of the negated existential quantifier (NOT EXISTS). As a result, certain queries (e.g., Example 6.5.9—"Get names of suppliers who supply all parts") cannot be expressed in QMF/QBE. The QBE language as originally defined [14.8] did include support for NOT EXISTS, but it was always somewhat troublesome; the basic problem was that there was no way to specify the order in which the various implicit quantifiers were to be applied, and unfortunately the order is significant (see Exercise 14.1).

EXERCISES

14.1 Let $f(x,y)$ be an arbitrary WFF with free variables x and y. Which of the following are true statements?

a) EXISTS x EXISTS y ($f(x,y)$) $\equiv$ EXISTS y EXISTS x ($f(x,y)$)

b) FORALL x ($f(x,y)$) $\equiv$ NOT EXISTS x (NOT $f(x,y)$)

c) EXISTS x FORALL y ($f(x,y)$) $\equiv$ FORALL y EXISTS x ($f(x,y)$)

d) FORALL x FORALL y ($f(x,y)$) $\equiv$ FORALL y FORALL x ($f(x,y)$)

14.2 Consider once again the query from Example 14.3.8 —"Get supplier numbers for suppliers who supply at least all those parts supplied by supplier S2"—for which a possible tuple calculus formulation is

```
SPX.S# WHERE FORALL SPY ( IF SPY.S# = 'S2' THEN
                           EXISTS SPZ ( SPZ.S# = SPX.S# AND
                                        SPZ.P# = SPY.P# ) )
```

What will this query return if supplier S2 currently supplies no parts at all?

14.3 It is important to understand that relational completeness is only a *basic* measure of expressive power. It is not necessarily a sufficient one. Can you think of any queries that cannot be formulated in a language that is only relationally complete (i.e., is no more powerful than the relational algebra or the relational calculus)?

14.4 There are two formally equivalent approaches to the manipulative part of the relational model, the calculus and the algebra. One implication of this point is that there are therefore two styles on which the design of a query language can be based. For example, QUEL is a calculus-based language, and so is QBE; by contrast, the language of the system PRTV [13.5] is algebra-based. Is SQL algebra-based or calculus-based?

14.5 Give tuple calculus solutions to Exercises 6.1–6.48 (where possible or appropriate).

14.6 Give domain calculus solutions to Exercises 6.1–6.48 (where possible or appropriate).

14.7 Give QBE solutions to the following subset of Exercises 6.1–6.48.

14.7.1 Get full details of all projects. (Exercise 6.1)

14.7.2 Get supplier numbers for suppliers who supply project J1, in supplier number order. (Exercise 6.3)

14.7.3 Get project numbers and cities where the city has an "o" as the second letter of its name. (Exercise 6.20)

14.7.4 Get all supplier-number / part-number / project-number triples such that the indicated supplier, part, and project are all colocated. (Exercise 6.6)

14.7.5 Get part numbers for parts supplied by a supplier in London. (Exercise 6.9)

14.7.6 Get part numbers for parts supplied by a supplier in London to a project in London. (Exercise 6.10)

14.7.7 Get part numbers for parts supplied to any project by a supplier in the same city as that project. (Exercise 6.12)

14.7.8 Get project numbers for projects supplied by at least one supplier not in the same city. (Exercise 6.13)

14.7.9 Get all pairs of part numbers such that some supplier supplies both the indicated parts. (Exercise 6.14)

14.7.10 Get supplier numbers for suppliers supplying at least one part supplied by at least one supplier who supplies at least one red part. (Exercise 6.25)

14.7.11 Get supplier numbers for suppliers with a status lower than that of supplier S1. (Exercise 6.26)

14.7.12 Construct a list of all cities in which at least one supplier, part, or project is located. (Exercise 6.41)

14.7.13 Change the color of all red parts to orange. (Exercise 6.43)

14.7.14 Delete all projects in Rome and all corresponding shipments. (Exercise 6.45)

14.7.15 Insert a new supplier (S10) into table S. The name and city are 'White' and 'New York', respectively; the status is not yet known. (Exercise 6.46)

REFERENCES AND BIBLIOGRAPHY

14.1 J. L. Kuhns. "Answering Questions by Computer: A Logical Study." *Report RM-5428-PR,* Rand Corp., Santa Monica, Calif. (1967).

14.2 E. F. Codd. "Relational Completeness of Data Base Sublanguages." In *Data Base Systems*: Courant Computer Science Symposia Series, Vol. 6. Englewood Cliffs, N.J.: Prentice-Hall (1972).

The paper that introduced the notion of relational completeness. It gives the original definitions of both the (tuple) relational calculus and the relational algebra. It also presents the details of the reduction algorithm sketched in Section 14.4, thereby proving that the algebra is at least as expressive as the calculus. (For the version of the calculus defined in the paper, incidentally, the converse is not true, because that version did not include any equivalent of the algebraic UNION operator.) The paper concludes with some brief arguments in favor of using the calculus over the algebra as the basis for a practical database language. The arguments are (paraphrasing):

■ Extendability: A calculus-based language is more suitable than an algebraic one for extension via the incorporation of arithmetic operators, built-in functions, etc.

■ Ease of capturing the user's intent (important for optimization, authorization, etc.): The calculus, because it permits the user to request data by its properties instead of by a sequence of manipulative operations, is a better basis than the algebra for this purpose.

■ Closeness to natural language: Codd recognizes that most users should not have to deal with either the algebra or the calculus per se. But the idea of requesting data by its properties is far more natural than that of having to devise an appropriate sequence of manipulative operations. Thus the calculus should prove more suitable as a target for some more user-friendly higher-level language.

However, it is not clear that any of these three arguments really stands up, given the formal equivalence of the two approaches.

14.3 E. F. Codd. "A Data Base Sublanguage Founded on the Relational Calculus." *Proc. 1971 ACM SIGFIDET Workshop on Data Description, Access and Control* (November 1971).

An introduction to and informal definition of a proposed tuple calculus language called "Data Sublanguage ALPHA." Serves as a good gentle introduction to the concepts of relational calculus.

14.4 M. Lacroix and A. Pirotte. "Domain-Oriented Relational Languages." *Proc. 3rd International Conference on Very Large Data Bases* (October 1977).

14.5 M. Lacroix and A. Pirotte. "ILL: An English Structured Query Language for Relational Data Bases." In *Architecture and Models in Data Base Management Systems* (ed., G. M. Nijssen). North-Holland (1977).

14.6 A. Pirotte and P. Wodon. "A Comprehensive Formal Query Language for a Relational Data Base." *R.A.I.R.O. Informatique / Computer Science* **11**, No. 2 (1977).

The "formal query language" FQL is based (like ILL) on the domain calculus but is much more formal (less "English-like") than ILL.

14.7 C. L. Chang. "DEDUCE—A Deductive Query Language for Relational Data Bases." In *Pattern Recognition and Artificial Intelligence* (ed., C. H. Chen). New York: Academic Press (1976).

14.8 M. M. Zloof. "Query By Example." *Proc. NCC* **44** (May 1975).

Zloof was the original inventor and designer of QBE. This paper was the first of many by Zloof on the subject.

ANSWERS TO SELECTED EXERCISES

14.1 a) True. b) True. c) False. d) True. Note that a sequence of *like* quantifiers can be written in any order, whereas for *unlike* quantifiers the order is significant. As an illustration, suppose that x and y are integers and f is the WFF "$y > x$". It should be clear that the WFF

```
FORALL x EXISTS y ( y > x )
```

is true, whereas the WFF

```
EXISTS y FORALL x ( y > x )
```

is false. Hence interchanging unlike quantifiers changes the WFF. In a calculus-based query language, therefore, interchanging unlike quantifiers in a WHERE clause will change the meaning of the query.

14.2 If supplier S2 currently supplies no parts, the query will return all supplier numbers appearing in relation SP.

14.3 We give a number of illustrations of types of query that cannot be handled. For purposes of reference, we number the illustrations 14.3.1, 14.3.2, etc.

14.3.1 First (as pointed out in Section 14.4), queries that involve arithmetic computation cannot be expressed in the "pure" algebra or calculus. For example, the following is not legal in pure calculus:

```
PX.P#, PX.WEIGHT * 454 WHERE PX.COLOR = 'Red'
```

By the same token, the pure algebra and calculus do not support simple computational functions such as SQRT (square root). For example, the following also would not be legal in pure calculus:

```
PX.P#, SQRT ( PX.WEIGHT ) WHERE PX.COLOR = 'Red'
```

(probably not a very sensible query, but it illustrates the point). Of course, such deficiencies are easily remedied.

14.3.2 The computations referred to in 14.3.1 above are what might be termed *row-wise* computations—they apply to values appearing within a single tuple or row. By contrast, the familiar built-in functions SUM, AVG, etc., represent *column-wise* computations—they apply to values appearing within a single attribute or column. It is clearly desirable to support column-wise computations also. Numerous examples have already been given in earlier chapters.

14.3.3 Most relational languages do support row- and column-wise computations, at least to a limited extent. However, we mention another class of query, very common in practice, that comparatively few systems today are capable of handling easily. We refer to that class as *quota queries*. An example of a quota query is "Get the three heaviest parts." Interestingly enough, Codd's ALPHA language [14.3] did include facilities for quota queries, but (as already stated) ALPHA per se was never implemented.

14.3.4 Next, consider the PART_STRUCTURE relation of Fig. 11.3. The query "Get part numbers for all parts that are components, *at any level*, of some given part—the result of which, PART_LIST say, is certainly a relation that can be derived from PART_STRUCTURE —cannot be expressed in the relational algebra (or calculus). In other words, PART_LIST is a relation that *cannot* be derived using only operations of the algebra. To see that this is so, let PSA, PSB, PSC, . . . , PSn be aliases for relation PART_STRUCTURE, and suppose the given part is part P1. Then:

a) The algebraic expression for the query "Get part numbers for all parts that are components, at the *first* level, of part P1" is:

```
( ( PSA )            WHERE PSA.MAJOR_P# = 'P1' )
                                  [ PSA.MINOR_P# ]
```

b) The algebraic expression for the query "Get part numbers for all parts that are components, at the *second* level, of part P1" is:

```
( ( PSA TIMES PSB ) WHERE PSA.MAJOR_P# = 'P1'
                    AND    PSB.MAJOR_P# = PSA.MINOR_P#
                                  [ PSB.MINOR_P# ]
```

c) The algebraic expression for the query "Get part numbers for all parts that are components, at the *third* level, of part P1" is:

```
( ( PSA TIMES PSB TIMES PSC )
              WHERE PSA.MAJOR_P# = 'P1'
              AND   PSB.MAJOR_P# = PSA.MINOR_P#
              AND   PSC.MAJOR_P# = PSB.MINOR_P#
                                   [ PSC.MINOR_P# ]
```

And so on. The algebraic expression for the query "Get part numbers for all parts that are components, at the nth level, of part P1" is:

```
( ( PSA TIMES PSB TIMES PSC TIMES ... TIMES PSn )
              WHERE PSA.MAJOR_P# = 'P1'
              AND   PSB.MAJOR_P# = PSA.MINOR_P#
              AND   PSC.MAJOR_P# = PSB.MINOR_P#
              AND   ....................
              AND   PSn.MAJOR_P# = ...            )
                                   [ PSn.MINOR_P# ]
```

(All of these result relations (a), (b), (c), . . . then need to be UNIONed together to construct the relation PART_LIST.)

The problem is, of course, that there is no way to write n such expressions if the value of n is unknown. Thus, the "parts explosion" query is a classic illustration of a problem that cannot be expressed in a language that is only relationally complete. What is needed is an extension to the relational algebra. See reference [12.1].

14.3.5 Finally, suppose the supplier relation S were to be replaced by a set of relations LS, PS, AS, . . . (one such relation for each distinct supplier city; the LS relation, for example, contains just the suppliers in London). Suppose too that we are unaware of exactly what supplier cities exist, and are therefore unaware of exactly how many such relations there are; and consider the query "Does supplier S1 exist in the database?" To express that query, we basically need to be able to say something like "Does there exist a *relation R* such that there exists a tuple t in R such that $t.S\# =$ 'S1'?" In other words, we need to be able to quantify *relation* variables; the query therefore cannot be expressed in the relational calculus, since the relational calculus only allows us to quantify *tuple* variables, not relation variables.

14.4 SQL is really a hybrid of both the algebra and the calculus. For example, it provides both the existential quantifier EXISTS (calculus) and the UNION operator (algebra). Interestingly, SQL was originally intended to be distinct from both the algebra and the calculus (see reference [4.5]); it was felt that the "nested subquery" construct was more user-friendly than both the explicit joins (etc.) of the algebra and the quantifiers of the calculus. As it turned out, however, the subquery construct was (obviously) inadequate by itself, and so it became necessary to extend the original language in a variety of ways. The situation now, ironically enough, is that the nested subquery facility could be eliminated entirely from the SQL language with effectively no loss of function. See reference [4.10] for further discussion of this point.

14.5 We have numbered the following solutions as 14.5.n, where 6.n is the number of the original exercise in Chapter 6. We assume that SX, SY, PX, PY, JX, JY, SPJX, SPJY, (etc.) are tuple variables ranging over relations S, P, J, SPJ, respectively; definitions of those range variables are not shown.

14.5.1 `JX.J#, JX.JNAME, JX.CITY`

An obvious shorthand would be to allow simply "JX" in the target list (as an abbreviation for what is shown).

14.5.2 `JX.J#, JX.JNAME, JX.CITY WHERE JX.CITY = 'London'`

14.5.3 Ignoring ordering:

```
SPJX.S# WHERE SPJX.J# = 'J1'
```

14.5.4 `SPJX.S#, SPJX.P#, SPJX.J#, SPJX.QTY WHERE SPJX.QTY >= 300`
`                                         AND    SPJX.QTY <= 750`

14.5.5 `PX.COLOR, PX.CITY`

14.5.6 `SX.S#, PX.P#, JX.J# WHERE SX.CITY = PX.CITY`
`                            AND    PX.CITY = JX.CITY`
`                            AND    JX.CITY = SX.CITY`

14.5.7 `SX.S#, PX.P#, JX.J# WHERE SX.CITY ~= PX.CITY`
`                            OR     PX.CITY ~= JX.CITY`
`                            OR     JX.CITY ~= SX.CITY`

14.5.8 `SX.S#, PX.P#, JX.J# WHERE SX.CITY ~= PX.CITY`
`                            AND    PX.CITY ~= JX.CITY`
`                            AND    JX.CITY ~= SX.CITY`

14.5.9 `SPJX.P# WHERE EXISTS SX ( SX.S# = SPJX.S# AND`
`                          SX.CITY = 'London' )`

14.5.10 `SPJX.P# WHERE EXISTS SX EXISTS JX`
`          ( SX.S# = SPJX.S# AND SX.CITY = 'London' AND`
`            JX.J# = SPJX.J# AND JX.CITY = 'London' )`

14.5.11 `SX.CITY, JX.CITY WHERE EXISTS SPJX ( SPJX.S# = SX.S# AND`
`                                     SPJX.J# = JX.J# )`

14.5.12 `SPJX.P# WHERE EXISTS SX EXISTS JX`
`                  ( SX.CITY = JX.CITY AND`
`                    SPJX.S# = SX.S# AND`
`                    SPJX.J# = JX.J# )`

14.5.13 `SPJX.J# WHERE EXISTS SX EXISTS PX`
`                  ( SX.CITY ~= PX.CITY AND`
`                    SPJX.S# = SX.S# AND`
`                    SPJX.P# = PX.P# )`

14.5.14 `SPJX.P#, SPJY.P# WHERE SPJX.S# = SPJY.S#`
`                       AND    SPJX.P# < SPJY.P#`

14.5.15–18 Cannot be done (they require the computational built-in functions SUM, AVG, etc.).

14.5.19 Cannot be done (it requires the "IS_NULL" operator; see Volume II).

14.5.20 `JX.J#, JX.CITY WHERE JX.CITY LIKE '_o%'`

We have assumed that the SQL "LIKE" operator is a legal comparison operator.

14.5.21 `JX.JNAME WHERE EXISTS SPJX ( SPJX.J# = JX.J# AND`
`                             SPJX.S# = 'S1' )`

14.5.22 `PX.COLOR WHERE EXISTS SPJX ( SPJX.P# = PX.P# AND`
`                             SPJX.S# = 'S1' )`

14.5.23 `SPJX.P# WHERE EXISTS JX ( JX.CITY = 'London' AND`
`                                JX.J# = SPJX.J# )`

14.5.24 `SPJX.J# WHERE EXISTS SPJY ( SPJX.P# = SPJY.P# AND`
`                                  SPJY.S# = 'S1' )`

14.5.25 `SPJX.S# WHERE EXISTS SPJY EXISTS SPJZ EXISTS PX`
`                  ( SPJX.P# = SPJY.P# AND`
`                    SPJY.S# = SPJZ.S# AND`
`                    SPJZ.P# = PX.P# AND`
`                    PX.COLOR = 'Red' )`

14.5.26 `SX.S# WHERE EXISTS SY ( SY.S# = 'S1' AND`
`                              SX.STATUS < SY.STATUS )`

14.5.27 `JX.J# WHERE FORALL JY ( JY.CITY >= JX.CITY )`

14.5.28–29 Cannot be done (they require the computational built-in functions).

14.5.30–31 Not applicable.

14.5.32 `SPJY.J# WHERE NOT EXISTS SPJX EXISTS SX EXISTS PX`
`                      ( SX.CITY = 'London' AND`
`                        PX.COLOR = 'Red' AND`
`                        SPJX.S# = SX.S# AND`
`                        SPJX.P# = PX.P# AND`
`                        SPJX.J# = SPJY.J# )`

14.5.33 `SPJX.J# WHERE FORALL SPJY ( IF SPJY.J# = SPJX.J#`
`                                 THEN SPJY.S# = 'S1' )`

14.5.34 `SPJX.P# WHERE FORALL JX ( IF JX.CITY = 'London' THEN`
`                                EXISTS SPJY`
`                                ( SPJY.P# = SPJX.P# AND`
`                                  SPJY.J# = JX.J# ) )`

14.5.35 `SPJX.S# WHERE FORALL JX EXISTS SPJY`
`                  ( SPJY.S# = SPJX.S# AND`
`                    SPJY.P# = SPJX.P# AND`
`                    SPJY.J# = JX.J# )`

14.5.36 `SPJX.J# WHERE FORALL SPJY ( IF SPJY.S# = 'S1' THEN`
`                                 EXISTS SPJZ`
`                                 ( SPJZ.J# = SPJX.J# AND`
`                                   SPJX.P# = SPJY.P# ) )`

14.5.37–40 Not applicable.

14.5.41 Ignoring ordering:

`     RANGE OF VX IS SX.CITY ; PX.CITY ; JX.CITY`
`     VX.CITY`

14.5.42–46 Not applicable.

14.5.47 `SPJX.P# WHERE EXISTS SX ( SX.S# = SPJX.S# AND`
`                                SX.CITY = 'London' )`
`              OR    EXISTS JX ( JX.J# = SPJX.J# AND`
`                                JX.CITY = 'London' )`

14.5.48 `JX.J# WHERE JX.CITY = 'London' OR`
`              EXISTS SPJX EXISTS SX ( SPJX.J# = JX.J# AND`
`                                      SPJX.S# = SX.S# AND`
`                                      SX.CITY = 'London' )`

14.6 We have numbered the following solutions as 14.6.*n*, where 6.*n* is the number of the original exercise in Chapter 6. We follow the same conventions as in Section 14.5 regarding the definition and naming of domain variables.

14.6.1 JX, NAMEX, CITYX
WHERE J (J#:JX, JNAME:NAMEX, CITY:CITYX)

14.6.2 JX, NAMEX, CITYX
WHERE J (J#:JX, JNAME:NAMEX, CITY:CITYX)
AND   CITYX = 'London'

14.6.3 Ignoring ordering:

SX WHERE SPJ (S#:SX, J#:'J1')

14.6.4 SX, PX, JX, QTYX
WHERE SPJ (S#:SX, P#:PX, J#:JX, QTY:QTYX)
AND   QTYX >= 300 AND QTYX <= 750

14.6.5 COLORX, CITYX WHERE P (COLOR:COLORX, CITY:CITYX)

14.6.6 SX, PX, JX WHERE EXISTS CITYX
(S (S#:SX, CITY:CITYX) AND
  P (P#:PX, CITY:CITYX) AND
  J (J#:JX, CITY:CITYX))

14.6.7 SX, PX, JX WHERE EXISTS CITYX EXISTS CITYY EXISTS CITYZ
(S (S#:SX, CITY:CITYX) AND
  P (P#:PX, CITY:CITYY) AND
  J (J#:JX, CITY:CITYZ)
  AND (CITYX ~= CITYY OR
        CITYY ~= CITYZ OR
        CITYZ ~= CITYX))

14.6.8 SX, PX, JX WHERE EXISTS CITYX EXISTS CITYY EXISTS CITYZ
(S (S#:SX, CITY:CITYX) AND
  P (P#:PX, CITY:CITYY) AND
  J (J#:JX, CITY:CITYZ)
  AND (CITYX ~= CITYY AND
        CITYY ~= CITYZ AND
        CITYZ ~= CITYX))

14.6.9 PX WHERE EXISTS SX
(SPJ (P#:PX, S#:SX) AND
  S (S#:SX, CITY:'London'))

14.6.10 PX WHERE EXISTS SX EXISTS JX
(SPJ (S#:SX, P#:PX, J#:JX)
  AND S (S#:SX, CITY:'London')
  AND J (J#:JX, CITY:'London')

14.6.11 CITYX, CITYY WHERE EXISTS SX EXISTS JY
(S (S#:SX, CITY:CITYX)
  AND J (J#:JY, CITY:CITYY)
  AND SPJ (S#:SX, J#:JY))

14.6.12 PX WHERE EXISTS SX EXISTS JX EXISTS CITYX
(S (S#:SX, CITY:CITYX)
  AND J (J#:JX, CITY:CITYX)
  AND SPJ (S#:SX, P#:PX, J#:JX))

14.6.13 JY WHERE EXISTS SX EXISTS CITYX EXISTS CITYY
  (SPJ (S#:SX, J#:JY)
    AND S (S#:SX, CITY:CITYX)
    AND J (J#:JY, CITY:CITYY)
    AND CITYX ~= CITYY)

14.6.14 PX, PY WHERE EXISTS SX
      (SPJ (S#:SX, P#:PX)
        AND SPJ (S#:SX, P#:PY)
        AND PX < PY)

14.6.15–18 Cannot be done (they require the computational built-in functions SUM, AVG, etc.).

14.6.19 Cannot be done (it requires the "IS_NULL" operator; see Volume II).

14.6.20 JX, CITYX WHERE J (J#:JX, CITY:CITYX)
        AND   CITYX LIKE '_o%'

We have assumed that the SQL "LIKE" operator is a legal comparison operator.

14.6.21 NAMEX WHERE EXISTS JX
          (J (J#:JX, JNAME:NAMEX)
            AND SPJ (S#:'S1', J#:JX))

14.6.22 COLORX WHERE EXISTS PX
            (P (P#:PX, COLOR:COLORX) AND
              SPJ (S#:'S1', P#:PX))

14.6.23 PX WHERE EXISTS JX
        (SPJ (P#:PX, J#:JX) AND
          J (J#:JX, CITY:'London'))

14.6.24 JX WHERE EXISTS PX
        (SPJ (P#:PX, J#:JX) AND
          SPJ (P#:PX, S#:'S1'))

14.6.25 SX WHERE EXISTS PX EXISTS SY EXISTS PY
        (SPJ (S#:SX, P#:PX) AND
          SPJ (P#:PX, S#:SY) AND
          SPJ (S#:SY, P#:PY) AND
          P (P#:PY, COLOR:'Red'))

14.6.26 SX WHERE EXISTS STATUSX EXISTS STATUSY
        (S (S#:SX, STATUS:STATUSX) AND
          S (S#:'S1', STATUS:STATUSY) AND
          STATUSX < STATUSY)

14.6.27 JX WHERE EXISTS CITYX
        (J (J#:JX, CITY:CITYX) AND
          FORALL CITYY (IF J (CITY:CITYY)
                         THEN CITYY >= CITYX))

14.6.28-29 Cannot be done (they require the computational built-in functions).

14.6.30-31 Not applicable.

14.6.32 JX WHERE J (J#:JX) AND
        NOT EXISTS SX EXISTS PX
            (SPJ (S#:SX, P#:PX, J#:JX) AND
              S (S#:SX, CITY:'London') AND
              P (P#:PX, COLOR:'Red'))

```
14.6.33 JX WHERE FORALL SX ( IF SPJ ( S#:SX, J#:JX )
                             THEN SX = 'S1' )
14.6.34 PX WHERE FORALL JX ( IF J ( J#:JX, CITY:'London' )
                             THEN SPJ ( P#:PX, J#:JX ) )
14.6.35 SX WHERE EXISTS PX FORALL JX
               ( SPJ ( S#:SX, P#:PX, J#:JX ) )
14.6.36 JX WHERE FORALL PX ( IF SPJ ( S#:'S1', P#:PX )
                             THEN SPJ ( P#:PX, J#:JX ) )
```

14.6.37–40 Not applicable.

14.6.41 Ignoring ordering:

```
      CITYX WHERE S ( CITY:CITYX )
            OR    P ( CITY:CITYX )
            OR    J ( CITY:CITYX )
```

14.6.42–46 Not applicable.

```
14.6.47 PX WHERE EXISTS SX ( SPJ ( S#:SX, P#:PX ) AND
                             S ( S#:SX, CITY:'London' ) )
        OR     EXISTS JX ( SPJ ( J#:JX, P#:PX ) AND
                           J ( J#:JX, CITY:'London' ) )
14.6.48 JX WHERE J ( J#:JX, CITY:'London' )
        OR     EXISTS SX ( S ( S#:SX, CITY:'London' ) AND
                           SPJ ( S#:SX, J#:JX ) )
```

14.7

14.7.1

J	J#	JNAME	CITY
P.			

14.7.2

SPJ	S#	P#	J#	QTY
P.	P.AO(1).		J1	

The "(1)" can be omitted if desired.

14.7.3

J	J#	JNAME	CITY
	P.		P. LIKE '_o%'

14.7.4

S	S#	CITY		P	P#	CITY		J	J#	CITY
	_SX	_CX			_PX	_CX			_JX	_CX

	S#	P#	J#
P.	_SX	_PX	_JX

14.7.5

SPJ	S#	P#		S	S#	CITY
	_SX	P.			_SX	London

14.7.6
```
SPJ | S# | P# | J# |            S   | S# |  CITY  |
----|-----|----|-----|           ----|-----|--------|
    | _SX | P. | _JX |               | _SX | London |

                                  J   | J# |  CITY  |
                                 ----|-----|--------|
                                     | _JX | London |
```

14.7.7
```
SPJ | S# | P# | J# |            S   | S# | CITY |
----|-----|----|-----|           ----|-----|------|
    | _SX | P. | _JX |               | _SX | _CX  |

                                  J   | J# | CITY |
                                 ----|-----|------|
                                     | _JX | _CX  |
```

14.7.8
```
SPJ | S# |   J#    |             S   | S# | CITY |
----|-----|---------|            ----|-----|------|
    | _SX | P._JX   |                | _SX | _CX  |

                                  J   | J# |  CITY  |
                                 ----|-----|--------|
                                     | _JX | ~_CX   |
```

14.7.9
```
SPJ | S# | P# |                     |     |     |
----|-----|-----|                 ----|-----|-----|
    | _SX | _PY |             P.      | _PY | _PZ |
    | _SX | _PZ |
```

14.7.10
```
SPJ | S# | P# |              P   | P# | COLOR |
----|-----|-----|             ----|-----|-------|
    | P.  | _PX |                 | _PY | Red   |
    | _SY | _PX |
    | _SY | _PY |
```

14.7.11
```
S   | S# | STATUS |
----|-----|--------|
    | P.  | < _T1  |
    | S1  |   _T1  |
```

14.7.12
```
S   | S# | CITY |        P   | P# | CITY |        J   | J# | CITY |
----|-----|------|       ----|-----|------|       ----|-----|------|
    | _SX | _CX  |           | _PY | _CY  |           | _JZ | _CZ  |

         |     |
     ----|-----|
  P.     | _CX |
  P.     | _CY |
  P.     | _CZ |
```

14.7.13
```
P   | P# | COLOR  |  COLOR   |
----|-----|--------|----------|
    |     | Red    | U.Orange |
```

14.7.14

First:
```
SPJ  | S# | P# |  J# | QTY |        J    |  J# | CITY |
-----|----|----|-----|-----|        -----|-----|------|
D.   |    |    | _JJ |     |             |  _JJ | Rome |
```

Then:
```
J    |  J# | JNAME  | CITY  |
-----|-----|--------|-------|
D.   |     |        | Rome  |
```

14.7.15
```
S    |  S#  | SNAME  | STATUS  |    CITY      |
-----|------|--------|---------|--------------|
I.   | S10  | White  |         | 'New York'   |
```

15
Relational
Systems

15.1 THE RELATIONAL MODEL: A SUMMARY

In the past few chapters we have discussed the relational model—i.e., the underlying theory of relational systems—in some considerable depth. However, we have nowhere defined exactly what a relational *system* is; in other words, we have not addressed the question of what exactly it is that constitutes such a system. In this chapter we turn our attention to that question. (The question has practical relevance, in view of the fact that just about every database product on the market today at least claims to be relational.)

We begin by reviewing the major aspects of the relational model (refer to Fig. 15.1).

Data structure:

        domains (atomic values)
        n-ary relations (attributes, tuples)

Data integrity:

    1. primary key values must not be null
    2. foreign key values must match primary key values (or be null)

Data manipulation:

        relational algebra (or relational calculus equivalents):
          union, intersection, difference, product
          select, project, join, divide
        relational assignment

Fig. 15.1 The relational model (in outline).

As Fig. 15.1 shows, the model consists of three major parts: a structural part, an integrity part, and a manipulative part. The structural part consists essentially of *n*-ary relations (together with their underlying domains), and nothing else; the significance of that "nothing else" is discussed in the next section. The integrity part consists of two general integrity rules, namely "entity integrity" and "referential integrity"; those two rules are discussed further in Section 15.4. Finally, the manipulative part provides a set of algebraic operators (or their calculus equivalents) for data manipulation *in all of its manifestations*. As explained in Chapter 13, the operators are not intended just for data retrieval. Rather, they permit the construction of arbitrary *relation-valued expressions*, and thereby provide a basis for investigation into numerous additional aspects of database systems, including, for example, database design (see Chapters 17 and 25), query optimization (see Chapter 16), view definition and database restructuring (see Chapter 8), and security and integrity (see Chapter 19).

Before we go any further, one point should be made absolutely clear: The relational model is *not* a panacea. In a sense, it might be thought of purely as a *minimum requirement*, in the sense that any modern database system ought at least to support the facilities prescribed by the model. But there are numerous other desirable features of such systems about which the relational model says nothing at all (or at least nothing direct, although it may indirectly influence the design of those features); examples include forms-based interfaces, support for multiple concurrent users, backup and recovery facilities, and so on. Even from the point of view of data access alone, the relational model is—as pointed out in earlier chapters—inadequate as it stands; additional facilities are needed to perform arithmetic operations, invoke built-in functions, etc. In particular, explicit update operations are obviously needed (see the discussion of this point at the end of Chapter 13). To repeat, the model represents a *minimum*.[1]

We might sum up the foregoing—at the risk of being severely misunderstood —by saying that *the relational model represents the assembly language of modern (and future) database systems*. By this statement, of course, we obviously do not mean that the model is at the same machine-dependent kind of level that conventional assembly languages normally are, but rather that database systems can build on the *abstract* machine that is the relational model in the same kind of way that

1.   In other words (to risk a sweeping generalization): A system is not necessarily good just because it supports the relational model; on the other hand, if it does not support that model, then it very likely is not "good"! Of course, this generalization, like most others, is obviously not entirely true. It would be absurd to suggest that older, prerelational systems are entirely without merit. Fundamentally, of course, what is important is not whether the system in question is relational or hierarchic or something else again—it is whether that system does whatever it was originally designed to do. Nevertheless, the generalization does contain a nugget of truth. It is certainly hard to imagine that anyone would consider designing a new system today that was *not* relational.

software systems in the past have built on the (much less abstract) machine defined by a given assembly language. The relational model is a foundation, not an end in itself. As such, it provides a common core of functions that will be needed in all future systems, just as assembly language provides a (very primitive) core of functions that are needed by all software systems today.

We are now ready to embark on our discussion of relational systems. In Section 15.2 we introduce the important concept of *essentiality*. Then in Section 15.3 we present a definition of "relational system." This is followed in Section 15.4 by an extended discussion of data integrity in current systems. Finally, in Section 15.5 we give a brief introduction to the range of relational systems available in the marketplace today. Note: For the remainder of this chapter, we deliberately revert (for the most part) to the comparatively informal terminology of records, fields, etc., instead of staying with the formal relational terms introduced in the last few chapters.

15.2 ESSENTIALITY

The only data structure provided in the relational model is the relation itself. In order to appreciate the significance of this fact, it is necessary to have at least a superficial understanding of one or more other data structures that are not relational. We therefore begin this section with a very brief tutorial on the *hierarchic* data structure, since that structure is probably the next easiest to understand. (This material will be treated in more detail in Chapter 22. It may be helpful to point out here that the hierarchic data structure is really nothing more than a slight abstraction of the parent/child *storage* structure described in Chapter 3.)

Consider the simple departments-and-employees database shown (in relational form) in Fig. 15.2.

DEPT	DEPT#	DNAME	BUDGET	EMP	EMP#	ENAME	DEPT#	SALARY
	D1	Sales	20M		E1	Lopez	D1	40K
	D2	Dvpmt	9M		E2	Cheng	D1	42K
	D3	Admin	18M		E3	Finzi	D3	30K
					E4	Saito	D3	35K
					E5	Jacob	D3	40K

Fig. 15.2 The departments-and-employees database (relational).

The database contains three department records and five employee records. Department D1 has two employees (E1 and E2), department D3 has three employees (E3, E4, and E5), and department D2 currently has no employees at all.

A hierarchic version of the same data is shown in Fig. 15.3.

```
--   -----   ---      --   -----   --      --   -----   ---
D1   Sales   20M      D2   Dvpmt   9M      D3   Admin   18M
--   -----   ---      --   -----   --      --   -----   ---
       |                                            |
       |                                            |
       |                                            |
--   -----   ---                             --   -----   ---
E1   Lopez   40K                             E3   Finzi   30K
--   -----   ---                             --   -----   ---
--   -----   ---                             --   -----   ---
E2   Cheng   42K                             E4   Saito   35K
--   -----   ---                             --   -----   ---
                                             --   -----   ---
                                             E5   Jacob   40K
                                             --   -----   ---
```

Fig. 15.3 The departments-and-employees database (hierarchic).

The hierarchic structure consists of three hierarchies, one for each of the three departments. Each hierarchy consists of:

- one department (DEPT) record, plus
- one EMP record for each employee in that department, plus
- *links* connecting all of those records together (shown as vertical lines in Fig. 15.3).

The links can be thought of as *chains of pointers*—a pointer from each DEPT record to the first EMP record for that DEPT, a pointer from that EMP record to the next for the same DEPT, and so on, and finally a pointer from the last EMP record for a given DEPT back to the original DEPT record.[2] In this hierarchic structure, DEPTs are said to be the *parent* records and EMPs the *child* records. In general, each parent record has zero or more corresponding child records, each child record has exactly one corresponding parent record. A child cannot exist in a hierarchy without its parent. Thus, if the user issues a request to delete a parent, then the DBMS must either automatically delete the children (if any) of that parent too, or it must reject the request if any such children exist.[3]

Note carefully that the EMP records in Fig. 15.3 do not include a DEPT# field. To find out what department a given employee is in, it is necessary to traverse the

---

2. The pointers may be physically represented in storage by actual pointers or by some functionally equivalent method. However, the user can always *think* of the pointers as physically existing, regardless of the actual implementation.

3. In other words, hierarchies can in principle support a delete rule of either DELETE CASCADES or DELETE RESTRICTED (see Chapter 12). In practice, however, hierarchic systems typically support DELETE CASCADES only, which in the case of departments-and-employees specifically is probably not what is required.

link from the EMP record to the corresponding DEPT record. Likewise, to find all employees in a given department, it is necessary to traverse the link from the DEPT record to the corresponding EMP records.

The two diagrams above (Figs. 15.2, 15.3) are of course *instance* diagrams— they show actual data values. By contrast, the (time-independent) *structure* of the two versions of the database is shown by the two structure diagrams in Fig. 15.4. In the hierarchic structure diagram, we have labeled the department/employee link explicitly as DEPTEMP, for purposes of subsequent reference. That link (shown as a single line in Fig. 15.3) must be understood to represent multiple chains of multiple pointers each, just as the record boxes in the same figure must be understood to represent multiple record occurrences. Note: The meaning of the remark in the figure "DEPTEMP essential" will be explained in a few moments.

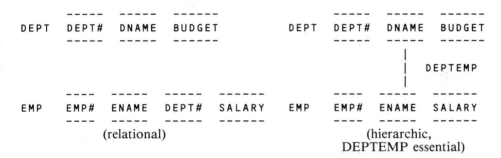

Fig. 15.4 Structure diagrams for departments-and-employees.

We now consider two sample queries against the departments-and-employees database. For each query we show a relational formulation (using SQL) and a hierarchic formulation (using a hypothetically extended version of SQL to cater for hierarchic structures).

Q1. Get employee numbers and employee names for employees with salary > 20K.

Relational: Hierarchic:

```
SELECT  EMP#, ENAME          SELECT  EMP#, ENAME
FROM    EMP                  FROM    EMP
WHERE   SALARY > 20K ;       WHERE   SALARY > 20K ;
```

Q2. Get employee numbers and employee names for employees with salary > 20K in department D3.

Relational: Hierarchic:

```
SELECT  EMP#, ENAME          SELECT  EMP#, ENAME
FROM    EMP                  FROM    EMP
WHERE   SALARY > 20K         WHERE   SALARY > 20K
AND     DEPT# = 'D3' ;       AND     (SELECT  DEPT#
                                      FROM     DEPT
                                      OVER     EMP ) = 'D3' ;
```

For query Q1 the two formulations are obviously identical. For query Q2, however, they are not. The relational formulation for Q2 still has the same basic form as for Q1 (SELECT – FROM – WHERE, with a simple restriction predicate in the WHERE clause); the hierarchic formulation, by contrast, has to make use of a new language construct, namely the "OVER" clause (which is our hypothetical SQL representation of a link-traversing operation). The predicate in that formulation is certainly not a simple restriction predicate.

The examples thus illustrate the important point that the hierarchic data structure fundamentally requires certain additional data access operators. Note carefully that those operators *are* additional; the operators needed for the relational structure are still needed as well, as query Q1 demonstrates. The links of the hierarchic data structure thus serve only to add *complexity*; they certainly do not add any *power* —there is nothing that can be represented by a hierarchy (i.e., by records and links) that cannot be represented by relations (i.e., by records) alone. And note, too, that analogous remarks apply, not only to all the other manipulative operators (INSERT, DELETE, etc.), but also to the definitional operators, the security operators, the integrity operators, etc., etc.[4]

It is sometimes suggested that the complexity problems of the hierarchic structure can be reduced, if not eliminated, by reinstating the field DEPT# in the EMP record. See Fig. 15.5. Given the revised hierarchy of that figure, query Q2 (hierarchic version) can now be formulated without using the OVER construct at all; in fact, the formulation becomes identical to the relational version. The reason is, of course, that the records (both DEPT and EMP) in that revised hierarchy are identical to their relational counterparts; the database is now the same as the relational version, except for the presence of the DEPTEMP link. However, that link is now entirely redundant; there is no information represented by link DEPTEMP that is not also represented by the field EMP.DEPT#, and the user can therefore ignore the link without any loss of function.

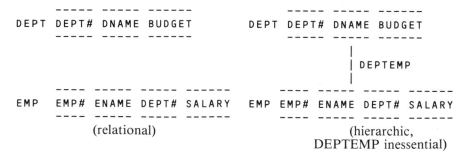

Fig. 15.5 Structure diagrams for departments-and-employees (field EMP.DEPT# reinstated in hierarchic version).

---

4. This point was touched on before in Section 6.7.

We can now explain the notion of *essentiality* [15.1]. A data object is *essential* if its loss would cause a loss of information (by which we mean, very precisely, that some relation would no longer be derivable). For example, in the relational version of departments-and-employees, all data objects (the two records and the seven fields) are essential in this sense. Likewise, in the original hierarchic version (Fig. 15.4), all data objects (the two records, the six fields, and the link) are again essential. But in the revised hierarchy of Fig. 15.5, the records and the fields are essential *but the link is inessential.* There is no information that can be derived from that revised hierarchy that cannot be derived from the records and fields alone.[5]

It is now possible to pin down the major difference between a relational database and any other kind of database, say a hierarchic database. In a relational database, the *only* essential data object is the relation itself (loosely speaking, the database is just records and fields). In other kinds of database, there must be at least one additional essential data object (such as an essential link). For if there is not, then the database is really a relational database that happens to have certain access paths exposed (and there is no requirement that the user use those access paths, and the question arises as to why they are exposed anyway when others are not). And it is those additional essential data objects that lead to much (not all) of the complexity of nonrelational databases.

Incidentally, we can now explain (as promised in Chapter 11) why it is significant that relations have no ordering. In an ordered file, the ordering itself might be essential in the sense defined above. For example, a file of temperature readings might be kept in the order in which those readings were taken; the ordering itself might thus carry information, which would be lost if the records were rearranged (just as information can be lost if someone drops a box of cards, if those cards do not include a sequence field). And essential ordering, like an essential link, requires additional operators to deal with it—for example, "select the nth record," "insert a record between records n and $n + 1$," and so on. For this reason it is not permitted in the relational model.

Aside: *In*essential ordering may be all right, however. A file is said to be inessentially ordered if it is ordered on the basis of the value(s) of some field(s)—for example, the employee file might be ordered by employee number, but no information would be lost if the records were shuffled around. Many relational systems do in fact support ordering in this sense. However, even inessential data constructs can cause problems, because they do still carry information even though they are inessential. For example, they may represent a security exposure. See reference [15.5] for further discussion of this point.

---

5. It might be argued that the opposite is the case: The DEPTEMP link is essential and the field EMP.DEPT# is inessential. But that argument misses the point, which is that, since some fields *must* be essential, and nothing else need be (since everything *can* be represented by fields), then why involve anything else?

15.3 DEFINITION OF A RELATIONAL SYSTEM

We are now (at last) in a position to define exactly what we mean by a *relational database management system* (relational DBMS, or relational system for short). The point is, *no* system today supports the relational model in its entirety (several come close, but most systems fall down on the integrity rules if nowhere else). On the other hand, it would be unreasonable to insist that a system is not relational unless it supports every last detail of the model. The fact is, not all aspects of the model are equally important; some of course are crucial, but others may be regarded merely as features that are "nice to have" (comparatively speaking). Following Codd [15.3], therefore, we define a system as *relational* if and only if it supports at least the following:

- Relational databases (i.e., databases that can be perceived by the user as tables, and nothing but tables);
- At least the operations select, project, and (natural) join, without requiring any predefinition of physical access paths to support those operations.

Of course, a system does not have to support the select, project, and join operators *explicitly* in order to qualify as relational. It is only the functionality of those operators that we are talking about here. For example, QUEL provides the functionality of all three of those operators, and more besides, via its RETRIEVE operator. More important, note that a system that does support relational databases, but not these three operators, does not qualify as a relational system under the definition. Likewise, a system that allows (say) the user to select records according to values of some field F only if that field F is indexed also does not qualify, because it is requiring predefinition of physical access paths.

We justify the definition as follows:

1. Although select, project, and join are less than the full algebra, they are an extremely useful subset. There are comparatively few practical problems that can be solved with the algebra that cannot be solved with select, project, and join alone.

2. A system that supports the relational data structure but not the relational operators does not provide the ease of use and productivity of a genuinely relational system.

3. A system that provides the relational operators but requires physical predefinition of access paths to support them does not provide the physical data independence of a true relational system.

4. To do a good job of implementing the relational operators—at least in a large mainframe environment—*requires* the system to do some optimization. A system that merely executed the exact operations requested by the user in a comparatively unintelligent fashion would almost certainly not have acceptable performance. Thus, to implement a system that realizes the potential of the relational model in an efficient manner is a highly nontrivial task. (Indeed, this

is one of the reasons that it took a comparatively long time for relational products to appear in the marketplace.)

Numerous systems currently available are indeed relational according to this definition (even though there are several aspects of the relational model that they do not support); for example, DB2 and SQL/DS are, and so is INGRES. But there are a number of systems on the market today that advertise themselves as "relational" that do not meet the criteria defined above. As we have tried to suggest, those criteria are useful as a means of drawing a sharp line between systems that are indeed genuinely relational and systems that are (at best) "relational-like." "Relational-like" systems do not truly provide the benefits of the relational model. The distinction is thus worth making, as it ensures that the label "relational" is not used in misleading ways.

Following Codd [15.3] again, we can take the foregoing ideas further and identify a *spectrum* of relational (and nonrelational) systems. See Fig. 15.6. The circles in that figure represent the relational model. Each circle is divided into three sectors, corresponding to the three parts (structural, integrity, manipulative) of the model. For each of the four categories of system, the degree of shading within a given sector indicates the degree to which systems in that category support the corresponding aspect of the model. To be more specific:

- A system that supports the tabular data structure (only) but not the set-level operators may be called *tabular*. It is not relational. (Note: Such systems were called "semirelational" in reference [12.1].) Inverted list systems typically fall into this category; see Chapter 21.

- A system that supports tables (only) and select, project, and join (but no other relational operators) is relational (but only minimally so). A number of microcomputer database systems fall into this "minimally relational" category.

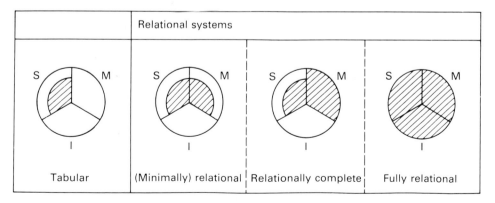

Fig. 15.6 System spectrum.

- A system that supports tables (only) and all of the operators of the relational algebra is said to be *relationally complete* (as already explained in Chapter 14). Many systems fall into this category today—for example, DB2, SQL/DS, INGRES, ORACLE, Rdb/VMS, etc., etc.

- Finally, a system that supports all aspects of the model, including in particular domains and the two general integrity rules, is said to be *fully relational*. As already indicated, no system (to this writer's knowledge) is fully relational today; however, several systems are beginning to come close, and we can expect to see fully relational systems appearing in the near future.

We conclude this section by repeating (in different terms) a point already made in the introduction to this chapter: The foregoing criteria are intended to be *minimal*. The fact that a given system is relational according to the definition does not in itself guarantee that the system in question is "a good system." However, the relational facilities do provide a good and solid basis on which to build the necessary features that go to make up such a "good" system.

15.4 ENFORCING THE RELATIONAL INTEGRITY RULES

Most current relational systems do not support the notion of primary or foreign keys at all, and therefore (of course) do not support the two relational integrity rules either. In this section, therefore, we present some "recipes" by which users can enforce the rules for themselves, in the absence of any direct system support for those rules.[6] (Note: The "user" here is probably the DBA.) To fix our ideas, we express the recipes in terms of SQL specifically, but the ideas apply with only minor revisions to many nonSQL systems also.

We begin by repeating the two rules from Chapter 12 (but using informal terms such as table, field, etc., instead of the formal terminology of that chapter):

1. *Entity integrity*:
   No field participating in the primary key of a base table is allowed to accept null values.

2. *Referential integrity*:
   If base table *T2* includes a foreign key *FK* matching the primary key *PK* of some base table *T1*, then every value of *FK* in *T2* must either (a) be equal to the value of *PK* in some record of *T1* or (b) be wholly null (i.e., each field value participating in that *FK* value must be null). *T1* and *T2* are not necessarily distinct.

Note that the rules apply specifically to base tables, not to views.

The rules as stated are fairly abstract. In any specific situation, they (and some

---

6.   The two integrity rules of the relational model represent important special cases of integrity rules in general. The topic of general integrity rules is discussed in detail in Chapter 19.

of their implications) can be expressed in more concrete terms using the "pseudoDDL" PRIMARY and FOREIGN KEY clauses discussed in Section 12.5. We repeat the syntax of those two clauses here. First, the PRIMARY KEY clause:

```
PRIMARY KEY ( primary-key )
```

Here "primary-key" is either a single field name, such as "S#", or a list of field names separated by commas, such as "S#,P#".

Second, the FOREIGN KEY clause:

```
FOREIGN KEY ( foreign-key IDENTIFIES target
              NULLS [ NOT ] ALLOWED
              DELETE OF target effect
              UPDATE OF target-primary-key effect )
```

Explanation:

1. "foreign-key" is the same as "primary-key" in the PRIMARY KEY clause—i.e., it is either a single field name or a list of field names separated by commas;

2. "target" is a table name;

3. "target-primary-key" specifies the "primary-key" for "target"; and

4. "effect" is CASCADES or RESTRICTED or NULLIFIES.

Now for the recipes. First, primary keys. For each table in the database, the user (i.e., DBA) should:

PK1. Specify NOT NULL for each field in the primary key (see Section 5.2).

PK2. Create a UNIQUE index over the combination of all fields in the primary key (see Section 5.3).

PK3. Ensure that this index is in existence whenever a record is inserted into the table or the primary key of a record in the table is updated. In practice, this typically means creating the index at the same time as the table is created, and "never" dropping that index.

PK4. Keep the PRIMARY KEY specifications from the pseudoDDL either as a comment in the catalog (see Section 7.3) or in some separate user-defined table (which can then logically be regarded as an extension to the catalog).

Note that the last of these recommendations means that it will be possible to interrogate the catalog regarding primary keys, even though the system itself has no knowledge of such keys.

Next, foreign keys. For each foreign key in the database, the DBA should:

FK1. Specify NOT NULL for each field in the foreign key, if and only if NULLS NOT ALLOWED applies to that foreign key.

FK2. Consider the merits of creating an index (probably not UNIQUE) over the combination of all fields in the foreign key. Such an index usually will be desirable for performance reasons, since it is likely that the foreign key and its matching primary key will often be used as the basis for join operations.

FK3. Use the authorization mechanism—see Part 4 of this book—to prohibit all on-line operations that could violate the constraints that apply to this foreign key. By "on-line operation" here we mean a SQL operation, such as INSERT or DE- LETE, that is issued by an end-user rather than by an application program. Spe- cifically, prohibit on-line:

- DELETE on the referenced table
- UPDATE on the referenced table primary key
- INSERT on the referencing table
- UPDATE on the referencing table foreign key

For example, consider the departments-and-employees database from Section 15.2. Here DEPT is the referenced table and EMP is the referencing table. An on- line SQL user cannot be allowed to INSERT an employee (for example), because there is no way to force that user to check that the department number for that employee does currently exist in the departments table. Similar remarks apply to the other prohibitions listed above.

FK4. Take the foreign key constraints as part of the requirements specification for database maintenance programs. Ideally, have exactly one such program for each foreign key (this does not mean that one program cannot deal with multiple foreign keys, only that one foreign key should not be maintained by multiple programs). Use the authorization mechanism to prevent all other programs from executing any operations that could violate those constraints (see paragraph FK3).

FK5. Keep the FOREIGN KEY specifications from the pseudoDDL either as a comment in the catalog or in some separate user-defined table (which again can then be regarded as a logical extension of the catalog). Note that—as in the case of the analogous rule for primary keys—this recommendation means that it will be possible to interrogate the catalog regarding foreign keys, even though the system itself has no knowledge of such keys.

Finally, as an independent (and conservative) measure:

FK6. Write a utility program to be run periodically to check for and report on any constraint violations. Note: If the FOREIGN KEY specifications are kept in the catalog (in stylized form), as recommended under paragraph FK5, then this utility can be generalized—i.e., driven off the catalog—instead of having to be specifically tailored to the particular foreign keys defined for a particular database.

A couple of additional remarks regarding paragraphs FK3 and FK4:

- First, on-line users will still be able to perform *some* SQL update operations. For example, inserting a new department record cannot cause any referential integrity problems. The same goes for deleting an employee, or changing a de- partment budget or an employee salary (etc.).

■ Second, on-line users will of course still be able to perform the other functions also, but *not via the SQL interface.* Instead, a user who (for example) wishes to insert a new employee will do so by invoking the appropriate installation-written application program and supplying the "new employee" details to that program. That program in turn will perform the necessary checks to ensure that (for example) the corresponding department already exists, before allowing the new employee record to be created. Thus the recipes do not really take any function away from the end-user; they merely impose additional responsibilities on the application programmer. Eventually, of course, when the systems themselves assume those responsibilities, the application programmer also will be able to devote more time to solving real application problems, instead of having to spend time remedying system deficiencies.

We conclude this section by remarking that systems like DB2 that do not support primary and foreign keys must nevertheless include *internal* support for those notions, because they are needed to maintain the integrity of the system's own catalog. In the catalog structure presented in Chapter 7, for example, field TBNAME of table SYSCOLUMNS is a foreign key matching field NAME (primary key) of table SYSTABLES. And if (for example) the user deletes a record from SYSTABLES (by issuing a DROP TABLE operation), then the system will automatically delete the matching records in SYSCOLUMNS also (in other words, the system supports a cascade delete rule with respect to the foreign key SYSCOLUMNS.TBNAME). Given the fact that such support must exist at the internal level of the system, it is hard to understand why the system designers did not see fit to support the same function at the external level also.

15.5   SOME CURRENT RELATIONAL PRODUCTS

We conclude this chapter with a representative list of relational products (current as of early 1985). All of these products are (to the best of the writer's knowledge) relational according to the definition presented in Section 15.3. The products were chosen because they are probably the ones the reader is most likely to encounter in practice—also for their own intrinsic interest, in certain cases. However, the list is certainly not exhaustive, nor is it intended to be. First, some SQL systems:

System	Vendor	Hardware	Software
DB2	IBM	IBM	MVS
SQL/DS	IBM	IBM	VM, DOS
QMF	IBM	IBM	(frontend for DB2 and SQL/DS)
AIM/RDB	Fujitsu	Fujitsu	OS IV F4

(cont.)

System	Vendor	Hardware	Software
ORACLE	ORACLE	IBM, DEC, DG, AT&T, MC68000, etc.	many
Shared Database System	Britton-Lee	IDM backend + IBM PC frontends	MS DOS
UNIFY	UNIFY	DEC, 8086, etc.	UNIX
SIR/SQL+	Scientific Information Retrieval	most	most
PDQ	Honeywell	Honeywell	GCOS 8
DG/SQL	DG	DG Eclipse	AOS/VS
QINT/SQL	QINT Database Systems	IBM PC, MC68000, etc.	MS DOS, UNIX, etc.

And here are some nonSQL systems (note, however, that here again the vendors of several of the following systems have promised to provide SQL interfaces to their product as soon as possible):

System	Vendor	Hardware	Software
INGRES	Relational Technology	DEC, AT&T, MC68000	VMS, UNIX
Rdb/VMS	DEC	DEC	VMS
RUBIX	Infosystems Technology	DEC, MC68000	UNIX
IDM	Britton-Lee	(the IDM is a backend machine)	—
DBC/1012	Teradata	(the DBC is a backend machine)	—
CA-UNIVERSE	Computer Associates	IBM	MVS, VM, DOS
IDMS/R	Cullinet	IBM	MVS, DOS
Encompass	TANDEM	TANDEM	Guardian
dBASE II, dBASE III	Ashton-Tate	IBM PC, etc.	MS DOS, CP/M
R:BASE	MicroRIM	IBM PC, etc.	MS DOS etc
NOMAD	D&B Computing Services	IBM	VM
INFORMIX	Relational Database Systems	DEC, IBM PC, etc.	UNIX, MS DOS

EXERCISES

15.1 Consider any DBMS you may have access to. Is it genuinely relational? If so, list aspects of the relational model (if any) that the system does not support.

15.2 Translate the primary and foreign key recipes given in Section 15.4 into specific recipes for any relational system you may have access to.

15.3 DB2, like most current relational systems, does not support primary keys, and therefore allows a table to include duplicate records. Discuss.

15.4 Devise a hierarchic representation for suppliers-and-parts. Consider what would be required of a hypothetical "hierarchic SQL" to support hierarchic versions of some of the SQL examples in Chapter 6.

REFERENCES AND BIBLIOGRAPHY

References [15.7–15.18] are concerned with view updating.

15.1 E. F. Codd and C. J. Date. "Interactive Support for Non-Programmers: The Relational and Network Approaches." In *Data Models*: *Data Structure Set vs. Relational* (ed., Randall Rustin): *Proc. 1974 ACM SIGMOD Workshop on Data Description, Access and Control*, Vol. II (May 1974).

The paper that first introduced the notion of essentiality (see Section 15.2). It also repeats from an earlier paper [17.4] Codd's original statement of objectives for the relational approach, which are as follows:

1. To provide a high degree of data independence;
2. To provide a community view of the data of spartan simplicity, so that a wide variety of users in an enterprise (ranging from the most computer-naive to the most computer-sophisticated) can interact with a common model (while not prohibiting superimposed user views for specialized purposes);
3. To simplify the potentially formidable job of the database administrator;
4. To introduce a theoretical foundation (albeit modest) into database management (a field sadly lacking [at that time] in solid principles and guidelines);
5. To merge the fact retrieval and file management fields in preparation for the addition at a later time of inferential services in the commercial world;
6. To lift database application programming to a new level—a level in which sets (and more specifically relations) are treated as operands instead of being processed element by element.

It is perhaps worth taking a moment to say something regarding objective number 4. Why exactly is a theoretical foundation desirable? One answer (not the only one) is that *it reduces the likelihood of surprise*—surprise for the user, that is. A system that is constructed in accordance with the prescriptions of a well-defined and well-understood abstract model will behave in a more predictable fashion than a system that has "just grown." The relational model thus serves as a focus for the design and construction of database systems, and also as a yardstick for checking the correctness of any given implementation. Volume II discusses these ideas in more detail.

15.2 C. J. Date. "An Introduction to the Unified Database Language (UDL)." *Proc. 6th International Conference on Very Large Data Bases* (October 1980).

UDL is a language that supports not only relations but also hierarchies and networks, all three in a consistent and uniform style. Its design is such as to stress both the essential similarities and the essential differences among the three approaches. It therefore serves to illustrate very clearly the claims made in Section 15.2 to the effect that the nonrelational structures add complexity but not power.

15.3 E. F. Codd. "Relational Database: A Practical Foundation for Productivity." *CACM* **25**, No. 2 (February 1982).

This is the paper that Codd presented on the occasion of his receiving the 1981 ACM Turing Award. It discusses the well-known "application backlog" problem: The demand for computer applications is growing fast—so fast that DP departments (whose responsibility it is to provide those applications) are lagging further and further behind in their ability to meet that demand. There are two complementary ways of attacking this problem:

1. Provide DP professionals with new tools to increase their productivity;

2. Allow end-users to interact directly with the database, thus bypassing the DP professional entirely.

Both approaches are needed, and in this paper Codd gives evidence to suggest that the necessary foundation for both is provided by relational technology.

The paper also discusses the performance of relational systems, and concludes with some comments on needed and likely future developments in the relational technology field (see references [15.4] and [15.6] for further elaboration of these last two topics).

15.4 C. J. Date. "Relational Database: Some Topics for Investigation." *Proc. GUIDE* **54**, Anaheim, California (May 1982) and elsewhere. Also available as *IBM Technical Report TR 03.193* (May 1982).

A brief discussion of some areas of relational technology in which developments are likely and/or required in the near future.

15.5 C. J. Date. "Some Relational Myths Exploded: An Examination of Some Popular Misconceptions Concerning Relational Database Management Systems." Part I, *InfoIMS* **4**, No. 2 (2nd Quarter 1984); Part II, *InfoIMS* **4**, No. 3 (3rd Quarter 1984); both available from PO Box 20651, San Jose, California 95160.

To quote from the abstract: Relational database management is one of the key technologies of the 1980s [and beyond], yet the field of relational technology still suffers from a great deal of misunderstanding and misrepresentation. Misconceptions abound. The purpose of this paper is to correct some of those misconceptions.

15.6 C. J. Date. "How Relational Systems Perform." *ComputerWorld:* InDepth article (February 13, 1984).

To quote from the abstract: Contrary to popular belief, relational systems are capable of performing at least as well as, and quite possibly better than, older (hierarchic or network) systems. This article explains why this is so.

15.7 A. L. Furtado and M. A. Casanova. "Updating Relational Views." In *Query Processing in Database Systems* (eds., W. Kim, D. Reiner, and D. Batory). New York: Springer Verlag (in press).

There are two basic approaches to the view update problem. One (the only one discussed in any detail in this book) attempts to provide a general mechanism that works regardless of the specific database involved; it is driven purely by the definitions of the views (and base relations) in question. References [15.8–15.18] below address themselves to this approach. The other, less ambitious, approach—the *abstract data type* approach—requires the database designer to specify, for each view, exactly what updates are allowed and what their semantics are, by (in effect) writing the procedural code to implement those updates in terms of the underlying base relations. This paper surveys work on each of the two approaches.

15.8 D. D. Chamberlin, J. N. Gray, and I. L. Traiger. "Views, Authorization, and Locking in a Relational Data Base System." *Proc. NCC* **44** (May 1975).

Includes a brief rationale for the approach to view updating in System R (and hence in DB2, etc.).

15.9 S. J. P. Todd. "Automatic Constraint Maintenance and Updating Defined Relations." *Proc. IFIP Congress* 1977.

15.10 A. L. Furtado, K. C. Sevcik, and C. S. dos Santos. "Permitting Updates Through Views of Data Bases." *Information Systems* **4**, No. 4 (1979).

15.11 I. M. Osman. "Updating Defined Relations." *Proc. NCC* **48** (1979).

15.12 C. R. Carlson and A. K. Arora. "The Updatability of Relational Views Based on Functional Dependencies." *Proc. 3rd IEEE International Conference on Computer Software and Applications* (November 1979).

15.13 F. Bancilhon and N. Spyratos. "Update Semantics of Relational Views." *ACM TODS* **6**, No. 4 (December 1981).

15.14 A. M. Keller. "Updates to Relational Databases Through Views Involving Joins." In *Improving Database Usability and Responsiveness* (ed., P. Scheuermann). New York: Academic Press (1982).

15.15 U. Dayal and P. A. Bernstein. "On the Correct Translation of Update Operations on Relational Views." *ACM TODS* **7**, No. 3 (September 1982).

15.16 S. Cosmadakis and C. H. Papadimitriou. "Updates of Relational Views." *Proc. 2nd ACM SIGACT-SIGMOD Symposium on Principles of Database Systems* (March 1983).

15.17 R. Fagin, J. D. Ullman, and M. Y. Vardi. "On the Semantics of Updates in Databases." *Proc. 2nd ACM SIGACT-SIGMOD Symposium on Principles of Database Systems* (March 1983).

15.18 A. M. Keller and J. D. Ullman. "On Complementary and Independent Mappings on Databases." *Proc. 1984 ACM SIGMOD International Conference on Management of Data* (June 1984).

ANSWERS TO SELECTED EXERCISES

15.1 We list some aspects of the relational model that SQL (i.e., IBM SQL specifically) does not adhere to, and use that list to make some additional points.

- Columns of a table are considered to be ordered left to right, at least in the "SELECT *" statement and the form of the INSERT statement in which column names are omitted.

- Composite columns or fields are not supported.
- Duplicate rows are allowed.
- Domain support is very primitive (basically, there are just two domains, namely numbers and strings).
- Primary keys are not supported (and hence Integrity Rule 1 is not supported).
- Foreign keys are not supported (and hence Integrity Rule 2 is not supported).
- UNION is allowed only between two SELECT *statements*, not between two SELECT expressions. Thus, for example, UNION is not permitted in a view definition, and the relational closure property breaks down (i.e., SQL does not have a direct equivalent of every conceivable nested algebraic expression).

A very significant consequence of SQL's lack of support for primary and foreign keys is that it does not support view updating correctly either, for the following reason. A view is a virtual relation. If the system is to be able to support updates against a virtual relation properly, it must be able to tell, for any given updated virtual record, precisely which real (base) record(s) that virtual record corresponds to. In other words, the system must be able to identify—that is, address—those underlying real records. *The system must therefore have an understanding of primary keys*, since (as explained in Chapter 12) it is primary keys that perform the record-level addressing function within the relational model. Since SQL does not have any such understanding, its view updating rules are necessarily ad hoc at best. The fact is, SQL sometimes allows views to be updated that logically ought not to be, and sometimes does not allow them to be updated when logically they could be!

The theory of view updating is in fact very much interwoven with the notion of primary keys, and, to a lesser extent, with the notion of foreign keys also—not that any such theory has ever been worked out in full detail (so far as this writer is aware), although many researchers have addressed the problem (see references [15.7–15.18]). We certainly do not address the problem here in detail either, but content ourselves with a few brief general statements:

- A projection of an updatable relation is updatable if and only if it includes the primary key of the underlying relation.
- A restriction of an updatable relation is always updatable—though it may be necessary to impose controls (akin to the "CHECK option" controls in SQL) to ensure that inserted and updated records satisfy the view-defining restriction predicate.
- A natural join of two updatable relations is updatable if it is taken over the primary key of one relation and a matching foreign key in the other—though the details are not always straightforward.

Yet another (comparatively slight) consequence of SQL's lack of knowledge of primary keys is that certain queries that are logically correct are rejected as invalid by SQL. For example:

```
SELECT  P.P#, P.WEIGHT, AVG (SP.QTY)
FROM    P, SP
WHERE   P.P# = SP.P#
GROUP   BY P.P# ;
```

This query is invalid because it includes the specification P.WEIGHT in the SELECT clause without at the same time including the same specification in the GROUP BY clause.

Such a specification in the GROUP BY clause is logically redundant, but must be included because SQL does not understand that P.WEIGHT is single-valued per part number—i.e., that parts have only one weight. (To use the terminology of Chapter 17, SQL is not aware of the *functional dependence* of P.WEIGHT on P.P#. See Section 17.2.) This may be only a minor annoyance, but it could be puzzling to the user.

15.3 It is true that SQL (i.e., DB2 SQL) allows a table to contain duplicate records. However, *there is no way, at least in interactive SQL, for the user to tell such duplicates apart.* For example, there is no way of deleting just one record out of a collection of duplicate records. (This fact in itself is a strong argument for disallowing such duplicates, incidentally.) To put this another way: In order to distinguish among duplicates, SQL would have to support *essential ordering*, so that terms like "first duplicate," "second duplicate," etc., had a meaning; but, of course, SQL—quite rightly—does not support such ordering.

16
Query
Optimization

16.1 INTRODUCTION

Query optimization presents both a challenge and an opportunity to relational systems: a challenge, because, as explained in Chapter 15, optimization is *required*—at least in the mainframe environment—if the system is ever to achieve acceptable performance; an opportunity, because it is precisely one of the strengths of the relational approach that relational expressions are at a sufficiently high semantic level that optimization is feasible in the first place. In a nonrelational system, by contrast, where user requests are expressed at a lower semantic level, any "optimization" has to be done manually by the human user ("optimization" in quotes, because the term is usually taken to mean *automatic* optimization). In such a system it is the user, not the system, who decides what record-level operations are needed and in what sequence those operations are to be executed—and if the user makes a bad decision, then there is nothing the system can do to improve matters.[1]

Incidentally, the advantage of optimization is not merely that users do not have to worry about how best to state their queries (i.e., how to phrase requests in order to get the best performance out of the system). On the contrary, there is a real possibility that the optimizer might actually do better than a human programmer, because a) the optimizer might have information available to it—regarding, for instance, current data values—that a programmer could not have, and b) it might be able to evaluate a wider range of alternatives than a programmer would be able to.

The overall purpose of the optimizer, then, is to choose an efficient strategy for evaluating a given relational expression. In this chapter we present a brief over-

---

1. Note, too, the implication that the user in a record-level system must have some programming expertise. That fact alone puts the system out of reach for many people who could otherwise benefit from it.

view of some of the fundamental principles and techniques of optimization. We also briefly discuss the specific approaches to optimization found in System R and INGRES. More detailed discussion on a variety of specific techniques can be found in the annotation to many of the references at the end of the chapter.

One final introductory point: We follow standard practice in labeling the subject "query optimization," although the name is both slightly misleading and somewhat of an overclaim. First, although we refer to the expression to be optimized as a query, it may of course have arisen in some context other than interactive interrogation of the database. More significant, there is usually no guarantee that the strategy chosen for implementing the query is actually *optimal* in any measurable sense; it may in fact be so, but usually all that is known for sure is that the "optimized" strategy is an *improvement* on the original unoptimized version. (In certain rather limited contexts, however, it may be possible to claim legitimately that the chosen strategy is optimal in a certain specific sense. See, for example, reference [16.20].)

16.2   A SIMPLE EXAMPLE

We begin with a simple example that illustrates the need for (and also some of the potential of) optimization. Consider the query "Get names of suppliers who supply part P2," for which a possible SQL formulation is:

```
SELECT  DISTINCT S.SNAME
FROM    S, SP
WHERE   S.S# = SP.S#
AND     SP.P# = 'P2' ;
```

Suppose the database contains 100 suppliers and 10,000 shipments, of which only 50 are for part P2, however. If the system were simply to execute the query in accordance with the hypothetical query evaluation algorithm given in Section 6.7— i.e., without performing any optimization at all—then the sequence of events would be as follows:

1. Compute the Cartesian product of relations S and SP. This step involves reading 10,100 tuples and constructing a relation containing 100 * 10,000 = 1,000,000 tuples (and therefore writing those 1,000,000 tuples back on to the disk).

2. Restrict the result of Step 1 as specified by the WHERE clause. This step involves reading 1,000,000 tuples but produces a relation consisting of only 50 tuples (which we can assume will be kept in main memory).

3. Project the result of Step 2 over SNAME to produce the desired final result (50 tuples at most).

The following procedure is equivalent to the one just described (in the sense that it produces the same final result) but is obviously much more efficient:

1. Restrict relation SP to just the tuples for part P2. This step involves reading 10,000 tuples but produces a relation consisting of only 50 tuples, which we can assume will be kept in main memory.

2. Join the result of Step 1 to relation S over S#. This step involves the retrieval of only 100 tuples. The result contains 50 tuples (still in main memory).

3. (Same as Step 3 before.) Project the result of Step 2 over SNAME to produce the desired final result (50 tuples at most).

   If we agree to take "number of tuple I/O's" as our performance measure,[2] it is clear that the second of these two procedures is something like 200 times better than the first. It would be better still if relation SP were indexed or hashed on P#— the number of tuples read in Step 1 would be reduced from 10,000 to just 50 (and the new procedure would then be 13,000 times better than the original). Likewise, an index or hash on S.S# would help with Step 2 (reducing 100 tuple I/O's to at most 50, another significant improvement). And of course numerous further improvements are possible.

   The foregoing example, simple though it is, is sufficient to give some idea as to why optimization is necessary. It should also give a preliminary hint of the kinds of improvement that may be possible in practice. In the next section we present a systematic approach to the optimization problem; in particular, we show how the overall problem can be divided into a number of more or less independent subproblems. That systematic approach serves as a convenient framework within which individual optimization strategies and techniques such as those of the two subsequent sections can be described and understood.

16.3　THE OPTIMIZATION PROCESS: AN OVERVIEW

Following [16.1], we can identify four broad stages in the overall optimization process, as follows:

1. Cast the query into some internal representation

2. Convert to canonical form

3. Choose candidate low-level procedures

4. Generate query plans and choose the cheapest

We now proceed to amplify each of these four stages.

1. *Cast the query into some internal representation*

   The first step in query processing is to convert the query to some internal representation, thus eliminating purely external-level considerations (such as quirks of the concrete syntax of the query language under consideration) and thereby paving the way for subsequent stages of the optimization process. The question obviously arises: On what formalism should the internal representation be based? Whatever formalism is chosen, it must of course be rich enough to represent all possible queries in the system's query language. It should also be as neutral as possible, in the sense that it should not prejudice any subsequent optimization choices. The internal

---

2. In practice, of course, it is *page* I/O's that count, not tuple I/O's.

form typically used is some kind of *abstract syntax tree* or *query tree*. For example, Fig. 16.1 below shows a possible query tree representation for the query from Section 16.2 ("Get names of suppliers who supply part P2").

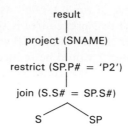

Fig. 16.1 Query tree for query "Get names of suppliers who supply part P2".

For our purposes, however, it is more convenient to assume that the internal representation employs one of the formalisms we are already familiar with—namely, the relational algebra or the relational calculus.[3] A query tree such as that of Fig. 16.1 can be regarded as just an encoded version of some expression of one of those two formalisms. To fix our ideas, we assume here that the formalism is the algebra specifically. The algebraic representation of the query of Fig. 16.1 might be:

    ((S JOIN SP) WHERE P# = 'P2') [SNAME]

(using the syntax of Chapter 13).

2. *Convert to canonical form*

Most languages allow all but the simplest of queries to be expressed in a variety of superficially distinct ways. For example, even a query as simple as the one discussed above—"Get names of suppliers who supply part P2"—can be expressed in at least seven apparently different ways[4] in SQL [4.10]. The next step in processing the query must therefore be to convert the internal representation into some equivalent *canonical form*,[5] with the objective of eliminating such superficial distinctions and (more important) finding a representation that is more efficient than the original in some specific way.

---

3.   As pointed out in Chapters 13 and 14, real query languages are invariably more powerful than the "pure" algebra and calculus, in that they at least include certain arithmetic operators, computational built-in functions, and so on. "Pure" algebra or calculus is therefore not adequate as it stands as a candidate for the internal representation, and needs to be extended appropriately. For simplicity, however, we ignore any such extensions here.

4.   Not counting trivial variations, such as replacing the condition "S.S# = SP.S#" by the condition "SP.S# = S.S#" or interchanging the two conditions on either side of the AND.

5.   The notion of canonical form is central to many branches of mathematics and related disciplines. It can be defined (somewhat loosely) as follows. Given a set Q of objects (say queries) and a notion of equivalence among those objects (say the notion that queries $q1$ and

We therefore proceed to transform the result of Stage 1 into some equivalent but more efficient form, using certain well-defined transformation rules. An important example of such a transformation rule is the one that allows any restriction predicate to be converted into an equivalent predicate in *conjunctive normal form*— that is, a predicate consisting of a set of restrictions that are ANDed together, where each restriction in turn consists of a set of simple comparisons connected only by ORs. For example, the WHERE-clause

```
WHERE p OR ( q AND r )
```

can be converted into the form

```
WHERE ( p OR q ) AND ( p OR r )
```

Conjunctive normal form is desirable for a number of reasons. For example, the query decomposition algorithm used in INGRES requires the input query predicate to be in conjunctive normal form, for reasons that should become clear in Section 16.5.

Here is another example of a transformation rule: The algebraic expression

```
( A JOIN B ) WHERE restriction-on-B
```

can be transformed into the equivalent but more efficient algebraic expression

```
( A JOIN (B WHERE restriction-on-B ) )
```

More generally, the expression

```
( A JOIN B) WHERE restriction-on-A AND restriction-on-B
```

is equivalent to the expression

```
( A WHERE restriction-on-A ) JOIN ( B WHERE restriction-on-B )
```

This was the rule we were using—tacitly—in the introductory example in Section 16.2, and that example showed clearly why such a transformation is desirable. Three more examples of such rules are given below; deciding exactly why they are desirable is left as an exercise for the reader. (We remark, however, that the rules are not independent of one another, in the following sense: Given a particular expression to transform, the application of one rule might generate an expression that is susceptible to transformation in accordance with one of the others. For example, it is unlikely that the original query will have been directly expressed in such

---

$q2$ are equivalent if and only if they produce the same result), subset C of Q is said to be a *set of canonical forms* for Q (under the stated definition of equivalence) if and only if every object q in Q is equivalent to just one object c in C. The object c is said to be the canonical form for the object q. All "interesting" properties that apply to an object q also apply to its canonical form c; thus it is sufficient to study just the small set C of canonical forms, not the large set Q, in order to prove a variety of "interesting" results.

a way as to require two successive projections—see rule 2 below—but such an
expression might arise internally as the result of applying certain other rules.)

1. A sequence of restrictions can be combined into a single restriction; i.e., the
   expression

   ```
   ( A WHERE restriction-1 ) WHERE restriction-2
   ```

   is equivalent to the expression

   ```
   A WHERE restriction-1 AND restriction-2
   ```

2. In a sequence of projections, all but the last can be ignored; i.e., the expression

   ```
   ( A [ attribute-list-1 ] ) [ attribute-list-2 ]
   ```

   is equivalent to the expression

   ```
   A [ attribute-list-2 ]
   ```

3. A restriction of a projection is equivalent to a projection of a restriction; i.e.,
   the expression

   ```
   ( A [ attribute-list-1 ] ) WHERE restriction-1
   ```

   is equivalent to the expression

   ```
   ( A WHERE restriction-1 ) [ attribute-list-1 ]
   ```

A complete list of such transformations is beyond the scope of this book. A
useful (not exhaustive) list can be found in reference [16.10].

Different *kinds* of transformation are also possible during this stage of query
processing. For example, the predicate

```
A.F1 > B.F2 AND B.F2 = 3
```

can be transformed into the simpler form

```
A.F1 > 3
```

(thereby replacing a join and a restriction by a simple restriction). Likewise, the
predicate

```
NOT ( p1 AND p2 )
```

can be converted to the equivalent form

```
( NOT p1 ) OR ( NOT p2 )
```

(such a conversion is performed in DB2, incidentally [16.13]). In this latter version
it is clear that, if predicate *p1* evaluates to *false*, then there is no need to evaluate
predicate *p2* at all.

As a final example, if the system is aware of the fact that SP.P# is a foreign key matching the primary key P.P#, the expression

```
( SP JOIN P ) [ S# ]
```

(representing supplier numbers for suppliers who supply at least one part) can be simplified to just

```
SP [ S# ]
```

(thereby eliminating a join entirely—a very significant improvement). This latter example illustrates what is sometimes called a *semantic* transformation [16.23]. By contrast, the transformations discussed previously have been more syntactic in nature.

For more ideas on the kinds of transformation that are possible, see references [16.1], [16.10], [16.11], [16.20], and [16.23], among others.

3. *Choose candidate low-level procedures*

Having converted the internal representation of the query into some more desirable (canonical) form, the optimizer must then decide how to evaluate the transformed query represented by that converted form. At this stage such considerations as the existence of indexes or other access paths, distribution of stored data values, physical clustering of records, etc., come into play (notice that we paid no heed to such matters in Stages 1 and 2 above).

The basic strategy is to consider the query expression as specifying a series of (comparatively) low-level operations (join, restriction, etc.), with certain interdependencies among them.[6] For each such low-level operation, the optimizer will have available to it a set of predefined, low-level implementation procedures. For example, there will be a set of procedures for implementing the restriction operation— one for the case where the restriction is an equality condition on a unique field, one where the restriction field is indexed, one where it is not indexed but the data is physically clustered on the restriction field, and so on. Each such procedure will have an associated cost measure. References [16.5], [16.6], [16.7], [16.18] and others describe a number of such low-level procedures and analyze their respective costs under a variety of assumptions.

Using information from the system catalog regarding the current state of the database (existence of indexes, cardinalities of relations, etc.), and using also the interdependency information referred to above, the optimizer will then choose one or more candidate procedures for implementing each of the low-level operations in the query expression. This process is sometimes referred to as *access path selection*

---

6. An example of such an interdependency is the following: The code to perform a projection operation will typically require its input tuples to be in a certain sequence (in order that it may perform duplicate elimination), which means that the immediately preceding operation in the series must produce its output tuples in that same sequence.

(see references [16.12] and [16.13]—though in those papers the term is used to cover both Stage 3 and Stage 4, as we define those two stages here).

4. *Generate query plans and choose the cheapest*

The final stage in the optimization process involves the construction of a set of candidate *query plans*, followed by a choice of the best—i.e., cheapest—of those plans. Each query plan is built by combining together a set of candidate implementation procedures, one such procedure for each of the low-level operations in the query. Note that there will normally be many reasonable plans—probably embarrassingly many—for any given query. In fact, it may not be a good idea to generate all possible plans, since there will be combinatorially many of them, and the task of choosing the cheapest may well become prohibitively expensive in itself;[7] some heuristic technique for keeping the generated set within reasonable bounds is highly desirable [16.1]. "Keeping the set within bounds" is usually referred to as *reducing the search space*, because it can be regarded as reducing the range ("space") of possibilities to be examined ("searched") by the optimizer to manageable proportions.

Choosing the cheapest plan naturally requires a method for assigning a cost to any given plan. Most systems use a cost formula that is basically an estimate of the number of disk I/O's involved, though some do take CPU utilization into account also (for example, System R does [16.12], and so does Commercial INGRES [16.27]). The problem is, all but the simplest queries require the generation of intermediate results during execution. In order to estimate the number of disk I/O's accurately, therefore, it is necessary to estimate the size of those intermediate results also, and unfortunately those sizes are highly dependent on actual data values. Accurate cost estimation is a difficult problem. Reference [16.1] discusses some approaches to it and contains references to current research in the area.

16.4   OPTIMIZATION IN SYSTEM R

In this section we consider some of the optimization techniques used in the SQL prototype system System R specifically. The discussion is based for the most part on material from reference [16.12]. Note: Much of what follows applies with only minor changes to the IBM products DB2 and SQL/DS. Reference [16.13] gives some additional information that is specific to DB2.

A query in System R (expressed in SQL) consists of a set of "SELECT-FROM-WHERE" blocks (*query blocks*), some of which may be nested inside others. The System R optimizer first decides on an order in which to execute those query blocks. It then seeks to minimize the total cost of the query by choosing the cheapest implementation for each individual block in the query. Note that this strategy (choos-

---

7.   This is less of a consideration (though still not negligible) in a system like System R, which does its optimization at compile time rather than run time.

ing block order first, then optimizing individual blocks) means that certain possible query plans will never be considered; in effect, it amounts to a technique for "reducing the search space" (see the remarks on this subject near the end of Section 16.3).

Note: In the case of *nested* blocks, the optimizer simply follows the nested order as specified by the user—i.e., the innermost block will be executed first. See reference [16.14] for criticism and further discussion of this strategy.

For a given query block, there are basically two cases to consider (the first of which can in fact be regarded as just a special case of the second):

1. For a block that involves just a restriction and/or projection of a single relation, the optimizer uses statistical information from the system catalog, together with formulas (given in reference [16.12]) for size estimates of intermediate results and for costs of low-level operations, to choose a strategy for constructing that restriction and/or projection. The statistics maintained in the catalog are summarized below.

- Number of tuples in each relation
- Number of pages occupied by each relation
- Percentage of pages occupied by each relation with respect to all pages in the relevant portion of the database
- Number of distinct data values for each index
- Number of pages occupied by each index

Note: These statistics are not updated every time the database is updated (because of the overhead such an approach would entail). Instead, they are updated in response to a special system utility—UPDATE STATISTICS in System R and SQL/DS, RUNSTATS in DB2—which can be executed at any time. As a result, however, the optimizer may in fact be basing its decisions on information that is at least partially obsolete.

2. For a block that involves two or more relations to be joined together, with (probably) local restrictions and/or projections on individual relations, the optimizer a) treats each individual relation as in Case 1, and b) decides on a sequence for performing the joins. The two operations a) and b) are not independent of one another. For example, a given strategy for accessing an individual relation A might well be chosen precisely because it produces tuples of A in the order in which they are needed to perform a subsequent join of A with some other relation B.

Given a set of relations to be joined, the optimizer chooses a pair to be joined first, then a third to be joined to the result of joining the first two, and so on. In other words, it always treats an expression such as

    A JOIN B JOIN C JOIN D

(not intended to be genuine SQL syntax) in strictly nested fashion, e.g., as

    ((A JOIN B) JOIN C) JOIN D

never, e.g., as

```
( A JOIN B ) JOIN (C JOIN D )
```

This approach can be seen as another strategy for reducing the search space. Heuristics for choosing the sequence of joins are given in reference [16.12].

Following reference [16.7], the System R optimizer chooses one of two methods for implementing any particular (binary) join, *A* JOIN *B* say. The two methods are the *nested loop* method and the *sort/merge* method. The choice between them is made on the basis of cost formulas, which again can be found in reference [16.12]. The two methods work as follows. First, the nested loop method is best described by the following pseudocode algorithm:

```
scan relation A sequentially (either via an index
                              or in "physical" sequence) ;
for each tuple of A do ;
    retrieve A-tuple ;
    scan relation B looking for tuples matching that A-tuple
                    (either via an index
                     or in "physical" sequence) ;
    for each such B-tuple do ;
        retrieve B-tuple ;
        construct joined (A, B)-tuple ;
    end ;
end ;
```

The sort/merge method basically consists of sorting the two relations into sequence on values of the joining attributes, and then applying the nested loop algorithm. However, certain improvements are now possible in that algorithm, compared with the general case. First, physical sequence will now definitely be the most efficient basis for the two scans. Second, the two scans can be synchronized, so that the complete join is constructed in a single pass over each of the two relations. This improved nested loop algorithm is usually referred to as a "merge" process, for obvious reasons.

One point that is stressed in reference [16.12] is that, in evaluating (for example) the nested join (*A* JOIN *B*) JOIN *C*, it is not necessary to compute the join of *A* and *B* in its entirety before computing the join of the result and *C*; on the contrary, as soon as any tuple of *A* JOIN *B* has been produced, it can immediately be passed to the process that joins such tuples with tuples of *C*. Thus it may never be necessary to materialize the complete relation "A JOIN B."

The paper [16.12] also includes a few observations on the cost of optimization. For a join of two relations, the cost is said to be approximately equal to the cost of between 5 and 20 database retrievals—a negligible overhead if the optimized query will subsequently be executed a large number of times. (Remember that System R is a compiling system—see Part 2 of this book—and hence that a SQL statement may be optimized once and then executed many times, perhaps many thousands of times.) Optimization of complex queries is said to require "only a few thousand bytes of storage and a few tenths of a second" on an IBM System 370 Model 158. "Joins of eight tables have been optimized in a few seconds."

16.5 OPTIMIZATION IN INGRES

We now turn our attention to some of the optimization techniques used in the INGRES prototype ("University INGRES"). Our discussion is based for the most part on material from references [16.15] and [16.16]. Further information on query optimization in INGRES—specifically in Commercial INGRES—can be found in a paper by Kooi and Frankforth in reference [16.26]. See also reference [16.27].

The general strategy for processing queries in INGRES is called *query decomposition*. The basic idea is to break a query involving multiple tuple variables down into a sequence of smaller queries involving one such variable each, using *detachment* and *tuple substitution* to achieve the desired decomposition:

- *Detachment* is the process of removing a component of the query that has just one variable in common with the rest of the query.

- *Tuple substitution* is the process of substituting for one of the variables in the query a tuple at a time.

Detachment is always applied in preference to tuple substitution (so long as there is a choice; see the example below). Eventually, however, the query will have been decomposed via detachment into a set of components that cannot be decomposed via detachment any further, and tuple substitution must be brought into play. The process of breaking the given query down into irreducible components via detachment is called *reduction*.

We give a simple example of the decomposition process (based on an example from reference [16.15]).

Initial query (Q0): Get names of London suppliers who supply some red part weighing less than 25 pounds in a quantity greater than 200.

```
Q0: RETRIEVE (S.SNAME) WHERE S.CITY   = "London"
                       AND   S.S#     = SP.S#
                       AND   SP.QTY   > 200
                       AND   SP.P#    = P.P#
                       AND   P.COLOR  = "Red"
                       AND   P.WEIGHT < 25
```

First we detach the "one-variable query" (actually a projection of a restriction) involving the variable P. That query is detachable because it has just one variable—namely P—in common with the rest of the query. Since it links up to the rest of the original query via the attribute P#, the detached query must retrieve exactly that P# attribute; i.e., attribute P# is the attribute that must appear in the target list in the detached version. We save that detached version as a query D1 that retrieves its result into a temporary relation P′, and replace P by P′ in the remaining query (which we now label Q1):

```
D1: RETRIEVE INTO P' (P.P#) WHERE P.COLOR  = "Red"
                            AND    P.WEIGHT < 25

Q1: RETRIEVE (S.SNAME) WHERE S.CITY = "London"
                       AND   S.S#   = SP.S#
                       AND   SP.QTY > 200
                       AND   SP.P#  = P'.P#
```

Next we detach the one-variable query involving variable SP similarly:

```
D2: RETRIEVE INTO SP' (SP.S#, SP.P#) WHERE SP.QTY > 200

Q2: RETRIEVE (S.SNAME) WHERE S.CITY = "London"
                       AND   S.S#   = SP'.S#
                       AND   SP'.P# = P'.P#
```

Next we detach the one-variable query involving S:

```
D3: RETRIEVE INTO S' (S.S#, S.SNAME)
                     WHERE S.CITY = "London"

Q3: RETRIEVE (S'.SNAME) WHERE S'.S#  = SP'.S#
                        AND   SP'.P# = P'.P#
```

Finally we detach the two-variable query involving SP′ and P′:

```
D4: RETRIEVE INTO SP" (SP'.S#) WHERE SP'.P# = P'.P#

Q4: RETRIEVE (S'.SNAME) WHERE S'.S# = SP".S#
```

The original query Q0 has been decomposed into three one-variable queries (D1, D2, and D3) and two two-variable queries (D4 and Q4). D1, D2, and D3 can be processed in any order (conceivably even in parallel). D4 and Q4 cannot be decomposed any further and must be processed by tuple substitution. For example, consider Q4. With our usual sample data, the set of supplier numbers in attribute SP″.S# will be the set (S1,S2,S4). Each of these three values will be substituted for SP″.S# in turn. Q4 will therefore be evaluated as if it had been written as follows:

```
RETRIEVE (S'.SNAME) WHERE S'.S# = "S1"
                    OR    S'.S# = "S2"
                    OR    S'.S# = "S4"
```

Reference [16.15] gives algorithms for reduction to irreducible components and for choosing the variable for tuple substitution. It is in that latter choice that most of the optimization per se resides; the paper [16.15] includes heuristics for making the cost estimates that drive the choice (INGRES will usually—but not always—try to choose the relation with the smallest cardinality as the one to do the substitution on). The principal objectives of the optimization process as a whole are to avoid having to build Cartesian products and to keep the number of tuples to be scanned to a minimum at each stage.

Note that the reduction process sketched above can be regarded as the application of certain syntactic transformation rules to expressions of the relational calculus. INGRES also applies another interesting transformation rule, which again we explain by example: The WHERE clause

```
WHERE S.CITY > P.CITY AND P.CITY > "Rome"
```

can be modified to the form

```
WHERE S.CITY > P.CITY AND P.CITY > "Rome" AND S.CITY > "Rome"
```

(thanks to an obvious transitivity principle). Since every additional restriction leads to a smaller intermediate relation, such terms should be added wherever possible [16.16].

Reference [16.15] does not discuss the optimization of one-variable queries. However, information regarding that level of optimization is provided in the INGRES overview paper [10.6]. Basically, it is similar to the analogous function in other systems (e.g., System R), involving the use of statistical information kept in the system catalog and the choice of a particular access path (e.g., a hash or index) for scanning the relation.

Reference [16.16] presents some experimental evidence (namely, measurements from a benchmark set of queries) that suggests that the optimization techniques described above are basically sound and in practice quite effective. Some specific conclusions from that paper are the following:

1. Reduction is the best first move.

2. If tuple substitution *must* be done first, then the best choice of variable to be substituted for is a joining variable.

3. Once tuple substitution has been applied to one variable in a two-variable query, it is an excellent tactic to modify the storage structure of the other relation (if necessary) into an indexed structure that provides clustering on the join attribute. (See the discussion of MODIFY in Chapter 10.) INGRES in fact very often applies this tactic.

16.6   IMPLEMENTING THE RELATIONAL OPERATORS

We conclude this chapter with a short description of some methods for implementing the major relational operators.[8] The methods (shown below in the form of pseudocode algorithms) correspond to what we referred to as "low-level procedures" in Section 16.3. Note: A few of the algorithms discussed have in fact already been touched on in previous sections. In particular, the nested loop and sort/merge algorithms for implementing the join operation were discussed briefly in Section 16.4.

The operations we consider are projection, join, and aggregation—where by

---

8.   I am indebted to Dave DeWitt for much of the material of this section.

"aggregation" we mean the application of some built-in function such as COUNT, SUM, or MAX. We do not discuss restriction because we have little to add to what has already been said on that subject in Sections 16.3–16.5. As for aggregation, there are two principal cases to consider:

1. GROUP BY omitted
2. GROUP BY included

Case 1 is straightforward: Basically, it involves scanning the entire relation over which the aggregation is to be done—except that, if the attribute to be aggregated is indexed, it may be possible to compute the result directly from the index without having to access the relation itself at all [16.13]. For example, the query

```
SELECT  AVG (QTY)
FROM    SP ;
```

can be answered directly from the QTY index, assuming such an index exists. For the rest of this section we take "aggregation" to mean Case 2 specifically. Here is an example of Case 2:

```
SELECT  P#, SUM (QTY)
FROM    SP
GROUP   BY P# ;
```

Projection, join, and Case 2 aggregation are all very similar to one another, in the following sense: In every case, we need to group tuples together on the basis of values of some attribute (possibly composite). In the case of projection, such grouping allows us to eliminate duplicates; in the case of join, it allows us to concatenate matching tuples; and in the case of aggregation, it allows us to compute the individual (i.e., per group) aggregate values. There are three basic techniques for performing such grouping:

1. Nested loops
2. Sort/merge
3. Hashing

Of course, each combination of relational operation and implementation algorithm has its own associated cost formula. Details of those formulas are straightforward and are left as an exercise for the reader.

Note: The name "nested loops" is a little misleading, in that (as will be seen) nested loops are in fact involved in all of the algorithms. However, the term is usually taken to mean what might be called the "plain" case, in which all possible tuple combinations are inspected (i.e., every tuple of the relation scanned in the outer loop is examined in conjunction with every tuple of the relation scanned in the inner loop).

Projection

Suppose the projection is to be taken over attribute A of relation R. Let the tuples of R be R[1], R[2], ..., R[n].

1. Nested loops

```
do i = 1 to n ;                                /* outer loop */
   if R[i] not marked "deleted" then
   do ;
      add R[i] to result ;
      do j = i + 1 to n ;                      /* inner loop */
         if R[j].A = R[i].A then
            mark R[j] "deleted" ;
      end ;
   end ;
end ;
```

2. Sort/merge

```
sort R on attribute A, storing sorted result as S ;
do i = 1 to n ;                                /* outer loop */
   add S[i] to result ;
   do j = i + 1 to n ;                         /* inner loop */
      if S[j].A > S[i].A then
      do ;
         i = j ;
         leave inner loop ;
      end ;
   end ;
end ;
```

3. Hashing

```
initialize hash table H to empty ;
do i = 1 to n ;                                    /* outer loop */
   dup = no ;
   k = hash(R[i]) ;                           /* k in range 1 to p, say */
   /* let there be h tuples S[1], ...,   S[h] stored at H[k] */
   do j = 1 to h ;                                  /* inner loop */
      if S[j].A = R[i].A then
      do ;
         dup = yes ;
         leave inner loop ;
      end ;
   end ;
   if dup = no then
   add R[i] to list of tuples at H[k] ;
end ;
/* now collect all result tuples together */
do k = 1 to p ;
   /* let there be h tuples S[1], ..., S[h] stored at H[k] */
   do j = 1 to h ;
      add S[j] to result ;
   end ;
end ;
```

Join

Suppose the join is to be taken over attribute A of relation R with attribute B of relation S. Let the tuples of R and S be, respectively, R[1], R[2], ..., R[m] and S[1], S[2], ..., S[n].

1. Nested loops

```
do i = 1 to m ;                         /* outer loop */
   do j = 1 to n ;                      /* inner loop */
      if R[i].A = S[j].B then
         add joined tuple R[i] * S[j] to result ;
   end ;
end ;
```

The foregoing should be regarded as a worst-case procedure. It assumes that relation S is neither indexed nor hashed on attribute B. Experiments by Bitton et al. [16.29] indicate that, if that assumption is in fact valid, matters will usually be improved by dynamically constructing such an index or hash before proceeding with the join. The pseudocode becomes:

```
/* (index case) */
/* build index X on S.B, then proceed as follows: */
do i = 1 to m ;                            /* outer loop *
   /* let there be k index entries X[1], ..., X[k] with   *
   /* indexed field value = R[i].A                        *
   do j = 1 to k ;                         /* inner loop *
      /* let tuple of S indexed by X[j] be S[j] */
      add joined tuple R[i] * S[j] to result ;
   end ;
end ;

/* (hash case) */
/* build hash table H on S.B, then proceed as follows: */
do i = 1 to m ;                            /* outer loop *
   k = hash(R[i]) ;
   /* let there be h tuples S[1], ..., S[h] stored at H[k]  *
   do j = 1 to h ;                         /* inner loop *
      if S[j].B = R[i].A then
         add joined tuple R[i] * S[j] to result ;
   end ;
end ;
```

2. Sort/merge (assuming one-to-many join)

```
sort R on attribute A, storing sorted result as X ;
sort S on attribute B, storing sorted result as Y ;
k = 1 ;
do i = 1 to m ;                         /* outer loop */
   do j = k to n ;                      /* inner loop */
      if Y[j].B = X[i].A then
         add joined tuple X[i] * Y[j] to result ;
```

```
        if Y[j].B > X[i].A then
        leave inner loop ;
      end ;
      k = j ;
  end ;
```

3. Hashing

```
/* same as hash version of nested loop algorithm, except */
/* that relation B is assumed to be stored hashed already */
```

Aggregation

Suppose the aggregation is to be performed over attribute A of relation R. Let the tuples of R be R[1], R[2], ..., R[n].

1. Nested loops

```
/* "plain" nested loops do not really make sense here */
/* (why not? exercise for the reader)                 */
```

2. Sort/merge

```
sort R on attribute A, storing sorted result as S ;
k = 1 ;
do i = 1 to n ;                           /* outer loop */
   do j = i + 1 to n ;                     /* inner loop */
      if S[j].A > S[i].A then
      do ;
         complete calculation of kth aggregate value;
         add kth aggregate value to result ;
         k = k + 1 ;
         leave inner loop ;
      end ;
   end ;
   i = j ;
end ;
```

3. Hashing

```
initialize hash table H to empty ;
do i = 1 to n ;                           /* outer loop */
   dup = no ;
   k = hash(R[i]) ;                /* k in range 1 to p, say */
   /* let there be h A-values A[1], ..., A[h] held at H[k] */
   do j = 1 to h ;                          /* inner loop */
      if A[j] = R[i].A then
      do ;
         dup = yes ;
         update jth aggregate value at H[k] ;
         leave inner loop ;
      end ;
   end ;
   if dup = no then
```

(cont.)

```
      do ;
         add R[i].A to list of A-values at H[k] ;
         initialize corresponding aggregate value at H[k] ;
      end ;
   end ;
   /* now collect all result values together */
   do k = 1 to p ;
      /* let there be h aggregate values at H[k] */
      do j = 1 to h ;
         add jth aggregate value to overall result ;
      end ;
   end ;
```

REFERENCES AND BIBLIOGRAPHY

16.1 Matthias Jarke and Juergen Koch. "Query Optimization in Database Systems." *ACM Comp. Surv.* **16**, No. 2 (June 1984).

An excellent tutorial. The paper gives a general framework for query evaluation, much like the one in Section 16.3 of the present chapter (which was influenced by this paper), but based on the relational calculus rather than the algebra. It then discusses a large number of optimization techniques within that framework: syntactic and semantic transformations, low-level operation implementation, and algorithms for generating query plans and choosing among them. A comprehensive set of syntactic transformation rules for calculus expressions is given. An extensive bibliography (not annotated) is also included.

The paper also briefly discusses certain other related issues: the optimization of higher-level query languages (i.e., languages that are more powerful than the algebra or calculus), optimization in a distributed database environment (see Chapter 24), and the role of database machines with respect to optimization.

Surveys of optimization techniques, less comprehensive than this one but with more formal and detailed treatment of certain specific aspects, can also be found in the books by Ullman [11.6] and Maier [11.7].

16.2 F. P. Palermo. "A Data Base Search Problem." In *Information Systems: COINS IV* (ed., J. T. Tou). New York: Plenum Press (1974).

One of the earliest papers on optimization. Starting from an arbitrary expression of the relational calculus, the paper shows how that expression can be reduced to an equivalent algebraic expression by means of Codd's reduction algorithm (see Chapter 14), and then introduces a number of improvements to that algorithm, among them the following:

- No tuple is ever retrieved more than once.

- Unnecessary values are discarded from a tuple as soon as that tuple is retrieved—"unnecessary values" being either values of attributes not referenced in the query or values used solely for selection purposes. This process is equivalent to projecting the relation over the "necessary" attributes, and thus not only reduces the space required for each tuple but may also reduce the number of tuples that need to be retained.

- The method used to build up the result relation is based on a "least growth principle," so that the result tends to grow slowly. This technique has the effect of reducing both the number of comparisons involved and the amount of intermediate storage required.

■ An efficient technique is employed in the construction of joins, involving the dynamic factoring out of values used in "join terms" (such as S.S# = SP.S#) into *semijoins* (which are effectively a kind of dynamically constructed secondary index), and the use of an internal representation of each join called an *indirect join* (which makes use of internal tuple reference numbers to identify the tuples that participate in the join). These techniques are designed to reduce the amount of scanning needed in the construction of the join, by ensuring for each join term that the tuples concerned are (logically) ordered on the values of the join attributes. They also permit the dynamic determination of a "best" sequence in which to access the required database relations.

Note: The term *semijoin* is frequently encountered in modern database literature with a meaning somewhat different from that originally ascribed to it by Palermo. See Section 24.4.

16.3 J. B. Rothnie, Jr. "An Approach to Implementing a Relational Data Management System." *Proc. 1974 ACM SIGMOD Workshop on Data Description, Access and Control* (May 1974).

16.4 J. B. Rothnie, Jr. "Evaluating Inter-Entry Retrieval Expressions in a Relational Data Base Management System." *Proc. NCC* **44** (May 1975).

Two more early optimization papers. They describe some techniques used in an experimental system called DAMAS (built at MIT) for implementing a calculus-based language—specifically, techniques for implementing what INGRES would call "two-variable queries" [16.15] within that system. Reference [16.4] is more tutorial in nature, reference [16.3] gives some experimental results and more internal details. The papers discuss, specifically, the implementation of expressions involving a single existentially quantified tuple variable in terms of simpler expressions known as "primitive Boolean conditions" or PBC's. A PBC is a predicate that can be established as *true* or *false* for a given tuple by examining that tuple in isolation—i.e., it is a simple restriction predicate. The DAMAS storage modules, which manage the stored database, support the following operations directly:

■ Get next tuple where *p* is *true*

■ Test the existence of a tuple such that *p* is *true*

■ Eliminate from consideration all tuples where *p* is *true*

(where *p* is a PBC). Using these operations, the system handles a retrieval involving *R1* (unquantified) and *R2* (existentially quantified) as follows. Note that the target of the retrieval must be some projection of *R1*.

Step 1. In the original predicate, set all terms involving *R2* to *true* and simplify. The result is a PBC, *p1* say. Tuples of *R1* not satisfying *p1* can be eliminated from further consideration.

Step 2. Get a (noneliminated) tuple from *R1*. Substitute values from that tuple in original predicate and simplify, yielding *p2*. Does there exist a tuple in *R2* such that *p2* is *true*?

Step 3A. (Yes) Fetch identified *R2* tuple. Extract target values from the *R1* tuple and append to result relation. Build *p3*, selecting all *R1* tuples containing the same value for target attributes, and use it to eliminate from consideration all *R1* tuples that would generate duplicates.(This elimination can be performed whenever a tuple is added to the result.) Also, substitute values from fetched *R2* tuple in original predicate and simplify, yielding *p4*. Get all *R1* tuples satisfying *p4* and append target values to result.

Step 3B. (No) Build *p5*, selecting all *R1* tuples that would yield (in Step 2) a PBC for which there cannot exist an *R2* tuple to make it *true* (because no *R2* tuple made *p2 true*). Eliminate those *R1* tuples.

Step 4. Repeat Steps 2–4 until no *R1* tuples remain.

The design of the foregoing algorithm is based on the principle that as much information as possible should be derived from each database access. In practice, however, it may prove more expensive to eliminate tuples from consideration (for example) than simply to examine and reject them. For this reason, certain steps of the algorithm may or may not be applied in a given situation. In DAMAS the choice of whether or not to apply those steps is left to the user, but the papers give some suggestions for automating that choice.

16.5 R. M. Pecherer. "Efficient Evaluation of Expressions in a Relational Algebra." *Proc. ACM Pacific Conference* (April 1975).

This paper begins by presenting a slightly revised version of the original algebra. The revisions are motivated by efficiency considerations. The implementation of individual operations of that revised algebra is then discussed. It is assumed that relations are stored as sorted files and that records can be retrieved only in the sequence in which they are stored. Performance bounds are given for each operator. The paper claims that, under the stated assumptions, the operators requiring the most careful attention are projection and division. For these two, it is concluded that the best approach is to sort the data before the operation; the paper shows that, for a large class of operations, intermediate results can be obtained in the desired order at no extra cost. The paper also considers the transformation of expressions into an equivalent, more efficient, form, using some of Palermo's techniques [16.2].

16.6 L. R. Gotlieb. "Computing Joins of Relations." *Proc. 1975 ACM SIGMOD International Conference on Management of Data* (May 1975).

Presents and compares a set of algorithms for implementing natural join. Note, however, that the sort/merge algorithm (see references [16.7–16.8]) is not considered.

16.7 M. W. Blasgen and K. P. Eswaran. "Storage and Access in Relational Databases." *IBM Sys. J.* **16**, No. 4 (1977).

Several techniques for handling queries involving restriction, projection, and join operations are compared on the basis of their cost in disk I/O. The techniques in question are basically those implemented in System R. The conclusions are that physical clustering of logically related items is a critical performance parameter, and that, in the absence of such clustering, methods that depend on sorting—the so-called sort/merge algorithms—seem to be the most generally satisfactory. (Of course, the effect of such sorting is precisely to produce the desired clustering dynamically.)

16.8 T. H. Merrett. "Why Sort/Merge Gives the Best Implementation of the Natural Join." *ACM SIGMOD Record* **13**, No. 2 (January 1983).

Presents a set of intuitive arguments to support the position statement of the title. The argument is basically that the join operation itself will be most efficient if the two relations are each sorted on values of the join attribute (because in that case merge is the obvious technique, and each data page will be retrieved exactly once, which is clearly optimal), and the cost of sorting the relations into that desired sequence—on a large enough machine—is likely to be less than the cost of any scheme for circumventing the fact that they are not so sorted. However, the author does admit that there may be some exceptions to his extreme position. For instance, one of the relations may be sufficiently small (e.g., it may be the result of a previous restriction operation) that direct access to the other relation via an index or a hash may be more efficient than sorting it.

16.9 David J. DeWitt et al. "Implementation Techniques for Main Memory Database Systems." *Proc. 1984 ACM SIGMOD International Conference on Management of Data* (June 1984).

Includes a description of an algorithm for implementing joins by means of *hashing* that might be useful (in certain circumstances) even in the absence of the very large main memory that is assumed in the paper. The algorithm involves a single pass over each of the relations to be joined (A and B, say). The first pass builds a hash table for relation A on values of A's join attribute; the entries in the table contain the join attribute value—possibly values of other A-attributes also—and a pointer to the corresponding tuple. (In the paper it is assumed that at least a large fraction of the hash table can be kept in main memory.) The second pass then scans relation B and applies the same hash function to B's join attribute. When a B tuple collides in the hash table with one or more A tuples, the algorithm checks to see that the values of the join attributes are indeed equal, and if so generates the appropriate joined tuple(s). The great advantage of this technique is that relations A and B do not need to be stored in any particular order, and hence that no sorting is necessary.

Note that an analogous hashing technique could also be used to perform grouping and duplicate elimination operations (in particular, it might be useful for projection). See Section 16.6.

16.10 J. M. Smith and P. Y.-T. Chang. "Optimizing the Performance of a Relational Algebra Database Interface." *CACM* **18,** No. 10 (October 1975).

Describes the algorithms used in the "Smart Query Interface for a Relational Algebra" (SQUIRAL). The techniques used include the following.

- Transforming the original algebraic expression into an equivalent but more efficient sequence of operations (along the lines indicated in Section 16.3).

- Assigning distinct operations in the transformed expression to distinct processes and exploiting concurrency and pipelining among them.

- Coordinating the sort orders of the temporary relations passed between those processes.

- Exploiting indexes and attempting to localize page references.

16.11 P. A. V. Hall. "Optimisation of a Single Relational Expression in a Relational Data Base System." *IBM J. R&D.* **20,** No. 3 (May 1976).

This paper describes some of the optimizing techniques used in the system PRTV [13.5]. PRTV, like SQUIRAL [16.10], begins by transforming the given algebraic expression into some more efficient form before evaluating it. A feature of PRTV is that the system does not automatically evaluate each expression as soon as it receives it; rather, it combines each new expression with those it has already accepted to build a larger and more complex expression, and defers actual evaluation until the last possible moment. Thus the "single relational expression" of the paper's title may actually represent an entire sequence of user operations. The optimizations described resemble those of SQUIRAL but go further in some respects; they include the following (in order of application).

- Restrictions are performed as early as possible.
- Sequences of projections are combined into a single projection.
- Redundant operations are eliminated.
- Expressions involving empty relations and trivial predicates are simplified.
- Common subexpressions are factored out.

The paper concludes with some experimental results and some suggestions for further investigations.

16.12 P. G. Selinger et al. "Access Path Selection in a Relational Database System." *Proc. 1979 ACM SIGMOD International Conference on Management of Data* (May 1979).

16.13 J. M. Cheng, C. R. Loosley, A. Shibamiya, and P. S. Worthington. "IBM Database 2 Performance: Design, Implementation, and Tuning." *IBM Sys. J.* **23**, No. 2 (1984).

Includes a brief description of optimization tactics in DB2 (query transformation techniques, the handling of nested query blocks, join methods, access path selection, and index-only processing). An example of the last of these is provided by the query

```
SELECT COUNT(*)
FROM    S ;
```

which DB2 will evaluate by counting the number of entries in some index on relation S (assuming, of course, that at least one such index exists), without accessing relation S itself at all.

The paper also includes much interesting material concerning other performance-oriented aspects of DB2.

16.14 Won Kim. "On Optimizing an SQL-Like Nested Query." *ACM TODS* **7**, No. 3 (September 1982).

As explained in Section 16.4, the implementation strategy chosen by the System R optimizer is dictated in part by the way the original query was formulated in terms of nested query blocks. However, any SQL query involving such nesting can always be reformulated in relational calculus terms without any such nesting, and it should be clear from the discussions in Section 16.3 that such reformulation is desirable as a preliminary step to subsequent optimization. Kim's paper provides an appropriate set of transformations for performing that reformulation task. Five types of nesting are identified and corresponding transformation algorithms described. Those algorithms are shown to improve the performance of nested queries by (typically) one to two orders of magnitude.

16.15 E. Wong and K. Youssefi. "Decomposition—A Strategy for Query Processing." *ACM TODS* **1**, No. 3 (September 1976).

16.16 K. Youssefi and E. Wong. "Query Processing in a Relational Database Management System." *Proc. 5th International Conference on Very Large Data Bases* (September 1979).

16.17 Robert Epstein. "Techniques for Processing of Aggregates in Relational Database Systems." University of California, Berkeley: *Electronics Research Laboratory Memorandum No. UCB/ERL M79/8* (21 February 1979).

Describes the algorithms used in University INGRES for dealing with the functions COUNT, SUM, AVG, etc., including in particular a number of optimizations that can be applied during such processing.

16.18 S. B. Yao. "Optimization of Query Evaluation Algorithms." *ACM TODS* **4,** No. 2 (June 1979).

A general model is developed of query evaluation that includes many known algorithms as special cases. The model includes the following set of low-level operations, together with an associated set of cost formulas:

1. Restriction indexing

2. Join indexing

3. Intersection

4. Record access

5. Sequential scan

6. Link scan

7. Restriction filter

8. Join filter

9. Sort

10. Concatenation

11. Projection

A given query processing algorithm expressed in terms of these low-level operations can be evaluated in accordance with the cost formulas. The paper identifies a set of *classes* of query processing algorithms and assigns a cost formula to each class. The problem of query optimization then becomes the problem of solving a simple set of cost equations to find a minimum cost, and then selecting the class of algorithm corresponding to that minimum cost.

16.19 Matthias Jarke and Juergen Koch. "Range Nesting: A Fast Method to Evaluate Quantified Queries." *Proc. 1983 ACM SIGMOD International Conference on Management of Data* (May 1983).

Defines a variation of the relational calculus that permits some additional (and useful) syntactic transformation rules to be applied, and presents algorithms for evaluating expressions of that calculus. The particular version of the calculus described allows range variables to be bound to expressions, instead of just to a named relation. The expressions in question involve exactly one free variable and an arbitrary number of existentially or universally quantified bound variables. (Actually, the version of the calculus defined in Chapter 14 is very close to Jarke and Koch's version.) The paper describes the optimization of a particular class of expressions of the revised calculus, called "perfect nested expressions." Methods are given for converting apparently complex queries—in particular, certain queries involving FORALL—into perfect expressions. The authors show that a large subset of the queries that arise in practice correspond to perfect expressions.

16.20 A. V. Aho, Y. Sagiv, and J. D. Ullman. "Efficient Optimization of a Class of Relational Expressions." *ACM TODS* **4,** No. 4 (December 1979).

The class of relational expressions referred to in the title of this paper is those expressions that involve only (equality-based) selection, projection, and (natural) join operations—

so-called *SPJ-expressions*. SPJ-expressions correspond to relational calculus queries involving only equality comparisons, AND connectors, and EXISTS quantifiers. The paper introduces *tableaus* as a means of symbolically representing SPJ-expressions. A tableau is a rectangular array, in which columns correspond to attributes and rows to predicates—specifically, to *membership predicates*, which state that a certain tuple of values must exist in a certain relation. Rows are logically connected by the appearance of common symbols in the rows concerned. For example, the tableau

```
 S#      STATUS      CITY       P#       COLOR
----------------------------------------------
         a1

----------------------------------------------
 b1      a1          London                       -- relation S
 b1                             b2                 -- relation SP
                                b2       Red       -- relation P
```

represents the query "Get status (a1) of suppliers (b1) in London who supply some red part (b2)." The top row of the tableau lists the names of all attributes mentioned in the query, the next row is the "summary" row (corresponding to the target list in a calculus query or the final projection in an algebraic expression), and the remaining rows (as already stated) represent membership predicates. We have tagged those rows in the example to indicate the relevant relations. Notice that the "b"s refer to bound variables and the "a"s to free variables; the summary row contains only "a"s.

Tableaus represent another candidate for a canonical formalism for queries (see Section 16.3), except of course that they are not general enough to represent all possible relational expressions. (In fact, they may be regarded as a syntactic variation on Query-By-Example, one that is however strictly less powerful than QBE.) The paper gives algorithms for reducing any tableau to another, semantically equivalent tableau in which the number of rows is reduced to a minimum. Since the number of rows (not counting the top two, which are special) is one more than the number of joins in the corresponding SPJ-expression, the converted tableau represents an optimal form of the query—optimal, in the very specific sense that the number of joins is minimized. (In the example above, of course, the number of joins is already the minimum possible for the query, and such optimization has no effect.) The minimal tableau can then be converted back if desired into some other representation for subsequent additional optimization.

The idea of minimizing the number of joins has applicability to queries formulated in terms of join views (in particular, queries formulated in terms of a "universal relation"; see references [17.25–17.32]). For example, suppose the user is presented with a view V that is defined as the join of relations S and SP over S#, and the user issues the query:

```
SELECT DISTINCT P#
FROM   V ;
```

A straightforward query processing algorithm would convert this query into the following:

```
SELECT DISTINCT P#
FROM   S, SP
WHERE  S.S# = SP.S# ;
```

As pointed out in Section 16.3, however, the following query produces the same result, and does not involve a join (i.e., the number of joins has been minimized):

```
SELECT DISTINCT P#
FROM     SP ;
```

We note that, since the algorithms for tableau reduction given in the paper take into account any explicitly stated functional dependencies among the attributes (see Chapter 17), they therefore provide a limited example of a *semantic* optimization technique.

16.21 Y. Sagiv and M. Yannakakis. "Equivalences Among Relational Expressions with the Union and Difference Operators." *JACM 27,* No. 4 (October 1980).

Extends the ideas of [16.20] to deal with queries that include the union and difference operations.

16.22 A. Makinouchi, M. Tezuka, H. Kitakami, and S. Adachi. "The Optimization Strategy for Query Evaluation in RDB/V1." *Proc. 7th International Conference on Very Large Data Bases* (September 1981).

RDB/V1 was the prototype forerunner of the Fujitsu product AIM/RDB (which is a SQL system). This paper describes the optimization techniques used in that prototype and briefly compares them with the techniques used in University INGRES and System R. One particular technique seems to be novel: the use of dynamically obtained MAX and MIN values to induce additional restriction predicates. This technique has the effect of simplifying the process of choosing a join order and improving the performance of the joins themselves. As a simple example of the latter point, suppose relations S and P are to be joined over city values. First relation S is sorted on attribute S.CITY. During the sort, the maximum and minimum values, HIGH and LOW say, of S.CITY are determined. Then the restriction predicate

```
LOW <= P.CITY AND P.CITY <= HIGH
```

can be used to reduce the number of tuples of P that need to be inspected in building the join.

16.23 J. J. King. "QUIST: A System for Semantic Query Optimization in Relational Databases." *Proc. 7th International Conference on Very Large Data Bases* (September 1981).

Semantic query optimization is the process of converting a specified query into another, qualitatively different query that is however guaranteed to produce the same result as the original one, thanks to the fact that the data is guaranteed to satisfy certain integrity constraints (see Chapter 19). For example, suppose the suppliers-and-parts database satisfies the (time-independent) constraint "All red parts must be stored in London," and consider the rather complex query (Q1) "Get suppliers who supply only red parts and are located in the same city as at least one of the parts they supply." The following query (Q2) is simpler than query Q1 but will obviously produce the same result: "Get London suppliers who supply only red parts." The paper describes a system called QUIST (standing for "query improvement through semantic transformation") that is capable of performing such query conversions. The converted query can of course then be optimized in any of the standard ways.

16.24 D. H. D. Warren. "Efficient Processing of Interactive Relational Database Queries Expressed in Logic." *Proc. 7th International Conference on Very Large Data Bases* (September 1981).

Presents a view of query optimization from a rather different perspective—namely, that of formal logic. The paper reports on techniques used in an experimental database system based on PROLOG. The techniques are apparently very similar to those of System R, although they were arrived at quite independently and with somewhat different objectives. The paper suggests that, in contrast to conventional query languages such as QUEL and SQL, logic-based languages such as PROLOG permit queries to be expressed in such a manner as to highlight:

a) what the essential components of the query are (namely, the logic goals);
b) what it is that links those components together (namely, the logic variables); and
c) what the crucial implementation problem is (namely, the order in which to try to satisfy the goals).

As a consequence, it is suggested that such a language is very convenient as a base for optimization. (Indeed, it could be regarded as yet another very suitable candidate for the internal representation of queries originally expressed in some other language. See Section 16.3.)

16.25 A. Rosenthal and D. Reiner. "An Architecture for Query Optimization." *Proc. 1982 ACM SIGMOD International Conference on Management of Data* (June 1982).

16.26 *IEEE Database Engineering* **5,** No. 3: Special Issue on Query Optimization (September 1982).

Contains thirteen short papers (from both academic and industrial environments) on various aspects of query optimization.

16.27 Lawrence A. Rowe and Michael Stonebraker. "The Commercial INGRES Epilogue." In Michael Stonebraker (ed.): *The INGRES Papers*: *The Anatomy of a Relational Database Management System*. Reading Mass.: Addison-Wesley (1985).

Describes the changes made to University INGRES to turn it into a commercial product. In particular, optimizer changes are described. The major differences between the University and Commercial INGRES optimizers are as follows:

1. The University optimizer used "incremental planning": i.e., it decided what to do first, did it, decided what to do next on the basis of the size of the result of the previous step, and so on. The Commercial optimizer decides on a complete plan before beginning execution, based on (good) estimates of intermediate result sizes.

2. The University optimizer handled two-variable (i.e., join) queries by tuple substitution (see Section 16.5). The Commercial optimizer supports a variety of preferred techniques for handling such queries, including in particular the sort-merge technique described in Section 16.4.

3. The University optimizer (like the System R optimizer) used statistical information from the catalog giving the number of tuples in each relation and number of pages occupied by each relation. The Commercial optimizer uses a much more sophisticated set of statistics, including minimum, maximum, and average values for each field, together with histogram information regarding the distribution of values in that field.

4. The University optimizer reduced the search space (see Section 16.3) by doing incremental planning, as noted under 1. above. The Commercial optimizer does a more

exhaustive search. However, the search process stops if the time spent on optimization exceeds the current best estimate of the time required to execute the query (for otherwise the overhead of doing the optimization might well outweigh the advantages).

16.28 W. Kim, D. Reiner, and D. Batory (eds.). *Query Processing in Database Systems*. New York: Springer-Verlag (in press).

16.29. Dina Bitton, David J. DeWitt, and Carolyn Turbyfill. "Benchmarking Database Systems: A Systematic Approach." *Proc. 9th International Conference on Very Large Data Bases* (November 1983).

17

Further
Normalization

17.1 INTRODUCTION

The subject of this chapter is different in kind from everything we have discussed in this book so far. The question to be addressed is the following: Given a body of data to be represented in a database, how do we decide on a suitable logical structure for that data? More precisely, how do we decide what relations are needed and what their attributes should be? This is the *database design* problem (more accurately, the *logical* database design problem; see Part 1 of this book for some brief notes on the distinction between logical and physical database design).

Consider the suppliers-and-parts database once again. The logical structure of that database—see the schema[1] of Fig. 4.2 in Chapter 4—does have a feeling of rightness about it; it is "obvious" that three relations (S, P, SP) are necessary, that (e.g.) COLOR belongs in relation P, STATUS in relation S, QTY in relation SP, and so on. But what is it that tells us these things are so? Some insight into this question can be gained by seeing what happens if the design is changed in some way. Suppose, for example, that attribute STATUS is moved out of relation S and into relation SP (intuitively the wrong place for it, since STATUS concerns sup-

---

1. Remember from Chapter 2 that the term "schema" simply means "data definition" or "data description." Database design really means *schema* design. By definition, when we design a database, we are interested in properties of the data that are *true for all time*, not with properties that merely happen to apply by chance at some specific instant. For example, the property "each part has one weight" is true for all time; by contrast, the property "every red part is stored in London" is just a fluke—it happens to be true given the sample values of Fig. 4.1, but it is not true for all time. The purpose of the schema is precisely to capture those properties that are true for all time (i.e., the *time-independent* properties). Throughout this chapter, therefore, we will be far more concerned with the "heading" or schema part of a relation than we will with the "body" or value part (see the definition of *relation* in Chapter 11 for an explanation of these terms).

pliers, not shipments). Figure 17.1 shows a partial tabulation for this revised SP relation (which we refer to as SP′ to avoid confusion).

```
                --   --   ---   ------
       SP'      S#   P#   QTY   STATUS
                --   --   ---   ------
                S1   P1   300      20
                S1   P2   200      20
                S1   P3   400      20
                S1   P4   200      20
                 .    .    .        .
                 .    .    .        .
```

Fig. 17.1 Partial tabulation of relation SP′

It is clear from the figure that relation SP′ involves a lot of redundancy—the fact that a given supplier has a certain status is stated as many times as there are shipments for that supplier. That redundancy leads to a variety of problems. For example, after an update, supplier S1 might be shown as having a status of 20 in one tuple and a status of 30 in another. So perhaps a good design principle is "one fact in one place" (i.e., avoid redundancy if possible). *The topic of this chapter, normalization theory, is basically a formalization of simple ideas such as this one* —a formalization, however, that has very practical application in the area of database design.

Recall from Chapter 11 that relations in a relational database are always normalized, in the sense that the underlying domains contain atomic values only. In Section 11.3 we showed by example how an unnormalized relation can be reduced to an equivalent normalized form. Normalization theory takes that simple basic idea much further. The fundamental point is that a given relation, even though it is normalized, may still possess certain undesirable properties (relation SP′ of Fig. 17.1 is a case in point); normalization theory allows us to recognize such cases and shows how such relations can be converted to a more desirable form. In the case of relation SP′, for example, the theory would tell us precisely what is wrong with that relation, and it would tell us how to break it down into two "more desirable" relations, namely the familiar relations S and SP (of course, we have ignored attributes SNAME and CITY in this simple example, so that the "more desirable" relation S would contain only the S# and STATUS attributes).

Normal Forms

Normalization theory is built around the concept of *normal forms*. A relation is said to be in a particular normal form if it satisfies a certain specified set of constraints. For example, a relation is said to be in *first normal form* (abbreviated 1NF) if and only if it satisfies the constraint that it contains atomic values only (thus every normalized relation is in 1NF, as already stated; it is this fact that accounts for the "first").

Numerous normal forms have been defined (refer to Fig. 17.2). Codd originally

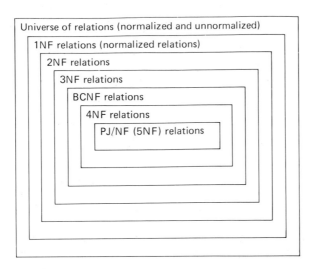

Fig. 17.2 Normal forms.

defined first, second, and third normal form (1NF, 2NF, 3NF) in reference [17.1]. Briefly, as the figure suggests, all normalized relations are in 1NF; some 1NF relations are also in 2NF; and some 2NF relations are also in 3NF. The motivation behind Codd's definitions was that 2NF was "more desirable" (in a sense to be explained) than 1NF, and 3NF in turn was more desirable than 2NF. That is, the database designer should generally aim for a design involving relations in 3NF, not relations that are merely in 2NF or 1NF.

To digress for a moment: The foregoing statement (that the designer should aim for 3NF) should *not* be construed as law. Sometimes there are good reasons for flouting the principles of normalization (see Section 17.8). The only hard requirement is that relations be in at least first normal form. Indeed, this is as good a place as any to make the point that database design can be an extremely complex task (at least in a "large database" environment; the design of "small" databases is usually fairly straightforward). Normalization theory is a useful aid in the process, but it is not a panacea; anyone designing a database is certainly advised to be familiar with the basic techniques of normalization as described in this chapter, but we do not mean to suggest that the design should necessarily be based on normalization principles alone. Chapter 25 includes a brief mention of a number of other design principles that have little or nothing to do with normalization as such.

To return to the topic of normal forms per se: Codd's original definition of 3NF [17.1] suffered from certain inadequacies, as we shall see in Section 17.4. A revised (stronger) definition, due to Boyce and Codd, was given in reference [17.4]— stronger, in the sense that any relation that was 3NF by the new definition was certainly 3NF by the old, but a relation could be 3NF by the old definition and not by the new. The new 3NF is now usually referred to as "Boyce/Codd normal form" (BCNF) in order to distinguish it from the old form.

Subsequently, Fagin [17.6] defined a new "fourth" normal form (4NF—"fourth" because at that time BCNF was still usually called "third"). More recently, Fagin again [17.9] defined yet another normal form which he called "projection-join normal form" (PJ/NF, also known as "fifth" normal form or 5NF). As Fig. 17.2 shows, some BCNF relations are also in 4NF, and some 4NF relations are also in 5NF.

The reader may very well be wondering by now whether there is any end to this progression, and whether there may be a 6NF, a 7NF, and so on ad infinitum. Although that is a good question to ask, we are obviously not in a position to give it any detailed consideration as yet. We content ourselves with the rather equivocal statement that there are indeed additional normal forms not shown in Fig. 17.2, but that 5NF is actually the "final" normal form in a special (but important) sense. We will return to this topic at the end of the chapter.

The reader is warned that we make little attempt at rigor in what follows; rather, we rely to a considerable extent on plain intuition. Indeed, part of the argument is that concepts such as BCNF, 4NF, etc., despite the somewhat esoteric terminology, are essentially very simple and commonsense ideas. Most of the references treat the material in a more formal and rigorous manner. A good tutorial can be found in reference [17.10].

The plan of the chapter is as follows. Section 17.2 introduces the simple but crucial concept of *functional dependence*, which provides the basis for Codd's original three normal forms and for Boyce/Codd normal form. The next two sections then describe, respectively, the original three normal forms and BCNF. Section 17.5 considers the question of alternative decompositions—that is, the question of choosing the "best" decomposition of a given relation into equivalent BCNF relations (when there is a choice). Sections 17.6 and 17.7 are concerned with 4NF and 5NF. Finally, Section 17.8 provides a summary of the overall normalization process and discusses a number of related issues.

One final introductory remark: As mentioned in the introduction to this part of the book, the various normal forms and associated ideas are not considered part of the relational model per se, but rather constitute a separate theory built on top of that model. Normalization theory thus serves to illustrate the important point that the theory of relational databases in general is a broad subject, much broader than just the underlying model alone.

17.2 FUNCTIONAL DEPENDENCE

As indicated in Section 17.1, we begin our treatment of normalization theory by defining the fundamental notion of *functional dependence* or *functional dependency* (the terms are used interchangeably).

■   Given a relation R, attribute Y of R is *functionally dependent* on attribute X of R—in symbols,

$R . X \rightarrow R . Y$

(read "*R.X functionally determines R.Y*")—if and only if each X-value in R has associated with it precisely one Y-value in R (at any one time). Attributes X and Y may be composite.

In the suppliers-and-parts database, for example, attributes SNAME, STATUS, and CITY of relation S are each functionally dependent on attribute S# of relation S, because, given a particular value for S.S#, there exists precisely one corresponding value for each of S.SNAME, S.STATUS, and S.CITY. In symbols,

```
S.S#  →  S.SNAME
S.S#  →  S.STATUS
S.S#  →  S.CITY
```

or, more succinctly,

```
S.S#  →  S.(SNAME,STATUS,CITY)
```

Note that if attribute X is a candidate key of relation R—in particular, if it is the *primary* key—then all attributes Y of relation R must necessarily be functionally dependent on X (follows from the definition of candidate key). The examples above involving relation S illustrate this point. Likewise, in relation SP we have:

```
SP.(S#,P#)  →  SP.QTY
```

Note, however, that there is no requirement in the definition of functional dependence (henceforth abbreviated FD) that X in fact be a candidate key of R; in other words, there is no requirement that a given X-value appear in only one tuple of R. We give an alternative definition of FD that makes this point more explicit:

- Given a relation R, attribute Y of R is functionally dependent on attribute X of R if and only if, whenever two tuples of R agree on their X-value, they must necessarily agree on their Y-value.

For example, relation SP′ of Fig. 17.1 satisfies the FD

```
SP'.S#  →  SP'.STATUS
```

(every SP′ tuple with a given S# value must have the same STATUS value).

We also define the concept of *full* functional dependence. Attribute Y of relation R is *fully* functionally dependent on attribute X of relation R if it is functionally dependent on X and not functionally dependent on any proper subset of X (that is, there does not exist any proper subset Z of the attributes constituting X such that Y is functionally dependent on Z). For example, in relation S, it is certainly true that attribute CITY is functionally dependent on the (composite) attribute (S#,STATUS):

```
S.(S#,STATUS)  →  S.CITY
```

However, this is not a *full* FD, because of course we also have the FD:

```
S.S#  →  S.CITY
```

(CITY is also functionally dependent on S# alone). Note that if Y is functionally dependent on X but not fully so, then X must be composite. From this point on we will normally take "functional dependence" to mean full functional dependence, unless we explicitly state otherwise. We will also abbreviate "full functional dependence" to just "full dependence" whenever there is no risk of ambiguity.

It is convenient to represent the FDs in a given relation by means of a *functional dependency diagram* (FD diagram). The FD diagrams for relations S, P, and SP are given in Fig. 17.3. We shall make frequent use of such diagrams in the sections that follow.

We conclude this section by emphasizing the point that functional dependence is a *semantic* notion. Recognizing the FDs is part of the process of understanding what the data means. The fact that CITY is functionally dependent on S#, for example, means that each supplier is located in precisely one city. To look at this another way: There is a constraint in the real world that the database represents, namely that each supplier is located in precisely one city; since it is part of the semantics of the situation, that constraint must somehow be observed in the database; the way to ensure that it is so observed is to specify it in the schema, so that the DBMS can enforce it; and the way to specify it in the schema is to declare the FD. Later we will see that the concepts of normalization lead to a very simple means of declaring such FDs (not all FDs, but probably the most important ones in practice).

17.3   FIRST, SECOND, AND THIRD NORMAL FORMS

We are now in a position to describe Codd's original three normal forms. We present a preliminary, very informal, definition of 3NF first in order to give some idea of the point we are aiming for. We then consider the process of reducing an arbitrary relation to an equivalent collection of 3NF relations, giving somewhat more precise definitions of the three forms as we go. However, we note at the outset that 1NF, 2NF, and 3NF are not very significant in themselves except as stepping-stones to BCNF (and beyond).

■   A relation R is in 3NF if and only if the nonkey attributes of R (if any) are

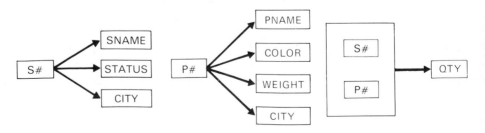

Fig. 17.3 Functional dependencies in relations S, P, SP.

a)   mutually independent, and

b)   fully dependent on the primary key of R.

We explain the terms "nonkey attribute" and "mutually independent" as follows.

- A *nonkey attribute* is any attribute that does not participate in the primary key of the relation concerned. Note: For simplicity we assume throughout this section that each relation has exactly one candidate key (i.e., a primary key and no alternate keys). This assumption is reflected in our definitions, which (we repeat) are not very rigorous. The case of a relation having two or more candidate keys is discussed in Section 17.4.

- Two or more attributes are *mutually independent* if none of the attributes concerned is functionally dependent on any of the others. Note that each such attribute can be updated independently of all of the rest.

For example, relation P (the parts relation) is in 3NF according to the foregoing definition: Attributes PNAME, COLOR, WEIGHT, and CITY are certainly all independent of one another (it is possible to change, e.g., the color of a part without simultaneously having to change its weight), and of course they are all fully dependent on P#, the primary key (the dependencies *must* be full, because P# is not composite).

The foregoing informal definition of 3NF may be interpreted, still more intuitively, as follows:

- A relation R is in third normal form (3NF) if and only if, for all time, each tuple of R consists of a primary key value that identifies some entity, together with a set of zero or more mutually independent attribute values that describe that entity in some way.

Again, relation P fits the definition.

Now we turn to the reduction process. First we give a definition of first normal form.

- A relation R is in *first normal form* (1NF) if and only if all underlying domains contain atomic values only.

This definition merely states that *any* normalized relation is in 1NF, which is of course correct. A relation that is only in first normal form (that is, a 1NF relation that is not also in 2NF, and therefore not in 3NF either) has a structure that is undesirable for a number of reasons. To illustrate the point, let us suppose that information concerning suppliers and shipments, rather than being split into two relations (S and SP), is lumped together into a single relation as follows:

```
FIRST ( S#, STATUS, CITY, P#, QTY )
```

Note that this is an extended version of relation SP′ from Section 17.1. The attributes have their usual meanings, except that for the sake of the example we

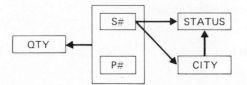

Fig. **17.4** Functional dependencies in the relation FIRST.

introduce an additional constraint, namely that STATUS is functionally dependent on CITY; the meaning of this constraint is that a supplier's status is determined by the location of that supplier (e.g., all London suppliers *must* have a status of 20). We ignore attribute SNAME for simplicity. The primary key of FIRST is the combination (S#,P#). The FD diagram is shown in Fig. 17.4.

Note that this FD diagram is "more complex" than the FD diagram for a 3NF relation. Informally, a 3NF diagram has arrows out of the primary key *only* (look at Fig. 17.3), whereas a non3NF diagram (such as the diagram for FIRST) has arrows out of the primary key *together with certain additional arrows*—and it is those additional arrows that cause all the trouble. In fact, relation FIRST violates both conditions (a) and (b) in the 3NF definition above—the nonkey attributes are not all mutually independent, because STATUS depends on CITY (one additional arrow), and they are not all fully dependent on the primary key, because STATUS and CITY are dependent on S# alone (two more additional arrows).

As a basis for illustrating some of the difficulties, Fig. 17.5 shows a sample tabulation (set of data values) for relation FIRST. The values shown are basically those of Fig. 4.1 (as usual), except that the status of supplier S3 has been changed from 30 to 10 to be consistent with the new constraint that CITY determines STATUS. The redundancies are obvious. For example, every tuple for supplier S1 shows CITY as London; likewise, every tuple for city London shows STATUS as 20.

The redundancies in relation FIRST lead to a variety of what are usually called "update anomalies"—that is, difficulties over the three update operations INSERT,

FIRST	S#	STATUS	CITY	P#	QTY
	S1	20	London	P1	300
	S1	20	London	P2	200
	S1	20	London	P3	400
	S1	20	London	P4	200
	S1	20	London	P5	100
	S1	20	London	P6	100
	S2	10	Paris	P1	300
	S2	10	Paris	P2	400
	S3	10	Paris	P2	200
	S4	20	London	P2	200
	S4	20	London	P4	300
	S4	20	London	P5	400

Fig. **17.5** Sample tabulation of FIRST.

DELETE, and UPDATE. To fix our ideas we concentrate first on the supplier city redundancy (caused by the FD FIRST.S# → FIRST.CITY). Problems occur with each of the three basic operations.

INSERT

We cannot enter the fact that a particular supplier is located in a particular city until that supplier supplies at least one part. Indeed, the tabulation of Fig. 17.5 does not show that supplier S5 is located in Athens. The reason is that, until S5 supplies some part, we have no appropriate primary key value. (Remember that, by Integrity Rule 1 of the relational model, no component of a primary key value can be null; in relation FIRST, primary key values consist of the combination of a supplier number and a part number.)

DELETE

If we delete the only FIRST tuple for a particular supplier, we destroy not only the shipment connecting that supplier to some part but also the information that the supplier is located in a particular city. For example, if we delete the FIRST tuple with S# value S3 and P# value P2, we lose the information that S3 is located in Paris. (The insertion and deletion problems are really two sides of the same coin.)

UPDATE

The city value for a given supplier appears in FIRST many times, in general. This redundancy causes update problems. For example, if supplier S1 moves from London to Amsterdam, we are faced with *either* the problem of searching FIRST to find every tuple connecting S1 and London (and changing it) *or* the possibility of producing an inconsistent result (the city for S1 may be given as Amsterdam in one tuple and London in another).

The solution to these problems is to replace the relation FIRST by the two relations

```
SECOND ( S#, STATUS, CITY )
```

and

```
SP ( S#, P#, QTY )
```

The FD diagrams for these two relations are given in Fig. 17.6; sample tabulations are given in Fig. 17.7. Note that information for supplier S5 has now been

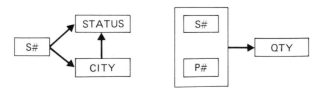

Fig. 17.6 Functional dependencies in the relations SECOND and SP.

included (in relation SECOND but not in relation SP). Relation SP is now in fact exactly as given in Fig. 4.1.

```
          --  ------  ------              --  --  ---
SECOND    S#  STATUS  CITY            SP  S#  P#  QTY
          --  ------  ------              --  --  ---
          S1      20  London              S1  P1  300
          S2      10  Paris               S1  P2  200
          S3      10  Paris               S1  P3  400
          S4      20  London              S1  P4  200
          S5      30  Athens              S1  P5  100
                                          S1  P6  100
                                          S2  P1  300
                                          S2  P2  400
                                          S3  P2  200
                                          S4  P2  200
                                          S4  P4  300
                                          S4  P5  400
```

Fig. 17.7 Sample tabulations of SECOND and SP.

It should be clear that this revised structure overcomes all the problems with update operations sketched earlier.

INSERT

We can enter the information that S5 is located in Athens, even though S5 does not currently supply any parts, by simply inserting the appropriate tuple into SECOND.

DELETE

We can delete the shipment connecting S3 and P2 by deleting the appropriate tuple from SP; we do not lose the information that S3 is located in Paris.

UPDATE

In the revised structure, the city for a given supplier appears once, not many times (the S#-CITY redundancy has been eliminated). Thus we can change the city for S1 from London to Amsterdam by changing it once and for all in the relevant SEC-OND tuple.

Comparing Figs. 17.6 and 17.4, we see that the effect of our structural revision has been to eliminate the *nonfull* dependencies, and it is that elimination that has resolved the difficulties. Intuitively, we may say that in relation FIRST the attribute CITY did not describe the entity identified by the primary key, namely a shipment; instead it described the *supplier* involved in that shipment. (Similarly for attribute STATUS, of course.) Mixing the two kinds of information in the same relation was what caused the problems in the first place.

We now give a definition of second normal form.

■ A relation *R* is in *second normal form* (2NF) if and only if it is in 1NF and every nonkey attribute is fully dependent on the primary key.

Relations SECOND and SP are both in 2NF (the primary keys are S# and the combination (S#,P#), respectively). Relation FIRST is not in 2NF. A relation that is in first normal form and not in second can always be reduced to an equivalent collection of 2NF relations. (Note, incidentally, that a 1NF relation that is not also in 2NF must have a composite primary key.) The reduction process consists of replacing the 1NF relation by suitable *projections*; the collection of projections so obtained is equivalent to the original relation, in the sense that the original relation can always be recovered by taking the (natural) *join* of those projections, so no information is lost in the reduction (which is highly important, of course). In other words, the process is reversible. In our example, SECOND and SP are projections of FIRST,[2] and FIRST is the join of SECOND and SP over S#.

The reduction of FIRST to SECOND and SP is an example of a *nonloss decomposition*.[3] In general, a relation R with attributes A, B, C that satisfies the FD

    $R.A \rightarrow R.B$

can always be "nonloss-decomposed" into its projections

    $R1(A,B)$ and $R2(A,C)$

(this result was first proved by Heath in reference [17.3] and is therefore sometimes referred to as Heath's theorem). Since no information is lost in the reduction process, any information that can be derived from the original structure can also be derived from the new structure. The converse is not true, however: The new structure can contain information (such as the fact that S5 is located in Athens) that could not be represented in the original. In this sense, the new structure may be regarded as a slightly more faithful representation of the real world.

The SECOND/SP structure still causes problems, however. Relation SP is satisfactory; as a matter of fact, relation SP is now in third normal form, and we shall ignore it for the remainder of this section. Relation SECOND, on the other hand, still suffers from a lack of mutual independence among its nonkey attributes. The FD diagram for SECOND is still "more complex" than a 3NF diagram. To be specific, the dependency of STATUS on S#, though it *is* functional, and indeed full, is *transitive* (via CITY): Each S# value determines a CITY value, and that CITY value in turn determines the STATUS value. In general, whenever the FDs

---

2. Except for the fact that SECOND may include tuples—such as the tuple for supplier S5 in Fig. 17.7—that have no counterpart in FIRST.
3. "Nonloss decomposition" is actually rather a strange term. The decomposition per se cannot lose information; the projection of a relation R on to some possibly composite attribute A contains exactly the same information as the original attribute $R.A$. However, joining the projections back together may cause the original relation R to reappear *together with some additional "spurious" tuples*. It can never produce anything *less* than R. (Exercise: Prove this statement.) A nonloss decomposition guarantees that the join produces exactly the original relation R—i.e., it guarantees that the *join* is nonloss (or *lossless*). A decomposition that is not nonloss (a "lossy" decomposition) loses information in the sense that the join may produce a superset of the original R, and there is no way of knowing which tuples in the superset are spurious and which genuine.

$R.A \rightarrow R.B$ and $R.B \rightarrow R.C$

both hold, then the (transitive) FD

$R.A \rightarrow R.C$

also holds. Transitive dependencies lead, once again, to update anomalies. (We now concentrate on the city/status redundancy, caused by the FD SECOND.CITY → SECOND.STATUS.)

INSERT

We cannot enter the fact that a particular city has a particular status—e.g., we cannot state that any supplier in Rome must have a status of 50—until we have some supplier actually located in that city. The reason is, again, that until such a supplier exists we have no appropriate (i.e., nonnull) primary key value.

DELETE

If we delete the only SECOND tuple for a particular city, we destroy not only the information for the supplier concerned but also the information that that city has that particular status. For example, if we delete the SECOND tuple for S5, we lose the information that the status for Athens is 30. (Once again, the insertion and deletion problems are two sides of the same coin.)

UPDATE

The status for a given city appears in SECOND many times, in general (the relation still contains some redundancy). Thus, if we need to change the status for London from 20 to 30, we are faced with *either* the problem of searching SECOND to find every tuple for London (and changing it) *or* the possibility of producing an inconsistent result (the status for London may be given as 20 in one tuple and 30 in another).

Again the solution to the problems is to replace the original relation (SECOND, in this case) by two projections, namely the projections

    SC (S#, CITY)

and

    CS (CITY, STATUS)

The FD diagrams for these two relations are given in Fig. 17.8; sample tabulations are given in Fig. 17.9. Note that status information for Rome has been included in relation CS. The reduction is reversible, once again, since SECOND is the join of SC and CS over CITY.

Fig. 17.8 Functional dependencies in the relations SC and CS.

```
      --  ------            ------  ------
SC    S#  CITY        CS    CITY    STATUS
      --  ------            ------  ------
      S1  London            Athens     30
      S2  Paris             London     20
      S3  Paris             Paris      10
      S4  London            Rome       50
      S5  Athens
```

Fig. 17.9 Sample tabulations of SC and CS.

It should be clear, again, that this revised structure overcomes all the problems with update operations sketched earlier. Detailed consideration of those problems is left to the reader. Comparing Figs. 17.8 and 17.6, we see that the effect of the further restructuring is to eliminate the transitive dependence of STATUS on S#, and again it is that elimination that has resolved the difficulties. Intuitively, we may say that in relation SECOND the attribute STATUS did not describe the entity identified by the primary key, namely a supplier; instead it described the city in which that supplier happened to be located. Once again, mixing the two kinds of information in the same relation was what caused the problems.

We now give a definition of third normal form.

■   A relation *R* is in *third normal form* (3NF) if and only if it is in 2NF and every nonkey attribute is nontransitively dependent on the primary key.

Relations SC and CS are both in 3NF (the primary keys are S# and CITY, respectively). Relation SECOND is not in 3NF. A relation that is in second normal form and not in third can always be reduced to an equivalent collection of 3NF relations. We have already indicated that the process is reversible, and hence that no information is lost in the reduction; however, the 3NF collection may contain information, such as the fact that the status for Rome is 50, that could not be represented in the original 2NF relation. Just as the SECOND/SP structure was a slightly better representation of the real world than the 1NF relation FIRST, so the SC/CS structure is a slightly better representation than the 2NF relation SECOND.

We conclude this section by stressing the point that the level of normalization of a given relation is a matter of semantics, not merely a matter of the data values that happen to appear in that relation at some particular time. It is not possible just to look at the tabulation of a given relation at a given time and to say whether or not that relation is in (say) 3NF—it is also necessary to know the meaning of the data, i.e., the dependencies, before such a judgment can be made. In particular, the DBMS cannot ensure that a relation is maintained in 3NF (or in any particular normal form other than first) without being informed of all relevant dependencies. For a relation in 3NF, however, all that is needed to inform the DBMS of those dependencies is an indication of the attribute(s) constituting the primary key (since the only dependencies will be those that are a consequence of the primary key—as stated earlier, "the only arrows are arrows out of the primary key"). For a relation not in 3NF, additional specifications would be necessary.

Note: Even given the dependencies, it is never possible to *prove* from a given tabulation that a relation is in 3NF (though it might be possible to prove that it is not). The best that can be done is to show that the given tabulation does not violate any of the dependencies; assuming it does not, then the tabulation is *consistent with the hypothesis* that the relation is in 3NF, but that fact of course does not guarantee that the hypothesis is true. And to show that a given tabulation does not violate any of the dependencies required by 3NF, it is sufficient to show that it does not contain any duplicate primary key values—hardly a demanding requirement. In fact, in a system that supports primary keys and therefore enforces primary key uniqueness, *every possible* tabulation will therefore be "consistent with the hypothesis" that the relation concerned is in 3NF.

17.4 BOYCE/CODD NORMAL FORM

As mentioned in Section 17.1, Codd's original definition of 3NF [17.1] suffered from certain inadequacies. To be precise, it did not deal satisfactorily with the case of a relation that

1. had multiple candidate keys, where

2. those candidate keys were composite, and

3. the candidate keys overlapped (i.e., had at least one attribute in common).

The original definition of 3NF was therefore subsequently replaced by a stronger definition to cater for this case also. However, since the new definition does actually define a normal form that is strictly stronger than the old 3NF, it is better to introduce a new name for it, instead of just continuing to call it 3NF; hence the term *Boyce/Codd normal form* (BCNF).[4] Note: The combination of conditions 1, 2, and 3 might not occur very often in practice. For a relation where 1, 2, and 3 do not apply, BCNF reduces to the old 3NF.

In order to define BCNF, it is convenient to introduce another term first. We define a (functional) *determinant* to be any attribute on which some other attribute is (fully functionally) dependent. For example, in relation FIRST (see the previous section), attributes S#, CITY, and (S#,P#) are all determinants. Now we define BCNF as follows.

■ A relation *R* is in *Boyce/Codd normal form* (BCNF) if and only if every determinant is a candidate key.

Observe that we are now talking in terms of *candidate* keys, not just the primary key. Note too that the BCNF definition is conceptually simpler than the old 3NF definition, in that it makes no explicit reference to first and second normal forms as such, nor to the concept of transitive dependence. Although (as already stated)

---

4. A definition of "third" normal form that was in fact equivalent to the BCNF definition was actually first given by Heath in 1971 [17.3].

BCNF is strictly stronger than 3NF, it is still the case that any given relation can be nonloss-decomposed into an equivalent collection of BCNF relations.

Before considering examples involving multiple candidate keys, let us convince ourselves that relations FIRST and SECOND, which were not in 3NF, are not in BCNF either; also that relations SP, SC, and CS, which were in 3NF, are also in BCNF. Relation FIRST contains three determinants, namely S#, CITY, and (S#,P#); of these, only (S#,P#) is a candidate key, so FIRST is not in BCNF. Similarly, SECOND is not in BCNF either, because the determinant CITY is not a candidate key. Relations SP, SC, and CS, on the other hand, are each in BCNF, because in each case the primary key is the only determinant in the relation.

We now consider an example involving two disjoint (nonoverlapping) candidate keys. Suppose that in the supplier relation.

```
S ( S#, SNAME, STATUS, CITY )
```

attributes S# and SNAME are both candidate keys (i.e., every supplier has a unique supplier number and also a unique supplier name). Assume, however (as earlier in the book), that attributes STATUS and CITY are mutually independent—i.e., the FD

```
S.CITY  →  S.STATUS
```

does *not* hold. Then the FD diagram for relation S is as shown in Fig. 17.10.

Relation S is in BCNF. Although it is true that the FD diagram is "more complex" than a 3NF diagram, it is nevertheless still the case that the only determinants are candidate keys; i.e., the only arrows are arrows out of those candidate keys. Note, however, that it would be desirable to specify the fact that SNAME is a candidate key in the schema, so that the DBMS can enforce the required uniqueness. For example (hypothetical syntax):

```
RELATION S ( S#, SNAME, STATUS, CITY )
          PRIMARY KEY ( S# )
          ALTERNATE KEY ( SNAME )
```

Now we present some examples in which the candidate keys overlap. Two candidate keys overlap if they involve two or more attributes each and have at least

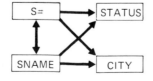

Fig. 17.10 Functional dependencies in relation S, if SNAME is a candidate key (and CITY → STATUS does not hold).

one attribute in common. For our first example, we suppose again that supplier names are unique, and we consider the relation

    SSP (S#, SNAME, P#, QTY)

The candidate keys are (S#,P#) and (SNAME,P#). Is this relation in BCNF? The answer is no, because it contains two determinants, S# and SNAME, that are not candidate keys for the relation (S# and SNAME are determinants because each of them determines the other). A partial tabulation of relation SSP is given in Fig. 17.11.

```
              --   -----   --   ---
       SSP   S#   SNAME   P#   QTY
              --   -----   --   ---
             S1   Smith   P1   300
             S1   Smith   P2   200
             S1   Smith   P3   400
             S1   Smith   P4   200
              .     .      .    .
```

Fig. 17.11 Sample tabulation of the relation SSP.

As the figure shows, relation SSP involves the same kind of redundancies as did relations FIRST and SECOND of Section 17.3, and hence is subject to the same kind of update anomalies. For example, changing the name of supplier S1 from Smith to Robinson leads, once again, either to search problems or to possibly inconsistent results. Yet SSP *is* in 3NF by the old definition, because that definition did not require an attribute to be fully dependent on the primary key if it was itself a component of some alternate key of the relation [17.1], and so the fact that SNAME is not fully dependent on (S#,P#)—assuming that combination to be the primary key—was ignored.

The solution to the SSP problems is, of course, to break the relation down into two projections, in this case the projections

    SS (S#, SNAME)   and   SP (S#, P#, QTY)

—or alternatively the projections

    SS (S#, SNAME)   and   SP (SNAME, P#, QTY)

All of these projections are in BCNF.

As a second example, we consider a relation SJT with attributes S (student), J (subject), and T (teacher). The meaning of an SJT tuple (s,j,t) is that student s is taught subject j by teacher t. Suppose in addition that the following constraints apply.

- For each subject, each student of that subject is taught by only one teacher.
- Each teacher teaches only one subject.
- Each subject is taught by several teachers.

A sample tabulation of this relation is given in Fig. 17.12.

```
          -----   -------   -----------
SJT    S        J          T
          -----   -------   -----------
          Smith   Math       Prof. White
          Smith   Physics    Prof. Green
          Jones   Math       Prof. White
          Jones   Physics    Prof. Brown
```

Fig. 17.12 Sample tabulation of the relation SJT.

What are the FDs in relation SJT? From the first constraint, we have a dependency of T on the composite attribute (S,J). From the second constraint, we have a dependency of J on T. Finally, the third "constraint" (scarcely a constraint in the usual sense of the term) tells us that there is *not* a dependency of T on J. So the FD diagram is as shown in Fig. 17.13.

Again we have two overlapping candidate keys, namely the combination (S,J) and the combination (S,T). Once again the relation is in 3NF and not in BCNF; and once again the relation suffers from certain update anomalies. For example, if we wish to delete the information that Jones is studying physics, we cannot do so without at the same time losing the information that Professor Brown teaches physics. The difficulties are caused by the fact that attribute T is a determinant but not a candidate key. Again we can get over the problems by replacing the original relation by two BCNF projections, in this case the projections

ST (S, T)   and   TJ (T, J)

It is left as an exercise for the reader to give tabulations of these two relations corresponding to the data of Fig. 17.12, to draw a corresponding FD diagram, to show that the two projections are indeed in BCNF[5] (what are the candidate keys?), and to check that this decomposition does in fact avoid the problems. (Note, however, that at the same time it introduces different problems. See the next section.)

Our third and final example of overlapping candidate keys concerns a relation EXAM with attributes S (student), J (subject), and P (position). The meaning of an EXAM tuple (s,j,p) is that student s was examined in subject j and achieved position p in the class list. For the purposes of the example, we assume that the following constraint holds.

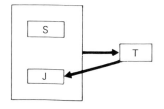

Fig. 17.13 Functional dependencies in the relation SJT.

5. As a matter of fact *any* binary relation must be in BCNF (why?).

- There are no ties; that is, no two students obtained the same position in the same subject.

Then the FDs are as shown in Fig. 17.14.

Again we have two overlapping candidate keys, namely (S,J) and (J,P). However, the relation is in BCNF, because those candidate keys are the only determinants. The reader should check that update anomalies such as those discussed earlier in this chapter do not occur with this relation. Thus overlapping candidate keys do not *necessarily* lead to problems in every case.

In conclusion, we see that the concept of BCNF eliminates certain problem cases that could occur—at least theoretically—under the old definition of 3NF. Moreover, BCNF is conceptually simpler than 3NF, in that it makes no reference to the concepts of 1NF, 2NF, primary key, or transitive dependence. Furthermore, the reference it does make to candidate keys can be replaced by a reference to the more fundamental notion of functional dependence (the definition given in [17.4] in fact makes this replacement). On the other hand, the concepts of primary key, transitive dependence, etc., are useful in practice, since they give some idea of the actual step-by-step process the designer must go through in order to reduce an arbitrary relation to an equivalent collection of BCNF relations. That process is summarized in Section 17.8.

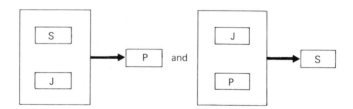

Fig. 17.14 Functional dependencies in the relation EXAM.

17.5 GOOD AND BAD DECOMPOSITIONS

During the reduction process it is frequently the case that a given relation can be decomposed in a variety of different ways. Consider the relation SECOND from Section 17.3 once again, with FDs

        SECOND.S# → SECOND.CITY

and

        SECOND.CITY → SECOND.STATUS

and therefore also (by transitivity)

        SECOND.S# → SECOND.STATUS

(see Fig. 17.15, in which the transitive FD is shown as a broken arrow). We showed
in Section 17.3 that the update anomalies encountered with SECOND could be overcome by replacing it by its decomposition into the two 3NF projections

```
SC ( S#, CITY )          and          CS ( CITY, STATUS )
```

(in fact, SC and CS are not only in 3NF but also in BCNF). Let us refer to this
decomposition as "decomposition A." As suggested at the beginning of this section,
decomposition A is not the only one possible. An alternative is decomposition B:

```
SC ( S#, CITY )          and          SS ( S#, STATUS )
```

(projection SC is the same for both A and B). Decomposition B is also nonloss,
and the two projections are again both in BCNF. But decomposition B is less satisfactory than decomposition A, for a number of reasons. For example, it is still
not possible (in B) to enter the information that a particular city has a particular
status unless some supplier is located in that city.

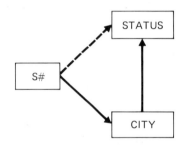

Fig. 17.15 Functional dependencies in the relation SECOND.

　　Let us examine this example a little more closely. First, note that the projections
in decomposition A correspond to the *solid* arrows in Fig. 17.15, whereas one of
the projections in decomposition B corresponds to the *broken* arrow. In decomposition A, the two projections are *independent* of one another, in the following
sense: Updates can be made to either one without regard for the other.[6] Provided
only that such an update is legal within the context of the projection concerned—
which means only that it must not violate the primary key uniqueness constraint
for that projection—then *the join of the two projections after the update will always
be a valid SECOND* (i.e., the join cannot possibly violate the FD constraints on
SECOND). In decomposition B, by contrast, updates to either of the two projections must be monitored to ensure that the FD

```
SECOND.CITY  →  SECOND.STATUS
```

6.　Actually this statement is an oversimplification. If attribute CITY of relation SC is regarded as a foreign key matching the primary key CITY of relation CS, then a certain amount
of cross-checking between the two projections will be required on updates after all. But this
fact is really a red herring—it does not invalidate the general point of the discussion.

is not violated (if two suppliers have the same city, then they must have the same status; consider, for example, what is involved in decomposition *B* in moving supplier S1 from London to Paris). In other words, the two projections are not independent of one another in decomposition *B*.

The basic problem is that, in decomposition *B*, the FD

```
CITY  →  STATUS
```

has become an *interrelational constraint*. In decomposition *A*, by contrast, it is the *transitive* FD

```
S#  →  STATUS
```

that is the interrelational constraint, and that constraint will be enforced automatically if the two *intra*relational constraints

```
S#  →  CITY
```

and

```
CITY  →  STATUS
```

are enforced. (Note: We drop the relation-name prefixes from these three FDs for brevity and simplicity.)

The concept of independent projections thus provides a guideline for choosing a particular decomposition when there is more than one possibility. Specifically, a decomposition in which the projections are independent in the sense described is generally preferable to one in which they are not. Rissanen [17.5] shows that projections *R1* and *R2* of a relation *R* are independent in this sense if and only if

1. every FD in *R* can be logically deduced from those in *R1* and *R2*, *and*
2. the common attributes of *R1* and *R2* form a candidate key for at least one of the pair.

Rissanen's theorem makes checking for independence a very simple operation. Consider decompositions *A* and *B* as defined earlier. In *A* the two projections are independent, because their common attribute CITY is the primary key for CS, and every FD in SECOND either appears in one of the two projections or is a logical consequence of those that do. In *B*, by contrast, the two projections are not independent, because the FD

```
CITY  →  STATUS
```

cannot be deduced from the FDs in those projections (though it is true that their common attribute, S#, is the primary key for both).

As an aside, we note that the third possibility, replacing SECOND by its two projections

```
SS ( S#, STATUS )     and     CS ( CITY, STATUS )
```

is not a valid decomposition, because it is not nonloss. (Exercise: Prove this statement.)

A relation that cannot be decomposed into independent components is said to be *atomic* [17.5]. We do not mean to suggest that a nonatomic relation should necessarily be decomposed into atomic components; for example, relations S and P of the suppliers-and-parts database are not atomic, but there seems little point in decomposing them further. Relation SP, by contrast, *is* atomic.

Note finally that the fact that an atomic relation cannot be (nonloss-)decomposed into independent components does not mean that it cannot be (nonloss-)decomposed at all. Consider relation SJT of Section 17.4, with FDs

$$(S , J) \rightarrow T$$

and

$$T \rightarrow J$$

(again we ignore the relation-name prefixes). As we saw, this relation (which is in 3NF but not in BCNF) can be nonloss-decomposed into its two projections

ST (S, T)   and   TJ (T, J)

However, those two projections are not independent, by Rissanen's theorem; the FD

$$(S , J) \rightarrow T$$

cannot be deduced from the FD

$$T \rightarrow J$$

(which is the only FD represented in the two projections). As a result, the two projections cannot be independently updated. (Exercise: Prove this statement.) In fact, relation SJT is atomic, even though it is not in BCNF. We are forced to the unpleasant conclusion that the two objectives of decomposing a relation into BCNF components and decomposing it into independent components may occasionally be in conflict; that is, it is not always possible to satisfy both objectives simultaneously.

17.6 FOURTH NORMAL FORM

Suppose we are given an *unnormalized* relation CTX containing information about courses, teachers, and texts. Each record in the relation consists of a course name, plus a repeating group of teacher names, plus a repeating group of text names (see Fig. 17.16 for an example of two such records). The intended meaning of a given CTX record is that the specified course can be taught by any of the specified teachers and uses all of the specified texts as references. We assume that, for a given course, there may exist any number of corresponding teachers and any number of corresponding texts; moreover, we also assume—perhaps not very realistically—that teachers and texts are quite independent of one another (that is, no matter who actually teaches any particular offering of the given course, the same texts are used). Finally, we also assume that a given teacher or a given text can be associated with any number of courses.

```
CTX    COURSE      TEACHER                    TEXT

       Physics     ⎰ Prof.  Green ⎱          ⎰ Basic Mechanics         ⎱
                   ⎱ Prof.  Brown ⎰          ⎱ Principles of Optics ⎰

       Math        ⎰ Prof.  Green ⎱          ⎰ Basic Mechanics  ⎱
                                             ⎰ Vector Analysis  ⎰
                                             ⎱ Trigonometry     ⎰
```

Fig. 17.16 Sample tabulation of CTX (unnormalized).

Now let us convert this structure into an equivalent normalized form. Observe first that there are no FDs in the data at all (apart from trivial ones such as COURSE → COURSE). The theory we have developed in this chapter so far therefore provides us with no formal basis by which to decompose the structure into projections; the only operation available to us of a normalizing nature is the elementary one of "flattening" the structure (as in Chapter 11), which for the data of Fig. 17.16 yields the tabulation shown in Fig. 17.17.

```
CTX    COURSE      TEACHER          TEXT

       Physics     Prof.  Green     Basic Mechanics
       Physics     Prof.  Green     Principles of Optics
       Physics     Prof.  Brown     Basic Mechanics
       Physics     Prof.  Brown     Principles of Optics
       Math        Prof.  Green     Basic Mechanics
       Math        Prof.  Green     Vector Analysis
       Math        Prof.  Green     Trigonometry
```

Fig. 17.17 Sample tabulation of CTX (normalized).

The meaning of the normalized version of CTX is as follows: A tuple (c,t,x) appears in CTX if and only if course c can be taught by teacher t and uses text x as a reference. Note that, for a given course, all possible combinations of teacher and text appear; that is, CTX satisfies the constraint

if   tuples $(c,t1,x1)$, $(c,t2,x2)$ both appear,
then   tuples $(c,t1,x2)$, $(c,t2,x1)$ both appear also.

It is apparent that relation CTX involves a good deal of redundancy, leading as usual to certain update anomalies. For example, to add the information that the math course can be taught by a new teacher (Professor White), it is necessary to create *three* new tuples, one for each of the three texts.[7] Nevertheless, CTX is in

_____

7. The reader may object that it is not necessary to include all teacher/text combinations for a given course; for example, two tuples are sufficient to show that the physics course has two teachers and two texts. The problem is, *which* two tuples? Any particular choice leads to a relation having a very unobvious interpretation and very strange update behavior. To

BCNF, since it is "all key" and there are no other functional determinants apart from the combination of all three attributes (COURSE,TEACHER,TEXT).

The existence of such "problem" BCNF relations has been recognized for some time. So far as relation CTX is concerned, it is intuitively clear that the difficulties are caused by the fact that teachers and texts are independent of one another; it is also easy to see that matters would be improved if CTX were replaced by its two projections

```
CT ( COURSE, TEACHER )        and        CX ( COURSE, TEXT )
```

(see Fig. 17.18). These two projections are both "all key" and are both in BCNF. However, it was not until 1977 that these intuitive ideas were put on a sound theoretical footing by Fagin's introduction of the notion of *multivalued dependencies*.[8]

```
        -------  ------------              -------  --------------------
CT      COURSE   TEACHER            CX     COURSE   TEXT
        -------  ------------              -------  --------------------
        Physics  Prof. Green               Physics  Basic Mechanics
        Physics  Prof. Brown               Physics  Principles of Optics
        Math     Prof. Green               Math     Basic Mechanics
                                           Math     Vector Analysis
                                           Math     Trigonometry
```

Fig. 17.18 Sample tabulations of CT and CX.

The decomposition of Fig. 17.18 is indeed correct, and desirable. However, as we have already indicated, that decomposition cannot be made on the basis of functional dependencies, because there are no FDs in the relation (other than trivial ones). Instead, it is made on the basis of a new kind of dependency, the *multivalued* dependency (MVD) mentioned above. Multivalued dependencies are a generalization of functional dependencies, in the sense that every FD is an MVD (but the converse is not true; i.e., there exist MVDs that are not FDs). There are two MVDs in relation CTX:

```
CTX.COURSE  → →  CTX.TEACHER
CTX.COURSE  → →  CTX.TEXT
```

---

see that this is so, the reader should try the experiment of making such a choice and then stating the meaning of the relation that results—i.e., stating the criteria for deciding whether some arbitrary proposed update (INSERT or DELETE or UPDATE) is or is not an acceptable operation against that relation.

8.   We stress the point that we are discussing a formal theory here (albeit in a fairly informal manner). From a practical standpoint, all we need do is recognize that when we are trying to normalize some unnormalized relation, *the first thing to do is to separate independent repeating groups*—a rule that makes obvious intuitive sense. In the example, the original unnormalized version of CTX should be converted into two unnormalized relations, CT (containing courses and repeating groups of teachers) and CX (containing courses and repeating groups of texts). Those two unnormalized relations can then be reduced to BCNF in the usual way, and the "problem" normalized version of CTX will simply not arise. But the theory gives us a formal basis for what would otherwise be a mere rule of thumb.

(Note the double-headed arrows. The dependency $R.A \to \to R.B$ is read as "attribute $R.B$ is *multidependent* on attribute $R.A$," or, equivalently, "attribute $R.A$ multidetermines attribute $R.B$.") For the moment we concentrate on the first of the two MVDs above, which means intuitively that, although a course does not have a *single* corresponding teacher—i.e., the functional dependence COURSE → TEACHER does *not* hold—nevertheless, each course does have a well-defined *set* of corresponding teachers. By "well-defined" we mean, more precisely, that for a given course c and a given text x, the set of teachers t matching the pair (c,x) in CTX depends on the value c alone—it makes no difference what particular value x we choose, provided only that c and x appear together in some CTX tuple. The second MVD (of TEXT on COURSE) is interpreted analogously.

We now give a definition of MVD.

- Given a relation R with attributes A, B, and C, the *multivalued dependence* (MVD)

  $$R.A \to \to R.B$$

  holds in R if and only if the set of B-values matching a given (A-value,C-value) pair in R depends only on the A-value and is independent of the C-value. As usual, A, B, and C may be composite.

Note that MVDs as we define them can exist only if the relation R has at least three attributes.[9]

It is easy to show (see [17.6]) that, given the relation $R(A,B,C)$, the MVD $R.A \to \to R.B$ holds if and only if the MVD $R.A \to \to R.C$ also holds. MVDs always go together in pairs in this way. For this reason it is common to represent both in a single joint statement, using the notation

$$R.A \to \to R.B \mid R.C$$

For example:

$$COURSE \to \to TEACHER \mid TEXT$$

(dropping the relation name prefixes).

An FD is an MVD in which the "set" of dependent values matching a given determinant value is actually always a single value; thus every FD is an MVD, but the converse is not true. To return now to our original normalization problem, we can see that the trouble with relations such as CTX is that they involve MVDs that are not also FDs. The two projections CT and CX do not involve any such MVDs, which is why they represent an improvement over the original relation. We would

---

9. The original definition (see reference [17.6]) does not require the relation to have at least three attributes. In our explanation we choose to ignore certain special cases, for reasons of simplicity—for example, the "trivial" MVD $R.X \to \to R.Y$ which always holds in the binary relation $R(X,Y)$, and certain nontrivial MVDs in which the left-hand side is the empty set. See reference [17.6] for details, also Exercise 17.5.

therefore like to replace CTX by those two projections, and a theorem proved by Fagin in reference [17.6] allows us to make exactly that replacement:

- Relation R, with attributes A, B, and C, can be nonloss-decomposed into its two projections $R1(A,B)$ and $R2(A,C)$ if and only if the MVDs $A \rightarrow \rightarrow B \mid C$ hold in R. (Note: This is a stronger version of Heath's theorem. See Section 17.3.)

Following reference [17.6], we can now define fourth normal form.

- A relation R is in *fourth normal form* (4NF) if and only if, whenever there exists an MVD in R, say $A \rightarrow \rightarrow B$, then all attributes of R are also *functionally* dependent on A. In other words, the only dependencies (FDs or MVDs) in R are of the form $K \rightarrow X$ (i.e., a functional dependency from a candidate key K to some other attribute X). Equivalently: R is in 4NF if it is in BCNF and all MVDs in R are in fact FDs.

Relation CTX is not in 4NF, since it involves an MVD that is not an FD at all, let alone an FD in which the determinant is a candidate key. The two projections CT and CX are both in 4NF, however. Thus 4NF is an improvement over BCNF, in that it eliminates another form of undesirable structure. Note: Fagin shows in reference [17.6] that 4NF is always achievable—that is, any relation can be nonloss-decomposed into an equivalent collection of 4NF relations—though the results of Section 17.5 show that it may not be desirable in some cases to carry the decomposition that far (or even as far as BCNF).

We conclude this section by remarking that Rissanen's work on independent projections [17.5], though couched in terms of FDs, is applicable to MVDs also. Remember that a relation $R(A,B,C)$ satisfying the FDs $A \rightarrow B$, $B \rightarrow C$ is better decomposed into its projections on (A,B) and (B,C) rather than into those on (A,B) and (A,C). The same holds true if the FDs are replaced by the MVDs $A \rightarrow \rightarrow B$, $B \rightarrow \rightarrow C$.

17.7   FIFTH NORMAL FORM

So far in this chapter we have tacitly assumed that the sole operation necessary or available in the decomposition process is the replacement of a relation (in a nonloss way) by two of its projections. This assumption has successfully carried us as far as 4NF. It comes perhaps as a surprise to discover that there exist relations that cannot be nonloss-decomposed into two projections but *can* be so decomposed into three or more. To coin an ugly but convenient term, we will describe such a relation as "*n*-decomposable" (for some $n > 2$)—meaning that the relation in question can be nonloss-decomposed into n projections but not into m projections for any $m < n$. A relation that can be nonloss-decomposed into two projections we will call "2-decomposable."

The phenomenon of *n*-decomposability (for $n > 2$) was first noted by Aho, Beeri, and Ullman [17.7]. The particular case $n = 3$ was also studied by Nicolas

[17.8]. Consider relation SPJ of Fig. 17.19. That relation is "all key" and involves no nontrivial FDs or MVDs, and is therefore in 4NF. The figure also shows a) the three binary projections SP, PJ, and JS of SPJ, and b) the effect of joining SP and PJ over P# and then joining that result and JS over (J#,S#). Note that the result of the first join is to produce a copy of the original SPJ relation plus one additional (spurious) tuple, and the effect of the second join is then to eliminate that tuple. (The net result is the same whatever pair of projections we choose for the first join, though the intermediate result is different in each case.)

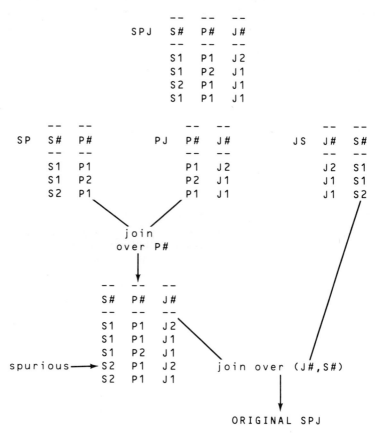

Fig. 17.19 SPJ is the join of all three of its (binary) projections but not of any two.

The example of Fig. 17.19 is of course expressed in terms of a set of specific data values that happen to exist at some specific time. However, the 3-decomposability of relation SPJ could be a more fundamental, time-independent property—i.e., a property satisfied by all legal values of the relation—*if* that relation satisfies a certain time-independent constraint. To understand what that constraint must be, observe first that the statement

SPJ is equal to the join of its three projections SP, PJ, and JS[10]

is precisely equivalent to the following statement:

if the pair $(s1,p1)$ appears in SP
and the pair $(p1,j1)$ appears in PJ
and the pair $(j1,s1)$ appears in JS
then the triple $(s1,p1,j1)$ appears in SPJ

(because the triple $(s1,p1,j1)$ obviously appears in the join of SP, PJ, and JS).[11]Since $(s1,p1)$ appears in SP if and only if $(s1,p1,j2)$ appears in SPJ (for some $j2$), and similarly for $(p1,j1)$ and $(j1,s1)$, we can rewrite this latter statement as a constraint on SPJ:

if $(s1,p1,j2)$, $(s2,p1,j1)$, $(s1,p2,j1)$ appear in SPJ
then $(s1,p1,j1)$ also appears in SPJ.

And if this final statement is true for all time—i.e., for all possible legal values of the relation—then we do have a time-independent constraint on SPJ (albeit rather a bizarre one). Notice the *cyclic nature* of that constraint. *A relation will be n-decomposable (for some n > 2) if and only if it satisfies some such cyclic constraint* [17.28].

Suppose, then, that relation SPJ does in fact satisfy that time-independent constraint. For brevity, let us agree to refer to that constraint as "constraint 3D" (for 3-decomposable). What does constraint 3D mean in real-world terms? Let us try to make it a little more concrete by giving an example. The constraint says that, in the portion of the real world that relation SPJ is supposed to represent, it is a fact that, *if* (for example)

a) Smith supplies monkey wrenches, and
b) monkey wrenches are used in the Manhattan project, and
c) Smith supplies the Manhattan project,

then

d) Smith supplies monkey wrenches to the Manhattan project.

Note that, as pointed out in Chapter 1 (Section 1.3), a), b), and c) together normally do *not* imply d); indeed, exactly this example was held up in that chapter as an illustration of "the connection trap." In the particular case at hand, however, we are saying that *there is no such trap*—because there is an additional real-world

---

10.   Aho, Beeri, and Ullman [17.7] give a generalized definition of join that allows us to speak unambiguously of the join of any number of relations. The generalized join of an ordered list of relations is formed by repeatedly replacing the first and second relations in the list by their natural join over like-named attributes, until the entire list has been reduced to a single relation.

11.   The converse of this statement, that if $(s1,p1,j1)$ appears in SPJ then $(s1,p1)$ appears in its projection SP (etc.) is obviously true for any degree-3 relation SPJ.

constraint in effect, namely constraint 3D, that makes the inference valid in this special case.

To return to the main topic of discussion: Because constraint 3D is satisfied if and only if the relation concerned is equal to the join of certain of its projections, we refer to that constraint as a *join dependency* (JD). A JD is a constraint on the relation concerned, just as an MVD or an FD is a constraint on the relation concerned. Join dependencies are defined as follows:

- Relation R satisfies the *join dependency* (JD)

  $$\star \ (\ X, \ Y, \ \ldots, \ Z \ )$$

  if and only if R is equal to the join of its projections on $X, Y, \ldots, Z$, where $X, Y, \ldots, Z$ are subsets of the set of attributes of R.

In the example, relation SPJ satisfies the JD *(SP,PJ,JS).

We have seen, then, that relation SPJ, with its JD *(SP,PJ,JS), can be 3-decomposed. The question is, *should* it be? The answer is probably yes. Relation SPJ suffers from a number of problems over update operations, problems that are removed when it is 3-decomposed. Some examples are shown in Fig. 17.20. Consideration of what happens after 3-decomposition is left as an exercise for the reader.

```
          --    --    --                        --    --    --
SPJ    S #   P #   J #            SPJ        S #   P #   J #
       --    --    --                        --    --    --
       S 1   P 1   J 2                        S 1   P 1   J 2
       S 1   P 2   J 1                        S 1   P 2   J 1
                                              S 2   P 1   J 1
                                              S 1   P 1   J 1
```

- If (S2,P1,J1) is inserted, (S1,P1,J1) must also be inserted
- Yet converse is not true

- Can delete (S2,P1,J1) without side effects
- If (S1,P1,J1) deleted, another tuple must also be deleted (which?)

Fig. 17.20 Examples of update problems in SPJ.

Fagin's theorem (Section 17.6), to the effect that $R(A,B,C)$ can be nonloss-decomposed into $R1(A,B)$ and $R2(A,C)$ if and only if the pair of MVDs $A \rightarrow \rightarrow B \mid C$ hold in R, can be restated as follows:

- $R(A,B,C)$ satisfies the JD *(AB,AC) if and only if it satisfies the pair of MVDs $A \rightarrow \rightarrow B \mid C$.

Since this theorem can be taken as a *definition* of MVD, it follows that an MVD is just a special case of a JD, or that JDs are a generalization of MVDs (rather as MVDs are a generalization of FDs). What is more, it is immediate from the JD definition that JDs are *the most general form of dependency possible* (using, of course, the term "dependency" in a very specialized sense). That is, there does not exist a still higher form of dependency such that JDs are merely a special case of that higher form—so long as we restrict our attention to dependencies that deal with a relation being decomposed via projection and reconstructed via join. (However, if we allow other operators in the decomposition/reconstruction process, then other types of dependency may come into play. We discuss this possibility very briefly at the end of the chapter.)

Returning now to our example, we can see that the problem with relation SPJ is that it involves a JD that is not an MVD (and hence not an FD either). We have also seen that it is possible, and probably desirable, to decompose such a relation into smaller components—namely, into the projections specified by the join dependency. The decomposition process can be repeated until all resulting relations are in *fifth normal form*.

- A relation R is in *fifth normal form* (5NF)—also called *projection-join normal form* (PJ/NF)—if and only if every join dependency in R is a consequence of the candidate keys of R. (We amplify the notion of a JD being "a consequence of the candidate keys" of a relation below.)

Relation SPJ is not in 5NF; it satisfies a certain join dependency, namely constraint 3D, that is certainly not a consequence of its sole candidate key (that key being the combination of all of its attributes). To state this differently, the fact that the combination (S#,P#,J#) is a candidate key certainly does not imply that the relation can be 3-decomposed. However, after 3-decomposition, the three projections SP, PJ, and JS are in 5NF, since they do not involve any (nontrivial) JDs at all.

Although it may not yet be obvious to the reader (because we have not yet explained what it means for a JD to be implied by candidate keys), it is a fact that any relation in 5NF is automatically in 4NF also, because an MVD is a special case of a JD. (Fagin shows in reference [17.9] that any MVD that is implied by a candidate key must in fact be an FD in which that candidate key is the determinant.) Fagin also shows in [17.9] that any given relation can be nonloss-decomposed into an equivalent collection of 5NF relations; that is, 5NF is always achievable.

We now explain what it means for a JD to be implied by (or to be a consequence of) candidate keys. First we consider a simple example. Suppose once again that the familiar supplier relation S has two candidate keys, S# and SNAME. Then that relation satisfies several join dependencies—for example, it satisfies the JD

    * ((S#, SNAME, STATUS), (S#, CITY))

That is, relation S is equal to the join of its projections on (S#,SNAME, STATUS) and (S#,CITY). This JD is implied by the fact that S# is a candidate key (by Heath's theorem). Likewise, relation S also satisfies the JD

    * ((S#, SNAME), (S# STATUS), (SNAME, CITY))

This JD is implied by the fact that S# and SNAME are *both* candidate keys. For the general case, Fagin [17.9] gives an algorithm by which it is possible, given a JD and a set of candidate keys, to test whether that JD is implied by those candidate keys (it is not always immediately obvious—witness the second example above). Thus, given a relation R, we can tell if R is in 5NF, provided we know the candidate keys *and all JDs* in R. However, discovering all the JDs may itself be a nontrivial operation. That is, whereas it is relatively easy to identify FDs and MVDs (because they have a fairly straightforward real-world interpretation), the same cannot be said for JDs (JDs, that is, that are not MVDs and not FDs), because the intuitive meaning of JDs may not be obvious. Hence the process of determining when a given relation is in 4NF but not 5NF (and so could probably be decomposed to advantage) is still unclear. It is tempting to suggest that such relations are pathological cases and likely to be rare in practice.

In conclusion, we note that it follows from the definition that 5NF is the *ultimate* normal form with respect to projection and join (which accounts for its alternative name, projection-join normal form). That is, a relation in 5NF is guaranteed to be free of update anomalies that can be eliminated merely by taking projections.[12] For, if a relation is in 5NF, the only join dependencies are those that are consequences of the candidate keys, and so the only valid decompositions are ones that are based on those candidate keys. (Each projection in such a decomposition will consist of one or more of those candidate keys, plus zero or more additional attributes.) For example, the supplier relation S is in 5NF. It *can* be further decomposed in several nonloss ways, as we saw above, but every projection in any such decomposition will still include a candidate key, and there therefore does not seem to be any particular advantage in that further reduction.

17.8 CONCLUDING REMARKS

This chapter has been concerned with the technique of *nonloss decomposition* as an aid to database design. The basic idea is as follows: Given some first normal form relation R[13] and some list of constraints (FDs, MVDs, and JDs) that apply to R, we systematically reduce R to a collection of smaller relations that are equivalent to R in a certain well-defined sense but are also in some way more desirable than R. Each step of the reduction process consists of taking projections of the relations resulting from the preceding step. The given constraints are used at each step to guide the choice of which projections to take next. The overall process can be stated informally as a set of rules, as follows.

1. Take projections of the original 1NF relation to eliminate any nonfull functional dependencies. This step will produce a collection of 2NF relations.

2. Take projections of those 2NF relations to eliminate any transitive functional dependencies. This step will produce a collection of 3NF relations.

---

12. Of course, it is not guaranteed to be free of *all possible* update anomalies.

13. The original 1NF relation may of course have been obtained by first "flattening" an unnormalized structure.

3. Take projections of those 3NF relations to eliminate any remaining functional dependencies in which the determinant is not a candidate key. This step will produce a collection of BCNF relations. Note: Rules 1–3 can be condensed into the single guideline "Take projections of the original relation to eliminate all FDs in which the determinant is not a candidate key."

4. Take projections of those BCNF relations to eliminate any multivalued dependencies that are not also functional dependencies. This step will produce a collection of 4NF relations. Note: In practice it is usual to eliminate such MVDs *before* applying Rules 1–3 above.

5. Take projections of those 4NF relations to eliminate any join dependencies that are not implied by the candidate keys—though perhaps we should add "if you can find them." This step will produce a collection of relations in 5NF.

The general objective of the reduction process is to reduce redundancy, and thereby to avoid certain "update anomalies." But it should be stressed once again that the normalization guidelines *are* only guidelines; sometimes there are good reasons for not normalizing "all the way." The classic example of a case where complete normalization may not be a good idea is provided by the name-and-address relation

```
NADDR ( NAME, STREET, CITY, STATE, ZIP )
```

in which we assume that, in addition to the FDs implied by NAME (which is the primary key), the following FD also holds:

```
ZIP → ( CITY, STATE )
```

This relation is not in 5NF (what form *is* it in?), and the normalization guidelines sketched above would suggest that we decompose it into the two projections

```
NSZ ( NAME, STREET, ZIP )
ZCS ( ZIP, CITY, STATE )
```

(primary keys NAME and ZIP, respectively). However, since STREET, CITY, and STATE are almost invariably required together (think of printing a mailing list), and since zipcodes do not change very often, it seems unlikely that such a decomposition would be worthwhile.[14]

We also repeat the point from the very beginning of this chapter that the topic of normalization is different in *kind* from that of the preceding chapters. The notions of dependency and normalization are *semantic* in nature (in fact, dependencies represent a special case of semantic integrity constraints—see Chapter 19). In other words, those notions are concerned with what the data *means*. By contrast, the relational algebra and relational calculus, and languages such as SQL that are based on those formalisms, are concerned only with data *values*; any interpretation of

---

14.   As a matter of fact, the dependency structure of relation NADDR is even worse than indicated above, since it also involves the FD (STREET,CITY,STATE) → ZIP.

those values is imposed from the outside (by the human user). Specifically, those formalisms and languages have no requirement that the relations they operate on be in any particular normal form other than first. The normalization guidelines should be regarded primarily as a *discipline* to help the database designer—a discipline by which the designer can capture a part, albeit a small part, of the semantics of the real world in a simple and straightforward manner.

We conclude this chapter by referring back to the remark in Section 17.1 to the effect that there do exist other normal forms, over and above those discussed in Sections 17.1–17.7. The fact is, the theory of normalization and related topics (now usually known as *dependency theory*) has grown into a very considerable field in its own right, with several distinct (though of course interrelated) aspects and with a very extensive literature. Research in the area is continuing and indeed flourishing. It is beyond the scope of this chapter to discuss such research in any depth; a good survey of the field can be found in reference [17.24]. We therefore mention only one specific aspect here (one chosen because its applicability to practical problems is perhaps more immediately apparent than that of some of the others).

Consider the supplier relation S once again. The normalization theory discussed in this chapter tells us that relation S is in a "good" normal form; indeed, it is in fifth normal form, and is therefore guaranteed to be free of anomalies that can be eliminated by taking projections. But why keep all suppliers in a single relation? What about a design in which London suppliers are kept in one relation (LS, say), Paris suppliers in another (PS, say), and so on? Would that be a good design or a bad one? Note that normalization theory (to the extent that we have discussed it so far) has absolutely nothing to say in answer to these questions.

One direction for normalization research therefore consists of examining the implications of reducing relations by some operation other than projection. In the example, the decomposition operator is (a limited form of) *restriction*. The corresponding recomposition operator is *union*. Thus, it might be possible to construct a "restriction-union" normalization theory, analogous *but orthogonal* to the projection-join normalization theory discussed in this chapter. To this writer's knowledge no such theory has ever been worked out in full detail, but some initial ideas can be found in a paper by Smith [17.21], where a new normal form called "(3,3)NF" is defined. (3,3)NF implies BCNF; however, a (3,3)NF relation need not be in 4NF, nor need a 4NF relation be in (3,3)NF, so that (as suggested above) reduction to (3,3)NF is orthogonal to reduction to 4NF (and 5NF). Further ideas on this topic appear in references [17.9] and [17.22–17.23].

EXERCISES

17.1 Figure 17.21 is a hierarchic (unnormalized) representation of a collection of information to be recorded in a company personnel database. The figure is read as follows.

- The company has a set of departments.
- Each department has a set of employees, a set of projects, and a set of offices.

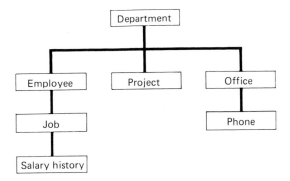

Fig. **17.21** A company database (unnormalized structure).

■ Each employee has a job history (set of jobs the employee has held). For each such job, the employee also has a salary history (set of salaries received while employed on that job).
■ Each office has a set of phones.

The database is to contain the following information.

■ For each department: department number (unique), budget, and the department manager's employee number (unique).
■ For each employee: employee number (unique), current project number, office number, and phone number; also, title of each job the employee has held, plus date and salary for each distinct salary received in that job.
■ For each project: project number (unique) and budget.
■ For each office: office number (unique), area in square feet, and numbers (unique) of all phones in that office.

Design an appropriate set of normalized relations to represent this information. State any assumptions you make concerning the dependencies involved.

17.2 A database used in an order-entry system is to contain information about customers, items, and orders. The following information is to be included.

■ For each customer:
Customer number (unique)
"Ship-to" addresses (several per customer)
Balance
Credit limit
Discount

■ For each order:
Heading information: customer number, ship-to address, date of order
Detail lines (several per order): item number, quantity ordered

■ For each item:
Item number (unique)
Manufacturing plants
Quantity on hand at each plant
Stock danger level for each plant
Item description

For internal processing reasons a "quantity outstanding" value is associated with each detail line of each order. This value is initially set equal to the quantity of the item ordered and is (progressively) reduced to zero as (partial) shipments are made.

Design a database for this data. As in the previous question, state any assumptions you make concerning semantic dependencies.

17.3 Suppose that in Exercise 17.2 only a very small number of customers, say one percent or less, actually have more than one ship-to address. (This is typical of real-life situations, in which it is frequently the case that just a few exceptions—usually rather important ones— fail to conform to some general pattern.) Can you see any drawbacks to your solution to Exercise 17.2? Can you think of any improvements?

17.4 A relation TIMETABLE is defined with the following attributes.

D   Day of the week (1–5)
P   Period within day (1–8)
C   Classroom number
T   Teacher name
S   Student name
L   Lesson identifier

The tuple (d,p,c,t,s,l) is an element of this relation if at time (d,p) student s is taught lesson l by teacher t in classroom c. You may assume that lessons are one period in duration and that every lesson has an identifier that is unique with respect to all lessons taught in the week. Reduce TIMETABLE to a more desirable structure.

17.5 Which of the following statements are true? For those that are false, produce a counterexample.

a) Any binary relation is in 3NF.

b) Any binary relation is in BCNF.

c) Any binary relation is in 4NF.

d) Any binary relation is in PJ/NF.

e) Relation $R(A,B,C)$ is equal to the join of its projections $R1(A,B)$ and $R2(A,C)$ if and only if the FD $A \rightarrow B$ holds in R.

f) If $R.A \rightarrow R.B$ and $R.B \rightarrow R.C$, then $R.A \rightarrow R.C$.

g) If $R.A \rightarrow R.B$ and $R.A \rightarrow R.C$, then $R.A \rightarrow R.(B,C)$.

h) If $R.B \rightarrow R.A$ and $R.C \rightarrow R.A$, then $R.(B,C) \rightarrow R.A$.

17.6 A database is to contain information concerning sales representatives, sales areas, and products. Each representative is responsible for sales in one or more areas; each area has one or more responsible representatives. Similarly, each representative is responsible for sales of one or more products, and each product has one or more responsible representatives. Every product is sold in every area; however, no two representatives sell the same product in the same area. Every representative sells the same set of products in every area for which that representative is responsible. Design a suitable relational structure for this data.

REFERENCES AND BIBLIOGRAPHY

As indicated in Section 17.8, the field of dependency theory (as the study of normal forms and related matters has come to be known) has expanded very greatly over the past few years.

The references below represent a short selected list, culled from an enormous range of published papers.

17.1 E. F. Codd. "Further Normalization of the Data Base Relational Model." In *Data Base Systems*, Courant Computer Science Symposia Series, Vol. 6. Englewood Cliffs, N.J.: Prentice-Hall (1972).

17.2 E. F. Codd. "Normalized Data Base Structure: A Brief Tutorial." *Proc. 1971 ACM SIGFIDET Workshop on Data Description, Access and Control* (November 1971).

17.3 I. J. Heath. "Unacceptable File Operations in a Relational Database." *Proc. 1971 ACM SIGFIDET Workshop on Data Description, Access and Control* (November 1971).

17.4 E. F. Codd. "Recent Investigations into Relational Data Base Systems." *Proc. IFIP Congress 1974* and elsewhere.

This paper reports on a somewhat miscellaneous collection of topics. In particular it gives "an improved definition of third normal form," which is in fact a definition of what is now known as Boyce/Codd normal form. Other topics discussed include views and view updating, data sublanguages, data exchange, and needed investigations.

17.5 J. Rissanen. "Independent Components of Relations." *ACM TODS* **2,** No. 4 (December 1977).

17.6 R. Fagin. "Multivalued Dependencies and a New Normal Form for Relational Databases." *ACM TODS* **2,** No. 3 (September 1977).

The new normal form was 4NF. We add a note here on *embedded* multivalued dependencies (EMVDs). Suppose we extend relation CTX of Section 17.6 to include an additional attribute DAYS, representing the number of days spent with the indicated TEXT by the indicated TEACHER on the indicated COURSE. Sample tabulation:

COURSE	TEACHER	TEXT	DAYS
Physics	Prof. Green	Basic Mechanics	5
Physics	Prof. Green	Principles of Optics	5
Physics	Prof. Brown	Basic Mechanics	6
Physics	Prof. Brown	Principles of Optics	4
Math	Prof. Green	Basic Mechanics	3
Math	Prof. Green	Vector Analysis	3
Math	Prof. Green	Trigonometry	4

The primary key here is the composite attribute (COURSE,TEACHER,TEXT), and we have the FD:

```
(COURSE,TEACHER,TEXT)  →  DAYS
```

Note that the relation *is* now in fourth normal form; it does not involve any MVDs that are not also FDs (refer back to the definitions of 4NF and MVD). However, it does include two *embedded* MVDs (of TEACHER on COURSE and TEXT on COURSE). An embedded MVD (of B on A, say) is said to hold in relation R if the "ordinary" MVD $A \rightarrow \rightarrow B$ holds in some projection of R. An ordinary MVD is a special case of an embedded MVD, but not all EMVDs are ordinary MVDs.

As the example illustrates, embedded MVDs cause redundancy, just like ordinary MVDs; however, that redundancy cannot be eliminated just by taking projections. The relation shown above cannot be nonloss-decomposed into projections at all (in fact, it is in fifth normal form as well as fourth). Instead, the two EMVDs would have to be stated as additional, explicit constraints on the relation. (Exercise: What would such constraints look like?)

17.7 A. V. Aho, C. Beeri, and J. D. Ullman. "The Theory of Joins in Relational Databases." *ACM TODS* **4**, No. 3 (September 1979). First published in *Proc. 19th IEEE Symp. on Foundations of Computer Science* (October 1977).

The paper that first pointed out that relations could exist that were not equal to the join of any two of their projections, but were equal to the join of three or more. The major objective of the paper was to present an algorithm, now generally called the *chase*, for determining whether or not a given collection of relations can be nonloss-joined, given a set of functional dependencies that apply to those relations. In other words, given a JD and a set of FDs, the algorithm determines whether the given JD is a logical consequence of the given FDs—an example of the *implication problem* (see reference [17.24]). The paper also discusses the question of extending the algorithm to deal with the case where the given dependencies are not FDs but MVDs.

17.8 J. M. Nicolas. "Mutual Dependencies and Some Results on Undecomposable Relations." *Proc. 4th International Conference on Very Large Data Bases* (1978).

Introduces the concept of "mutual dependency." A mutual dependency is actually a special case of the general join dependency—i.e., a JD that is not an MVD or FD—that happens to involve exactly three projections (like the JD example given in Section 17.7). It has nothing to do with the concept of mutual dependence discussed in Section 17.3.

17.9 R. Fagin. "Normal Forms and Relational Database Operators." *Proc. 1979 ACM SIGMOD International Conference on Management of Data.*

This is the paper that introduced the concept of projection/join normal form (PJ/NF, or 5NF). However, it is also much more than that. It can be regarded as the definitive statement of what might be termed "classical" normalization theory—i.e., the theory of nonloss decomposition based on projection as the reduction operator and (natural) join as the corresponding reconstruction operator. Among other things, the paper provides insight into the nature of BCNF, 4NF, and 5NF by giving definitions of those three normal forms that deliberately stress the parallels among them, as follows (paraphrasing slightly):

1. A relation R is in BCNF if and only if every FD in R is a consequence of the candidate keys of R.

2. A relation R is in 4NF if and only if every MVD in R is a consequence of the candidate keys of R.

3. A relation R is in 5NF if and only if every JD in R is a consequence of the candidate keys of R.

The update anomalies discussed in the present chapter are precisely anomalies that are caused by FDs (or MVDs or JDs) that are not consequences of candidate keys.

17.10 W. Kent. "A Simple Guide to Five Normal Forms in Relational Database Theory." *CACM* **26**, No. 2 (February 1983).

Includes the following intuitively attractive characterization of "3NF" (more accurately BCNF): *Each field must represent a fact about the key, the whole key, and nothing but the key* (slightly paraphrased).

17.11 P. A. Bernstein. "Synthesizing Third Normal Form Relations from Functional Dependencies." *ACM TODS* **1**, No. 4 (December 1976).

In this chapter we have discussed techniques for decomposing large relations into smaller ones. In this paper, Bernstein considers the converse problem of using small relations to construct larger ones. The problem is not actually characterized in this way in the paper; rather, it is described as the problem of synthesizing relations given a set of attributes and a set of corresponding FDs (with the constraint that the synthesized relations must be in 3NF). However, since attributes and FDs have no meaning outside the context of some containing relation, it would be more accurate to regard the primitive construct as a binary relation involving an FD, rather than as a pair of attributes plus an FD.

Aside: It would equally well be possible to regard the given set of attributes and FDs as a *universal relation*—see references [17.25–17.32]—that satisfies a given set of dependencies, in which case the "synthesis" process can alternatively be perceived as a process of *decomposing* that universal relation into 3NF projections. But we stay with the original "synthesis" interpretation for the purposes of the present discussion.

The synthesis process, then, is one of constructing *n*-ary relations from binary relations, given a set of FDs that apply to those binary relations, and given the objective that all constructed relations be in third normal form. (The higher normal forms had not been defined when this work was done.) Algorithms are presented for performing this task.

One objection to the approach (recognized by Bernstein) is that the manipulations performed by the synthesis algorithm are necessarily purely syntactic in nature and take no account of semantics. For instance, given the FDs

```
R.A  →  R.B
S.B  →  S.C
T.A  →  T.C
```

the third may or may not be redundant (i.e., implied by the first and second), depending on the meaning of R, S, and T. As an example of where it is not, take A as employee number, B as office number, C as department number; take R as "office of employee," S as "department owning office," T as "department of employee"; and consider the case of an employee working in an office belonging to a department not the employee's own. The synthesis algorithm simply assumes that (e.g.) S.C and T.C are one and the same (in fact, it does not recognize relation names at all); it thus relies on the existence of some external mechanism—namely, human intervention—for avoiding semantically invalid manipulations. In the case at hand, it would be the responsibility of the person defining the original FDs to use distinct attribute names (C1 and C2, say) in place of S.C and T.C.

17.12 W. W. Armstrong. "Dependency Structures of Data Base Relationships." *Proc. IFIP Congress 1974.*

The paper that first formalized the theory of FDs. The theory provides a set of axioms—now usually called *Armstrong's axioms*—that precisely characterize all possible FD structures within a relation. The axioms can be stated in a variety of equivalent ways, one of the simplest of which is as follows (A, B, and C are attributes, possibly composite, of some relation R, and all FDs are to be understood as applying within the context of R):

1. If B is a subset of A, then $A \rightarrow B$.

2. $A \to (B,C)$ if and only if $A \to B$ and $A \to C$.

3. If $A \to B$ and $B \to C$, then $A \to C$.

These axioms are *complete*, in the sense that, given a set S of FDs, all FDs implied by S can be derived from S using the axioms. They are also *sound*, in the sense that no additional FDs (i.e., FDs not implied by S) can be so derived. (Aside: Be aware that the term "complete" is used by some authors to mean both complete *and* sound in the foregoing sense.)

The paper also gives a precise characterization of candidate keys.

17.13 C. Beeri, R. Fagin, and J. H. Howard. "A Complete Axiomatization for Functional and Multivalued Dependencies." *Proc. 1977 ACM SIGMOD International Conference on Management of Data.*

Extends the work of Armstrong [17.12] to include MVDs as well as FDs.

17.14 E. Sciore. "A Complete Axiomatization of Full Join Dependencies." *JACM* **29**, No. 2 (April 1982).

17.15 R. G. Casey and C. Delobel. "Decomposition of a Data Base and the Theory of Boolean Switching Functions." *IBM J. R&D* **17**, No. 5 (September 1973).

Shows that for any given normalized relation the set of FDs (called functional relations in this paper) can be represented by a "Boolean switching function," and moreover that that function is unique in the following sense: The original FDs can be specified in many superficially different (but actually equivalent) ways, each one in general giving rise to a superficially different Boolean function—but all such functions can be reduced by the laws of Boolean algebra to the same canonical form. The problem of decomposing the original relation is then shown to be logically equivalent to the well-understood Boolean algebra problem of finding "a covering set of prime implicants" for the Boolean function corresponding to that relation together with its FDs. Hence the original problem can be transformed into an equivalent problem in Boolean algebra, and well-known techniques can be brought to bear on it.

This paper was the first of several to draw parallels between normalization theory and a variety of other disciplines. See, for example, references [17.18] and [17.19].

17.16 C. Delobel and D. S. Parker. "Functional and Multivalued Dependencies in a Relational Database and the Theory of Boolean Switching Functions." *Tech. Report No. 142,* Dept. Maths. Appl. et Informatique, Univ. de Grenoble, France (November 1978).

Extends the results of [17.15] to include MVDs as well as FDs.

17.17 D. S. Parker and C. Delobel. "Algorithmic Applications for a New Result on Multivalued Dependencies." *Proc. 5th International Conference on Very Large Data Bases* (October 1979).

Applies the results of [17.16] to various problems, such as the problem of testing for a nonloss decomposition.

17.18 R. Fagin. "Functional Dependencies in a Relational Database and Propositional Logic." *IBM J. R&D* **21**, No. 6 (November 1977).

Shows that Armstrong's axioms [17.12] are strictly equivalent to the system of implicational statements in propositional logic. In other words, the paper defines a mapping between FDs and propositional statements, and then shows that a given FD f is a consequence of a given set S of FDs if and only if the proposition corresponding to f is a logical consequence of the set of propositions corresponding to S.

17.19 Y. Sagiv and R. Fagin. "An Equivalence Between Relational Database Dependencies and a Subclass of Propositional Logic." *IBM Research Report RJ2500* (March 1979).

Extends the results of [17.18] to include MVDs as well as FDs.

17.20 Y. Sagiv, C. Delobel, D. S. Parker, and R. Fagin. "An Equivalence Between Relational Database Dependencies and a Subclass of Propositional Logic." *JACM* **28**, No. 3 (June 1981).

Combines references [17.18] and [17.19].

17.21 J. M. Smith. "A Normal Form for Abstract Syntax." *Proc. 4th International Conference on Very Large Data Bases* (1978).

The paper that introduced (3,3)NF.

17.22 David Maier and Jeffrey D. Ullman. "Fragments of Relations." *Proc. 1983 ACM SIGMOD International Conference on Management of Data* (May 1983).

Classical normalization theory is concerned with "vertical" decomposition of relations —i.e., decomposition by projection. By contrast, this paper proposes a theory of "horizontal" decomposition—i.e., decomposition by restriction. The ideas are similar to but more general than those of reference [17.21].

17.23 R. Fagin. "A Normal Form for Relational Databases That Is Based on Domains and Keys." *ACM TODS* **6**, No. 3 (September 1981).

Proposes a normal form called "domain-key normal form" (DK/NF), in which the notions of FD, MVD, and JD are not mentioned at all. A relation R is in DK/NF if and only if every constraint on R is a logical consequence of the *domain constraints* and *key constraints* that apply to R. A domain constraint is simply a constraint to the effect that values of a certain attribute lie within some prescribed set of values; a key constraint is a constraint to the effect that a certain attribute (possibly composite) is a candidate key. Enforcing constraints on a DK/NF relation is thus conceptually simple, since it is sufficient to enforce just the domain and key constraints and the others will then be enforced automatically. The paper shows that any DK/NF relation is necessarily in 5NF (and therefore in 4NF, etc.), and indeed also in (3,3)NF (see reference [17.21]). However, DK/NF is not always achievable, nor has the question "Exactly when *can* it be achieved?" been answered.

17.24 R. Fagin and M. Y. Vardi. "The Theory of Data Dependencies—A Survey." *IBM Research Report RJ4321* (June 1984).

Provides a brief history of the subject of dependency theory and then summarizes the major achievements in three specific areas within the overall field (and in so doing provides a good selected list of relevant references). The three areas are 1) the implication problem, 2) the universal relation model, and 3) acyclic schemas. The *implication problem* is the problem of determining, given a set of dependencies D and some specific dependency d, whether d is a logical consequence of D. The *universal relation model* and *acyclic schemas* (also known as acyclic *schemes*) are discussed below in the annotation to references [17.25–17.32] and reference [17.34], respectively.

17.25 C. S. Carlson and R. S. Kaplan. "A Generalized Access Path Model and Its Application to a Relational Data Base System." *Proc. 1976 ACM SIGMOD International Conference on Management of Data* (June 1976).

This appears to have been the first paper to discuss the "universal relation" model (not however under that name; in any case, the term "universal relation" has differing interpretations, and indeed has been the source of much confusion). Numerous subsequent papers have discussed the idea [17.26–17.32]. The basic concept is quite straightforward, however, and from a practical standpoint quite appealing: Users frame their database requests, not in terms of relations and joins among those relations, but rather in terms of attributes alone. For example:

```
SELECT STATUS
WHERE   COLOR = 'Red' ;
```

("Get status for suppliers who supply at least one red part"). At this point the idea of the "universal relation model" forks into two distinct interpretations:

1. One suggestion (that of the present paper) is that the system should somehow determine for itself what logical access paths to follow (in particular, what joins to perform) in order to answer the query. This approach is critically dependent on proper naming of attributes. Thus, for example, the two supplier number attributes (in relations S and SP respectively) *must* be given the same name; conversely, the supplier name and part name attributes (in relations S and P respectively) must *not* be given the same name. If either of these two rules is violated, there will be certain queries that the system will be unable to handle properly.

2. The other (less ambitious) approach is simply to regard all queries as being formulated in terms of a *predefined* set of joins—in effect, a predefined view consisting of "the" join of all relations in the database.

While there is no question that either approach would greatly simplify the expression of many queries arising in practice—and indeed some such approach is essential to the support of any natural-language frontend—it is also clear that the user must have the ability to specify logical access paths explicitly as well, in general. To see that this must be so, consider the query

```
SELECT STATUS
WHERE   COLOR ~= 'Red' ;
```

Does this mean "Get status of suppliers who supply a part that is not red" or "Get status of suppliers who do not supply a red part"? Whichever it is, there has to be some way of formulating the other. Come to that, the first example above is also susceptible to an alternative interpretation: "Get status for suppliers who supply *only* red parts." And here is a third example: "Get names of suppliers who are colocated." Here again it seems that an explicit join will be necessary (because it involves a join of relation S with itself).

Another aspect of the "universal relation" idea is discussed briefly in the annotation to reference [17.26] below.

17.26 W. Kent. "Consequences of Assuming a Universal Relation." *ACM TODS* **6**, No. 4 (December 1981).

The discipline of normalization tacitly assumes that it is possible to define an initial universal relation, involving all attributes relevant to the database under consideration, and then shows how that relation can be replaced by successively smaller and smaller projections until some "good" structure is reached. Kent suggests that this initial assumption is unrealistic and difficult to justify, on both practical and theoretical grounds.

See also the correspondence following the publication of this paper (references [17.27], [17.28] below).

17.27 J. D. Ullman. "On Kent's "Consequences of Assuming a Universal Relation"." *ACM TODS* **8**, No. 4 (December 1983).

17.28 W. Kent. "The Universal Relation Revisited." *ACM TODS* **8**, No. 4 (December 1983).

17.29 Jeffrey D. Ullman. "The U.R. Strikes Back." *Proc. 1st ACM SIGACT-SIGMOD Symposium on Principles of Database Systems* (March 1982).

17.30 David Maier, Jeffrey D. Ullman, and Moshe Y. Vardi. "On the Foundations of the Universal Relation Model." *ACM TODS* **9**, No. 2 (June 1984). An earlier version of this paper, under the title "The Revenge of the JD," appeared in *Proc. 2nd ACM SIGACT-SIGMOD Symposium on Principles of Database Systems* (March 1983).

17.31 R. Fagin, A. O. Mendelzon, and J. D. Ullman. "A Simplified Universal Relation Assumption and Its Properties." *ACM TODS* **7**, No. 3 (September 1982).

Conjectures that the "real world" can always be represented by means of a universal relation that satisfies precisely one JD plus a set of FDs, and explores some of the consequences of that hypothesis.

17.32 David Maier and Jeffrey D. Ullman. "Maximal Objects and the Semantics of Universal Relation Databases." *ACM TODS* **8**, No. 1 (March 1983).

Maximal objects represent an approach to the ambiguity problem that arises in universal relation systems when the underlying structure is not acyclic (see reference [17.34]). A maximal object corresponds to a predeclared subset of the attributes of the universal relation for which the underlying structure *is* acyclic. Such objects are then used to guide the interpretation of queries that would otherwise be ambiguous.

17.33 Marco A. Casanova, Ronald Fagin, and Christos H. Papadimitriou. "Inclusion Dependencies and Their Interaction with Functional Dependencies." *Proc. 1st ACM SIGACT-SIGMOD Symposium on Principles of Database Systems* (March 1982).

Inclusion dependencies (INDs) represent a formalization of Integrity Rule 2 of the relational model. For example, the IND

```
SP.S# << S.S#
```

(not the notation used in the paper) states that the set of values appearing in attribute SP.S# must be a subset (not necessarily a proper subset) of the set of values appearing in attribute S.S#. The paper provides a sound and complete set of axioms for INDs, which we may state (a little loosely) as follows:

1. $R.A << R.A$.

2. If $R.(A,B) << S.(C,D)$, then $R.A << S.C$ and $R.B << S.D$.

3. If $R.A << S.B$ and $S.B << T.C$, then $R.A << T.C$.

17.34 Ronald Fagin. "Acyclic Database Schemes (of Various Degrees): A Painless Introduction." *IBM Research Report RJ3800* (April 1983).

Section 17.7 of this chapter showed how a certain ternary relation SPJ that satisfied a certain cyclic constraint could be nonloss-decomposed into its three binary projections. The resulting database structure (i.e., schema, called scheme in this paper) is said to be *cyclic*, because each of the three relations has an attribute in common with each of the other two. (If the structure is depicted as a *hypergraph*, in which edges represent individual relations and the node that is the intersection of two edges corresponds precisely to the attributes in common to those two edges, then it should be clear why the term "cyclic" is used.) By contrast, most of the structures that arise in practice tend to be acyclic. Acyclic structures enjoy a number of formal properties that do not apply to database structures in general. In this paper, Fagin presents and explains a list of such properties.

A helpful way to think about acyclicity is the following: Just as the theory of normalization can help in determining when *a single relation* should be restructured in some way, so the theory of acyclicity can help in determining when a *collection* of relations should be restructured in some way.

ANSWERS TO SELECTED EXERCISES

17.1 The diagram shows all direct functional dependencies involved, both those implied by the wording of the exercise and those corresponding to reasonable semantic assumptions (stated explicitly below). The attribute names are intended to be self-explanatory.

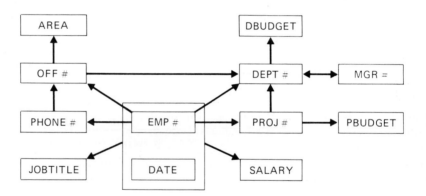

For *multivalued* dependencies, see Step 1 below. We assume there are no join dependencies that are not FDs or MVDs.

Semantic assumptions

- No employee is the manager of more than one department at a time.
- No employee works in more than one department at a time.
- No employee works on more than one project at a time.
- No employee has more than one office at a time.
- No employee has more than one phone at a time.
- No employee has more than one job at a time.
- No project is assigned to more than one department at a time.
- No office is assigned to more than one department at a time.

Step 0

First observe that the original hierarchic structure can be regarded as an unnormalized relation DEPT0:

```
DEPT0 ( DEPT#, DBUDGET, MGR#, XEMP0, XPROJ0, XOFFICE0 )
```

in which DEPT# is the primary key (indicated by italics), DBUDGET and MGR# are self-explanatory, and the domains corresponding to attributes XEMP0, XPROJ0, and XOFFICE0 are *relation-valued* and clearly require further explanation. (Recall from Chapter 11 that a relation-valued domain is a domain whose elements are relations—possibly even unnormalized relations—instead of simple atomic values.)

Let us concentrate for the moment on the relation-valued domain corresponding to XPROJ0. Define the composite domain PB to be the set of all PROJ#-PBUDGET pairs (i.e., the Cartesian product of the simple domains underlying PROJ# and PBUDGET). Then the XPROJ0 value corresponding to any given DEPT# value is some subset of the set of pairs in composite domain PB. The (relation-valued) domain corresponding to XPROJ0 is thus *the set of all possible subsets* of domain PB—the so-called *power set* of domain PB. (We are ignoring the fact that there is an FD from PROJ# to PBUDGET, which means that in practice some subsets of domain PB are not legal values for attribute XPROJ0.)

Analogous remarks apply to XEMP0, XOFFICE0, and indeed to all attributes in the example whose underlying domains are relation-valued; in each case, the domain is the power set of a composite domain defined as the set of all possible tuples of some particular type (and those tuples are not necessarily normalized—i.e., they may contain repeating groups). We shall indicate each such relation-valued attribute by a prefix X. Thus the given hierarchy can be represented as the following "nest" of normalized and unnormalized relations. Note: We use italics to indicate fields that are "unique and within parent," or are globally unique if no such parent exists.

```
DEPT0 ( DEPT#, DBUDGET, MGR#,
        XEMP0 ( EMP#, PROJ#, OFF#, PHONE#,
                XJOB0 ( JOBTITLE,
                        XSALHIST0 ( DATE, SALARY ) ) ),
        XPROJ0 ( PROJ#, PBUDGET ),
        XOFFICE0 ( OFF#, AREA, XPHONE0 ( PHONE# ) ) )
```

Step 1

We now reduce this unnormalized relation DEPT0 to a collection of 1NF relations. This preliminary reduction process is explained by Codd [11.1] as follows. Starting with the relation at the top of the hierarchy, we take its primary key and expand each of the immediately subordinate relations by inserting that primary key. The primary key of each such expanded relation is the combination of the field that gave "uniqueness within parent" before expansion, together with the primary key copied down from the parent relation. Now we strike out from the parent relation all relation-valued attributes (i.e., those attributes defined on relation-valued domains), remove the top node of the hierarchy, and repeat the same sequence of operations on each remaining subhierarchy. We obtain the following collection of 1NF relations. Note that we have lost all relation-valued attributes. Moreover, by considering each subhierarchy separately, we have immediately eliminated all MVDs that are not also FDs.

```
DEPT1 ( DEPT#, DBUDGET, MGR# )
EMP1 ( DEPT#, EMP#, PROJ#, OFF#, PHONE# )
JOB1 ( DEPT#, EMP#, JOBTITLE )
SALHIST1 ( DEPT#, EMP#, JOBTITLE, DATE, SALARY )
PROJ1 ( DEPT#, PROJ#, PBUDGET )
```

```
OFFICE1 ( DEPT#, OFF#, AREA )
PHONE1 ( DEPT#, OFF#, PHONE# )
```

Step 2

We now reduce the 1NF relations to an equivalent 2NF collection by eliminating nonfull dependencies. We consider the 1NF relations one by one.

DEPT1:   This relation is already in 2NF.

EMP1:   First observe that DEPT# is actually redundant as a component of the primary key for this relation. We may take EMP# alone as the primary key, in which case the relation is in 2NF as it stands.

JOB1:   Again, DEPT# is not required as a component of the primary key. Since DEPT# is functionally dependent on EMP#, we have a nonkey attribute (DEPT#) that is not fully functionally dependent on the primary key (the combination EMP#-JOBTITLE), and hence JOB1 is not in 2NF. We can replace it by

```
JOB2A ( EMP#, JOBTITLE )
```

and

```
JOB2B ( EMP#, DEPT# )
```

However, JOB2A is a projection of SALHIST2 (see below), and JOB2B is a projection of EMP1 (renamed as EMP2 below), so both of these relations can be discarded.

SALHIST1: As with JOB1, we can project out DEPT# entirely. Moreover, JOBTITLE is not required as a component of the primary key; we can take the combination EMP#-DATE as the primary key, to obtain the 2NF relation

```
SALHIST2 ( EMP#, DATE, JOBTITLE, SALARY )
```

PROJ1:   As with EMP1, we can consider DEPT# as a nonkey attribute; the relation is then in 2NF as it stands.

OFFICE1:   Similar remarks apply.

PHONE1:   We can project out DEPT# entirely, since the relation (DEPT#,OFF#) is a projection of OFFICE1 (renamed as OFFICE2 below). Also, OFF# is functionally dependent on PHONE#, so we can take PHONE# alone as the primary key, to obtain the 2NF relation

```
PHONE2 ( PHONE#, OFF# )
```

Note that this relation is not necessarily a projection of EMP2 (phones or offices may exist without being assigned to employees), so that we cannot discard this relation.

Hence our collection of 2NF relations is

```
DEPT2 ( DEPT#, DBUDGET, MGR# )
EMP2 ( EMP#, DEPT#, PROJ#, OFF#, PHONE# )
SALHIST2 ( EMP#, DATE, JOBTITLE, SALARY )
PROJ2 ( PROJ#, DEPT#, PBUDGET )
OFFICE2 ( OFF#, DEPT#, AREA )
PHONE2 ( PHONE#, OFF# )
```

Step 3

Now we reduce the 2NF relations to an equivalent 3NF set by eliminating transitive dependencies. The only 2NF relation not already in 3NF is the relation EMP2, in which OFF# and DEPT# are both transitively dependent on the primary key EMP#—OFF# via PHONE#, and DEPT# via PROJ# *and* via OFF# (and hence via PHONE#). The 3NF relations (projections) corresponding to EMP2 are

```
EMP3 ( EMP#, PROJ#, PHONE# )
X ( PHONE#, OFF# )
Y ( PROJ#, DEPT# )
Z ( OFF#, DEPT# )
```

However, X is PHONE2, Y is a projection of PROJ2, and Z is a projection of OFFICE2. Hence our collection of 3NF relations is simply

```
DEPT3 ( DEPT#, DBUDGET, MGR# )
EMP3 ( EMP#, PROJ#, PHONE# )
SALHIST3 ( EMP#, DATE, JOBTITLE, SALARY )
PROJ3 ( PROJ#, DEPT#, PBUDGET )
OFFICE3 ( OFF#, DEPT#, AREA )
PHONE3 ( PHONE#, OFF# )
```

Each of these 3NF relations is in fact in BCNF, and indeed in 4NF (because of the way we performed the reduction to 1NF in Step 1). By our assumption concerning lack of any additional JDs they are also in 5NF, so the decomposition is complete. Note that in DEPT3 we have two candidate keys, DEPT# and MGR#.

We remark also that, given certain (reasonable) additional semantic constraints, this collection of relations is *strongly redundant* [11.1], in that the projection of relation PROJ3 over (PROJ#,DEPT#) is at all times equal to a projection of the join of EMP3 and PHONE3 and OFFICE3.

Note finally that it is possible to "spot" the 3NF relations from the FD diagram (how?).

17.2 The diagram on page 406 shows all direct FDs involved.

Semantic assumptions

- No two customers have the same ship-to address.
- Each order is identified by a unique order number.
- Each detail line within an order is identified by a line number, unique within the order.

4NF (5NF) relations

```
CUST ( CUST#, BAL, CREDLIM, DISCOUNT )
SHIPTO ( ADDRESS, CUST# )
ORDHEAD ( ORD#, ADDRESS, DATE )
ORDLINE ( ORD#, LINE#, ITEM#, QTYORD, QTYOUT )
```

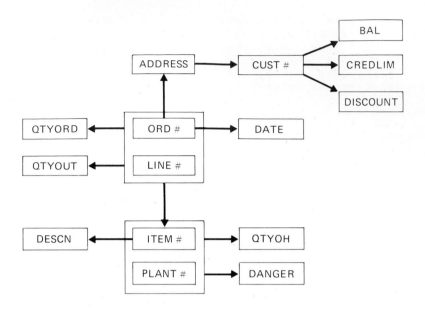

```
ITEM ( ITEM#, DESCN )
IP ( ITEM#, PLANT#, QTYOH, DANGER )
```

17.3 Consider the processing that must be performed by a program handling orders. We assume that the input order specifies customer number, ship-to address, and details of the items ordered (item numbers and quantities).

```
SELECT * FROM CUST WHERE CUST# = input.CUST# ;
check balance, credit limit, etc. ;
SELECT * FROM SHIPTO WHERE ADDRESS = input.ADDRESS
                      AND   CUST#   = input.CUST#
/* this checks the ship-to address */ ;
if everything is OK then process the order ;
```

If 99 percent of customers actually have only one ship-to address, it would be rather inefficient to put that address in a relation other than CUST (if we consider only that 99 percent, ADDRESS is in fact functionally dependent on CUST#). We can improve matters as follows. For each customer we designate one valid ship-to address as that customer's *primary* address. For the 99 percent, of course, the primary address is the only address. Any other addresses we refer to as *secondary*. Relation CUST can then be redefined as

```
CUST ( CUST#, ADDRESS, BAL, CREDLIM, DISCOUNT )
```

and relation SHIPTO can be replaced by

```
SECOND ( ADDRESS, CUST# )
```

Here CUST.ADDRESS refers to the primary address, and SECOND contains all secondary addresses (and corresponding customer numbers). These relations are both in 4NF. The order-processing program now looks like this:

```
SELECT * FROM CUST WHERE CUST# = input.CUST# ;
check balance, credit limit, etc. ;
if CUST.ADDRESS ~= input.ADDRESS then
SELECT * FROM SECOND WHERE ADDRESS = input.ADDRESS
                        AND   CUST#  = input.CUST#
/* this checks the ship-to address */ ;
if everything is OK then process the order ;
```

The advantages of this approach include the following:

- Processing is simpler and marginally more efficient for 99 percent of customers.
- If the ship-to address is omitted from the input order, the primary address could be used by default.
- Suppose that the customer can have a different discount for each ship-to address. With the original approach (shown as the answer to the previous exercise), the DISCOUNT attribute would have to be moved to the SHIPTO relation, making processing still more complicated. With the revised approach, however, the primary discount (corresponding to the primary address) can be represented by an appearance of DISCOUNT in CUST, and secondary discounts by a corresponding appearance of DISCOUNT in SECOND. Both relations are still in 4NF, and processing is again simpler for 99 percent of customers.

To sum up: Isolating exceptional cases seems to be a valuable technique for obtaining the best of both worlds—i.e., combining the advantages of 4NF with the simplification in retrieval that can occur if the restrictions of 4NF are violated.

17.4 The diagrams below illustrate the most important functional dependencies.

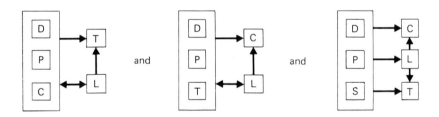

A possible collection of 4NF relations is

```
RELATION SCHED ( L, T, C, D, P )
         PRIMARY KEY ( L )
         ALTERNATE KEY ( T, D, P )
         ALTERNATE KEY ( C, D, P )

RELATION STUDY ( S, L )
         PRIMARY KEY ( S, L )
```

This reduction is not unique.

17.5

a) True.

b) True.

c) False (but "almost true"). A binary relation $R(X, Y)$ can be nonloss-decomposed into its two unary projections $R1(X)$, $R2(Y)$ if and only if R is equal to the Cartesian product of $R1$ and $R2$ (remember that $R1$ JOIN $R2$ is equivalent to $R1$ TIMES $R2$ if $R1$ and $R2$ have no common attribute). Such a relation satisfies the special, but nontrivial, MVD $\emptyset \to \to X \mid Y$ (where $\emptyset$ represents the empty set), and is thus not in 4NF.

d) False—see c).

e) False (true if "$A \to B$" is changed to "$A \to \to B$"). The "if" part is true. Counter-example for the "only if" part:

R	A	B	C		R1	A	B		R2	A	C
	a1	b1	c1			a1	b1			a1	c1
	a1	b2	c1			a1	b2			a1	c2
	a1	b1	c2								
	a1	b2	c1								

R is the join of R1 and R2, yet $A \to B$ does not hold in R, and neither does $A \to C$.

f) True.

g) True.

h) True.

17.6 First we introduce three relations

```
REPS        ( REP#,  ... )
AREAS       ( AREA#, ... )
PRODUCTS  ( PROD#, ... )
```

with the obvious interpretation. Second, we can represent the relationship between sales representatives and sales areas by a relation

```
RA ( REP#, AREA# )
```

and the relationship between sales representatives and products by a relation

```
RP ( REP#, PROD# )
```

(both of these are many-to-many relationships).

Next, we are told that every product is sold in every area. So if we introduce a relation

```
AP ( AREA#, PROD# )
```

to represent the relationship between areas and products, then we have the constraint (C):

```
FORALL AX FORALL PX EXISTS APX ( APX.AREA# = AX.AREA# AND
                                 APX.PROD# = PX.PROD# )
```

(where AX, PX, APX are tuple variables for relations AREAS, PRODUCTS, AP, respectively). Note that constraint C implies that relation AP is not in 4NF (see Exercise 17.5(c)).

No two representatives sell the same product in the same area. In other words, given an (AREA#,PROD#) combination, there is exactly one responsible sales representative (REP#), so we can introduce a relation

```
APR ( AREA#, PROD#, REP# )
```

in which (to make the FD explicit)

```
APR.(AREA#,PROD#) → APR.REP#
```

(of course, specification of the combination (AREA#,PROD#) as primary key is sufficient to express this FD). Now, however, relations RA, RP, and AP are all redundant, since they are all projections of APR; they can therefore all be dropped. In place of constraint C, we now need constraint C1:

```
FORALL AX FORALL PX EXISTS APRX ( APRX.AREA# = AX.AREA# AND
                                  APRX.PROD# = PX.PROD# )
```

(where APRX is a tuple variable for relation APR). Constraint C1 certainly needs to be stated explicitly if it is to be enforced by the DBMS—see Chapter 19—but should be stated explicitly in any case since it represents part of the semantics of the situation and needs to be understood by the user.

Also, since every representative sells all of that representative's products in all of that representative's areas, we have the additional constraint C2:

```
APR.REP# → → APR.AREA# | APR.PROD#
```

(an MVD; relation APR is not in 4NF). Again the constraint should be stated explicitly.

Thus the final design consists of relations REPS, AREAS, PRODUCTS, and APR, together with explicit constraints C1 and C2. This exercise illustrates very clearly the point that, in general, the normalization discipline is adequate to represent *some* semantic aspects of a given problem (basically, dependencies that are a consequence of candidate keys, where by "dependencies" we mean FDs, MVDs, or JDs), but that explicit statement of additional dependencies may also be needed for other aspects, and some aspects cannot be represented in terms of such dependencies at all. It also illustrates the point (once again) that it is not always desirable to normalize "all the way" (relation APR is in BCNF but not in 4NF).

Part 4
The Database
Environment

So far in this book we have concentrated for the most part on the *data access* functions of a database system—not unreasonably, since data access is of course the principal reason for using the system in the first place. However, data access alone is certainly not the whole of the story (at least, not if the system in question is "large" or multi-user). Indeed, as indicated briefly in Chapters 1 and 2 of this book, a complete system will necessarily provide a number of additional functions, over and above the simple data access facilities discussed prior to this point. Such additional functions can be divided into two broad categories—those provided by the base DBMS itself, and those provided by some frontend system or built-in application or other auxiliary component:

- The additional functions provided by the base DBMS itself generally have to do with various aspects of *data control* or *data protection*. Controls must be provided to protect the database against a variety of possible threats (both deliberate and accidental). The necessary controls include *recovery*, *concurrency*, *security*, and *integrity* controls. Recovery and concurrency controls are discussed in Chapter 18, and security and integrity controls are discussed in Chapter 19.

- The other additional functions subdivide into a number of more or less separate categories — report writing, business graphics, application generation, and many others. Such functions are considered briefly in Chapter 20.

18

Recovery and Concurrency

18.1 INTRODUCTION

The problems of recovery and concurrency in a database system are heavily bound up with the notion of *transaction processing*. (The reader may recall that this term was mentioned in Chapter 9—the chapter on embedded SQL—as part of a brief discussion of the SQL COMMIT and ROLLBACK operations.) In this chapter, therefore, we first explain what a transaction is, what the term *transaction processing* (or transaction *management*) means, and what exactly the functions of COMMIT and ROLLBACK are. We then go on to discuss the problems of recovery and concurrency that the transaction concept is intended to solve. To fix our ideas, we base most of our examples and discussions on a SQL system specifically (where it makes any difference; actually, the ideas are very general and apply to numerous other systems—relational or otherwise—with comparatively little change).

Note: We assume for the most part throughout this chapter that we are in a "large" or mainframe environment. "Small" DBMS's typically provide little or no support for recovery and concurrency—the question of concurrency simply does not arise, and recovery is considered to be a user problem (the user has to make backup copies of the database and must redo work manually if a failure occurs).

18.2 TRANSACTION RECOVERY

As indicated in Section 18.1, we begin our discussions by introducing the fundamental notion of *transaction*. A transaction is a *logical unit of work*. Consider the following example (a generalized version of Example 6.6.4 from Chapter 6, cast into embedded-SQL form): Change the supplier number of supplier Sx from 'Sx' to 'Sy' (where Sx and Sy are parameters). For the sake of the example, we assume—realistically enough—that the system does not provide any foreign-key support, so that application code must be written to perform the necessary "cascade" of the UPDATE from relation S to relation SP.

```
TRANEX: PROC OPTIONS ( MAIN ) ;

        /* declarations omitted */

        EXEC SQL WHENEVER SQLERROR GO TO UNDO ;

        GET LIST ( SX, SY ) ; /* get values from end-user */
        EXEC SQL UPDATE S
                 SET    S# = :SY
                 WHERE  S# = :SX ;
        EXEC SQL UPDATE SP
                 SET    S# = :SY
                 WHERE  S# = :SX ;
        EXEC SQL COMMIT ;
        GO TO FINISH ;
UNDO:   EXEC SQL ROLLBACK ;
FINISH: RETURN ;

END /*  TRANEX */ ;
```

The point of the example is that what is presumably perceived by the end-user as a single, atomic operation—"Change a supplier number from Sx to Sy"—in fact involves *two* UPDATEs to the database. What is more, the database will probably not even be consistent between those two UPDATEs; to be specific, it may temporarily contain some shipment records that have no corresponding supplier record. Thus a transaction, or logical unit of work, is not necessarily just a single database operation; rather, it is a *sequence* of several such operations (in general) that transforms a consistent state of the database into another consistent state, without necessarily preserving consistency at all intermediate points.

Now, it is clear that what must *not* be allowed to happen in the example is for one of the two UPDATEs to be executed and the other not (because that would leave the database in an inconsistent state). Ideally, of course, we would like a cast-iron guarantee that both UPDATEs will be executed. Unfortunately, it is impossible to provide any such guarantee—there is always a chance that things will go wrong, and go wrong moreover at the worst possible moment. For example, a system crash might occur between the two UPDATEs, or the program itself might abnormally terminate between the two with (say) an overflow error.[1] But a system that supports *transaction processing* does provide the next best thing to such a guarantee. Specifically, it guarantees that if the transaction executes some updates and then a failure occurs (for whatever reason) before the transaction reaches its normal termination, *then those updates will be undone.* Thus the transaction *either* executes in its entirety *or* is totally canceled (i.e., made as if it never executed at all). In this

---

1. System crash is referred to in the next section as a *global* (or *system*) failure. By contrast, a program failure such as overflow is referred to as a *local* failure.

way a sequence of operations that is fundamentally not atomic can be made to look as if it really were atomic from the end-user's point of view.

The COMMIT and ROLLBACK operations are the key to providing this atomicity (or semblance of atomicity). The COMMIT operation signals *successful end-of-transaction*: It tells the system that a logical unit of work has successfully completed, the database is (or should be) in a consistent state again, and all of the updates made by that unit of work can now be "committed" or made permanent. The ROLLBACK operation, by contrast, signals *unsuccessful* end-of-transaction: It tells the system that something has gone wrong, the database might be in an inconsistent state, and all of the updates made by the logical unit of work must be "rolled back" or undone. (By "update" here, of course, we include INSERT and DELETE operations as well as UPDATE operations per se.)

In the example, therefore, we issue a COMMIT if we get through the two UPDATEs successfully, which will commit the changes in the database and make them permanent. If anything goes wrong, however—i.e., if either UPDATE raises the SQLERROR condition—then we issue a ROLLBACK instead, to undo any changes made so far.

- Note 1: We have shown the COMMIT and ROLLBACK operations explicitly, for the sake of the example. As mentioned in Section 9.4, however, the system— at least in the case of SQL specifically—will automatically issue a COMMIT for any program that reaches normal termination, and will automatically issue a ROLLBACK for any program that does not (regardless of the reason; in particular, if a program terminates abnormally because of a *system* failure, a ROLLBACK will be issued on its behalf when the system is restarted—see Section 18.3). In the example, therefore, we could have omitted the explicit COMMIT, but not the explicit ROLLBACK.

- Note 2: A realistic application program should not only update the database (or attempt to) but should also send some kind of message back to the end-user indicating what has happened. For example, program TRANEX above might send the message "Renumbering complete" if the COMMIT is reached, or the message "Error—no renumbering done" otherwise. Message-handling, in turn, has additional implications for recovery. See reference [18.1] or Volume II.

The reader may be wondering how it is possible to undo an update. The answer is that the system maintains a *log* or *journal*, on tape or (nowadays more commonly) on disk,[2] on which details of all update operations—in particular, before and after values of the updated item—are recorded. Thus, if it becomes necessary to undo

---

2.   This remark is an oversimplification. Actually the log consists of two portions, an active or on-line portion and an archive or off-line portion. The on-line portion is the portion used during normal system operation to record details of updates as they are performed, and is normally held on disk. When the on-line portion becomes full, its contents are transferred to the off-line portion, which (because it is always processed sequentially) is usually held on tape.

some particular update, the system can use the corresponding log entry to restore the updated item to its previous value.

Synchronization Points

Executing either a COMMIT or a ROLLBACK operation establishes what is called—among other things—a *synchronization point* (abbreviated synchpoint). A synchpoint represents the boundary between two consecutive transactions; it thus corresponds to the end of a logical unit of work, and hence to a point at which the database is (or should be) in a state of consistency. The *only* operations that establish a synchpoint are COMMIT, ROLLBACK, and program initiation. (Remember, however, that COMMIT and ROLLBACK may often be implicit.) When a synchpoint is established:

- All updates made by the program since the previous synchpoint are committed (COMMIT) or undone (ROLLBACK).
- All database positioning is lost (all open cursors are closed).
- All record locks are released (see Section 18.5 for a discussion of locks).

Note carefully that COMMIT and ROLLBACK terminate the *transaction*, not the program. In general, a single program execution will consist of a sequence of several transactions, running one after another, with each COMMIT or ROLL-BACK operation terminating one transaction and starting the next.[3] However, it is true that very often one program execution will correspond to just one transaction; and if it does, of course, then it will frequently be possible to code that program without any explicit COMMIT or ROLLBACK statements at all.

In conclusion, therefore, we can now see that transactions are not only the unit of work but also the unit of *recovery*. For if a transaction successfully COMMITs, then the system must guarantee that its updates will be permanently established in the database, even if the system crashes the very next moment. It is quite possible, for instance, that the system may crash after the COMMIT has been honored but before the updates have been physically written to the database (they may still be waiting in a main storage buffer and so be lost at the time of the crash). Even if that happens, the system's restart procedure will still install those updates in the database; it is able to discover the values to be written by examining the relevant entries in the log.[4] Thus the restart procedure will recover any units of work (transactions) that completed successfully but did not manage to get their updates physically written prior to the crash; hence, as stated earlier, transactions are indeed the

---

3. Loosely speaking. It would be more accurate to say that the next transaction is started by *the first recoverable operation following* the COMMIT or ROLLBACK—where a "recoverable operation" is any operation, such as UPDATE, that can subsequently be undone if necessary.

4. It follows, therefore, that the log must be physically written before COMMIT processing can complete. This rule is known as the *Write-Ahead Log Protocol*.

unit of recovery. Later in this chapter we will see that they are the unit of *concurrency* also.

18.3   SYSTEM AND MEDIA RECOVERY

The system must be prepared to recover, not only from purely local failures such as the occurrence of an overflow condition within a single transaction, but also from "global" failures such as a power failure on the CPU. A local failure, by definition, affects only the transaction in which the failure has actually occurred; such failures have already been adequately discussed in Section 18.2. A global failure, by contrast, affects several—quite likely all—of the transactions in progress at the time of the failure, and hence has significant system-wide implications. In this section, we briefly consider what is involved in recovering from a global failure.

Such failures fall into two broad categories:

- *System failures* (e.g., power failure), which affect all transactions currently in progress but do not physically damage the database.
- *Media failures* (e.g., head crash on the disk), which do cause damage to the database, or to some portion of it, and affect at least those transactions currently using that portion.

Note: System and media failures are also known as soft and hard crashes, respectively. We proceed to discuss each case in somewhat more detail.

System Failure

The critical point regarding system failure is that *the contents of main storage are lost* (in particular, the database buffers are lost). The precise state of any transaction that was in progress at the time of the failure is therefore no longer known; such a transaction can therefore never be successfully completed, and so must be *undone* (rolled back) when the system restarts. Furthermore—as indicated briefly at the end of Section 18.2—it may also be necessary at restart time to *redo* certain transactions that did successfully complete prior to the crash but did not manage to get their updates transferred from the database buffers to the physical database.

The question arises: How does the system know at restart time which transactions to undo and which to redo? The answer is as follows. At certain prescribed intervals—typically whenever some specified number of entries have been written to the log—the system automatically "takes a checkpoint." Taking a checkpoint involves a) physically writing the contents of the database buffers out to the physical database, and b) physically writing a special *checkpoint record* out to the physical log. The checkpoint record gives a list of all transactions that were in progress at the time the checkpoint was taken. To see how this information is used, consider Fig. 18.1, which is meant to be read as follows:

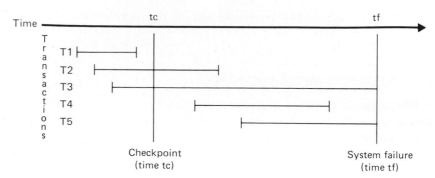

Fig. 18.1 Five transaction categories.

- A system failure has occurred at time *tf*.
- The most recent checkpoint prior to time *tf* was taken at time *tc*.
- Transactions of type *T1* were completed prior to time *tc*.
- Transactions of type *T2* started prior to time *tc* and completed after time *tc* and before time *tf*.
- Transactions of type *T3* also started prior to time *tc* but did not complete by time *tf*.
- Transactions of type *T4* started after time *tc* and completed before time *tf*.
- Finally, transactions of type *T5* also started after time *tc* but did not complete by time *tf*.

It should be clear that, when the system is restarted, transactions of types *T3* and *T5* must be undone, and transactions of types *T2* and *T4* must be redone. Note, however, that transactions of type *T1* do not enter into the restart process at all, because their updates were physically written to the database at time *tc*.

At restart time, therefore, the system goes through the following procedure in order to identify all transactions of types *T2–T5*:

1. Start with two lists of transactions, the UNDO-list and the REDO-list. Set the UNDO-list equal to the list of all transactions given in the checkpoint record; set the REDO-list to empty.

2. Search forward through the log, starting from the checkpoint record.

3. If a "start of transaction" log entry is found for transaction *T*, add *T* to the UNDO-list.

4. If a "commit" log entry is found for transaction *T*, move *T* from the UNDO-list to the REDO-list.

5. When the end of the log is reached, the UNDO- and REDO-lists identify, respectively, transactions of types *T3* and *T5*, and transactions of types *T2* and *T4*.

The system now works backward through the log, undoing the transactions in the UNDO-list; then it works forward again, redoing the transactions in the REDO-list. Finally, when all such recovery activity is complete (and only then), the system is ready to accept new work.

Media Failure

A media failure is a failure (such as a disk head crash or a disk controller failure) in which some portion of the database has been physically destroyed. Recovery from such a failure basically involves reloading (or *restoring*) the database from a backup copy (or *dump*), and then using the log—both active and archive portions, in general—to redo all transactions that completed since that backup copy was taken. There is no need to undo transactions that were still in progress at the time of the failure, since by definition all updates of such transactions have been "undone" (destroyed) anyway.

The need to be able to perform media recovery thus implies the need for a *dump/restore utility*. The dump portion of that utility is used to make backup copies of the database on demand. (Such copies can be kept on tape or other archival storage; it is not necessary that they be on direct access.) The restore portion of the utility—which may in fact be nothing more than the standard database *load* utility—is then used to recreate the database after a media failure from a specified backup copy.

18.4   THREE CONCURRENCY PROBLEMS

Most DBMS's (at least, most mainframe DBMS's) are multiple-user systems; that is, they are systems that allow any number of transactions to access the same database at the same time. In such a system, some kind of *concurrency control mechanism* is needed to ensure that concurrent transactions do not interfere with each other's operation. For without such a mechanism, there are numerous problems that can arise; we explain some of those problems in this section, then go on to show in the next section how those problems can be solved, using a concurrency control mechanism known as *locking*. Note: Locking is not the only possible approach to the concurrency control problem, but it is far and away the one most commonly encountered in practice. Some other approaches are described in references [18.10–18.11].

There are essentially three ways in which things can go wrong—three ways, that is, in which a transaction, though correct in itself, can nevertheless produce the wrong answer because of interference on the part of some other transaction (in the absence of a suitable control mechanism, of course). Note, incidentally, that the interfering transaction may also be correct in itself. It is the *interleaving* of operations from the two correct transactions that produces the overall incorrect result. The three problems are:

1. The *lost update* problem,
2. The *uncommitted dependency* problem, and
3. The *inconsistent analysis* problem.

We consider each in turn.

The Lost Update Problem

Consider the situation illustrated in Fig. 18.2. That figure is intended to be read as follows: Transaction *A* retrieves some record *R* at time *t1*; transaction *B* retrieves that same record *R* at time *t2*; transaction *A* updates the record (on the basis of the values seen at time *t1*) at time *t3*; and transaction *B* updates the same record (on the basis of the values seen at time *t2*, which are the same as those seen at time *t1*) at time *t4*. Transaction *A*'s update is lost at time *t4*, because transaction *B* overwrites it without even looking at it.

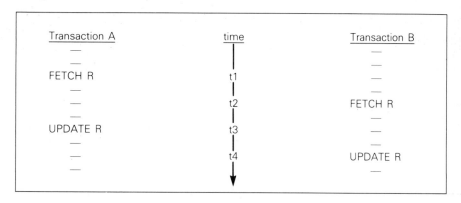

Fig. 18.2 Transaction *A* loses an update at time *t4*.

The Uncommitted Dependency Problem

The uncommitted dependency problem arises if one transaction is allowed to retrieve (or, worse, update) a record that has been updated by another transaction but has not yet been committed by that other transaction. For if it has not yet been committed, there is always a possibility that it never will be committed but will be rolled back instead—in which case the first transaction will have seen some data that now no longer exists (and in a sense "never" existed). Consider Figs. 18.3 and 18.4.

In the first example (Fig. 18.3), transaction *A* sees an uncommitted update (also called an uncommitted change) at time *t2*. That update is then undone at time *t3*. Transaction *A* is therefore operating on a false assumption—namely, the assumption that record *R* has the value seen at time *t2*, whereas in fact it has whatever value it had prior to time *t1*. As a result, transaction *A* may well produce incorrect

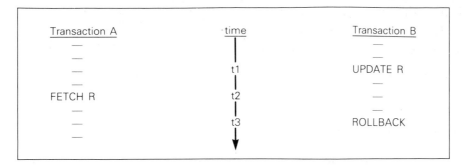

Fig. 18.3 Transaction *A* becomes dependent on an uncommitted change at time *t2*.

output. Note, incidentally, that the ROLLBACK of transaction *B* may be due to no fault of *B*'s—it could, for example, be the result of a system crash. (And transaction *A* may already have terminated by that time, in which case the crash would not cause a ROLLBACK to be issued for *A* also.)

The second example (Fig. 18.4) is even worse. Not only does transaction *A* become dependent on an uncommitted change at time *t2*, but it actually loses an update at time *t3*—because the ROLLBACK at time *t3* causes record *R* to be restored to its value prior to time *t1*. This is another version of the lost update problem.

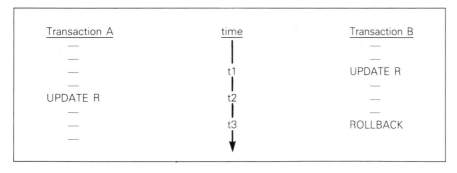

Fig. 18.4 Transaction *A* updates an uncommitted change at time *t2*, and loses that update at time *t3*.

The Inconsistent Analysis Problem

Consider Fig. 18.5, which shows two transactions *A* and *B* operating on account (ACC) records: Transaction *A* is summing account balances, transaction *B* is transferring an amount 10 from account 3 to account 1. The result produced by *A* (110) is obviously incorrect; if *A* were to go on to write that result back into the database, it would actually leave the database in an inconsistent state. We say that *A* has seen an inconsistent state of the database and has therefore performed an inconsistent

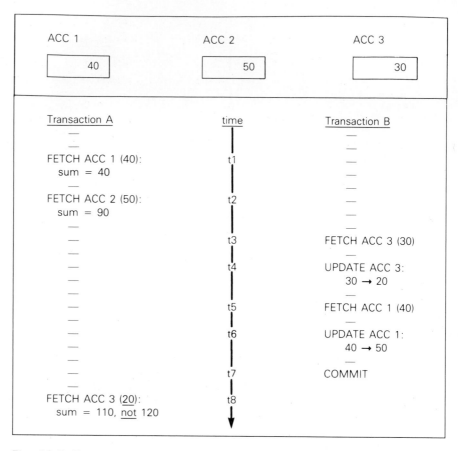

Fig. 18.5 Transaction *A* performs an inconsistent analysis.

analysis. Note the difference between this example and the previous one: There is no question here of *A* being dependent on an uncommitted change, since *B* COM-MITs all its updates before *A* sees ACC 3.

18.5   LOCKING

The basic idea of locking is simple: When a transaction needs an assurance that some object that it is interested in—typically a database record—will not change in some unpredictable manner while its back is turned (as it were), it *acquires a lock* on that object. The effect of the lock is to "lock other transactions out of" the object, and thus in particular to prevent them from changing it. The first transaction is thus able to carry out its processing in the certain knowledge that the object in question will remain in a stable state for as long as that transaction wishes it to.

We now give a more detailed explanation of the way locking works.

1. First, we assume the existence of two kinds of lock, namely *exclusive locks* (X locks) and *shared locks* (S locks), defined as indicated in the next two paragraphs.[5]

2. If transaction *A* holds an exclusive (X) lock on record *R*, then a request from transaction *B* for a lock of either type on *R* will cause *B* to go into a wait state. *B* will wait until *A*'s lock is released.

3. If transaction *A* holds a shared (S) lock on record *R*, then:

    a) a request from transaction *B* for an X lock on *R* will cause *B* to go into a wait state (and *B* will wait until *A*'s lock is released);

    b) a request from transaction *B* for an S lock on *R* will be granted (that is, *B* will now also hold an S lock on *R*).

These first three paragraphs can conveniently be summarized by means of a *compatibility matrix* (Fig. 18.6). That matrix is interpreted as follows: Consider some record *R*; suppose transaction *A* currently holds a lock on *R* as indicated by the entries in the column headings (dash = no lock); and suppose some distinct transaction *B* issues a request for a lock on *R* as indicated by the entries down the left-hand side (for completeness we again include the "no lock" case). An N indicates a *conflict* (*B*'s request cannot be satisfied and *B* goes into a wait state), a Y indicates compatibility (*B*'s request is satisfied). The matrix is obviously symmetric.

To continue with the explanations:

4. Transaction requests for record locks are normally implicit (at least in most modern systems). When a transaction successfully retrieves a record, it automatically acquires an S lock on that record. When a transaction successfully updates a record, it automatically acquires an X lock on that record. (If the transaction al-

	X	S	—
X	N	N	Y
S	N	Y	Y
—	Y	Y	Y

Y = yes (requests compatible)

N = no (requests not compatible)

Fig. 18.6 Lock type compatibility matrix.

---

5. We assume throughout this section that X and S are the only kinds of lock available. In practice other kinds of lock do exist, but the details are beyond the scope of this introductory text. We assume also that the record is the only "lockable object"; in practice, again, other lockable objects do exist. A far more extensive discussion of the whole subject of concurrency control in general, and locking in particular, can be found in Volume II. See also the references at the end of the chapter.

ready holds an S lock on the record, as it will in a SQL FETCH . . . UPDATE sequence, then the UPDATE will "promote" the S lock to X level.)

5. X locks are held until the next synchpoint. S locks are also normally held until that time (but see reference [18.9]).

Now we are in a position to see how locking solves the three problems described in the previous section. Again we consider them one at a time.

The Lost Update Problem

Fig. 18.7 is a modified version of Fig. 18.2, showing what would happen to the interleaved execution of that figure under the locking scheme described above. Transaction A's UPDATE at time $t3$ is not accepted, because it is an implicit request for an X lock on R, and such a request conflicts with the S lock already held by transaction B; so A goes into a wait state. For analogous reasons, B goes into a wait state at time $t4$. Now both transactions are unable to proceed, so there is no question of any update being lost. Locking thus solves the lost update problem by reducing it to another problem! —but at least it does solve the original problem. The new problem is called *deadlock*. The problem of deadlock is discussed at the end of this section.

The Uncommitted Dependency Problem

Figs. 18.8 and 18.9 are, respectively, modified versions of Figs. 18.3 and 18.4, showing what would happen to the interleaved executions of those figures under the locking mechanism described above. Transaction A's operation at time $t2$ (FETCH in Fig. 18.8, UPDATE in Fig. 18.9) is not accepted in either case, because it is an

Transaction A	time	Transaction B
—		—
—		—
FETCH R	t1	—
(acquire S lock on R)		—
—		—
—	t2	FETCH R
—		(acquire S lock on R)
—		—
UPDATE R	t3	—
(request X lock on R)		—
wait		—
wait	t4	UPDATE R
wait		(request X lock on R)
wait		wait
wait		wait
wait		wait

Fig. 18.7 No update is lost, but deadlock occurs at time *t4*.

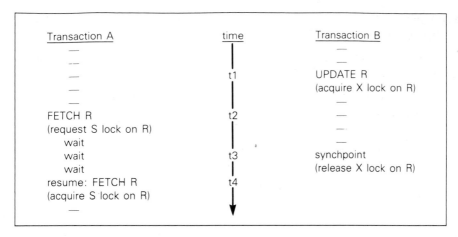

Fig. 18.8 Transaction A is prevented from seeing an uncommitted change at time *t2*.

implicit request for a lock on R, and such a request conflicts with the X lock already
held by B; so A goes into a wait state. It remains in that wait state until B reaches
a synchpoint (either COMMIT or ROLLBACK), when B's lock is released and A
is able to proceed; and at that point A sees a *committed* value (either the pre-B
value, if B terminates with a ROLLBACK, or the post-B value otherwise). Either
way, A is no longer dependent on an uncommitted update.

The Inconsistent Analysis Problem

Fig. 18.10 is a modified version of Fig. 18.5, showing what would happen to the
interleaved execution of that figure under the locking mechanism described above.
Transaction B's UPDATE at time *t6* is not accepted, because it is an implicit request

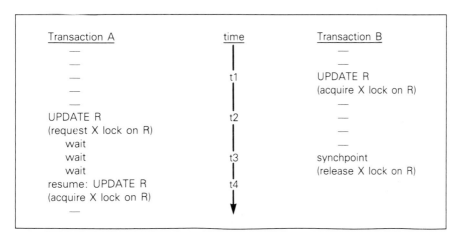

Fig. 18.9 Transaction A is prevented from updating an uncommitted change at
time *t2*.

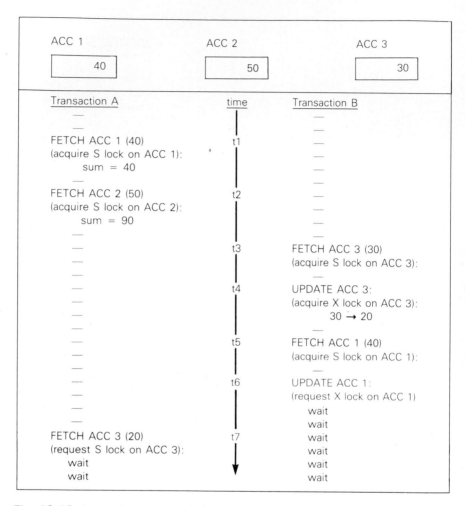

Fig. 18.10 Inconsistent analysis is prevented, but deadlock occurs at time *t7*.

for an X lock on ACC 1, and such a request conflicts with the S lock already held by *A*; so *B* goes into a wait state. Likewise, transaction *A*'s FETCH at time *t7* is also not accepted, because it is an implicit request for an S lock on ACC 3, and such a request conflicts with the X lock already held by *B*; so *A* goes into a wait state also. Again, therefore, locking solves the original problem (the inconsistent analysis problem, in this case) by forcing a deadlock. As already mentioned, deadlock is discussed below.

Deadlock

We have now seen how locking can be used to solve the three basic problems of concurrency. Unfortunately, however, we have also seen that locking can introduce problems of its own, principally the problem of deadlock. Two examples of dead-

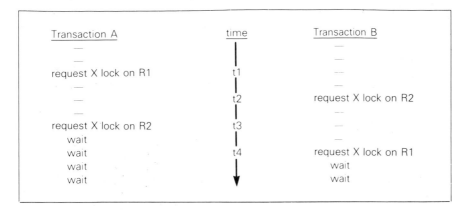

Fig. 18.11 An example of deadlock.

lock were given above. Fig. 18.11 shows a slightly more generalized version of the problem. *R1* and *R2* in that figure are intended to represent any lockable objects (e.g., database records).

Deadlock is a situation in which two or more transactions are in a simultaneous wait state, each one waiting for one of the others to release a lock before it can proceed. Fig. 18.11 shows a deadlock involving two transactions, but deadlocks involving three, four, . . . transactions are also possible, at least in theory.[6] If a deadlock occurs, the system must detect it and break it. Detecting the deadlock involves detecting a cycle in the graph of "who is waiting for whom"—see Exercise 18.2. Breaking the deadlock involves choosing one of the deadlocked transactions— i.e., one of the transactions in the cycle in the graph—as the *victim* and rolling it back, thereby releasing its locks and so allowing some other transaction to proceed.

Observe that the victim has "failed" and been rolled back *through no fault of its own*. Some systems will automatically restart such a transaction from the beginning, on the assumption that the conditions that caused the deadlock in the first place will probably not arise again. Other systems simply send a "deadlock victim" return code back to the application; it is then up to the program to deal with the situation in some graceful manner. The first of these two approaches is clearly preferable from the application programmer's point of view. But even if the programmer does sometimes have to get involved, it is *always* desirable to conceal the problem from the end-user, for obvious reasons.

18.6 CONCLUDING REMARKS

In this chapter we have presented a necessarily brief introduction to the topic of *transaction management*. A transaction is a logical unit of work—also a unit of recovery and a unit of concurrency. Transaction management is the task of super-

---

6. Experiments with System R seemed to show that in practice deadlocks would almost never involve more than two transactions (see Volume II).

vising the execution of transactions in such a way that each transaction can be considered as an all-or-nothing proposition, given the possibility of arbitrary failures on the part of individual transactions or on the part of the system itself, and given also the fact that multiple independent transactions may be executing concurrently and accessing the same data. In fact, the overall function of the system might well be defined as *the reliable execution of transactions*.

In conclusion, we observe that we have tacitly been assuming an application programming environment throughout this chapter. However, all of the concepts discussed apply equally to the end-user environment also (though they may be somewhat more concealed in that environment). For example, consider the case of DB2 specifically, where the end-user has the ability to enter SQL statements interactively, either through DB2I or through QMF. Normally, each such interactive SQL statement is treated as a transaction in its own right; the DB2 frontend system (DB2I or QMF, as the case may be) will automatically issue a COMMIT on the user's behalf after the SQL statement has been executed. However, facilities do exist for the end-user to inhibit those automatic COMMITs, and instead to execute a whole series of SQL statements (followed by an explicit COMMIT) as a single transaction. The practice is not generally recommended, however, since it is likely to cause portions of the database to remain locked (and therefore inaccessible to other users) for excessively lengthy periods of time. In such an environment, moreover, it is possible for *end-users* to deadlock with one another, which is another good argument for prohibiting the practice (see the remarks on concealing deadlock from the end-user at the end of the previous section).

EXERCISES

18.1 An interleaved execution of some set of transactions is considered to be correct if and only if it is *serializable*—i.e., if and only if it produces the same result as some (arbitrary) serial execution of those same transactions, for arbitrary input (see reference [18.7]). Let transactions T1, T2, and T3 be defined to perform the following operations:

(T1) Add one to A

(T2) Double A

(T3) Display A on the screen and then set A to one

(where A is some item in the database).

    a) Suppose transactions T1, T2, T3 are allowed to execute concurrently. If A has initial value zero, how many possible correct results are there? Enumerate them.

    b) Suppose the internal structure of T1, T2, T3 is as indicated below:

```
T1                          | T2                         | T3
----------------------------+----------------------------+----------------------------
F1: FETCH A INTO t1         | F2: FETCH A INTO t2        | F3: FETCH A INTO t3
    t1 := t1 + 1            |     t2 := t2 * 2           |     display t3
U1: UPDATE A FROM t1        | U2: UPDATE A FROM t2        | U3: UPDATE A FROM 1
                            |                            |
```

If the transactions execute *without* any locking, how many possible interleaved executions are there?

c) With the given initial value for A (zero), are there any interleaved executions of T1, T2, T3 that in fact produce a "correct" result and yet are not serializable?

d) Are there any interleaved executions of T1, T2, T3 that are in fact serializable but could not be produced if the system enforced the locking scheme described in Section 18.5 (i.e., if all transactions obeyed the "two-phase locking protocol" [18.7])?

18.2 The following list represents the sequence of events in an interleaved execution of a set of transactions T1, T2, . . . , T12. (Note: A, B, . . . H are intended to be items in the database, not cursors.)

```
time  t0        . . . . . . . . . .
time  t1    (T1)    :  FETCH  A
time  t2    (T2)    :  FETCH  B
  -         (T1)    :  FETCH  C
  -         (T4)    :  FETCH  D
  -         (T5)    :  FETCH  A
  -         (T2)    :  FETCH  E
  -         (T2)    :  UPDATE  E
  -         (T3)    :  FETCH  F
  -         (T2)    :  FETCH  F
  -         (T5)    :  UPDATE  A
  -         (T1)    :  COMMIT
  -         (T6)    :  FETCH  A
  -         (T5)    :  ROLLBACK
  -         (T6)    :  FETCH  C
  -         (T6)    :  UPDATE  C
  -         (T7)    :  FETCH  G
  -         (T8)    :  FETCH  H
  -         (T9)    :  FETCH  G
  -         (T9)    :  UPDATE  G
  -         (T8)    :  FETCH  E
  -         (T7)    :  COMMIT
  -         (T9)    :  FETCH  H
  -         (T3)    :  FETCH  G
  -         (T10)   :  FETCH  A
  -         (T9)    :  UPDATE  H
  -         (T6)    :  COMMIT
  -         (T11)   :  FETCH  C
  -         (T12)   :  FETCH  D
  -         (T12)   :  FETCH  C
  -         (T2)    :  UPDATE  F
  -         (T11)   :  UPDATE  C
  -         (T12)   :  FETCH  A
  -         (T10)   :  UPDATE  A
  -         (T12)   :  UPDATE  D
  -         (T4)    :  FETCH  G
time  tn        . . . . . . . . .
```

Assume that (as explained in Section 18.5) "FETCH R" acquires an S lock on R, and "UPDATE R" promotes that lock to X level. Assume also that all locks are held until the next synchpoint. Are there any deadlocks at time *tn*?

REFERENCES AND BIBLIOGRAPHY

Most of the following references treat the material considerably more rigorously than we have done in the body of the chapter.

18.1 James Gray. "Notes on Data Base Operating Systems." In *Operating Systems: An Advanced Course* (eds., R. Bayer, R. M. Graham, and G. Seegmuller). New York: Springer-Verlag (1978). Also available as *IBM Research Report RJ 2188* (February 1978).

The best single source for material on transaction management. It covers just about everything in the other references below (not always in as much detail as those other references, of course), with only one significant exception, namely concurrency control techniques that are not based on locking [18.10,18.11]. Strongly recommended.

One very important idea, not mentioned in the body of this chapter, that is well described in this paper is the principle of *two-phase commit*. We explain this idea by means of an example. Consider a transaction that updates both an IMS database and a DB2 database (such a transaction is perfectly legal, by the way, as mentioned in Section 4.3). If the transaction completes successfully, then *all* of its updates, to both IMS data and DB2 data, must be committed; conversely, if it fails, then *all* of its updates must be rolled back (in other words, it must not be possible for the IMS updates to be committed and the DB2 updates rolled back, or conversely—for then the transaction would no longer be atomic).

It follows that it does not make sense for the transaction to issue, say, a COMMIT to IMS and a ROLLBACK to DB2; and even if it issued the same instruction to both, the system could still fail in between the two, with unfortunate results. Instead, therefore, the transaction issues a single *system-wide* COMMIT (or ROLLBACK). That COMMIT or ROLLBACK is handled by a system component called the *Coordinator*, whose task it is to guarantee that both "resource managers" (i.e., IMS and DB2, in the example) commit or roll back the updates they are responsible for *in unison*—and furthermore to provide that guarantee *even if the system fails in the middle of the process*. The two-phase commit protocol is the key to providing that guarantee, and this is the way it works. Assume for simplicity that the transaction completes successfully, so that the system-wide operation is COMMIT, not ROLLBACK. On receiving the COMMIT request, the Coordinator goes through the following two-phase process:

1. First, it requests all resource managers to get ready to "go either way" on the transaction. In practice, this means that each resource manager must physically write all log entries for local resources used by the transaction to its own local log. If the resource manager succeeds in doing this, it replies "OK" to the Coordinator, otherwise it replies "NOT OK."

2. When the Coordinator has received replies from all of the resource managers, it physically writes an entry to *its* log, recording its decision regarding the transaction. If all replies are "OK," that decision is "commit"; if any reply is "NOT OK," the decision is "rollback." Either way, the Coordinator then informs each resource manager of its decision, and *each resource manager must then commit or rollback the transaction locally, as instructed*. Note that each resource manager *must* do what it is told in Phase 2.

The switch from Phase 1 to Phase 2 is marked by the appearance of the decision record in the Coordinator's log.

Now, if the system fails at some point during the overall process, the restart procedure will look for the decision record in the Coordinator's log. If it finds it, then the two-phase commit process can pick up where it left off. If it does not find it, then it assumes that the decision was "rollback," and again the process can complete appropriately.

We remark that the data communications manager (DC manager) can be regarded as a resource manager in the foregoing sense. That is, messages can be regarded as a recoverable resource, just like database records. Gray has a lot to say in his paper regarding message recovery also, but the details are beyond the scope of this book.

One final snippet from the paper: Gray suggests that a typical (large) system generates about four log tapes each day, for a total of about 200 megabytes of log data per day. A typical (small) transaction produces about 500 bytes of log data.

18.2 Jim Gray. "The Transaction Concept: Virtues and Limitations." *Proc. 7th International Conference on Very Large Data Bases* (September 1981).

A concise statement of various transaction-related concepts and problems (including a variety of implementation issues). One particular problem addressed is the following: It follows from the definition that transactions cannot be nested inside one another, because each COMMIT or ROLLBACK terminates one transaction and starts another. Is there nevertheless some way of allowing transactions to be composed of smaller "sub-transactions"? The answer is a limited "yes"; in fact, some such facility is implemented in both Commercial INGRES [10.1] and System R [18.5] (although not in DB2). Such a concept seems a little closer to the notion of transactions as that term is usually understood in the real world.

18.3 Theo Haerder and Andreas Reuter. "Principles of Transaction-Oriented Database Recovery." *ACM Comp. Surv.* **15,** No. 4 (December 1983).

A very clear and careful presentation of the principles of recovery. The paper provides a consistent terminological framework for describing a wide variety of recovery schemes and logging techniques in a uniform way, and classifies and describes a number of existing systems in accordance with that framework.

The paper includes some interesting empirical figures regarding frequency of occurrence and typical (acceptable) recovery times for the three kinds of failure (local, system, media) in a typical large system:

Type of failure	Frequency of occurrence	Recovery time
Local	10-100 per minute	Same as transaction execution time
System	Several per week	Few minutes
Media	Once or twice per year	1-2 hours

18.4 R. A. Lorie. "Physical Integrity in a Large Segmented Database." *ACM TODS* **2,** No. 1 (March 1977).

18.5 Jim Gray et al. "The Recovery Manager of the System R Data Manager." *ACM Comp. Surv.* **13,** No. 2 (June 1981).

References [18.4] and [18.5] are both concerned with the recovery features of System R. Reference [18.5] provides an overview of the entire recovery subsystem; reference [18.4] describes a specific aspect, called the *shadow page* mechanism, in detail. The basic idea behind shadow pages is simple: When an (uncommitted) update is first written to the database, the system does not overwrite the existing page but stores a new page somewhere else on the disk. The old page is then the "shadow" for the new one. Committing the update involves updating the database directory to point to the new page and discarding the shadow; rolling back the update, on the other hand, involves reinstating the shadow page and discarding the new one.

Although conceptually simple, the shadow page scheme suffers from the serious drawback that it destroys any physical clustering that may previously have existed in the data. For this reason the scheme was not used in the DB2 product [18.6].

18.6 R. A. Crus. "Data Recovery in IBM Database 2." *IBM Sys. J.* **23,** No. 2 (1984).

Describes the DB2 recovery mechanism in detail (and in so doing provides yet another good description of recovery techniques in general). In particular, the paper explains how DB2 recovers from a system crash during the recovery process itself, while some transaction is in the middle of a rollback. This problem requires special care to ensure that uncommitted updates from the transaction being rolled back are in fact undone (the opposite of the lost update problem, in a sense).

18.7 K. P. Eswaran, J. N. Gray, R. A. Lorie, and I. L. Traiger. "The Notions of Consistency and Predicate Locks in a Data Base System." *CACM* **19,** No. 11 (November 1976).

This is the paper that put the subject of concurrency control on a sound theoretical footing. It begins by introducing the important notion of *serializability* (not however under that name). Serializability is proposed as the *criterion for correctness*. That is, the interleaved execution of a set of transactions is considered to be correct if and only if it is serializable—i.e., if and only if it produces the same result as some *serial* execution of the same transactions, running them one at a time. The argument goes as follows:

- First, individual transactions are assumed to be correct—i.e., they convert a consistent state of the database into another consistent state.

- Second, running the transactions one at a time in any serial order is therefore also correct—"any" serial order because individual transactions are assumed to be independent of one another.

- Third, an interleaved execution is therefore correct if and only if it is equivalent to some serial execution—i.e., if and only if it is serializable.

The paper then goes on to prove an important theorem, which we state briefly as follows: *If all transactions obey the "two-phase locking protocol," then all possible interleaved executions are serializable.* The two-phase locking protocol has two parts:

1. Before operating on any item, a transaction must acquire at least a shared lock on that item.

2. After releasing a lock, a transaction must never go on to acquire any more locks.

The transaction therefore has two phases, a lock acquisition phase and a lock releasing phase. (Note: In practice the second phase is usually compressed into the single operation of COMMIT at end-of-transaction.) The protocol is therefore known as the two-phase locking protocol (as already mentioned), and the theorem is called the *two-phase locking theorem.*

Two-phase locking is nothing to do with two-phase commit, incidentally—they just have similar names.

18.8 J. N. Gray, R. A. Lorie, and G. R. Putzolu. "Granularity of Locks in a Large Shared Data Base." *Proc. 1st International Conference on Very Large Data Bases* (September 1975).

The term "granularity" refers to the size of the objects that can be locked. For example, it may be possible to lock entire tables (coarse granularity) as well as individual records (fine granularity). Locking an entire table will dispense with the need for record-level locks for the table in question (loosely speaking). The advantage of a coarse granularity is that there are fewer locks, and hence less overhead in testing, setting, and maintaining those locks. The disadvantage, of course, is that there will be less concurrency. Since different transactions obviously have different characteristics and different requirements, it is desirable that the system provide a range of different locking granularities (as indeed many systems do). This paper presents an implementation mechanism for such a multiple-granularity system, using a protocol based on *intent locking*.

18.9 J. N. Gray, R. A. Lorie, G. R. Putzolu, and I. L. Traiger. "Granularity of Locks and Degrees of Consistency in a Shared Data Base." In *Proc. IFIP TC-2 Working Conference on Modelling in Data Base Management Systems* (ed., G. M. Nijssen). North-Holland (1976).

The paper that first described the concept of *isolation level* (under the name "degrees of consistency"). It also proposes an implementation approach based on the *intent locking protocol* introduced in reference [18.8]. The isolation level of a given transaction has to do with the amount of interference that transaction is prepared to tolerate from other (concurrent) transactions. Generally speaking, the higher the isolation level, the less the interference (and the lower the concurrency); the lower the isolation level, the more the interference (and the higher the concurrency). DB2, for example, supports two levels, called "cursor stability" (CS) and "repeatable read" (RR). Under CS, if a transaction T1

a) obtains addressability to some record *R* by setting a cursor to point to it, and thus

b) acquires an S lock on *R*, and then

c) relinquishes its addressability to *R* without updating it, and so

d) does not promote its S lock to X level, then

e) that S lock can be released without having to wait for the next synchpoint. But note that now

f) some other transaction T2 can update *R* and commit the change. If transaction T1 now comes back and looks at *R* again, it will see the change. T1 therefore may not see a consistent state of the database.

Under RR, record-level S locks are held until the next synchpoint, like X locks. The problem sketched above therefore cannot occur. Note: That problem is *not* the only problem that can occur under CS—it just happens to be the easiest one to explain. The example suggests that RR is needed only in the comparatively unlikely case that a given transaction needs to look at the same record twice. On the contrary, there are arguments to suggest that RR is *always* a better choice than CS (see reference [18.1]). Note that a transaction running under CS is in fact violating the two-phase locking protocol [18.7]. The fact is, given a transaction operating under CS, it is *always* theoretically possible to define a second transaction that could execute interleaved with the first in such a way as to cause the first to produce an incorrect result. The counterargument, of course, is that CS gives more concurrency than RR (probably but not necessarily).

18.10 H. T. Kung and J. T. Robinson. "On Optimistic Methods for Concurrency Control." *ACM TODS* **6,** No. 2 (June 1981).

18.11 P. A. Bernstein and N. Goodman. "Timestamp-Based Algorithms for Concurrency Control in Distributed Database Systems." *Proc. 6th International Conference on Very Large Data Bases* (October 1980).

These two papers [18.10,18.11] describe some approaches to concurrency control that are not based on locking.

- The so-called *optimistic* methods [18.10] are based on the assumption that conflict (in the sense of two transactions requesting simultaneous access to the same object) is likely to be quite rare in practice. The methods operate by allowing transactions to run to completion completely unhindered, and then checking at COMMIT time to see whether a conflict did in fact occur. If it did, the offending transaction is simply started again from the beginning. No updates are ever written to the database prior to successful completion of COMMIT processing, so such restarts do not require any updates to be undone.

- The timestamping methods are based on the idea that, if transaction *A* starts execution before transaction *B*, then the system should behave as if *A* actually executed in its entirety before *B* started (as in a genuine serial execution). Thus *A* should never be allowed to see any of *B*'s updates; likewise, *A* should never be allowed to update anything that *B* has already seen. Such controls can be enforced as follows. For any given database request, the system compares the timestamp of the requesting transaction with the timestamp of the transaction that last retrieved or updated the requested record. If there is a conflict, then the requesting transaction can simply be restarted (with a new timestamp), as in the optimistic methods.

As the title of reference [18.11] suggests, timestamping was originally introduced in the context of a distributed system (where it was felt that locking imposed intolerable overheads, because of the messages needed to test and set locks, etc.). It is almost certainly not appropriate in a nondistributed system. Indeed, there is considerable skepticism as to its practicality in distributed systems also. Optimistic methods, by contrast, are definitely applicable to nondistributed systems; in fact, they have already been implemented in a number of commercial products, including in particular the "Fast Path" version of IMS [22.1].

ANSWERS TO SELECTED EXERCISES

18.1

a) There are six possible correct results, corresponding to the six possible serializations of the three transactions:

```
Initially  :  A = 0
T1-T2-T3   :  A = 1
T1-T3-T2   :  A = 2
T2-T1-T3   :  A = 1
T2-T3-T1   :  A = 2
T3-T1-T2   :  A = 4
T3-T2-T1   :  A = 3
```

Of course, the six possible correct results are not all distinct. As a matter of fact, it so happens in this particular example that the possible correct results are independent of the initial state of the database, owing to the nature of transaction T3.

b) There are 90 possible distinct interleaved executions. We may represent the possibilities as follows. (Fi, Fj, Fk stand for the three FETCH operations F1, F2, F3, not necessarily in that order; similarly, Up, Uq, Ur stand for the three UPDATE operations U1, U2, U3, again not necessarily in that order.)

```
Fi-Fj-Fk-Up-Uq-Ur : 3 * 2 * 1 * 3 * 2 * 1 = 36 possibilities
Fi-Fj-Up-Fk-Uq-Ur : 3 * 2 * 2 * 1 * 2 * 1 = 24 possibilities
Fi-Fj-Up-Uq-Fk-Ur : 3 * 2 * 2 * 1 * 1 * 1 = 12 possibilities
Fi-Up-Fj-Fk-Uq-Ur : 3 * 1 * 2 * 1 * 2 * 1 = 12 possibilities
Fi-Up-Fj-Uq-Fk-Ur : 3 * 1 * 2 * 1 * 1 * 1 =  6 possibilities
                                    TOTAL = 90 combinations
```

c) Yes. For example, the interleaved execution F1-F2-F3-U3-U2-U1 produces the same result (one) as two of the six possible serializations of T1, T2, T3 (exercise: check this statement), and thus happens to be "correct" for the given initial value of zero. But it must be clearly understood that this "correctness" is a mere fluke, and results purely from the fact that the initial data value happened to be zero and not something else. As a counterexample, consider what would happen if the initial value of A were ten instead of zero. Would the result of the interleaved execution shown above still be the same as one of the genuinely correct results? (What *are* the genuinely correct results in this case?) If not, then the execution F1-F2-F3-U3-U2-U1 is not serializable.

d) Yes. For example, the interleaved execution F1-F3-U1-U3-F2-U2 is serializable (it is equivalent to the serialization T1-T3-T2), but it cannot be produced if T1, T2, and T3 all obey the two-phase locking protocol. For, under that protocol, operation F3 will acquire an S lock on A on behalf of transaction T3; operation U1 in transaction T1 will thus not be able to proceed until that lock has been released, and that will not happen until transaction T3 terminates (in fact, transactions T3 and T1 will deadlock when operation U3 is reached).

This exercise illustrates very clearly the following important point. Given a set of transactions and an initial state of the database: 1) Let ALL be the set of all possible interleaved executions of those transactions; 2) let "CORRECT" be the set of all interleaved executions of those transactions that are guaranteed to produce a correct final state or at least happen to do so from the given initial state; 3) let SERIALIZABLE be the set of all serializable executions of those transactions; and 4) let PRODUCIBLE be the set of all executions producible under the two-phase locking protocol. Then, in general,

```
PRODUCIBLE < SERIALIZABLE < "CORRECT" < ALL
```

(where "A < B" means "A is a subset of B").

18.2 At time *tn* no transactions are doing any useful work at all! There is one deadlock, involving transactions T2, T3, T9, and T8; in addition, T4 is waiting for T9, T12 is waiting for T4, and T10 and T11 are both waiting for T12. We can represent the situation by means of a graph (the *Wait-For Graph*), in which the nodes represent transactions and a directed edge from node T*i* to node T*j* indicates that T*i* is waiting for T*j*. Edges are labeled with the name of the database item and level of lock they are waiting for.

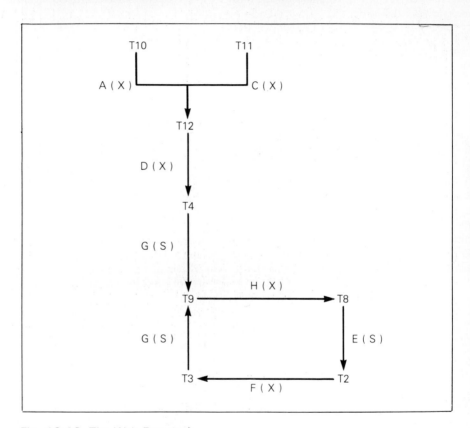

Fig. 18.12 The Wait-For graph.

19

Security
and Integrity

19.1 INTRODUCTION

The terms "security" and "integrity" are very frequently heard together in database contexts, though the two concepts are actually quite distinct. *Security* refers to the protection of data against unauthorized disclosure, alteration, or destruction; *integrity* refers to the accuracy or validity of data. In other words:

- Security involves ensuring that users are *allowed* to do the things they are trying to do.

- Integrity involves ensuring that the things they are trying to do are *correct*.

There are some similarities too, of course: In both cases, the system needs to be aware of certain *constraints* that users must not violate; in both cases those constraints must be specified (typically by the DBA) in some suitable language, and must be maintained in the system catalog or dictionary; and in both cases the DBMS must monitor user interactions in some way to ensure that the constraints are in fact observed. In this chapter we examine such ideas in some detail. Sections 19.2–19.4 are concerned with security and Sections 19.5–19.6 with integrity.

The sections on security (19.2–19.4) are based for the most part (where it makes any difference) on SQL specifically, but a brief explanation of the INGRES approach (which does differ somewhat from that of SQL) is given in Section 19.7. The sections on integrity (19.5–19.6) are *not* based on SQL, nor on any other implemented database language, since no system, SQL-based or otherwise, currently provides very much in the way of integrity support.[1] Instead, those sections are

---

1. The DEC system Rdb/VMS, which became generally available after this chapter was originally written, does provide a set of integrity control facilities rather similar to—though not as extensive as—the hypothetical facilities we describe in Section 19.6.

based on a hypothetical language derived from the tuple relational calculus of Chapter 14. However, INGRES does provide a little more integrity support than most systems, and for that reason a brief discussion of the INGRES approach is again included in Section 19.7.

19.2   SECURITY: GENERAL CONSIDERATIONS

There are numerous aspects to the security problem, among them the following:

- Legal, social, and ethical aspects (for example, does the person making the request, say for a customer's credit, have a legal right to the requested information?);

- Physical controls (for example, should the computer or terminal room be locked or otherwise guarded?);

- Policy questions (for example, how does the company decide who should be allowed access to what?);

- Operational problems (for example, if a password scheme is used, how are the passwords themselves kept secret?);

- Hardware controls (for example, does the CPU provide any security features, such as storage protection keys or a privileged operation mode?);

- Operating system security (for example, does the underlying operating system erase the contents of storage and data files when they are finished with?);

and finally

- Issues that are the specific concern of the database system itself. For obvious reasons, we limit ourselves for the most part to consideration of issues in this last category only.

The unit of data for security purposes—that is, the "data object" that may need to be individually protected—can range all the way from an entire collection of tables on the one hand, to a specific data value at a specific row-and-column position within a specific table on the other. A given user will typically have different access rights or *authorities* on different objects (e.g., SELECT authority only on one table, SELECT and UPDATE authority on another, and so on). Also, of course, different users may have different rights on the same object; e.g., user *A* could have SELECT authority (only) on some given table, while another user *B* could simultaneously have both SELECT and UPDATE authority on that same table.

In the case of SQL specifically, there are two more or less independent features of the system that are involved in the provision of security: 1) the view mechanism, which (as mentioned at the end of Chapter 8) can be used to hide sensitive data from unauthorized users, and 2) the authorization subsystem, which allows users having specific rights selectively and dynamically to grant those rights to other users, and subsequently to revoke those rights, if desired. Both features are discussed in Section 19.3.

Of course, all decisions as to which rights should be granted to which users are policy decisions, not technical ones. As such, they are clearly outside the jurisdiction of the DBMS per se; all that the DBMS can do is enforce those decisions once they are made. In order that the DBMS should be able to perform this function properly:

1. The results of those decisions must be made known to the system (this is done in SQL by means of the GRANT and REVOKE statements), and must be remembered by the system (this is done by saving them in the catalog, in the form of *authorization constraints*).

2. There must be a means of checking a given access request against the applicable authorization constraints. (By "access request" here we mean the combination of requested operation plus requested object plus requesting user.) In DB2 specifically, that checking is done by the Bind component at the time the request is compiled; in an interpretive system, of course, it must be done at the time the request is executed.

3. In order that it may be able to decide which constraints are applicable to a given request, the system must be able to recognize the source of that request—that is, it must be able to recognize which particular user a particular request is coming from. For that reason, when users sign on to the system, they are typically required to supply, not only their user ID (to say who they are), but also a *password* (to prove they are who they say they are). The password is supposedly known only to the system and to legitimate users of the user ID concerned.

19.3 SECURITY IN SQL

Views and Security

To illustrate the use of views for security purposes, we present a series of examples.

1. For a user permitted access to supplier records, but only for suppliers located in Paris:

```
CREATE VIEW PARIS_SUPPLIERS
     AS SELECT S#, SNAME, STATUS, CITY
        FROM   S
        WHERE  CITY = 'Paris' ;
```

Users of this view see a "horizontal subset"—or (better) a row subset or *value-dependent* subset—of the base table S.

2. For a user permitted access to all supplier records, but not to supplier ratings (i.e., STATUS values):

```
CREATE VIEW S#_NAME_CITY
     AS SELECT S#, SNAME, CITY
        FROM   S ;
```

Users of this view see a "vertical subset"—or (better) a column subset or *value-independent* subset—of the base table S.

3. For a user permitted access to supplier records for suppliers in Paris (only), but not to supplier ratings:

```
CREATE VIEW PARIS_S#_NAME_CITY
    AS SELECT S#, SNAME, CITY
       FROM   S
       WHERE  CITY = 'Paris' ;
```

Users of this view see a row-and-column subset of the base table S.

4. For a user permitted access to catalog entries (i.e., SYSTABLES entries) for tables created by that user only:

```
CREATE VIEW MY_TABLES
    AS SELECT *
       FROM    SYSTABLES
       WHERE   CREATOR = USER ;
```

USER is a special SQL keyword that refers to a system variable whose value (in the example) is the user ID for the user who uses the view. For example, if user Janice issues the statement

```
SELECT *
FROM    MY_TABLES ;
```

then the system will effectively convert that statement into

```
SELECT *
FROM    SYSTABLES
WHERE   CREATOR = 'Janice' ;
```

Like the view in the first example above, this view represents a "horizontal subset" of the underlying base table. In the present case, however, different users here see different subsets (in this particular example, in fact, no two users' subsets overlap). Such subsets are sometimes described as *context-dependent*.

5. For a user permitted access to average shipment quantities per supplier, but not to any individual quantities:

```
CREATE VIEW AVQ ( S#, AVGQTY )
    AS SELECT S#, AVG (QTY)
       FROM    SP
       GROUP   BY S# ;
```

Users of this view see a *statistical summary* of the underlying base table SP.

As the examples illustrate, the view mechanism of SQL provides an important measure of security "for free" ("for free" because the view mechanism is included in the system for other purposes anyway, as explained in Chapter 8). What is more, many authorization checks—even value-dependent checks—can be applied at compile time (bind time) instead of at execution time, a significant performance benefit. However, the view-based approach to security does suffer from some slight awkwardness on occasion—in particular, if some particular user needs different rights over different subsets of the same table at the same time.

GRANT and REVOKE

The view mechanism allows the database to be conceptually divided up into pieces in various ways so that sensitive information can be hidden from unauthorized users. However, it does not allow for the specification of the operations that *authorized* users may execute against those pieces. That function is performed by the SQL statements GRANT and REVOKE, which we now discuss. Note: The GRANT and REVOKE statements represent the principal user interface to what is usually called the *authorization subsystem*.

First, in order to be able to perform any operation at all in SQL, the user must hold the appropriate *authority* for that operation; otherwise, the operation will be rejected with an appropriate error message or exception code. For example, to execute the statement

```
SELECT *
FROM    S ;
```

successfully, the user must hold SELECT authority on table S.

Different systems will typically recognize a wide range of different authorities, many of which will however be very specific to the system in question. In DB2, for example, there are authorities relating to specific system utilities, specific database buffers, specific operator commands, and so forth. In this section we restrict our attention to just those authorities that can be taken as typical of the ones supported by database systems in general. Most of those typical authorities, not unnaturally, have to do with access to data (base tables and views, in the case of a relational system). Before describing those data access authorities, however, we first explain how the entire authorization subsystem is initialized, using the DB2 procedure as a typical example of that initialization process.

When DB2 is first installed, part of the installation procedure involves the designation of one specially privileged user as the *system administrator* for that installed system. ("System administrator" is the DB2 term for what elsewhere in this book we refer to as the DBA. The system administrator is identified to DB2 by a user ID, of course, just like everyone else.) That privileged user is automatically given a special authority called SYSADM. SYSADM authority means that the holder can perform every operation that the system supports. Initially, therefore, there is one user who can do everything—in particular, he or she can grant rights to other users—and nobody else can do anything at all.

Now suppose that the system administrator grants the right to create some object—say a view or a base table—to some other user U, and suppose that U in fact goes on to create such an object. User U will then automatically be given full rights on that object, including in particular the right to grant such rights to another user.

Of course, "full rights" here does not include rights that do not make sense. For example, if user *U* has SELECT authority (only) on base table *T*, and if *U* creates some view *V* that is based on *T*, then *U* certainly does not receive UPDATE authority on *V*.

Granting rights is done by means of the GRANT statement. Here are some examples:

```
GRANT SELECT ON TABLE S TO CHARLEY ;

GRANT SELECT, UPDATE ( STATUS, CITY ) ON TABLE S
                                 TO JUDY, JACK, JOHN ;

GRANT ALL ON TABLE S, P, SP TO WALT, TED ;

GRANT SELECT ON TABLE P TO PUBLIC ;

GRANT INDEX ON TABLE S TO PHIL ;
```

PUBLIC is a special keyword, standing for "all users of the system" (see the fourth GRANT above). In general, the rights that apply to tables (both base tables and views) are as follows:

```
SELECT
UPDATE    (can be column-specific)
DELETE
INSERT
```

The remaining two apply to base tables only:

```
ALTER    (right to execute ALTER TABLE on the table)
INDEX    (right to execute CREATE INDEX on the table)
```

If user *U1* grants some authority to some other user *U2*, user *U1* can subsequently *revoke* that authority from user *U2*. Revoking authority is done by means of the REVOKE statement. Here are some examples:

```
REVOKE SELECT ON TABLE S FROM CHARLEY ;

REVOKE UPDATE ON TABLE S FROM JOHN ;

REVOKE INSERT, DELETE ON TABLE SP FROM NANCY, JACK ;

REVOKE ALL ON TABLE S, P, SP FROM SAM ;
```

In DB2, revoking a given authority from a given user causes all application plans bound by that user and dependent on that authority to be flagged as "invalid," and hence causes an automatic rebind on the next invocation of each such plan. (The process is essentially analogous to what happens when an object such as an index is dropped. In fact, REVOKE can logically be regarded as a special form of DROP—"drop authorization"; likewise, GRANT can be regarded as the corresponding "create authorization." Note however that there is no "alter authorization''; but of course authorizations can be queried, because they are kept in the system catalog.)

There is one final topic to mention in this section, namely *the GRANT option*. If user *U1* has the right to grant some authority *A* to another user *U2*, then (by definition) user *U1* also has the right to grant that authority *A* to user *U2* "with the GRANT option" (by specifying WITH GRANT OPTION in the GRANT statement). Passing the GRANT option along from *U1* to *U2* in this way means that *U2* in turn now has the right to grant that authority *A* to some third user *U3*. And therefore, of course, *U2* also has the right to pass the GRANT option along to *U3* as well, etc., etc. For example:

User *U1*:

```
GRANT SELECT ON TABLE S TO U2 WITH GRANT OPTION ;
```

User *U2*:

```
GRANT SELECT ON TABLE S TO U3 WITH GRANT OPTION ;
```

User *U3*:

```
GRANT SELECT ON TABLE S TO U4 WITH GRANT OPTION ;
```

And so on. If user *U1* now issues

```
REVOKE SELECT ON TABLE S FROM U2 ;
```

then the revocation will *cascade* (that is, *U2*'s GRANT to *U3* and *U3*'s GRANT to *U4* will also be revoked automatically). For further details of this process, see references [19.4,19.5].

19.4   OTHER ASPECTS OF SECURITY

Views and the GRANT/REVOKE mechanism are by no means all there is to database security. In this section we briefly sketch a number of other relevant considerations. Note: Most of the following ideas are amplified in Volume II. See also the references at the end of the chapter.

1. There is no point in the DBMS providing an extensive set of security controls if it is possible to bypass those controls. For instance, DB2's security mechanism would be almost useless if (for example) it were possible to access DB2 data from a conventional MVS program via conventional VSAM calls (remember from Chapter 4 that DB2 databases are built on top of VSAM files). For this reason, DB2 works in harmony with its various companion systems—MVS and VSAM, in particular—to guarantee that the *total* system is secure. The details are beyond the scope of this chapter.

2. It is important not to assume that the security system is perfect. A would-be infiltrator who is sufficiently determined will usually find a way of breaking through the controls, especially if the payoff for doing so is high. In situations where the

data is sufficiently sensitive, therefore, or where the processing performed on the data is sufficiently critical, an *audit trail* becomes a necessity. If, for example, data discrepancies lead to a suspicion that the data has been tampered with, the audit trail can be used to examine what has been going on and to verify that matters are under control (or, if they are not, to help pinpoint the wrongdoer).

An audit trail can be thought of as a special file or database in which the system automatically keeps track of all operations performed by users on the regular database.[2] A typical entry in the audit trail might contain the following information:

operation (e.g., UPDATE)
terminal from which the operation was invoked
user who invoked the operation
date and time of the operation
database, table, record, and field affected
old value of the field
new value of the field

In some cases, the very fact that an audit trail is being maintained may be sufficient in itself to deter a would-be infiltrator.

3. Another level of security can be provided by *data encryption*. The basic idea here is that data can be physically stored on the disk (and transmitted along the communication lines) in a scrambled or encrypted form, so that anyone who tries to access it other than through the official channels will see just an unintelligible jumble of bits. Ideally, the effort involved on the part of a snooper in decrypting such a jumble should far outweigh the advantage to be gained in doing so. See references [19.2–19.3] and [19.7–19.10].

4. Finally, in DB2 at any rate, the entire security mechanism is optional. It can be disabled if desired at system installation time. If it is, then anyone can do anything (anything that makes sense, that is; for example, no user would ever be allowed to drop a catalog table).

19.5   INTEGRITY: GENERAL CONSIDERATIONS

As explained in Section 19.1, the term "integrity" refers to the accuracy or correctness of the data in the database. Systems today are typically rather weak on integrity—most integrity checking today is still done by user-written procedural code.[3] It would obviously be preferable to be able to specify integrity constraints

---

2. In some systems, the audit trail is integrated with the recovery log; in others the two are distinct.

3. Many systems that claim to provide data integrity are actually using the term to mean *concurrency control* instead. As explained in Chapter 18, it is possible in a shared system for two concurrently executing transactions, each one correct in itself, to interfere with one another in such a manner as to produce an overall result that is incorrect. Systems that provide

in some more declarative fashion and thereby have the system do the checking instead. Indeed, it has been suggested that the specification of integrity constraints could account for as much as 80 percent of a typical database definition (i.e., conceptual schema); thus a system that supported such specifications would relieve application programmers of a significant burden. At the same time, it would also enable those programmers to become considerably more productive. Integrity support is an important area for development.

An integrity constraint can be regarded as a *predicate* that all correct states of the database are required to satisfy. A simple example of such a predicate might be

```
S.STATUS > 0
```

("status values must be positive"). If the user attempts to execute an operation that would violate the constraint, the system must then either reject the operation or possibly (in more complicated situations) perform some compensating action on some other part of the database to ensure that the overall result is still a correct state. (An example of this latter case is provided by the "cascading" form of the foreign key delete rule. See Chapter 12.) Thus, any language for specifying integrity constraints should include, not only the ability to specify arbitrary predicates, but also facilities for specifying such compensating actions when appropriate. In the next section we will show by example what such a language might look like.

Several specific examples of integrity constraints have in fact been discussed in this book already:

- *Domain constraints*, which are implied by the fact that a particular attribute (or field) is defined on a particular domain. A domain constraint simply states that values of the attribute in question are required to belong to the set of values constituting the underlying domain. Such a constraint can be regarded as an extended form of the familiar constraint in programming languages to the effect that values of a given variable are required to be of a given data type.

- *Primary and foreign key constraints* (discussed in detail in Chapters 12 and 15).

- *Functional, multivalued, and join dependencies* (discussed in Chapter 17). Note that the term "dependency" can be regarded as simply another name for "constraint"; for example, the FD S.S# → S.CITY is equivalent to the following constraint (i.e., predicate):

```
FORALL SX FORALL SY ( IF SX.S# = SY.S#
                      THEN SX.CITY = SY.CITY )
```

(where SX and SY are tuple variables that range over relation S).

We briefly mention also a couple more special cases that some current systems do in fact support—namely, format constraints and range constraints. Each is really

---

"integrity" in this sense typically guarantee merely that such interference cannot occur; they do not concern themselves with the question as to whether individual transactions are correct in themselves.

a limited form of domain constraint (remember that most systems do not provide general domain support). A *format* constraint might specify (for example) that values of the field SS# (social security number) are required to conform to the format

999-99-9999

(where each 9 stands for an arbitrary decimal digit and the hyphens stand for themselves). A *range* constraint might specify (for example) that values of the field SALARY are required to lie in the range 10,000–100,000 dollars.

19.6 A HYPOTHETICAL INTEGRITY LANGUAGE

Our hypothetical integrity language consists of two statements, CREATE CONSTRAINT and DROP CONSTRAINT. We do not give detailed definitions of those statements here—indeed, further definitional work would be needed before they could seriously be considered as a candidate for implementation—but content ourselves rather with a moderately extensive set of examples to show the kind of features that such statements would need to provide. As usual, we use SX, . . ., PX, . . ., SPX, . . ., to represent tuple variables ranging over S, P, SP, respectively, and (also as usual) we use S, P, SP as default range variables where there is no ambiguity in so doing.

1. Status values must be positive:

```
CREATE CONSTRAINT C1
        CHECK S.STATUS > 0
        ELSE reject operation ;
```

In general, the CREATE CONSTRAINT statement must specify:

- The name of the constraint ("C1" in the example);
- The constraint itself (CHECK clause);
- The *violation response*, indicating what to do if the check fails (ELSE clause). If the ELSE clause is omitted, the specification "reject operation (with a suitable return code)" will be assumed in what follows.

Additional clauses are also required in some situations (see Examples 3 and 5–7 below).

When the CREATE CONSTRAINT is executed, the system checks to see whether the current state of the database satisfies the specified constraint. If it does not, the CREATE CONSTRAINT is rejected; otherwise it is accepted (i.e., saved in the catalog) and enforced from that time on. Enforcement in the example at hand requires the DBMS to monitor all INSERT operations on table S and all UPDATE operations on field S.STATUS.

An example of DROP CONSTRAINT:

```
DROP CONSTRAINT C1 ;
```

2. An example to illustrate the point that constraints can be arbitrarily complex. Assume that relation SP includes an additional set of attributes MONTH, DAY, YEAR (each CHAR(2)), representing the date of the shipment in question:

```
CREATE CONSTRAINT C2
       CHECK IS_INTEGER (SP.YEAR)
       AND   IS_INTEGER (SP.MONTH)
       AND   IS_INTEGER (SP.DAY)
       AND   NUM (SP.YEAR) BETWEEN 0 AND 99
       AND   NUM (SP.MONTH) BETWEEN 1 AND 12
       AND   NUM (SP.DAY) > 0
       AND   IF NUM (SP.MONTH) IN (1,3,5,7,8,10,12)
             THEN NUM (SP.DAY) < 32
       AND   IF NUM (SP.MONTH) IN (4,6,9,11)
             THEN NUM (SP.DAY) < 31
       AND   IF NUM (SP.MONTH) = 2
             THEN NUM (SP.DAY) < 30
       AND   IF NUM (SP.MONTH) = 2 AND NUM (SP.YEAR) ~= 0 AND
                MOD ( NUM (SP.YEAR), 4 ) = 0
             THEN NUM (SP.DAY) < 29 ;
```

We have assumed the existence of two built-in functions: IS_INTEGER, which tests a character string to see if it represents a legal decimal integer value, and NUM, which converts a character string that represents a decimal value to internal numeric form. Of course, the foregoing constraint would be much better specified at the domain level (since it applies to all dates, not just shipment dates), but we are not assuming here that the system supports domains.

3. Status values must never decrease:

```
CREATE CONSTRAINT C3
       BEFORE UPDATE OF S.STATUS FROM NEW_STATUS
       CHECK  NEW_STATUS > S.STATUS ;
```

Constraint C3 applies, not to any particular state of the database, but rather to the *transition* between two states. Note that this constraint requires an explicit *trigger condition* (BEFORE clause) to specify when the checking is to be done; the trigger condition was left implicit in the first two examples above. Variable NEW_STATUS is a parameter.

4. The average status value must be greater than 25:

```
CREATE CONSTRAINT C4
       CHECK IF EXISTS S () THEN AVG ( S.STATUS ) > 25 ;
```

Constraint C4 involves, not just a single record as in constraints C1–C3, but rather the entire set of records in table S. The condition "IF EXISTS S ()" is required because if table S is empty the average is not well-defined. (In SQL specifically it is defined to be *null*, and null is not greater than 25.)

5. Every London supplier must supply part P2:

```
CREATE CONSTRAINT C5
       AT      COMMIT
       CHECK FORALL S ( IF S.CITY = 'London' THEN
                        EXISTS SP ( SP.S# = S.S# AND SP.P# = 'P2' ) )
       ELSE  ROLLBACK ;
```

In this example both the trigger condition—AT COMMIT—and the violation response—ROLLBACK—must be specified explicitly. The constraint has to be checked at COMMIT time, because otherwise it would never be possible to INSERT a new S record for a supplier in London, since there could not possibly exist an SP record at the time of the INSERT saying that the new supplier already supplies part P2.[4] However, the constraint implies that any transaction that does INSERT such a new London supplier must then go on to create at least one shipment connecting that supplier to part P2; for if it does not, then the database will not satisfy the constraint at COMMIT time, and the transaction will be rolled back, by virtue of the violation response (ELSE clause).

It follows from this example that, although a correct transaction transforms a correct state of the database into another correct state, it may temporarily generate an incorrect state on the way. (Of course, no other transaction will actually see such an incorrect state, if the locking protocol described in Chapter 18 is followed.) Note, therefore, that a transaction can be regarded, not only as a unit of work and a unit of recovery and a unit of concurrency, but also as a unit of *integrity*.

6. Field S# is the primary key for table S:

```
CREATE CONSTRAINT C6
       BEFORE INSERT OF S FROM NEW_S,
              UPDATE OF S.S# FROM NEW_S.S#
       CHECK  NEW_S.S# IS NOT NULL
              AND NOT EXISTS SX ( SX.S# = NEW_S.S# ) ;
```

This example shows that primary key constraints *can* be expressed in our general integrity language. However, the general formulation is intolerably clumsy; the special-case syntax introduced in Chapter 12—"PRIMARY KEY (S#)"—is clearly a much better alternative. Note too that it is better both for the user *and for the system*, because it allows the system to recognize the special case and thus implement it in a special-case way—obviously a good thing for a constraint that is so fundamental.[5] Analogous remarks apply, but with even more force, to foreign key constraints also (see the next example).

7. Field S# is a foreign key in table SP, matching the primary key of table S:

---

4.   Assuming, of course, that the referential constraint between tables SP and S is enforced.

5.   Indeed, it is more than just a "good thing." As explained earlier in this book, the system must have knowledge of primary keys—and also foreign keys, in some cases—in order to perform various other functions (such as view updating) properly. Thus, special-casing primary and foreign key constraints is not merely desirable—it is *essential* if those functions are to be supported other than in an ad hoc manner.

```
CREATE CONSTRAINT C7A
        AFTER INSERT OF SP, UPDATE OF SP.S#
        CHECK EXISTS S ( S.S# = SP.S# ) ;

CREATE CONSTRAINT C7B
        BEFORE DELETE OF S, UPDATE OF S.S#
        CHECK  NOT EXISTS SP ( SP.S# = S.S# ) ;
```

Constraint C7A says that it is illegal to insert an SP record or change the S# value in an SP record if no corresponding S record exists after the operation. Constraint C7B says that it is illegal to delete an S record or change the S# value in an S record if any corresponding SP record currently exists—i.e., it corresponds to the foreign key rules

```
DELETE OF S RESTRICTED
UPDATE OF S.S# RESTRICTED
```

(to use the syntax of Chapters 12 and 15). Suppose instead we wanted to represent the CASCADES versions of those rules:

```
DELETE OF S CASCADES
UPDATE OF S.S# CASCADES
```

These can be represented as follows:

```
CREATE CONSTRAINT C7C
        BEFORE DELETE OF S
        CHECK  NOT EXISTS SP ( SP.S# = S.S# )
        ELSE   DELETE SP WHERE SP.S# = S.S# ;

CREATE CONSTRAINT C7D
        BEFORE UPDATE OF S.S# FROM NEW_S.S#
        CHECK  NOT EXISTS SP ( SP.S# = S.S# )
        ELSE   UPDATE SP.S# FROM NEW_S.S#
               WHERE SP.S# = S.S# ;
```

These two constraints (C7C and C7D) illustrate the point very clearly that the CHECK . . . ELSE . . . portion of the CREATE CONSTRAINT statement really represents a *triggered procedure*. A triggered procedure is a procedure that is to be invoked when a specified trigger condition occurs. In the case at hand, the purpose of those triggered procedures is to carry out certain compensating actions (if necessary) to ensure that the database remains in a state of integrity after the complete set of operations has been performed. In previous examples the procedure was rather simpler, usually taking the form "if some predicate is not satisfied then reject the original operation"—but in general, of course, a triggered procedure could be arbitrarily complex.[6]

We remark in passing that the CHECK portion of constraints C7C and C7D is actually superfluous (since the effect of the ELSE portion is to make the predicate

---

6.   Triggered procedures are applicable to many other problems in addition to the problem of integrity under consideration here. See Volume II for further discussion.

true even if it is not true initially), and hence that the term "constraint" is not really very apt. We also repeat the point that the purpose of the example is only to show that foreign key constraints *can* be formulated in a general integrity language; we do not mean to suggest that in practice they should be. On the contrary, we strongly believe that some special-case syntax such as that of Chapters 12 and 15 should be used, for reasons that have already been adequately discussed.

So much for our examples. For interest, we conclude this section with a brief summary of the integrity features of SQL (as implemented in DB2). The following is an exhaustive list of those features:

- Data type checking: Fields are constrained to contain only values of the correct data type.

- NOT NULL: Can be specified for any field.

- UNIQUE: Uniqueness can be enforced for any field or field combination via a UNIQUE index.

- CHECK option: Can be specified for certain updatable views (see Chapter 8); if it is, it guarantees that records inserted or updated through the view will satisfy the view-defining predicate.[7]

- VALIDPROC: For any base table, a *validation procedure* can be specified. That procedure will be given control each time a record of the table is inserted or updated, and can therefore perform a variety of integrity checks (for example, range or format checks) on that record. However, (a) validation procedures are subject to numerous restrictions—for instance, they cannot issue any SQL operations—and (b) in any case, a validation procedure consists by definition of procedural code (very much so, since it must be written in Assembler Language), whereas the whole point of an integrity mechanism of the kind we have been describing is to allow integrity constraints to be specified declaratively.

19.7   SECURITY AND INTEGRITY IN INGRES

In this section we briefly describe the security and integrity aspects of INGRES, since INGRES employs an implementation approach that is rather different from that described so far in this chapter. First, security. Unlike SQL, INGRES does not

---

7. Actually the CHECK option is something of an anomaly in DB2. It is strange that such an option exists for views but not for base tables. Of course, the effect of a "base table CHECK option" can be achieved by defining a view that is identical to the base table in question. For example:

```
CREATE VIEW V AS SELECT *
                 FROM    S
                 WHERE   STATUS > 0
                 WITH    CHECK OPTION ;
```

If all updates intended for base table S are actually made through view V instead, then DB2 will in fact enforce the base table constraint "status values must be positive."

make use of views for security enforcement (although of course INGRES does support views for other purposes). Instead, any given user request is automatically modified before execution in such a way that it cannot possibly violate any authorization constraint. For example, suppose user U is allowed to see parts stored in London (only), and suppose user U issues the request:

```
RETRIEVE ( P.P#, P.WEIGHT )
WHERE       P.COLOR = "Red"
```

INGRES will automatically modify the query to the form:

```
RETRIEVE ( P.P#, P.WEIGHT )
WHERE       P.COLOR = "Red"
AND         P.CITY = "London"
```

And of course this modified query cannot possibly violate the security constraint. Note, incidentally, that the modification process is "silent"—user U is not informed that the system has in fact executed a query that is somewhat different from the original request. The argument is that that fact in itself might be sensitive (user U might not even be allowed to know that there are any parts not stored in London).

The process of *query modification* just outlined is actually identical to the technique used for the implementation of views (see Chapter 8). So one advantage of the INGRES scheme is that it is very easy to implement—most of the necessary code exists in the system already. Another advantage is that it is comparatively efficient —the security enforcement overhead occurs at query interpretation time rather than execution time. Yet another advantage is that some of the awkwardnesses that can occur with the SQL mechanism (when a given user needs different authorities over different portions of the same table) do not arise. However, one disadvantage is that not all security constraints can be handled in this simple fashion. As a trivial counterexample, suppose user U is not allowed to access table P at all. Then no simple "modified" form of the RETRIEVE shown above can be produced that can preserve the illusion that table P does not exist. Instead, an explicit error message— "You are not allowed to access this table"—must necessarily be generated.

Security constraints are expressed in INGRES by means of the DEFINE PERMIT statement—syntax as follows:

```
DEFINE PERMIT operation(s)
       ON      table [ ( field-commalist ) ]
       TO      user
   [ AT        terminal(s) ]
   [ FROM      time1 TO time2 ]
   [ ON        day1  TO day2 ]
   [ WHERE     predicate ]
```

Note that it is thus possible not only to limit a given user's access to a given table to some specific set of operations on some specific row-and-column subset of that table, but also to insist that all such access be made from some specific terminal(s) and/or at some specific time(s) on some specific day(s). Here is an example:

```
DEFINE PERMIT RETRIEVE, REPLACE
        ON     S ( SNAME, CITY )
        TO     Joe
        AT     TTA4
        FROM   9:00 TO 17:30
        ON     SAT TO SUN
        WHERE  S.STATUS < 50
        AND    S.S# = SP.P#
        AND    SP.P# = P.P#
        AND    P.COLOR = "Red"
```

Note that the "AT terminal", "FROM time TO time", and "ON day TO day" clauses allow context-sensitive constraints to be expressed. In addition, INGRES provides a system variable called USERNAME (analogous to USER in SQL) to allow constraints to be formulated that are sensitive to the user context also.

Security constraints are kept in the INGRES catalog under numeric identifiers (0, 1, 2, etc.). Those identifiers can be discovered by querying the catalog (a special HELP command is provided to assist in this process, though the conventional QUEL RETRIEVE statement can also be used). Thus, to delete the constraint defined above, it is first necessary to find out the applicable identifier. Suppose that identifier is 27. Then the statement

```
DESTROY PERMIT S 27
```

will remove the constraint from the system.

Turning now to integrity: The INGRES approach to integrity is very similar to its approach to security. Integrity constraints are defined by means of the DEFINE INTEGRITY statement—syntax as follows:

```
DEFINE INTEGRITY
        ON     table
        IS     predicate
```

For example:

```
DEFINE INTEGRITY
        ON     S
        IS     S.STATUS > 0
```

Suppose user U attempts the following REPLACE:

```
REPLACE S ( STATUS = S.STATUS - 10 )
WHERE   S.CITY = "London"
```

Then INGRES will automatically modify the statement to:

```
REPLACE S ( STATUS = S.STATUS - 10 )
WHERE   S.CITY = "London"
AND     ( S.STATUS - 10 ) > 0
```

And of course this modified operation cannot possibly violate the integrity constraint. (Note: As in the security case, the modification process is "silent.") The advantages and disadvantages of this scheme are very similar to those already sketched earlier in our discussion of the INGRES security mechanism. Note in particular that not all integrity constraints can be enforced in this simple way. As a matter of fact, INGRES supports only constraints that can be expressed by means of a pure restriction predicate. However, even that limited support represents (as stated in Section 19.1) more than is found in most current systems.

Like security constraints, integrity constraints are kept in the INGRES catalog under numeric identifiers (which can be discovered by means of the HELP INTEGRITY statement). Those identifiers are used in the DESTROY operation to remove a constraint from the system. For example:

```
DESTROY INTEGRITY S 18
```

We conclude this section by remarking that INGRES, like a number of other modern systems, does provide certain additional integrity support—in particular, it provides a limited form of referential integrity support—through some of its built-in applications (i.e., via certain frontend systems). See Chapter 20.

19.8 CONCLUDING REMARKS

In this chapter we have discussed the need for security and integrity in a database system. We can distinguish between the two concepts, somewhat glibly, as follows:

- Security means protecting the database against unauthorized users;
- Integrity means protecting it against authorized users.

Security and integrity both involve a) the definition of appropriate constraints, b) a specification of what to do if those constraints are violated, and c) system monitoring of user operations to detect any such violations. We have described a number of approaches to these problems. In the case of security, we have discussed:

- Use of the view mechanism (which has the advantage that many constraints can be checked at compile time);
- The GRANT and REVOKE statements of SQL;
- The INGRES technique of query modification.

In the case of integrity we have discussed:

- A hypothetical language for the expression of general integrity constraints;
- A variety of special cases (domain constraints, primary and foreign key constraints, functional, multivalued, and join dependencies, and format and range constraints);
- The query modification approach (again).

By way of conclusion, we stress the point once again that, whereas many systems are in fact quite strong on security, no system (at the time of writing) is really completely satisfactory in the area of integrity. It is to be hoped that this state of affairs will not persist for very much longer.

EXERCISES

19.1 Base table STATS is defined as follows:

```
CREATE TABLE STATS
       ( USERID       CHAR(8),
         SEX          CHAR(1),
         DEPENDENTS   DECIMAL(2),
         OCCUPATION   CHAR(20),
         SALARY       DECIMAL(7),
         TAX          DECIMAL(7),
         AUDITS       DECIMAL(2) ) ;
```

Write SQL statements to give:

a) User Ford SELECT authority over the entire table.

b) User Smith INSERT and DELETE authority over the entire table.

c) Each user SELECT authority over that user's own record (only).

d) User Nash SELECT authority over the entire table and UPDATE authority over the SALARY and TAX fields (only).

e) User Todd SELECT authority over the USERID, SALARY, and TAX fields (only).

f) User Ward SELECT authority as for Todd and UPDATE authority over the SALARY and TAX fields (only).

g) User Pope full authority (SELECT, UPDATE, INSERT, DELETE) over records for preachers (only).

h) User Jones SELECT authority as for Todd and UPDATE authority over the TAX and AUDITS fields (only).

i) User King SELECT authority for maximum and minimum salaries per occupation class, but no other authority.

19.2 Give INGRES versions of your answers to Exercise 19.1, parts a)–i), where possible or appropriate.

19.3 For each of parts a)–i) under Exercise 19.1, write SQL statements to remove the indicated authority from the user concerned.

19.4 Using the integrity language of Section 19.6, write CREATE CONSTRAINT statements for the following constraints on the suppliers-parts-projects database:

a) The only legal part colors are red, blue, and green.

b) All red parts weigh less than 50 pounds.

c) No two projects can be located in the same city.

d) At most one supplier can be located in Athens at any one time.

e) No shipment can have a quantity more than double the average of all such quantities.

f) The highest-status supplier must not be located in the same city as the lowest-status supplier.

g) Every project must be located in a city in which there is at least one supplier.

h) Every project must be located in a city in which there is at least one supplier of that project.

19.5 Again using the constraint language of Section 19.6, write a suitable set of primary and foreign key constraints for the suppliers-parts-projects database. For each constraint give also a formulation in terms of the special-case syntax of Chapter 12.

REFERENCES AND BIBLIOGRAPHY

For a more extensive overview of security and integrity in general, see Volume II or the book by Fernandez et al. [19.1]. For an overview (much more detailed) of security specifically, see the book by Denning [19.2]. The remaining references listed below are technical papers, either tutorials or research contributions, on various specific aspects of security and integrity.

We remark that certain of the nonrelational systems do support some forms of integrity—specifically referential integrity—by virtue of their data structure. (They do not support all possible referential constraints, but they do support some of the most important cases.) See Part 5 of this book.

19.1 E. B. Fernandez, R. C. Summers, and C. Wood. *Database Security and Integrity*. Reading, Mass.: Addison-Wesley (1981).

19.2 D. E. Denning. *Cryptography and Data Security*. Reading, Mass.: Addison-Wesley (1983).

19.3 D. E. Denning and P. J. Denning. "Data Security." *ACM Comp. Surv.* **11**, No. 3 (September 1979).

A tutorial, covering not only "access control" (essentially the principal topic of Sections 19.2–19.4 of the present chapter) but also data encryption (see references [19.7–19.10]), "flow controls" (methods for preventing data from flowing from one file of a high level of confidentiality to another of a lower level), and "inference controls" (the special problem of statistical databases: see Volume II).

19.4 P. P. Griffiths and B. W. Wade. "An Authorization Mechanism for a Relational Data Base System." *ACM TODS* **1**, No. 3 (September 1976).

Describes the GRANT and REVOKE mechanism originally proposed for System R. The scheme actually implemented in DB2 and SQL/DS is based on that mechanism, though significantly different in detail.

19.5 R. Fagin. "On an Authorization Mechanism." *ACM TODS* **3**, No. 3 (September 1978).

An extended corrigendum to [19.4]. Under certain circumstances the mechanism of [19.4] would revoke an authority that ought not to be revoked. This paper corrects that flaw.

19.6 M. R. Stonebraker and E. Wong. "Access Control in a Relational Data Base Management System by Query Modification." *Proc. ACM National Conference 1974*.

The paper that introduced the INGRES query modification mechanism. See also reference [19.12].

19.7 U.S. Department of Commerce / National Bureau of Standards. Data Encryption Standard. *Federal Information Processing Standards Publication 46* (1977 January 15).

Defines the official Data Encryption Standard (DES), to be used by federal agencies and anyone else who wishes to do so. The encryption/decryption algorithm is suitable for implementation on a chip, which means that devices that incorporate it can operate at a high data rate. A number of such devices are currently available.

19.8 W. Diffie and M. E. Hellman. "New Directions in Cryptography." *IEEE Transactions on Information Theory IT-22* (November 1976).

The paper that laid the theoretical groundwork for the new "public-key" encryption schemes. Ordinary encryption schemes such as the DES [19.7] require the encryption key to be kept secret. The public-key schemes use two different keys, one for encryption and one for decryption, and only the decryption key need be kept secret (and it is not possible to deduce the decryption key from the encryption key). In such schemes, therefore, anyone can generate encrypted messages, but no one—not even the message originator—is able to decrypt those messages except their intended recipient.

19.9 R. L. Rivest, A. Shamir, and L. Adleman. "A Method for Obtaining Digital Signatures and Public-Key Cryptosystems." *CACM* **21**, No. 2 (February 1978).

Describes the best-known of the public-key encryption schemes, the so-called prime number scheme.

19.10 A. Lempel. "Cryptology in Transition." *ACM Comp. Surv.* **11**, No. 4: Special Issue on Cryptology (December 1979).

A good tutorial on cryptography and cryptanalysis.

19.11 K. P. Eswaran and D. D. Chamberlin. "Functional Specifications of a Subsystem for Data Base Integrity." *Proc. 1st International Conference on Very Large Data Bases* (September 1975).

Describes a proposed set of integrity facilities for SQL: ASSERT and DROP ASSERTION statements (analogous to our CREATE CONSTRAINT and DROP CONSTRAINT statements, but without an ELSE clause); a DEFINE TRIGGER statement (analogous to our CREATE CONSTRAINT *with* an ELSE clause), and a corresponding DROP TRIGGER statement; and an ENFORCE INTEGRITY statement to force the evaluation of "AT COMMIT"-type constraints without actually causing a COMMIT. Note: The SQL term TRIGGER corresponds to our triggered *procedure*, not our trigger *condition*.

19.12 M. R. Stonebraker. "Implementation of Integrity Constraints and Views by Query Modification." *Proc. 1975 ACM SIGMOD International Conference on Management of Data* (May 1975).

19.13 M. M. Zloof. "Security and Integrity Within the Query-By-Example Data Base Management Language." *IBM Research Report RC 6982* (February 1978).

The original Query-By-Example language included facilities for specifying both security and integrity constraints in the usual QBE tabular style. For example (security):

```
S                    | SNAME | STATUS  |  CITY   |
---------------------|-------|---------|---------|
I.AUTH (U.)    Joe  |       | < 50    | ~Paris  |
```

User Joe can update supplier names, status values, and cities (but not supplier numbers), only where the status is less than 50 and the city is not Paris. And here is an integrity example:

```
S                    | S# | SNAME | STATUS  |  CITY   |
---------------------|----|-------|---------|---------|
I.CONSTR (I.,U.)    |    |       | > 0     |         |
```

Status values must be positive.

Note, however, that these facilities are not implemented in the version of QBE supported in the QMF product.

ANSWERS TO SELECTED EXERCISES

19.1

a) `GRANT SELECT ON TABLE STATS TO FORD ;`

b) `GRANT INSERT, DELETE ON TABLE STATS TO SMITH ;`

c)
```
CREATE VIEW MY_REC
    AS SELECT *
       FROM    STATS
       WHERE   USERID = USER ;

GRANT SELECT ON TABLE MY_REC TO PUBLIC ;
```

d)
```
GRANT SELECT, UPDATE ( SALARY, TAX )
    ON TABLE STATS TO NASH ;
```

e)
```
CREATE VIEW UST
    AS SELECT USERID, SALARY, TAX
       FROM    STATS ;

GRANT SELECT ON TABLE UST TO TODD ;
```

f)
```
CREATE VIEW UST
    AS SELECT USERID, SALARY, TAX
       FROM    STATS ;

GRANT SELECT, UPDATE ( SALARY, TAX )
    ON TABLE UST TO WARD ;
```

g)
```
CREATE VIEW PREACHERS
    AS SELECT *
       FROM    STATS
       WHERE   OCCUPATION = 'Preacher' ;

GRANT ALL ON TABLE PREACHERS TO POPE ;
```

ALL normally includes ALTER and INDEX, but these operations do not apply to views.

h)
```
CREATE VIEW UST
    AS SELECT USERID, SALARY, TAX
       FROM    STATS ;

CREATE VIEW UTA
    AS SELECT USERID, TAX, AUDITS
       FROM    STATS ;

GRANT SELECT ON TABLE UST TO JONES ;

GRANT UPDATE ( TAX, AUDITS ) ON TABLE UTA TO JONES ;
```

i)
```
CREATE VIEW SALBOUNDS ( OCCUPATION, MAXSAL, MINSAL )
    AS SELECT OCCUPATION, MAX (SALARY), MIN (SALARY)
       FROM    STATS
       GROUP   BY OCCUPATION ;

GRANT SELECT ON SALBOUNDS TO KING ;
```

19.2

a) DEFINE PERMIT RETRIEVE ON STATS TO FORD

b) DEFINE PERMIT APPEND, DELETE ON STATS TO SMITH

c) DEFINE PERMIT RETRIEVE ON STATS TO USERNAME
                    WHERE   STATS.USERID = USERNAME

d) DEFINE PERMIT RETRIEVE ON STATS TO NASH

   DEFINE PERMIT REPLACE ON STATS (SALARY, TAX) TO NASH

e) DEFINE PERMIT RETRIEVE ON STATS (USERID, SALARY, TAX)
                                             TO TODD

f) DEFINE PERMIT RETRIEVE ON STATS (USERID, SALARY, TAX)
                                             TO WARD

   DEFINE PERMIT REPLACE ON STATS (SALARY, TAX) TO WARD

g) DEFINE PERMIT ALL ON STATS TO POPE
             WHERE   STATS.OCCUPATION = "Preacher"

   ALL is shorthand for RETRIEVE, REPLACE, APPEND, DELETE.

h) DEFINE PERMIT RETRIEVE ON STATS (USERID, SALARY, TAX)
                                             TO JONES

   DEFINE PERMIT REPLACE ON STATS (TAX, AUDITS) TO JONES

i) Cannot be done.

19.3

a) REVOKE SELECT ON TABLE STATS FROM FORD ;

b) REVOKE INSERT, DELETE ON TABLE STATS FROM SMITH ;

c) REVOKE SELECT ON TABLE MY_REC FROM PUBLIC ;

   Or perhaps simply:

   DROP VIEW MY_REC ;

   For d) through i) below we generally ignore the possibility of simply dropping the view (if applicable).

d) REVOKE SELECT, UPDATE ON TABLE STATS FROM NASH ;

e) REVOKE SELECT ON TABLE UST FROM TODD ;

f) REVOKE SELECT, UPDATE ON TABLE UST FROM WARD ;

g) REVOKE ALL ON PREACHERS FROM POPE ;

h) REVOKE SELECT ON TABLE UST FROM JONES ;

   REVOKE UPDATE ON TABLE UTA FROM JONES ;

i) REVOKE SELECT ON TABLE SALBOUNDS FROM KING ;

19.4

a) CREATE CONSTRAINT CA
      CHECK P.COLOR = 'Red'
      OR   P.COLOR = 'Blue'
      OR   P.COLOR = 'Green' ;

b) CREATE CONSTRAINT CB
      CHECK IF P.COLOR = 'Red' THEN P.WEIGHT < 50 ;

c) CREATE CONSTRAINT CC
      BEFORE INSERT J FROM NEW_J,
            UPDATE J.CITY FROM NEW_J.CITY
      CHECK NOT EXISTS JX (JX.CITY = NEW_J.CITY) ;

d) CREATE CONSTRAINT CD
      BEFORE INSERT S FROM NEW_S,
            UPDATE S.CITY FROM NEW_S.CITY
      CHECK IF NEW_S.CITY = 'Athens' THEN
            NOT EXISTS SX (SX.CITY = 'Athens') ;

e) CREATE CONSTRAINT CE
      CHECK NOT EXISTS SPX (SPX.QTY >
                       2 * AVG (SPY.QTY)) ;

f) CREATE CONSTRAINT CF
      CHECK FORALL SX FORALL SY
          (IF SX.STATUS = MAX (SZ.STATUS) AND
            SY.STATUS = MIN (SZ.STATUS)
        THEN SX.CITY ~= SY.CITY) ;

g) CREATE CONSTRAINT CG
      CHECK FORALL J EXISTS S (S.CITY = J.CITY) ;

h) CREATE CONSTRAINT CH
      CHECK FORALL J EXISTS S EXISTS SPJ
                      (S.CITY = J.CITY AND
                      SPJ.S# = S.S# AND
                      SPJ.J# = J.J#) ;

20
The Database
Product Family

20.1 INTRODUCTION

We have stressed the point several times already in this book that the DBMS alone is not a "total solution" to the problems of the enterprise, nor was it ever intended to be. The problems we are referring to are, of course, problems of *information management*—i.e., problems of storing, accessing, manipulating, controlling, presenting, and otherwise using information. To repeat, the DBMS does not solve all of these problems; but it does provide a foundation for solving them, by providing an extensive repertoire of basic functions to support the various higher-level software components—report writers, business graphics systems, and the like—that do more directly address them. (Those higher-level components are sometimes described as *decision support* tools, because their primary purpose is to make information available on demand and thereby to assist in the overall decision-making process.)

We see, therefore, that the DBMS should be regarded, not as an end in itself, but rather as the cornerstone of a family of interrelated systems. In this chapter we take a brief look at some of the components of that family. Our discussions are necessarily very superficial, for reasons of space; our primary purpose is simply to explain what the components are, rather than to describe in great detail how they work (indeed, such a description could easily fill another book).

The components in question are mostly what we have been calling *built-in applications* in earlier parts of this book (though "built-in" may not be quite accurate, since they need not necessarily come from the vendor of the DBMS per se). They subdivide—not always in a very clearcut way—into a number of separate categories, as follows:

- Data communications
- Data dictionary

- Data access
- Data presentation
- Application generation
- Other

Of these various categories:

- The *data communications* function is provided (as explained in Chapter 2) by the DC manager component. The DC manager is responsible for controlling the transfer of messages between terminal users and the DBMS. Most of the functions of the DC manager are beyond the scope of this book.

- The *data dictionary* (or at least the catalog) has also been mentioned several times in this book already, and we have nothing further to add here—except to note that (in addition to all of its other uses) the dictionary is important during the database design phase, and some systems provide a database design aid component that is integrated with the dictionary.

- The "other" category includes such tools as statistical packages, word processors, spreadsheet programs, and expert systems of various kinds. For obvious reasons, all of these tools may need to be integrated with the underlying DBMS to a greater or lesser extent. For example, it should be possible to incorporate database data into a business letter that is being prepared on a word processor; it should be possible to apply the functions of a statistical package to database data; and so on. Additional "other" components include database application testing tools, micro-to-mainframe upload and download programs, and many others. Of course the list is completely open-ended.

The remaining categories—data access, data presentation, and application generation—are the subject of Sections 20.2, 20.3, and 20.4, respectively. In order to impose some semblance of unity on what is an essentially diverse collection of topics, we take most of our examples from a single system, namely Commercial INGRES [20.1]. However, the reader should clearly understand that most currently available systems provide facilities analogous to those of INGRES in most of the areas we describe (not always in so nicely integrated a manner, however).

20.2   DATA ACCESS

The term "data access" refers to the process of locating and retrieving some requested set of data. By contrast, the term "data presentation" (the topic of the next section) refers to the process of displaying that data to the user in some appropriate fashion. In a nutshell: Data access means the query, data presentation means the result (loosely speaking). Up to this point we have not bothered to distinguish very carefully between the two, but now it becomes necessary to do so. One reason (not the only one) for stressing the distinction is that it may be possible to issue a given query once and display the result of that query several times in several different ways (such a facility is provided by the IBM product QMF, for example). We discuss data access in this section and data presentation in the next.[1]

Some common styles of data access are the following:

- Command-driven interfaces (query languages)
- Menu- and forms-driven interfaces
- Natural language interfaces

Of these, query languages have of course been extensively discussed in this book already. Menu- and forms-driven interfaces and natural language are discussed briefly later in this section. Other possibilities for the data access interface, not discussed in this book in any detail, include:

- Icon-based interfaces. An *icon* is a pictorial representation of some object (for example, a truck or car in a vehicles database, though of course the picture is likely to be much more abstract in many cases). Queries are formulated by "touching" icons in some sequence with the screen cursor. Reference [20.10] describes an icon-based system.

- "Pointing" interfaces, in which the screen cursor movement is achieved by means of a mouse or a touch-sensitive screen. Such interfaces are typically used in conjunction with the icon-based interfaces just discussed.

- Voice input systems (still in the realms of research rather than a commercial reality at the time of writing). Note that natural language support is likely to be a prerequisite for voice input.

Menu- and Forms-driven Interfaces

We illustrate the ideas of menu- and forms-driven interfaces by discussing the INGRES facilities specifically [20.1]. A *form* in INGRES is basically just a screen-display version of a familiar paper form. Such a form can be used for both input to the system and output to the user. The INGRES forms system works as follows (in outline).

- First, INGRES automatically creates a *default* form for every table (base table or view) described in the catalog. As an example, the default form for the parts table P might look as shown in Fig. 20.1. Note that it consists essentially of a

---

1. Of course, any mechanism for data access must include *some* facility for presenting results to the user; however, that presentation facility need only be quite primitive. For example, compare the built-in query component of DB2 (namely DB2I) with the end-user query product QMF. Both of those products support SQL queries against a DB2 database. However, the output from a query in DB2I is stored simply as a string of text in a conventional MVS file, and must subsequently be displayed by means of a conventional text editor; the output from a query in QMF, by contrast, is displayed directly by QMF as a customized and formatted report, with page numbers, explanatory headings, subtotals, and other additional material.

simple heading line, together with a set of display fields corresponding to the fields of the table, in the order in which those fields were defined when the table was created. Each display field is labeled with the name of the corresponding database field and has a width that is determined from the data type of that database field. Note: The line at the bottom of the figure is not part of the form but is the associated menu of operations that the user of the form can execute. The combination of form and menu is called a *frame* (see Section 20.4 for further discussion of frames).

```
TABLE IS  p


p#:          pname:                      color:

weight:        city:




Help    Go    Query    End :
```

Fig. 20.1 Default form for table P.

■   By calling up a copy of the default form on the screen and filling in some of the blank entries, the user can use that form to formulate simple queries concerning table P. Various control keys can be used during this process to step from field to field across the screen. As an example, Fig. 20.2 shows a formulation for the query "Get blue parts that weigh more than 10 pounds." After formulating a query, the user will choose the "Go" option from the menu, and INGRES will then retrieve the required records and display them one at a time in the same format (i.e., by means of the default form, but with all values filled in). The user can thus examine the records at leisure (this process is sometimes known as *database browsing*).

The INGRES component that supports the process just described is called "Query By Forms" (QBF). As the example shows, QBF allows the user to issue simple queries against an INGRES database without requiring any knowledge of QUEL, the formal INGRES query language. QBF queries can involve base tables or views; joins of multiple tables; certain combinations of AND and OR; and the usual comparison operators (equals, less than, etc.). The ability to query joins is particularly attractive, of course; for example, a query such as "Find suppliers who supply at least one part in a quantity greater than 200" is very easy to formulate through QBF. Note, however, that the join must be predefined to QBF via a process

```
┌─────────────────────────────────────────────────────────────┐
│                                                               │
│   TABLE IS p                                                  │
│                                                               │
│   p#:        pname:                      color:  Blue         │
│                                                               │
│   weight:  >10 city:                                          │
│                                                               │
│                                                               │
│                                                               │
│   Help    Go    Query    End :                                │
│                                                               │
└─────────────────────────────────────────────────────────────┘
```

Fig. 20.2 Sample query using the default form for P.

called QDEF (query definition). The person defining the join need not (and very likely will not) be the person who performs the subsequent queries, however.

Aside: At first glance QBF may look somewhat like Query-By-Example; however, it is in fact rather different, as can be seen from the way it handles update operations (to be discussed). Query-By-Example—at least as currently implemented in QMF—is really nothing more than an ordinary command-driven query language that happens to be dressed up in an appealing syntactic style. Of course, this remark is not intended as a disparagement of QBE; on the contrary, considered *as* a command-driven language, QBE is a very attractive proposition. Nevertheless, the fact remains that QBF represents an entirely different *style* of database access (although in principle there is no reason why QBE should not follow that style also).

QBF also supports simple update and data entry operations. Suppose, for example, that the user wishes to browse through all parts in London and possibly update some of them. The relevant part records can be retrieved and displayed one by one, using the mechanism already described; and, during that process, the user can at any time delete the record currently being displayed, or change it by simply overtyping values on the screen.[2] This process is sometimes called *database editing*.

As for data entry, that can be done by (again) filling in values on the form, and storing the records so created one at a time. After storing each record, QBF will optionally redisplay the field values from that record on the next form, so that only values that are different from those in the previous record need to be entered each time. In this way the data entry process can be made very fast (in fact, this is the normal way of doing data entry in INGRES).

2. Incidentally, QBF even allows joins to be updated in this manner. However, the effect of such updates on the underlying base tables is not "automatically" understood by INGRES but has to be specified by the person defining the join as part of the QDEF process (see later). The reason for this state of affairs is, of course, that INGRES (like DB2) has no knowledge of primary and foreign keys, and (as explained in Chapter 15) such knowledge is required if the system is to support such updates unaided.

As can be seen from the foregoing discussion, the QBF mechanism is very easy to use, and indeed quite powerful. However, the default forms are perhaps a little utilitarian (though no doubt adequate in simple cases). For that reason INGRES provides a number of facilities for the creation of forms that are more carefully tailored to the needs of specific applications:

- First (as indicated earlier), it is possible to create a form that corresponds to a join instead of just to a single base table. For such a form it is also possible to specify whether or not the join may be updated, and if so what the effect of such updates should be.

- Second, it is also possible to have multiple rows displayed on a single form, instead of being limited to one row per form as described above. This facility is particularly useful in connection with one-to-many joins, where several rows from the "many" table can be shown together with a single row from the "one" table on the same form. For such a form INGRES provides automatic scrolling through the rows of the "many" table for each row of the "one" table.

- Third, forms of considerable sophistication can be created by means of another INGRES component, the *Visual Forms Editor* (VIFRED). Using VIFRED, the user can create a new form from scratch, or can edit an existing form (default or user-created).

We briefly sketch the possibilities available with VIFRED. Suppose the user wishes to edit some form—say the default form for table P from Fig. 20.1. On request, VIFRED will display that form on the screen. The user can then use VIFRED editing commands to rearrange items on the screen, to add, change, or delete headings, footings, and similar explanatory text, and to add, change, or delete display fields. In the case of fields, the user can specify:

- The label to be used on the display (which need not be the same as the name of the field in the database);

- Whether the field is to be displayed in a box frame, and/or in reverse video, and/or blinking, and/or underlined, and/or in a different brightness from the rest of the form;

- Whether the field is for "display only" or the user of the form is to be allowed to enter a value into the field;

- Whether the value from the previous record should be displayed in this field (useful for data entry);

- Whether a value is mandatory for this field on data entry;

- An integrity check to be applied when the form user supplies new values for this field;[3]

- A message to display if that integrity check is violated;

---

3. Such integrity checks can include a limited form of referential constraint checking.

- A default value to be supplied for the field if the user of the form omits to supply a value on data entry.

All INGRES forms, default or user-created, are stored in the system catalog.

Natural Language Interfaces

Natural language interfaces have been the subject of research for some considerable time, but it is only comparatively recently that corresponding products have begun to appear in the marketplace. We briefly describe two natural language systems here—RENDEZVOUS [20.2–20.4], an experimental system developed by Codd at IBM Research, and INTELLECT [20.6], a system originally developed by Harris at Dartmouth College (under the name ROBOT [20.5]) and now commercially available from Artificial Intelligence Corporation (AIC). Note: Other companies, including IBM, also market INTELLECT under license from AIC (not always under the INTELLECT name, however).

First RENDEZVOUS. In outline, RENDEZVOUS operates as follows. First, it transforms the original natural language query into an expression of the relational calculus (actually an expression in a formal query language called DEDUCE [14.7]). In doing this, it makes use of what is usually called a *knowledge base*. Since some kind of knowledge base is found in all natural language systems, we digress for a moment to discuss its function very briefly.

The knowledge base is what enables the system to "understand" natural language queries. It includes (among several other things):

- copies of certain of the tables from the database catalog;
- tables of commonly occurring data values;
- a set of phrase transformation rules, which allow the system to perform substitutions such as replacing "how many" by "count"; and
- a *lexicon*, which is a table defining certain natural language words (English words, in the case of RENDEZVOUS) that are likely to be used in queries. Such words fall into two broad classes—those that are specific to the database to be queried (such as *supplier, part, shipment*), and those that are more general (such as *find, have, with*).

Part of the process of installing a natural language system must be to generate at least the database-specific portion of the lexicon, and possibly other portions of the knowledge base also, such as database-specific phrase transformation rules. In some cases, the system may subsequently be capable of adding new terms to the knowledge base on its own initiative (for example, after learning from some user that "London" is the name of a city—see the example below).

To return to RENDEZVOUS specifically: The process of transforming the original query into a calculus expression is actually done in a fragmentary fashion. In general, there will be pieces of the original query that RENDEZVOUS can understand and pieces that it cannot. For those latter pieces, RENDEZVOUS will attempt to extract the meaning from the user by means of a *clarification dialog*. For example:

```
User:      HOW MANY LONDON PARTS ARE THERE?
System:    THE WORD 'LONDON' IS UNFAMILIAR. IS IT ONE OF THE
           FOLLOWING:

           1 PART NUMBER        4 PART WEIGHT
           2 PART NAME          5 PART CITY
           3 PART COLOR         6 NONE OF THE ABOVE

           SELECT BY NUMBER THE CLOSEST CATALOG ITEM
User:      5
```

Once RENDEZVOUS has completed its internal formulation of a relational calculus expression, it then transforms that expression back into English for approval by the user:

```
System:    THIS IS WHAT THE SYSTEM UNDERSTANDS YOUR QUERY TO BE:

           COUNT THE NUMBER OF PARTS STORED IN LONDON.

           IS THE SYSTEM'S UNDERSTANDING

               1 CORRECT AND COMPLETE
               2 NOT YET COMPLETE
               3 INCORRECT

           SELECT EXACTLY ONE ITEM BY NUMBER

User:      1

System:    THE ANSWER TO YOUR QUERY IS:

           THERE ARE 3 PARTS STORED IN LONDON.
```

As Cuff remarks in [20.7], the dialogs in RENDEZVOUS (clarification dialogs and also other kinds, not discussed here) tend to have a rather plodding quality, with the result that the entire interaction may become somewhat cumbersome from the user's point of view. For example, the user may be asked to make choices where one of the alternatives is "obviously" (from a human point of view) much less likely than the other (is London a color?). On the other hand, straightforward queries do seem to be dealt with smoothly, and the system seems to be quite robust.

We turn now to the INTELLECT system. The internal structure of INTELLECT is significantly different from that of RENDEZVOUS in a number of respects. First, INTELLECT does not indulge in clarification dialog. Instead, it employs its built-in knowledge of English syntax to generate an initial set of feasible (at least syntactically feasible) interpretations of the original query. (By contrast, RENDEZVOUS does not have a deep understanding of English syntax. To quote [20.2], it cannot even "distinguish a noun from a verb!" Of course, this lack of emphasis on syntax was a deliberate design decision [20.2].)

Next, if it now has many possible interpretations for the query, INTELLECT *searches the database* in an attempt to discover the user's intended meaning. In this way it can (for example) learn that "London" is the name of a city, and thereby discover what the query "How many London parts are there?" means, without having to ask the user for that information. Note that in a sense, therefore, INTELLECT uses the database itself as a dynamic extension to the lexicon.

Like RENDEZVOUS, INTELLECT will—optionally—"echo back" a formal English statement of its interpretation of the original query to the user. Unlike RENDEZVOUS, however, it does not then offer the user the option of revising that interpretation; the purpose of the "echo" is simply to make clear to the user exactly what query it is that the system is responding to.

Comparing the two approaches (RENDEZVOUS and INTELLECT), we can observe that the INTELLECT idea of examining the database is preferable to the RENDEZVOUS scheme of interrogating the user, in that (obviously) it involves less effort on the part of the user. On the other hand, searching the database is likely to be expensive if the database is large (even if the searching is restricted to indexed fields). Moreover, the RENDEZVOUS approach is more suitable to implementation on an intelligent workstation—i.e., personal computer—that is physically remote from the central system, because there is no need to access the database (except for the catalog, which can be locally cached) until the time comes to execute the final and completed version of the query. Indeed, suitability for such remote implementation was one of RENDEZVOUS's original objectives [20.3].

We conclude this brief discussion of natural language interfaces with a few miscellaneous observations:[4]

1. Note that RENDEZVOUS and INTELLECT (like all other natural language systems known to this writer) are both read-only. Update operations are not supported.

2. As mentioned earlier, part of the process of installing a natural language system must be to generate at least the database-specific portion of the lexicon. In practice, it seems that lexicon generation is likely to be quite difficult, and to require highly specialized skills, for all but rather simple databases.

3. Natural language systems tend to be expensive, in the sense that they typically require a lot of main memory.

4. Finally, icon-based and pointing interfaces (using a mouse or a touch-sensitive screen) seem to be just as easy to use in practice as natural language systems, and they are much easier to build and are faster.

---

4. I am indebted to Larry Rowe for most of these comments.

20.3   DATA PRESENTATION

Techniques of data presentation include the following:

- Simple tabular reports
- Tailored reports
- Business graphics
- Pictorial displays (icon output)
- Voice output

Of this list, simple tabular reports are what we have been showing in all examples in this book prior to this chapter, and pictorial and voice output still lie (at the time of writing) primarily in the province of experimental systems. The remaining two possibilities, tailored reports and business graphics, form the principal topic of the rest of this section.

Report Writers

The term "report" is used to mean a set of formatted output from the database, either on the screen or on paper ("hard copy"). A *report writer* (or report *generator*) is a software component that supports the production of such reports. In this subsection we use the INGRES report writer to illustrate the kind of facilities typically found in report writers in general.

The user invokes the INGRES report writer by issuing the command

```
REPORT name
```

where "name" is either

1. the name of the table (possibly a view) from which the report is to be produced, or

2. the name of a *report specification* which in turn includes either

   - the name of that table, or

   - a QUEL RETRIEVE statement (possibly parameterized), in which case the report is produced from the *derived* table that is the result of that RETRIEVE. Values for the parameters (if the RETRIEVE is parameterized) are supplied in the REPORT command.

In case 1, INGRES automatically generates a *default* report specification for the table in question, so in fact there is always a report specification (default or user-generated) to control the details of how the finished report will look. All report specifications are kept in the INGRES catalog.

Suppose it is desired to produce a report showing supplier cities, suppliers in those cities, the parts they supply, and the corresponding quantities. Suppose too—without loss of generality—that an appropriate table (actually a view) exists containing precisely the required information:

```
DEFINE VIEW CITYSHIPS
     ( CITY      = S.CITY,
       SUPPLIER = S.S#,
       PART     = SP.P#,
       QUANTITY = SP.QTY )
     WHERE S.S# = SP.S#
```

Then the command

```
REPORT CITYSHIPS
```

(using the INGRES default report specification) will produce the "default report" shown in Fig. 20.3.

```
14-AUG-84                                              11:41:19
                    Report on Table: Cityships

City               Supplier            Part            Quantity

London             S1                  P1              300
                   S1                  P2              200
                   S1                  P3              400
                   S1                  P4              200
                   S1                  P5              100
                   S1                  P6              100
                   S4                  P2              200
                   S4                  P4              300
                   S4                  P5              400
Paris              S2                  P1              300
                   S2                  P2              400
                   S3                  P2              200

                            - 1 -
```

Fig. 20.3 A default report.

Default reports are adequate in many cases, but sometimes it is desirable to produce a report that is more carefully tailored to some specific requirement. Tailored reports require a user-generated report specification. User-generated specifications can be created in two ways:

1. They can be created interactively through the forms-based system "Report By Forms" (RBF). This is the simplest method.

2. They can be written using the report writer's "report definition language", which does provide certain additional facilities not supported under method 1 but which also requires some degree of conventional programming expertise.

The interactive RBF interface is to the report writer what VIFRED is to QBF. In other words, RBF is an interactive editor for forms (like VIFRED); however, the

forms it is designed to edit are, specifically, the forms that make up a report specification. In fact, the starting point for RBF is always one of INGRES's own default
specifications—the user is not allowed to create a new report specification from
scratch, but instead must work by editing one of the default specifications. A pictorial representation of the relationship between the INGRES report writer and RBF
is shown in Fig. 20.4 (opposite).

Using RBF, the user can specify display formats (etc.) for the data in the desired
report. In particular, the user might designate CITY as a break column, and CITY,
SUPPLIER, and PART (in that major-to-minor order) as sort columns, using an
RBF *report structure form:*

```
                       Sorting         Sorting       Break
                       Sequence        Order         Column?
        Column name    (0 - 127)       ('a'/'d')     ('y'/'n')
        ===========    =========       =========     =========

        City              1               a             y
        Supplier          2               a
        Part              3               a
        Quantity          0
```

Next, the user can call up an RBF *column options form* for each of these four
columns and make entries in those four forms as follows (we show the forms for
the CITY and QUANTITY columns only, slightly simplified as usual). First CITY:

```
Column name: City

When to print values: b

Lines to skip on break: 1

Selection criteria at run time: n

Aggregation/break combinations to calculate for column.
Enter 'x' to select.

Aggregate     Over Report     Over Breaks     Over Pages
==============================================================
Count         |               |               |
==============================================================
```

The "b" ("When to print values") means "Print on control breaks". The "n"
("Selection criteria at run time") means "None". If the user had specified "v"
(Value) or "r" (Range of values), the report writer would prompt for a (range of)
CITY value(s) each time a report is produced using this specification; in this way,

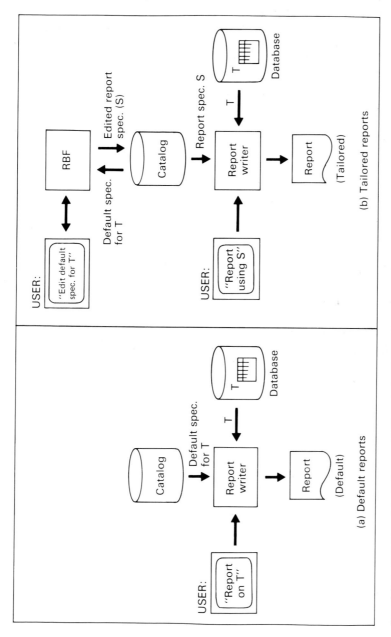

Fig. 20.4 Relationship between RBF and the INGRES report writer.

473

tailored reports for specific individual cities could be produced. Notice that the only aggregate option offered is "Count", because CITY is a character string column and counting is the only aggregation that makes sense. In fact we have chosen not to specify any aggregation for CITY at all.

Now the column options form for QUANTITY. Here we have requested totaling ("Sum") to be performed for each value of the break column (i.e., for each CITY value) and also for the report as a whole:

```
Column name: Quantity

Selection criteria at run time: n

Aggregation/break combinations to calculate for column.
Enter 'x' to select.

Aggregate      Over Report      Over Breaks      Over Pages
===========================================================
Count          |                |                |
Sum            |      x         |      x         |
Average        |                |                |
Minimum        |                |                |
Maximum        |                |                |
===========================================================
```

The resulting report is shown in Fig. 20.5.

Business Graphics

The graphics component of INGRES—"Graph By Forms" or GBF—is somewhat analogous to the report writing component, except that the final "report" consists of a picture (i.e., a two-dimensional graph) rather than a simple table of rows and columns. For many kinds of data, a graph is a much more effective means of communication than a conventional report. As a trivial illustration, compare the bar chart in Fig. 20.6 with the same data in conventional report form (Fig. 20.5).

GBF supports four types of graph: bar charts, pie charts, scatter graphs, and line plots. In all cases, the data to be graphed consists of a table, derived in some way from the tables of the underlying database; GBF requires the user to define a query whose result is precisely the table in question. That table must have either two or three columns (referred to generically as the X, Y, and Z columns). For example, here is a QUEL query corresponding to the bar chart shown above:

```
RANGE OF CS IS CITYSHIPS

RETRIEVE ( X = CS.PART,
           Y = SUM (CS.QUANTITY BY CS.CITY, CS.PART),
           Z = CS.CITY )
```

```
14-AUG-84                                                          11:46:07
                        Report on Table: Cityships

City                 Supplier              Part              Quantity

London               S1                    P1                     300
                     S1                    P2                     200
                     S1                    P3                     400
                     S1                    P4                     200
                     S1                    P5                     100
                     S1                    P6                     100
                     S4                    P2                     200
                     S4                    P4                     300
                     S4                    P5                     400
-----------------------------------------------------------------------------
Totals: London
Sum:                                                             2200
-----------------------------------------------------------------------------

Paris                S2                    P1                     300
                     S2                    P2                     400
                     S3                    P2                     200
-----------------------------------------------------------------------------
Totals: Paris
Sum:                                                              900
-----------------------------------------------------------------------------
Grand Totals: REPORT
Sum:                                                             3100
=============================================================================
                                  - 1 -
```

Fig. 20.5 A tailored report.

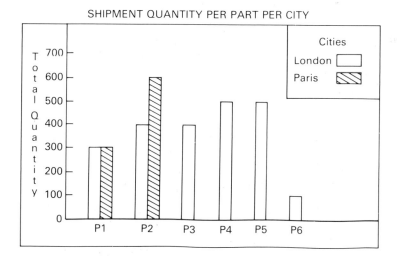

Fig. 20.6 Example of a bar chart.

In general, the query can be specified via a QBF-like operation (if it is sufficiently simple), or via an explicit QUEL operation otherwise. The meanings of the three columns X, Y, and Z depend on the type of graph, as follows:

- Bar chart: X represents the independent variable (the labels on the bars); Z (if present) represents labels of "sub-bars" within each bar ("City" in the example above); Y represents the dependent variable (the bar or "sub-bar" heights).
- Pie chart: X represents the independent variable (the labels on the slices), Y represents the dependent variable (the slice areas). Z should not be present for this type of graph.
- Scatter graph: X and Y represent (X,Y)-coordinates. For each value of Z, GBF will optionally attempt to find the straight line most closely fitting the set of (X,Y) points ("linear regression").
- Line plot: X and Y again represent (X,Y)-coordinates. For each value of Z, GBF will assume that the set of (X,Y) points represents a continuous function, and will approximate that function by connecting adjacent points by means of a straight-line segment.

After specifying the query that defines the table to be graphed, the user can run that query and get GBF to create a default *graph specification* to control the display of the resulting graph. Subsequently, the user can modify that default graph specification, much as the user can modify a default report specification under RBF. Following are some of the changes the user can apply to the default graph specification:

- Bar charts: The fill patterns for the bars can be changed.
- Scatter graphs: The displayed character representing individual (X,Y)-points can be changed (on an individual Z-value basis). Linear regression can be requested.
- Line plots: The character used to draw connecting lines can be changed (on an individual Z-value basis).
- All graphs except pie charts: Axis origins can be changed. Axis scales can be set to logarithmic (base 10). Axes can be labeled and/or can have specific values marked, in a variety of fonts and font sizes. A grid can be superimposed on the graph.
- All graphs: Placement details, title, and legend can be adjusted.

Like report specifications, graph specifications are kept in the INGRES catalog.

20.4   APPLICATION GENERATION

The availability of the various generalized (built-in) applications described in Sections 20.2 and 20.3 certainly reduces the need for special-purpose, user-written application programs. Indeed, it may even be possible to avoid having to write any such programs at all in some installations. Usually, however, it will still be necessary to develop at least a few applications that are specialized to the installation's own particular needs. Even then, it may still be possible to avoid programming in the traditional sense (i.e., programming in a conventional language such as COBOL or PL/I), if the system includes a suitable *application generator*.

Application generators are *rapid application development tools*. They can be regarded as an advance over the conventional high-level languages (COBOL, PL/I, etc.), just as those languages are an advance over assembler language and assembler language in turn was an advance over machine code. For this reason, application generators are sometimes referred to as *fourth generation* tools—machine code, assembler language, and high-level languages representing the first three generations—and the user interface to an application generator is accordingly sometimes called a *fourth generation language* (4GL). However, we choose not to adopt this terminology in this book, since it does not seem to have any very precise definition.

The user of an application generator—i.e., the application designer—is thus presented with a very high-level application development language, in which the primitive operations include not only the usual arithmetic and control flow facilities of conventional languages, but also facilities for database definition and access, terminal screen layout definition, screen input/output, screen data manipulation, and so on. Furthermore, the process of actually developing an application is typically done—at least in part—not by writing code in any conventional manner, but rather by conducting some kind of interactive dialog with the system. We illustrate these general ideas by (once again) using the facilities of INGRES as a concrete example; however, the reader is warned that different application generators differ very considerably from one another at the detail level, and hence that the facilities of INGRES should not necessarily be regarded as typical.

The INGRES application generator is called "Applications By Forms" (ABF). ABF supports the development of *forms-based* applications—that is, applications that communicate with the end-user by means of forms displayed on the screen. QBF, RBF, GBF, and VIFRED are all special cases of forms-based applications. (So is ABF itself, for that matter.) Any such application can be regarded as consisting of a hierarchical arrangement of *frames*, where each frame in turn consists of a *form* and an associated *menu*. See Fig. 20.7.

The hierarchy of Fig. 20.7 is interpreted as follows. Frame 1 represents the entry point to the application—i.e., it is the frame displayed when the user first invokes the application. Frames 1.1–1.3 represent three possible successor frames (corresponding to three possible menu choices on frame 1—for example, "Produce sales

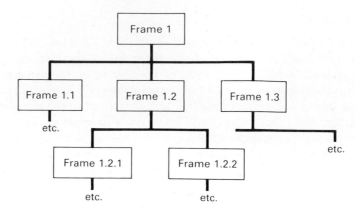

Fig. 20.7 Structure of a forms-based application.

report," "Enter new order," or "Update customer information," in a SALES application). Likewise, frames 1.2.1–1.2.2 represent two possible successor frames to frame 1.2, and so on. Note, incidentally, that several frames can share the same form, thus presenting a consistent set of interfaces to the application user at run time.

As an aside, we note that the entire INGRES system is in fact presented to the user as one large forms-based application in the above sense. The user initially invokes INGRES by entering the command:

```
INGRES database-name
```

INGRES responds by displaying the "INGRES subsystem interface" frame. Options on that frame then allow the user to do any of the following:

- Invoke QBF or RBF or GBF or ABF or VIFRED;
- Perform data definition operations such as creating or destroying tables;
- Issue QUEL operations;
- Run saved queries or reports or graphs;

and so on. And each of these options in turn leads to further, more detailed frames for the operation(s) in question.

To return to the main thread of our discussion: In order to create a forms-based application, therefore, the application designer needs to be able to specify:

1. The frames involved in the application;
2. For each such frame, the form and menu items to be displayed;
3. For each such menu item, the sequence of operations to be performed if the application user selects that item. Note that, for a given menu item, the sequence of operations will include (but will not in general be limited to) the operation of invoking the frame to be displayed next.

There are four possible types of frame: user-specified frames, QBF frames, report frames, and GBF frames. The purposes of the four types are as follows:

- *User-specified* frames[5] are frames that are completely specific to the application in question (such as Frame 1, the entry frame, in the SALES application sketched above). For each such frame, the designer specifies the name of the frame, the name of the associated form, the menu, and the set of operations corresponding to each menu item (see the discussion of OSL below). If the associated form does not yet exist, the designer can create it using VIFRED, without leaving the ABF environment. The designer can also use QBF, again without leaving the ABF environment, if it becomes necessary to interrogate the database while building the application.

- *QBF* frames allow the application to make use of the built-in QBF code. Suppose, for example, that one of the menu choices the application offers to its user is "ad hoc query." Then, instead of writing explicit code to perform that function, the designer can simply incorporate the QBF code into the application directly. For a QBF frame, the designer specifies the name of the frame, the corresponding form (which can be created via VIFRED), and the name of the table on which QBF is to operate.

- *Report* frames allow the application to make use of the INGRES report writer. The designer specifies the name of the frame, a form for the acquisition of run-time parameters for the report (if any), and the corresponding report specification (which can be built via RBF).

- Finally, *GBF* frames allow the application to make use of the built-in GBF code. These frames are analogous to the report frames just discussed.

In the case of a user-specified frame, the application designer must also (as already stated) define the *operations* corresponding to each menu item in the frame. This function is performed by means of the ABF *Operation Specification Language* (OSL). OSL can be regarded as a very high-level programming language. Some idea of its power can be obtained from the following brief outline of some of its most important statements.

- Database statements:

OSL includes almost all of the database function of QUEL. In particular, it allows values to be retrieved from the database directly into a form for display; it also allows values entered into a form by the application user to be used to update the database or to condition further database retrievals.

- Form control statements:

Form control statements control what appears on the screen. For example, the "clear" statement clears one or more fields on the screen, the "message" statement

---

5. "User" here refers to the application designer, not to the application end-user.

displays a single-line message at the foot of the screen, the assignment statement assigns the value of some expression to a field on the screen, and so on. Mention should also be made of the "validate" statement, which is used to cause the validation checks specified for the form (via VIFRED—see Section 20.2) to be applied.

- Control flow statements:

Examples of control flow statements include various forms of "if" statement, statements to call another (user-specified) frame, statements to call one of the INGRES-supplied frames (such as a QBF frame), statements to return to the previous frame, and statements to call a user-specified procedure. (User-specified procedures can be written in any of the INGRES languages—BASIC, C, COBOL, FORTRAN, and Pascal—and can include embedded QUEL statements. Note, however, that such procedures should not be needed very often in practice, because most of the relevant functions are directly available from within OSL itself.)

The application designer creates OSL text by means of a standard operating system editor, which can be invoked directly from ABF. User-specified procedures (if necessary) are created in the same fashion.

At any point during construction of the application, the designer can ask ABF to *run* the current version, even though it may still be incomplete. ABF will then invoke all the necessary compilers, etc. to convert the application to (temporarily) executable form, and will then try to execute it. Syntax errors will be diagnosed. If a call is encountered to a frame or procedure that does not yet exist, ABF will display a message, together with a trace of the control flow to that point. The application designer can then request execution to continue from a different point or can stop the run. When errors are discovered, the designer can use ABF to make corrections to frames and procedures, and can then try to execute the application again.

Finally, when the application is executing successfully, the designer can *install* it on the host system. Installation involves creating an "executable image" of the application (which is done via an appropriate ABF form) and defining a host system command by which that "image" can be invoked. Thereafter the application can be invoked directly from the host system level, instead of having to access it through ABF.

We conclude this section with a brief mention of *application packages*. Application packages exploit the fact that many applications tend to fall into a small number of rather stereotyped patterns. For example, the account maintenance procedures for bank *A* are unlikely to differ very significantly from those for bank *B*. As a consequence, it is feasible to provide prewritten, generalized programs or "packages" to perform commonly required functions such as account maintenance. Such packages can be tailored to some installation's specific requirements by simply providing values for some small number of parameters. When available (and suitable), such packages probably represent the most cost-effective form of "application generator" of all. Of course, the distinction between a package and a generator may not be very clearcut.

EXERCISES

20.1 Distinguish among the following:
a) command-driven interfaces;
b) menu- and forms-driven interfaces;
c) natural language interfaces;
d) icon-based interfaces;
e) "pointing" interfaces.

20.2 Define the following terms:
a) database browsing;
b) database editing;
c) report writer;
d) application generator;
e) fourth generation language.

20.3 State the principal functions of QBF, RBF, GBF, ABF, and VIFRED.

20.4 What are the relative advantages and disadvantages of natural language interfaces?

20.5 What do you understand by the terms *knowledge base* and *lexicon*?

REFERENCES AND BIBLIOGRAPHY

20.1 Information regarding the INGRES forms systems (QBF, RBF, GBF, ABF, and VIFRED) is available from Relational Technology Inc., 1080 Marina Village Parkway, Alameda, Calif. 94501.

20.2 E. F. Codd. "Seven Steps to Rendezvous with the Casual User." In *Data Base Management* (eds., J. W. Klimbie and K. L. Koffeman). *Proc. IFIP TC-2 Working Conference on Data Base Management*. North-Holland (1974).

20.3 E. F. Codd et al. "RENDEZVOUS Version 1: An Experimental English Language Query Formulation System for Casual Users of Relational Data Bases." *IBM Research Report RJ 2144* (January 1978).

20.4 E. F. Codd. "How About Recently? (English Dialog with Relational Data Bases Using RENDEZVOUS Version 1)." In *Databases: Improving Usability and Responsiveness* (ed., B. Shneiderman). New York: Academic Press (1978).

20.5 Larry R. Harris. "The ROBOT System: Natural Language Processing Applied to Data Base Query." *Proc. ACM Annual Conf.* (December 1978).

20.6 Information regarding INTELLECT is available from Artificial Intelligence Corporation, 100 5th Avenue, Waltham, MA 02254.

20.7 Rodney N. Cuff. "Database Query Using Menus and Natural Language Fragments." Man-Machine Systems Laboratory, Department of Electrical Engineering Science, University of Essex, UK (April 1982).

20.8 I. D. Hill. "Wouldn't It Be Nice If We Could Write Computer Programs in Ordinary English—Or Would It?" *BCS Comp. Bulletin* (June 1972).

Discusses (in an entertaining and nontechnical manner) some of the problems involved in attempting to understand natural language.

20.9 James Martin. *Application Development Without Programmers*. Englewood Cliffs, N.J.: Prentice-Hall (1982).

Argues strongly that the application development process needs to be made dramatically more efficient (i.e., by becoming more automated), and presents a survey of currently available tools and techniques for achieving such an improvement.

20.10 Christopher F. Herot. "Spatial Management of Data." *ACM TODS* **5**, No. 4 (December 1980).

Describes the implementation of an experimental system—the Spatial Data Management System (SDMS)—with an icon-based interface.

20.11 M. M. Zloof. "Office-By-Example: A Business Language that Unifies Data and Word Processing and Electronic Mail." *IBM Sys. J.* **21**, No. 3 (1982).

Describes a very elegant extension of Query-By-Example to handle not only database query and update, but also database browsing and editing, document processing and text editing, electronic mail, application development, etc., all in a highly integrated and "user-friendly" fashion.

20.12 L. A. Rowe and K. Shoens. "A Forms Application Development System." *Proc. 1982 ACM SIGMOD International Conference on Management of Data* (June 1982).

20.13 K. Shoens. "A Forms Application Development System." Ph.D. Dissertation, EECS Dept., U.C. Berkeley (November 1982).

References [20.12, 20.13] describe the prototype forerunner of the Commercial INGRES forms-based systems [20.1].

Part 5
Nonrelational
Systems

In this part of the book we briefly examine three representative nonrelational systems: an inverted list system (DATACOM/DB), a hierarchic system (IMS), and a network system (IDMS). These three systems can be regarded as typical of the three major nonrelational approaches to database—namely, the inverted list, hierarchic, and network approaches. Though obviously very different from one another at the detail level, nonrelational systems such as the three just mentioned do nevertheless share a number of common characteristics, among them the following:

1. First, they have all been in existence longer—in some cases much longer—than the current relational products.

2. Second, they were *not* developed on the basis of a predefined abstract data model (the previous point notwithstanding). Instead, any such models were defined after the event by a process of abstraction or induction from existing implementations.[1] The relational model was the first example of a data model that was defined prior to any implementation (indeed, it was the first example of a data model, period).

3. Nonrelational systems are at a lower level of abstraction than relational systems. In particular, they are all basically record-at-a-time systems (except as indicated in paragraph 6 below). This state of affairs is a direct consequence of the fact that the systems were originally designed some considerable time ago. Comparing a relational system and a nonrelational system is in many ways analogous to comparing a modern programming language such as Ada or APL to an older one such as

---

1. At the time of writing, the hierarchic approach is still the only one (apart from the relational) ever to have been subjected to any *formal* analysis, so far as this writer is aware. See reference [22.5].

COBOL; as time goes by, the level of abstraction increases in database systems just as it does in programming languages (and for very similar reasons).

4. To pursue the point of the previous paragraph a little further: The "data models" for the various nonrelational systems can be regarded as abstractions of certain of the underlying storage structures (and associated operators) discussed in Chapter 3. Loosely speaking, the inverted list model is an abstraction of the indexed file organization discussed in Section 3.4, and the hierarchic and network models are abstractions of the pointer chain (parent/child) file organization discussed in Section 3.6 (with certain elements of hashing and indexing thrown in). If a relational system is to a nonrelational system what Ada or APL is to COBOL, then a nonrelational system is to a file management system what COBOL is to Assembler Language.

5. As a result of their record-at-a-time orientation, nonrelational systems are all fundamentally *programming* systems; the user in every case is an application programmer, typically using COBOL, who has to navigate manually through the database. Any "optimization" is generally performed by the user, not by the system.

6. End-users are supported by means of on-line application programs, either system-supplied (i.e., built-in) or installation-written. Incidentally, it is significant that just about every nonrelational system known to this writer—with the noteworthy exception of IMS—is currently being extended to include some kind of "relational" frontend (i.e., a built-in application to support interactive "relational" access to a nonrelational database). We place "relational" in quotes because it is certainly not the case that those frontends all provide the kind of function that can and should be expected of a true relational system.

7. Even if a nonrelational system can be extended to include a relational frontend, as suggested in the previous paragraph, there will still be a significant difference between such a system and a "pure" relational system, namely as follows: In a nonrelational system, users can always access the database through the nonrelational (record-at-a-time) interface. (Such access is impossible in a pure relational system, of course.) As a result, it might be possible to *subvert the system* in the nonrelational case—e.g., by bypassing certain security or integrity controls, or by creating or updating a database in such a way as to make it impossible to provide a pure relational view of that database.

This part of the book consists of three chapters, one for each of the three systems discussed. In each case we start with a little background information on the approach (inverted list, hierarchic, or network) typified by the system in question, and then attempt to define the underlying data model for that approach, before getting into details of the system per se. We then give an overview of the system and describe its basic data definition and data manipulation operators; we also briefly touch on the storage structure in each case. At that point the chapters diverge to discuss features that are highly specific to the particular system under consideration; the IMS chapter, for example, discusses "logical databases" and "secondary data structures.'' In the case of DATACOM/DB and IDMS we offer a brief description of recent developments that move those products in the direction of relational support.

Needless to say, we omit a lot of detail in each of these chapters, and we also simplify considerably in many places (in particular by not using genuine syntax, in most cases).

21

An Inverted
List System:
DATACOM/DB

21.1 BACKGROUND

DATACOM/DB is a product of Applied Data Research, Inc. (ADR) for IBM main-frames running either DOS or MVS [21.1]. It may be regarded as a typical example of an inverted list DBMS. Other products in the same general category as DATA-COM/DB include ADABAS from Software AG [21.2], Model 204 from Computer Corporation of America [21.3], and System 1022 from Software House [21.4]. In this chapter we present a reasonably detailed overview of DATACOM/DB, in order to give some idea of what it is that constitutes a typical inverted list system.

As indicated in the introduction to this part of the book, no one has ever defined an abstract "inverted list data model" (so far as this writer is aware). However, Section 21.2 below describes in an informal manner what such an abstract model might be like. The rest of the chapter then goes on to describe DATACOM/DB specifically.

Note: The reader may find the following helpful as a guide to understanding systems like DATACOM/DB. Many relational systems—though certainly not all—can be thought of as inverted list systems at the internal (i.e., physical) level. DB2 in particular can be thought of in such a way. In other words, the Stored Data Manager component of DB2 (see Chapter 4) provides essentially an "inverted list" set of functions—with the important difference that those functions are not exposed to the human user, but are instead used by other, higher-level DB2 components whose purpose in turn is to provide the true human interface (namely SQL). Thus an inverted list DBMS might loosely be regarded as a system comparable to the low-level component of a relational DBMS such as DB2, in which users operate directly at the record-at-a-time level instead of at the relational level.

21.2   THE INVERTED LIST MODEL

Data Structure

An inverted list database is similar to a relational database—but a relational database at a low level of abstraction, a level at which the stored tables themselves *and also certain access paths to those stored tables* (in particular, certain indexes) are directly visible to the user. (Remember that "user" here means an application programmer specifically.) Like a relational database, an inverted list database contains a collection of files or tables, and those files or tables are divided into rows (records) and columns (fields) as in the relational case. However, there are of course some significant differences:

1. First, the rows of an inverted list table, unlike the rows of a relational table, are considered to be *ordered* in some physical sequence. Note that this physical sequence is independent of any additional orderings that may be imposed on the table by means of indexes (see paragraph 3 below).

2. Next, an ordering may also be defined for the *total database*, in which (for example) all the rows of table A are considered to precede all the rows of table B, or the rows of tables A and B are considered to be interleaved in some specific way. We refer to this ordering as the *database sequence*. The physical sequence for a given table will of course be a subsequence of the overall database sequence.

3. For a given table, any number of *search keys* can be defined. A search key is an arbitrary field or field combination over which an index is to be built.[1] Such indexes permit both direct and sequential access on the basis of search key values; in particular, of course, they support sequential access via an ordering that may be different from the underlying physical sequence. Note that access via a search key and access via a nonindexed field are different operations (indeed, access via a nonindexed field is not even possible in some systems).

Data Manipulation

The data manipulation operators in any record-level system (inverted list or otherwise) are crucially dependent on the notion of *record addressing*. In general, the operators in such a system will fall into two broad classes:

1. Operators that establish addressability to some record in the database.

2. Operators that operate on the record at some previously established address.

We refer to operators in the first of these two categories variously as *search*, *locate*, or *find* operators. Those operators in turn fall into two subsidiary classes:

---

1.   Indexes are thus not "transparent to the user" in an inverted list system. Of course, the user is not responsible for maintaining those indexes; on the contrary, index maintenance is handled by the DBMS, just as it is in a relational system.

1.1 Operators that locate a record "out of the blue"—i.e., direct search operators.

1.2 Operators that locate a record in terms of its position relative to some previously established address—i.e., relative search operators.

Examples of all of these cases follow.

- An example of Case 1.1—direct search operators—is "Locate the first record in physical sequence in table T." The system finds the requested record and returns its address in some designated area A.

- An example of Case 1.2—relative search operators—is "Locate the first record in physical sequence in table T following the record whose address is given in area A." The system finds the requested record and returns its address in that same area A.

- An example of Case 2—operators that operate on the record at some previously established address—is "Delete the record whose address is given in area A."

We refer to areas such as A in these examples as "database address areas." A program can maintain addressability to any number of records at the same time by supplying enough database address areas.

Note carefully that, in the case of the search operators, the system needs to know the *access path* by which it is to locate the desired record, so that it can understand what is meant by terms such as "first" and "next." The access path in the examples above was physical sequence for table T. The other available access paths in an inverted list database are provided by the total database sequence and the defined indexes (i.e., the search keys). The access path for a given search operation is specified as follows:

- In the case of a direct search operator (e.g., "locate first"), it is specified as one of the operands to the operation.

- In the case of a relative search operator (e.g., "locate next"), it is *not* specified as an operand. Instead, what happens is the following. When any search operator (direct or relative) is executed, the system returns, not only the address of the record found, but also certain control information to identify the access path that was used to locate that record. (Both the address and the control information are returned in the same database address area A.) Thus, when a relative search operator specifies a particular area A to identify the start point for the search, it is also implicitly specifying the access path along which that search is to be done. The access path information in A must not be changed by the user.

It is normally not possible to go part way down one access path and then veer off on another.

Here then are some examples of typical inverted list operations (T is a table in the database, K is a search key for T, and A is a database address area):

- LOCATE FIRST: Find the first record of T in physical sequence, and return its address (plus access path ID) in A.

- LOCATE FIRST WITH SEARCH KEY EQUAL: Find the first record of T in K sequence having a specified value for K, and return its address (plus access path ID) in A.

- LOCATE NEXT: Find the first record of T following the record identified by A (using the access path identified by A), and return its address in A.

- LOCATE NEXT WITH SEARCH KEY EQUAL: Find the first record of T following the record identified by A having the same value for K as that record (using the access path identified by A, which must be "K sequence"), and return its address in A.

- LOCATE FIRST WITH SEARCH KEY GREATER: Find the first record of T following the record identified by A and having a higher value for K than that record (using the access path identified by A, which must be "K sequence"), and return its address in A.

- RETRIEVE: Retrieve the record identified by A.

- UPDATE: Update the record identified by A.

- DELETE: Delete the record identified by A.

- STORE: Store a new record and return its address in A.

Data Integrity

No general integrity rules are included in the inverted list model. Some systems do provide some limited integrity support, allowing certain constraints—e.g., field uniqueness constraints—to be specified declaratively and enforced automatically, but most constraints will normally have to be enforced by the user (i.e., by installation-written procedural code). In particular, referential integrity is typically the user's responsibility.

21.3 AN OVERVIEW OF DATACOM/DB

We now proceed with our detailed examination of DATACOM/DB specifically. DATACOM/DB is the database management component of "ADR/DATACOM RIME," ADR's "Relational Information Management Environment" (of which a little more at the end of this section). As mentioned in Section 21.1, DATACOM/DB runs on IBM mainframes under both the DOS and MVS operating systems. It provides a CALL-level interface for application programs written in any of the following languages: COBOL, PL/I, FORTRAN, RPG II, and System/370 Assembler Language.[2] End-users are of course supported by appropriate application programs,

---

2. In the case of COBOL (only), ADR also provides an interface called DATACOM/DL (also known as COBOL/DL), which consists essentially of a set of extensions to COBOL that are expanded via a preprocessor macro pass into conventional DATACOM/DB CALLs.

and several such applications are provided by ADR as part of the Relational Information Management Environment mentioned above.

A DATACOM/DB system can support up to 999 databases. Each database is defined by adding an appropriate set of descriptors to the ADR dictionary (DATADICTIONARY). The definition process is performed interactively through a forms-based interface. The descriptors for a given database specify (in effect) the DATACOM/DB versions of all three of the ANSI/SPARC levels—internal, conceptual, and external—though the three are not always clearly distinguished. In particular, of course, the descriptors specify the tables, fields, and search keys[3] involved in the database.

The unit of access to a DATACOM/DB database is not the field, however, but the *element*. An element can be thought of as a "subrecord"; it consists of an arbitrary collection of contiguous fields from the record in question. Note the contiguity requirement. For example, given the usual supplier record S(S#,SNAME,STATUS,CITY), there are ten possible elements that can be defined—one covering the entire record, two involving three fields each, three involving two fields each, and four involving a single field each. Each element can be individually protected against unauthorized access. Retrieval operations can access any subset of the elements of the record, subject of course to the authorization controls just mentioned.

The remainder of this chapter has the following structure. Following this brief overview section, Section 21.4 explains the DATACOM/DB data definition process in a little more detail. At the same time, it also necessarily introduces some aspects of the DATACOM/DB storage structure (since the user's view of the database is definitely affected by the storage structure, as we will see). Section 21.5 then discusses some of the most important DATACOM/DB data manipulation operations. Finally, Section 21.6 describes the *Compound Boolean Selection* feature (CBS), a comparatively recent addition to the DATACOM/DB base product.

We do not have room in this book for a detailed discussion of such aspects of DATACOM/DB as recovery, concurrency, etc. We content ourselves instead with the following brief comments. First, the system does provide a set of recovery and concurrency controls, more or less along the lines discussed in Chapter 18. It also provides a set of security controls, both at the element level (as already mentioned) and also at the table and database levels. As for integrity, DATACOM/DB requires most integrity controls to be provided by user-written code; however, it is possible to specify for any given table that a certain search key, the "master key," must have DUPLICATES NOT ALLOWED (see Section 21.4).

We conclude this section with a brief survey of the products that, along with DATACOM/DB itself, together constitute the ADR "Relational Information Management Environment." Those products include the following:

---

3.   The DATACOM/DB term for search key is simply *key*. In this book, however (as explained in Chapter 11), we generally reserve the unqualified term "key" to mean the primary key specifically. DATACOM/DB does not have a notion of primary key per se.

- DATADICTIONARY (already mentioned)
- DATACOM/DL (already mentioned)
- DATACOM/DC (a DC manager)
- DATAQUERY (a relational query/update frontend, for both interactive and batch use)
- DATAREPORTER (a batch report writer)
- DATAENTRY (a generalized interactive data entry application)
- DATADESIGNER (a logical database design aid)
- IDEAL (an application development system, with relational operators for database access)

21.4 DATA DEFINITION

As explained in Section 21.2, indexing in an inverted list system such as DATA-COM/DB is visible to the user. Any discussion of the DATACOM/DB logical data structure must therefore necessarily include some description of the corresponding physical storage structure also. Briefly, a DATACOM/DB database can be thought of as a collection of stored records, each stored record belonging to exactly one table, together with *a single* (B-tree) *index over all of the records in the database.* That single index actually supports *all* of the search keys in all of the tables in the database. By way of example, we give a DATACOM/DB version of the suppliers-and-parts database (with numerous details omitted, as usual).

Aside: For simplicity, we do not show genuine DATACOM/DB syntax. In fact, as mentioned in Section 21.3, data definition in DATACOM/DB is actually done interactively, via a forms-based interface to the ADR dictionary (DATADICTION-ARY). For present purposes, however, it is obviously more convenient to show the definitions in a conventional linear manner.

First, the suppliers table:

```
ADD TABLE S        TABLEID = 1
     FIELDS        S#       = CL5
                   SNAME    = CL20
                   STATUS   = H
                   CITY     = CL15
     ELEMENTS      S        = ( S#,SNAME,STATUS,CITY )
                   S#       = ( S# )
                   SNAME    = ( SNAME )
                   STATUS   = ( STATUS )
                   CITY     = ( CITY )
     SEARCH KEYS   S#       = ( S# )      KEYID = 1
                   CITY     = ( CITY )    KEYID = 5
     MASTER KEY    S#       DUPLICATES NOT ALLOWED
                            UPDATES        ALLOWED
     NATIVE KEY    S#
```

Explanation:

- The TABLEID clause gives a unique internal identifier to the table (namely 1, in the example).
- The FIELDS portion of the definition specifies the four fields of the table and their data types (DATACOM/DB supports the standard IBM System/370 data types: CL5 is a character string of length 5, H is halfword binary, etc.).
- The ELEMENTS portion defines five elements—one for each field in isolation and one for the combination of all four fields. For simplicity, we have given each element the same name as the object from which it is derived.
- The SEARCH KEYS portion defines two search keys, S# (based on the S# field) and CITY (based on the CITY field); for simplicity, again, we have given each search key the same name as the field from which it is derived. The significance of the KEYID specifications will be explained in a moment.
- Finally, the MASTER KEY and NATIVE KEY clauses specify that the search key S# is both the "master key" and the "native key" for the suppliers table. Every table is required to have exactly one master key and exactly one native key (they do not have to be identical, though they are in our example). The significance of these two keys is as follows:

  - The master key can optionally be specified "unique" (DUPLICATES NOT ALLOWED) and nonupdatable (UPDATES NOT ALLOWED).[4]
  - The native key controls the physical clustering of records of the table in storage (see later).

Now the parts table:

```
ADD TABLE P      TABLEID = 2
    FIELDS       P#      = CL6
                 PNAME   = CL20
                 COLOR   = CL6
                 WEIGHT  = H
                 CITY    = CL15
    ELEMENTS     P       = ( P#,PNAME,COLOR,WEIGHT,CITY )
                 P#      = ( P# )
                 PNAME   = ( PNAME )
                 COLOR   = ( COLOR )
                 WEIGHT  = ( WEIGHT )
                 CITY    = ( CITY )
    SEARCH KEYS  P#      = ( P# )     KEYID = 2
                 COLOR   = ( COLOR )  KEYID = 4
                 CITY    = ( CITY )   KEYID = 5
    MASTER KEY   P#      DUPLICATES NOT ALLOWED
                         UPDATES        ALLOWED
    NATIVE KEY   P#
```

---

4. In our example we ignore the (unfortunate) DATACOM/DB restriction that if updates are allowed then duplicates must be allowed also.

Now we can explain the KEYID specification. Observe that the CITY search keys for both tables have been given the same search key ID, namely 5. *As far as DATACOM/DB is concerned, they are therefore the same search key.* The CITY index entries for suppliers in a particular city, say London, will be physically adjacent to the CITY index entries for parts in that same city (see the explanation of index structure below). As a result, queries of the form "Find suppliers and parts that are colocated" (which will have to make use of the index) will be reasonably efficient.

Finally the shipments table:

```
ADD  TABLE  SP        TABLEID  =  3
     FIELDS           S#       =  CL5
                      P#       =  CL6
                      QTY      =  F
     ELEMENTS         SP       =  ( S#,P#,QTY )
                      S#       =  ( S# )
                      P#       =  ( P# )
                      QTY      =  ( QTY )
     SEARCH  KEYS     S#       =  ( S# )         KEYID  =  1
                      P#       =  ( P# )         KEYID  =  2
                      SHIP#    =  ( S#,P# )      KEYID  =  3
     MASTER  KEY      SHIP#    DUPLICATES  NOT  ALLOWED
                               UPDATES             ALLOWED
     NATIVE KEY       S#
```

Note the SEARCH KEYS, MASTER KEY, and NATIVE KEY specifications here—in particular, note the search key IDs, and note the fact that S# is specified as the native key. Since S# is also the native key for table S, supplier and shipment records will be physically clustered together on the basis of matching supplier numbers. For example, shipment records for supplier S1 will be stored physically close to the supplier record for supplier S1. Furthermore, the supplier and shipment records for supplier S1 will precede and be close to those for supplier S2, those for S2 will precede and be close to those for supplier S3, and so on.

We are now in a position to explain the structure of the (single) DATACOM/DB index. Conceptually, that index is built on a single hypothetical composite field, made up as follows:

$$search\ key\ ID\ +\ search\ key\ value\ +\ table\ ID$$

Each index entry contains a value for this hypothetical field, together with a pointer to a corresponding record in the database. In our example, the search key IDs and table IDs are as follows:

```
search key IDs:  S#      1
                 P#      2
                 SHIP#   3
                 COLOR   4
                 CITY    5
```

```
table IDs:   S        1
             P        2
             SP       3
```

The overall sequence of index entries is thus as indicated below (assuming the usual set of sample data values):

```
search
key        value   table    pointer
------     ------  -------   ----------------------------------
  S#         S1      S        pointer to S record for S1
  S#         S1      SP       pointer to 1st SP record for S1
  S#         S1      SP       pointer to 2nd SP record for S1
  .          .       .               . . . . .
  S#         S1      SP       pointer to last SP record for S1
  S#         S2      S        pointer to S record for S2
  S#         S2      SP       pointer to 1st SP record for S2
  .          .       .               . . . . .
  .          .       .               . . . . .
  S#         S5      .        pointer to S record for S5
  P#         P1      P        pointer to P record for P1
  P#         P1      SP       pointer to 1st SP record for P1
  .          .       .               . . . . .
  .          .       .               . . . . .
  .          .       .               . . . . .
  P#         P6      SP       pointer to last SP record for P6
  SHIP#      S1/P1   SP       pointer to SP record for S1/P1
  .          .       .               . . . . .
  SHIP#      S4/P5   SP       pointer to SP record for S4/P5
  COLOR      Blue    P        pointer to 1st P record for Blue
  .          .       .               . . . . .
  .          .       .               . . . . .
  COLOR      Red     P        pointer to last P record for Red
  CITY       Athens  S        pointer to 1st S record for Athens
  .          .       .               . . . . .
  .          .       .               . . . . .
  CITY       Rome    P        pointer to last P record for Rome
```

Points arising:

1. This single index does indeed provide the functionality of separate indexes on S.S#, SP.S#, SP.(S#,P#), etc.
2. Note that the index includes multiple entries for a given record, in general.
3. As already explained, the index entries for (e.g.) S.S# and SP.S# are interleaved in such a way as to provide a form of inter-file clustering (in the index entries themselves, that is, not in the data). Access via the index to a given S record and its corresponding SP records will thus be reasonably fast, because the relevant index entries (at least) will be physically close together. Analogous re-

marks apply to the index entries for P.P# and SP.P# and to the index entries for S.CITY and P.CITY.

4. Furthermore (again as already explained), a given S record and its corresponding SP records will also be stored physically close together, because S# has been defined as the native key for both tables. Analogous remarks do *not* apply to P records and their corresponding SP records, nor to S and P records for the same city (data can be physically clustered in one and only one way, of course).

5. Since every table must have at least one search key (because every table must have both a master key and a native key, not necessarily distinct), every record in the database is represented at least once in the index. Thus the index provides a total ordering over all records in the database, and programs can exploit that ordering in a variety of ways. Note, however, that (as already pointed out), a given record may appear multiple times in that total ordering.

21.5 DATA MANIPULATION

As explained in Section 21.2, the manipulative operators in an inverted list system such as DATACOM/DB fall into two broad classes, those that establish addressability ("search operators") and those that operate on the record at a previously established address. In addition, the search operators can be further subdivided into direct search operators and relative search operators. The following list is a brief summary of the principal DATACOM/DB operators, grouped in accordance with the foregoing classification. The list is not intended to be exhaustive; in particular, it does not include the operators of the Compound Boolean Selection feature (discussed in Section 21.6).

Direct search operators:

GSETP —locate (and read) first record in physical sequence
LOCKX —locate first record with specified search key equal to specified value
LOCKY —locate first record with specified search key equal to or greater than specified value
REDKY —same as LOCKX + REDLE
RDUKY —same as LOCKX + RDULE

Relative search operators:

GETPS —locate (and read) next record in physical sequence
LOCNX —locate next record
LOCBR —locate previous record (backward search)
LOCNE —locate next record with same search key value
LOCNK —locate first record with greater search key value
LOCKL —locate first record with same or lower search key value (backward search)
REDNX —same as LOCNX + REDLE

RDUNX—same as LOCNX + RDULE
REDNE —same as LOCNE + REDLE
RDUNE —same as LOCNE + RDULE

Operators that operate on a previously located record:

REDLE —read located record
RDULE —read located record for update (set exclusive lock)
DELET —delete located record
UPDAT —update located record
RELES —release exclusive lock
(ADDIT —store new record;
            does not establish addressability)

Each operator takes three operands (among others that we choose to ignore): a request area, an I/O area, and an element list (in general—but not all operands are needed for all operations). The request area corresponds to what we called the database address area in Section 21.2; it is used to hold position and access path information, and also a return code from the most recent operation using this request area (blank means the operation was successful). The I/O area and element list are required for retrieval (GSETP, GETPS, REDxx, RDUxx), UPDAT, and ADDIT operations; the I/O area serves the obvious purpose, and the element list indicates the elements of the record that are to be retrieved, updated, or stored.

We now present a small set of manipulative examples (as usual ignoring many details and making use of a much simplified syntax).

21.5.1 Direct retrieval.   Get the supplier record for supplier S4.

```
LOCKX using request-area-1
       ( table = S,
         search-key = S#,
         value = 'S4' ) ;
REDLE using request-area-1
       ( element-list = S ) ;
```

Or simply:

```
REDKY using request-area-1
       ( table = S,
         search-key = S#,
         value = 'S4',
         element-list = S ) ;
```

21.5.2 Sequential retrieval.   Get part numbers for parts supplied by supplier S4.

```
LOCKY using request-area-1
       ( table = SP,
         search-key = S#,
         value = 'S4' ) ;
```

```
while "record found" on request-area-1
do ;
    REDLE using request-area-1
          ( element-list = P# ) ;
    LOCNE using request-area-1 ;
end ;
```

21.5.3 Sequential retrieval.   Get part numbers for parts supplied by suppliers in London.

```
LOCKY using request-area-1
      ( table = S,
        search-key = CITY,
        value = 'London' ) ;
while "record found" on request-area-1
do ;
    REDLE using request-area-1
          ( element-list = S# ) ;
    LOCKY using request-area-2
          ( table = SP,
            search-key = S#,
            value = S# value read in preceding REDLE ) ;
    while "record found" on request-area-2
    do ;
        REDLE using request-area-2
              ( element-list = P# ) ;
        LOCNE using request-area-2 ;
    end ;
    LOCNE using request-area-1 ;
end ;
```

21.5.4 Sequential retrieval.   Get part numbers for parts supplied by suppliers with status 20. (Compare previous example.)

```
GSETP using request-area-1
      ( table = S,
        element-list = S#, STATUS ) ;
while "record found" on request-area-1
do ;
    if STATUS = 20 then
    do ;
        LOCKY using request-area-2
              ( table = SP,
                search-key = S#,
                value = S# value read in preceding REDLE ) ;
        while "record found" on request-area-2
        do ;
            REDLE using request-area-2
                  ( element-list = P# ) ;
            LOCNE using request-area-2 ;
        end ;
    end ;
```

```
         GETPS using request-area-1
                ( element-list = S#, STATUS ) ;
  end ;
```

Since STATUS has not been defined as a search key, searching for suppliers with status 20 has to be done by an exhaustive scan. We choose to perform that scan in physical sequence, for reasons of performance.

21.5.5 Update. Add 10 to the status for supplier S4.

```
LOCKX using request-area-1
      ( table = S,
        search-key = S#,
        value = 'S4' ) ;
RDULE using request-area-1
      ( element-list = STATUS ) ;
set STATUS = STATUS + 10 in I/O area ;
UPDAT using request-area-1
      ( element-list = STATUS ) ;
```

Before a record can be updated (or deleted), it must first be retrieved with one of the RDU*xx* operations ("read for update").

21.5.6 Storing a new record. Store a new supplier record (supplier number S6, name Robinson, status 35, city unknown).

```
move 'S6', 'Robinson', 35 to I/O area for request-area-1 ;
ADDIT using request-area-1
      ( element-list = S#, SNAME, STATUS ) ;
```

The CITY field will be set to blanks in the new record.

21.6 THE COMPOUND BOOLEAN SELECTION FEATURE

The Compound Boolean Selection feature (CBS) is a comparatively recent extension to the DATACOM/DB base product. The general objective of CBS is to provide increased flexibility and increased data independence at the application programming interface; indeed, it can be regarded as a step toward converting DATACOM/DB into a true relational DBMS. A good way of explaining CBS (at perhaps rather a superficial level) is to compare it with embedded SQL (see Chapter 9). The major CBS operations, and their embedded SQL equivalents, are as follows:

■ SELFR—"select first"

SELFR is analogous to a combination of the embedded SQL operations DECLARE CURSOR, OPEN, and FETCH. Thus, one of the operands of SELFR is a *query* (not a CBS term), defining a set of records; that set is opened or "activated" (also not a CBS term), and the first record of that active set is retrieved. The defining query consists of a table name, a restriction predicate, and an optional ordering specification.[5]

- SELNR—"select next"

SELNR is analogous to FETCH in embedded SQL, though it does also provide certain additional functions (to be discussed).

- SELSM—"select same"

SELSM retrieves the current record (again). Embedded SQL has no equivalent of this function.

- UPDAT/DELET—"update"/"delete"

UPDAT and DELET are analogous in the CBS context to the embedded SQL operations UPDATE CURRENT and DELETE CURRENT, respectively.

- SELPR—"release set"

SELPR is analogous to CLOSE in embedded SQL.

These operations clearly provide more function than the basic data manipulation facilities described in Section 21.5. First, access paths—that is, *logical* access paths—do not have to be predefined but can be specified dynamically via the SELFR operation. Second, those logical access paths can be defined in terms of arbitrary restriction predicates, involving any fields—they are not limited to simple predicates of the form "search key equal (or greater than or equal) to value." (In fact, there is no reliance on predefined search keys at all.) Third, the ordering of those logical access paths can also be specified dynamically. On the other hand, the fact that the predicate in a path definition must be a simple restriction—in particular, the fact that it cannot involve a join—means that DATACOM/DB still does not qualify as a true relational system in the sense of Chapter 15.

The CBS feature provides a number of further facilities in addition to those sketched above. First, the SELFR can optionally include the following specifications (not genuine CBS syntax):

- UNIQUE (specifiable only if ordering is specified)

Records with the same value for the ordering field(s) as the record most recently retrieved will be skipped over during subsequent retrieval requests.

- COUNT

The cardinality of the active set is returned.

- *n* (quota)

5.   The query is actually specified by means of a "request qualification area" parameter to the CBS call. The details are complex and are beyond the scope of this text.

Subsequent retrieval requests will return "not found" after the first n records of the active set have been retrieved. This facility can be used—in conjunction with the dynamic ordering facility—to implement such retrievals as "Get the three heaviest parts" (for example).

■ FOR UPDATE

An exclusive lock will be applied to each record as it is retrieved. FOR UPDATE is required if the retrieved record is subsequently to be updated or deleted. The lock will be released automatically on the next retrieval if the record has not in fact been updated or deleted. Note: FOR UPDATE can be specified on SELNR and SELSM as well as on SELFR.

Second, SELNR ("select next") can specify a "skip count." A skip count of $+n$ causes SELNR to retrieve the record n positions after the current record in the active set. Similarly, a skip count of $-n$ causes it to retrieve the record n positions before the current record. Skip counts of 0 and -32768 cause SELNR to retrieve the first record and the last record, respectively. SELFR initializes the skip count to $+1$.

Third, it is also possible to establish certain "interrupt limits" in SELFR. An example of an interrupt limit is "number of I/O's." If that number is exceeded during SELFR execution, control is returned to the application program with an appropriate return code in the request area. At that point the program can issue any one of the following operations: SELPR, which cancels the SELFR entirely (no active set is established); SELST, which stops execution of the SELFR but accepts the partially built active set as a basis for subsequent processing (SELNR, etc.); or SELCN, which continues building the active set (the interrupt counters are all reset, and may subsequently cause another interrupt during further execution of the same SELFR).

We conclude this section, and this chapter, by observing that the CBS feature clearly implies the existence of a query optimization component within the DATACOM/DB system. Detailed characteristics of that optimizer are unknown at the time of writing.

EXERCISES

21.1 Define a DATACOM/DB version of the suppliers-parts-projects database.

21.2 Using your answer to Exercise 21.1 as a basis, give DATACOM/DB solutions to the following. Use operators of the Compound Boolean Selection feature where appropriate.

    a) Get S# values for suppliers who supply project J1.

    b) Get S# values for suppliers who supply project J1 with a red part.

    c) Get P# values for parts supplied to all projects in London.

    d) Get J# values for projects not supplied with any red part by any London supplier.

e) Get P# values for parts supplied by at least one supplier who supplies at least one part supplied by supplier S1.

f) Get all pairs of CITY values such that a supplier in the first city supplies a project in the second city.

g) Change the color of all red parts to orange.

h) The quantity of P1 supplied to J1 by S1 is now to be supplied by S2 instead (in addition to any quantity of P1 that S2 already supplies to J1). Make all the necessary changes.

REFERENCES AND BIBLIOGRAPHY

21.1 Information on DATACOM/DB and the Relational Information Management Environment (RIME) is available from Applied Data Research, Inc., Rte. 206 and Orchard Rd., CN-8, Princeton, New Jersey 08540.

21.2 Information on ADABAS is available from Software AG, 11800 Sunrise Valley Drive, Reston, Virginia 22091.

21.3 Information on Model 204 is available from Computer Corporation of America, Four Cambridge Center, Cambridge, Massachusetts 02142.

21.4 Information on System 1022 is available from Software House, 1105 Massachusetts Avenue, Cambridge, Massachusetts 02138.

22

A Hierarchic
System:
IMS

22.1 BACKGROUND

The name "IMS" is an acronym for "Information Management System." IMS is
an IBM program product for the MVS environment (like DB2, though of course
unlike DB2 it is hierarchic, not relational). It was one of the first database systems
to become commercially available—the first version of the system ("IMS/360 Version 1") was released in 1968—and at the time of writing it is easily one of the top
two or three products, if not *the* top product, in the mainframe marketplace, both
in terms of number of systems installed and also in terms of user commitment. We
therefore use it as our example of the hierarchic approach.

Note: The full name of the current version of IMS is "Information Management System / Virtual Storage" (IMS/VS), and IBM manuals invariably refer to
it by this full name. However, we will continue to use the abbreviated form "IMS"
in this book.

Hierarchic systems, like inverted list systems, were not originally constructed
on the basis of a predefined abstract data model; rather, such a model was defined
after the event by a process of abstraction from implemented systems (mainly from
IMS, in fact). As suggested in the introduction to this part of the book, however,
it is convenient to discuss the abstract model first—even if such a discussion must
necessarily be somewhat hypothetical—before embarking on a description of the
details of IMS per se. Section 22.2 is therefore devoted to a discussion (fairly informal) of such a hypothetical model.

22.2 THE HIERARCHIC MODEL

Hierarchic Data Structure

A hierarchic database consists of an ordered set of *trees*—more precisely, an ordered
set consisting of multiple *occurrences* of a single *type* of tree. We discuss types first,
then go on to discuss occurrences later.

A *tree type* consists of a single "root" record type, together with an ordered set of zero or more dependent (lower-level) subtree types. A subtree type in turn also consists of a single record type—the root of the subtree type—together with an ordered set of zero or more lower-level dependent subtree types, and so on. The entire tree type thus consists of a hierarchic arrangement of record types. In addition, of course, record types are made up of field types in the usual way.

As an example, consider the *education database*[1] of Fig. 22.1, which contains information about the internal education system of a large industrial company. The company in question maintains an education department whose function is to run a number of training courses for the employees of the company; each course is offered at a number of different locations within the organization, and the database contains details both of offerings already given and of offerings scheduled to be given in the future. The database contains the following information:

- For each course: course number, course title, details of all immediate prerequisite courses, and details of all offerings;

- For each prerequisite course for a given course: course number for that prerequisite course;

- For each offering of a given course: offering number, date, location, details of all teachers, and details of all students;

- For each teacher of a given offering: employee number and name;

- For each student of a given offering: employee number, name, and grade.

The tree type for the education database has COURSE as its root record type and has two subtree types, rooted in the PREREQ and OFFERING record types respectively (and note that this set of two subtree types is ordered—that is, the PREREQ subtree type definitely precedes the OFFERING subtree type, as the fig-

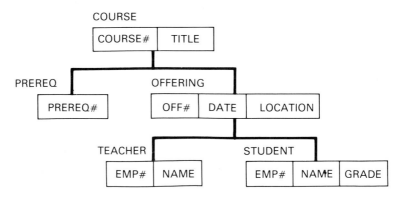

Fig. 22.1 Structure of the education database.

---

1. We deliberately depart for a while from our standard suppliers-and-parts example.

ure suggests). The subtree type rooted in PREREQ is "root only"; by contrast, the
subtree type rooted in OFFERING in turn has two lower-level subtree types, both
root only, rooted in the TEACHER and STUDENT record types respectively. Again
the subtree types are ordered.

The database thus contains five record types: COURSE, PREREQ, OFFER-
ING, TEACHER, and STUDENT. COURSE (as already stated) is the root record
type, the others are *dependent* record types. Furthermore, COURSE is said to be
the *parent* record type for record types PREREQ and OFFERING, and PREREQ
and OFFERING are said to be *child* record types for record type COURSE. Likewise, OFFERING is the parent record type for TEACHER and STUDENT, and
TEACHER and STUDENT are child record types for OFFERING. The connection
between a given child (type) and its corresponding parent (type) is called a *link*
(type). Note: It is (as always) normal to drop the qualifiers "type" and "occurrence" whenever it is possible to do so without risk of ambiguity, though for the
purposes of the present section we will continue to be specific (usually).

At this point it may be helpful to point out the principal (indeed, crucial) difference between a hierarchic structure such as that of Fig. 22.1 and the equivalent
relational structure. That difference is as follows: *In a hierarchic database, certain
information that would be represented in a relational database by foreign keys is
represented instead by parent-child links.* In the education database, for example,
the connection between OFFERINGs and COURSEs is represented, not by a
COURSE# field in the OFFERING record, but rather by the COURSE-OFFERING
link.[2] This difference in structure naturally leads to a difference in the operators
also, as we will see.

So much for types; now we turn our attention to *occurrences*. The root/parent/
child (etc.) terminology just introduced for types carries over into occurrences too.
Thus, each tree occurrence consists of a single root record occurrence, together with
an ordered set of zero or more occurrences of each of the subtree types immediately
dependent on the root record type. Each of those subtree occurrences in turn also
consists of a single record occurrence—the root of the subtree occurrence—together
with an ordered set of zero or more occurrences of each of the subtree types immediately dependent on that root record type, and so on. In other words, for any
given occurrence of any given parent record type, there are *n* occurrences of each
of its child record types (*n* greater than or equal to zero). For an illustration, see
Fig. 22.2, which shows a single tree from the education database of Fig. 22.1—
more accurately, of course, a single tree *occurrence*.

We explain the tree of Fig. 22.2 as follows. By definition, that tree contains a
single COURSE occurrence (the root of the tree). That COURSE has two subordinate PREREQs and three subordinate OFFERINGs (more accurately, that

2. Note, however, that in general not all such connections will be represented by links; on
the contrary, some will still be represented by fields, as in a relational database. For example,
field PREREQ.PREREQ# in Fig. 22.1 is a foreign key in the conventional relational sense.
The reader is referred back to Section 15.2 for further discussion of this point.

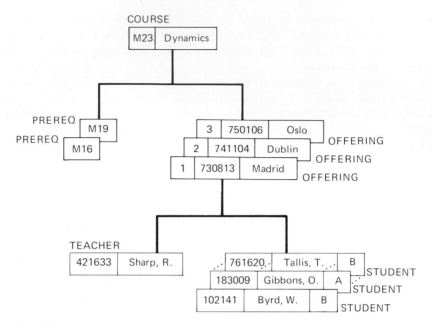

Fig. 22.2 Sample tree for the education database.

COURSE *occurrence* has an *ordered set* of two subordinate PREREQ *occurrences* and an *ordered set* of three subordinate OFFERING *occurrences*). We say that the COURSE is a parent (occurrence), with two PREREQ children and three OFFER-ING children (i.e., child occurrences). Likewise, the first OFFERING is also a parent, with one TEACHER child and several STUDENT children (only three shown). The other two OFFERINGs have no TEACHER or STUDENT children at present. Furthermore, each parent (occurrence) is considered to be the parent in as many links (i.e., link occurrences) as that parent has children; the COURSE record in Fig. 22.2, for example, is the parent in two occurrences of the COURSE-PREREQ link and the parent in three occurrences of the COURSE-OFFERING link. Conversely, each child (occurrence) is the child in exactly one link (occurrence).

In addition to the foregoing, there is one term that applies to occurrences and not to types—the term "twin." All occurrences of a given child type that share a common parent occurrence are said to be *twins*. Thus, for example, the three OF-FERINGs in Fig. 22.2 are twins (even though there are three of them). Note by contrast that the PREREQs in that figure are not twins of those OFFERINGs, because, although they have the same parent as those OFFERINGs, they are of a different type.

The reader will have observed the frequency with which the concept of ordering was mentioned during the foregoing explanations. In fact, the notion of ordering is critical to the hierarchic data structure. Consider some (sub)tree type T, with root record type R and subtree types $S1, S2, \ldots, Sn$ (in that order). Let t be an occurrence of T, with root r (an occurrence of R) and subtrees $s1, s2, \ldots, sn$ (occur-

rences of *S1, S2, . . ., Sn*, respectively). Then we define the *hierarchic sequence* for
t—recursively—to be that sequence obtained by taking record *r* first, followed by
all of the records of *s1* in hierarchic sequence, followed by all of the records of *s2*
in hierarchic sequence, . . . , followed by all of the records of *sn* in hierarchic sequence. For example, the hierarchic sequence for the tree of Fig. 22.2 is as follows:

```
COURSE        M23
PREREQ        M16
PREREQ        M19
OFFERING        1
TEACHER     421633
STUDENT     102141
STUDENT     183009
        . . . . . . . . . .
STUDENT     761620
OFFERING        2
OFFERING        3
```

(i.e., top-to-bottom, left-to-right order).

Note that each individual tree in the database can be regarded as a subtree of
a hypothetical "system" root record. As a result, *the entire database can be considered as a single tree.* It follows that the notion of hierarchic sequence defined
above applies to the entire database as well as to each individual (sub)tree. That is,
the notion of hierarchic sequence defines a *total ordering* for the set of all records
in the database, and databases can and should be regarded as being (logically) stored
in accordance with that total ordering. (This idea is particularly important in IMS,
because many of the IMS manipulative operators are defined in terms of that sequence. See Section 22.5.)

We conclude this subsection with a brief note on IMS terminology. In explaining
the hierarchic data structure, we have wherever possible used common and fairly
standard terms, such as "tree," "record," and so on. However, IMS uses "segment" in place of the more familiar "record," and refers to an entire tree of
segments—somewhat confusingly—as a "database record." The terms "tree,"
"subtree," and "link" are not used in IMS at all; however, they are convenient,
and we will continue to use them in this chapter.

Hierarchic Data Manipulation

A hierarchic data manipulation language consists of a set of operators for processing data represented in the form of trees. Examples of such operators include
the following:

- An operator to locate a specific tree in the database—for example, an operator
to locate the tree for course M23 (see Fig. 22.2);

- An operator to move from one such tree to the next—for example, an operator
to step from the tree for course M23 to the tree that follows it in the hierarchic
sequence of the database;

- Operators to move from record to record within such a tree by moving up and

down the various hierarchic paths—for example, an operator to step from the
COURSE record for course M23 to the first OFFERING record for that course;

- Operators to move from record to record in accordance with the hierarchic
  sequence of the database—for example, an operator to step from a TEACHER
  record for a particular OFFERING to a STUDENT record for that OFFERING
  or for some subsequent OFFERING;

- An operator to insert a new record at a specified position within such a tree—
  for example, an operator to insert a new OFFERING into the tree for course
  M23;

- An operator to delete a specified record—for example, an operator to delete a
  particular OFFERING from the tree for course M23;

and so on. Note that (as suggested by the examples) such operators are typically all
record-level; it is true that certain systems do support certain set-level operators also,
but such operators are outside the scope of "the hierarchic model," as that term is
usually understood.

Hierarchic Data Integrity

The hierarchic model includes "automatic" support for certain forms of referential
integrity, by virtue of the following rule: *No child is allowed to exist without its
parent*. (The rule refers to occurrences, of course, not types.) For example, if a given
parent is deleted, the system will automatically delete the entire (sub)tree that is
rooted at that parent. Likewise, a child cannot be inserted unless its parent already
exists. In terms of the rules of Section 12.5, therefore, we can say—a little loosely
—that the hierarchic data structure automatically enforces the following rules:

```
NULLS NOT ALLOWED
DELETE ... CASCADES
UPDATE ... CASCADES
```

IMS in particular supports certain additional constraints by means of its logical
database and secondary indexing facilities. See Sections 22.7 and 22.8.

22.3   AN OVERVIEW OF IMS

We turn now to IMS specifically. First, the definitional aspects. There are two principal definitional constructs in IMS, the *database description* (DBD) and the *program communication block* (PCB). We explain those two constructs in outline as
follows.

1. An IMS database is of course a hierarchic database,[3] in the sense of Section
22.2; it consists of a hierarchic arrangement of *segments* (i.e., records), and each

---

3.   At least from the user's point of view. Under some circumstances, however, the physical
(stored) structure may be more network-like.

segment in turn consists of a collection of *fields*. Each such database is defined by means of a DBD, which specifies (among other things) the hierarchic structure of that database.

2. However, users deal not with databases directly, but with *views* of those databases ("view" is not an IMS term). A given user's view of a given database consists basically of a "subhierarchy," derived from the underlying hierarchy by omitting certain segments and/or certain fields. Such a view is defined by means of a PCB, which specifies (among other things) the hierarchic structure of that view.

We can thus see that, *very* approximately, a DBD is the IMS equivalent of "CREATE TABLE" and a PCB is the IMS equivalent of "CREATE VIEW"—with the significant difference that CREATE TABLE and CREATE VIEW are dynamic operations and can be performed at any time, whereas DBD and PCB definition are static operations and require the execution of an IMS utility. Furthermore, the simple explanation above ignores two very important points:

- First, a given IMS database can be either *physical* or *logical*. A physical database has a DBD that directly describes the representation of that database in physical storage. A logical database, by contrast, has a DBD that describes the representation of that database in terms of one or more other (physical) databases; i.e., a "logical" DBD is defined in terms of one or more underlying "physical" DBDs. The referential integrity rules for a logical database are significantly more complex than those for a physical database. (The simple rule given in Section 22.2, to the effect that no record (segment) can exist without its parent, tacitly assumed that the database in question was physical, in IMS terms.)

- Second, if the DBD corresponding to a given PCB defines a database having one or more *secondary indexes*, then it is possible for that PCB to specify, not just a subhierarchy of the underlying hierarchy, but a *secondary data structure*. A secondary data structure is still a hierarchy, but a hierarchy in which the participant segments have been rearranged, possibly drastically. Note: A secondary index in IMS is a significantly more complex object than the secondary indexes discussed in Chapter 3 of this book.

As a result of these two considerations, the true IMS picture is considerably more complicated than our initial brief explanation might have suggested. For further details, see Sections 22.7 and 22.8.

We turn now to data manipulation. IMS is invoked via a CALL interface called DL/I (Data Language/I) from application programs written in PL/I, COBOL, or System/370 Assembler Language. Note, therefore, that (as usual in nonrelational systems) the user in IMS is definitely an *application programmer*; we restrict our use of the term "user" accordingly in this chapter. *End*-users are of course supported by means of appropriate on-line application programs.

Note: The full IMS system includes not only the DBMS component that is the principal topic of this chapter, but also a data communications (DC) component; in other words, IMS is a DB/DC system, to use the terminology of Chapter 2. Facilities are provided a) to permit the user to define the mappings between byte string messages and the physical layout of those messages on the terminal ("Message Formatting Services"), and b) to allow programs to send and receive such messages ("DL/I DC calls," so called to distinguish them from DL/I database calls). However, all such facilities are beyond the scope of this text.

The remainder of this chapter has the following structure. After this preliminary overview section, Section 22.4 explains IMS data definition (i.e., the DBD and PCB constructs); note, however, that the more complex aspects—logical databases and secondary indexing—are not discussed at all until Sections 22.7 and 22.8. Section 22.5 describes IMS data manipulation (i.e., the DL/I database calls). Section 22.6 then presents a necessarily brief introduction to IMS storage structures. Next, as already indicated, Sections 22.7 and 22.8 describe the logical database and secondary index features omitted from Section 22.3. Finally, Section 22.9 presents a few concluding remarks.

There is no room in this chapter for a detailed discussion of the topics of Part 4 of this book (recovery, concurrency, etc.). We content ourselves with the following brief comments:

- *Recovery*. The recovery features of IMS are both extensive and sophisticated, and include all of the aspects (transaction, system, and media recovery) discussed in Chapter 18.

- *Concurrency*. IMS concurrency control is based on record (segment) locking, though certain additional controls are also provided. However, IMS does not automatically support full two-phase locking [18.7] but rather a protocol that more nearly resembles the "cursor stability" (CS) protocol of DB2 (see the annotation to reference [18.9]).

- *Security*. Just as views can be used to hide information in a relational system such as DB2, so PCBs can be used (though not so flexibly) to hide information in IMS. PCBs are also used to specify the DL/I operations (get, insert, etc.) the user is allowed to execute on the "view." In addition, IMS provides a range of facilities (password checking, etc.) to ensure that specific transactions can be invoked only by specific end-users and/or from specific terminals.

- *Integrity*. IMS will optionally enforce certain field uniqueness constraints (see Section 22.4). In addition (as already indicated), certain referential integrity constraints are supported directly by the hierarchic data structure itself (together with certain explicit insert/update/delete rules, in the case of logical databases; see Section 22.7).

Further details of the foregoing can be found in Volume II.

IMS also possesses a fairly extensive family of related products in the sense of Chapter 20, as is only to be expected for a system that has been available for as long as IMS has. Such products include a data dictionary, query interfaces (both interactive and batch), an application generator, design aids, testing and debugging aids, measurement and tuning tools, and many other facilities. Such products are available from several other vendors in addition to IBM.

To conclude this section, we stress the point that our treatment of IMS in this chapter is necessarily very superficial. Many details are simply ignored. As a result, our explanations may make the system appear unrealistically straightforward! The fact is, IMS is an extremely complex system—complex, that is, not only internally, but externally too; the user interface to IMS is *extremely* complicated. And needless to say it is precisely the details—the numerous special cases, exceptions, interdependencies, etc. that the user has to learn and deal with—that give rise to all the complexity. Indeed, one of Codd's motivations for developing the relational model in the first place was precisely to escape from the complexities of systems such as IMS [22.6].

22.4 DATA DEFINITION

As explained in the previous section, there are two major definitional constructs in IMS, the database description (DBD) and the program communication block (PCB). We discuss the DBD first. Figure 22.3 shows a possible DBD for the education database. (We remind the reader that we are ignoring numerous details in this chapter; in particular, Fig. 22.3 does not show details of how the database is mapped to physical storage. However, some of those details will be discussed briefly in Section 22.6.)

We explain Fig. 22.3 as follows.

- Statement 1 merely assigns the name EDUCPDBD ("education physical DBD") to the DBD.

```
 1     DBD        NAME=EDUCPDBD
 2     SEGM       NAME=COURSE,BYTES=36
 3     FIELD      NAME=(COURSE#,SEQ),BYTES=3,START=1
 4     FIELD      NAME=TITLE,BYTES=33,START=4
 5     SEGM       NAME=PREREQ,PARENT=COURSE,BYTES=3
 6     FIELD      NAME=(PREREQ#,SEQ),BYTES=3,START=1
 7     SEGM       NAME=OFFERING,PARENT=COURSE,BYTES=21
 8     FIELD      NAME=(OFF#,SEQ),BYTES=3,START=1
 9     FIELD      NAME=DATE,BYTES=6,START=4
10     FIELD      NAME=LOCATION,BYTES=12,START=10
11     SEGM       NAME=TEACHER,PARENT=OFFERING,BYTES=24
12     FIELD      NAME=(EMP#,SEQ),BYTES=6,START=1
13     FIELD      NAME=NAME,BYTES=18,START=7
14     SEGM       NAME=STUDENT,PARENT=OFFERING,BYTES=24
15     FIELD      NAME=(EMP#,SEQ),BYTES=6,START=1
16     FIELD      NAME=NAME,BYTES=18,START=7
17     FIELD      NAME=GRADE,BYTES=1,START=25
```

Fig. 22.3 DBD (many details omitted) for the education database.

- Statement 2 defines the root segment as having the name COURSE and a length of 36 bytes.

- Statements 3–4 define the fields that go to make up COURSE. Each is given a name, a length in bytes, and a start position within the segment. Field COURSE# is defined (via the SEQ specification) to be the sequence field for COURSEs, which means that a) COURSE# values are unique within the database, and b) COURSEs (and therefore trees) will be sequenced within the database in ascending course number order.

  Two asides regarding segments and fields: First, IMS does not support any field data types, in the usual sense of that term; instead, all fields are considered simply as byte strings (all field comparisons are performed bit by bit from left to right). Second, IMS also allows segments to have nonunique or omitted sequence fields. However, details of those possibilities are beyond the scope of this book.

- Statement 5 defines PREREQ as a 3-byte segment that is a child of COURSE. Statement 6 defines the single field of PREREQ, namely field PREREQ#. That field is defined as the sequence field for PREREQ, which means that a) PREREQ# values are unique within COURSE, and b) for each occurrence of COURSE, PREREQs will be sequenced in ascending prerequisite number order (in other words, the SEQ specification defines "twin sequence" for PREREQ).

- Statements 7–10 are analogous to statements 5–6. The sequence field for OFFERINGs is OFF# (offering number).

- Statements 11–13 define TEACHER (a child of OFFERING) and its fields. Statements 14–17 define STUDENT similarly.

We turn now to "user views" and the PCB. Any particular user view is a subhierarchy of the underlying DBD hierarchy, derived from that underlying hierarchy in accordance with the following three rules:

1. Any field type can be omitted.
2. Any segment type can be omitted.
3. If a given segment type is omitted, then all of its children must be omitted too.

Rule 3 implies that the root of the PCB hierarchy must be the same as the root of the DBD hierarchy. Consider the education database of Fig. 22.1 once again. Ignoring Rule 1, there are basically ten user views that can be derived from that database. One is shown in Fig. 22.4. What are the others?

Those segments and fields included in the user view—segments COURSE, OFFERING, and STUDENT, with their constituent fields, in the case of Fig. 22.4— are said to be "sensitive." A user of the view will not be aware of the existence of any other segments or fields. Thus the IMS "user view" mechanism, like the view mechanism in a relational system, protects the user from certain kinds of growth in the database. It also provides a degree of control over data security.

Figure 22.5 shows a PCB for the user view of Fig. 22.4—except that, purely

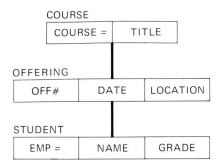

Fig. 22.4 Sample user view of the education database.

for the sake of the example, we have excluded the LOCATION field from the OF-FERING segment. Sensitive segments and sensitive fields are specified by SENSEG and SENFLD statements, respectively; if no SENFLDs are specified for a given SENSEG, all fields of that segment are assumed to be sensitive by default. The PROCOPT entries in the SENSEG statements specify the types of operation the user will be permitted to perform on the corresponding segments; possible values include G ("get"), I ("insert"), R ("replace"), D ("delete"), or any combination. The PCB statement simply identifies the underlying DBD.

```
1      PCB        DBDNAME=EDUCPDBD
2      SENSEG     NAME=COURSE,PROCOPT=G
3      SENSEG     NAME=OFFERING,PARENT=COURSE,PROCOPT=G
4      SENFLD     NAME=OFF#,START=1
5      SENFLD     NAME=DATE,START=4
6      SENSEG     NAME=STUDENT,PARENT=OFFERING,PROCOPT=G
```

Fig. 22.5 PCB for the user view of Fig. 22.4 (excluding the LOCATION field).

22.5 DATA MANIPULATION

The IMS data manipulation language (DL/I) is invoked from the host language (PL/I, COBOL, or System/370 Assembler Language) by means of ordinary sub-routine calls. Here is an example of such a call, in which the host is PL/I:

```
CALL PLITDLI ( SIX, GU, EDPCB, STUDENT_AREA, CSSA, OSSA, SSSA ) ;
```

This call is intended to retrieve a specific STUDENT segment from the edu-cation database. The arguments are interpreted as follows:

- PLITDLI ("PL/I to DL/I") identifies the entry point into IMS from a PL/I program.

- SIX represents a PL/I numeric variable whose value (presumably six) represents a count of the number of arguments in the call (excluding the count argument itself).

- GU represents a PL/I character string variable whose value (presumably 'GU') specifies the DL/I operation to be performed (the operation GU stands for "get unique": see later).

- EDPCB ("education PCB") represents a PL/I structure corresponding to the PCB for the user view against which the operation is to be performed. This argument is explained in more detail below.

- STUDENT_AREA represents a PL/I character string variable into which the desired STUDENT segment is to be retrieved. In other words, STUDENT_AREA represents the *I/O area* for the call.

- CSSA, OSSA, and SSSA represent PL/I character string variables whose values in turn are "segment search arguments" or *SSAs*. An SSA consists of a segment name, an optional set of "command codes" (see later), and an optional restriction predicate. Typical SSAs might be:

```
CSSA:    COURSE   WHERE TITLE = 'Dynamics'
OSSA:    OFFERING WHERE DATE  > '750101'
SSSA:    STUDENT  WHERE GRADE = 'A'
```

(not genuine IMS syntax). A "get unique" with these three SSAs will retrieve the first STUDENT in hierarchic sequence for which the grade is A and the offering date is greater than 750101 and the course title is Dynamics.

To explain the EDPCB argument, we remind the reader once again of certain facilities of embedded SQL—namely, *cursors* and the *SQL Communication Area* (SQLCA). Briefly, a cursor is a database position holder, and the SQLCA is a feedback area (see Chapter 9 for more information). *EDPCB can be regarded as the IMS equivalent of a cursor and a corresponding feedback area in combination.*[4] In IMS, a program does not have just one feedback area as it does in SQL, but rather one feedback area for each "cursor" (i.e., each PCB—note that one IMS program can have any number of PCBs, just as one SQL program can have any number of cursors). And each feedback area includes, not only a return code ("STATUS," analogous to SQLCODE in the SQLCA) and related information, but also the program's current position for the PCB in question—current position, that is, within the user view corresponding to that PCB. From the perspective of IMS, in fact, each cursor/feedback-area combination is considered to be simply an internalized form of the corresponding external PCB, and it is therefore actually referred to (somewhat confusingly) as a PCB. In this section we will follow IMS usage and take "PCB" to refer to the internalized form.

We now embark on a brief explanation of the major DL/I operations. First we summarize those operations:

- Get unique (GU):   Direct retrieval
- Get next (GN):   Sequential retrieval

---

4. It can also be regarded as the IMS equivalent of a request area in DATACOM/DB.

- Get next within parent (GNP): Sequential retrieval under current parent
- Get hold (GHU, GHN, GHNP): As above but allow subsequent DLET/ REPL
- Insert (ISRT): Insert new segment
- Delete (DLET): Delete existing segment
- Replace (REPL): Update existing segment

To simplify our examples we choose not to use the genuine DL/I call syntax in this book, but rather the hypothetical syntax illustrated by the following example:[5]

```
GU COURSE    WHERE TITLE = 'Dynamics' ,
   OFFERING WHERE DATE  > '750101' ,
   STUDENT  WHERE GRADE = 'A' ;
```

—a "get unique" operation with a "path" of three SSAs. Simplifying the IMS rules considerably, we may say that a) "get unique" and "insert" operations require SSAs specifying the entire hierarchic path from the root down; b) "get next" and "get next within parent" operations may or may not involve SSAs, and if they do, then the SSAs must again specify a hierarchic path, but one that can start at any level, not necessarily at the root; and c) "delete" and "replace" operations do not involve SSAs at all. We now give examples of all of these possibilities, all expressed in terms of the education database of Fig. 22.1. For simplicity, we assume that the "user view" consists of the entire database—i.e., all segments and fields are sensitive.

22.5.1 Direct retrieval. Get the first offering for Stockholm.

```
GU COURSE ,
   OFFERING WHERE LOCATION = 'Stockholm' ;
```

This example illustrates a) the use of an SSA without a predicate and b) a path of SSAs that stops short of the lowest level. If no predicate is specified, any segment of the indicated type is considered to satisfy the SSA. Note that "first" in the problem statement means *first in hierarchic sequence.* "Get unique" is really a misnomer—the operation is really "get *first*."

Incidentally, this "get unique," like all other DL/I operations, should in practice be followed by an appropriate test on the STATUS field of the PCB (a blank STATUS value means the operation completed satisfactorily, a nonblank value means some exceptional condition occurred). We will generally ignore such testing in our examples.

22.5.2 Path call. Get the first Stockholm offering and also its parent course.

```
GU COURSE * D ,
   OFFERING WHERE LOCATION = 'Stockholm' ;
```

5. Note that this simplified syntax omits all mention of both the PCB and the I/O area.

Normally a DL/I retrieval operation such as GU retrieves only the segment at the lowest level of the path. In Example 22.5.1, for instance, only an OFFERING is retrieved. However, it is also possible to retrieve any *ancestor* of that lowest segment in addition,[6] by specifying the "command code" D in the applicable SSA(s). Command codes (there may be more than one) follow the segment name in the SSA and are separated from it by an asterisk.

22.5.3 Sequential retrieval.   Get all Stockholm offerings.

```
GU COURSE ;
do until no more OFFERINGs ;
    GN OFFERING WHERE LOCATION = 'Stockholm' ;
end ;
```

The operation of GN ("get next") is defined in terms of the *current database position* ("current position" for short). That position, in turn, is defined to be the segment last accessed by a "get" operation (of any type) or an "insert" operation.[7] In the example, therefore, the GU operation establishes an initial position, namely the first COURSE in the database. The first iteration of the loop then retrieves the first Stockholm OFFERING following that position, and establishes that OFFERING as the new current position; the second iteration then retrieves the second Stockholm OFFERING, and so on. The loop will be repeated until all OFFERINGs in the database have been scanned, at which point an appropriate nonblank STATUS value will be returned in the PCB.

Notice that the "path" of SSAs—actually a single SSA—in the GN in this example starts at a segment lower than the root. Note too that "next" in "get next" means (of course) "next in hierarchic sequence."

22.5.4 Sequential retrieval within a parent.   Get all Stockholm offerings for course M23.

```
GU COURSE WHERE COURSE# = 'M23' ;
do until no more OFFERINGs under current COURSE ;
    GNP OFFERING WHERE LOCATION = 'Stockholm' ;
end ;
```

The operation of GNP ("get next within parent") is defined in terms of both the current database position (as for GN) and also the *current parent position*. That current parent position, in turn, is defined to be the segment last accessed by "get unique" or "get next" (*not* "get next within parent") or "insert." In the example, therefore, the GU operation establishes the COURSE segment for course M23 as both the current database position and the current parent position. The first iter-

---

6. An ancestor of a given segment is either the parent of that segment or an ancestor of that parent.

7. More accurately, the program has multiple current positions, one for each PCB. Since our hypothetical syntax omits all reference to the PCB, we will usually assume for simplicity that there is in fact just one current position.

ation of the loop then retrieves the first Stockholm OFFERING under that COURSE and establishes that OFFERING as the new current database position, but does not change the current parent position; the second iteration then retrieves the second Stockholm OFFERING under that COURSE, and so on. The loop will be repeated until all OFFERINGs under that COURSE have been scanned, at which point (again) an appropriate nonblank STATUS value will be returned in the PCB.

22.5.5 Sequential retrieval within a parent.   Get all grade A students for course M23.

```
GU COURSE WHERE COURSE# = 'M23' ;
do until no more STUDENTs under current COURSE ;
   GNP STUDENT WHERE GRADE = 'A' ;
end ;
```

"Get next within parent" is really a misnomer—the operation is really "get next within *ancestor*," as this example illustrates. The code will retrieve all grade A STUDENTs *for all OFFERINGs* for COURSE M23.

22.5.6 Sequential retrieval across segment types.   Get any student taught by employee 421633 as a teacher.

```
GU COURSE ;
do until no more OFFERINGs ;
   GN OFFERING ;
   GNP TEACHER WHERE EMP# = '421633' ;
   if TEACHER found then
   do ;
      GNP STUDENT ;
      leave loop ;
   end ;
end ;
```

The GU is the by now familiar "initial position" call. In the loop, the GN establishes an OFFERING as the current parent position, and the GNP then searches to see whether the specified employee taught that offering; these two operations are repeated until an offering taught by the specified employee has been found. Then another GNP is executed to retrieve the first STUDENT under the current parent OFFERING (we assume for simplicity that such a STUDENT exists). Note, therefore, that we are explicitly taking advantage of the fact that STUDENTs follow TEACHERs in hierarchic sequence (for any given OFFERING, that is).

22.5.7 Use of command code F.   Get the teacher (we assume there is only one) of the first offering of any course attended by employee 183009 as a student.

```
GU COURSE ;
do until no more OFFERINGs ;
   GN OFFERING ;
   GNP STUDENT WHERE EMP# = '183009' ;
   if STUDENT found then
```

```
    do ;
        GNP TEACHER * F ;
        leave loop ;
    end ;
end ;
```

This code is essentially similar to the code in the previous example, except for the presence of the F command code. Without that command code, the GNP for TEACHER would fail, because it would search *forward* from the current STUDENT, and (as explained in the previous example) TEACHERs precede STUDENTs with respect to the hierarchic sequence. What is needed is a means for stepping *backward* under the current parent, and that is what the F command code provides—it causes IMS to start its search at the *first occurrence* of the specified segment type under the current parent, regardless of the current database position. (Note that an F command code was unnecessary in Example 22.5.6 but would not have been wrong.)

22.5.8 Use of command code V.   Get the teacher (we assume there is only one) of the first offering of any course attended by employee 183009 as a student (same as Example 22.5.7).

```
GU STUDENT WHERE EMP# = '183009' ;
GN OFFERING * V ,
    TEACHER * F ;
```

Before we can explain this example properly, it is first necessary to amplify slightly the concept of "current database position." Basically, current database position is defined as the segment last accessed via a "get" or "insert" operation. In addition, however, each *ancestor* of the current position—that is, each segment in the path from the current position to the corresponding root—is also considered to be *the current segment of the applicable segment type*. In the example, therefore, the GU operation establishes a STUDENT—STUDENT x, say—as the current position (and therefore, of course, the current STUDENT); in addition, it also establishes the parent of x—OFFERING y, say—as the current OFFERING, and the parent of that OFFERING—COURSE z, say—as the current COURSE.

An SSA with a V command code directs IMS not to move away from the current segment of the type named in the SSA in attempting to satisfy the call. In the example, the GN will therefore not move away from OFFERING y in searching for the required TEACHER. In other words, the GN is equivalent to a "get next within parent" for TEACHERs under OFFERING y—except that OFFERING y is *not* the current parent.

This code is obviously much simpler than the code of the previous example. It is also more efficient. As a general rule, it is always preferable to use command code V rather than a GNP operation if possible. However, there are certain situations (details beyond the scope of this book) where it is not possible.

22.5.9 Segment insertion.   Insert a new student for offering 8 of course M23 (student employee number 275404, grade blank).

```
build new STUDENT segment in I/O area
     (EMP# = '275404', GRADE = ' ') ;
ISRT COURSE WHERE COURSE# = 'M23' ,
     OFFERING WHERE OFF# = '  8' ,
     STUDENT ;
```

22.5.10 Segment deletion.   Delete offering 8 of course M23.

```
GHU COURSE WHERE COURSE# = 'M23' ,
     OFFERING WHERE OFF# = '  8' ;
DLET ;
```

The segment to be deleted must first be retrieved via one of the "get hold" operations—"get hold unique" (GHU), "get hold next" (GHN), or "get hold next within parent" (GHNP). The DLET operation can then be executed (unless the user decides not to delete the segment after all, in which case processing simply continues as usual, e.g., with another "get hold" operation).

22.5.11 Segment update.   Change the location of offering 8 of course M23 to Helsinki.

```
GHU COURSE WHERE COURSE# = 'M23' ,
     OFFERING WHERE OFF# = '  8' ;
change OFFERING segment in I/O area
     (LOCATION = 'Helsinki') ;
REPL ;
```

As with "delete," the segment to be updated ("replaced") must first be retrieved via one of the "get hold" operations. It is then modified in the I/O area, and the REPL operation executed (again, unless the user decides not to update the segment after all). The sequence field cannot be updated.

22.5.12 Use of multiple PCBs.   Get all offerings of all prerequisite courses of course M23.

```
GU COURSE WHERE COURSE# = 'M23' (using PCB-1) ;
do until "not found" on PCB-1 ;
   GN COURSE * V ,
      PREREQ (using PCB-1) ;
   GU COURSE WHERE COURSE# = PCB-1.PREREQ# (using PCB-2) ;
   do until "not found" on PCB-2 ;
      GN COURSE * V ,
         OFFERING (using PCB-2) ;
   end ;
end ;
```

This problem requires the ability to maintain two independent positions in the database simultaneously, and therefore needs two PCBs. One PCB, PCB-1, is used to scan the PREREQs of the given course; the other, PCB-2, is used to scan the OFFERINGs of the course corresponding to the PREREQ currently identified by the first PCB. The outer loop position (maintained by PCB-1) must not change while the inner loop (controlled by PCB-2) is executed. Note that our simplified syntax breaks down on this example, because of the need to be able to specify PCBs explicitly.

22.6   STORAGE STRUCTURE

IMS provides a very wide variety of physical storage structures, and it is certainly not our intent to cover them in detail here. However, some brief notes on the possibilities may prove useful, and in particular may pave the way for an understanding of the next two sections.

1. First, each "physical database" is represented in storage by a *stored* database (note that physical databases are the only kind we have discussed in this chapter so far in any detail). Each segment of a physical database is represented by a stored segment in the stored database. A stored segment consists of stored versions of the segment's data fields, together with a stored *prefix* (hidden from the user) containing pointers, flags, and other control information. Where the various storage structures differ is in the manner in which they represent the hierarchic sequence of the database—i.e., the manner in which stored segments are tied together to form trees and trees are tied together to form the complete database.

2. Next, IMS provides two principal storage structures, hierarchic sequential (HS) and hierarchic direct (HD). The difference between them (as stated above) lies in the way they represent the database sequence—broadly speaking, HS uses physical contiguity and HD uses pointers. HS is intended for situations in which most access is sequential, HD is intended for situations in which most access is direct (though of course both structures can be used for both kinds of access, in general).

3. Each of the two principal structures has two principal variants—HS is supported by the hierarchic sequential and hierarchic indexed sequential access methods (HSAM and HISAM), HD is supported by the hierarchic direct and hierarchic indexed direct access methods (HDAM and HIDAM).

4. *HSAM*: In HSAM the hierarchic sequence of the database is represented entirely by physical contiguity, as on a magnetic tape (indeed, an HSAM database may actually be on tape). For an example, see Fig. 22.6 (where we assume that the next course after M23 in the education database is M27—M24, M25, and M26 do not exist). The only operations that can be used on an HSAM database are ISRT (allowed only when the database is first being built) and GU/GN/GNP (allowed only for an existing database). It follows that the most common use of HSAM involves the conventional old-master/new-master technique used in traditional sequential file processing; in other words, updating is done by reading an existing version of the database and writing a new one. HSAM is thus scarcely a *database* structure at all, in the conventional sense of that term.

5. *HISAM*: HISAM provides indexed access to root segments, physical sequential access from roots to dependent segments. The index is on the root segment sequence

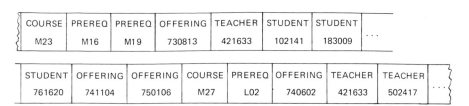

COURSE	PREREQ	PREREQ	OFFERING	TEACHER	STUDENT	STUDENT	
M23	M16	M19	730813	421633	102141	183009	...

STUDENT	OFFERING	OFFERING	COURSE	PREREQ	OFFERING	TEACHER	TEACHER	
761620	741104	750106	M27	L02	740602	421633	502417	...

Fig. 22.6 Part of the education database (HSAM).

field, and provides (of course) both sequential and direct access on the basis of values of that field. See Fig. 22.7.

6. The two HD structures both use pointers to tie segments together. For any given parent-child link, either "hierarchic" pointers or "child/twin" pointers can be used. With hierarchic pointers, each segment simply points to the next in hierarchic sequence; with child/twin pointers, each parent points to its first child of each type, and each child points to its next twin. Child/twin pointers give better direct access performance than hierarchic pointers but take up more space on the disk. Hierarchic pointers may give slightly better sequential performance than child/twin pointers. Figures 22.8 and 22.9 show how the tree for course M23 would be stored a) if hierarchic pointers were used exclusively (Fig. 22.8), b) if child/twin pointers were used exclusively (Fig. 22.9).

7. *HDAM*: HDAM provides hash access to root segments, pointer access from roots to dependent segments. The hash is on the root segment sequence field, and provides (of course) direct but not sequential access on the basis of values of that field. Note: Sequential access can be provided by means of a secondary index—see Section 22.8.

8. *HIDAM*: HIDAM provides indexed access to root segments, pointer access from roots to dependent segments. The index is on the root segment sequence field, and provides (of course) both sequential and direct access on the basis of values of that field.

9. For completeness, we briefly mention the other IMS storage structures, which are as follows:

- Simple HSAM and simple HISAM (SHSAM and SHISAM), which are variants of HSAM and HISAM in which the database contains only a single type of segment (i.e., is root only).
- Data Entry Databases (DEDBs), which can be regarded as an extended form of HDAM oriented specifically to high performance and high availability.
- Main Storage Databases (MSDBs), which are root-only databases that are kept entirely in primary (virtual) storage during processing.

Figure 22.10 is an attempt to summarize the most important of the foregoing ideas.

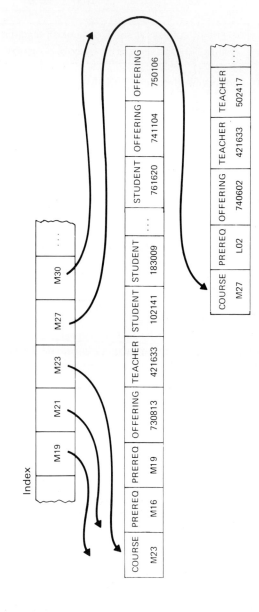

Fig. 22.7 Part of the education database (HISAM).

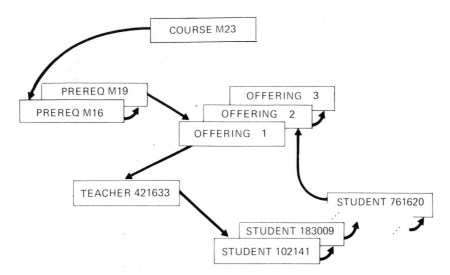

Fig. 22.8 Hierarchic pointers (example).

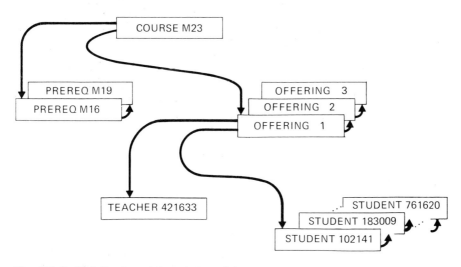

Fig. 22.9 Child/twin pointers (example).

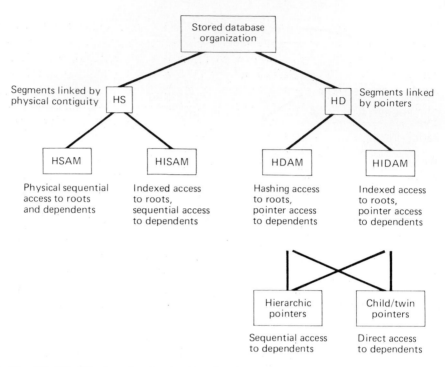

Fig. 22.10 The four basic storage structures.

22.7 LOGICAL DATABASES

A logical database, like a physical database, consists of a hierarchic arrangement of segments. However, the segments in question, though accessible via that logical database, really belong to one or more underlying physical databases. The purpose of the logical database is to allow the user to see the data in a hierarchic arrangement that differs—possibly quite significantly—from the arrangement in the underlying physical database(s).

A logical database is defined by means of a logical DBD. From the first paragraph above, it is clear that there must be some similarities between a logical DBD and a PCB. It is certainly true that both constructs define a (hierarchic) logical view of data that is different from the (hierarchic) physical structure of that data. But of course there are numerous differences as well. Some of the most important are as follows:

■ A logical DBD can be defined over multiple (physical) DBDs, whereas a PCB must be defined over a single (physical or logical) DBD.

■ A view defined by a logical DBD can differ much more considerably from the underlying physical structure than can a view defined by a PCB.[8]

---

8. Except that a PCB can define a "secondary data structure"—see Section 22.8—which can in fact be significantly different from the underlying physical structure.

■   Unlike the view defined by a PCB,[9] the view defined by a logical DBD is directly
    supported by its own physical pointer chains (etc.). That is, a logical database
    in IMS is in fact a very physical construct. Although the data segments "really"
    belong to one or more physical databases, the pointers (etc.) that define the
    logical database really belong to that logical database. Creating a new logical
    database is thus a nontrivial operation (certainly much more nontrivial than
    creating a view in a relational system), involving as it does a major reorgani-
    zation and restructuring of the physical data.

    We illustrate these ideas by means of an IMS version of our familiar suppliers-
and-parts example. A possible IMS representation of suppliers-and-parts, involving
two physical databases (the suppliers database and the parts database), is shown in
Fig. 22.11.

    The parts database is root-only; it contains a single segment type (segment type
P), which is in fact identical to the usual P relation. The suppliers database, by
contrast, contains two segment types—segment type S, which is identical to the
usual S relation, and segment type SP (a child of S), which contains a QTY field
and also a *pointer* field. The purpose of the pointer (which is not explicitly visible
to the user, by the way) is to identify, for any given SP occurrence, the appropriate
P occurrence in the parts database. See Fig. 22.12.

    Now a logical database—the suppliers-and-parts logical database—can be de-
fined, with the structure shown in Fig. 22.13.[10] Note that this logical database involves certain redundancies: Specifically, the name, color, weight, and city for a
given part will be duplicated in every logical SP segment occurrence for that part.
However, those redundancies are of course not reflected in the underlying physical
databases.

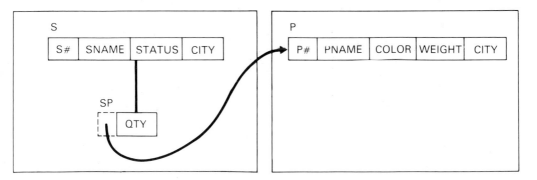

Fig. 22.11 Suppliers-and-parts as two physical databases.

---

9.   Again, we are ignoring here the possibility that the view defined by the PCB is in fact
a secondary data structure.

10.   For reasons beyond the scope of this book, the SP segment in the logical database will
actually include two copies of the P# field.

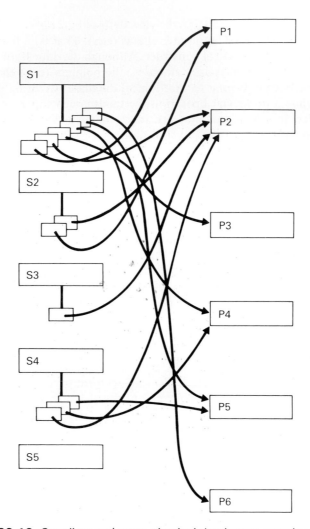

Fig. 22.12 Suppliers-and-parts physical databases: sample values.

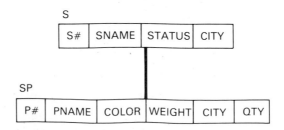

Fig. 22.13 The suppliers-and-parts logical database.

Terminology: Segment SP is of course a child of segment S in the suppliers physical database. *It is also considered to be a child of segment P in the parts physical database.* We say that S is the *physical* parent of SP and P is the *logical* parent; equivalently, we say that SP is a *physical child* of S and a *logical* child of P. A given segment can have at most two parents; the possibilities are a) no parents at all, b) physical parent only, and c) both physical parent and logical parent.[11] Also, two child segment occurrences (of the same type) having the same physical parent occurrence are said to be *physical twins*, and two child segment occurrences (of the same type) having the same logical parent occurrence are said to be *logical* twins.

The suppliers-and-parts logical database of Fig. 22.13, in which parts are subordinate to suppliers, simplifies the formulation of queries such as "Get parts supplied by supplier S1." However, it is not much good for the converse query "Get suppliers who supply part P1" (exercise: why not?). We can overcome this difficulty by means of a second logical database, the parts-and-suppliers logical database, in which suppliers are subordinate to parts. First we introduce another segment type, PS say, into the parts physical database (see Fig. 22.14). PS is a physical child of P and a logical child of S. Then we define the parts-and-suppliers logical database as shown in Fig. 22.15.

Segments PS (in the parts physical database) and SP (in the suppliers physical database) are examples of what IMS calls *paired segments*. Note that the PS occurrence that connects a given P to a given S is identical (except for the pointer) to the SP occurrence that connects the given S to the given P. For example, the PS occurrence connecting P1 to S1 is basically the same as the SP occurrence connecting S1 to P1. Thus the structure of Fig. 22.14 involves (once again) a certain amount of redundancy. However, a) that redundancy will only be perceived, not real, if one of the paired segments is "virtual"; b) even if both segments are "physical," the redundancy will at least be controlled (i.e., managed by IMS instead of by the user). For details, see the IMS manuals [22.1].

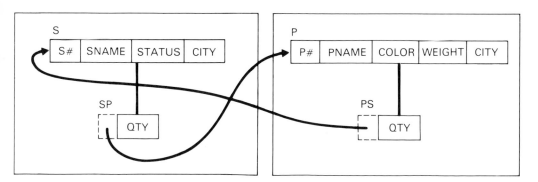

Fig. 22.14 Suppliers-and-parts as two physical databases (symmetric version).

11. It follows that it is difficult to represent a database such as suppliers-parts-projects in IMS.

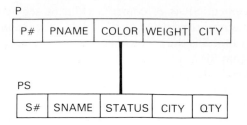

Fig. 22.15 The parts-and-suppliers logical database.

Referential integrity: For every segment that participates in a "logical relationship"—that is, for every segment that is a logical parent, or a logical child, or a physical parent that has a physical child that is also a logical child—the physical DBD for that segment must specify an insert rule, a delete rule, and a replace rule. Those rules govern the effect of ISRT, DLET, and REPL operations on the segment concerned—also, in many cases, on various related segments. Each rule can be any one of "physical," "logical," or "virtual".[12] It is certainly not our intention here to describe the rules in detail, but we briefly discuss the possibilities for the suppliers-and-parts logical database of Fig. 22.13. For that database:

- Inserting a shipment for a nonexistent supplier (i.e., a supplier not already represented in the suppliers physical database) is impossible.

- Inserting a shipment for a nonexistent part (i.e., a part not already represented in the parts physical database):

  a) fails if the insert rule for P is "physical";
  b) succeeds otherwise, and automatically inserts the part also (note that the shipment includes all of the necessary part information).

- Inserting a shipment for an existing part always succeeds. In addition:

  a) if the insert rule for P is "virtual," the values of PNAME, COLOR, WEIGHT, and CITY for that part are replaced by the values from the new shipment, which in turn means that they are also simultaneously replaced (logically) in all existing shipments for that part;
  b) otherwise, the values of PNAME, COLOR, WEIGHT, and CITY for that shipment are replaced (logically) by the values from the existing part.

- Deleting a supplier automatically deletes all shipments for that supplier.

- Deleting a part (i.e., via the parts physical database—it is not directly accessible via the suppliers-and-parts logical database):

---

12.   Or (in the case of the delete rule only) "bidirectional virtual." The "bidirectional virtual" rule is applicable only to databases that participate in a "bidirectional logical relationship" such as that illustrated in Fig. 22.14.

a) fails if the delete rule for P is "physical" and the part has any corresponding shipments;

b) succeeds otherwise, in the sense that the part is logically removed from the parts physical database. However, it remains accessible from the suppliers-and-parts logical database so long as there are any shipments that refer to it.

- If the delete rule for P is "virtual," then deleting the last shipment referring to a given part causes that part to be physically removed from the parts physical database also.

- Field S.S# cannot be updated.

- Field P.P# cannot be updated (i.e., via the parts physical database—it is not directly accessible via the suppliers-and-parts logical database).

- Field SP.P# cannot be updated. Note that there is of course no "SP.S#" field, so the question of updating such a field does not arise.

- Updating fields SP.PNAME, SP.COLOR, SP.WEIGHT, and SP.CITY:

  a) fails if the replace rule for P is "physical";

  b) succeeds otherwise, in which case the updates are actually applied to the corresponding part, which in turn means that they are instantaneously applied (logically) to all other shipments for that part.

- Updating fields P.PNAME, P.COLOR, P.WEIGHT, and P.CITY (i.e., via the parts physical database—they are not directly accessible via the suppliers-and-parts logical database):

  a) fails if the replace rule for P is "logical";

  b) succeeds otherwise, in which case the updates are instantaneously applied (logically) to all shipments for that part.

We remark that the above rules represent both less and more than the foreign key rules of Section 12.5. Detailed comparisons are left as an exercise for the interested reader. Note too that the foregoing discussion treats the rules only in the context of the simplest possible kind of logical database. For details of what happens in more complex cases (such as the database of Fig. 22.14) the reader is referred to the IMS manuals [22.1].

22.8 SECONDARY INDEXES

In Chapter 3 we defined a secondary index as an index on a field other than the primary key. At that point, however, we were tacitly assuming that the file to be indexed was no more complex than a conventional "flat" sequential file. In IMS, of course, the file (i.e., database) is more complex—it is hierarchic, and the concept of secondary indexing needs to be extended accordingly. Thus, all of the following are possibilities in IMS:

- An index that indexes any given segment, root or dependent, on the basis of any field of that segment;
- An index that indexes any given segment, root or dependent, on the basis of any field of any dependent (at any level) of that segment.

In all cases, the "field" on which the index is based can actually be a combination of several fields (not necessarily contiguous) from the relevant segment.

To illustrate the possibilities, we return to the education database of Section 22.2. The following list outlines some of the many indexes that could be constructed for that database:

1. An index to COURSEs on field COURSE.TITLE
2. An index to COURSEs on field OFFERING.LOCATION
3. An index to OFFERINGs on field OFFERING.LOCATION
4. An index to OFFERINGs on field TEACHER.EMP#

We consider each of these four cases in some detail.

1. Indexing the root on a field not the sequence field

Secondary indexes are very definitely *not* "transparent to the user" in IMS. On the contrary, IMS will use a particular secondary index only if the DL/I call explicitly instructs it to do so. For example, suppose an index to COURSEs has been constructed on the basis of TITLE values. Then the definition of COURSE in the education database DBD must include an "XDFLD" statement, of the form

```
XDFLD    NAME=XTITLE,SRCH=TITLE
```

(say), to indicate that a reference in some DL/I call to the name XTITLE means that IMS is to use the TITLE index in responding to that call. For example, the DL/I call:

```
GU COURSE WHERE TITLE = 'Dynamics' ;
```

will *not* use the index, but the following DL/I call will:

```
GU COURSE WHERE XTITLE = 'Dynamics' ;
```

A secondary index also allows the database in question to be processed in a *secondary processing sequence*—namely, the sequence defined by that index. (The *primary* processing sequence is the sequence of trees in the underlying physical database—that is, it is the sequence defined by ascending values of the root segment sequence field, loosely speaking.) Requesting a secondary sequence is done by naming the appropriate secondary index in the PCB. "Get unique" and "get next" operations will then operate in terms of that secondary sequence. *Recommendation*: Whenever any given index is being used, the sequence requested in the PCB should be the sequence defined by that index; for otherwise the sequence that applies to GU and GN operations will not be the sequence represented by the index, and those operations will therefore be *extremely* inefficient.

2. Indexing the root on a field in a dependent

Suppose we wish to find all courses that have an offering in Stockholm. Assume we are not concerned with the problem of eliminating duplicate COURSEs. Then the following code will suffice:

```
position to start of primary sequence ;
do until no more OFFERINGs ;
   GN COURSE * D ,
      OFFERING WHERE LOCATION = 'Stockholm' ;
end ;
```

This code is not particularly efficient, however, since it consists essentially of a sequential scan of the entire database in primary sequence. A more efficient solution to the problem can be achieved by means of an index to COURSEs on the basis of OFFERING.LOCATION values. Suppose such an index is constructed, and the corresponding XDFLD statement (part of the definition of the COURSE segment in the education DBD) is

```
XDFLD   NAME=XLOC,SRCH=LOCATION,SEGMENT=OFFERING
```

(meaning that the user can instruct IMS to use the index on the LOCATION field of the OFFERING segment by specifying the name XLOC in the DL/I call). Suppose also that the secondary sequence defined by that index has been requested in the PCB. Then we can write

```
position to start of secondary (i.e., LOCATION) sequence ;
do until no more COURSEs ;
   GN COURSE WHERE XLOC = 'Stockholm' ;
end ;
```

And this code will probably be much more efficient, because it uses the index to go directly to just the OFFERINGs required.

Note, incidentally, that the index in this example contains as many index entries as there are OFFERINGs in the education database. Each index entry points to a COURSE segment. If there are m COURSEs altogether, and an average of n OF-FERINGs per COURSE, then there will be $m * n$ entries in the index, of which (on average) n will point to any given COURSE. The secondary sequence defined by this index is (of course) ascending LOCATION sequence. If the database is processed in this sequence, then (on average) each COURSE, together with all of its dependents, will appear n times, once for each of its OFFERINGs. In other words, when seen via the index, the database appears n times larger than it really is. (Furthermore, the n appearances of a given tree will probably not all be grouped together.)

3. Indexing a dependent on a field in that dependent

As indicated at the beginning of this section, the indexed segment does not have to be the root of the underlying database. If it is not, however, the effect is to

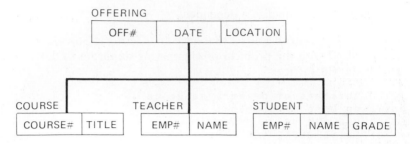

Fig. 22.16 Indexing OFFERINGs on LOCATION: secondary data structure.

restructure the hierarchy so that it *becomes* the root in the structure seen by the user. As an example, we consider the case of indexing OFFERINGs on the basis of LOCATION values. Figure 22.16 shows the *secondary data structure* that results when the user specifies the secondary sequence corresponding to this index in the PCB.[13]

The rules for defining a secondary data structure are as follows:

- The indexed segment becomes the root.

- Ancestors of that segment become the leftmost dependents of the root, in reverse order. (If COURSE had a parent CATEGORY in the education database, CATEGORY would be a *child* of COURSE in the secondary structure.)

- Dependents of the indexed segment appear exactly as in the underlying database, except that they are to the right of the dependents introduced by the rule of the previous paragraph.

- No other segments are included. (In the example, PREREQs are omitted.)

The SENSEG statements in the PCB must define the secondary structure in accordance with these rules. Note, therefore, that here we have a situation in which the view defined by the PCB is not just a simple subhierarchy of the hierarchy defined by the underlying DBD.[14]

As an illustration of a possible use for this facility, we extend our Stockholm courses example as follows. Suppose we wish to find, not only courses with an offering in Stockholm, but also the teachers of those Stockholm offerings. The index of the previous subsection (indexing COURSEs on OFFERING.LOCATION) is not particularly helpful here; it will enable us to find qualifying courses easily enough, but there is no immediate way of knowing which of the many subordinate

---

13.   We are assuming that the secondary processing sequence is being used (the normal case). If it is not, the restructuring described in this section does not occur.

14.   Secondary data structures are subject to severe update restrictions, as is probably only to be expected. For example, it is not possible to insert or delete COURSEs using the structure of Fig. 22.16. Full details of such restrictions are beyond the scope of this book.

teachers for those courses are in fact the teachers for the Stockholm offerings. But with the secondary structure of Fig. 22.16, we can write:

```
position to start of secondary (i.e., LOCATION) sequence ;
do until no more OFFERINGs ;
   GN OFFERING WHERE XLOC = 'Stockholm' ,
      COURSE ;
   do until no more TEACHERs ;
      GN OFFERING * V ,
         TEACHER ;
   end ;
end ;
```

Note that, in the hierarchy of Fig. 22.16, each OFFERING will have *exactly one* COURSE child.

4. Indexing a dependent on a field in a lower-level dependent

This, the last of the four possibilities, does not really illustrate any new points, but we include it for completeness. As our example, we consider the case of indexing OFFERINGs on the basis of TEACHER.EMP# values. The secondary data structure will be the same as that of Fig. 22.16; however, a) OFFERINGs will now be accessible via the "XD field" XEMP# (say), corresponding to the real field TEACHER.EMP#, and b) sequencing will be defined in terms of values of that XD field instead of LOCATION values. We present a single coding example. The problem is: "Find all Stockholm offerings taught by employee 876225."

```
position to start of secondary (i.e., TEACHER.EMP#) sequence ;
do until no more OFFERINGs ;
   GN OFFERING WHERE XEMP# = '876225'
               AND LOCATION = 'Stockholm' ;
end ;
```

22.9 CONCLUDING REMARKS

In this chapter, we have sketched a (hypothetical) hierarchic data model, and have described the major features of IMS (easily the most important example of the hierarchic approach). We stress the point once again that we have omitted a very great amount of detail from that description. By way of conclusion, we now offer the following critical comments on hierarchic systems in general.

First, refer back to the discussion of secondary indexing in Section 22.8. In that section we presented a particular problem—"Find courses with offerings in Stockholm"—and showed a solution to that problem involving a particular index. Then we modified the problem slightly—"Find corresponding teachers too"—and showed a solution to that modified problem involving a different index and a secondary data structure. Observe from this example how *a slight change in the problem can lead to a major change in the solution*. This *perturbation effect* can be attributed to the fact that secondary indexes represent an attempt to provide symmetry of access to a data structure that is fundamentally not symmetric. That is, access via an indexed field is made to look like access via the root segment sequence field, which implies that the indexed field has to *become* the root segment sequence field, which implies in turn that the hierarchy may need to be restructured.

Let us abstract the foregoing argument a little. The essential point is that a hierarchic structure has a *built-in bias*; it is good for some applications but bad for others.[15] As a result, some kind of logical restructuring mechanism becomes desirable, so that the data can be logically rearranged into whatever hierarchic form is best suited for the application at hand. And of course that is exactly what the IMS secondary indexing facility is, a logical restructuring mechanism.[16] So too is the logical database facility, and so also is the PCB facility (to a lesser extent).

We have thus shown that a hierarchic system requires a restructuring mechanism, and that secondary indexes (etc.) provide such a mechanism in IMS. But the question is: Is such a restructuring facility sufficiently flexible to satisfy the range of demands that users are likely to make on it? There are several arguments that suggest that the answer to this question is probably *no*:

- First, the number of possible hierarchies rises combinatorially with the number of records (segments). Two records can be arranged into two different hierarchies; three can be arranged into 12 different hierarchies; four, into 88; and so on (exercise for the reader). In any real environment, therefore, it is virtually certain that not all possible hierarchies will be directly supported, simply because there are so many of them. In IMS in particular, certain hierarchies *cannot* be directly supported, because of various IMS restrictions (for example, the root of a logical database must be the root of a physical database).

- Second, there are some applications for which no single hierarchy is directly suitable anyway. Example 22.5.12 is a case in point, and the suppliers-parts-projects database is another.

- Next, there is no good theory available (so far as this writer is aware) on which to base such a restructuring mechanism. In IMS in particular, the restructuring is quite ad hoc, with the result that users (not just the DBA, but also application programmers and probably end-users too) have to be aware of a large number of apparently arbitrary rules, restrictions, and interdependencies.

- In IMS also, the restructuring mechanism is cumbersome and not very dynamic. It is a nontrivial operation to define a new logical database or new secondary

---

15.   The relational structure, by contrast, has no such bias—instead, it is rather neutral. For a given application, the necessary bias is provided by the relational operators, which effectively allow the user to *impose* a "hierarchic" structure (or any other kind of structure that may be desired) on the data dynamically, at run time.

16.   Of course it is a performance aid also, but performance is not the point at issue here.

data structure over existing data. As a result, such operations must definitely be performed by an IMS specialist—certainly not by an end-user.

Note carefully that all of the foregoing are arguments against hierarchies as a *logical* structure, not as a physical structure. There is no question that a hierarchic physical structure might be the best performer for certain applications (though of course not for all applications). But another criticism of hierarchic systems, or at least of IMS specifically, is precisely that there is no clear distinction between the logical and physical levels of the system. Secondary indexes, for example, are both a physical-level (performance-oriented) construct and a logical-level (data-structuring) construct in IMS. Similarly for logical databases, and similarly for numerous other IMS features.

Finally, some criticisms regarding IMS specifically:

- The choice as to whether or not to use a secondary index is in the hands of the user (i.e., application programmer), instead of being under the control of the system. This is unfortunate, since not only do programs that use a secondary index thereby lose some measure of data independence, but also system performance may be critically dependent on a judicious choice of when and when not to use some particular index.

- Suppose we restrict our attention to two-level hierarchies only, for simplicity. Such a hierarchy, by definition, is best suited to representing a one-to-many relationship, such as the relationship of courses to offerings. A many-to-many relationship, such as that between suppliers and parts, can be considered as a combination of two one-to-many relationships (suppliers to shipments, parts to shipments), and can therefore be handled by two hierarchies that are inverses of one another (as shown in Section 22.7)—though the details are scarcely straightforward. But a many-to-many-to-many relationship, such as that involving suppliers, parts, and projects, cannot be represented in IMS in any reasonably direct manner at all, owing to the restriction that a given child segment can have at most two parents. (Suppliers-parts-projects can be regarded as a combination of *three* one-to-many relationships—suppliers to shipments, parts to shipments, and projects to shipments.)

- The insert/delete/replace rules for segments that participate in a logical relationship are extremely complex, particularly with respect to the implications that a rule for one segment may have for operations on another. In some cases, in fact, defining a new logical database over one or more existing physical databases may invalidate programs that previously operated successfully on those existing databases. Furthermore, the rules are asymmetric, and do not provide all the function needed; yet they do provide some function for which the need is (to say the least) debatable. Nevertheless, the fact remains that IMS does provide some support in this area, whereas many relational systems currently do not.

EXERCISES

22.1 Figure 22.17 represents an IMS database that contains information about published papers in a number of selected subject areas. The segments contain the following fields:

- Subject: subject classification number (unique), name of subject
- Paper: title, abstract, number of pages
- Details: publishing house, journal name, volume number, issue number, date of publication (note that a given paper may be published several times in several different places)
- Author: author name, address (note that a given paper may have several coauthors)

  Define an appropriate DBD for this information.

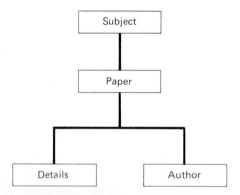

Fig. 22.17 The publications database.

22.2 Define a PCB (all segments and fields sensitive) for the publications database. This PCB is to be used for both retrieval and update operations (all kinds).

22.3 Write DL/I operations (hypothetical syntax) for the following:

a) Get all authors of papers on the subject of "Information Retrieval" (you may assume that this subject name is unique).

b) Get all papers for which Grace or Hobbs is (one of) the author(s).

c) Get all subjects on which Bradbury has published a paper.

d) Get the name of the paper and date of first publication for all papers published by Owen.

e) Get all authors who have had a paper published by the Cider Press since 1969.

f) Get all authors who have coauthored a paper with Bradman.

g) A paper on the subject of science fiction, entitled "Computers in SF," was published on 1 January 1985 by the Galactic Publishing Corporation. The author's name is Hal. Add this information to the database. (You may assume that the subject "Science Fiction" is already represented.)

h) For all papers currently available from more than one source, delete all details segments except the most recent.

22.4 Restructure the publications database as two physical databases, so that logical databases can be defined that are specifically suited to responding to both of the following queries: a) Find the authors of a given paper; b) find all papers by a given author. What logical databases can the user see with your design?

22.5 A secondary index is to be built for the publications database. What structure does the user see:

a) if the subject segment is indexed on author name;

b) if the paper segment is indexed on author name;

c) if the author segment is indexed on author name?

22.6 Using the secondary structure of Exercise 22.5 b), get all papers by Adams.

22.7 If the publications database contains:

100 subject segments,

average of 100 paper segments per subject,

average of 1.5 details segments per paper,

average of 1.2 author segments per paper,

how many segments of each type are seen in the secondary structure of Exercise 22.5 b)?

REFERENCES AND BIBLIOGRAPHY

22.1 Information on IMS is available from IBM Corporation, Armonk, New York 10504.

22.2 W. C. McGee. "The IMS/VS System." *IBM Sys. J.* **16**, No. 2 (June 1977).

An extensive tutorial on both database and data communications aspects.

22.3 D. Kapp and J. F. Leben. *IMS Programming Techniques: A Guide to Using DL/I.* New York: Van Nostrand Reinhold (1978).

22.4 D. C. Tsichritzis and F. H. Lochovsky. "Hierarchical Data Base Management: A Survey." *ACM Comp. Surv.* **8**, No. 1 (March 1976).

Includes a brief tutorial not only on IMS but also on System 2000 (another hierarchic system).

22.5 Dines Bjørner and Hans Henrik Løvengreen. "Formalization of Database Systems—And a Formal Definition of IMS." *Proc. 8th International Conference on Very Large Data Bases* (September 1982).

An attempt to define a formal data model for IMS. Note, however, that the following IMS features (among others) are not included:

- Command codes
- "Advanced features" such as multiple positioning
- Logical databases
- Access method dependent features
- Database positioning after an exception
- "Get hold" calls
- Inserted segment positioning other than FIRST

22.6 E. F. Codd. Interview in *Data Base Newsletter* **10,** No. 2 (March 1982). Available from Database Research Group Inc., 129 Tremont St., Suite 500, Boston, MA 02108.

22.7 C. J. Date. "Why Is It So Difficult to Provide a Relational Interface to IMS?" *InfoIMS* **4,** No. 4 (4th Quarter 1984), PO Box 20651, San Jose, California 95160.

To quote from the abstract: Several commercial DBMSs—but not however IMS—now claim to provide an interface by which users can obtain relational access to existing (i.e., nonrelational) data. This paper shows that there are certain inherent (and possibly insuperable) difficulties in trying to provide such an interface. It illustrates those difficulties by considering the specific case of attempting to provide a SQL interface to IMS.

ANSWERS TO SELECTED EXERCISES

```
22.1 DBD      NAME=PUBSDBD
     SEGM     NAME=SUBJECT,BYTES=45
     FIELD    NAME=(SUB#,SEQ),BYTES=7,START=1
     FIELD    NAME=SUBNAME,BYTES=38,START=8
     SEGM     NAME=PAPER,PARENT=SUBJECT,BYTES=762
     FIELD    NAME=(PAPER#,SEQ),BYTES=4,START=1
     FIELD    NAME=TITLE,BYTES=256,START=5
     FIELD    NAME=ABSTRACT,BYTES=500,START=261
     FIELD    NAME=PAGES,BYTES=2,START=761
     SEGM     NAME=DETAILS,PARENT=PAPER,BYTES=118
     FIELD    NAME=(DATE,SEQ),BYTES=6,START=1
     FIELD    NAME=HOUSE,BYTES=19,START=7
     FIELD    NAME=JOURNAL,BYTES=88,START=26
     FIELD    NAME=VOLUME,BYTES=3,START=114
     FIELD    NAME=ISSUE,BYTES=2,START=117
     SEGM     NAME=AUTHOR,PARENT=PAPER,BYTES=50
     FIELD    NAME=(AUTHNAME,SEQ),BYTES=16,START=1
     FIELD    NAME=AUTHADDR,BYTES=34,START=17

22.2 PCB      DBDNAME=PUBSDBD
     SENSEG   NAME=SUBJECT,PROCOPT=GIRD
     SENSEG   NAME=PAPER,PARENT=SUBJECT,PROCOPT=GIRD
     SENSEG   NAME=DETAILS,PARENT=PAPER,PROCOPT=GIRD
     SENSEG   NAME=AUTHOR,PARENT=PAPER,PROCOPT=GIRD

22.3
 a) GU SUBJECT WHERE SUBNAME = 'Information Retrieval' ;
    do until no more AUTHORs ;
       GNP AUTHOR ;
    end ;

 b) position to start of database ;
    do until no more AUTHORs ;
       GN PAPER * D ,
          AUTHOR WHERE AUTHNAME = 'Grace'
                 OR AUTHNAME = 'Hobbs' ;
    end ;
```

```
c) position to start of database ;
   do until no more AUTHORs ;
      GN SUBJECT * D ,
         PAPER ,
         AUTHOR WHERE AUTHNAME = 'Bradbury' ;
   end ;
d) position to start of database ;
   do until no more AUTHORS ;
      GN AUTHOR WHERE AUTHNAME = 'Owen' ;
      GN PAPER * VD ,
         DETAILS * F ;
   end ;
e) position to start of database ;
   do until no more DETAILS ;
      GN DETAILS WHERE HOUSE = 'Cider Press' ;
      do until no more AUTHORs ;
         GN PAPER * V ,
            AUTHOR ;
      end ;
   end ;
f) position to start of database ;
   do until no more AUTHORs ;
      GN AUTHOR WHERE AUTHNAME = 'Bradman' ;
      GN PAPER * V ,
         AUTHOR * F ;
      do until no more AUTHORs ;
         GN PAPER * V ,
            AUTHOR ;
      end ;
   end ;
g) build PAPER segment in I/O area ;
   ISRT SUBJECT WHERE SUBNAME = 'Science Fiction' ,
         PAPER ;
   build DETAILS segment in I/O area ;
   ISRT PAPER * V ,
         DETAILS ;
   build AUTHOR segment in I/O area ;
   ISRT PAPER * V ,
         AUTHOR ;
h) position to start of database ;
   do until no more PAPERs ;
      GN PAPER ;
      set count = 0 ;
      do until no more DETAILS ;
         GN PAPER * V ,
            DETAILS ;
         if not found leave inner loop ;
         set count = count + 1 ;
      end ;
```

(Continued)

```
      do while count > 1 :
         GHN PAPER * V ,
               DETAILS * F ;
         DLET ;
      end ;
   end ;
```

22.5 The user sees:

(a)

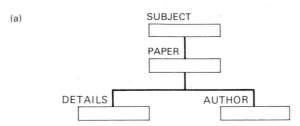

In this case the hierarchic structure is unchanged.

(b)

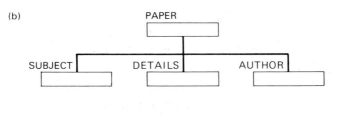

(c)

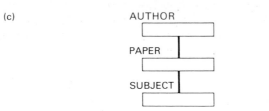

In all three cases a), b), and c), the structure is seen in AUTHNAME sequence, with as many trees as there are AUTHOR occurrences in the original database. See also the answer to Exercise 22.7.

22.6 position to start of secondary (i.e., AUTHNAME) sequence ;
   do until no more PAPERs ;
      GN PAPER WHERE XAUTH = 'Adams' ;
   end ;

We assume that XAUTH is the XD field for PAPER corresponding to the indexed field AUTHNAME.

22.7 PAPER   : 12000
      SUBJECT : 12000
      DETAILS : 18000
      AUTHOR : 14400

23

A Network
System:
IDMS

23.1 BACKGROUND

IDMS (Integrated Database Management System) is a product of Cullinet Software, Inc. [23.1]. It runs on IBM mainframes under most of the standard IBM operating systems (DOS, MVS, etc.). It is probably the best known example of what is usually referred to as a "CODASYL system" (or sometimes "DBTG system")— that is, a system based on the proposals of the Data Base Task Group (DBTG) of the Programming Language Committee (subsequently renamed the COBOL Committee) of the "Conference on Data Systems Languages" (CODASYL), the organization responsible for the definition of COBOL. The DBTG final report [23.2] was produced in 1971, and several systems based on it were built during the 1970s, among them IDMS.

The DBTG report contained proposals for three distinct database languages: a schema data description language (schema DDL), a subschema data description language (subschema DDL), and a data manipulation language (DML). The purpose of the three languages was as follows:

- The schema DDL was a language for describing a network-structured database. The DBTG term "schema" corresponds very approximately to the ANSI/ SPARC term "conceptual schema," but the DBTG schema DDL is really much more "internal" than "conceptual" in nature—i.e., it includes many constructs that are quite storage-oriented, such as definitions of physical access paths.

- The subschema DDL was a language for defining an external view of the database (the DBTG "subschema" corresponds to the ANSI/SPARC external schema).

- The DML consisted of a set of (record-level) operators for manipulating a network database defined by means of the two data description languages. The user in DBTG is assumed to be an application programmer; thus, a given DML will have a syntax compatible with that of some programming language. The DML defined in [23.2] was intended for use with COBOL.

In 1984 the ANSI Database Committee X3H2 (the same body that is currently at work on a proposed relational standard [4.9]) produced a document [23.5] defining a proposed standard network database language (NDL) very loosely based on the original DBTG specifications. Note that, at the time of writing, that document represents a *proposed* standard only, not an actual one. Furthermore, the reader is warned that the languages of DBTG, IDMS, and X3H2 differ quite significantly from one another on points of detail; they should really be regarded as three distinct languages, or at least three distinct dialects (and this remark applies both to the two DDLs and to the DML). In this chapter we base most of our examples and discussions on the IDMS dialects specifically.

One further preliminary remark: In 1983 Cullinet announced an extended version of IDMS called IDMS/R ("IDMS/Relational"). IDMS/R includes all of the original CODASYL-style facilities of the base IDMS product, together with certain new relational facilities; in fact, "IDMS/R" is now the official name for the entire product, replacing the old "IDMS" name. In this chapter, however, we are primarily concerned with the base CODASYL facilities, and it is convenient to continue to use the name "IDMS" to refer to those facilities specifically. Toward the end of the chapter we will briefly describe the new relational features of IDMS/R.

As in the two previous chapters, we precede our discussion of the system per se with a short discussion of the underlying data model. Once again that discussion is necessarily somewhat hypothetical, since IDMS and systems like it were not in fact designed in terms of any such predefined model; on the contrary (as in the case of hierarchic systems), the model was defined after the event by a process of abstraction—principally from the DBTG specifications, in the case of networks. In fact, this writer is not aware of the existence of any *formal* definition of such a model at all, though the specifications of X3H2 [23.5] perhaps come close. Furthermore, the hypothetical model we do discuss is very much simplified in comparison with the "model" actually implemented in IDMS and systems like it, because we choose to stress only those features (such as links) that may be regarded as truly crucial to the network approach. Other features (such as areas and repeating groups) we simply ignore. The interested reader is referred to [23.1], [23.2], and [23.5] for details of such features.

23.2   THE NETWORK MODEL

Network Data Structure

The network data structure can be regarded as an extended form of the hierarchic data structure defined in the previous chapter. The principal distinction between the two is as follows: In a hierarchic structure, a child record has exactly one parent;

in a network structure, a child record can have any number of parents[1] (possibly zero). We make these ideas a little more precise as follows.

A network database consists of two sets, a set of *records* and a set of *links*— more accurately, a set of multiple occurrences of each of several types of record, together with a set of multiple occurrences of each of several types of link. Each link type involves two record types, a *parent* record type and a *child* record type.[2] Each occurrence of a given link type consists of a single occurrence of the parent record type, together with an *ordered set* of multiple occurrences of the child record type. Given a particular link type L with parent record type P and child record type C:

1. Each occurrence of P is the parent in *exactly* one occurrence of L;
2. Each occurrence of C is a child in *at most* one occurrence of L.

In addition, of course, record types are made up of field types in the usual way. Note: From now on we will (as usual) drop the "type" and "occurrence" qualifiers whenever it seems safe to do so.

As an example, we show in Fig. 23.1 how the suppliers-and-parts database could be represented in network form. The database contains three record types, namely S, P, and SP. S and P are identical to their relational counterparts; SP, by contrast, contains only a QTY field. In place of the two foreign keys SP.S# and SP.P#, we have two link types, namely S-SP and P-SP:

---

1.   To jump ahead of ourselves a little: This distinction means that every relationship that is represented by a foreign key in a relational structure can in principle be represented by a link in a network structure. In a hierarchic structure, by contrast, some such relationships can be represented by links, but some must still be represented by foreign keys (as explained in Chapter 22). Even in a network structure, of course, there is no guarantee that *all* such relationships will in fact be represented by links; indeed, it is probable that they will not, because:

a) There are likely to be so many of them;

b) In any case, most systems do not support links having the same record type as both parent and child, implying that (e.g.) the foreign key MGR_EMP# in the relation EMP (EMP#, ENAME, MGR_EMP#, SALARY) cannot be replaced by a link;

and (perhaps most significant in practice)

c) It is a nontrivial operation to add a new link to an existing database (see Exercise 23.6).

2.   "Link," "parent," and "child" are not CODASYL terms. The CODASYL terminology is as follows: Links are called *sets* (a particularly unfortunate choice, since it is often necessary to use the same term "set" in its more usual mathematical sense, even in a CODASYL context); parents are called *owners*; and children are called *members*. In this section we choose to stay with the link/parent/child terminology, in order to stress the essential similarities and essential differences between hierarchies and networks. We will switch to the CODASYL terminology when we discuss IDMS specifically.

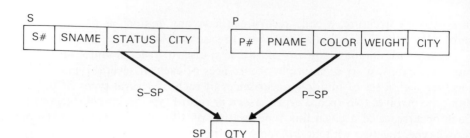

Fig. 23.1 The suppliers-and-parts database: network version (data structure).

1. Each occurrence of S-SP consists of a single occurrence of S, together with one occurrence of SP for each shipment by the supplier represented by that S occurrence;

2. Each occurrence of P-SP consists of a single occurrence of P, together with one occurrence of SP for each shipment of the part represented by that P occurrence.

Some sample occurrences (corresponding to the usual set of sample data values) are shown in Fig. 23.2. Note that, for a given S occurrence, the SP occurrences appear in part number order; likewise, for a given P occurrence, the SP occurrences appear in supplier number order.

Each occurrence of a link represents a one-to-many relationship between the parent occurrence and the corresponding child occurrences. The means by which each parent occurrence is connected to the corresponding child occurrences is irrelevant so far as the user is concerned. One way of making those connections (the method illustrated in Fig. 23.2) is via a chain of pointers that originates at the parent occurrence, runs through all the child occurrences, and finally returns to the parent occurrence. In practice, the connections may be physically represented by pointers or by some alternative (but functionally equivalent) method; however, the user can always think in terms of the pointer chain representation without any loss of generality.

A note on the figures: Drawing link occurrences as chains of pointers, as in Fig. 23.2, is a generally accepted convention. The technique for drawing link *types* illustrated in Fig. 23.1 is based on another widely accepted convention, due to Bachman [23.3], called "data structure diagrams" (or sometimes "Bachman diagrams"). The data structure diagram for a given link is very similar to the IMS diagram for such a link; the only differences are that a) the link is labeled with its name (links are anonymous in IMS), and b) the link is directed to indicate which is the parent and which the child (in a network diagram, unlike an IMS diagram, it is not always possible to show the parent as being above the child).

There is no restriction on how record types can be combined into link types:

1. The child record type in one link type *L1* can be the parent record type in another link type *L2* (as in a hierarchy).

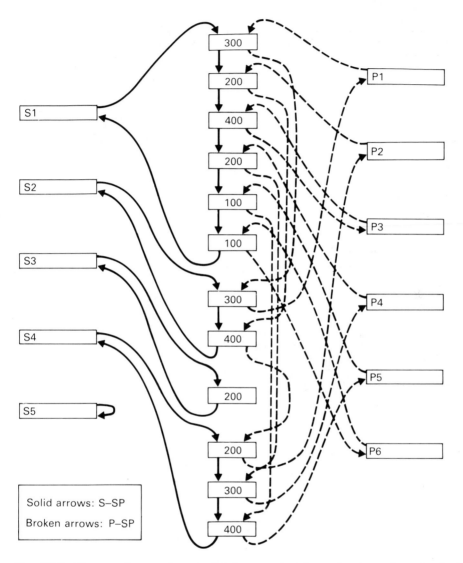

Fig. 23.2 The suppliers-and-parts database: network version (sample values).

2. A given record type *P* can be the parent record type in any number of link types.

3. A given record type *C* can be the child record type in any number of link types.

4. There can be any number of link types with the same record type *P* as parent and the same record type *C* as child; and if *L1* and *L2* are two link types with the same parent type *P* and the same child type *C*, then the arrangement of

parents and children in the two links will in general be quite different. For example, Ci may be a child of Pj in $L1$ but a child of Pk in $L2$.

5. Record types X and Y may be parent and child types respectively in link type $L1$, but child and parent types respectively in link type $L2$.

6. A given link type may have the same record type as both parent and child.

Of the foregoing possibilities, only number 3 is illustrated by the suppliers-and-parts example. For examples of numbers 1, 2, and 4 (and 3 again), see Exercises 23.1–23.3 at the end of the chapter. Note that most systems (including in particular IDMS) do not support number 6.

One final point regarding data structure: Let us agree to call a record type that is not a child in any link a *root* record type. Then, just as in the hierarchic model it is convenient to regard all occurrences of the (single) root as being children of a hypothetical "system" record, so in the network model it may be convenient to regard all occurrences of a given root as children of a hypothetical "system" record in what we will call a "system link." In fact, it may be convenient to regard each root as the child in several distinct system links, each one imposing a different ordering over occurrences of that root. Note that each system link has *exactly one* *occurrence*. (In fact, a system link is basically nothing more than a conventional sequential file.) Figure 23.3 shows an extended form of the suppliers-and-parts database, in which system links S-FILE and P-FILE have been introduced for the S and P record types, respectively. We might assume, purely for the sake of the example, that S-FILE is ordered on the basis of S.CITY values, and P-FILE is ordered on the basis of P.COLOR values.

It is sometimes desirable to introduce system links for nonroot record types also.

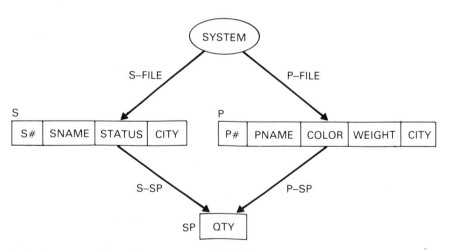

Fig. 23.3 The suppliers-and-parts database: network version (extended to include two system links).

Network Data Manipulation

A network data manipulation language consists of a set of operators for processing data represented in the form of records and links. Examples of such operators include the following:

■ An operator to locate a specific record, given a value for some field in that record—for example, an operator to locate the S record for supplier S1;

■ An operator to move from a parent to its first child in some link—for example, an operator to step from the S record for supplier S1 to the SP record for supplier S1 and part P1 (via the S-SP link);

■ An operator to move from one child to the next in some link—for example, an operator to step from the SP record for supplier S1 and part P1 to the SP record for supplier S1 and part P2 (via the S-SP link);

■ An operator to move from a child to its parent within some link—for example, an operator to step from the SP record for supplier S1 and part P2 to the P record for part P2 (via the P-SP link);

■ An operator to create a new record—for example, an operator to create an S record for a new supplier;

■ An operator to destroy an existing record—for example, an operator to destroy the S record for an existing supplier;

■ An operator to update an existing record—for example, an operator to change the status for an existing supplier;

■ An operator to connect an existing (child) record into a link—for example, an operator to connect a particular SP record into the S-SP and P-SP links;

■ An operator to disconnect an existing (child) record from a link—for example, an operator to disconnect a particular SP record from the S-SP and P-SP links;

■ An operator to disconnect an existing (child) record from one occurrence of a given link (type) and reconnect it into another—for example, an operator to disconnect a particular SP record from the S-SP link with parent S1 and reconnect it into the S-SP link with parent S2;

and so on. Note that (as suggested by the examples) such operators are typically all *record-level*, as in the inverted list and hierarchic models.

Network Data Integrity

Like the hierarchic model, the network model includes "built-in" support for certain forms of referential integrity, by virtue of its primary data structure, the link. For example, it is possible (but not required) to enforce the rule that a child cannot be inserted unless its parent already exists. We defer discussion of the details to Section 23.5; here we simply note that, for a given link, it is possible to achieve an effect that is approximately (but only approximately) equivalent to the following foreign key rules:[3]

```
NULLS ALLOWED or NULLS NOT ALLOWED
DELETE ... CASCADES or RESTRICTED or NULLIFIES
UPDATE ... CASCADES
```

(to use the terminology of Section 12.5 once again).

23.3 AN OVERVIEW OF IDMS

As explained in Section 23.1, the complete IDMS product now includes a base CO-DASYL (network) DBMS, together with certain relational extensions to that base. In this chapter, however, we are primarily concerned with the CODASYL aspects of the system; we therefore ignore the relational features entirely until we reach Sections 23.7 and 23.8. Please note too that, as with our discussions of IMS, we are forced to omit a very great amount of detail (on both CODASYL and relational aspects); some comparatively major topics will simply not be discussed at all.

An IDMS database is defined by a *schema*, written in the IDMS schema data description language (schema DDL). The schema for a given database defines the records in the database, the "elements" (fields) they contain, and the "sets" (links) in which they participate as either "owner" (parent) or "member" (child). Once written, the schema is compiled by the schema DDL compiler, and the output from the compilation is stored in the IDMS dictionary.

Users do not interact with the database per se but rather with a *user view* of that database, defined by a *subschema*. However, the view defined by a subschema is not actually all that different from the "view" defined by the underlying schema; the only really significant difference is that certain schema sets and/or records and/ or fields can be excluded from the subschema. (Of course, "sets," "records," and "fields" here refer to types, not occurrences.) In other words, a subschema is *a simple subset of the schema*, loosely speaking.

Subschemas are written in the IDMS subschema DDL. Once written, they are compiled by the subschema DDL compiler, and again the output is stored in the IDMS dictionary.

As for data manipulation, IDMS (like IMS and DATACOM/DB) is basically invoked by means of a host language CALL interface. However, users do not have to code the calls directly; instead, IDMS provides a set of DML statements (such as FIND, GET, STORE), with a syntax that resembles the syntax of the host language, together with preprocessors to translate those DML statements into the appropriate host language calling sequences. Preprocessors are provided for the following host languages: COBOL, PL/I, FORTRAN, and System/370 Assembler Language.

---

3.   In the case of IDMS specifically, not all of the possibilities shown are fully supported. See Example 23.5.10.

The remainder of this chapter has the following structure. After this preliminary overview section, Section 23.4 explains IDMS data definition (i.e., the schema and subschema), and Section 23.5 describes the IDMS DML. Next, Section 23.6 presents a brief overview of the IDMS storage structure. Sections 23.7 and 23.8 then describe certain extensions to the base system; Section 23.8 discusses the *Logical Record Facility* (LRF) and Section 23.9 discusses the *Automatic System Facility* (ASF). Finally, Section 23.9 presents a few concluding remarks.

As in the case of IMS (Chapter 22), we do not have room in this book for a detailed discussion of such aspects of IDMS as recovery, concurrency, etc. We content ourselves instead with the following brief comments. First, IDMS does indeed provide full recovery and concurrency controls, very much along the lines of DB2 and IMS. Second, it enforces security constraints through the subschema mechanism, which can be used not only to hide information but also to restrict the range of operations the user is allowed to perform. As for integrity, IDMS can optionally be made to enforce certain field uniqueness constraints (see Section 23.4) and certain referential constraints (see Section 23.5).

IDMS also possesses an extensive and well-integrated family of related products in the sense of Chapter 20. Those products include a DC frontend (IDMS-DC), an integrated data dictionary (IDD, already mentioned a couple of times above), an on-line query interface (OLQ), a natural language interface (OnLine English[4]), an application generator (Application Development System / OnLine), a report writer (CULPRIT), and many others.

23.4 DATA DEFINITION

Figure 23.4 shows a possible schema for the suppliers-and-parts database of Fig. 23.3. We remind the reader that we are ignoring numerous details in this chapter; in particular, Fig. 23.4 omits most of the details having to do with how the database is mapped to physical storage. However, some of those details will be discussed briefly in Section 23.6.

We explain this schema as follows.

- Linc 1 merely assigns the schema a name.

- Line 2 defines the existence of a record type S.

- Lines 3–4 define the *location mode* for record type S. In general, a record's location mode tells IDMS how to choose a storage location in the database for a new occurrence of the record type in question. The possibilities are CALC, VIA, plus some other alternatives not discussed at this point.

  - CALC means hashing; the new record is stored at a location determined by hashing the specified "CALC key" (S# in the case at hand; we ignore the

---

4. OnLine English is in fact the INTELLECT product (see Chapter 20), marketed under license from AIC.

```
 1    SCHEMA NAME IS SUPPLIERS-AND-PARTS.

 2    RECORD NAME IS S.
 3    LOCATION MODE IS CALC USING S#
 4                         DUPLICATES NOT ALLOWED.
 5       02 S#    PIC X(5).
 6       02 SNAME PIC X(20).
 7       02 STATUS PIC 999 USAGE COMP-3.
 8       02 CITY   PIC X(15).

 9    RECORD NAME IS P.
10    LOCATION MODE IS CALC USING P#
11                         DUPLICATES NOT ALLOWED.
12       02 P#    PIC X(6).
13       02 PNAME PIC X(20).
14       02 COLOR PIC X(6).
15       02 WEIGHT PIC 999 USAGE COMP-3.
16       02 CITY   PIC X(15).

17    RECORD NAME IS SP.
18    LOCATION MODE IS VIA S-SP SET.
19       02 QTY    PIC 99999 USAGE COMP-3.

20    SET NAME IS S-SP.
21    ORDER IS NEXT.
22    OWNER IS S.
23    MEMBER IS SP OPTIONAL MANUAL.

24    SET NAME IS P-SP.
25    ORDER IS NEXT.
26    OWNER IS P.
27    MEMBER IS SP OPTIONAL MANUAL.

28    SET NAME IS S-FILE.
29    ORDER IS SORTED.
30    OWNER IS SYSTEM.
31    MEMBER IS S MANDATORY AUTOMATIC
32                ASCENDING KEY IS CITY.

33    SET NAME IS P-FILE.
34    ORDER IS SORTED.
35    OWNER IS SYSTEM.
36    MEMBER IS P MANDATORY AUTOMATIC
37                ASCENDING KEY IS COLOR.
```

Fig. 23.4 Schema (many details omitted) for suppliers-and-parts.

fact that "#" is not a legal character in an IDMS name). The CALC key may optionally be specified to be unique (DUPLICATES NOT ALLOWED, line 4).

- VIA means "store the new record near its owner in the specified set" (see line 18 for an example).

- Lines 5–8 define the fields of record type S.

- Lines 9–16 define record type P similarly.

- Lines 17–19 define record type SP similarly, except that the location mode for SP is defined to be VIA S-SP SET, which means that each SP occurrence will be stored physically close to the corresponding S occurrence (i.e., on the same page, or one that is nearby).

- Line 20 defines the existence of a set type called S-SP.

- Line 21 defines the sequence of member (SP) record occurrences within any given occurrence of the set S-SP. ORDER IS NEXT means that the sequence is program-controlled; that is, any program that creates a new member must (procedurally) specify the connection point for that new member. Other possibilities are FIRST (a new member appears in front of all existing members), LAST (a new member appears behind all existing members), PRIOR (another version of program-controlled ordering), and SORTED (ordering based on values of some field in the member record). In the case at hand, we want SP occurrences within a given S-SP occurrence to be kept in part number order; since P# is not a field of the record SP, that ordering cannot be specified as SORTED and so must be maintained by some application program, which is why we specified NEXT. See Example 23.5.8.

- Line 22 specifies the owner record type for S-SP.

- Line 23 specifies the member record type for S-SP. It also includes the "connect option" MANUAL (the alternative is AUTOMATIC) and the "disconnect option" OPTIONAL (the alternative is MANDATORY). We defer explanation of these options to Section 23.5. However, we note in passing that, in the case of S-SP (and P-SP) specifically, MANDATORY AUTOMATIC would be much more appropriate in practice than OPTIONAL MANUAL. We choose OPTIONAL MANUAL purely to serve as a basis for certain examples in Section 23.5.

- Lines 24–27 define set type P-SP similarly.

- Lines 28–32 define a *system-owned set* called S-FILE. System-owned sets correspond to the "system links" of Section 23.2. The set type S-FILE has exactly one occurrence, with a hypothetical SYSTEM record as owner and all S record occurrences as members, in ascending CITY order (by virtue of the specifications ORDER IS SORTED and ASCENDING KEY IS CITY; CITY is the "sort control key" for set S-FILE). The connect and disconnect options have been specified as AUTOMATIC and MANDATORY, respectively.

- Lines 33–37 define the system-owned set P-FILE similarly.

We turn now to user views and the subschema. Any particular user view is a substructure of the underlying schema structure, derived from that underlying structure in accordance with the following rules:

1. Any field type can be omitted.
2. Any record type can be omitted.

3. Any set type can be omitted.

4. If a given record type is omitted, then all set types in which that record type participates (as either owner or member) must be omitted also.

Figure 23.5 shows a possible subschema for the suppliers-and-parts database, in which only two record types are visible, some fields are omitted, and some sets are omitted.

```
1      ADD  SUBSCHEMA NAME  IS  S-AND-P-ONLY
2           OF  SCHEMA NAME  IS  SUPPLIERS-AND-PARTS.

3      ADD  RECORD  S.
4      ADD  RECORD  P
5           ELEMENTS  ARE
6                   P#
7                   COLOR
8                   CITY.

9      ADD  SET  S-FILE.
10     ADD  SET  P-FILE.
```

Fig. 23.5 Possible subschema for the suppliers-and-parts schema (many details omitted).

23.5 DATA MANIPULATION

Preliminaries

For definiteness, we base all our examples and discussions in this section on COBOL, since COBOL is the language most widely used with IDMS. We also assume for simplicity that the subschema is identical to the schema, in the sense that the program has unrestricted access to all sets, records, and fields defined in the schema. Our examples are of course based on the suppliers-and-parts database (schema of Fig. 23.4).

A program issuing IDMS DML operations must contain an IDMS *record description* for each subschema record type it intends to process. That description causes an area of storage to be reserved for records of the specified type; the name of that storage area and the names of its constituent fields are identical to those for the record type in question. Suppose, for example, that the program includes a record description for the supplier record type S. Then (e.g.) to create a new supplier record occurrence, the program could issue the following statements:

```
MOVE  'S13'  TO  S#  IN  S
MOVE  'Johnson'  TO  SNAME  IN  S
MOVE  45  TO  STATUS  IN  S
MOVE  'Warsaw'  TO  CITY  IN  S
STORE  S
```

The four MOVEs initialize the four fields in the record area in storage; the STORE then creates the new record in the database from the values in those four fields. Note: The original DBTG proposals [23.2] referred to the totality of all such record areas as the *User Work Area* (UWA), and we will occasionally make use of that term in this section.

An IDMS program must also include an *IDMS Communications Block* (ICB). The function of the ICB is similar to that of the SQLCA in DB2—that is, it provides feedback information to the program. In particular, it includes a field called ER-ROR-STATUS, which should be checked after each DML operation; a value of 0000 means that the operation completed satisfactorily, a nonzero value means that some exceptional condition occurred. As usual, we will not normally bother to show such checking in our examples.

Note: In practice, the IDMS preprocessors provide facilities to simplify a) the process of constructing the ICB and UWA and b) the process of testing for and dealing with ERROR-STATUS exceptions. Such facilities are beyond the scope of this chapter, however.

Currency

Before we can examine the statements of the DML in any detail, it is necessary to discuss the fundamental concept of *currency*. The concept of currency is analogous to the notion of "current position" in IMS or "current of cursor" in SQL—i.e., it is a generalization of the familiar notion of current position within a file. However, it is rather more complicated than the SQL or IMS concepts. The basic idea is as follows: For each program operating under its control—i.e., for each "run unit," to use the CODASYL term—IDMS maintains a table of *currency indicators*. A currency indicator is an object whose value at any given time is either *null* (meaning that it currently identifies no record) or the address of a record in the database (called a *database key* in IDMS; a database key is basically the same as what we called a record ID or RID in Chapter 3). In other words, a currency indicator is a *database pointer*. The currency indicators for a given run unit identify the record (occurrence) most recently accessed by that run unit for each of the following:[5]

■ Each type of record

For a record type R, the most recently accessed R occurrence is referred to as "the current record of type R" or "the current R occurrence."

■ Each type of set

For a set type S, the most recently accessed record occurrence that participates in an occurrence of S may be either an owner occurrence or a member occurrence. Whichever it is, it is referred to as "the current record of set type S." Note that "the current record of set type S" also uniquely identifies a unique *set* occurrence—namely, the unique occurrence of set type S that contains the current record of set

---

5. "Most recently accessed" is not strictly accurate here. See Examples 23.5.5 and 23.5.6 below.

type *S*. That uniquely identified set occurrence is referred to as "the current occurrence of set type *S*" or "the current *S* occurrence."

- Any type of record

The most recently accessed record occurrence, no matter what its type and no matter what sets it participates in, is referred to as "the current record of the run unit" (usually abbreviated to just "current of run unit"). "Current of run unit" is the most important currency of all, as will shortly be made clear.

As an example, consider the following sequence of operations:

```
MOVE 'S4' TO S# IN S
FIND CALC S
FIND FIRST SP WITHIN S-SP
FIND OWNER WITHIN P-SP
```

The effect of these four statements is as follows. The MOVE initializes the UWA field S# IN S. The FIND CALC then locates the corresponding S record occurrence—namely, the S occurrence for supplier S4. The FIND FIRST ... WITHIN then locates the first SP record occurrence within the S-SP set occurrence owned by supplier S4—namely, the SP occurrence for S4 and P2 (see Fig. 23.2). Last, the FIND OWNER then locates the owner record for that SP occurrence within the set P-SP—namely, the P occurrence for part P2. At the end of the sequence, therefore, that P occurrence is the current of run unit. As an exercise, try to complete the rest of the table:

Current of run unit   P 'P2'
Current S occurrence
Current P occurrence
Current SP occurrence
Current record of set S-SP
Current record of set P-SP
Current S-SP occurrence
Current P-SP occurrence

The complete table is given in the Answers section at the end of the chapter.

Statements

We now embark on our explanation of the major DML statements. First a brief overview:

■ FIND	Locates an existing record occurrence and establishes it as current of run unit (updating other currency indicators as appropriate)
■ GET	Retrieves current of run unit
■ OBTAIN	Same as FIND followed by GET
■ MODIFY	Updates current of run unit

- ■ CONNECT   Connects current of run unit into current occurrence of specified set
- ■ DISCONNECT   Disconnects current of run unit from specified set
- ■ ERASE   Deletes current of run unit
- ■ STORE   Creates a new record occurrence and establishes it as current of run unit (updating other currency indicators as appropriate)

The importance of the notion "current of run unit" is apparent from this summary. So too is the importance of the FIND statement—it is logically required before each of the other statements, except for STORE (and OBTAIN, which we do not discuss any further in this section). The FIND statement has several variants, the most important of which we illustrate in Examples 23.5.1–23.5.6 below.

23.5.1 FIND CALC.   Find the supplier record for supplier S4.

```
MOVE 'S4' TO S# IN S
FIND CALC S
```

FIND CALC can be used if and only if the record type in question has been defined with a location mode of CALC. IDMS finds the required record by taking the value supplied in the UWA field corresponding to the CALC key and hashing it. The record found becomes the current of run unit, the current of its record type, and the current of all sets in which it participates as either owner or member (this remark applies to all forms of FIND and will not be repeated every time).

23.5.2 FIND OWNER.   Find the owner of the current occurrence of set P-SP.

```
FIND OWNER WITHIN P-SP
```

In general, FIND OWNER finds the owner in the specified set type of the current occurrence of that set type. Note: The FIND will fail if the specified set type does not include "owner linkage." See Section 23.6.

23.5.3 FIND member.   Get part numbers for parts supplied by supplier S4.

```
MOVE 'S4' TO S# IN S
FIND CALC S
FIND FIRST SP WITHIN S-SP
while SP found
PERFORM
    FIND OWNER WITHIN P-SP
    GET P
    (add P# IN P to result list)
    FIND NEXT SP WITHIN S-SP
END-PERFORM
```

Two versions of "FIND member" are illustrated in this example. The FIND FIRST locates the first SP occurrence within the current occurrence of set S-SP (namely, the S-SP occurrence owned by supplier S4). Then, on each iteration of the loop, the FIND OWNER and GET find and retrieve the corresponding part, and the FIND NEXT then locates the next SP occurrence for supplier S4. In general, FIND NEXT locates the next record within the current occurrence of the specified set, relative to the position defined by the current record of that set.

If and only if the specified set type has "prior linkage" (see Section 23.6), then the specification FIRST (or NEXT) in "FIND member" can be replaced by the specification LAST (or PRIOR). If and only if the specified set type has "mode chain" (again, see Section 23.6), then the specification FIRST (or NEXT, etc.) can be replaced by an integer n or the name of a program variable having an integer value n, representing a request for the nth member in the set.

23.5.4 FIND member USING.   Get part numbers for red parts.

```
MOVE 'Red' TO COLOR IN P
FIND FIRST P WITHIN P-FILE USING COLOR IN P
while P found
PERFORM
    GET P
    (add P# IN P to result list)
    FIND NEXT P WITHIN P-FILE USING COLOR IN P
END-PERFORM
```

"FIND FIRST member USING" locates the first member of the current occurrence of the specified set having the same value for the specified field as the corresponding field in the UWA. Similarly, "FIND NEXT member USING" locates the next record within the current occurrence of the specified set, relative to the position defined by the current record of that set, having the same value for the specified field as the corresponding field in the UWA. In the example, the specified set happens to have owner SYSTEM, and therefore has only one occurrence; that single occurrence is considered to be the current occurrence at all times.

Note: "FIND member USING" can be used only if the specified set type is defined with ORDER IS SORTED, and the USING field is defined as the sort control key for that set type. Also, the comments under Example 23.5.3 regarding LAST, PRIOR, n, etc. in "FIND member" apply also to "FIND member USING."

23.5.5 FIND CURRENT.   Establish the current record of type P as the current of run unit (note that this record is not necessarily the current of run unit already).

```
FIND CURRENT P
```

FIND CURRENT differs from the FIND formats so far described in that its *only* function is to update the table of currency indicators; it does not require any access to the database (since the record in question must already have been located by some previous operation, by definition). FIND CURRENT is frequently required to establish some record found earlier in the program as current of run unit, immediately prior to (say) a MODIFY operation. The possible FIND CURRENT formats are:

```
FIND CURRENT record
FIND CURRENT OF set
FIND CURRENT OF RUN UNIT
```

23.5.6 FIND DB-KEY. For each supplier who supplies part P4, find another part supplied by the same supplier, and print the supplier number and part number. For simplicity assume that each supplier that supplies P4 does in fact supply at least one other part.

First attempt (*** INCORRECT ***):

```
 1 MOVE 'P4' TO P# IN P
 2 FIND CALC P
 3 PERFORM "forever"
 4     FIND NEXT SP WITHIN P-SP
 5     IF SP not found
 6         leave outer loop
 7     IF SP found
 8         FIND OWNER WITHIN S-SP
 9         GET S
10         PERFORM "forever"
11             FIND NEXT SP WITHIN S-SP
12             FIND OWNER WITHIN P-SP
13             GET P
14             IF P# IN P NOT = 'P4'
15                 leave inner loop
16             END-IF
17         END-PERFORM
18         (print S# IN S and P# IN P)
19     END-IF
20 END-PERFORM
```

As indicated, the code above is not correct—it contains a logical error (quite apart from the assumption mentioned in the problem statement, which of course would not be justified in practice). Try finding the error before reading the explanation below. It is probably a good idea to "execute" the procedure on the sample data of Fig. 23.2.

The error is as follows. When the FIND OWNER in line 12 is executed, it establishes a P occurrence as the current of run-unit—also as the current record of all sets in which it participates (as either owner or member), including in particular set P-SP. This fact in turn means that the current occurrence of set P-SP becomes the one owned by that P occurrence. Thus, when the FIND NEXT in line 4 is executed on the next iteration of the outer loop (in an attempt to find the next supplier of P4), *the P-SP occurrence referenced in that statement will no longer be the one owned by P4*. To avoid this situation, we must do the following:

1. Following successful execution of the FIND NEXT in line 4, we must save the address (database key) of the SP record just found. This can be done by inserting the statement

```
ACCEPT SP-ADDR FROM SP CURRENCY
```

between lines 4 and 5 in the above code. The effect of this statement is to save the database key of the SP record just found in the program variable SP-ADDR.

2. Immediately before attempting to execute the FIND NEXT in line 4 again, we must manually restore the currency indicator for SP to the desired value (i.e., to the value that we saved in SP-ADDR). This can be done by inserting the statement

```
FIND SP DB-KEY IS SP-ADDR
```

between lines 19 and 20 in the above code. The effect of this statement is to find the SP record with database key as given by the program variable SP-ADDR (and thus of course to update all currency indicators accordingly). Like FIND CURRENT, FIND DB-KEY does not actually require any access to the database.

The technique illustrated by this example (saving and restoring currency indicators via ACCEPT and FIND DB-KEY) is needed very frequently in practice. Further examples of its use are given in Examples 23.5.8 and 23.5.9 below.

23.5.7 MODIFY. Add 10 to the status value for supplier S4.

```
MOVE 'S4' to S# IN S
FIND CALC S
GET S
ADD 10 TO STATUS IN S
MODIFY S
```

23.5.8 STORE and CONNECT. Create an SP record relating supplier S4 to part P3 (shipment quantity 1000), and connect it into the S-SP occurrence for S4 and the P-SP occurrence for P3.

```
MOVE 'S4' TO S# IN S
FIND CALC S
ACCEPT S-SP-ADDR FROM S-SP CURRENCY
FIND LAST SP WITHIN S-SP
while SP found PERFORM
    ACCEPT S-SP-ADDR FROM S-SP CURRENCY
    FIND OWNER WITHIN P-SP
    GET P
    IF P# IN P < 'P3'
        leave loop
    END-IF
    FIND PRIOR SP WITHIN S-SP
END-PERFORM
MOVE 'P3' TO P# IN P
FIND CALC P
ACCEPT P-SP-ADDR FROM P-SP CURRENCY
FIND LAST SP WITHIN P-SP
while SP found PERFORM
    ACCEPT P-SP-ADDR FROM P-SP CURRENCY
    FIND OWNER WITHIN S-SP
    GET S
```

```
      IF S# IN S < 'S4'
         leave loop
      END-IF
      FIND PRIOR SP WITHIN P-SP
   END-PERFORM
   MOVE 1000 TO QTY IN SP
   FIND DB-KEY IS S-SP-ADDR
   FIND DB-KEY IS P-SP-ADDR
   STORE SP
   CONNECT SP TO S-SP
   CONNECT SP TO P-SP
```

This example is not straightforward! The code assumes that:

1. The connect options for S-SP and P-SP are specified as MANUAL. If instead they are AUTOMATIC, the two explicit CONNECT statements above will be unnecessary (and in fact illegal); the rest of the code, however, will remain unchanged. A connect option of AUTOMATIC means that, when a new occurrence of the member record type is first stored, it will automatically be connected into the current occurrence of the set (at the position dictated by the ORDER specification for that set—see paragraph 2 below). AUTOMATIC is probably more reasonable in the case of suppliers-and-parts specifically, since it is unlikely that we would want to allow an SP occurrence in the database *not* to be connected into some S-SP occurrence and some P-SP occurrence. The AUTOMATIC connect option thus corresponds very roughly to the "NULLS NOT ALLOWED" foreign key rule of Section 12.5. (Though there are several subtle differences, beyond the scope of this book. See Volume II.)

2. The order options for S-SP and P-SP are specified as NEXT. ORDER IS NEXT means that, when the CONNECT is done, the new record is to be connected into the set at the point immediately following the position identified by the current record of the set.

3. Sets S-SP and P-SP have been specified with both "prior linkage" and "owner linkage" (as mentioned under Examples 23.5.2 and 23.5.3 above).

Note also the need for the various ACCEPT CURRENCY and corresponding FIND DB-KEY statements in this example. The STORE statement establishes the SP record just stored as the current of run-unit but *not* as the current of S-SP or the current of P-SP (because it is not automatically connected into those sets). The FIND DB-KEY statements are needed in order to establish the correct current positions within those sets, as required by paragraph 2 above; note that those statements do not specify a record type, because the record type identified by the specified database key can be either owner or member, in general (for example, if supplier S4 currently supplies no parts, then the variable S-SP-ADDR will identify an S record, otherwise it will identify an SP record). Finally, the CONNECT statements connect the SP record just stored into sets S-SP and P-SP appropriately. Note, incidentally, that the FIND DB-KEY statements *must* precede the STORE statement (why?).

23.5.9 DISCONNECT.   Disconnect the SP record relating supplier S4 and part P3 from the occurrences of sets S-SP and P-SP that contain it.

```
MOVE 'S4' TO S# IN S
FIND CALC S
PERFORM "forever"
    ACCEPT S-SP-ADDR FROM S-SP CURRENCY
    FIND NEXT SP WITHIN S-SP
    FIND OWNER WITHIN P-SP
    GET P
    IF P# IN P = 'P3'
       leave loop
    END-IF
    FIND DB-KEY IS S-SP-ADDR
END-PERFORM
FIND CURRENT SP
DISCONNECT SP FROM S-SP
DISCONNECT SP FROM P-SP
```

The foregoing code assumes that the disconnect options for S-SP and P-SP are specified as OPTIONAL. If instead they are MANDATORY, the DISCONNECT statements above will fail. A disconnect option of MANDATORY means that, once an occurrence of the member record type has been connected into some occurrence of the set, it can never be disconnected from the set again unless it is deleted from the database entirely (see the next example). In practice, of course, MANDATORY is more likely than OPTIONAL in the specific case of sets S-SP and P-SP.

23.5.10 ERASE.   Delete the S occurrence for supplier S4.

The question here is, of course, what to do about the fact that there happen to be some SP occurrences for supplier S4. The answer to that question depends on the format of the ERASE statement. There are four possible formats:

```
MOVE 'S4' TO S# IN S
FIND CALC S
ERASE S [ PERMANENT | SELECTIVE | ALL ]
```

The four formats behave as follows:

- No qualification

The current of run unit is deleted only if it is not the owner of any nonempty set occurrence (corresponds roughly to a foreign key rule of DELETE RESTRICTED; but note that the rule applies to *all* sets for which the record type is the owner—it cannot be varied on a set-by-set basis).

- PERMANENT

The current of run unit is deleted, together with MANDATORY member occurrences of any set occurrences of which it is the owner—OPTIONAL member occurrences being merely disconnected, not deleted (corresponds roughly to a foreign key rule of DELETE CASCADES in the MANDATORY case and DELETE NULLIFIES in the OPTIONAL case).

■ SELECTIVE

The effect is the same as for PERMANENT, except that OPTIONAL members not participating as members in any other set occurrence are deleted, not just disconnected (corresponds roughly to DELETE CASCADES, but note that SELECTIVE effectively allows the program to *override* the static schema specifications).

■ ALL

The current of run unit is deleted, together with all member occurrences of any set occurrence of which it is the owner, regardless of disconnect options (DELETE CASCADES again, except that again the program is overriding the schema specifications).

In each case, if *any* deleted member occurrence is itself the owner of another set occurrence, then the effect is as if the original ERASE (with the appropriate qualification) had been applied directly to that member occurrence.

23.6   STORAGE STRUCTURE

As with our discussion of IMS in Chapter 22, it is certainly not our intent to cover all possible IDMS storage structures in detail in this chapter. However, there are a few general remarks that can usefully be made.

1. First, as in IMS, each stored record includes a hidden prefix, containing (principally) pointers to represent the record's participation as owner or member in various sets, as described in the next few paragraphs.

2. Next, IDMS provides two principal storage representations for the set construct, namely *chained sets* and *indexed sets*. The representation for a given set is specified in the schema, via the MODE clause (not shown in Fig. 23.4): MODE IS CHAIN or MODE IS INDEX.

3. MODE IS CHAIN means that the set is stored essentially as described in Section 23.2—i.e., with a chain of pointers for each set occurrence, linking the owner to the first member, the first member to the second member, . . . , and the last member back to the owner. The chain may optionally be specified as two-way: *prior linkage*. Prior linkage means that the owner also points back to the last member, the last member also points back to the previous member, . . . , and the first member also points back to the owner. *Owner linkage* may also optionally be specified, meaning that each member also includes a pointer to the owner (does not apply to system-owned sets; see paragraph 6 below). As noted in Section 23.5, prior linkage is required for FIND PRIOR and FIND LAST, and owner linkage is required for FIND OWNER.

4. MODE IS INDEX means that each occurrence of the set uses an index instead of a pointer chain to identify (and sequence) the members in that occurrence. Note, therefore, that there are as many occurrences of the index as there are occurrences of the set; see Fig. 23.6, which represents the occurrence of set S-SP for supplier S1 as it would appear in storage if MODE IS INDEX were specified. (For simplicity we have shown the index entries as if each required a separate index record, though in practice they would probably all be contained within just one such record.) Note that the owner and index records are chained by means of next, prior, and owner pointers. In addition, the index records point to the members (of course), and the members also point to the index records; in addition, the members may (optionally) point direct to the set owner. However, such owner linkage is *not* required to support FIND OWNER on an indexed set.

5. Note that MODE IS INDEX does not necessarily imply ORDER IS SORTED. Member sequence within the set is represented by entry sequence within the index, and that sequence in turn can be any of the usual IDMS possibilities—NEXT, PRIOR, FIRST, LAST, or SORTED. For ORDER IS SORTED, the index is multi-level (basically a form of B-tree). In the other cases it is single-level.

6. MODE IS INDEX is used in particular to implement system-owned sets in IDMS. For such a set, of course, there is exactly one occurrence of the owner record (supplied by IDMS and not directly visible to the user), and hence exactly one occurrence of the index.

7. The location mode VIA SET has an extended interpretation if the set in question is defined with MODE IS INDEX and ORDER IS SORTED, as follows: In addition to causing each member record to be stored close to the corresponding owner, it

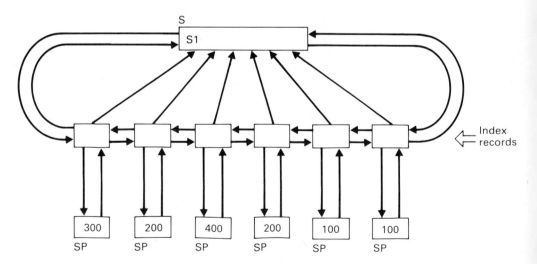

Fig. 23.6 Sample occurrence of an indexed set.

also causes all member records for a particular owner to be stored in a physical order that approximates their logical order. In the particular case where the set in question is system-owned, this facility is similar to the "clustering index" feature of DB2 (see Chapter 5).

8. Finally, we remind the reader of the location mode option CALC (hashing). A difference between IMS and IDMS is that hashing access can be provided to *any* record type in IDMS—it is not restricted to root records only, as it is in IMS.

23.7   THE LOGICAL RECORD FACILITY

The IDMS Logical Record Facility (LRF) provides a "flat record view" layer on top of an IDMS database. In other words, LRF is a mechanism that allows the application programmer to be unaware of the detailed structure of the underlying database and to operate in terms of "logical records" instead—where a logical record (type) is essentially just a virtual table, in relational terms. For example, LRF could be used on the suppliers-and-parts database of Fig. 23.1 to define the following logical record (or view)—

```
SCP ( S#, SCITY, PCITY, P# )
```

—representing supplier number and city plus part number and city for suppliers and parts that are colocated.[6] Then the programmer could perform operations against that view such as the following:

- OBTAIN the FIRST (or NEXT) SCP record WHERE SCITY = 'London'
- MODIFY or ERASE the SCP record most recently OBTAINed
- STORE a new SCP record

Note that the user in LRF is still an application programmer, not an end user. Note too that the user still operates in terms of one (virtual) record at a time.

In discussing LRF, it is important to distinguish carefully between two DMLs, the *application programming DML* and the *view definition DML* (not LRF terms). We refer to them as U-DML and D-DML for short (U for user and D for DBA or definer):

- U-DML is the DML the application programmer uses to operate on the view. The statements OBTAIN, MODIFY, ERASE, and STORE mentioned above are statements of that DML (in fact, they are basically the *only* statements of that DML).

- D-DML is the DML the database administrator uses to define the view and to define the semantics of U-DML operations on the view. D-DML consists bas-

---

6. Actually the SCP logical record would appear in LRF to contain two group items called S and P, each of which in turn contained two elementary items—S# and CITY in S and P# and CITY in P. LRF does not actually provide field renaming as our example suggests.

ically of a somewhat extended version of the regular IDMS DML (actually it looks rather like U-DML plus some additional statements).

In outline, then, LRF works as follows:

1. Views (i.e., logical records) are defined by the DBA as part of the relevant subschema.

2. Users can operate on such views by means of the U-DML operations, which (unlike the regular IDMS DML operations) can include a WHERE clause. Such WHERE clauses can involve arbitrary Boolean combinations of simple comparisons, with parentheses if necessary to force a desired order of evaluation. The simple comparisons in turn can involve the usual comparison operators and also certain string matching operators, and the comparands can consist of arbitrary arithmetic expressions in which the operands can be constants, program variables, or database fields. A comparison can also be a "keyword"—that is, a term defined by the DBA as a shorthand for a longer, more detailed predicate. For example:

```
OBTAIN NEXT SCP WHERE FRENCH
```

Here FRENCH might be a DBA-defined keyword standing for the predicate

```
    SCITY = 'Paris'
OR  SCITY = 'Nice'
OR  SCITY = 'Marseille'
OR  SCITY = 'Amiens'
```

3. Each view is derived from the records of the underlying database by means of a DBA-written procedure, or rather by means of several such procedures (see paragraphs 4 and 5 below), expressed in D-DML. D-DML effectively allows the (procedural) definition of views that are derivable via certain combinations of the relational select, "project," and join operations ("project" in quotes because duplicates are not eliminated). It does not of course provide the select, project, and join operations directly.[7] Note, too, that not all select/project/join views are derivable; for example, it is not possible to define a view that involves a join of a table with itself.

4. As indicated in paragraph 3, the DBA actually provides several procedures (or "paths," to use the LRF terminology) for each view. The purpose of the procedures is basically to tell IDMS what it has to do to support U-DML operations on the view. In the case of the view SCP shown above, for example, the following procedure might be specified for the U-DML operation

```
OBTAIN ... SCP WHERE SCITY = x
```

---

7. Cartesian product is effectively implemented by simply concatenating the names of the records concerned in the definition of the logical record in the subschema. Likewise, "projection" is effectively implemented by simply omitting fields from the definitions of those records in the subschema. Only restriction is implemented purely by executable D-DML code.

(where "..." stands for FIRST or NEXT, and *x* is a parameter; the D-DML pseudocode shown below is intended to be similar but not identical to genuine D-DML code):

```
/* Entry point for FIRST invocation : */
OBTAIN FIRST S WITHIN S-FILE WHERE CITY = x
while S found PERFORM
    extract S.S#, S.CITY
    OBTAIN FIRST P WITHIN P-FILE WHERE CITY = x
    while P found PERFORM
        extract P.P#, P.CITY
        return S.S#, S.CITY, P.CITY, P.P# to user
        /* Entry point for NEXT invocation : */
        OBTAIN NEXT P WITHIN P-FILE WHERE CITY = x
    END-PERFORM
    OBTAIN NEXT S WITHIN S-FILE WHERE CITY = x
END-PERFORM
```

Each time the programmer issues the U-DML OBTAIN operation shown above, LRF will invoke this procedure to construct the required next record. Note that LRF is able to remember the point it left off execution of the procedure on the previous invocation, so it knows what "next" means in this context.

5. In general, the DBA must provide a "path" or procedure for each distinct operation that the user is to be allowed to perform on the view. In particular, the DBA may have to provide several distinct *retrieval* procedures for a given view. In the case of view SCP, for example, retrieval by supplier number may best be implemented by a procedure involving FIND CALC on the S record; retrieval by part number may best be implemented by a procedure involving FIND CALC on the P record; retrieval by an equality condition on SCITY may best be implemented by a procedure involving FIND USING on the S-FILE system-owned set; and so on. Thus the complete definition for the view SCP might look something like the following:

```
ADD SUBSCHEMA NAME IS ...

ADD RECORD S
    ELEMENTS ARE S# CITY.

ADD RECORD P
    ELEMENTS ARE P# CITY.

ADD SET S-SP etc.

ADD LOGICAL RECORD NAME IS SCP
    ELEMENTS ARE S P.

ADD PATH-GROUP OBTAIN SCP
    SELECT FOR FIELDNAME-EQ S#
        OBTAIN S WHERE CALCKEY EQ S# OF REQUEST
        ... etc ...
```

(Continued)

```
SELECT FOR FIELDNAME-EQ P#
    OBTAIN P WHERE CALCKEY EQ P# OF REQUEST
    ... etc ...
SELECT FOR FIELDNAME-EQ SCITY
    OBTAIN ...
    ... etc ...
SELECT FOR FRENCH
    OBTAIN ...
    ... etc ...

ADD PATH-GROUP MODIFY SCP
    SELECT ...
    ... etc ...

ADD PATH-GROUP STORE SCP
    SELECT ...
    ... etc ...

ADD PATH-GROUP ERASE SCP
    SELECT ...
    ... etc ...
```

For a given user request, LRF will search through the D-DML procedures in sequence as written and will take the first it finds that matches the request. If it finds no match, it will reject the request. Thus, for example, if users are not to be allowed to access SCP records by SCITY value, it is sufficient for the DBA simply not to supply a retrieval procedure for that kind of access.

Having thus briefly sketched the way LRF works, we are now in a position to analyze it and compare it with a relational view mechanism such as that described in Part 2 of this book. We offer the following comments.

1. First, of course, LRF is not relational, because the U-DML does not support the relational operators (neither does the D-DML, come to that). In addition, the views seen by the user may include duplicate records and may involve repeating groups and/or "redefined" fields and/or essential ordering (see Section 15.2 for a discussion of essential ordering).

2. However, if the underlying IDMS database is sufficiently disciplined and does not (for example) rely on essential ordering, then LRF could—and indeed probably should—be used to provide a "true" relational view of that database (the previous point notwithstanding). For example, it could be used to define a relational view of the network version of suppliers-and-parts (Fig. 23.1) that consisted precisely of the familiar relations S, P, and SP. Of course, the U-DML operations would still be record-at-a-time, but at least the structure would be relational.

3. Note that each view definition requires the construction of a new subschema, a rather static kind of operation. Note too that it is not possible to construct "views on views"—i.e., to refer to existing views in D-DML procedures.

4. The views definable in D-DML are not arbitrary derived relations—they are basically just restrictions of Cartesian products, with certain fields optionally omitted. In particular, it is not possible to construct a view that involves a union or difference operation.

5. Of course, a view *can* be a join, since a join is just a restriction of a product. Furthermore, LRF allows the user to perform updates on a join view. However, LRF per se has no knowledge of what "update of join" means in any kind of general sense; instead, the meaning of such an operation (just like the meaning of every other U-DML operation) must be spelled out by the DBA in the form of a D-DML procedure. In other words, "update of join" and similar operations still require someone to write ad hoc, procedural application code—but that someone is the DBA instead of the user. (Note that IDMS, like most current relational products, has no clear notion of primary and foreign keys. As a result, any view updating mechanism must necessarily be ad hoc, as explained in the Answers section in Chapter 15.)

6. It follows from the previous paragraph that it is not sufficient to tell the user what views are available and what U-DML operations can be performed on those views; it is of course also necessary to explain the *meaning* of those views and operations, which in some cases will amount to explaining the underlying structure of the database. For example, consider the following LRF view of suppliers-and-parts:

```
SQP ( S#, QTY, P# )
```

(with the conventional "shipment" interpretation). Depending on how the DBA chooses to write the D-DML procedures, a U-DML ERASE operation on a record of SQP might a) be disallowed, or b) delete the corresponding supplier, with or without that supplier's shipments, or c) delete the corresponding part, with or without that part's shipments, or d) just delete the shipment, or e) take any of many other possible actions. Furthermore, each of these possibilities has interactions with the SCP view shown at the beginning of the section. And all of this needs to be explained to the user.[8]

Of course, remarks analogous to the foregoing apply to the relational view mechanism also, but with this significant difference: In the relational case, the underlying database and the view—and the mapping between them—are all based on the same (relational) model of data, which therefore provides a framework in which the explanations can make sense. In LRF the different levels are based on different models.

---

8. It is the responsibility of the DBA to provide the necessary explanations by including extensive comments in the subschema along with the logical record definitions. An IDMS utility is provided to generate an explanatory report for the user from such comments.

7. Note that the requirement that the DBA provide a procedure for each and every operation that the user is to be able to perform means that a) the user *is* able to issue only those predefined operations, and (more important) b) *the DBA is hand-optimizing those predefined operations.* Note too that by "hand-optimizing predefined operations" we do not mean, for example, hand-optimizing a generic join operation—we mean hand-optimizing each and every join operation separately. Also, of course, if the physical structure of the database is changed, then reoptimization (i.e., reprogramming by the DBA) will be necessary.

8. Finally, we cannot resist pointing out that implementing a mechanism like LRF in terms of the implicit currency indicators of CODASYL must be significantly more complicated than implementing a similar mechanism in a system with explicit position holders (i.e., cursors). In fact, LRF users are advised not to mix LRF operations and regular CODASYL DML operations in the same program, because the regular operations will affect the currency indicators that control the LRF operations behind the scenes. For similar reasons, LRF users cannot dynamically switch from one path to another before the first is exhausted (i.e., before a "not found" condition has occurred). In the following sequence of U-DML operations, for example, the second OBTAIN NEXT will produce an unpredictable result:[9]

```
OBTAIN NEXT SCP WHERE S# = 'S1'
OBTAIN NEXT SCP WHERE SCITY = 'London'
```

These same currency difficulties are probably also the source of the limitation that views cannot be defined in terms of other views.

23.8 THE AUTOMATIC SYSTEM FACILITY

Disclaimer: Not all of the function described in this section is supported at the time of writing.

The Automatic System Facility (ASF) is the justification for the "R" in "IDMS/R." It is the component that provides (most of) the relational function of the system. It may be regarded as a frontend to the base IDMS product, supporting simple relational definitional and manipulative operations through a set of forms-based interfaces. Functionally, in fact, it somewhat resembles the forms-based QBF and definitional interfaces (only) of INGRES, as described in Chapter 20. It runs under the IDMS data communications component IDMS-DC.

Before we go any further, it may perhaps be helpful to point out what ASF is not. It is not a command-driven query language processor. Nor is it a report writer. Furthermore, it does not support the use of relational operators in application programs. Instead:

---

9. Unless the first happens to give "not found." In this case the currency indicators will be set to null, with the result that the second OBTAIN NEXT will be interpreted as OBTAIN FIRST.

- The interactive query / report writer function is provided by the existing OnLine Query product OLQ. Relations created through ASF can be accessed through OLQ. However, OLQ does not support the full set of relational operators—in particular, it does not support join—and neither does it allow update. It does however allow the result of a query to be saved as a table in the database.

- The batch report writer function is provided through the existing report writer product CULPRIT.

- Since relations are implemented as LRF logical records (see below), application programs can access them using the operators of "U-DML." Applications can also be written to operate directly against the underlying database using conventional IDMS DML, as described in Section 23.5. Note, however, that all such access is basically one-record-at-a-time (in both cases).

In addition, the forms generated automatically by ASF can be customized if desired by means of the IDMS application generator ADS/OnLine, much as QBF forms can be customized via VIFRED in INGRES.

The primary purpose of ASF is to support the definition of, and subsequent access to, new (relational) databases. However, *it can also be used to provide a relational view of, and relational processing of, existing network databases.*[10] We defer consideration of this latter possibility (relational access to networks) to the end of this section.

As indicated above, ASF is implemented on top of LRF, just as LRF is implemented on top of the base DBMS. In other words, ASF supports relations[11] by treating them as LRF logical records, and LRF supports logical records by mapping them to (sub)schema records via access procedures expressed in "D-DML," as explained in Section 23.7. In the case of ASF, however, those access procedures are not written by the DBA but are generated automatically by ASF from specifications provided by the person defining the relation. See Fig. 23.7.

A given "relational record" (i.e., table) can be *stored* or it can be a *view*. A view of course is derived from one or more other tables (stored tables and/or views); in IDMS/R, unlike most other relational systems, a stored table can also be derived in the same sense.[12] A derived stored table has a defining query associated with it (just as a view does, of course), specified at the time the table is defined. When the table is "populated," the query is executed and the result is stored as the current value of the table. The table can subsequently be repopulated whenever the user desires ("populate" is a command on one of the ASF forms).

A stored table that is not derived is said to be a *basic* stored table.

---

10.   "Relational" should really be in quotes here, because the data structure shown to the user may not be a genuine relation—it may involve essential ordering, repeating groups, etc.

11.   Or "relational records," to use the ASF term. We will generally use the more familiar terms "table" and "relation" in this section.

12.   Derived stored tables are not supported at the time of writing.

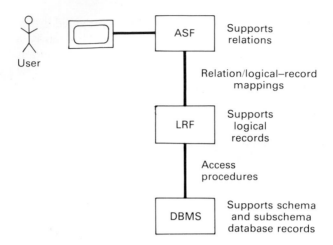

Fig. 23.7 ASF is implemented on top of LRF.

Creating a Basic Stored Table

Suppose, then, that the user wishes to create a new basic stored table. Through the appropriate ASF definitional forms, the user will specify:

1. The fact that this is a basic stored table (not a derived one and not a view);
2. The table name and field names;
3. The field data types (the possibilities are TEXT, NUMERIC, and CURRENCY—i.e., dollars and cents);
4. Optional integrity constraints on the table (details unclear at the time of writing, but probably limited to simple restriction predicates);
5. Optional "keys" (i.e., fields or field combinations to be indexed; note that there is no way to specify a CALC key). Each such "key" can optionally be specified to be UNIQUE.

When the definition is complete, the user issues the ASF "generate" command. ASF then does all of the following:

- Adds a definition of the new stored record type to the "relational schema." The relational schema is an internal-level description of the relational database ("internal" in the ANSI/SPARC sense); it contains definitions of all the records, CODASYL "indexed sets," etc. that appear in the stored form of the database. The initial relational schema is created when IDMS/R is first installed (it does not have to be defined by the DBA, unlike a network schema).

- Adds a definition of an indexed set to the relational schema for each defined "key."

- Creates a subschema defining the table as an LRF logical record, with corresponding OBTAIN, MODIFY, STORE, and ERASE access procedures. Those procedures make use of the defined "keys" (and hence indexes) as appropriate.

- Compiles the subschema.
- Generates code to support forms-based access (via the subschema) to the new table.

The user can now load data into the table, run simple restriction queries (only) on it, and update it, all very much as in QBF in INGRES. Note clearly however that all such operations are by definition *single-table* operations.

Creating a View

The operations available for defining a view are basically restrict, "project" (in quotes because as usual there is no question of eliminating duplicates), and join (but the join can involve a maximum of five ANDed join predicates, meaning that at most six tables can be joined; furthermore, no two of those tables can be the same). The names of fields in the view can differ from the names of the corresponding fields in the underlying table(s).

Part of the view definition process involves the specification of a) whether updates are allowed on the view, and b) if they are, what their effect is on the underlying tables. In the particular case of a view V that is a join of two tables (possibly views) $T1$ and $T2$, the possibilities are as follows:[13]

- Inserting a record into V can cause (the applicable portions of) the record to be inserted into both, either, or neither of $T1$ and $T2$;
- Updating a field in V can either cause or not cause a corresponding update to a field in $T1$ or $T2$ (whichever is applicable);
- Deleting a record from V can cause (the applicable portions of) the record to be deleted from both, either, or neither of $T1$ and $T2$.

Updates to views are monitored to ensure that inserted or changed records satisfy the view-defining predicate. Note in particular that the "update of join" mechanism just described could be used to enforce certain referential integrity constraints—*provided* all updates are made through appropriate views and not directly on the underlying stored tables. We shall have more to say regarding this possibility in the next section.

When the definition of the view is complete, the user issues the ASF "generate" command (as in the case of a stored table). ASF then does the following:

- Creates a subschema defining the view as an LRF logical record, with corresponding access procedures as indicated by the view-defining expression and the update specifications.

---

13.   This feature is not supported at the time of writing (currently, only row-and-column-subset views can be updated).

- Compiles the subschema.
- Generates code to support forms-based access (via the subschema) to the new view.

The user can now operate on the view in all the usual ways, just as if it were a stored table, subject of course to any specified update constraints. Note once again that all such operations are by definition single-table operations—but here the "single table" can be a (predefined) join of up to six tables, any of which can in turn be a (predefined) join, etc.

Creating a Derived Stored Table

Creating a derived stored table is very similar to creating a view, with the added step of "populating" the table (done as a separate step after the "generate" operation). Thereafter the table then behaves like a basic stored table, except that it can be "repopulated" on request at any time.

Further Definitional Operations

ASF supports several further data definition operations in addition to the various table creation operations discussed above. First, of course, any existing table can be deleted ("dropped," to use the SQL term). Second, columns can be added to and removed from both stored tables and views. Third, "key" specifications (and therefore indexes) can also be added and removed. Finally, any of the following can be changed (again, for both stored tables and views, except where the change would be meaningless):

- Field names, lengths, and data types
- "Key" specifications
- Integrity constraints
- Derivation predicates

(The full implications of some of these changes are very unclear at the time of writing. Some cases—for example, changing the data type of a field—will almost certainly require the table in question to be unloaded and reloaded.)

Following any such definitional changes to a given table, the user is required to reissue the "generate" command. ASF will then modify the schema and subschema appropriately, restructure the database if necessary, and rebuild the forms-based application code. If the user makes changes to one table that affect other tables derived from it, ASF will flag those derived tables as "invalid." It *will* change the source-code definitions of those derived tables to bring them into line with the changes to the table(s) from which they are derived, but it will not automatically go through the "regenerate" procedure for them. The purpose of propagating the changes at the source-code level is to simplify the subsequent "regenerate" procedure, if the user does decide to request that procedure, but not to automate it.

Any application programs that have been developed against the now changed tables will *not* automatically be invalidated; it is the user's responsibility to change such programs manually and then recompile them (if necessary).

Creating an ASF View of a Network Database

In order to construct an ASF view of an existing network database as a collection of relations, the DBA must go through the following steps:

1. Copy all the network definitions—for CODASYL records, CODASYL sets, etc. —over from the network schema into the relational schema. (Note: It is the DBA's responsibility to ensure that the two schemas are kept in synch once the copying has been done.)

2. Write a (CODASYL-style) subschema for each desired relation (i.e., view), specifying all the CODASYL records, CODASYL sets, etc., involved in the definition of that relation (view).

3. Construct an ASF view definition for each desired relation (view), specifying the derivation of that relation in terms of CODASYL records and CODASYL sets. The source records in a given derivation can be either network records or relational records, in general; in the case at hand, of course, they will be network records. For network records, an additional form of join predicate can be specified in the derivation condition: "SET setname," meaning that each member record is to be joined to its owner record in the designated CODASYL set.

4. Issue "generate" for each such view.[14]

Finally, the foregoing raises the possibility of tuning an existing IDMS/R *relational* database by adding CODASYL-style (chained) owner-member sets to link existing tables together. (Such sets would almost certainly be inessential, MANDATORY, and AUTOMATIC.) The DBA would then have to modify the source-level (ASF) view definitions to exploit those sets (i.e., by changing the derivation predicates to specify "SET setname"), and then reissue the "generate" command

---

14.   Of course, the views defined by this procedure will only be as "relational" as the original network structure permits. For example, they may (as pointed out earlier) involve repeating groups, essential ordering, and similar nonrelational constructs. Also, given the limitations on updating views in ASF, they may not be updatable; and even if they are, there are likely to be certain difficulties. For example, foreign keys may not be updatable, because such updates correspond to a DISCONNECT plus a (re)CONNECT at the underlying database level, and membership is very likely to have been specified as MANDATORY. (Given the relation SP(S#,P#,QTY) as a relational view of the network database of Fig. 23.1, how could a shipment for part P1 be updated to become a shipment for part P2 instead, if membership were MANDATORY?) And another question: What are the semantics of a relational STORE operation if the "relation" involves essential ordering? (Analogous questions arise for MODIFY and ERASE, of course.)

for those views. Such tuning may well be desirable and appropriate in certain situations.

23.9   CONCLUDING REMARKS

In this chapter, we have sketched a hypothetical network data model (abstracted from the CODASYL DBTG proposals), and we have described the major features of IDMS, a well-known example of the CODASYL approach. We stress the point once again that we have omitted a very great amount of detail from that description. By way of conclusion, we now offer the following critical comments on network systems in general, and CODASYL systems and IDMS in particular.

Network Systems in General

Networks are complicated. The structure is complex; see Exercise 23.3 for an illustration of this point (if further illustration is needed). The operators are complex; and note that they would still be complex, even if they functioned at the set level instead of just on one record at a time (see reference [15.2] for evidence and further discussion of this claim). And, as explained in Chapter 15, this increase in complexity (compared with relational systems) does not lead to any corresponding increase in functionality.

It is usually claimed, however, that network systems do at least provide good performance. However, good performance is by no means a foregone conclusion in such a system, for at least the following two reasons:

- First, the network data structure tends to *fragment information*. For example, the supplier number for a particular shipment in the network structure of Fig. 23.1 is not part of the shipment record, but is instead part of the supplier record that is the owner of the shipment in a certain CODASYL set. As a result, it is possible that a given application can require significantly more I/O on a network structure than it would on an equivalent inverted list structure.

- Second, as pointed out at several points in this chapter and elsewhere, much of the optimization in such a system is likely to be done manually, either by application programmers or by the DBA.

In fact, many of the criticisms of hierarchic systems made in Chapter 22 apply to network systems also.

CODASYL and IDMS

CODASYL in particular is considerably more complex than the hypothetical network model presented in Section 23.2 (though we omitted much of that additional complexity in our discussions in Sections 23.3–23.5). The concept of currency is an especially rich source of complexity (and error, we might add). Likewise, the complexity of the manual CONNECT process for essential sets—see Example 23.5.8— is sufficiently severe to suggest that sets should almost always be inessential in practice, which in turn raises the question of why the CODASYL set construct should be visible at all at the logical level.

In the case of IDMS specifically, application programs are not very data independent: FIND CALC works if and only if the named record type has CALC location mode; FIND PRIOR and LAST work if and only if the named set type has prior linkage; FIND OWNER works only if the named set type has owner linkage (unless it is an indexed set); FIND USING works if and only if the named set type has SORTED order and the named field is the sort control key; DISCONNECT works if and only if the named set type has a disconnect option of MANUAL; and so on (this is not an exhaustive list).

LRF

A number of criticisms of LRF were made in Section 23.7, and there is no need to repeat the points here. Now that the ASF frontend is available, LRF should be regarded primarily as a stepping stone (i.e., implementation vehicle) to that frontend. However, LRF does also allow (record-level) application programs to be written against databases defined through ASF, and such programs will of course still be needed in many situations.

ASF

To repeat from the introduction to Section 23.8: ASF is basically a forms-based system for defining relations and performing simple manipulative operations on them. It is not intended to be a report-writing or command-driven query language system, nor does it support the use of relational operations in application programs. It may be regarded as a *minimally relational* system according to the classification presented in Chapter 15, in that it does support the select, project, and join operators (with the limitations noted in Section 23.8). It does not support:[15]

- Duplicate elimination
- Union or difference operations
- Aggregate operations (SUM, AVG, etc.) and grouping
- Dynamic ordering (as in SQL "ORDER BY")
- Set-level update operations (e.g., "UPDATE WHERE")

Nor does it support a truly dynamic, ad hoc join operation; instead, joins are specified definitionally, as part of the definition of a view (or derived stored table). Accessing the view (or issuing "populate" for the derived stored table) then causes the predefined join to be executed.

We now turn our attention to the question of referential integrity. Like most other relational products at the time of writing, IDMS/R does not have the nec-

---

15.   The third and fourth items in this list are supported by OnLine Query, however.

essary knowledge of primary and foreign keys to approach this question in a systematic and "automatic" manner. Instead, the approach seems to be basically as follows. For a given pair of tables that are connected in a primary-key/foreign-key relationship, the DBA must:

1. Construct a view of the tables concerned, joining the tables together on the basis of that primary/foreign key match;
2. Next, specify the set of updates the user is allowed to perform on that view;
3. Finally, specify the effects of those allowed updates on the underlying tables.[16]

In other words, referential integrity support appears to be bundled in with the view mechanism. In this writer's opinion such a bundling is an architectural mistake, for the following reasons among others:

1. The "same" rules will have to be specified for multiple views. Consider suppliers and parts, for example. Suppose we want to specify (the equivalent of) DELETE CASCADES for shipments with respect to suppliers. Then we can certainly define a view SSP as the join of S and SP (over supplier numbers), and define the effect of DELETE—or rather ERASE—against that view appropriately. But suppose we also need a view SSPP, defined as the join of S and SP and P (over supplier numbers and part numbers). Presumably, then, we will have to define the effect of DELETE against this view analogously. (For why should SSP be updatable and SSPP not?)
2. "Same" was in quotes in the previous paragraph for the obvious reason that the rules may in fact be defined differently for different views over the same data—though it is hard to imagine why that would be a good thing.
3. What if the user updates the stored tables directly, without going through the view?

The fundamental point is that referential integrity constraints (and corresponding triggered procedures) are more logically a property of the *base data*, not of some particular user's view of that base data. They should therefore be specified once and for all as part of the definition of that base data.

Finally, what about performance? As usual in a relational system, the answer to this question must depend to a large extent on the quality of the system optimizer. Although we did not say so explicitly in Section 23.8, the ASF component that generates LRF access procedures is of course a relational optimizer. Note that optimization is therefore done at "generate" time (analogous to BIND time in DB2), not at run time, which is definitely a point in IDMS/R's favor.

Now, since it cascades through LRF, the sophistication of the ASF optimizer is

---

16.   We remind the reader that "update of join" is currently not supported, so that referential integrity is in fact currently not supported either.

automatically bounded by the sophistication of LRF. For example, LRF selects a strategy for responding to a particular request by means of a simple sequential search through the strategies available to it, which is obviously not as flexible as a scheme that evaluates multiple alternatives and chooses the cheapest. Suppose, for example, that table T has two indexed fields A and B; suppose also that the strategy "access via the A index" precedes the strategy "access via the B index" in the (ASF-generated) LRF list of strategies. Then a predicate involving both A and B will always use the A index, never the B index (and never both). Furthermore, a predicate that could be evaluated by access to the index(es) alone, without any access to the data at all, can never be recognized as such by LRF.

Following on from the previous point: It is also not clear that the classification of strategies recognized by LRF is fine-grained enough to discriminate adequately between different kinds of query—for example:

1. To distinguish between a predicate of the form "condition AND condition" and one of the form "condition OR condition"; or

2. To distinguish between a predicate of the form "field $> =$ value" (for which an index is probably a good choice) and one of the form "field $\sim =$ value" (for which an index is probably a bad choice); or

3. To allow different queries involving the "same" relational operators to have those operators applied in different sequences;

and so on. Furthermore, note that the optimizer is definitely *not* intelligent enough to take automatic advantage of CODASYL links (if such links exist). For if such a link does exist, then the DBA must explicitly tell the optimizer to use it, via the join predicate "SET setname" (see the subsection on creating an ASF view of a network database in Section 23.8). And if the DBA does specify link X (say) as such an access path, the optimizer will presumably *always* use that link, even though it may well not be optimal in all cases.

Note finally that at the time of writing the optimization process does not make any use of database statistics (table cardinalities, index selectivities, clustering information, etc.). Nor can it involve any dynamic sorting (which is unfortunate, since dynamically sorting one or both tables is frequently the best technique for implementing a join).

EXERCISES

23.1 Draw a data structure diagram for a network version of the education database of Chapter 22, in which the foreign keys TEACHER.EMP#, STUDENT.EMP#, and PREREQ.PREREQ# are each replaced by a link.

23.2 Write a schema for the education database of Exercise 23.1.

23.3 Suppose in the education database of Exercise 23.1 that courses have prerequisites as indicated in the following table:

```
-------        -------
COURSE#        PREREQ#
-------        -------
  C1             C2
  C1             C4
  C2             C4
  C3             C6
  C5             C3
  C5             C6
  C6             C1
```

Draw an occurrence diagram for this data corresponding to the schema given in your answer to Exercise 23.1.

23.4 Write a schema for a network version of the suppliers-parts-projects database.

23.5 Using your answer to Exercise 23.4 as a basis, write DML procedures for the following:

a) Get S# values for suppliers who supply project J1.

b) Get S# values for suppliers who supply project J1 with part P1.

c) Get P# values for parts supplied to all projects in London.

d) Get J# values for projects not supplied with any red part by any London supplier.

e) Get P# values for parts supplied by at least one supplier who supplies at least one part supplied by supplier S1.

f) Get all pairs of CITY values such that a supplier in the first city supplies a project in the second city.

g) Change the color of all red parts to orange.

h) The quantity of P1 supplied to J1 by S1 is now to be supplied by S2 instead (in addition to any quantity of P1 that S2 already supplies to J1). Make all the necessary changes.

23.6 Suppose that a new set type *OM* (owner *O*, member *M*) is added to the database. To what extent can existing programs remain unaffected by this addition? You should consider each of the following cases (and each combination of cases, where combinations make sense):

a) *O* and *M* both new record types (additions)

b) *O* and *M* both old (existing) record types

c) *O* old and *M* new

d) *O* new and *M* old

e) *M* AUTOMATIC with respect to *OM*

f) *M* MANUAL with respect to *OM*

g) *M* MANDATORY with respect to *OM*

h) *M* OPTIONAL with respect to *OM*

i) *OM* essential (see Chapter 15)

j) *OM* inessential (again, see Chapter 15)

REFERENCES AND BIBLIOGRAPHY

23.1 Information on IDMS is available from Cullinet Software Inc., Westwood, Mass. 02090.

23.2 Data Base Task Group of CODASYL Programming Language Committee. *Report* (April 1971).

23.3 C. W. Bachman. "Data Structure Diagrams." *Data Base* (journal of ACM SIGBDP) **1**, No. 2 (Summer 1969).

23.4 C. W. Bachman. "The Programmer as Navigator." *CACM* **16**, No. 11 (November 1973).

Contains the lecture Bachman gave on the occasion of his receiving the 1973 Turing Award. Bachman contrasts the earlier view of data processing, in which the computer was central and data was considered as flowing through the machine as it was processed, with the more modern view, in which the database is the major resource and the computer is merely a tool for accessing it. The term "navigation" (nowadays *manual* navigation, to distinguish it from the automatic navigation found in relational systems) is used to describe the process of traveling through the database, following explicit paths from one record to the next in the search for some required piece of data.

23.5 X3H2 (American National Standards Database Committee). *Draft Proposed Network Database Language NDL*. Document X3H2-84-100 (August 1984). ANSI Inc., 1430 Broadway, New York, NY 10018.

ANSWERS TO SELECTED EXERCISES

The currency table in Section 23.5 should be completed as follows:

Current of run unit	P 'P2'
Current S occurrence	S 'S4'
Current P occurrence	P 'P2'
Current SP occurrence	SP linking S4 and P2
Current record of set S-SP	ditto (member)
Current record of set P-SP	P 'P2' (owner)
Current S-SP occurrence	owned by S 'S4'
Current P-SP occurrence	owned by P 'P2'

23.1 See Fig. 23.8 on page 580.

23.2
```
SCHEMA NAME IS EDUCATION-DATABASE.

RECORD NAME IS COURSE.
LOCATION MODE IS CALC USING COURSE# DUPLICATES NOT ALLOWED.
    02 COURSE# PIC X(3).
    02 TITLE   PIC X(33).

RECORD NAME IS PREREQ.
LOCATION MODE IS VIA HASPRE SET.
```

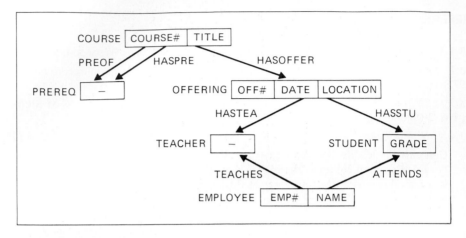

Fig. 23.8 Network version of the education database.

```
RECORD NAME IS OFFERING.
LOCATION MODE IS VIA HASOFFER SET.
     02 OFF#      PIC X(3).
     02 DATE      PIC X(6).
     02 LOCATION PIC X(12).

RECORD NAME IS TEACHER.
LOCATION MODE IS VIA HASTEA SET.

RECORD NAME IS STUDENT.
LOCATION MODE IS VIA HASSTU SET.
     02 GRADE     PIC X.

RECORD NAME IS EMP.
LOCATION MODE IS CALC USING EMP# DUPLICATES NOT ALLOWED.
     02 EMP#      PIC X(6).
     02 NAME      PIC X(18).

SET NAME IS HASPRE.
ORDER IS NEXT.
OWNER IS COURSE.
MEMBER IS PREREQ MANDATORY AUTOMATIC.

SET NAME IS PREOF.
ORDER IS NEXT.
OWNER IS COURSE.
MEMBER IS PREREQ MANDATORY AUTOMATIC.

SET NAME IS HASOFFER.
ORDER IS SORTED.
OWNER IS COURSE.
MEMBER IS OFFERING MANDATORY AUTOMATIC
        ASCENDING KEY IS OFF# DUPLICATES NOT ALLOWED.
```

```
SET NAME IS HASTEA.
ORDER IS NEXT.
OWNER IS OFFERING.
MEMBER IS TEACHER MANDATORY AUTOMATIC.

SET NAME IS HASSTU.
ORDER IS NEXT.
OWNER IS OFFERING.
MEMBER IS STUDENT MANDATORY AUTOMATIC.

SET NAME IS TEACHES.
ORDER IS NEXT.
OWNER IS EMP.
MEMBER IS TEACHER MANDATORY AUTOMATIC.

SET NAME IS ATTENDS.
ORDER IS NEXT.
OWNER IS EMP.
MEMBER IS STUDENT MANDATORY AUTOMATIC.

SET NAME IS COURSE-FILE.
ORDER IS SORTED.
OWNER IS SYSTEM.
MEMBER IS COURSE MANDATORY AUTOMATIC
          ASCENDING KEY IS COURSE#.

SET NAME IS EMP-FILE.
ORDER IS SORTED.
OWNER IS SYSTEM.
MEMBER IS EMP MANDATORY AUTOMATIC
          ASCENDING KEY IS EMP#.
```

23.3 See Fig. 23.9 on page 582.

23.4 SCHEMA NAME IS S-P-J.

```
RECORD NAME IS S.
LOCATION MODE IS CALC USING S# DUPLICATES NOT ALLOWED.
      02 S#      PIC X(5).
      02 SNAME   PIC X(20).
      02 STATUS PIC 999 USAGE COMP-3.
      02 CITY    PIC X(15).

RECORD NAME IS P.
LOCATION MODE IS CALC USING P# DUPLICATES NOT ALLOWED.
      02 P#      PIC X(6).
      02 PNAME   PIC X(20).
      02 COLOR   PIC X(6).
      02 WEIGHT PIC 999 USAGE COMP-3.
      02 CITY    PIC X(15).

RECORD NAME IS J.
LOCATION MODE IS CALC USING J# DUPLICATES NOT ALLOWED.
      02 J#      PIC X(4).
```

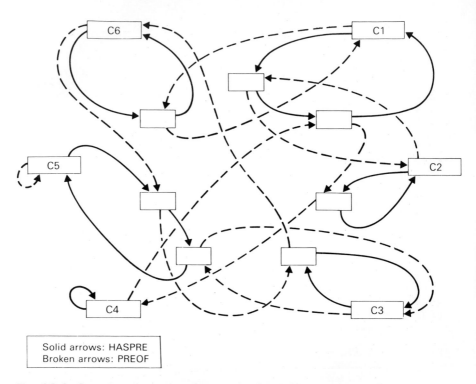

Solid arrows: HASPRE
Broken arrows: PREOF

Fig. 23.9 Sample occurrence diagram for COURSEs and PREREQs.

```
       02 JNAME   PIC X(20).
       02 CITY    PIC X(15).

RECORD NAME IS SPJ.
LOCATION MODE IS VIA S-SPJ SET.
       02 QTY     PIC 99999 USAGE COMP-3.

SET NAME IS S-SPJ.
ORDER IS NEXT.
OWNER IS S.
MEMBER IS SPJ MANDATORY AUTOMATIC.

SET NAME IS P-SPJ.
ORDER IS NEXT.
OWNER IS P.
MEMBER IS SPJ MANDATORY AUTOMATIC.

SET NAME IS J-SPJ.
ORDER IS NEXT.
OWNER IS J.
MEMBER IS SPJ MANDATORY AUTOMATIC.

SET NAME IS S-FILE.
ORDER IS SORTED.
```

```
OWNER IS SYSTEM.
MEMBER IS S MANDATORY AUTOMATIC ASCENDING KEY IS S#.

SET NAME IS P-FILE.
ORDER IS SORTED.
OWNER IS SYSTEM.
MEMBER IS P MANDATORY AUTOMATIC ASCENDING KEY IS P#.

SET NAME IS J-FILE.
ORDER IS SORTED.
OWNER IS SYSTEM.
MEMBER IS J MANDATORY AUTOMATIC ASCENDING KEY IS J#.
```

Part 6
Some Current
Developments

The field of database research and development is certainly still growing. As suggested in earlier parts of this book, however, much of that growth is occurring not so much at the level of the base DBMS itself, but rather at some higher level of the system—for example, at the level of the user interface (natural language support, etc.). Of course, there are still many significant problems to be solved, even at the base DBMS level—for example, in the areas of integrity control and optimization. Nevertheless, much current database R & D activity simply takes the DBMS per se as a *given*, using it just as a foundation on which to construct some more sophisticated or more functionally complete system. (Of course, it is normally assumed that the underlying DBMS is relational.) Thus, the DBMS per se can be thought of as merely a component—certainly a crucial one, but one that in some respects can be regarded as comparatively low-level—of some more comprehensive system. Examples of such systems include forms-based systems; natural language systems; expert systems; statistical and graphics systems; and systems that provide integrated spreadsheet and word processing functions as well as database access.

The foregoing remarks notwithstanding, there are of course many important areas in which fundamental database research is still actively being pursued. In this final part of the book, we present a brief introduction to two such areas (rather important ones): *distributed systems* and *semantic modeling*. Note, however, that even in these two areas a) some of the research activity is again well above the base DBMS level, and furthermore b) a few early products are already beginning to appear.

24
Distributed
Systems

24.1 INTRODUCTION

The term "distributed system" does not have a single, universally accepted interpretation. However, it is possible to give a broad definition that does fit most cases reasonably well:

- A *distributed system* is any system involving multiple sites connected together into some kind of communications network, in which a user (end-user or application programmer) at any site can access data stored at any site.

Each *site*, in turn, can be thought of as a database system in its own right: It has its own database and its own DBA function, its own terminals and users, its own local storage, and its own CPU, running its own local DBMS (in general). It also has its own local DC manager with the responsibility (among other things) for controlling the exchange of messages with other sites in the overall distributed system.

An example of such a system is shown in Fig. 24.1. The example represents a simple distributed banking system, with two sites, one in Los Angeles and one in San Francisco.[1] Account records for the Los Angeles area are kept in the local database at the Los Angeles site and account records for the San Francisco area are kept in the local database at the San Francisco site, and the two local databases are linked together to form a single "global" or distributed database. The advantages of such an arrangement should be clear: It combines efficiency of processing (the data is stored close to the point where it is most frequently used) with increased accessibility (it is possible to access a Los Angeles account from San Francisco and vice versa, via the communications link). Other advantages are discussed in Section 24.2.

---

1. Of course, genuine distributed systems usually involve more than just two sites.

587

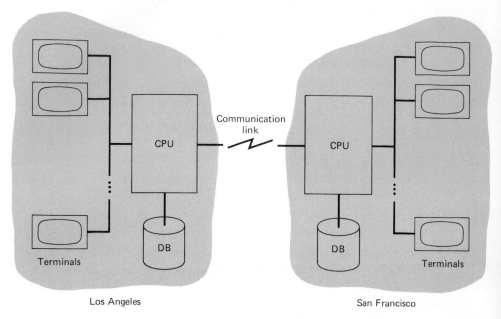

Fig. 24.1 Example of a distributed system.

In this chapter we will assume for the most part that:

1. The system is *homogeneous*, in the sense that each site is running (its own copy of) the same DBMS;

2. Each site is *autonomous*, in the sense that it relies scarcely at all on any kind of centralized service or control; and

3. The communications network is *slow*—i.e., the sites are geographically dispersed and are linked by a "long-haul" network (telephone lines), in which the data rate is typically 50K–100K bits per second or less (often much less).

Most current distributed database research in fact makes the same set of assumptions. Note assumption 2, the autonomy assumption, in particular. One important consequence of that assumption is that "local applications"—i.e., applications that access only data stored at their own local site—should indeed genuinely be local. Indeed, it is more helpful in many ways to think of a distributed system as a *partnership* among a set of independent but cooperating centralized systems, rather than as some kind of monolithic and indivisible object. By the same token, a distributed database can best be thought of as the union of a set of individual centralized databases.

Toward the end of the chapter we will briefly describe other kinds of distributed system in which assumptions 1–3 do not hold.

24.2 OBJECTIVES AND RATIONALE

A major objective of distributed systems is to provide what is usually called *location transparency*—meaning that users should not need to know at which site any given piece of data is stored, but should be able to behave as if the entire database were stored at their own local site. A request for some remote piece of data should cause the system to find that data automatically (by consulting the catalog). The advantages of such transparency are obvious: It simplifies the logic of application programs, and it allows data to be moved from one site to another as usage patterns change, without necessitating any reprogramming. In fact, of course, location transparency is nothing more than another aspect of physical data independence, as that concept applies to a distributed system.

A second objective is to support *data fragmentation*. A system supports data fragmentation if a given logical object, say the complete accounts file, can be divided up into pieces (*fragments*) for physical storage purposes. In fact, we were tacitly assuming such support in our banking example in Section 24.1, since we were storing Los Angeles account records in Los Angeles and San Francisco account records in San Francisco; the fragments in that example consisted of, respectively, a restriction of the total accounts file (relation) to just those records having location "Los Angeles" and a restriction to just those records having location "San Francisco." Alternatively, we might have decided (if the application were a little different) to store checking account records in Los Angeles and savings account records in San Francisco; the fragments here would again be restrictions. In other circumstances we might have decided to store account numbers and balances in Los Angeles and account numbers and customer names in San Francisco; the fragments here would be projections, not restrictions. In general, a fragment could be any arbitrary subrelation that is derivable from the original relation by means of restriction and projection operations (except that, in the case of projection, it should preserve the primary key of that original relation).

A system that supports data fragmentation should also support *fragmentation transparency*—i.e, users should be able to behave in all cases as if the relation were not fragmented at all (data independence again). In other words, users should be presented with a *view* of the data in which the fragments are combined together by means of suitable join and union operations. Note: The twin objectives of data fragmentation and fragmentation transparency together constitute one of the reasons why distributed database systems are almost invariably relational: Relations are easy to fragment, and the fragments are easy to recombine (by contrast, consider what would be involved in performing the analogous functions in IMS or IDMS). The fact is, there are several reasons why relational technology is particularly suitable for distributed systems, and fragmentation is one of them (by no means the strongest, incidentally; we shall meet other, more persuasive, reasons in Sections 24.3 and 24.5). In the particular case of fragmentation, however, note the implication that the system needs to be able to support updates against certain join and union views.

Another objective for distributed systems (much more difficult to achieve than the previous ones) is to support *data replication*, and its corollary, *replication transparency*. The basic idea here is that a given logical object, say a given account record, may be represented at the physical level by many distinct copies (replicas) of the same stored object, at many distinct sites. For example, a given account record could be stored in both the Los Angeles database and the San Francisco database. One advantage of such an arrangement is that retrievals can be directed to the nearest replica. The corresponding disadvantage is of course that updates must be directed to *all* replicas. (Note: In a system that supports data fragmentation, the unit of replication will be the fragment, rather than the complete logical relation.) Replication transparency then means that users should not need to be aware of replication, but should be able to behave as if every logical object were represented by a single stored object (yet another aspect of physical data independence).

Note that location, fragmentation, and replication transparency together imply that *a distributed system should look like a centralized system to the user.* The problems of distributed systems are (or should be) system problems, not user problems. Distribution per se does not have any effect on (for example) the user's view of the data, or on the specific language used, or on logical database design. It does, however, have a very definite effect on such matters as recovery, concurrency, and physical database design. Solutions to these latter problems in a centralized context are frequently inappropriate in a distributed context because the internal-level structure is so different. See Section 24.3.

Following are some of the advantages of distributed systems.

Local autonomy

The enterprise served by the system is almost certainly logically distributed (into divisions, departments, projects, etc.), and is quite likely to be physically distributed as well (into plants, factories, laboratories, etc.). Distributing the system allows individual groups within the enterprise to exercise local control over their own data, with local accountability, and more generally makes them less dependent on some remote data processing center that by definition will not be so deeply involved in purely local issues. At the same time, of course, it allows those local groups to access data at other locations when necessary.

Capacity and incremental growth

A common reason for installing a distributed system in the first place is simply that there may not exist any single machine with adequate capacity for the application in hand. Once installed, moreover, a distributed system can grow more gracefully than a nondistributed one: If it becomes necessary to expand the system because the volume of data has expanded or the volume of processing against it has increased, then it should be easier to add a new site to an existing distributed system —provided sites are fairly autonomous—than to replace an existing centralized system by a larger one.

Reliability and availability

A distributed system offers greater reliability than a centralized one in that it is not an all-or-nothing proposition—it can continue to function (at a reduced level) in the face of failure of an individual site or individual communication link between sites. And if data is replicated, availability is improved also, because a given data object remains available so long as at least one copy of that object is available.

Efficiency and flexibility

As pointed out in Section 24.1, data in a distributed system can be stored close to its normal point of use, thus reducing both response times and communication costs (most access is local). And if the usage pattern changes, then data can be dynamically moved or replicated, or existing replicas can be deleted. Furthermore, the inherent parallelism in a multisite network can lead to improved throughput and possibly improved response times in some situations.

The principal *dis*advantages of distributed systems are the subject of the next section.

24.3 PROBLEMS OF DISTRIBUTED SYSTEMS

We are now in a position to understand some of the problem areas in distributed systems. The basic point is that, as mentioned in Section 24.1, networks—at least, long-haul networks—are *slow*. ARPANET, for example, has an effective data rate of at most 1250 bytes per second [24.8]; contrast this with the typical disk drive, which has a data rate of the order of 1–2 *million* bytes per second. Thus, an overriding objective in distributed systems is *to minimize the number and volume of messages*. This objective in turn gives rise to problems in a number of subsidiary areas, among them the following (the list is not intended to be exhaustive):

- Query processing
- Update propagation
- Concurrency
- Recovery
- Catalog management

Query Processing

There are two broad points to be made under this heading.

- First, consider the query "Find London suppliers of red parts." Suppose the user is at site A in the network and the data is at site B. Suppose too that n records satisfy the request. If the system is relational, the query will involve basically two messages—one to send the request from A to B, and one to return the result set of n records from B to A. If, on the other hand, the system is not relational but record-at-a-time, the query will involve $2n$ messages—n from A to B requesting the next record, and n from B to A to return that next record. The example illustrates the point that a relational system is thus likely to out-perform a nonrelational one (for any request returning more than a single record) by possibly orders of magnitude.

- Second, *optimization* is even more important in a distributed system than it is in a centralized one. The basic point is that there will be many possible strategies for processing a given query (in general). For example, a request for a join of a relation Ra stored at site A and a relation Rb stored at site B could be carried out by moving Ra to B or by moving Rb to A or by moving both to a third site C (etc.). A detailed example is presented in Volume II, involving the query mentioned above ("Find London suppliers of red parts"); the example gives six superficially plausible strategies for processing the query (under a certain set of detailed assumptions), and then shows that the response time for the six strategies varies from one second (the best) to two and a third *days*. Optimization is thus clearly crucial; and that fact in turn can be seen as an even more compelling argument in favor of a relational system (the whole point is that relational operations are optimizable, whereas record-at-a-time operations are not).

Update Propagation

The basic problem with data replication, as pointed out in Section 24.2, is that an update to any given logical data object must be propagated to all stored copies of that object. A difficulty that arises immediately is that some site holding a copy of the object may be unavailable (because of a site or network failure) at the time of the update. The obvious strategy of propagating updates immediately to all copies may thus be unacceptable, because it implies that the update (and therefore the transaction) will fail if any one of those copies is currently unavailable. In fact, data is *less* available under this strategy than in the nonreplicated case (at least for update transactions), thereby contradicting one of the advantages claimed for distributed systems in the previous section.

A possible solution to this problem is to designate exactly one copy of each object as the *primary* copy. The primary copies of different objects will be at different sites, in general. Update operations are deemed to be complete as soon as the primary copy has been updated (control is returned and the transaction can continue execution). The site holding the primary copy is responsible for broadcasting the update to all other sites after applying the initial update; those other sites can then update their copies in parallel with the continuing transaction execution (or at some later time). Of course, this primary copy strategy leads to several further problems, most of them beyond the scope of this chapter; note in particular that it runs counter to the autonomy objective mentioned in Section 24.1 (a transaction may fail because a remote copy of an object is unavailable, even though a local copy may be available).

We remark in passing that it may be difficult to maintain fragmentation transparency for certain update transactions. For example, updating the location value for an account record from Los Angeles to San Francisco might mean that the record in question has to be moved from one fragment to another. But this problem has nothing to do with update propagation per se.

Concurrency

Concurrency control in most distributed systems is based on locking, just as it is in most nondistributed systems. In a distributed system, however, requests to test, set, and release locks become *messages* (assuming that the object under consideration is at a remote site), and messages mean overhead. For example, consider a transaction T that needs to update an object for which there exist replicas at n remote sites. If each site is responsible for locks on objects stored at that site (as it will be under the autonomy assumption), then a straightforward implementation will require $5n$ messages:

   n lock requests
   n lock grants
   n update messages
   n acknowledgments
   n unlock requests

The total time for the update could thus easily be two or more orders of magnitude greater than in a centralized system.

The usual solution to this problem is (again) to adopt the primary copy strategy outlined in the previous subsection. For a given object X, the site holding the primary copy of X will handle all locking operations involving X (remember that the primary copies of different objects will be at different sites, in general). Under this strategy the set of all copies of an object can be considered as a single object for locking purposes, and the total number of messages will be reduced from $5n$ to $2n+3$ (one lock request, one lock grant, n updates, n acknowledgments, and one unlock request). But notice once again that this solution entails a (severe) loss of autonomy—a transaction can fail if a primary copy is unavailable, even if the transaction is read-only and a local copy is available.

Another problem with locking in a distributed system is that it can lead to *global deadlock*. In order to explain this point, it is first necessary to distinguish between *transactions* and *agents*. A single transaction can involve the execution of code at any number of sites. An *agent* is the "representative" of a transaction at a site; i.e., it is the process that executes on behalf of some transaction at some site. Now consider the following example:

- The agent of transaction *T1* at site *A* is waiting for the agent of transaction *T2* at site *A* to release a lock;

- The agent of transaction *T2* at site *A* is waiting for the agent of transaction *T2* at site *B* to complete;

- The agent of transaction *T2* at site *B* is waiting for the agent of transaction *T1* at site *B* to release a lock;

- The agent of transaction *T1* at site *B* is waiting for the agent of transaction *T1* at site *A* to complete.

See Fig. 24.2.

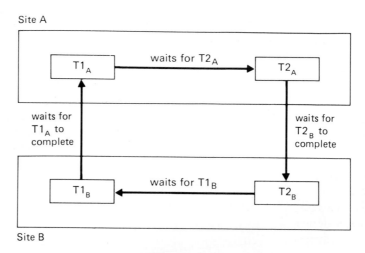

Fig. 24.2 Example of global deadlock.

The problem with a deadlock such as the one in this example is that neither site can detect it using only information that is internal to that site. In other words, there are no cycles in the two local Wait-For graphs, but a cycle will appear if those two graphs are joined together. It follows that global deadlock detection incurs further communication overhead, because it requires the joining together of individual local graphs.

Recovery

The reader may recall the notion of *two-phase commit*, discussed in the annotation to reference [18.1] in Chapter 18. Briefly, two-phase commit protocols are required whenever a single transaction interacts with multiple autonomous resource managers; the purpose of such protocols is to ensure that all the resource managers concerned "go the same way" on the transaction—i.e., either they all accept it (commit it) or they all reject it (roll it back), thus guaranteeing that the transaction is genuinely all-or-nothing. We do not repeat the details here, but content ourselves with the following observations:

1. Two-phase commit is particularly important in a distributed system, where distinct resource managers are typically at distinct sites and are hence particularly vulnerable to independent failure.

2. In the interests of site autonomy, the Coordinator function (see reference [18.1])
   is not assigned to one distinguished site in the network but is instead performed
   by different sites for different transactions (normally by the site at which the
   transaction in question is initiated).

3. The two-phase commit process requires the Coordinator to communicate with
   every participant site—which means more messages and more overhead.

4. If site *B* acts as a participant in a two-phase commit process coordinated by
   site *A*, then site *B must* do what it is told by *A* (commit or rollback, whichever
   applies)—another loss of local autonomy.

Catalog Management

In a distributed system, the system catalog will include not only the usual catalog
data regarding relations, indexes, users, etc., but also all the necessary control information to enable the system to provide the desired location, fragmentation, and
replication transparency. The question arises: Where and how should the catalog
itself be stored? Here are some of the possibilities:

1. *Centralized*: The total catalog is stored exactly once, at a single central site.

2. *Fully replicated*: The total catalog is stored in its entirety at every site.

3. *Partitioned*: Each site maintains its own catalog for objects stored at that site.
   The total catalog is the union of all of those disjoint local catalogs.

4. *Combination of (1) and (3)*: Each site maintains its own local catalog, as in (3);
   in addition, a single central site maintains a unified copy of all of those local
   catalogs, as in (1).

Each of these approaches has problems. Approach (1) obviously suffers from a
severe loss of autonomy. So does Approach (2), in that every catalog update has to
be propagated to every site. Approach (3) makes nonlocal operations very expensive
(finding a remote object will require access to half the sites, on average). Approach
(4) is more efficient than Approach (3) (finding a remote object requires only one
remote catalog access) but is critically dependent on the availability of the central
site (as is Approach (1), of course). In practice, therefore, systems usually do not
use *any* of these four approaches! See Section 24.4 for details of the approaches
that are used in specific systems.

24.4 SOME SAMPLE SYSTEMS

In this section we consider very briefly three sample distributed systems (all of them
research prototypes rather than commercial products): SDD-1, R*, and Distributed
INGRES. SDD-1 was developed at Computer Corporation of America and was
probably the first true distributed system anywhere [24.6–24.10]. R* (pronounced
"R star") is a distributed version of System R and was developed in IBM Research
[24.11–24.14]. Distributed INGRES is a distributed version of the University

INGRES system and was developed at the University of California at Berkeley [24.15–24.17]. All of these systems are operational at the time of writing, but the research is not yet considered complete (at least in the latter two cases). We examine the systems in the light of the ideas presented in the preceding two sections.

SDD-1

SDD-1 runs on a collection of DEC PDP-10s, interconnected via the ARPANET. It provides full location, fragmentation, and replication transparency. Its query optimizer makes extensive use of an operator called *semijoin*, which we explain as follows.[2] Given two relations A and B, the expression "A semijoin B" is defined to be equivalent to the join of A and B, projected back on to the attributes of A. In other words, the semijoin operation yields that subset of the tuples of A that match at least one tuple in B (under the joining condition). For example, the semijoin of the supplier relation S and the shipment relation SP (over supplier numbers) is the set of S tuples for suppliers who supply at least one part—namely, the set of S tuples for suppliers S1, S2, S3, and S4, given our usual sample data values. Notice that the expressions "A semijoin B" and "B semijoin A" are not equivalent.

The advantage of using semijoins in query processing is that it may have the effect of reducing the volume of data shipped across the network. For example, suppose that the supplier relation S is stored at site A and the shipment relation SP is stored at site B, and the query is "Compute the natural join J of S and SP over S#." Instead of shipping the entire relation S to B (say), we can do the following:

- Compute the projection (TEMP1) of SP over S# at B.
- Ship TEMP1 to A.
- Compute the semijoin (TEMP2) of TEMP1 and S over S# at A.
- Ship TEMP2 to B.
- Compute the semijoin of TEMP2 and SP over S# at B. The result is equal to the desired natural join J.

This procedure will obviously reduce the total amount of data movement across the network if and only if

```
size (TEMP1) + size (TEMP2) < size (S)
```

where the "size" of a relation is the cardinality of that relation multiplied by the width of an individual tuple (in bits, say). The optimizer thus clearly needs to be able to estimate the size of intermediate results such as TEMP1 and TEMP2.

The SDD-1 update propagation algorithm is "update all copies immediately" (there is no notion of a primary copy). Concurrency control is based on a technique called timestamping, instead of on locking; the objective is to avoid the message overhead associated with locking, but the price seems to be that there is not in fact

---

2.   The term "semijoin" first appeared (with a somewhat different meaning) in a paper by Palermo [16.2].

very much concurrency. The details are beyond the scope of this book, though the annotation to reference [18.11] does describe the basic idea very briefly; see Volume II or reference [24.9] for more information. Recovery is based on a *four*-phase commit protocol; the intent is to make the process more resilient than the conventional two-phase commit protocol to a failure at the Coordinator site, but the details are (again) beyond the scope of this book. Finally, the catalog is managed by treating it as if it were ordinary user data: It can be arbitrarily fragmented, and the fragments can be arbitrarily replicated and distributed, just like any other data. The advantages of this approach are obvious. The disadvantage is, of course, that since the system has no a priori knowledge of the location of any given piece of the catalog, it is necessary to maintain a higher-level catalog—the *directory locator*— to provide exactly that information! The directory locator is fully replicated (i.e., a copy is stored at every site).

R*

R* consists of multiple cooperating copies of System R, running on a set of IBM mainframes that communicate via CICS/ISC (see Section 24.5). The current version provides location transparency, but no fragmentation and no replication, and therefore no fragmentation or replication transparency either. The question of update propagation does not arise, for the same reason. Concurrency control is based on locking (note that there is only one copy of any object to be locked; the question of a primary copy also does not arise). Recovery is based on two-phase commit, but with certain improvements that have the effect of reducing the number of messages required (see reference [24.12]).

Perhaps the most novel aspects of R* are those that have to do with catalog management and the associated problems of compilation and optimization. In order to discuss these aspects, it is first necessary to say something about *object naming*. R* distinguishes between an object's *printname*, which is the name by which the object is usually referenced externally (e.g., in a SQL SELECT statement), and its *system-wide name*, which is a globally unique internal identifier for the object. System-wide names have four components:

- Creator ID (the ID of the user who created the object)
- Creator site ID (the ID of the site at which the CREATE operation was entered)
- Local name (the name of the object as assigned by its creator)
- Birth site ID (the ID of the site at which the object is initially stored)

For example, the system-wide name

    ARTHUR @ HURSLEY . STATS @ GREENOCK

identifies an object (say a base table) with local name STATS, created by the user called ARTHUR at the HURSLEY site and first stored at the GREENOCK site. That object may subsequently be moved to some other site, say the CROYDON site; however, its system-wide name will not change as a consequence.

As already indicated, users normally refer to objects by printnames. A print-name consists of a simple unqualified name—either the "local name" component of the system-wide name (such as STATS in the example above), or a *synonym* for that system-wide name, introduced via the SQL statement CREATE SYNONYM. In the first case, default name completion rules allow the system to expand the local name to its full system-wide form in an obvious manner. In the second case, the system determines the system-wide name by interrogating the relevant *synonym table*. Synonym tables can be thought of as the first component of the catalog; each site maintains a set of such tables for each user known at that site, mapping the synonyms known to that user to their corresponding system-wide names.

Now consider some particular site S. That site will maintain a local catalog entry for every object X for which it is the *birth* site, and a local catalog entry for every object Y for which it is the *current* site (i.e., the site at which Y is currently stored). Consider a user reference to some printname Z. By the name completion rules or by reference to the local synonym tables, R* can determine the system-wide name for Z, and hence can identify Z's birth site. It can then interrogate the local catalog at that site. If Z is still stored there, then the required object has been found. Other-wise, the catalog entry for Z at that site will point to Z's current site, and R* can then go to that site for the desired object. Thus any desired object can be found in at most two remote accesses.

Now we turn to compilation and optimization. Suppose a SQL statement is submitted at site S. Compilation proceeds as follows [24.14]:

1. The SQL compiler at site S gathers together all of the catalog entries (both local and remote) for all objects referenced by that statement.

2. It then generates an overall access strategy for the statement, using techniques described in reference [24.13]. (Note: Those techniques can be regarded as a natural extension of the techniques used in the nondistributed version of System R, as described in Chapter 16. One difference between them and the approach used in SDD-1 is that the R* techniques do not assume that CPU cost is neg-ligible compared with communication costs.)

3. The strategy generated in Step 2 will involve multiple sites (in general). Site S sends each such site the relevant portion of the overall strategy.

4. Each site then completes the compilation process for its own portion of the strategy and stores the compiled code in its own local catalog. It also makes entries in that catalog to record the dependencies of that code on local objects (e.g., on local indexes).

This last step is necessary for reasons (once again) of local autonomy: It must be possible to drop a local object, say an index, without having to refer to any remote site. Dropping such an object may invalidate some local compiled code (which will therefore be automatically recompiled on its next invocation), but should not invalidate the entire strategy.

Distributed INGRES

Distributed INGRES consists of multiple copies of University INGRES, running on multiple interconnected machines (DEC PDP-11s). It supports location transparency (like SDD-1 and R*); it also supports data fragmentation (via restriction but not projection), with fragmentation transparency, and data replication for such fragments, with replication transparency. Unlike SDD-1 and R*, Distributed INGRES does not necessarily assume that the communication network is slow; on the contrary, it is designed to handle both "slow" (long-haul) networks and local (i.e., comparatively fast) networks (see Section 24.5). The query optimizer understands the difference between the two cases. The query optimization algorithm is basically an extension of the decomposition strategy described in Chapter 16; it is described in detail in reference [24.16].

As for update propagation, Distributed INGRES provides two algorithms: a "performance" algorithm, which works by updating a primary copy and then returning control to the transaction (leaving the propagated updates to be performed in parallel by a set of slave processes); and a "reliable" algorithm, which updates all copies immediately (see reference [24.17]). Concurrency control is based on locking in both cases. Recovery is based on two-phase commit (with certain improvements that are beyond the scope of this book, as in the case of R*; again, see reference [24.17]).

	SDD-1	R*	Distributed INGRES
relational	yes	yes	yes
location transparency	yes	yes	yes
fragmentation transparency	yes	no	yes (restriction)
replication transparency	yes	no	yes
update propagation	immediate	(no)	primary copy and immediate
concurrency control	timestamping	locking	locking
recovery control	4-phase commit	2-phase commit	2-phase commit

Fig. 24.3 Major characteristics of SDD-1, R*, and Distributed INGRES.

Finally, catalog management. Distributed INGRES uses a combination of full replication for certain portions of the catalog—basically the portions containing a logical description of the relations visible to the user and a description of how those relations are fragmented—together with purely local catalog entries for other portions, such as the portions describing local physical storage structures, local database statistics (used by the optimizer), and security and integrity constraints.

Figure 24.3 is an attempt to summarize some of the major points of the foregoing discussion.

24.5   OTHER TYPES OF DISTRIBUTED SYSTEM

Our discussions so far in this chapter have been based on a number of assumptions: the long-haul assumption (networks are slow), the homogeneity assumption (the same DBMS is running at every site), and the autonomy assumption (sites are independent). We have also assumed that systems should provide at least location transparency, if not fragmentation and replication transparency also. In this section we briefly examine the possibility of relaxing any or all of these assumptions (note that they are basically all independent of one another).

Relaxing the Location Transparency Requirement

There are a number of systems available in the marketplace that can reasonably be considered as distributed systems, even though they may provide only limited location transparency. For example:

- The InterSystems Communication facility (ISC) of CICS (CICS/ISC) allows a program, or rather agent, at one site to invoke an agent at another site [24.18]. However, the invoking agent is required to specify the identity of that other site, and so to that extent knowledge of the data distribution is built into the application logic; but the application can conceal that knowledge from the end-user. (Note: CICS/ISC also provides a number of other distributed system features that are beyond the scope of this chapter.)

- The INGRES/NET product [24.19] allows any Commercial INGRES user (end-user or application programmer) at any site A to "invoke" an INGRES database at any site B (A and B not necessarily distinct). It is true that the user at site A does need to know the identity of site B at "invoke" time; thereafter, however, all operations on the possibly remote database—QUEL operations or forms-based operations (see Chapter 20)—behave just as if the database were local, i.e., as if A and B were the same site (see Fig. 24.4). INGRES/NET thus does provide a limited form of location transparency.

Of course, a system that does not provide location transparency will certainly not provide fragmentation or replication transparency either.

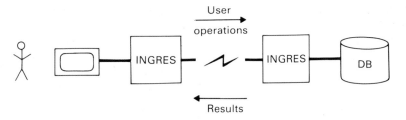

Fig. 24.4 INGRES/NET.

Local Area Networks vs. Long-Haul Networks

Not all networks are "long-haul." A local area network (LAN) such as the Ethernet can achieve quite respectable data rates (of the order of, say, 10 million bits per second). Furthermore, such networks are typically much more reliable than the long-haul networks. Each of these considerations can have dramatic implications for the internal architecture of a distributed system. We briefly sketch the facilities of the Tandem system [24.20], which, though not exclusively LAN-based, is nevertheless probably one of the best known examples of a system designed for LANs. Note, however, that in the case of Tandem specifically the "dramatic implications" just mentioned affect the operating system rather than the DBMS per se.

- Each Tandem machine actually consists of several CPUs (at least two), each with its own main storage, but all sharing a common set of disk drives. The CPUs are interconnected via a high-speed bus (13M bytes per second).

- Several Tandem machines can be interconnected via either a LAN or a long-haul network.

- All communication between processes is by means of messages. The Tandem GUARDIAN operating system supports exactly the same interprocess communication protocols, regardless of whether the processes concerned are executing on the same CPU, or on different CPUs in the same machine, or at different sites in a local area network, or at different sites in a long-haul network.

- *All* Tandem databases can thus automatically be regarded as distributed, even if there is only a single machine in the system. The ENCOMPASS database management system, which runs on top of GUARDIAN, is thus automatically a distributed DBMS. Note, however, that ENCOMPASS per se is in fact unaware of whether the network is a LAN or a long-haul network, though it is aware of whether data is local or remote.

- ENCOMPASS provides complete location transparency. It also provides a limited form of fragmentation (restriction by primary key ranges), together with the corresponding necessary fragmentation transparency. It does not provide any data replication.

Heterogeneous Systems

A heterogeneous system is a distributed system in which different DBMS's are running at different sites—more precisely, a system in which the DBMS's at different sites support different data models and/or different database operations. Now, there does not seem to be much advantage to building a heterogeneous system from scratch; but there is no question that it would be nice to be able to interconnect a set of preexisting centralized DBMS's into a distributed system, and of course the resulting system would almost certainly be heterogeneous, simply because of the plethora of different centralized DBMS's already installed.

The heterogeneous system problem is a very difficult one, however, because it includes as a subproblem the problem of conversion between different data models, for which no general solution is known.[3] The best that can be done is to attempt to solve it in a variety of special cases in an ad hoc manner. There are two broad approaches to such special-case solutions, typified by IBM's InterSystem Communications facility ISC [24.18] and CCA's MULTIBASE [24.21] respectively:

- ISC is a set of protocols by which any systems conforming to those protocols (not necessarily just IBM systems, incidentally) can communicate with one another. The IBM data communications manager CICS supports a large subset of those protocols (CICS/ISC, already mentioned earlier in this section). As a result, it is possible (for example) for a site running the IMS database manager under CICS to communicate with another site running DB2 or SQL/DS under CICS. Note, however, that CICS/ISC merely provides the *communication* facilities (i.e., it permits the exchange of messages); *interpretation* of those messages is left to the application programs concerned. In other words, CICS/ISC provides a base upon which a heterogeneous system might be built, but it does not itself constitute such a system.

- MULTIBASE is a frontend system, supporting retrieval operations (only) against a heterogeneous set of backend DBMS's. It requires a) a global schema, expressed in a language called DAPLEX [25.9], defining the information content of the entire distributed database; b) a set of local schemas, also expressed in DAPLEX, defining the information content of each individual database separately; and c) a set of local schemas expressed in the DDL of the local DBMS (of course). Queries are issued in DAPLEX, using the DAPLEX global schema (see Fig. 24.5).

Once a query is received, the *global data manager* (GDM) converts it into a set of subqueries against the local DAPLEX schemas. At each site, a *local database interface* (LDI) module then converts DAPLEX subqueries into operations that the DBMS at that site understands. Each LDI module is specific to its own local DBMS, of course. Also, the DBA is required to describe each local DBMS to

---

3. Even if such a solution were known, many systems do not in fact conform to a well-defined data model anyway, as explained in Part 5 of this book.

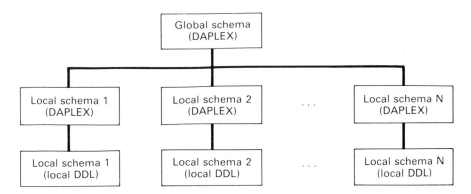

Fig. 24.5 MULTIBASE schema architecture.

the GDM, so that the GDM may be aware of features of DAPLEX that cannot be supported by the local DBMS in question.

Relaxing the Autonomy Requirement

There are of course many situations in which local autonomy for every site may not be necessary or even desirable. Typically such situations involve some kind of master/slave arrangement, in which each individual site in the network has its own specific role to play within the overall system. We briefly describe two particular cases of such a general arrangement. Note: The two cases are architecturally very similar; the difference lies mainly in how they are perceived by the user.

- *Micro/mainframe links*: Here there is typically a single centralized DBMS, running on a conventional mainframe and managing some kind of corporate database; in addition, users have their own microprocessors running (ideally) some trimmed-down version of the mainframe software, and the micros are connected to the mainframe via some kind of communications link (LAN or telephone lines). Data can be extracted from the mainframe database and shipped to any one of the micros for local processing ("download"); conversely, data can be shipped from a micro to the mainframe for incorporation into the mainframe database ("upload"). The Cullinet Information Database (IDB) and GOLDENGATE products together provide a good example of such a system [24.22].

- *Backend machines*: Here there is typically a single backend "database machine" that is responsible for managing the database,[4] together with one or more frontend "host machines" performing conventional computational tasks and linked to the backend via an I/O channel (normally). See Fig. 24.6.

---

4. It should be mentioned that the term "database machine," like the term "distributed system," has no universally accepted definition; different writers use it to mean very different things.

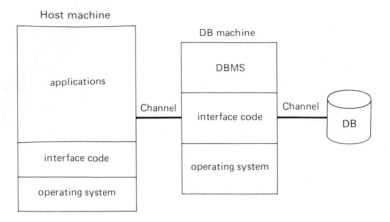

Fig. 24.6 Structure of a system with a database machine.

The emphasis in such a system is on offloading the database function from the host(s) on to the backend machine, thereby freeing the host(s) for other work. The backend machine is dedicated to the database function; it consists basically of a conventional processor (though in some cases it may include some specialized hardware of some kind), running just a single "application," namely the DBMS. Note that such a system can be regarded as a special case of a distributed system, in which the entire database happens to be stored at one site and all applications execute at another. Two well-known examples of such backend machines are the Britton-Lee IDM [24.23] and the Teradata DBC/1012 [24.24]. They are both relational, incidentally; previous attempts to build backend machines were not commercial successes, almost certainly because they were not relational and therefore could not meet performance requirements (as the arguments of this chapter—especially Section 24.3—should have led us to expect).

24.6 CONCLUDING REMARKS

We have presented a brief discussion of distributed database systems. First we made a set of (widely accepted) assumptions, namely:

1. The *homogeneity* assumption (i.e. each site is running a copy of the same DBMS);

2. The *autonomy* assumption (i.e., each site is as independent as possible);

3. The *long-haul network* assumption (i.e., communication between sites is slow).

We then showed that these assumptions (the last one especially) led to problems in a number of areas, the following among them:

1. Query processing;

2. Update propagation;

3. Concurrency control;

4. Recovery control;

5. Catalog management.

We discussed the approaches taken to these problems in a number of prototype systems: SDD-1, R*, and Distributed INGRES. We also explored the effects of relaxing the initial assumptions. In particular, we showed that a system incorporating a database machine can be regarded as a simple distributed database system in which the autonomy assumption is relaxed.

EXERCISES

24.1 Define a) location transparency; b) fragmentation transparency; c) replication transparency.

24.2 Why are distributed database systems almost invariably relational?

24.3 What are the advantages of distributed systems?

24.4 Explain the following terms:

a) primary copy update strategy;

b) primary copy locking strategy;

c) global deadlock;

d) two-phase commit;

e) semijoin.

24.5 Describe the R* object naming scheme.

REFERENCES AND BIBLIOGRAPHY

For a more extensive overview of distributed systems and also of database machines, see Volume II.

24.1 Stefano Ceri and Giuseppe Pelagatti. *Distributed Databases: Principles and Systems.* New York: McGraw-Hill (1984).

The best single source for information on distributed database research and development as of about 1983.

24.2 P. A. Bernstein, J. B. Rothnie, Jr., and D. A. Shipman (eds.). Tutorial: Distributed Data Base Management. IEEE Computer Society, 5855 Naples Plaza, Suite 301, Long Beach, Calif. 90803 (1978).

A collection of papers from various sources, grouped under the following headings:

- Overview of relational database management
- Distributed database management overview
- Approaches to distributed query processing

- Approaches to distributed concurrency control
- Approaches to distributed database reliability

24.3 J. N. Gray. "A Discussion of Distributed Systems." *Proc. Congresso AICA* **79,** Bari, Italy (October 1979). Also available as *IBM Research Report RJ2699* (September 1979).

A sketchy but good overview/tutorial.

24.4 J. B. Rothnie, Jr., and N. Goodman. "A Survey of Research and Development in Distributed Database Management." *Proc. 3rd International Conference on Very Large Data Bases* (October 1977). Also published in [24.2].

A very useful survey. The field is discussed under the following headings:

- Synchronizing update transactions
- Distributed query processing
- Handling component failures
- Directory management
- Database design

24.5 B. G. Lindsay et al. "Notes on Distributed Databases." *IBM Research Report RJ2571* (July 1979).

This paper is divided into five chapters:

1. Replicated data
2. Authorization and views
3. Introduction to distributed transaction management
4. Recovery facilities
5. Transaction initiation, migration, and termination

24.6 J. B. Rothnie, Jr., et al. "Introduction to a System for Distributed Databases (SDD-1)." *ACM TODS* **5,** No. 1 (March 1980).

24.7 E. Wong. "Retrieving Dispersed Data from SDD-1: A System for Distributed Databases." In [24.2].

24.8 Philip A. Bernstein et al. "Query Processing in a System for Distributed Databases (SDD-1)." *ACM TODS* **6,** No. 4 (December 1981).

24.9 P. A. Bernstein, D. W. Shipman, and J. B. Rothnie, Jr. "Concurrency Control in a System for Distributed Databases (SDD-1)." *ACM TODS* **5,** No. 1 (March 1980).

24.10 M. M. Hammer and D. W. Shipman. "Reliability Mechanisms for SDD-1: A System for Distributed Databases." *ACM TODS* **5,** No. 4 (December 1980).

24.11 R. Williams et al. "R*: An Overview of the Architecture." *Proc. International Conference on Database Systems,* Jerusalem, Israel (1982). Also available as *IBM Research Report RJ3325* (December 1981).

24.12 C. Mohan and B. G. Lindsay. "Efficient Commit Protocols for the Tree of Processes Model of Distributed Transactions." *Proc. 2nd ACM SIGACT-SIGOPS Symposium on Principles of Distributed Computing* (1983).

24.13 P. G. Selinger and M. E. Adiba. "Access Path Selection in Distributed Data Base Management Systems." In S. M. Deen and P. Hammersley (eds.): *Proc. International Conference on Data Bases,* Aberdeen, Scotland (July 1980). Heyden and Sons Ltd. (1980).

24.14 D. Daniels et al. "An Introduction to Distributed Query Compilation in R*." In *Distributed Data Bases* (ed., H.-J. Schneider): *Proc. 2nd International Symposium on Distributed Data Bases* (September 1982). North-Holland (1982).

24.15 M. R. Stonebraker and E. J. Neuhold. "A Distributed Data Base Version of INGRES." In [24.2].

24.16 R. Epstein, M. Stonebraker, and E. Wong. "Distributed Query Processing in a Relational Data Base System." *Proc. 1978 ACM SIGMOD International Conference on Management of Data* (June 1978).

24.17 M. R. Stonebraker. "Concurrency Control and Consistency of Multiple Copies in Distributed INGRES." *IEEE Transactions on Software Engineering,* Vol. SE-5, No. 3 (May 1979).

24.18 Information regarding CICS and ISC is available from IBM Corporation, Armonk, New York 10504.

24.19 Information regarding INGRES/NET is available from Relational Technology Inc., 1080 Marina Village Parkway, Alameda, Calif. 94501.

24.20 Information regarding GUARDIAN and ENCOMPASS is available from Tandem Computers Inc., 19333 Vallco Parkway, Cupertino, Calif. 95014.

24.21 Terry Landers and Ronni L. Rosenberg. "An Overview of MULTIBASE." In *Distributed Data Bases* (ed., H.-J. Schneider): *Proc. 2nd International Symposium on Distributed Data Bases* (September 1982). North-Holland (1982).

24.22 Information regarding IDB and GOLDENGATE is available from Cullinet Software Inc., Westwood, Mass. 02090.

24.23 Information regarding the IDM is available from Britton-Lee Inc., 14600 Winchester Blvd., Los Gatos, Calif. 95030.

24.24 Information regarding the DBC/1012 is available from Teradata Corporation, 12945 West Jefferson Boulevard, Los Angeles, CA 90066   DBC/1012 is a registered trademark of Teradata Corporation.

25
Semantic
Modeling

25.1 WHAT IS THE PROBLEM?

At the time of writing, most database systems—relational or otherwise—really have only a very limited understanding of what the data in the database *means*: They typically "understand" certain simple atomic data values, and certain many-to-one relationships among those values, *but very little else* (any more sophisticated interpretation is left to the human user). And it would be nice if systems could understand a little more, so that they could respond a little more intelligently to user interactions. As a trivial example, it would be nice if DB2 understood that part weights and shipment quantities, though of course both numeric values, were different in kind—i.e., *semantically* different—so that (e.g.) a request to join parts and shipments on the basis of matching weights and quantities could at least be questioned, if not rejected outright. (The notion of domains is relevant to this particular example, of course.) In this, the final chapter of the book, we address the problem of incorporating more meaning into the system—i.e., the problem of *semantic modeling*.

Before going any further, we stress the point that existing data models are not totally devoid of all semantic aspects; consider, for example, the primary and foreign key aspects of the relational model, which are certainly not purely syntactic constructs. To put this another way, the "extended" models to be discussed in the present chapter are only slightly more semantic than the earlier models; to paraphrase [25.14], capturing the meaning of the data is a never-ending task, and we can expect to see continuing developments in this area as our understanding continues to evolve. The term *semantic data model*, sometimes used to refer to one or other of the "extended" models, is thus not particularly apt. On the other hand, "semantic modeling" *is* an appropriate label for the overall activity of attempting to represent meaning. In this chapter we present a short introduction to some of the ideas underlying that activity.

25.2   THE OVERALL APPROACH

We can characterize the overall approach to the semantic modeling problem as follows.

1. First, we try to identify a set of *semantic* concepts that appear to be useful in talking informally about the real world. Examples of such concepts are *entity*, *property*, and *association*. Informally, we might agree that the real world consists of entities that possess properties, are connected together in associations, etc.

2. Next, we devise a set of corresponding *symbolic* (formal) objects to represent those semantic concepts. For example, the extended relational model RM/T (to be discussed in Section 25.4) provides *E-relations* to represent entities, *P-relations* to represent properties, etc.

3. We also devise a set of *integrity rules* to go along with those symbolic objects. For example, the extended relational model RM/T provides an integrity rule (*property integrity*) that says that every entry in a P-relation must have a corresponding entry in an E-relation (to reflect the fact that every property must be a property of some entity).

4. Finally, we also develop a set of *operators* for manipulating those symbolic objects. For example, RM/T provides the *PROPERTY* operator, which can be used to join together an E-relation and all of its corresponding P-relations, and thus to collect together all of the properties for a given entity.

The objects, rules, and operators of paragraphs 2–4 above together constitute an "extended" data model ("extended," that is, if those constructs are truly a superset of those of some one of the basic models, such as the basic relational model; but there is not really a clear distinction between what is extended and what is basic in this context). Note that, as in the case of the relational model, the operators and integrity rules are just as much part of the model as the basic objects are.

Figure 25.1 lists a few useful semantic concepts (actually semantic *objects*—it does not attempt to show what the corresponding integrity rules and operators might be like), and gives an informal definition and some examples in each case. The examples are deliberately chosen to illustrate the point that a given object in the real world may well be regarded as an entity by some people, as a property by others, and as an association by still others, etc. It is a goal of semantic modeling—not yet fully achieved—to support such flexibility of interpretation.

25.3   THE ENTITY/RELATIONSHIP MODEL

One of the earliest proposals in the semantic modeling area—not the first, but certainly one of the most influential—was Chen's "entity/relationship model" [25.10]. (Some other early proposals are documented in references [25.1–25.9].) The terms "entity/relationship approach" and "entity/relationship modeling" are now frequently encountered in articles on database design and related topics. Before we try

Concept	Informal definition	Examples
ENTITY	A distinguishable object (of some particular type)	Supplier, Part, Shipment Employee, Department Person Composition, Concerto Orchestra Purchase order, Order line
PROPERTY	A piece of information that describes an entity	Supplier number Shipment quantity Employee department Person height Concerto type Purchase order date
ASSOCIATION	A many-to-many(-to-many, etc.) relationship among entities	Shipment (supplier-part) Assignment (employee-department) Recording (composition-orchestra-conductor)
SUBTYPE	Entity type Y is a subtype of entity type X if and only if every Y is necessarily an X	Employee is a subtype of Person Concerto is a subtype of Composition

Fig. 25.1 Some useful semantic concepts.

to explain in any detail exactly what those terms mean, a few preliminary remarks are in order:

1. First, the terms do not in fact have a single, well-defined meaning but are instead interpreted in many different ways [25.11–25.12]. Of course, it is true that the whole database field is bedeviled by inaccurate and conflicting terminology, but this particular area is worse than most. The reader is warned. In this section we will be guided by Chen's own definitions in [25.10]; even those are often very imprecise, however, and we stress the point that the explanations in this section are therefore rather vague and contain a number of loose ends.

2. It is not even clear that the entity/relationship "model" is truly a data model in the sense in which we have been using that term in this book [25.13]. On the contrary, it seems that to many people it is nothing more than a collection of data structures (actually a collection of relations of various kinds); in other words, the manipulative and integrity aspects are virtually ignored. Certainly the term "entity/relationship modeling" is usually taken simply to mean the process of deciding the

structure (only) of the database. Indeed, Chen's original paper [25.10] itself tends to support this interpretation. In this chapter, however, we will assume that the operators and integrity rules are indeed intended to be regarded as components of the model.

3. The entity/relationship approach is best thought of as *a thin layer on top of the basic relational model* (it is not an alternative to the relational model, as some people seem to think). As already indicated, the fundamental data object is still the *n*-ary relation. The operators are still the operators of the relational algebra.[1] It is in the area of integrity that the two approaches differ from each other somewhat: The entity/relationship model provides a set of *built-in* integrity rules, corresponding to some—but probably not all—of the foreign key rules discussed in Chapter 12 of this book. Thus, where a "pure" relational system would require the user to formulate certain foreign key rules explicitly, an entity/relationship system would require only that the user state that a given relation represented (say) a many-to-many relationship between certain other relations, and certain foreign key rules would then be implicitly understood.

4. Along with the entity/relationship model per se, reference [25.10] also introduced a diagramming technique ("entity/relationship diagrams") for representing logical database structure in a pictorial manner. Such diagrams are useful as a documentation aid, not least during the database design process. The popularity of "entity/relationship modeling" as an approach to database design can probably be attributed more to the existence of that diagramming technique than to any other cause (see later).

We now describe Chen's proposals [25.10] in some detail. First, he defines an entity as "a thing which can be distinctly identified" and a relationship as "an association among entities" (one-to-one or many-to-one or many-to-many; note that in Fig. 25.1, by contrast, we specifically defined an association to be many-to-many). The first question that arises, then, is the following: Is a relationship an entity? A relationship clearly is "a thing which can be distinctly identified," but later sections of the paper seem to reserve the term "entity" to mean an entity that is definitely *not* a relationship. We will follow that usage in this section, since it seems to be a crucial characteristic of the entity/relationship model, at least as that model was originally defined; we note in passing, however, that the opposite assumption—i.e., that a relationship is just a special case of an entity—is clearly preferable in practice, as noted in Chapter 1 of this book.

Entities and relationships are represented in the database by *entity relations* and *relationship relations*, respectively. Primary keys are required in both cases. In the case of a relationship, the primary key is assumed to be the combination of the foreign keys identifying the entities (and/or relationships?) involved in the rela-

---

1.   Reference [25.10] is not very specific, but actually it seems to propose a set of operators that are strictly less powerful than the relational algebra; for example, there is apparently no union and no explicit join.

tionship.[2] Entities and relationships may also have *attributes*; once again, Chen is ambivalent as to the meaning of the term—at first he defines an attribute to be a property that is not the primary key, nor any component thereof (contrast the relational definition of the same term), but later he seems to use it in the standard relational sense.

Chen then goes on to classify entities into *regular entities* and *weak entities* (and entity relations into regular and weak entity relations accordingly). A weak entity is an entity that is existence-dependent on some other entity, in the sense that it cannot exist if that other entity does not also exist. For example, the order lines for a given purchase order might be weak entities—they cannot exist if the purchase order itself does not exist (in particular, if a given purchase order is deleted, all order lines for that purchase order must be deleted too). A regular entity is an entity that is not a weak entity. Relationships—and relationship relations—are then classified into regular and weak categories in a similar manner. An understanding of the classification scheme is not required for an appreciation of the overall ideas of the entity/relationship model, however, and in this brief description we ignore it from this point on.

We now consider the entity/relationship diagramming technique mentioned earlier in this section. Figure 25.2 (which is based on a figure from reference [25.10]) is an entity/relationship diagram for the operational data of a simple manufacturing company (compare the example of operational data in Chapter 1 of this book). Observe that:

- Each entity type is shown as a rectangular box, labeled with the name of the entity type in question.

- Each relationship type is shown as a diamond-shaped box, labeled with the name of the relationship type in question.

- Attributes are not shown (but presumably could be).

- Each relationship box is connected by lines to the entity boxes (and/or relationship boxes?) for the entities (and/or relationships?) participating in the relationship in question.

- Each such line is labeled "one" or "many" to indicate whether the relationship is one-to-one, many-to-one, etc. Note: We take "one" to mean exactly one. "Many" means n, where n may be one, two, and so on; whether it may be zero is not clear—additional definition required.

From an entity/relationship diagram such as that of Fig. 25.2, it is possible a) to assign primary keys to entities and relationships, and thus b) to begin to write a

---

2. The term "foreign key" is not used, however. Note too that many examples can be found in which the assumption breaks down. For example, consider the relation SPD (S#,P#, DATE,QTY), representing shipments of certain parts by certain suppliers on certain dates; assume that the same supplier can ship the same part more than once, but not more than once on the same date. Then the primary key is the combination (S#,P#,DATE); yet we may choose to regard suppliers and parts as entities but dates not.

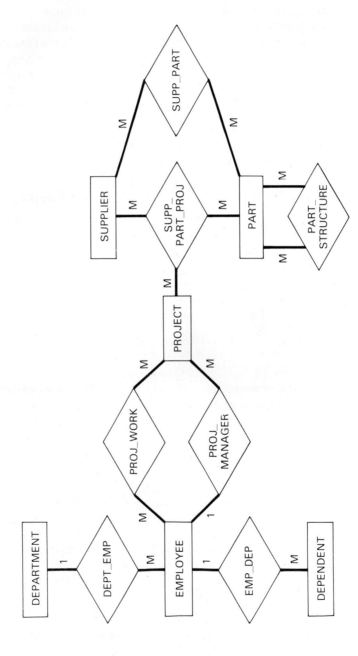

Fig. 25.2 Entity/relationship diagram (example).

corresponding database definition. Details of this process are straightforward and are left as an exercise for the reader.

Finally, we turn to the entity/relationship operators and integrity rules. As stated earlier, the operators are basically the same as those of the relational model, and we have nothing further to say regarding them here. As for the integrity rules, it would be nice to be able to explain them in terms of the foreign key rules defined in Chapter 12; unfortunately, however, it is not plain from reference [25.10] exactly what the entity/relationship rules are. The following possibilities are definitely supported:

```
NULLS NOT ALLOWED
DELETE  ... CASCADES
UPDATE  ... CASCADES
```

It could be argued (with a charitable interpretation of the paper) that the other possibilities—namely,

```
NULLS ALLOWED
DELETE  ... RESTRICTED or NULLIFIES
UPDATE  ... RESTRICTED or NULLIFIES
```

—are supported also, but the situation really is not clear. Indeed, Chen admits in the paper that his rules "may not be complete."

25.4 THE EXTENDED RELATIONAL MODEL RM/T

Overview

The extended relational model RM/T was first defined by Codd in reference [25.14]. An extended description of certain aspects of RM/T, incorporating a number of refinements and improvements developed by Codd and the present author since the original publication of [25.14], is given in Volume II. This section forms a brief introduction to some of the material discussed in more detail in Volume II. The reader is warned that the treatment below is necessarily very superficial; for more information, see [25.14] or Volume II.

An immediate difference between RM/T and the entity/relationship model discussed in the previous section is that RM/T makes no unnecessary distinctions between entities and relationships; a relationship is regarded merely as a special kind of entity. A second difference is that the structural and integrity aspects of the model are more extensive, and are defined much more precisely, in RM/T. A third difference is that RM/T includes its own special operators, over and above the operators of the basic relational model (note, however, that much additional work remains to be done in this third area). In outline, then, the model works as follows:

- First, entities (of all kinds) are represented by *E-relations* and *P-relations*, both of which are special forms of the general *n*-ary relation; E-relations are used to record the fact that certain entities exist, and P-relations are used to record certain properties of those entities.

- Second, a variety of relationships can exist among entities—for example, entity types *T1* and *T2* might be linked together in an association (many-to-many relationship), or entity type *T1* might be a subtype of entity type *T2* (every instance of *T1* might necessarily also be an instance of *T2*). RM/T includes a formal catalog structure (details beyond the scope of this section) by which such relationships can be made known to the system; the system is therefore capable of enforcing the various integrity constraints that are implied by the existence of such relationships.

- Third, a number of high-level operators are provided to facilitate the manipulation of the various RM/T objects (E-relations, P-relations, catalog relations, etc.).

The Entity Classification Scheme

RM/T divides entities into three categories:

- *Kernel entities*: Kernel entities are entities that have independent existence; they are "what the database is really all about." In other words, kernels are entities that are neither characteristic nor associative (see below); for example, suppliers, parts, purchase orders, employees, and departments would typically all be kernel entities.

- *Characteristic entities*: A characteristic entity is an entity whose sole function is to describe or "characterize" some other entity. For example, an order line might be a characteristic of a purchase order. Characteristics are existence-dependent on the entity they describe. The entity described may be kernel, characteristic, or associative.

- *Associative entities*: An associative entity is an entity whose function is to represent a many-to-many (or many-to-many-to-many, etc.) relationship among two or more other entities. For example, a shipment is an association between a supplier and a part. The entities associated may each be kernel, characteristic, or associative.

A major purpose of this classification scheme is to impose some structure on what would otherwise be a comparatively unstructured collection of information, and thereby to introduce some discipline into the integrity enforcement scheme (see later).

In addition to the foregoing, entities (regardless of their classification) can have *properties*; for example, parts have weights, departments have budgets, shipments have quantities. In particular, any entity (again, regardless of its classification) may have a property whose function is to identify or *designate* some other related entity; for example, each employee will typically designate some corresponding department entity. Entities such as employees in this example are said to be *designative*. A designation thus represents a many-to-one relationship between two entities.[3]

---

3. A characteristic entity is in fact a special case of a designative entity; it is really nothing more than a designating entity that happens to be existence-dependent on the entity it des-

Surrogates

By definition, any database contains representatives of certain real-world entities (e.g., suppliers, parts, and shipments, in the case of the suppliers-and-parts database). Since entities are distinguishable in the real world, their representatives in the database must also be distinguishable. In the basic relational model, this identification function is performed by user-defined, user-controlled primary keys ("user keys" for short). In RM/T, by contrast, it is performed by *system*-controlled primary keys, or *surrogates*.

The advantages of surrogates are discussed at length in Volume II and reference [25.14]; for present purposes, it is sufficient to understand that, in RM/T, *all primary and foreign keys are surrogates*. The basic idea is as follows. When the user creates a new entity representative in the database—e.g., when the user issues the SQL statement

```
INSERT
INTO    S ( S#, SNAME, STATUS, CITY )
VALUES ('S1','Smith',20,'London') ;
```

—the system generates a new surrogate value (*alpha*, say) for the new entity (supplier S1, in the example). The value *alpha* is unique with respect to all surrogate values that exist or ever have existed in the database; furthermore, it is guaranteed never to change. All references *inside the system* to supplier S1 will be via the value *alpha*. (References outside the system, on the other hand, will probably continue to be via the value S1.)

E-relations

The database contains one E-relation for each entity type. The E-relation for a given entity type is a unary (single-column) relation that lists the surrogates for all entities of that type currently existing in the database. The primary purpose of an E-relation is thus to record the existence of the entities in question, and hence to serve as a central reference point for all other entries in the database that concern those entities in any way. By way of example, let us consider an RM/T version of suppliers-and-parts. The database will include three E-relations, which might look as follows:

S	S¢		P	P¢		SP	SP¢
	alpha			gamma			zeta
	beta			delta			eta
				epsilon			theta
							iota
							kappa

---

ignates. Thus, order lines are characteristics of purchase orders—they designate purchase orders and are existence-dependent on them. Employees, by contrast, are *not* characteristics of departments—although they designate departments, they are not existence-dependent on them.

(the database currently contains two suppliers, three parts, and five shipments). Each E-relation is given the same name as the corresponding entity type; the single attribute in each case has a name that is obtained by appending a trailing "¢" to the relation name. (In fact, all attributes whose values are surrogates—i.e., all primary and foreign keys—are given names that include a trailing "¢", for reasons that are beyond the scope of this section.)

We will continue with the suppliers-and-parts example in the next subsection.

P-relations

The property types for a given entity type are represented by a set of P-relations. In the case of suppliers, for example, we might have the three P-relations:

```
SKN ( S¢, S#, SNAME )
ST  ( S¢, STATUS )
SC  ( S¢, CITY )
```

The precise manner in which properties are grouped into P-relations is left to the discretion of the database designer; at one extreme all properties might be bundled together into a single P-relation, at the other extreme each property might have a (binary) P-relation of its own. To continue the suppliers-and-parts example: For the two suppliers *alpha* and *beta* (who we assume are actually suppliers S1 and S2), the P-relations might look as follows:

SKN	S¢	S#	SNAME	ST	S¢	STATUS	SC	S¢	CITY
	alpha	S1	Smith		alpha	20		alpha	London
	beta	S2	Jones		beta	10		beta	Paris

Similarly for parts (details left as an exercise for the reader). What about shipments? Shipments are of course an associative entity type; for a given shipment, the properties to be represented in the database are as follows:

- the surrogate for the relevant supplier (S¢)
- the surrogate for the relevant part (P¢)
- the relevant quantity (QTY)

Note that there is no longer any need for shipments to have a supplier number or part number property: The supplier and part for a given shipment are identified by surrogates, not by user keys.[4] For simplicity let us assume that all three properties are represented in a single P-relation:

```
SPSPQ ( SP¢, S¢, P¢, QTY )
```

---

4. Similar remarks apply to designations (not illustrated by the suppliers-and-parts example). For example, employees would typically have a DEPT¢ property, not a DEPT# property. Likewise for characteristics; as pointed out earlier, a characteristic entity is really just a designating entity that happens to be existence-dependent on the entity it designates.

Possible sample values:

SPSPQ	SP¢	S¢	P¢	QTY
	zeta	alpha	gamma	300
	eta	alpha	delta	200
	theta	alpha	epsilon	400
	iota	beta	gamma	300
	kappa	beta	delta	400

Subtypes and Supertypes

Any given entity is of at least one entity type; but an entity may be of several types simultaneously. For example, if some employees are programmers (and all programmers are employees), then we might say that PROGRAMMER is a subtype of the EMPLOYEE supertype. All properties of employees apply automatically to programmers, but the converse is not true (e.g., programmers may have a property "primary programming language," which does not apply to employees in general). Likewise, a) all designations by employees are automatically designations by programmers, but the converse is not true; b) all associations in which employees participate are automatically associations in which programmers participate, but the converse is not true.

Note furthermore that some programmers may be application programmers and some may be system programmers; thus we might say that APPLICATION_PROGRAMMER and SYSTEM_PROGRAMMER are subtypes of the PROGRAMMER supertype (and so on). A given entity type and its immediate subtypes, their immediate subtypes, and so on, together constitute the *type hierarchy* for the entity type in question. See Fig. 25.3 for an example.[5]

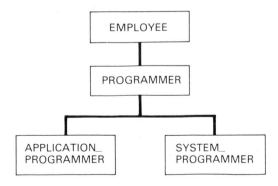

Fig. 25.3 Example of a type hierarchy.

---

5. Of course, type hierarchies should not be confused with the IMS-style hierarchies of the hierarchic data model. In Fig. 25.3, for example, there is no suggestion that for one EMPLOYEE there are multiple corresponding PROGRAMMERs; on the contrary, for one instance of EMPLOYEE there is *at most one* corresponding PROGRAMMER, representing that same EMPLOYEE in his or her PROGRAMMER role.

Here are some possible E- and P-relations for the EMPLOYEE and PRO-GRAMMER entity types (only):

EMPLOYEE	EMPLOYEE¢	EMPLOYEE_PROPS	EMPLOYEE¢	EMP#	ENAME
	lambda		lambda	E1	Lopez
	mu		mu	E2	Cheng
	nu		nu	E3	Finzi
	xi		xi	E4	Saito
	omicron		omicron	E5	Jacob

PROGRAMMER	PROGRAMMER¢	PROGRAMMER_PROPS	PROGRAMMER¢	LANG
	lambda		lambda	COBOL
	xi		xi	PL/I
	omicron			

Note in this example that Jacob (surrogate *omicron*) is a programmer who has presumably not yet been trained in any programming language.

Integrity Rules

RM/T includes a number of new integrity rules. They are numbered 3–8, since Rules 1 and 2 of the basic relational model still apply. We remark however that Rules 4–8 can all be seen as special cases of the existing Rule 2 (referential integrity). See [25.14] or Volume II for further discussion.

3. *Entity integrity in RM/T*: E-relations accept insertions and deletions but not updates.

4. *Property integrity*: If a tuple t appears in a P-relation P, then the (surrogate) primary key value of t must appear in the E-relation corresponding to P.

5. *Characteristic integrity*: A characteristic entity cannot exist in the database unless the entity it describes is also in the database.

6. *Association integrity*: An associative entity cannot exist in the database unless each entity participating in the association is also in the database (except where it is explicitly stated that such a participant may legally be specified as "unknown").

7. *Designation integrity*: A designative entity cannot exist in the database unless the entity it designates is also in the database (except where it is explicitly stated that the designated entity may legally be specified as "unknown").

8. *Subtype integrity*: Whenever a surrogate, say e, appears in the E-relation for an entity of type E, e must also appear in the E-relation for any entity type E' for which E is a subtype.

Operators

What distinguishes RM/T from most other proposals in the semantic modeling area is that it includes not only a set of objects and rules as described above, but also a corresponding set of operators. Those operators permit (among other things) the definition of widely varying user views over a common underlying database; moreover, they allow those definitions to be comparatively independent of the precise structure of that database. For example, suppose that the suppliers-and-parts database is represented by E- and P-relations as sketched above. Using only the operators of the basic relational model, it would be possible to provide user views of suppliers, parts, and shipments as the familiar three *n*-ary relations S (degree 4), P (degree 5), and SP (degree 3), in which all surrogates are concealed and only user keys show through.[6] However:

1. Each of those three view definitions would have to be thought out and formulated independently;
2. Each would involve several distinct relational algebra operations;
3. Moreover, each would be highly sensitive to changes in the RM/T-level definition of the database; consider the effect of breaking the supplier P-relation SKN into two, one each for S# and SNAME, for example.

RM/T, by contrast, provides a single operator, the PROPERTY operator, whose effect is to gather together *all* the immediate properties for a specified entity type into a single *n*-ary relation, regardless of how many properties there are, regardless of how those properties are grouped into P-relations, and regardless of the naming structure of those P-relations. Thus the three view definitions could each involve just that one operator, and the problems 1–3 outlined above would not arise.

Having said that, we should now stress the point (already mentioned in the introduction to this section) that the operators of RM/T as currently defined must be regarded as preliminary only; a considerable amount of additional definitional work is needed before they can be regarded as being in any final kind of form. For that reason we do not discuss them any further here. The interested reader is referred to Volume II or reference [25.14] for more information.

25.5 CONCLUDING REMARKS

We have presented a brief introduction to the general idea of, and some specific approaches to, the problem of semantic modeling. The ultimate objective of that activity is to make database systems more intelligent. However, the reader should realize that an extended model such as RM/T can be useful as an aid to systematic database design, even in the absence of direct system support for that model—just as the basic relational model has similarly been used for some time as a primitive design aid in systems such as IMS that do not directly support relational databases at all. A design methodology based on RM/T is sketched in reference [4.4].

---

6. Note once again the necessity for being able to update certain kinds of join view.

For similar reasons, the ideas of semantic modeling are also directly applicable to data dictionary systems (indeed, the data dictionary can be regarded in some respects as "the database designer's database"; it is after all a database in which the database designer records his or her design decisions [25.15]). The study of semantic modeling should thus be regarded, not merely as an academic exercise, but rather as a discipline that a) has immediate practical relevance today, and b) may possibly have far-reaching effects on database system architecture in the future.

EXERCISES

25.1 Draw an entity/relationship diagram for the education database from Chapter 22, or any other database with which you may be familiar.

25.2 Define the following RM/T terms:

a) kernel;

b) characteristic;

c) association;

d) designation;

e) surrogate;

f) E-relation;

g) P-relation;

h) entity subtype.

25.3 Sketch an RM/T version of the education database from Chapter 22, or any other database with which you may be familiar.

REFERENCES AND BIBLIOGRAPHY

See also some of the references in Chapter 2—especially the ISO working document on the conceptual schema [2.5].

25.1 J. R. Abrial. "Data Semantics." In J. W. Klimbie and K. L. Koffeman (eds.): *Data Base Management*. North-Holland (1974).

25.2 P. Hall, J. Owlett, and S. J. P. Todd. "Relations and Entities." In J. W. Klimbie and K. L. Koffeman (eds.): *Data Base Management*. North-Holland (1974).

The paper that first introduced the idea of surrogates (incorporated later into RM/T).

25.3 B. Sundgren. "The Infological Approach to Data Bases." In J. W. Klimbie and K. L. Koffeman (eds.): *Data Base Management*. North-Holland (1974).

The "infological approach" is an approach to semantic modeling that has been successfully used (for database design, at least) for a number of years in Scandinavia.

25.4 H. A. Schmid and J. R. Swenson. "On the Semantics of the Relational Data Base Model." *Proc. 1975 ACM SIGMOD International Conference on Management of Data* (May 1975).

This paper proposed a "basic semantic model" that predated Chen's work on the entity/relationship model but in fact was very similar to that model (except in terminology, of course; Schmid and Swenson use *independent object*, *dependent object*, and *association* in place of Chen's terms *regular entity*, *weak entity*, and *relationship*, respectively).

25.5 J. M. Smith and D. C. P. Smith. "Database Abstractions: Aggregation." *CACM* **20,** No. 6 (June 1977).

25.6 J. M. Smith and D. C. P. Smith. "Database Abstractions: Aggregation and Generalization." *ACM TODS* **2,** No. 2 (June 1977).

The proposals of these two papers [25.5,25.6] had a significant influence on RM/T, especially in the area of subtypes and supertypes.

25.7 M. M. Hammer and D. J. McLeod. "The Semantic Data Model: A Modelling Mechanism for Database Applications." *Proc. 1978 ACM SIGMOD International Conference on Management of Data* (June 1978).

25.8 W. Kent. *Data and Reality.* North-Holland (1978).

See the annotation to this reference in Chapter 2.

25.9 D. Shipman. "The Functional Data Model and the Data Language DAPLEX." *ACM TODS* **6,** No. 1 (March 1981).

25.10 P. P.-S. Chen. "The Entity-Relationship Model—Toward a Unified View of Data." *ACM TODS* **1,** No. 1 (March 1976).

25.11 P. P.-S. Chen. "A Preliminary Framework for Entity-Relationship Models." In *Entity-Relationship Approach to Information Modeling and Analysis* (ed., P. P.-S. Chen). ER Institute, PO Box 617, Saugus, Calif. 91350 (1981).

25.12 W. Kent. "A Taxonomy of Entity-Relationship Models." Unpublished paper.

25.13 E. F. Codd. "Data Models in Database Management." *Proc. Workshop on Data Abstraction, Databases and Conceptual Modelling. ACM SIGART Newsletter* No. 74 (January 1981); *ACM SIGMOD Record* **11,** No. 2 (February 1981); *ACM SIGPLAN Notices* **16,** No. 1 (January 1981).

A short and informal paper on the following topics:

1. What is a data model?
2. Purposes of a data model
3. History of data model development
4. Common misunderstandings
5. The future

25.14 E. F. Codd. "Extending the Database Relational Model to Capture More Meaning." *ACM TODS* **4,** No. 4 (December 1979).

The paper that first defined RM/T. In addition to the aspects discussed briefly in the present chapter, the paper includes proposals for including time considerations and various kinds of data aggregation in the overall activity of semantic modeling.

25.15 Frank W. Allen, Mary E. S. Loomis, and Michael V. Mannino. "The Integrated Dictionary-Directory System." *ACM Comp. Surv.* **14,** No. 2 (June 1982).

A tutorial on the data dictionary, with a brief survey of available products.

List of Acronyms

We list below some of the more important acronyms introduced in the text, together with their meanings.

ABF	Applications By Forms (INGRES)
ANSI/SPARC	literally, American National Standards Institute / Systems Planning and Requirements Committee; used to refer to the three-level architecture described in Chapter 2
ASF	Automatic System Facility (IDMS/R)
BCNF	Boyce/Codd normal form
CBS	compound boolean selection (DATACOM/DB)
CICS	Customer Information Control System (IBM)
CODASYL	literally, Conference on Data Systems Languages; used to refer to the DBTG proposals
DATACOM/DB	DATACOM / database (ADR)
DB/DC	database/data communications
DBA	database administrator
DBD	database description (IMS)
DBMS	database management system
DBRM	database request module (DB2)
DBTG	Data Base Task Group
DB2	Database 2 (IBM)
DB2I	DB2 Interactive
DC	data communications
DDL	data definition language
DEDB	data entry database (IMS)
DES	data encryption standard
DK/NF	domain-key normal form
DL/I	data language / I (IMS)
DML	data manipulation language
EMVD	embedded MVD
EQUEL	embedded QUEL
FD	functional dependency
GBF	Graph By Forms (INGRES)
GN	get next (IMS)

GNP	get next within parent (IMS)
GU	get unique (IMS)
HDAM	hierarchic direct access method (IMS)
HIDAM	hierarchic indexed direct access method (IMS)
HISAM	hierarchic indexed sequential access method (IMS)
HSAM	hierarchic sequential access method (IMS)
IDM	Intelligent Database Machine (Britton-Lee)
IDMS	Integrated Database Management System (Cullinet)
IDMS/R	IDMS / Relational
IMS	Information Management System (IBM)
IMS/DC	IMS / data communications
INGRES	Interactive Graphics and Retrieval System (RTI)
ISC	InterSystem Communications (IBM)
JD	join dependency
LAN	local area network
LRF	Logical Record Facility (IDMS)
MSDB	main storage database (IMS)
MVD	multivalued dependency
OSL	Operation Specification Language (INGRES)
PCB	Program Communication Block (IMS)
PJ/NF	projection-join normal form
QBE	Query-By-Example (QMF)
QBF	Query By Forms (INGRES)
QMF	Query Management Facility (IBM)
QUEL	query language (INGRES)
R*	"R star" (distributed System R)
RBF	Report By Forms (INGRES)
RID	record ID
RIME	Relational Information Management Environment (DATACOM/DB)
RM/T	relational model / Tasmania
SDD-1	System for Distributed Databases-1
SHISAM	simple HISAM (IMS)
SHSAM	simple HSAM (IMS)
SQL	structured query language (DB2, etc.)
SSA	segment search argument (IMS)
TSO	time-sharing option (MVS)
UDL	unified database language
UWA	user work area (CODASYL)
VIFRED	Visual Forms Editor (INGRES)
XD	indexed (IMS)
X3H2	ANSI database committee
1NF	first normal form
2NF	second normal form
3NF	third normal form
4GL	fourth generation language
4NF	fourth normal form
5NF	fifth normal form (same as PJ/NF)

Index